v.

(versus)

Case Law, Concepts, & American Society

First Edition

By Alan S. Nemeth

University of Maryland

cognella™
San Diego, CA

Bassim Hamadeh, CEO and Publisher
Christopher Foster, General Vice President
Michael Simpson, Vice President of Acquisitions
Jessica Knott, Managing Editor
Kevin Fahey, Cognella Marketing Manager
Jess Busch, Senior Graphic Designer
Melissa Barcomb, Acquisitions Editor
Sarah Wheeler, Project Editor
Stephanie Sandler, Licensing Associate

First published in the United States of America in 2012 by Cognella, Inc.

16 15 14 13 12 1 2 3 4 5

Printed in the United States of America

ISBN: 978-1-60927-685-0

cognella™

www.cognella.com 800.200.3908

Table of Contents

This book would not have been possible without the many long hours

and support provided by my wife, Rose.

Thank you.

Introduction
Law & Society in America

The title of the book is "*v.*," which is representative of the v., "versus," in case names, such as *Marbury v. Madison*, *Roe v. Wade*, etc. Rather than reading about the law and legal concepts through the author's interpretations, this book relies primarily on actual court opinions to lay out the concepts and highlight their effects on society. As a result, this book is heavy on cases and original documents and short on prose. It uses the cases and documents as a guide through which the reader can view issues of law and their interplay with society and vice versa.

There are many ways to discuss law and society. One can review different topics, such as governmental control, societal change, and how the law drives each. One can review various theories of law and society, the mechanisms of law, the history of law, groups affecting and affected by the law, and so on. This book will instead review American law and society through various different fields of law by examining the legal concepts and case law within those fields. The concepts and cases selected are by no means an exhaustive list. Multiple volumes and more than three years of law school would be necessary to cover every possible legal concept affecting our society. This book is merely designed to be representative of some of the most important legal issues currently affecting our society.

The allure of the law is that it is dynamic and ever-changing despite its well-established framework. Legislatures create the law. Courts interpret that law through the cases brought before them. Society follows the law as its foundation and rules of behavior. It is that simple. The beauty of the law is that as new laws are implemented, society is forced to change or modify its previously established behavior. For example, when legislatures across the country began banning smoking in buildings, smokers were compelled to change their smoking habits due to the change in the law. Change, however, is not unidirectional. Society can demand changes in the law as it evolves and matures over time. The civil rights laws are an example of this. Protests against racial discrimination fostered public interest in the civil rights movement, which eventually forced a change in the law through legislation and court decisions.

Just as law and society change over time, so too do the fields of law in which an attorney can practice. According to HG.org, an online legal information site, there are currently over 260 legal specialties and sub-specialties. These range from the more common fields of corporate law, criminal law, family law, personal injury, wills & trusts, employment law, intellectual property law, tax law, property/real estate law, and so on, to the lesser known fields of veterans law, construction law, election law, administrative/regulatory law, education law, admiralty/maritime law, etc. There are also the newer and growing fields of animal law, environmental law, elder law, health law, cyberspace/e-commerce law, gaming law, disability law, fashion law, and more.

Throughout the book, when possible, the vote count of the Supreme Court justices is included with the case cite. For example in *Kulko*, the Court voted 6–3 in favor of the decision, which the reader can see in the parentheses next to "Supreme Court of the United States."

KULKO v. SUPERIOR COURT OF CALIFORNIA
Supreme Court of the United States (6–3)
436 U.S. 84 (1978)

The vote count gives the reader a sense of how closely the Court was divided or united on the issues presented to it in each case. As will be seen throughout the book, the outcome of a particular case often rests on the vote of one justice—a justice who is appointed by the president of the United States and confirmed by the U.S. Senate. Most importantly, however, the vote count serves to remind the reader of the importance of the political process in relation to the law and society. Elections are about more than just getting a particular candidate into office. Elections help to shape the future direction that society will take, since elected officials affect more than mere legislation. They leave a legacy for years to come through the appointment and confirmation of the Supreme Court justices whom they select, as well as judges throughout the judicial system.

The concepts included under the umbrella of law and society pervade every aspect of daily life. From the moment one wakes up in the morning until the moment one goes to sleep at night, an individual is affected by the law. People come into contact with the law in the jobs/professions they perform, in the products they buy, in the entertainment they enjoy, and in the way they choose to live their lives. This book is designed to provide a broad overview of some of the many common legal concepts touching everyday life. There is much more to law and society than one volume can hold. It is this author's hope, however, that the cases and concepts included herein will provide a good basic introduction to some common legal concepts and the societal issues that they affect.

Chapter 1
Animal Law

Animal law is a relatively new, yet rapidly growing field of law. It cuts across a wide variety of legal subject matter, including essentially every chapter heading in this book, as well as other established fields, such as environmental law, administrative law, and disability law. According to the Animal Legal Defense Fund, as of this writing, at least 136 law schools throughout the United States and Canada offer classes in animal law, and 36 bar associations have animal law sections or committees. The American Bar Association also has an animal law committee. In September 2011, the ABA published *Careers in Animal Law*. With that publication, the ABA recognized animal law as "[o]ne of the fastest growing legal disciplines" and defined animal law as "protecting and improving the lives of animals through city ordinances, state and federal laws, international treaties, and cases that impact animals."

Animal law is a very broad field of law, but it can be defined simply as the laws and regulations affecting animals. Animal law concerns itself with issues facing domestic animals, farm animals, animals in the wild, endangered species, marine animals, animals used in research, animals used in entertainment, etc., as well as with the relationship between humans and animals. Additionally, animal law examines the link between animal cruelty and violence against humans.

Besides the actual application of law to specific cases and situations, some of the larger or philosophical questions that animal law delves into include:

- What is an animal? (Statutes define animals differently from state to state and from law to law.)
- What rights do animals have? (Do they have the right to be free from cruelty and mistreatment?)
- What rights should they have? (Should they have the right to live their lives as they would without human intervention? Should an animal have the right not to be forced to perform in a circus?)
- Should different animals have different rights? (Does a primate deserve more rights than an amphibian, since they are more like humans? Does a dog or a cat have more rights than a snake, since they are "cuter" and "cuddlier?")

- Should animals be treated differently in different situations? (Is a mouse kept as a pet different from a mouse that is found running around a pantry?)

- Are animals property? (Should they be treated the same way a couch or a car or a diamond necklace are treated? Are they like any other piece of property?)

- Should animals be considered something other than property? (Does the fact that they are feeling and sentient beings mean anything? Does the fact that people feel that animals are a part of their families change the way that they should be legally viewed? Should animals follow the path of humans who were once treated as property—women, children, slaves—in the development of rights and legal standing?)

According to a March 4, 2009 Congressional Research Service paper, "Brief Summaries of Federal Animal Protection Statutes" (by Henry Cohen), there were over 90 federal statutes relating to animals. More have been passed since then. The Supreme Court has even weighed in on the animal law issue. Most recently, in *U.S. v. Stevens,* 130 S. Ct. 1577, 559 US __, 176 (2010), the Court found a federal statute that banned depictions of animal cruelty to be unconstitutional.

Every state has animal cruelty laws—some stronger than others. A number of states have already passed and others are considering passing legislation to provide protection to animals in domestic abuse situations, since an abusive spouse will often hurt or threaten to hurt the family pets as a way of further abusing or getting back at his/her spouse. Legislation has been proposed to allow judges to grant joint custody and visitation rights to family pets in the case of a divorce, instead of treating the family pet as just another piece of property. The majority of states have passed legislation allowing for pet trusts—trusts that benefit pets after the death of their owners. None of these laws would be applicable to mere property. So, it seems that law and/or society do already recognize animals as something other than "property," at least in certain states and in certain situations.

The cruel treatment of farm animals has been addressed in recent years. Animal welfare groups have increasingly made society aware of the cruel living conditions under which various farm animals have been forced to live (and, in most cases, still do). Several state legislatures have responded to the subsequent growth in public interest by banning particular farming practices, such as the use of battery cages (small cramped cages in which egg-laying hens are forced to live), gestation crates (small enclosures for pregnant pigs which do not allow the pigs room to move around), and veal crates (similar small enclosures for calves destined to become veal). This legislation has required the factory farming industry to change its commonly accepted practices and is a clear example of how society can affect a change in the law.

As society becomes more aware of these issues, market forces and the force of law will further precipitate change in the current practices of factory farms. For example, as laws against the use of battery cages proliferate, not only will egg producers not be able to use battery cages in the states that have banned them, but they will no longer be able to sell eggs derived from battery cages interstate to states whose laws have banned the sale of eggs produced in battery cages. Additionally, as more consumers both individually and through large organizations (such as governments, corporations, and universities) choose to buy cage-free eggs over traditional battery cage eggs, supply and demand will force farms to amend their mode of operating or risk losing revenue and ultimately their businesses.

Recent animal law issues explore the intertwining between animal law and another relatively new field of law—that of fashion law. There have been cases where a designer or clothes manufacturer has claimed to be using faux fur on its clothing line when, in fact, it was not faux but real fur. This sort of case can raise a whole host of issues, including animal protection, consumer protection, false advertising, and perhaps even issues in tort (if someone is allergic to fur and s/he suffers an injury due to the fur, because s/he thought s/he was buying faux fur). This type of case is not relegated to the attention of animal welfare activists. In December 2010, President Obama signed the Truth in Fur Labeling Act, which closed a loophole and now requires garments under $150 to be properly labeled—if a garment contains fur, it must be clearly labeled as such and with the country and animal of origin of the fur.

The following cases (*People v. Voelker* and *People v. Garcia*) represent but a very small sampling of issues involved in the study or practice of animal law.

> *People v. Voelker* raises a number of issues, including cruelty and free speech.

PEOPLE v. VOELKER

Criminal Court of the City of New York, Kings County
658 N.Y.S.2d 180 (1997)

ESTHER M. MORGENSTERN, J.

Can a defendant insulate himself from prosecution on First Amendment grounds by televising the criminal acts of decapitating three live, conscious iguanas in violation of the State's anti-cruelty statute?

Defendant was arrested on October 2, 1996 and charged with three counts of overdriving, torturing and injuring animals pursuant to section 353 of the Agriculture and Markets Law. These charges stem from a videotaped incident wherein defendant is alleged to have cut off the heads of three live, conscious iguanas without justification.

* * *

The complaint in this case alleges, in pertinent part, that on or about and between February 6, 1996 and August 2, 1996 at 85 Havemeyer Street, apartment 1L, in Brooklyn, the defendant allegedly cut off the heads of three live, conscious iguanas without justification. The complaint alleges further that Assistant District Attorney Todd Davis (hereinafter deponent) is in possession of and has viewed a videotape showing the defendant committing the acts alleged. Additionally, the complaint alleges that deponent was informed:

* * *

> "by Frank Fitzgerald that informant recorded said videotape on August 9, 1996, from a television broadcast by Manhattan Neighborhood Network of the show entitled 'Sick and Wrong,' 566*566 and that informant saw the same incident broadcast on an earlier edition of the show, `Sick and Wrong,' aired on August 2, 1996."

Defendant maintains that an essential element of Agriculture and Markets Law § 353 is an "unjustifiable act" toward an animal, and that the allegation that defendant cut off the heads of three live iguanas, "without justification," is conclusory and insufficient. Defendant contends that killing the animals in this case was justified and necessary and that any pain or suffering was temporary, unavoidable and without criminal intent.

The People maintain that the term "without justification" means just what it says, that defendant cut off the heads of three animals without apparent justification. Thus, the allegations in the accusatory instrument provide reasonable cause to believe that the defendant committed the offense charged and establish, if true, every element of the offense charged.

The People maintain further that defendant's alleged "justification defense" does not support the motion to dismiss and that the issue of justification is a question of fact to be determined at trial. Additionally, the People argue that defendant's acts were unjustified in that defendant violated the State's anti-cruelty statute by cutting off the heads of three conscious iguanas and that the mere fact that defendant thereafter allegedly cooked and consumed these animals does not justify defendant's actions.

DISCUSSION

* * *

The Constitutional Issue

Defendant also moves for dismissal upon the ground that Agriculture and Markets Law § 353 is being unconstitutionally applied in that the motivation for the prosecution of defendant is that he chose to televise an act that is normally relegated to the back room of a restaurant, and that such content-based restrictions on speech are unconstitutional.

There is no question that government action that stifles speech on account of its message, or that requires the utterance of a particular message favored by the government, contravenes an individual's rights under the First Amendment. (*Turner Broadcasting Sys. v. Federal Communications Commn.*, 512 US 622 [1994].) However, it is well established that a content-neutral restriction on speech will be upheld if "'it furthers an important or substantial governmental interest; if the governmental interest is unrelated to the suppression of free expression; and if the incidental restriction on alleged First Amendment freedoms is no greater than is essential to the furtherance of that interest.'" (*Turner Broadcasting Sys. v. Federal Communications Commn., supra*, at 662, quoting *United States v. O'Brien*, 391 US 367, 377 [1968].)

Contrary to defendant's contention, this court holds that the animal cruelty statute at issue is not a content-based restriction on speech. Rather, it is a restriction against torturing, injuring, maiming, mutilating or killing animals. The statute is not directed at any form of communication. Furthermore, the People correctly point out that although the statute might prohibit the torturing of an animal as a form of expression, such a statute would not be unconstitutional where it serves a legitimate governmental interest (*Barnes v. Glen Theatre*, 501 US 560, 567 [1991]), and that the United States Supreme Court has indicated that a neutral anti-cruelty statute which is limited to the Government's legitimate interest in the prevention of cruelty to animals may be upheld despite its effect on religious observance. (*Church of Lukumi Babalu Aye v. Hialeah*, 508 US 520, 538 [1993].)

Moreover, defendant is not being prosecuted because he televised the decapitation of the iguanas. The televising of the decapitations merely provided law enforcement officials with a way to observe defendant engage in criminal activity. A defendant cannot shelter himself from prosecution by the mere televising of a criminal act. Taking defendant's argument to its logical conclusion, a defendant could televise any criminal act and seek to shield himself from prosecution on First Amendment grounds. Such an argument defies common sense and cannot be sustained.

The court holds that Agriculture and Markets Law § 353 is not being unconstitutionally applied in this case. Accordingly, defendant's motion to dismiss is denied on this ground.

People v. Garcia discusses a common issue, not only within an animal law context, but within the legal field in general. That is, how does one define terms? In this case, the term being examined is "companion animal."

PEOPLE v. GARCIA

Appellate Division of the Supreme Court of the State of New York, First Department
29 A.D.3d 255 (2006)

CATTERSON, J.

The earliest known domestic animal appears to be the dog, a companion to mankind as early as 15,000 B.C. Goats, sheep, pigs and cows followed in domestication in the next 10,000 years. Horses, however, did not succumb to the lure of mankind's presence until 4000 B.C. The domestication of fish is believed to have begun much later, in China during the Tang Dynasty, around 620 A.D. The common goldfish (Carassius auratus), a member of the carp family that was first domesticated in China, is now the most commonly kept aquarium fish. The goldfish's leap from domesticated fish to family pet and companion may have happened as early as 1368 during the Ming Dynasty. The goldfish's popularity in the West began as the first public aquarium opened in London in 1853. Keeping goldfish as companions and pets in the United States has been popular since that time.

Agriculture and Markets Law § 353-a (1), "Aggravated cruelty to animals," represents the Legislature's recognition that man's inhumanity to man often begins with inhumanity to those creatures that have formed particularly close relationships with mankind. (Assembly Mem in Support of L 1999, ch 118, 1999 McKinney's Session Laws of NY, at 1585.) The scope of section 353-a (1) is a question of first impression for the Appellate Division, and the instant case compels the conclusion that its reach is broad.

On August 2, 2003, Emelie Martinez was living in an apartment with the defendant, her three children, Juan Torres, Crystal and Emaleeann, and Jesus Rabassa, an 18-year-old high school student. Juan was nine years old, Crystal eight and Emaleeann five. Also living in the apartment were two dogs, a cat, and three goldfish named after the children, Junior, Crystal and Emma.

At about 3:00 A.M., Martinez awoke on the sofa to find the defendant standing over her, holding the fish tank. She asked him what he was doing. The defendant threw the fish tank into the television set, saying, "That could have been you." The fish tank shattered, as did the television screen and a portion of a glass wall unit. The defendant also destroyed Juan's VCR by ripping it out and throwing it against the wall unit.

Eventually, the defendant and Martinez began cleaning up the mess. Juan came out of his room, with the girls behind him, crying. The defendant turned to Juan and said, "You want to see something awesome?" and stomped on Juan's fish, killing the fish. Martinez had to calm the children before she could continue cleaning up the mess.

* * *

The trial court also convicted the defendant of aggravated cruelty to animals, a felony. The court determined that the pet goldfish of Martinez and her children was a companion animal within the meaning of Agriculture and Markets Law § 353-a (1) and § 350 (5), and that the statute is not unconstitutionally vague.

"ALL CREATURES GREAT AND SMALL"[*]

The defendant argues that his "stomping of young Juan's pet goldfish" is a misdemeanor pursuant to Agriculture and Markets Law § 353 (unjustifiable killing of any animal, whether wild or tame), and not a felony because a fish is not a "companion animal" and his "stomping" did not constitute "aggravated cruelty" within the meaning of the statute.

Agriculture and Markets Law § 353-a (1) provides:

> "A person is guilty of aggravated cruelty to animals when, with no justifiable purpose, he or she intentionally kills or intentionally causes serious physical injury to a companion animal with aggravated cruelty. For purposes of this section, 'aggravated cruelty' shall mean conduct which: (i) is intended to cause extreme physical pain; or (ii) is done or carried out in an especially depraved or sadistic manner."

The term "companion animal" is defined in section 350 (5):

> "'Companion animal' or 'pet' means any dog or cat, and shall also mean any other domesticated animal normally maintained in or near the household of the owner or person who cares for such other domesticated animal. 'Pet' or 'companion animal' shall not include a 'farm animal' as defined in this section."

The defendant contends that a fish is not a companion animal because it is not domesticated and because there is no reciprocity or mutuality of feeling between a fish and its owner, such as there is between a dog or a cat and its owner.

In the absence of a definition in the statute, the defendant, citing 4 Am Jur 2d, Animals § 2 (at 346 [Lawyers Coop Publ 1995]), defines "domesticated animals" as those that "no longer possess the disposition or inclination to escape," and claims that "if dropped in a pond and offered the opportunity to swim away, a goldfish will do so without any hesitation and not look back." He maintains that the statute's reference to "any other" domesticated animal limits "companion animal[s]" to those that are similar to dogs or cats, that is, those with a degree of sentience sufficiently elevated to enable them to enter into a relationship of mutual affection with a human being. Furthermore, "[b]eloved household pets (fish) may be, but 'companion animals' in the same vein as dogs or cats they are not."

The defendant's contention that all household pets are equal but some are more equal than others is manifestly not derived from the statute. The Legislature simply did not require a reciprocity of affection in the definition of "companion animal." To the contrary, the statutory language is consistent with the People's contention that, "domesticated" is commonly understood to mean "to adapt (an animal or plant) to life in intimate association with and to the advantage of humans." Thus, a goldfish such as the one herein is a domesticated rather than a wild animal within the common meaning of the term. Moreover, the goldfish was, as the statute requires, "normally maintained in or near the household of the owner or person who cares for [it]." Indeed, acknowledging that the goldfish is one of the most common household pets, defense counsel stipulated at trial that there are "millions of fish owners throughout the country."

The defendant's argument that goldfish are not domesticated animals because given the opportunity they would leave home is without merit. While this trait arguably distinguishes fish from dogs and, probably to a lesser extent cats, it fails to take into account that many other animals commonly considered pets, such as hermit crabs, gerbils, hamsters, guinea pigs and rabbits, would depart for less confining venues and greener pastures if given the opportunity. Loyalty, if that is what it is, is merely another characteristic urged by defendant—but not included by the Legislature—as a defining feature of a companion animal.

* * *

While the defendant maintains that the statute's definition of "companion animal" is unconstitutionally vague, we find, as did the trial court, the statute sufficiently clear to apprise a person of ordinary intelligence that the sort of conduct in which the defendant engaged comes within the statute's prohibition. (*See United States v. Harriss*, 347 US 612, 617 [1954].)

The defendant further asserts that because the fish's death was instantaneous, it was not accompanied by "extreme physical pain" or accomplished with "especial[]" depravity or sadism, and that therefore the killing was not accomplished with any heightened level of cruelty. The trial court correctly observed that the legislative history of the statute indicates that the crime was established in recognition of the correlation between violence against animals and subsequent violence against human beings. (*People v. Garcia,* 3 Misc 3d 699, 702 [Sup Ct, NY County 2004].) Thus, it must be inferred that the Legislature's concern was with the state of mind of the perpetrator rather than that of the victim.

* * *

[*] "All things bright and beautiful, all creatures great and small, all things wise and wonderful: The Lord God made them all." (Cecil F. Alexander, Hymns For Little Children [1848].)

The following concurrence from *Bueckner v. Hamel* is included, as it provides a sense of the growing societal recognition of the importance of animals to the lives of individuals in our society.

BUECKNER v. HAMEL

Court of Appeals of Texas, Houston (1st Dist.)
886 S.W.2d 368 (1994)

ANDELL, Justice, concurring.

I agree that the majority's analysis and disposition of this case is correct. I write separately, however, to address what I consider to be a more substantial basis for affirming this award, namely, the intrinsic or special value of domestic animals as companions and beloved pets. The issue is whether bereaved pet owners must accept the market value of their pets as the measure of actual damages for their pets' wrongful killing, or if they have the option of accepting either the market value or the special value. I consider the general rule of market value to be inadequate for assessing damages for the loss of domestic pets. For the reasons in the following analysis, I would hold that the pet owners have the option of accepting either measure of damages. Hence, I would affirm, but on different grounds.

In this case, Bueckner challenges the sufficiency of the evidence to support the award of $1450 in actual damages to compensate Hamel and Collins for the loss of their beloved pets. The trial court's findings consisted of five separate categories of value: (1) market value; (2) pecuniary value to Hamel and Collins; (3) value to Hamel and Collins of prospective litters of puppies; (4) *intrinsic value* of the dogs to Hamel and Collins and the *value of the dogs as companions* to Hamel and Collins; and (5) special value to Hamel and Collins *as beloved pets*.

* * *

The majority cites *Arrington v. Arrington*, 613 S.W.2d 565, 569 (Tex.Civ.App.—Fort Worth 1981, no writ), for the proposition that animals are treated as property in the eyes of the law. I agree that this is an established principle of law. But animals are not *merely* property. *Arrington* was a divorce case. Among many other items of "property" to be divided, it involved the question of which spouse would be the "managing conservator" of their pet dog, Bonnie Lou. The court decided that issue on the grounds that Bonnie Lou was the property of Mrs. Arrington. But the court spoke in terms that show how our society loves and appreciates dogs as domestic pets, or even as family members:

> *Bonnie Lou is a very fortunate little dog with two humans to shower upon her attentions and genuine love frequently not received by human children from their divorced parents.* All too often children of broken homes are used by their parents to vent spite on each other or they use them as human ropes in a post divorce tug-of-war. In trying to hurt each other they often wreak immeasurable damage on the innocent pawns they profess to love. *Dogs involved in divorce cases are luckier than children in divorce cases—they do not have to be treated as humans.* The office of "managing conservator" was created for the benefit of human children, not canine.

A dog, for all its admirable and unique qualities, is not a human being and is not treated in the law as such. A dog is personal property, ownership of which is recognized under the law. There was testimony that Bonnie Lou was given to Mrs. Arrington over ten years ago.

> Mr. Arrington agreed to Mrs. Arrington's custody of the dog if he could have reasonable visitation. He does not complain of lack of visitation; only that he was not appointed managing conservator. We overrule point of error no. 7 with the *hope that both Arringtons will continue to enjoy the companionship of Bonnie Lou for years to come* within the guidelines set by the trial court. *We are sure there is enough love in that little canine heart to "go around."* Love is not a commodity that can be bought and sold—or decreed. It should be shared and not argued about.
>
> *Id.* (emphasis added; citations omitted).

This language is strikingly different from that used in disposing of inanimate property. This could only have been because animals are so different from other types of property. The Arringtons contended for the companionship of Bonnie Lou. While their conflict was easy to resolve under simple property concepts, simple property concepts cannot reflect the complex reality of the relationships between humans and their pets. Because of the characteristics of animals in general and of domestic pets in particular, I consider them to belong to a unique category of "property" that neither statutory law nor caselaw has yet recognized.

Many people who love and admire dogs as family members do so because of the traits that dogs often embody. These represent some of the best of human traits, including loyalty, trust, courage, playfulness, and love. This cannot be said of inanimate property. At the same time, dogs typically lack the worst human traits, including avarice, apathy, pettiness, and hatred.

Scientific research has provided a wealth of understanding to us that we cannot rightly ignore. We now know that mammals share with us a great many emotive and cognitive characteristics, and that the higher primates are very similar to humans neurologically and genetically. It is not simplistic, ill-informed sentiment that has led our society to observe with compassion the occasionally televised plights of stranded whales and dolphins. It is, on the contrary, a recognition of a kinship that reaches across species boundaries.

The law must be informed by evolving knowledge and attitudes. Otherwise, it risks becoming irrelevant as a means of resolving conflicts. Society has long since moved beyond the untenable Cartesian view that animals are unfeeling automatons and, hence, *mere* property. The law should reflect society's recognition that animals are sentient and emotive beings that are capable of providing companionship to the humans with whom they live. In doing so, courts should not hesitate to acknowledge that a great number of people in this country today treat their pets as family members. Indeed, for many people, pets are the *only* family members they have.

Losing a beloved pet is not the same as losing an inanimate object, however cherished it may be. Even an heirloom of great sentimental value, if lost, does not constitute a loss comparable to that of a living being. This distinction applies even though the deceased living being is a nonhuman.

Bueckner contends that under existing Texas case law, if an animal has a market value, then that market value *alone* constitutes the proper measure of damages for the killing of the animal. No Texas Supreme Court case cited by either party, nor any that I have found, has held precisely on this point. I would disagree with *Redmon* and with any other appellate cases that are restrictive on this issue and hold that Hamel and Collins could recover *either* the market value *or* the special or intrinsic value of their beloved pets. Accordingly, I would affirm if the finding of $1825 in actual damages is supported by *either* the evidence of the market or pecuniary value of Freckles and Muffin *or* the evidence of the intrinsic or special value of Freckles and Muffin.

As stated above, I concur in the analysis and disposition of the majority opinion. I hasten to add, however, that testimony that an animal is a beloved companion should generally be considered sufficient to justify a finding of damages well beyond the market value of the animal and its yet-unborn progeny.

[Footnotes Omitted.]

Administrative/Regulatory Law

Animal law is a good example of an area of the law where administrative and regulatory law can be important. Legislatures pass laws but then rely upon administrative agencies to establish rules and regulations to put those laws into effect. Generally, it is considered that regulations are comprised of rules. Examples of where animal law can be impacted through administrative and regulatory law can be found within the Department of Agriculture and the Department of the Interior. Each of these agencies has its own regulatory powers and Freedom of Information Act (FOIA) processes. Furthermore, each of these agencies has its own processes for enforcing its rules and regulations and adjudicating any issues that fall under its purview. Once a party exhausts all of the opportunities to adjudicate her/his claim within the agency, s/he can then take her/his case to a court for a determination.

As mentioned, legislatures pass laws but then rely upon agencies to put into place the rules and regulations to implement those laws. The concept behind the delegation of rulemaking is that the agencies are the experts in their particular fields and will be in a better position than the legislature to craft the specific details to carry out the law. An agency can only act within the powers that it has been granted. Anything beyond those granted powers is considered *ultra vires*, or beyond the scope of its powers. If one believes that an agency is acting *ultra vires*, one can challenge the agency in court.

There are specific procedures that each agency must follow when creating rules. Any proposed rule must be published, there must be a period for the public to comment on the rule, and the final decision regarding the rule must be based on the whole record. One can research rules and regulations at both Regulations.gov (www.regulations.gov) and the Federal Register (http://www.gpoaccess.gov/fr/).

A sample proposed rule from the Fish and Wildlife Service of the Department of the Interior as posted on the Federal Register site follows.

[Federal Register: May 5, 2011 (Volume 76, Number 87)]

[Proposed Rules]
[Page 26085-26145]
From the Federal Register Online via GPO Access [wais.access.gpo.gov]
[DOCID:fr05my11-34]

[[Page 26085]]

Vol. 76

Thursday,

No. 87

May 5, 2011

Part III

Department of the Interior

Fish and Wildlife Service

---

50 CFR Part 17
Endangered and Threatened Wildlife and Plants; Proposed Rule To Revise the List of Endangered and Threatened Wildlife for the Gray Wolf (Canis lupus) in the Eastern United States, Initiation of Status Reviews for the Gray Wolf and for the Eastern Wolf (Canis lycaon); Proposed Rule

---

DEPARTMENT OF THE INTERIOR

Fish and Wildlife Service

50 CFR Part 17

[Docket No. FWS-R3-ES-2011-0029; 92220-1113-000; ABC Code: C6]
RIN 1018-AX57

Endangered and Threatened Wildlife and Plants; Proposed Rule To Revise the List of Endangered and Threatened Wildlife for the Gray Wolf (Canis lupus) in the Eastern United States, Initiation of Status Reviews for the Gray Wolf and for the Eastern Wolf (Canis lycaon)

AGENCY: Fish and Wildlife Service, Interior.

ACTION: Proposed rule, initiation of status reviews.

SUMMARY: We, the U.S. Fish and Wildlife Service (Service or USFWS) are re-evaluating the listing of the Minnesota population of gray wolves (Canis lupus) and propose to revise it to conform to current statutory and policy requirements. We propose to identify the Minnesota population as a Western Great Lakes (WGL) Distinct Population Segment (DPS) of the gray wolf and to remove this DPS from the List of Endangered and Threatened Wildlife. We propose these actions because the best available scientific and commercial information indicates that the WGL DPS does not meet the definitions of threatened or endangered under the Act.

This proposed rule, if made final, would remove the currently designated critical habitat for the gray wolf in Minnesota and Michigan and the current special regulations for gray wolves in Minnesota. We also propose to revise the range of the gray wolf (the species C. lupus) by removing all or parts of 29 eastern states that we now recognize were not part of the historical range of the gray wolf. New information indicates that these areas should not have been included in the original listing of the gray wolf.

In this proposed rule, we recognize recent taxonomic information indicating that the gray wolf subspecies Canis lupus lycaon should be elevated to the full species C. lycaon. Given that a complete status review of this newly recognized species has never been conducted, we are initiating a rangewide review of the conservation status of C. lycaon in the United States and Canada. This rule also constitutes the initiation of our five-year review of the status of gray wolves under section 4(c)(2) of the Act, as well as the initiation of status reviews specific to gray wolves in the Pacific Northwest and Mexican wolves in the Southwest United States and Mexico.

DATES: Comment submission: We will accept comments received or postmarked on or before July 5, 2011.

Public hearings: We will hold two public hearings on this proposed rule scheduled on May 18, 2011 and on June 8, 2011. Informational meetings will be held from 6 p.m. to 7:15 p.m., followed by the public hearings from 7:30 p.m. to 9 p.m.

ADDRESSES: Comment submission: You may submit comments by one of the following methods:

Electronically: Go to the Federal eRulemaking Portal: http://www.regulations.gov. In the Enter Keyword or ID box, enter FWS-R3-ES-2011-0029, which is the docket number for this rulemaking. Then, in the Search panel at the top of the screen, under the Document Type heading, click on the Proposed Rules link to locate this document. You may submit a comment by clicking on "Submit a Comment."

By hard copy: Submit by U.S. mail or hand-delivery to: Public Comments Processing, Attn: FWS-R3-ES-2011-0029; Division of Policy and Directives Management; U.S. Fish and Wildlife Service; 4401 N. Fairfax Drive, MS 2042-PDM; Arlington, VA 22203.

We will post all comments on http://www.regulations.gov. This generally means that we will post any personal information you provide us (see the Public Comments section below for more information).

Public hearings: We have scheduled an informational meeting followed by a public hearing in Ashland, Wisconsin, on May 18, 2011, at the Northern Great Lakes Center, 29270 County Highway G. We have scheduled an informational meeting followed by a public hearing in Augusta, Maine, on June 8, 2011, at the Augusta Civic Center, 16 Cony Street. See the Public Hearings section below for more details.

FOR FURTHER INFORMATION CONTACT: Laura Ragan, 612-713-5350. Direct all questions or requests for additional information to: GRAY WOLF QUESTIONS, U.S. Fish and Wildlife Service, Federal Building, 1 Federal Drive, Ft. Snelling, Minnesota 55111-4056. Additional information is also available on our Web site at http://www.fws.gov/midwest/wolf.

Individuals who are hearing-impaired or speech-impaired may call the Federal Relay Service at 1-800-877-8337 for TTY assistance.

The Freedom of Information Act (FOIA)

> The following is from the introductory paragraph to the U.S. Department of Agriculture's FOIA Reference Guide (http://www.dm.usda.gov/foia_guide.htm).

The Freedom of Information Act (FOIA), which can be found in Title 5 of the United States Code, section 552, was enacted in 1966 and provides that any person has the right to request access to federal agency records or information. All agencies of the United States government are required to disclose records upon receiving a written request for them, except for those records that are protected from disclosure by the nine exemptions and three exclusions of the FOIA. This right of access is enforceable in court. The federal FOIA does not, however, provide access to records held by state or local government agencies, or by private businesses or individuals. All states have their own statutes governing public access to state and local records; state agencies should be consulted for further information about them.

Chapter 2
Civil Procedure

Civil Procedure is simply the set of rules that must be followed throughout the life of a civil lawsuit, from its commencement all the way through to the appeals process. There are different rules for criminal procedure, as will be discussed in Chapter 10. Rule 1 of the Federal Rules of Civil Procedure states "[t]he Federal Rules apply generally to all civil actions in the district courts of the United States. Federal courts, and the attorneys who appear before them, are required to construe and administer the Rules in a manner that achieves the just, speedy, and inexpensive determination of each civil action."

This chapter will focus on the Federal Rules of Civil Procedure (http://www.uscourts.gov/uscourts/RulesAndPolicies/rules/2010%20Rules/Civil%20Procedure.pdf), which cover actions in Federal courts. Each state has its own rules of procedure for its state courts, but those rules will generally be similar in nature to the Federal Rules. Attorneys practicing in state and local courts must be well-versed in those state and local rules.

To provide a sense of what is covered in the Federal Rules of Civil Procedure, the eleven titles (or parts) are included below.

Title I.	Scope of Rules; Form of Action
Title II.	Commencing an Action; Service of Process, Pleadings, Motions, And Orders
Title III.	Pleadings and Motions
Title IV.	Parties
Title V.	Disclosures and Discovery
Title VI.	Trials
Title VII.	Judgment
Title VIII.	Provisional and Final Remedies
Title IX.	Special Proceedings
Title X.	District Courts and Clerks: Conducting Business; Issuing Orders
Title XI.	General Provisions

Some particular examples of civil procedure rules include:

- Rule 3, under Title II, which covers the commencement of a lawsuit.
- Rule 4, under Title II, which covers the rules around the service of process.
- Rule 11(b), under Title III, which discusses complaints that are frivolous or filed in bad faith.
- Rule 12(b), under Title III, which discusses certain defenses to a lawsuit, such as improper venue, lack of jurisdiction, and insufficient process.
- Rules 26–37, under Title V, which lay out the rules for discovery, including those for depositions, interrogatories, production of documents and other information, and requests for physical and mental examinations.
- Rule 84, under Title XI, which includes various forms that can be used throughout a Federal civil case. Some examples of these forms are included at the end of this chapter.

The following is a brief overview of the life of a civil lawsuit.

1. **Cause of action.** Simply stated, there must be an issue to sue about. Even though there may be a legitimate cause of action, the plaintiff-to-be must, however, determine whether it is worth his or her time to pursue the case. Can the case be proven? In what court should the suit be filed? How much will it cost? Is the plaintiff willing to settle? Might there be any counterclaims? Does the plaintiff want any information that may come out during the course of the case to not be made public? How much can the plaintiff win? And, if s/he does win, can s/he collect on the judgment? These questions and more should all be considered prior to filing suit.

2. **File a complaint.** Once the decision to sue has been made, the plaintiff needs to file a complaint with the court. The complaint basically lays out the claim(s) or reason(s) for which the defendant is being sued.

3. **Service of process.** This lets the defendant know that a suit has been filed against him or her. Usually a copy of the complaint will be served along with a summons to appear in court.

4. **Defendant responds.** The defendant will have to respond within a certain period of time or risk losing the case by default. The defendant can respond in a variety of ways, including filing a motion to dismiss, filing an answer, and filing a countersuit.

5. **Discovery.** Discovery is a key part in the life of a lawsuit. It is through discovery that evidence can be obtained, that each party can learn information about the other party, that documents can be gathered, etc. Discovery helps both parties to prepare their cases and often reveals and/or provides information that will lead to a settlement of the case. Discovery can take many forms, including interrogatories (a set of written questions), depositions (a process whereby attorneys question parties and witnesses under oath with a court reporter present to record

the testimony), requests for the production of documents, and requests for examinations (to determine the physical and mental condition of a party).

6. **Jury Selection.** If the case has not yet been closed by summary judgment (when there is no dispute as to the facts of the case, the court can make a decision based solely on the pleadings and by applying the applicable law) or through a settlement, a trial date is set, and the case moves forward. If a jury trial has been selected, jury selection will take place. In federal court, the 7th Amendment guarantees the right to a jury trial for a civil case. The right, however, to a jury trial in a civil case has not been applied to states, so parties to a civil suit may not have the right to a jury trial in a particular state. Jury selection includes both the venire and the process of voir dire.

   a. Venire—The venire is simply the list from which potential jurors are drawn. This could include voting registration lists, driver's license lists, etc.

   b. Voir Dire—Voir dire is the process by which the court and the attorneys involved in a case question jurors in order to make the final jury selection. Sample voir dire questions are included at the end of this chapter. Attorneys can dismiss potential jurors through "for cause" challenges (for which they need a reason, such as bias, previous knowledge of the case, knowledge of a party to the case, etc.) or through peremptory challenges (for which they do not need to define a specific reason, although attorneys cannot use race and gender as their reason to use a peremptory challenge). The number of peremptory challenges is limited.

   > If conducted properly, voir dire can inform litigants about potential jurors, making reliance upon stereotypical and pejorative notions about a particular gender or race both unnecessary and unwise. Voir dire provides a means of discovering actual or implied bias and a firmer basis upon which the parties may exercise their peremptory challenges intelligently. *J.E.B v. Alabama*, 511 U.S. 127 (1994).

7. **Trial.** This part of the life of a lawsuit is pretty well-known. Everyone has seen trials on TV and in the movies. Trials include opening and closing statements, presentation of evidence, examination of witnesses, and so on.

8. **Jury Deliberation.** Once the trial ends, the jury receives the case. Prior to the onset of deliberation, the jury receives instructions. Attorneys can propose instructions for the jury, but it will be the judge who decides how to instruct the jury. Generally, the judge will summarize the case, discuss the law to be applied, and explain what the burden of proof is and upon which party that burden falls. The jury must then apply the law, as it has been instructed, to the facts and testimony presented in court.

9. **Post-trial motions.** After the reading of the verdict, attorneys for both parties have several options that they can pursue, including a motion to overturn the jury's verdict and a motion for a new trial. These are discussed under Rule 50 of the Federal Rules.

10. **Judgment.** Judgments will vary depending on the type of case and the outcome being sought by the plaintiff.

11. **Enforcing the judgment.** Just because the court rules in a particular way does not necessarily mean that the plaintiff will get what s/he was awarded. If a plaintiff gets a million dollar judgment against someone without sufficient assets, all s/he has is a moral victory. If a defendant does have assets and s/he refuses to pay, the plaintiff can take action to seize assets in an attempt to recover the damages awarded by the court. If the judgment for the plaintiff is an injunction and the defendant fails to abide by that injunction, the court can sanction the defendant with fines and jail time.

12. **Appeal.** The losing party can appeal to a higher court, assuming there are grounds on which to base an appeal. On appeal, the attorneys file briefs with the appellate court, which discuss the issues at hand. If court rules allow, oral arguments may follow. The appellate decision is based on the record of the case established at trial. No new evidence is presented on an appeal. The appellate court can affirm, reverse, or modify the lower court's ruling based solely on the briefs submitted to it or after hearing the case argued in front of it. Often, a case is remanded to the lower court for further proceedings based on the appellate court's decision.

Service of Process and Personal Jurisdiction–Transient or Tag Jurisdiction

Generally, a person comes under the jurisdiction of a state's courts if s/he is properly served while in that state—even if the person was just visiting or traveling through. If, however, there was fraud or force that caused the person to be in that state, personal jurisdiction will not attach.

> *Wyman v. Newhouse* addresses the issue of fraud in the service of process.

WYMAN v. NEWHOUSE

Circuit Court of Appeals, Second Circuit

93 F.2d 313 (1937)

MANTON, Circuit Judge.

This appeal is from a judgment entered dismissing the complaint on motion before trial. The action is on a judgment entered by default in a Florida state court, a jury having assessed the damages. The recovery there was for money loaned, money advanced for appellee, and for seduction under promise of marriage.

Appellee's answer pleads facts supporting his claim that he was fraudulently enticed into the Florida jurisdiction, appellant's state of residence, for the sole purpose of service of process.

* * *

The affidavits submitted by the appellee deemed to be true for the purpose of testing the alleged error of dismissing the complaint established that he was a resident of New York and never lived in Florida. On October 25, 1935, while appellee was in Salt Lake City, Utah, he received a telegram from the appellant, which read: "Account illness home planning leaving. Please come on way back. Must see you." Upon appellee's return to New York he received a letter from appellant stating that her mother was dying in Ireland; that she was leaving the United States for good to go to her mother; that she could not go without seeing the appellee once more; and that she wanted to discuss her affairs with him before she left. Shortly after the receipt of this letter, they spoke to each other on the telephone, whereupon the appellant repeated, in a hysterical and distressed voice, the substance of her letter. Appellee promised to go to Florida in a week or ten days and agreed to notify her when he would arrive. This he did, but before leaving New York by plane he received a letter couched in endearing terms and expressing love and affection for him, as well as her delight at his coming. Before leaving New York, appellee telegraphed appellant, suggesting arrangements for their accommodations together while in Miami, Fla. She telegraphed him at a hotel in Washington, D. C., where he was to stop en route, advising him that the arrangements requested had been made. Appellee arrived at 6 o'clock in the morning at the Miami Airport and saw the appellant standing with her sister some 75 feet distant. He was met by a deputy sheriff who, upon identifying appellee, served him with process in a suit for $500,000. A photographer was present who attempted to take his picture.

* * *

These facts and reasonable deductions therefrom convincingly establish that the appellee was induced to enter the jurisdiction of the state of Florida by a fraud perpetrated upon him by the appellant in falsely representing her mother's illness, her intention to leave the United States, and her love and affection for him, when her sole purpose and apparent thought was to induce him to come within the Florida jurisdiction so as to serve him in an action for damages. Appellant does not deny making these representations. All her statements of great and undying love were disproved entirely by her appearance at the airport and participation in the happenings there. She never went to Ireland to see her mother, if indeed the latter was sick at all.

* * *

This judgment is attacked for fraud perpetrated upon the appellee which goes to the jurisdiction of the Florida court over his person. A judgment procured fraudulently, as here, lacks jurisdiction and is null and void. *Lucy v. Deas*, 59 Fla. 552, 52 So. 515. *Thompson v. Thompson*, 226 U.S. 551, 33 S.Ct. 129, 57 L.Ed. 347. A fraud affecting the jurisdiction is equivalent to a lack of jurisdiction. *Dunlap & Co. v. Cody*, 31 Iowa 260, 7 Am.Rep. 129; *Duringer v. Moschino*, 93 Ind. 495, 498; *Abercrombie v. Abercrombie*, 64 Kan. 29, 67 P. 539. The appellee was not required to proceed against the judgment in Florida. His equitable defense in answer to a suit on the judgment is sufficient. A judgment recovered in a sister state, through the fraud of the party procuring the appearance of another, is not binding on the latter when an attempt is made to enforce such judgment in another state. *Gray v. Richmond Bicycle Co.*, 167 N.Y. 348, 355, 60 N.E. 663, 82 Am.St.Rep. 720. There is a dictum to the contrary in *Capwell v. Sipe*, 51 F. 667, 668 (C.C.N.D.Ohio), where the defendant was sued in the foreign court while within the jurisdiction attending another case. His objection to service of process was overruled. There is authority to like effect in *Vastine v. Bast*, 41 Mo. 493. But we think the weight of authority is against such view. In *Jaster v. Currie*, 198 U.S. 144, 25 S.Ct. 614, 49 L.Ed. 988, to which appellant refers, the court decided only that the defendant had not been enticed into the jurisdiction by fraud and, therefore, that case is not helpful. *Smith v. Apple*, 6 F.2d 559 (C.C.A.8) and *Cragin v. Lovell*, 109 U.S. 194, 3 S.Ct. 132, 27 L.Ed. 903, deal with irregularities in procedure not voiding the judgment.

The appellee was not required to make out a defense on the merits to the suit in Florida. We are not here concerned with such rule, applicable to alleged fraud in the proceedings after valid jurisdiction of the person and the subject matter has been obtained. Here the court did not duly acquire jurisdiction and no such defense to the merits need be shown. An error made in entering judgment against a party over whom the court had no jurisdiction permits a consideration of the jurisdictional question collaterally. The complaint was properly dismissed.

Judgment affirmed.

> The service of process on an individual while s/he is temporarily within a state is discussed in *Burnham v. Superior Court of California, County of Marin.*

BURNHAM v. SUPERIOR COURT OF CALIFORNIA, COUNTY OF MARIN

Supreme Court of United States (9–0)
495 U.S. 604 (1990)

Justice SCALIA

The question presented is whether the Due Process Clause of the Fourteenth Amendment denies California courts jurisdiction over a nonresident, who was personally served with process while temporarily in that State, in a suit unrelated to his activities in the State.

I

Petitioner Dennis Burnham married Francie Burnham in 1976 in West Virginia. In 1977 the couple moved to New Jersey, where their two children were born. In July 1987 the Burnhams decided to separate. They agreed that Mrs. Burnham, who intended to move to California, would take custody of the children. Shortly before Mrs. Burnham departed for California that same month, she and petitioner agreed that she would file for divorce on grounds of "irreconcilable differences."

In October 1987, petitioner filed for divorce in New Jersey state court on grounds of "desertion." Petitioner did not, however, obtain an issuance of summons against his wife and did not attempt to serve her with process. Mrs. Burnham, after unsuccessfully demanding that petitioner adhere to their prior agreement to submit to an "irreconcilable differences" divorce, brought suit for divorce in California state court in early January 1988.

In late January, petitioner visited southern California on business, after which he went north to visit his children in the San Francisco Bay area, where his wife resided. He took the older child to San Francisco for the weekend. Upon returning the child to Mrs. Burnham's home on January 24, 1988, petitioner was served with a California court summons and a copy of Mrs. Burnham's divorce petition. He then returned to New Jersey.

Later that year, petitioner made a special appearance in the California Superior Court, moving to quash the service of process on the ground that the court lacked personal jurisdiction over him because his only contacts with California were a few short visits to the State for the purposes of conducting business and visiting his children. The Superior Court denied the motion, and the California Court of Appeal denied mandamus relief, rejecting petitioner's contention that the Due Process Clause prohibited California courts from asserting jurisdiction over him because he lacked "minimum contacts" with the State. The court held it to be "a valid jurisdictional predicate for *in personam* jurisdiction" that the "defendant [was] present in the forum state and personally served with process." App. to Pet. for Cert. 5. We granted certiorari. 493 U. S. 807 (1989).

II

A

* * *

The question we must decide today is whether due process requires a similar connection between the litigation and the defendant's contacts with the State in cases where the defendant is physically present in the State at the time process is served upon him.

B

Among the most firmly established principles of personal jurisdiction in American tradition is that the courts of a State have jurisdiction over nonresidents who are physically present in the State. The view developed early that each State had the power to hale before its courts any individual who could be found within its borders, and that once having acquired jurisdiction over such a person by properly serving him with process, the State could retain jurisdiction to enter judgment against him, no matter how fleeting his visit. See, *e. g.*, *Potter v. Allin*, 2 Root 63, 67 (Conn. 1793); *Barrell v. Benjamin*, 15 Mass. 354 (1819). That view had antecedents in English common-law practice, which sometimes allowed "transitory" actions, arising out of events outside the country, to be maintained against seemingly nonresident defendants who were present in England. See, *e. g.*, *Mostyn v. Fabrigas*, 98 Eng. Rep. 1021 (K. B. 1774); *Cartwright v. Pettus*, 22 Eng. Rep. 916 (Ch. 1675). Justice Story believed the principle, which he traced to Roman origins, to be firmly grounded in English tradition: "[B]y the common law[,] personal actions, being transitory, may be brought in any place, where the party defendant may be found," for "every nation may … rightfully exercise jurisdiction over all persons within its domains." J. Story, Commentaries on the Conflict of Laws §§ 554, 543 (1846). See also *id.*, §§ 530-538; *Picquet v. Swan*, *supra*, at 611–612 (Story, J.) ("Where a party is within a territory, he may justly be subjected to its process, and bound personally by the judgment pronounced, on such process, against him").

* * *

Decisions in the courts of many States in the 19th and early 20th centuries held that personal service upon a physically present defendant sufficed to confer jurisdiction, without regard to whether the defendant was only briefly in the State or whether the cause of action was related to his activities there. *** Although research has not revealed a case deciding the issue in every State's courts, that appears to be because the issue was so well settled that it went unlitigated. See R. Leflar, American Conflicts Law § 24, p. 43 (1968) ("The law is so clear on this point that there are few decisions on it"); Note, Developments in the Law—State Court Jurisdiction, 73 Harv. L. Rev. 909, 937-938 (1960). Opinions from the courts of other States announced the rule in dictum. *** Most States, moreover, had statutes or common law rules that exempted from service of process individuals who were brought into the forum by force or fraud, see, *e. g.*, *Wanzer v. Bright*, 52 Ill. 35 (1869), or who were there as a party or witness in unrelated judicial proceedings, see, *e. g.*, *Burroughs v. Cocke & Willis*, 56 Okla. 627, 156 P. 196 (1916); *Malloy v. Brewer*, 7 S. D. 587, 64 N. W. 1120 (1895). These exceptions obviously rested upon the premise that service of process conferred jurisdiction. See *Anderson v. Atkins*, 161 Tenn. 137, 140, 29 S. W. 2d 248, 249 (1930). Particularly striking is the fact that, as far as we have been able to determine, *not one* American case from the period (or, for that matter, not one American case until 1978) held, or even suggested, that in-state personal service on an individual was insufficient to confer personal jurisdiction. Commentators were also seemingly unanimous on the rule. ***

This American jurisdictional practice is, moreover, not merely old; it is continuing. It remains the practice of, not only a substantial number of the States, but as far as we are aware *all* the States and the Federal Government—if one disregards (as one must for this purpose) the few opinions since 1978 that have erroneously said, on grounds similar to those that petitioner presses here, that this Court's due process decisions render the practice unconstitutional. *** We do not know of a single state or federal statute, or a single judicial decision resting upon state law, that has abandoned in-state service as a basis of jurisdiction. Many recent cases reaffirm it. ***

C

Despite this formidable body of precedent, petitioner contends, in reliance on our decisions applying the *International Shoe* standard, that in the absence of "continuous and systematic" contacts with the forum, see n. 1, *supra*, a nonresident defendant can be subjected to judgment only as to matters that arise out of or relate to his contacts with the forum. This argument rests on a thorough misunderstanding of our cases.

* * *

The short of the matter is that jurisdiction based on physical presence alone constitutes due process because it is one of the continuing traditions of our legal system that define the due process standard of "traditional notions of fair play and substantial justice."

* * *

Because the Due Process Clause does not prohibit the California courts from exercising jurisdiction over petitioner based on the fact of in-state service of process, the judgment is

Affirmed.

[Footnotes Omitted.]

Personal (In Personam) Jurisdiction

In order for a court to hear a case, the court needs to have appropriate jurisdiction over the defendant. The cases in the previous section discuss jurisdiction over a person when that person is served with process while physically in the particular state in which a case has been filed. What happens, however, if a case is brought in a particular state and the defendant is not physically in that state to be served? Can a court attain jurisdiction over that defendant? The following cases lay out the rules for establishing in personam jurisdiction in such situations.

International Shoe is an important case in the history of determining a court's ability to maintain jurisdiction over a defendant. This case lays out the foundation upon which future jurisdiction cases were decided.

INTERNATIONAL SHOE CO. v. WASHINGTON

Supreme Court of the United States

326 U.S. 310 (1945)

Mr. Chief Justice STONE delivered the opinion of the Court.

The questions for decision are (1) whether, within the limitations of the due process clause of the Fourteenth Amendment, appellant, a Delaware corporation, has by its activities in the State of Washington rendered itself amenable to proceedings in the courts of that state to recover unpaid contributions to the state unemployment compensation fund exacted by state statutes, Washington Unemployment Compensation Act, Washington Revised Statutes, § 9998-103a through § 9998-123a, 1941 Supp., and (2) whether the state can exact those contributions consistently with the due process clause of the Fourteenth Amendment.

* * *

The facts as found by the appeal tribunal and accepted by the state Superior Court and Supreme Court, are not in dispute. Appellant is a Delaware corporation, having its principal place of business in St. Louis, Missouri, and is engaged in the manufacture and sale of shoes and other footwear. It maintains places of business in several states, other than Washington, at which its manufacturing is carried on and from which its merchandise is distributed interstate through several sales units or branches located outside the State of Washington.

Appellant has no office in Washington and makes no contracts either for sale or purchase of merchandise there. It maintains no stock of merchandise in that state and makes there no deliveries of goods in intrastate commerce. During the years from 1937 to 1940, now in question, appellant employed eleven to thirteen salesmen under direct supervision and control of sales managers located in St. Louis. These salesmen resided in Washington; their principal activities were confined to that state; and they were compensated by commissions based upon the amount of their sales. The commissions for each year totaled more than $31,000. Appellant supplies its salesmen with a line of samples, each consisting of one shoe of a pair, which they display to prospective purchasers. On occasion they rent permanent sample rooms, for exhibiting samples, in business buildings, or rent rooms in hotels or business buildings temporarily for that purpose. The cost of such rentals is reimbursed by appellant.

The authority of the salesmen is limited to exhibiting their samples and soliciting orders from prospective buyers, at prices and on terms fixed by appellant. The salesmen transmit the orders to appellant's office in St. Louis for acceptance or rejection, and when accepted the merchandise for filling the orders is shipped f.o.b. from points outside Washington to the purchasers within the state. All the merchandise shipped into Washington is invoiced at the place of shipment from which collections are made. No salesman has authority to enter into contracts or to make collections.

The Supreme Court of Washington was of opinion that the regular and systematic solicitation of orders in the state by appellant's salesmen, resulting in a continuous flow of appellant's product into the state, was sufficient to constitute doing business in the state so as to make appellant amenable to suit in its courts. But it was also of opinion that there were sufficient additional activities shown to bring the case within the rule frequently stated, that solicitation within a state by the agents of a foreign corporation plus some additional activities there are sufficient to render the corporation amenable to suit brought in the courts of the state to enforce an obligation arising out of its activities there. *** The court found such additional activities in the salesmen's display of samples sometimes in permanent display rooms, and the salesmen's residence within the state, continued over a period of years, all resulting in a substantial volume of merchandise regularly shipped by appellant to purchasers within the state. The court also held that the statute as applied did not invade the constitutional power of Congress to regulate interstate commerce and did not impose a prohibited burden on such commerce.

* * *

Appellant also insists that its activities within the state were not sufficient to manifest its 'presence' there and that in its absence the state courts were without jurisdiction, that consequently it was a denial of due process for the state to subject appellant to suit. It refers to those cases in which it was said that the mere solicitation of orders for the purchase of goods within a state, to be accepted without the state and filled by shipment of the purchased goods interstate, does not render the corporation seller amenable to suit within the state. ***And appellant further argues that since it was not present within the state, it is a denial of due process to subject it to taxation or other money exaction. It thus denies the power of the state to lay the tax or to subject appellant to a suit for its collection.

Historically the jurisdiction of courts to render judgment in personam is grounded on their de facto power over the defendant's person. Hence his presence within the territorial jurisdiction of court was prerequisite to its rendition of a judgment personally binding him. *Pennoyer v. Neff*, 95 U.S. 714, 733, 24 L.Ed. 565. But now that the *capias ad respondendum* has given way to personal service of summons or other form of notice, due process requires only that in order to subject a defendant to a judgment in personam, if he be not present within the territory of the forum, he have certain minimum contacts with it such that the maintenance of the suit does not offend 'traditional notions of fair play and substantial justice.'

* * *

Since the corporate personality is a fiction, although a fiction intended to be acted upon as though it were a fact, *Klein v. Board of Tax Supervisors*, 282 U.S. 19, 24, 51 S.Ct. 15, 16, 75 L.Ed. 140, 73 A.L.R. 679, it is clear that unlike an individual its 'presence' without, as well as within, the state of its origin can be manifested only by activities carried on in its behalf by those who are authorized to act for it. To say that the corporation is so far 'present' there as to satisfy due process requirements, for purposes of taxation or the maintenance of suits against it in the courts of the state, is to beg the question to be decided. For the terms 'present' or 'presence' are used merely to symbolize those activities of the corporation's agent within the state which courts will deem to be sufficient to satisfy the demands of due process. L. Hand, J., in *Hutchinson v. Chase & Gilbert*, 2 Cir., 45 F.2d 139, 141. Those demands may be met by such contacts of the corporation with the state of the forum as make it reasonable, in the context of our federal system of government, to require the corporation to defend the particular suit which is brought there. An 'estimate of the inconveniences' which would result to the corporation from a trial away from its 'home' or principal place of business is relevant in this connection. *Hutchinson v. Chase & Gilbert, supra*, 45 F.2d 141.

'Presence' in the state in this sense has never been doubted when the activities of the corporation there have not only been continuous and systematic, but also give rise to the liabilities sued on, even though no consent to be sued or authorization to an agent to accept service of process has been given. *** Conversely it has been generally recognized that the casual presence of the corporate agent or even his conduct of single or isolated items of activities in a state in the corporation's behalf are not enough to subject it to suit on causes of action unconnected with the activities there. *** To require the corporation in such circumstances to defend the suit away from its home or other jurisdiction where it carries on more substantial activities has been thought to lay too great and unreasonable a burden on the corporation to comport with due process.

While it has been held in cases on which appellant relies that continuous activity of some sorts within a state is not enough to support the demand that the corporation be amenable to suits unrelated to that activity, *** there have been instances in which the continuous corporate operations within a state were thought so substantial and of such a nature as to justify suit against it on causes of action arising from dealings entirely distinct from those activities. ***

Finally, although the commission of some single or occasional acts of the corporate agent in a state sufficient to impose an obligation or liability on the corporation has not been thought to confer upon the state authority to enforce it, *Rosenberg Bros. & Co. v. Curtis Brown Co.*, 260 U.S. 516, 43 S.Ct. 170, 67 L.Ed. 372, other such acts, because of their nature and quality and the circumstances of their commission, may be deemed sufficient to render the corporation liable to suit. *Cf. Kane v. New Jersey*, 242 U.S. 160, 37 S.Ct. 30, 61 L.Ed. 222; *Hess v. Pawloski, supra*; *Young v. Masci, supra*. True, some of the decisions holding the corporation amenable to suit have been supported by resort to the legal fiction that it has given its consent to service and suit, consent being implied from its presence in the state through the acts of its authorized agents. ***

It is evident that the criteria by which we mark the boundary line between those activities which justify the subjection of a corporation to suit, and those which do not, cannot be simply mechanical or quantitative. The test is not merely, as has sometimes been suggested, whether the activity, which the corporation has seen fit to procure through its agents in another state, is a little more or a little less. *** Whether due process is satisfied must depend rather upon the quality and nature of the activity in relation to the fair and orderly administration of the laws which it was the purpose of the due process clause to insure. That clause does not contemplate that a state may make binding a judgment in personam against an individual or corporate defendant with which the state has no contacts, ties, or relations. *Cf. Pennoyer v. Neff, supra*; *Minnesota Commercial Men's Ass'n v. Benn*, 261 U.S. 140, 43 S.Ct. 293, 67 L.Ed. 573.

But to the extent that a corporation exercises the privilege of conducting activities within a state, it enjoys the benefits and protection of the laws of that state. The exercise of that privilege may give rise to obligations; and, so far as those obligations arise out of or are connected with the activities within the state, a procedure which requires the corporation to respond to a suit brought to enforce them can, in most instances, hardly be said to be undue. ***

Applying these standards, the activities carried on in behalf of appellant in the State of Washington were neither irregular nor casual. They were systematic and continuous throughout the years in question. They resulted in a large volume of interstate business, in the course of which appellant received the benefits and protection of the laws of the state, including the right to resort to the courts for the enforcement of its rights. The obligation which is here sued upon arose out of those very activities. It is evident that these operations establish sufficient contacts or ties with the state of the forum to make it reasonable and just according to our traditional conception of fair play and substantial justice to permit the state to enforce the obligations which appellant has incurred there. Hence we cannot say that the maintenance of the present suit in the State of Washington involves an unreasonable or undue procedure.

We are likewise unable to conclude that the service of the process within the state upon an agent whose activities establish appellant's 'presence' there was not sufficient notice of the suit, or that the suit was so unrelated to those activities as to make the agent an inappropriate vehicle for communicating the notice. It is enough that appellant has established such contacts with the state that the particular form of substituted service adopted there gives reasonable assurance that the notice will be actual.

* * *

Nor can we say that the mailing of the notice of suit to appellant by registered mail at its home office was not reasonably calculated to apprise appellant of the suit.

* * *

Affirmed.

In the following case, *Kulko v. Superior Court of California*, Ezra Kulko was a citizen of New York. Kulko allowed his children, who lived with him, to move to California to live with their mother, Kulko's ex-wife, Sharon. Sharon filed a suit in California regarding the divorce, custody, and support. In this case, the Court examines whether California court has jurisdiction over Ezra. Contrast this to the *Burnham* case.

KULKO v. SUPERIOR COURT OF CALIFORNIA

Supreme Court of the United States (6-3)
436 U.S. 84 (1978)

MR. JUSTICE MARSHALL delivered the opinion of the Court.

The issue before us is whether, in this action for child support, the California state courts may exercise *in personam* jurisdiction over a nonresident, nondomiciliary parent of minor children domiciled within the State. For reasons set forth below, we hold that the exercise of such jurisdiction would violate the Due Process Clause of the Fourteenth Amendment.

* * *

II

The Due Process Clause of the Fourteenth Amendment operates as a limitation on the jurisdiction of state courts to enter judgments affecting rights or interests of nonresident defendants.

* * *

A

* * *

Finally, in holding that personal jurisdiction existed, the court below carefully disclaimed reliance on the fact that appellant had agreed at the time of separation to allow his children to live with their mother three months a year and that he had sent them to California each year pursuant to this agreement. As was noted below, 19 Cal. 3d, at 523-524, 564 P. 2d, at 357, to find personal jurisdiction in a State on this basis, merely because the mother was residing there, would discourage parents from entering into reasonable visitation agreements. Moreover, it could arbitrarily subject one parent to suit in any State of the Union where the other parent chose to spend time while having custody of their offspring pursuant to a separation agreement. As we have emphasized:

"The unilateral activity of those who claim some relationship with a nonresident defendant cannot satisfy the requirement of contact with the forum State ... [I]t is essential in each case that there be some act by which the defendant purposefully avails [him]self of the privilege of conducting activities within the forum State ..." *Hanson v. Denckla*, *supra*, at 253.

The "purposeful act" that the California Supreme Court believed did warrant the exercise of personal jurisdiction over appellant in California was his "actively and fully consent[ing] to Ilsa living in California for the school year ... and ... sen[ding] her to California for that purpose." *** We cannot accept the proposition that appellant's acquiescence in Ilsa's desire to live with her mother conferred jurisdiction over appellant in the California courts in this action. A father who agrees, in the interests of family harmony and his children's preferences, to allow them to spend more time in California than was required under a separation agreement can hardly be said to have "purposefully availed himself" of the "benefits and protections" of California's laws. ***

* * *

B

* * *

The circumstances in this case clearly render "unreasonable" California's assertion of personal jurisdiction. There is no claim that appellant has visited physical injury on either property or persons within the State of California. Cf. *Hess v. Pawloski*, 274 U. S. 352 (1927). The cause of action herein asserted arises, not from the defendant's commercial transactions in interstate commerce, but rather from his personal, domestic relations. It thus cannot be said that appellant has sought a commercial benefit from solicitation of business from a resident of California that could reasonably render him liable to suit in state court; appellant's activities cannot fairly be analogized to an insurer's sending an insurance contract and premium notices into the State to an insured resident of the State. Cf. *McGee v. International Life Insurance Co.*, 355 U. S. 220 (1957). Furthermore, the controversy between the parties arises from a separation that occurred in the State of New York; appellee Horn seeks modification of a contract that was negotiated in New York and that she flew to New York to sign. As in *Hanson v. Denckla*, 357 U. S., at 252, the instant action involves an agreement that wa s entered into with virtually no connection with the forum State. See also n. 6, *supra*.

Finally, basic considerations of fairness point decisively in favor of appellant's State of domicile as the proper forum for adjudication of this case, whatever the merits of appellee's underlying claim. It is appellant who has remained in the State of the marital domicile, whereas it is appellee who has moved across the continent. Cf. *May v. Anderson*, 345 U. S. 528, 534-535, n. 8 (1953). Appellant has at all times resided in New York State, and, until the separation and appellee's move to California, his entire family resided there as well. As noted above, appellant did no more than acquiesce in the stated preference of one of his children to live with her mother in California. This single act is surely not one that a reasonable parent would expect to result in the substantial financial burden and personal strain of litigating a child-support suit in a forum 3,000 miles away, and we therefore see no basis on which it can be said that appellant could reasonably have anticipated being "haled before a [California] court," *Shaffer v. Heitner*, 433 U. S., at 216. To make jurisdiction in a case such as this turn on whether appellant bought his daughter her ticket or instead unsuccessfully sought to prevent her departure would impose an unreasonable burden on family relations, and one wholly unjustified by the "quality and nature" of appellant's activities in or relating to the State of California. *International Shoe Co. v. Washington*, 326 U. S., at 319.

* * *

IV

We therefore believe that the state courts in the instant case failed to heed our admonition that "the flexible standard of *International Shoe*" does not "heral[d] the eventual demise of all restrictions on the personal jurisdiction of state courts." *Hanson v. Denckla*, 357 U. S., at 251. In *McGee v. International Life Ins. Co.*, we commented on the extension of *in personam* jurisdiction under evolving standards of due process, explaining that this trend was in large part "attributable to the … increasing nationalization of commerce … [accompanied by] modern transportation and communication [that] have made it much less burdensome for a party sued to defend himself in a State where he engages in economic activity." 355 U. S., at 222–223. But the mere act of sending a child to California to live with her mother is not a commercial act and connotes no intent to obtain or expectancy of receiving a corresponding benefit in the State that would make fair the assertion of that State's judicial jurisdiction.

Accordingly, we conclude that the appellant's motion to quash service, on the ground of lack of personal jurisdiction, was erroneously denied by the California courts. The judgment of the California Supreme Court is, therefore,

Reversed.

[Footnotes Omitted.]

Asahi builds on the principles first outlined in *International Shoe.* It involves a Japanese company, without ties to California, that faced suit in California for defective tire valves. Should jurisdiction be imposed on Asahi Metal?

ASAHI METAL INDUSTRY CO., LTD. v. SUPERIOR COURT OF CALIFORNIA, SOLANO COUNTY

Supreme Court of the United States (9–0)
480 U.S. 102 (1987)

Justice O'CONNOR

This case presents the question whether the mere awareness on the part of a foreign defendant that the components it manufactured, sold, and delivered outside the United States would reach the forum State in the stream of commerce constitutes "minimum contacts" between the defendant and the forum State such that the exercise of jurisdiction "does not offend 'traditional notions of fair play and substantial justice.'" *International Shoe Co. v. Washington*, 326 U.S. 310, 316, 66 S.Ct. 154, 158, 90 L.Ed. 95 (1945), quoting *Milliken v. Meyer*, 311 U.S. 457, 463, 61 S.Ct. 339, 342, 85 L.Ed. 278 (1940).

I

On September 23, 1978, on Interstate Highway 80 in Solano County, California, Gary Zurcher lost control of his Honda motorcycle and collided with a tractor. Zurcher was severely injured, and his passenger and wife, Ruth Ann Moreno, was killed. In September 1979, Zurcher filed a product liability action in the Superior Court of the State of California in and for the County of Solano. Zurcher alleged that the 1978 accident was caused by a sudden loss of air and an explosion in the rear tire of the motorcycle, and alleged that the motorcycle tire, tube, and sealant were defective. Zurcher's complaint named, *inter alia*, Cheng Shin Rubber Industrial Co., Ltd. (Cheng Shin), the Taiwanese manufacturer of the tube. Cheng Shin in turn filed a cross-complaint seeking indemnification from its codefendants and from petitioner, Asahi Metal Industry Co., Ltd. (Asahi), the manufacturer of the tube's valve assembly. Zurcher's claims against Cheng Shin and the other defendants were eventually settled and dismissed, leaving only Cheng Shin's indemnity action against Asahi.

* * *

In relation to the motion, the following information was submitted by Asahi and Cheng Shin. Asahi is a Japanese corporation. It manufactures tire valve assemblies in Japan and sells the assemblies to Cheng Shin, and to several other tire manufacturers, for use as components in finished tire tubes. Asahi's sales to Cheng Shin took place in Taiwan. The shipments from Asahi to Cheng Shin were sent from Japan to Taiwan. Cheng Shin bought and incorporated into its tire tubes 150,000 Asahi valve assemblies in 1978; 500,000 in 1979; 500,000 in 1980; 100,000 in 1981; and 100,000 in 1982. Sales to Cheng Shin accounted for 1.24 percent of Asahi's income in 1981 and 0.44 percent in 1982. Cheng Shin alleged that approximately 20 percent of its sales in the United States are in California. Cheng Shin purchases valve assemblies from other suppliers as well, and sells finished tubes throughout the world.

*** An affidavit of a manager of Cheng Shin whose duties included the purchasing of component parts stated: " 'In discussions with Asahi regarding the purchase of valve stem assemblies the fact that my Company sells tubes throughout the world and specifically the United States has been discussed. I am informed and believe that Asahi was fully aware that valve stem assemblies sold to my Company and to others would end up throughout the United States and in California.'" 39 Cal.3d 35, 48, n. 4, 216 Cal.Rptr. 385, 392, n. 4, 702 P.2d 543, 549-550, n. 4 (1985). An affidavit of the president of Asahi, on the other hand, declared that Asahi " 'has never contemplated that its limited sales of tire valves to Cheng Shin in Taiwan would subject it to lawsuits in California.'" *Ibid*. The record does not include any contract between Cheng Shin and Asahi. Tr. of Oral Arg. 24.

* * *

II

A

The Due Process Clause of the Fourteenth Amendment limits the power of a state court to exert personal jurisdiction over a nonresident defendant. "[T]he constitutional touchstone" of the determination whether an exercise of personal jurisdiction comports with due process "remains whether the defendant purposefully established 'minimum contacts' in the forum State." *** Most recently we have reaffirmed the oft-quoted reasoning of *Hanson v. Denckla*, 357 U.S. 235, 253, 78 S.Ct. 1228, 1239, 2 L.Ed.2d 1283 (1958), that minimum contacts must have a basis in "some act by which the defendant purposefully avails itself of the privilege of conducting activities within the forum State, thus invoking the benefits and protections of its laws." *Burger King*, 471 U.S., at 475, 105 S.Ct., at 2183. "Jurisdiction is proper … where the contacts proximately result from actions by the defendant *himself* that create a 'substantial connection' with the forum State." *Ibid.*, quoting *McGee v. International Life Insurance Co.*, 355 U.S. 220, 223, 78 S.Ct. 199, 201, 2 L.Ed.2d 223 (1957) (emphasis in original).

Applying the principle that minimum contacts must be based on an act of the defendant, the Court in *World-Wide Volkswagen Corp. v. Woodson*, 444 U.S. 286, 100 S.Ct. 559, 62 L.Ed.2d 490 (1980) [*Author's note: In World-Wide Volkswagen, the plaintiffs bought a car in New York from World-Wide (a New York Corporation),were injured in an accident in Oklahoma, and filed a products-liability suit in Oklahoma.*] rejected the assertion that a *consumer's* unilateral act of bringing the defendant's product into the forum State was a sufficient constitutional basis for personal jurisdiction over the defendant. It had been argued in *World-Wide Volkswagen* that because an automobile retailer and its wholesale distributor sold a product mobile by design and purpose, they could foresee being haled into court in the distant States into which their customers might drive. The Court rejected this concept of foreseeability as an insufficient basis for jurisdiction under the Due Process Clause. *Id.*, at 295–296, 100 S.Ct., at 566. The Court disclaimed, however, the idea that "foreseeability is wholly irrelevant" to personal jurisdiction, concluding that "[t]he forum State does not exceed its powers under the Due Process Clause if it asserts personal jurisdiction over a corporation that delivers its products into the stream of commerce with the expectation that they will be purchased by consumers in the forum State." *Id.*, at 297–298, 100 S.Ct., at 567 (citation omitted). The Court reasoned:

"When a corporation 'purposefully avails itself of the privilege of conducting activities within the forum State,' *Hanson v. Denckla*, 357 U.S. [235,] 253 [78 S.Ct. 1228, 1239, 2 L.Ed.2d 1283 (1958)], it has clear notice that it is subject to suit there, and can act to alleviate the risk of burdensome litigation by procuring insurance, passing the expected costs on to customers, or, if the risks are too great, severing its connection with the State. Hence if the sale of a product of a manufacturer or distributor … is not simply an isolated occurrence, but arises from the efforts of the manufacturer or distributor to serve, directly or indirectly, the market for its product in other States, it is not unreasonable to subject it to suit in one of those States if its allegedly defective merchandise has there been the source of injury to its owners or to others." *Id.*, at 297, 100 S.Ct., at 567.

In *World-Wide Volkswagen* itself, the state court sought to base jurisdiction not on any act of the defendant, but on the foreseeable unilateral actions of the consumer. Since *World-Wide Volkswagen*, lower courts have been confronted with cases in which the defendant acted by placing a product in the stream of commerce, and the stream eventually swept defendant's product into the forum State, but the defendant did nothing else to purposefully avail itself of the market in the forum State. Some courts have understood the Due Process Clause, as interpreted in *World-Wide Volkswagen*, to allow an exercise of personal jurisdiction to be based on no more than the defendant's act of placing the product in the stream of commerce. Other courts have understood the Due Process Clause and the above-quoted language in *World-Wide Volkswagen* to require the action of the defendant to be more purposefully directed at the forum State than the mere act of placing a product in the stream of commerce.

The reasoning of the Supreme Court of California in the present case illustrates the former interpretation of *World-Wide Volkswagen*. The Supreme Court of California held that, because the stream of commerce eventually brought some valves Asahi sold Cheng Shin into California, Asahi's awareness that its valves would be sold in California was sufficient to permit California to exercise jurisdiction over Asahi consistent with the requirements of the Due Process Clause. The Supreme Court of California's position was consistent with those courts that have held that mere foreseeability or awareness was a constitutionally sufficient basis for personal jurisdiction if the defendant's product made its way into the forum State while still in the stream of commerce. See *Bean Dredging Corp. v. Dredge Technology Corp.*, 744 F.2d 1081 (CA5 1984); *Hedrick v. Daiko Shoji Co.*, 715 F.2d 1355 (CA9 1983).

* * *

***The "substantial connection," *Burger King*, 471 U.S., at 475, 105 S.Ct., at 2184; *McGee*, 355 U.S., at 223, 78 S.Ct., at 201, between the defendant and the forum State necessary for a finding of minimum contacts must come about by *an action of the defendant purposefully directed toward the forum State*. *Burger King, supra*, 471 U.S., at 476, 105 S.Ct., at 2184; *Keeton v. Hustler Magazine, Inc.*, 465 U.S. 770, 774, 104 S.Ct. 1473, 1478, 79 L.Ed.2d 790 (1984). The placement of a product into the stream of commerce, without more, is not an act of the defendant purposefully directed toward the forum State. Additional conduct of the defendant may indicate an intent or purpose to serve the market in the forum State, for example, designing the product for the market in the forum State, advertising in the forum State, establishing channels for providing regular advice to customers in the forum State, or marketing the product through a distributor who has agreed to serve as the sales agent in the forum State. But a defendant's awareness that the stream of commerce may or will sweep the product into the forum State does not convert the mere act of placing the product into the stream into an act purposefully directed toward the forum State.

Assuming, *arguendo*, that respondents have established Asahi's awareness that some of the valves sold to Cheng Shin would be incorporated into tire tubes sold in California, respondents have not demonstrated any action by Asahi to purposefully avail itself of the California market. Asahi does not do business in California. It has no office, agents, employees, or property in California. It does not advertise or otherwise solicit business in California. It did not create, control, or employ the distribution system that brought its valves to California. Cf. *Hicks v. Kawasaki Heavy Industries*, 452 F.Supp. 130 (MD Pa.1978). There is no evidence that Asahi designed its product in anticipation of sales in California. Cf. *Rockwell International Corp. v. Costruzioni Aeronautiche Giovanni Agusta*, 553 F.Supp. 328 (ED Pa.1982). On the basis of these facts, the exertion of personal jurisdiction over Asahi by the Superior Court of California exceeds the limits of due process.

B

The strictures of the Due Process Clause forbid a state court to exercise personal jurisdiction over Asahi under circumstances that would offend " 'traditional notions of fair play and substantial justice.' " *International Shoe Co. v. Washington*, 326 U.S., at 316, 66 S.Ct., at 158; quoting *Milliken v. Meyer*, 311 U.S., at 463, 61 S.Ct., at 342.

We have previously explained that the determination of the reasonableness of the exercise of jurisdiction in each case will depend on an evaluation of several factors. A court must consider the burden on the defendant, the interests of the forum State, and the plaintiff's interest in obtaining relief. It must also weigh in its determination "the interstate judicial system's interest in obtaining the most efficient resolution of controversies; and the shared interest of the several States in furthering fundamental substantive social policies." *World-Wide Volkswagen*, 444 U.S., at 292, 100 S.Ct., at 564 (citations omitted).

A consideration of these factors in the present case clearly reveals the unreasonableness of the assertion of jurisdiction over Asahi, even apart from the question of the placement of goods in the stream of commerce.

Certainly the burden on the defendant in this case is severe. Asahi has been commanded by the Supreme Court of California not only to traverse the distance between Asahi's headquarters in Japan and the Superior Court of California in and for the County of Solano, but also to submit its dispute with Cheng Shin to a foreign nation's judicial system. The unique burdens placed upon one who must defend oneself in a foreign legal system should have significant weight in assessing the reasonableness of stretching the long arm of personal jurisdiction over national borders.

When minimum contacts have been established, often the interests of the plaintiff and the forum in the exercise of jurisdiction will justify even the serious burdens placed on the alien defendant. In the present case, however, the interests of the plaintiff and the forum in California's assertion of jurisdiction over Asahi are slight. All that remains is a claim for indemnification asserted by Cheng Shin, a Taiwanese corporation, against Asahi. The transaction on which the indemnification claim is based took place in Taiwan; Asahi's components were shipped from Japan to Taiwan. Cheng Shin has not demonstrated that it is more convenient for it to litigate its indemnification claim against Asahi in California rather than in Taiwan or Japan.

Because the plaintiff is not a California resident, California's legitimate interests in the dispute have considerably diminished. The Supreme Court of California argued that the State had an interest in "protecting its consumers by ensuring that foreign manufacturers comply with the state's safety standards." 39 Cal.3d, at 49, 216 Cal.Rptr., at 392, 702 P.2d, at 550. The State Supreme Court's definition of California's interest, however, was overly broad. The dispute between Cheng Shin and Asahi is primarily about indemnification rather than safety standards. Moreover, it is not at all clear at this point that California law should govern the question whether a Japanese corporation should indemnify a Taiwanese corporation on the basis of a sale made in Taiwan and a shipment of goods from Japan to Taiwan. *** The possibility of being haled into a California court as a result of an accident involving Asahi's components undoubtedly creates an additional deterrent to the manufacture of unsafe components; however, similar pressures will be placed on Asahi by the purchasers of its components as long as those who use Asahi components in their final products, and sell those products in California, are subject to the application of California tort law.

World-Wide Volkswagen also admonished courts to take into consideration the interests of the "several States," in addition to the forum State, in the efficient judicial resolution of the dispute and the advancement of substantive policies. In the present case, this advice calls for a court to consider the procedural and substantive policies of other *nations* whose interests are affected by the assertion of jurisdiction by the California court. The procedural and substantive interests of other nations in a state court's assertion of jurisdiction over an alien defendant will differ from case to case. In every case, however, those interests, as well as the Federal interest in Government's foreign relations policies, will be best served by a careful inquiry into the reasonableness of the assertion of jurisdiction in the particular case, and an unwillingness to find the serious burdens on an alien defendant outweighed by minimal interests on the part of the plaintiff or the forum State. "Great care and reserve should be exercised when extending our notions of personal jurisdiction into the international field." *United States v. First National City Bank,* 379 U.S. 378, 404, 85 S.Ct. 528, 542, 13 L.Ed.2d 365 (1965) (Harlan, J., dissenting). See Born, Reflections on Judicial Jurisdiction in International Cases, to be published in 17 Ga.J. Int'l & Comp. L. 1 (1987).

Considering the international context, the heavy burden on the alien defendant, and the slight interests of the plaintiff and the forum State, the exercise of personal jurisdiction by a California court over Asahi in this instance would be unreasonable and unfair.

III

Because the facts of this case do not establish minimum contacts such that the exercise of personal jurisdiction is consistent with fair play and substantial justice, the judgment of the Supreme Court of California is reversed, and the case is remanded for further proceedings not inconsistent with this opinion.

It is so ordered.

[Footnotes omitted.]

In *Calder v. Jones*, the actress Shirley Jones filed a libel claim against the defendants for an article that appeared in the National Enquirer. Jones sued in California. The defendants were Florida residents. Should in personam jurisdiction apply to the defendants?

CALDER v. JONES

Supreme Court of the United States (9–0)
465 U.S. 783 (1984)

Justice REHNQUIST delivered the opinion of the Court.

Respondent Shirley Jones brought suit in California Superior Court claiming that she had been libeled in an article written and edited by petitioners in Florida. The article was published in a national magazine with a large circulation in California. Petitioners were served with process by mail in Florida and caused special appearances to be entered on their behalf, moving to quash the service of process for lack of personal jurisdiction. The superior court granted the motion on the ground that First Amendment concerns weighed against an assertion of jurisdiction otherwise proper under the Due Process Clause. The California Court of Appeal reversed, rejecting the suggestion that First Amendment considerations enter into the jurisdictional analysis. We now affirm.

Respondent lives and works in California. She and her husband brought this suit against the National Enquirer, Inc., its local distributing company, and petitioners for libel, invasion of privacy, and intentional infliction of emotional harm. The Enquirer is a Florida corporation with its principal place of business in Florida. It publishes a national weekly newspaper with a total circulation of over 5 million. About 600,000 of those copies, almost twice the level of the next highest State, are sold in California. Respondent's and her husband's claims were based on an article that appeared in the Enquirer's October 9, 1979 issue. Both the Enquirer and the distributing company answered the complaint and made no objection to the jurisdiction of the California court.

Petitioner South is a reporter employed by the Enquirer. He is a resident of Florida, though he frequently travels to California on business. South wrote the first draft of the challenged article, and his byline appeared on it. He did most of his research in Florida, relying on phone calls to sources in California for the information contained in the article. Shortly before publication, South called respondent's home and read to her husband a draft of the article so as to elicit his comments upon it. Aside from his frequent trips and phone calls, South has no other relevant contacts with California.

Petitioner Calder is also a Florida resident. He has been to California only twice—once, on a pleasure trip, prior to the publication of the article and once after to testify in an unrelated trial. Calder is president and editor of the Enquirer. He "oversee[s] just about every function of the Enquirer." *J.A.*, at 24. He reviewed and approved the initial evaluation of the subject of the article and edited it in its final form. He also declined to print a retraction requested by respondent. Calder has no other relevant contacts with California.

* * *

The allegedly libelous story concerned the California activities of a California resident. It impugned the professionalism of an entertainer whose television career was centered in California. The article was drawn from California sources, and the brunt of the harm, in terms both of respondent's emotional distress and the injury to her professional reputation, was suffered in California. In sum, California is the focal point both of the story and of the harm suffered. Jurisdiction over petitioners is therefore proper in California based on the "effects" of their Florida conduct in California. *World-Wide Volkswagen Corp. v. Woodson*, 444 U.S. 286, 297-298, 100 S.Ct. 559, 567–568, 62 L.Ed.2d 490 (1980); Restatement (Second) of Conflicts of Law § 37.

Petitioners argue that they are not responsible for the circulation of the article in California. A reporter and an editor, they claim, have no direct economic stake in their employer's sales in a distant State. Nor are ordinary employees able to control their employer's marketing activity. The mere fact that they can "foresee" that the article will be circulated and have an effect in California is not sufficient for an assertion of jurisdiction. *World-Wide Volkswagen Corp. v. Woodson*, 444 U.S., at 295, 100 S.Ct., at 566; *Rush v. Savchuk*, 444 U.S., at 328–329, 100 S.Ct., at 577–578. They do not "in effect appoint the [article their] agent for service of process." *World-Wide Volkswagen Corp. v. Woodson*, 444 U.S., at 296, 100 S.Ct., at 566. Petitioners liken themselves to a welder employed in Florida who works on a boiler which subsequently explodes in California. Cases which hold that jurisdiction will be proper over the manufacturer, *Buckeye Boiler Co. v. Superior Court*, 71 Cal.2d 893, 80 Cal.Rptr. 113, 458 P.2d 57 (1969); *Gray v. American Radiator & Standard Sanitary Corp.*, 22 Ill.2d 432, 176 N.E.2d 761 (1961), should not be applied to the welder who has no control over and derives no direct benefit from his employer's sales in that distant State.

Petitioners' analogy does not wash. Whatever the status of their hypothetical welder, petitioners are not charged with mere untargeted negligence. Rather, their intentional, and allegedly tortious, actions were expressly aimed at California. Petitioner South wrote and petitioner Calder edited an article that they knew would have a potentially devastating impact upon respondent. And they knew that the brunt of that injury would be felt by respondent in the State in which she lives and works and in which the *National Enquirer* has its largest circulation. Under the circumstances, petitioners must "reasonably anticipate being haled into court there" to answer for the truth of the statements made in their article. *** An individual injured in California need not go to Florida to seek redress from persons who, though remaining in Florida, knowingly cause the injury in California.

Petitioners are correct that their contacts with California are not to be judged according to their employer's activities there. On the other hand, their status as employees does not somehow insulate them from jurisdiction. Each defendant's contacts with the forum State must be assessed individually. See *Rush v. Savchuk*, 444 U.S., at 332, 100 S.Ct., at 579 ("The requirements of *International Shoe* … must be met as to each defendant over whom a state court exercises jurisdiction"). In this case, petitioners are primary participants in an alleged wrongdoing intentionally directed at a California resident, and jurisdiction over them is proper on that basis.

* * *

We hold that jurisdiction over petitioners in California is proper because of their intentional conduct in Florida calculated to cause injury to respondent in California. The judgment of the California Court of Appeal is

Affirmed

[Footnotes omitted.]

In Personam Jurisdiction and the Internet

> The final case regarding in personam jurisdiction regards the Internet. With websites being available virtually everywhere, does that automatically subject a defendant to in personam jurisdiction in every state in which a website can be accessed?

BOSCHETTO v. HANSING

United States Court of Appeals, Ninth Circuit

539 F.3d 1011 (2008)

BETTY B. FLETCHER, Circuit Judge:

This appeal presents a question that remains surprisingly unanswered by the circuit courts: Does the sale of an item via the eBay Internet auction site provide sufficient "minimum contacts" to support personal jurisdiction over a nonresident defendant in the buyer's forum state? Plaintiff-Appellant Paul Boschetto ("Boschetto") was the winning bidder for a 1964 Ford Galaxie sold on eBay by the Defendant-Appellee, Jeffrey Hansing ("Hansing") for $34,106. Boschetto arranged for the car to be shipped from Wisconsin to California, but upon arrival it failed to meet his expectations or the advertised description. Boschetto sued in federal court; his complaint was dismissed for lack of personal jurisdiction. We now affirm.

I. FACTUAL BACKGROUND AND PROCEDURAL HISTORY

Boschetto lives in San Francisco, California. Defendant-Appellee Jeffrey D. Hansing resides in Milton, Wisconsin. *Id.* Defendants-Appellees Frank-Boucher Chrysler Dodge-Jeep, Gordie Boucher Ford and Boucher Automotive Group ("Boucher Defendants") are private corporations with their principal places of business in Wisconsin. The Boucher Defendants operate a website that advertises their auto dealerships although it is not alleged that this website was connected in any way with the transaction at issue in this case. Hansing is an employee of one of the Boucher Defendants, Frank Boucher Chrysler Dodge-Jeep. The complaint avers that on August 1, 2005, all Defendants "owned and advertised [] a 1964 Ford Galaxie 500 XL 427/425 hp 'R Code' in awesome condition, not restored, rust free chrome in excellent condition, recently rebuilt and ready to be driven, with clear title, and a vehicle warranty number of 4E68R149127."

The car was advertised for sale on the eBay Internet auction site; a copy of a portion of the eBay listing was attached to Boschetto's complaint. *Id.* The eBay listing indicated that the item was located in Janesville, Wisconsin. Boschetto bid $34,106 for the Galaxie on August 8, 2005, and was notified through eBay that same day that he was the winning bidder. *Id.* Boschetto and Hansing communicated via email to arrange for delivery of the vehicle from Wisconsin to California. Boschetto ultimately hired a transport company to pick up the car in Wisconsin; it arrived in California on September 15, 2005. *Id.*

Upon delivery, Boschetto discovered that the car was not an "R Code" as advertised, and noted a variety of other problems, including a motor that would not turn over, rust, and extensive dents on the body of the vehicle. *Id.* Boschetto contacted eBay and Hansing in an attempt to rescind the purchase, but those efforts failed. *Id.* He filed a complaint in United States District Court, Northern District of California on February 23, 2006. Boschetto alleged four state law causes of action (violation of the California Consumer Protection Act; breach of contract; misrepresentation; and fraud), and pled jurisdiction pursuant to the federal diversity statute, 28 U.S.C. § 1332(a).

All Defendants moved to dismiss based on lack of personal jurisdiction. On July 13, 2006, the district court granted the motion. The district court reasoned that the lone jurisdictionally relevant contact with California, an eBay sale consummated with a California purchaser, was insufficient to establish jurisdiction over any of the Defendants. Although Hansing used eBay to market the automobile, the district court observed that "eBay acted not as a 'distribution center' but rather as a virtual forum for the exchange of goods," and that in a standard eBay transaction—like the one at issue in this appeal—the item goes to whomever is the highest bidder, and so "the eBay seller does not purposefully avail himself of the privilege of doing business in a forum state absent some additional conduct directed at the forum state." *Id.*

The district court also rejected Boschetto's request to conduct additional discovery relevant to jurisdiction. *Id.* Noting its "broad discretion" to permit or deny such discovery, the court found that Boschetto's request for further discovery was premised on "speculat[ion] without any support" that the additional discovery would yield jurisdictionally relevant information. *Id.* Judgment was entered on July 17, 2006 and this timely appeal followed.

II. PERSONAL JURISDICTION

* * *

A. The district court correctly dismissed Boschetto's complaint for lack of personal jurisdiction.

We apply a three-part test to determine whether the exercise of specific jurisdiction over a nonresident defendant is appropriate:

> (1) The non-resident defendant must purposefully direct his activities or consummate some transaction with the forum or resident thereof; or perform some act by which he purposefully avails himself of the privilege of conducting activities in the forum, thereby invoking the benefits and protections of its laws;
> (2) the claim must be one which arises out of or relates to the defendant's forum-related activities; and
> (3) the exercise of jurisdiction must comport with fair play and substantial justice, i.e. it must be reasonable.

Id. at 802 (citing *Lake v. Lake*, 817 F.2d 1416, 1421 (9th Cir.1987)). The plaintiff bears the burden on the first two prongs. *Id.* If the plaintiff establishes both prongs one and two, the defendant must come forward with a "compelling case" that the exercise of jurisdiction would not be reasonable. *Id.* (quoting *Burger King Corp. v. Rudzewicz*, 471 U.S. 462, 476–78, 105 S.Ct. 2174, 85 L.Ed.2d 528 (1985)). But if the plaintiff fails at the first step, the jurisdictional inquiry ends and the case must be dismissed. *See Pebble Beach Co. v. Caddy*, 453 F.3d 1151, 1155 (9th Cir. 2006) ("[Plaintiff's] arguments fail under the first prong. Accordingly, we need not address [the remaining two prongs].").

* * *

Here, Boschetto fails at step one of the test for specific jurisdiction, as the lone transaction for the sale of one item does not establish that the Defendants purposefully availed themselves of the privilege of doing business in California. The arrangement between Boschetto and Hansing which is, at bottom, a contract for the sale of a good, is insufficient to have created a substantial connection with California. Hansing (and assuming arguendo that they had any involvement in the transaction, the Boucher Defendants) did not create any ongoing obligations with Boschetto in California; once the car was sold the parties were to go their separate ways. Neither Boschetto's complaint nor his affidavit in opposition to dismissal point to any continuing commitments assumed by the Defendants under the contract. *Id.* Nor did performance of the contract require the Defendants to engage in any substantial business in California. On Boschetto's version of the facts, funds were sent to Wisconsin and arrangements were made to pick up the car there and have it delivered to California. This was, as the district court observed, a "one-shot affair." *See CompuServe, Inc. v. Patterson*, 89 F.3d 1257, 1265 (6th Cir.1996). As the Supreme Court has expressly cautioned, a contract alone does not automatically establish minimum contacts in the plaintiff's home forum. ***

Ignoring the limited nature of the transaction at issue, Boschetto attaches special significance to the fact that the transaction was consummated via eBay, noting that the eBay listing could have been viewed by anyone in California (or any other state for that matter) with Internet access. But the fact that eBay was used as the conduit for this sale does not affect the jurisdictional outcome, at least not on the particular facts presented here.

In *Cybersell, Inc. v. Cybersell, Inc.*, 130 F.3d 414, 419 (9th Cir.1997), we discussed with approval a sliding scale analysis that looks to how interactive an Internet website is for purposes of determining its jurisdictional effect. ("In sum, the common thread, well stated by the district court in *Zippo*, is that the 'likelihood that personal jurisdiction can be constitutionally exercised is directly proportionate to the nature and quality of the commercial activity that an entity conducts over the Internet.'") (quoting *Zippo Mfg. Co. v. Zippo Dot Com*, 952 F.Supp. 1119, 1124 (W.D.Pa. 1997)). The plaintiff in *Cybersell* relied on the fact that the defendant operated a website, accessible in the forum state, that contained allegedly infringing trademarks. 130 F.3d at 416. The defendant's website advertised its services but did not allow parties to transact business via the site. *Id.* at 419. Noting the lack of interactivity on the defendant's website, the court concluded that the defendant had "done no act and consummated no transaction, nor has it performed any act by which it purposefully availed itself of the privilege of conducting activities, in Arizona, thereby invoking the benefits and protections of Arizona law." *Id.*

The *Cybersell* analysis, while persuasive where the contact under consideration is the website itself, is largely inapplicable in this case. Here, eBay was used to create a listing for the sale of a good. Based on a superficial application of *Cybersell*, the eBay listing process and the sale it engenders is "interactive." *Id.* (noting the lack of evidence suggesting that defendant's website resulted in any business generation). But, as the district court noted, "the issue is not whether the court has personal jurisdiction over the intermediary eBay but whether it has personal jurisdiction over an individual who conducted business over eBay." In *Cybersell* and related cases where the Internet site actually belongs to and is operated by the defendant, the nature of the website has jurisdictional significance because the website allows the defendant to maintain some ongoing contact with the forum state (as well as every other state that can access the site). *See Zippo*, 952 F.Supp. at 1125–26 ("We are being asked to determine whether Dot Com's conducting of electronic commerce with Pennsylvania residents constitutes the purposeful availment of doing business in Pennsylvania."). Here, the eBay listing was not part of broader e-commerce activity; the listing temporarily advertised a good for sale and that listing closed once the item was sold, thereby extinguishing the Internet contact for this transaction within the forum state (and every other forum).

Moreover, Boschetto does not allege that any of the Defendants are using eBay to conduct business generally. He does not allege that Defendants conduct regular sales in California (or anywhere else) via eBay. Based on his own affidavit he named the Boucher Defendants based on a "good faith belief" that Hansing may have been acting as their agent during the sale. But he does not go on to allege—on information and belief or otherwise—that either Hansing or the Boucher Defendants are regular users of the eBay sales platform to sell their cars.

This is a distinction with a difference, as the cases that have found that jurisdiction was proper based on eBay sales relied heavily on the fact that the defendant was using the platform as a broader vehicle for commercial activity. See, e.g., *Crummey v. Morgan*, 965 So.2d 497, 500 (Ct.App.La. 2007) (evidence of two prior sales to Louisiana residents in prior year); *Dedvukaj v. Maloney*, 447 F.Supp.2d 813, 822-23 (E.D.Mich.2006) ("Although the Court's research has not disclosed any personal jurisdiction cases involving the use of eBay auctions as a commercial seller's primary marketing vehicle, it is clear from the record that Defendants' use of eBay is regular and systemic."); *Malcolm v. Esposito*, 2003 WL 23272406 at *4 (Va.Cir.Ct. Dec. 12, 2003) ("Defendants are commercial sellers of automobiles who, at the time the BMW was sold, were represented on eBay as 'power sellers' with 213 transactions.").

At bottom, the consummation of the sale via eBay here is a distraction from the core issue: This was a one-time contract for the sale of a good that involved the forum state only because that is where the purchaser happened to reside, but otherwise created no "substantial connection" or ongoing obligations there. *See McGee*, 355 U.S. at 223, 78 S.Ct. 199. The Supreme Court has, in the past, sounded a note of caution that traditional jurisdictional analyses are not upended simply because a case involves technological developments that make it easier for parties to reach across state lines. *World-Wide Volkswagen v. Woodson*, 444 U.S. 286, 293, 100 S.Ct. 580, 62 L.Ed.2d 490 (1980) ("[W]e have never accepted the proposition that state lines are irrelevant for jurisdictional purposes, nor could we, and remain faithful to the principles of interstate federalism embodied in the Constitution."). The use of eBay no doubt made it far easier to reach a California buyer, but the ease with which Boschetto was contacted does not determine whether the nature and quality of the Defendants' contacts serve to support jurisdiction. That is not to say that the use of eBay digs a virtual moat around the defendant, fending off jurisdiction in all cases. Where eBay is used as a means for establishing regular business with a remote forum such that a finding of personal jurisdiction comports with "traditional notions of fair play and substantial justice," *International Shoe Co.*, 326 U.S. at 316, 66 S.Ct. 154, then a defendant's use of eBay may be properly taken into account for purposes of establishing personal jurisdiction. *See Crummey*, 965 So.2d at 500; *Dedvukaj*, 447 F.Supp.2d at 822–23; *Malcolm*, 2003 WL

23272406 at *4. But on the facts of this case—a one-time transaction—the use of eBay as the conduit for that transaction does not have any dispositive effect on jurisdiction.

* * *

III. CONCLUSION

The sale of one automobile via the eBay website, without more, does not provide sufficient "minimum contacts" to establish jurisdiction over a nonresident defendant in the forum state. Likewise, given the total absence of any evidence or allegations that the conduct here involved more than just this one sale, the district court did not abuse its discretion by refusing to allow jurisdictional discovery.

[Footnotes Omitted.]

Forum Non Conveniens

Even though a court has proper jurisdiction over a case, it may choose to not hear the case if, for example, the venue in which the plaintiff filed the lawsuit provides an undue hardship on the defendant or witnesses and/or evidence might not be readily available in the chosen forum. Issues of public policy may also enter into a court's decision to not hear a case pursuant to the doctrine of forum non conveniens.

Gulf Oil v. Gilbert provides an overview of forum non conveniens.

GULF OIL v. GILBERT

Supreme Court of the United States

330 U. S. 501 (1947)

MR. JUSTICE JACKSON delivered the opinion of the Court.

The questions are whether the United States District Court has inherent power to dismiss a suit pursuant to the doctrine of *forum non conveniens* and, if so, whether that power was abused in this case.

The respondent-plaintiff brought this action in the Southern District of New York, but resides at Lynchburg, Virginia, where he operated a public warehouse. He alleges that the petitioner-defendant, in violation of the ordinances of Lynchburg, so carelessly handled a delivery of gasoline to his warehouse tanks and pumps as to cause an explosion and fire which consumed the warehouse building to his damage of $41,889.10, destroyed merchandise and fixtures to his damage of $3,602.40, caused injury to his business and profits of $20,038.27, and burned the property of customers in his custody under warehousing agreements to the extent of $300,000. He asks judgment of $365,529.77, with costs and disbursements, and interest from the date of fire. The action clearly is one in tort.

The petitioner-defendant is a corporation organized under the laws of Pennsylvania, qualified to do business in both Virginia and New York, and it has designated officials of each state as agents to receive service of process. When sued in New York, the defendant, invoking the doctrine of *forum non conveniens,* claimed that the appropriate place for trial is Virginia, where the plaintiff lives and defendant does business, where all events in litigation took place, where most of the witnesses reside, and where both state and federal courts are available to plaintiff, and are able to obtain jurisdiction of the defendant.

The case, on its merits, involves no federal question, and was brought in the United States District Court solely because of diversity in citizenship of the parties. Because of the character of its jurisdiction and the holdings of and under *Erie Railroad Co. v. Tompkins,* 304 U. S. 64, the District Court considered that the law of New York as to *forum non conveniens* applied, and that it required the case to be left to Virginia courts. It therefore dismissed.

The Circuit Court of Appeals disagreed as to the applicability of New York law, took a restrictive view of the application of the entire doctrine in federal courts, and, one judge dissenting, reversed. The case is here on certiorari.

* * *

II

The principle of *forum non conveniens* is simply that a court may resist imposition upon its jurisdiction even when jurisdiction is authorized by the letter of a general venue statute. These statutes are drawn with a necessary generality, and usually give a plaintiff a choice of courts, so that he may be quite sure of some place in which to pursue his remedy. But the open door may admit those who seek not simply justice, but perhaps justice blended with some harassment. A plaintiff sometimes is under temptation to resort to a strategy of forcing the trial at a most inconvenient place for an adversary, even at some inconvenience to himself.

Many of the states have met misuse of venue by investing courts with a discretion to change the place of trial on various grounds, such as the convenience of witnesses and the ends of justice. The federal law contains no such express criteria to guide the district court in exercising its power. But the problem is a very old one affecting the administration of the courts as well as the rights of litigants, and, both in England and in this country, the common law worked out techniques and criteria for dealing with it.

Wisely, it has not been attempted to catalogue the circumstances which will justify or require either grant or denial of remedy. The doctrine leaves much to the discretion of the court to which plaintiff resorts, and experience has not shown a judicial tendency to renounce one's own jurisdiction so strong as to result in many abuses.

If the combination and weight of factors requisite to given results are difficult to forecast or state, those to be considered are not difficult to name. An interest to be considered, and the one likely to be most pressed, is the private interest of the litigant. Important considerations are the relative ease of access to sources of proof; availability of compulsory process for attendance of unwilling, and the cost of obtaining attendance of willing, witnesses; possibility of view of premises, if view would be appropriate to the action, and all other practical problems that make trial of a case easy, expeditious, and inexpensive. There may also be questions as to the enforceability of a judgment if one is obtained. The court will weigh relative advantages and obstacles to fair trial. It is often said that the plaintiff may not, by choice of an inconvenient forum, "vex," "harass," or "oppress" the defendant by inflicting upon him expense or trouble not necessary to his own right to pursue his remedy. But, unless the balance is strongly in favor of the defendant, the plaintiff's choice of forum should rarely be disturbed.

Factors of public interest also have place in applying the doctrine. Administrative difficulties follow for courts when litigation is piled up in congested centers instead of being handled at its origin. Jury duty is a burden that ought not to be imposed upon the people of a community which has no relation to the litigation. In cases which touch the affairs of many persons, there is reason for holding the trial in their view and reach, rather than in remote parts of the country where they can learn of it by report only. There is a local interest in having localized controversies decided at home. There is an appropriateness, too, in having the trial of a diversity case in a forum that is at home with the state law that must govern the case, rather than having a court in some other forum untangle problems in conflict of laws, and in law foreign to itself.

The law of New York as to the discretion of a court to apply the doctrine of *forum non conveniens,* and as to the standards that guide discretion is, so far as here involved, the same as the federal rule. *** It would not be profitable therefore to pursue inquiry as to the source from which our rule must flow.

III

Turning to the question whether this is one of those rather rare cases where the doctrine should be applied, we look first to the interests of the litigants.

The plaintiff himself is not a resident of New York, nor did any event connected with the case take place there, nor does any witness with the possible exception of experts live there. No one connected with that side of the case save counsel for the plaintiff resides there, and he has candidly told us that he was retained by insurance companies interested presumably because of subrogation. His affidavits and argument are devoted to controverting claims as to defendant's inconvenience, rather than to showing that the present forum serves any convenience of his own, with one exception. The only justification for trial in New York advanced here is one rejected by the district court and is set forth in the brief as follows:

"This Court can readily realize that an action of this type, involving as it does a claim for damages in an amount close to $400,000, is one which may stagger the imagination of a local jury which is surely unaccustomed to dealing with amounts of such a nature. Furthermore, removed from Lynchburg, the respondent will have an opportunity to try this case free from local influences and preconceived notions which make it difficult to procure a jury which has no previous knowledge of any of the facts herein."

This unproven premise that jurors of New York live on terms of intimacy with $400,000 transactions is not an assumption we easily make. Nor can we assume that a jury from Lynchburg and vicinity would be "staggered" by contemplating the value of a warehouse building that stood in their region, or of merchandise and fixtures such as were used there, nor are they likely to be staggered by the value of chattels which the people of that neighborhood put in storage. It is a strange argument on behalf of a Virginia plaintiff that the community which gave him patronage to make his business valuable is not capable of furnishing jurors who know the value of the goods they store, the building they are stored in, or the business their patronage creates. And there is no specification of any local influence, other than accurate knowledge of local conditions, that would make a fair trial improbable. The net of this is that we cannot say the District Court was bound to entertain a provincial fear of the provincialism of a Virginia jury. That leaves the Virginia plaintiff without even a suggested reason for transporting this suit to New York.

Defendant points out that not only the plaintiff, but every person who participated in the acts charged to be negligent, resides in or near Lynchburg. It also claims a need to interplead an alleged independent contractor which made the delivery of the gasoline and which is a Virginia corporation domiciled in Lynchburg, that it cannot interplead in New York. There also are approximately 350 persons residing in and around Lynchburg who stored with plaintiff the goods for the damage to which he seeks to recover. The extent to which they have left the community since the fire and the number of them who will actually be needed is in dispute. The complaint alleges that defendant's conduct violated Lynchburg ordinances. Conditions are said to require proof by firemen and by many others. The learned and experienced trial judge was not unaware that litigants generally manage to try their cases with fewer witnesses than they predict in such motions as this. But he was justified in concluding that this trial is likely to be long, and to involve calling many witnesses, and that Lynchburg, some 400 miles from New York, is the source of all proofs for either side, with possible exception of experts. Certainly to fix the place of trial at a point where litigants cannot compel personal attendance and may be forced to try their cases on deposition is to create a condition not satisfactory to court, jury, or most litigants. Nor is it necessarily cured by the statement of plaintiff's counsel that he will see to getting many of the witnesses to the trial, and that some of them "would be delighted to come to New York to testify." There may be circumstances where such a proposal should be given weight. In others, the offer may not turn out to be as generous as defendant or court might suppose it to be. Such matters are for the District Court to decide in exercise of a sound discretion.

The court likewise could well have concluded that the task of the trial court would be simplified by trial in Virginia.

If trial was in a state court, it could apply its own law to events occurring there. If in federal court by reason of diversity of citizenship, the court would apply the law of its own state in which it is likely to be experienced. The course of adjudication in New York federal court might be beset with conflict of laws problems all avoided if the case is litigated in Virginia, where it arose.

We are convinced that the District Court did not exceed its powers or the bounds of its discretion in dismissing plaintiff's complaint and remitting him to the courts of his own community. The Circuit Court of Appeals took too restrictive a view of the doctrine as approved by this Court. Its judgment is

Reversed.

[Footnotes Omitted.]

Sample Choice of Venue Clause

> To avoid issues of jurisdiction, parties to a contract often include a section that specifically addresses which state will have jurisdiction over any disputes related to the contract. Below is an example.

Governing Law and Venue. This Agreement shall be governed by and construed in accordance with the laws of the [STATE] as those laws are applied to contracts entered into and to be performed entirely in [STATE] by [STATE] residents, notwithstanding the actual state or country of residence or incorporation of [COMPANY] or Customer and without regard to choice of law principles. Any legal suit, action or proceeding arising out of or relating to this Agreement shall be commenced in a court of competent jurisdiction located within the [STATE], and each party irrevocably submits to the personal jurisdiction and venue of such court in any suit, action or proceeding. For purposes of establishing jurisdiction in [STATE] under this Agreement, each party hereby waives, to the fullest extent permitted by applicable law, any claim that: (i) it is not personally subject to the jurisdiction of such court; (ii) it is immune from any legal process with respect to it or its property; and (iii) any such suit, action or proceeding is brought in an inconvenient forum. No action, regardless of form, arising out of this Agreement may be brought by Customer more than one year after the cause of action has occurred.

Sample Forms from the Federal Rules of Civil Procedure

The following are some commonly used templates. Additional forms can be seen at http://www.uscourts.gov/uscourts/RulesAndPolicies/rules/2010%20Rules/Civil%20Procedure.pdf, "Appendix of Forms."

Form 1. Caption. *(Use on every summons, complaint, answer, motion, or other document.)*

United States District Court
for the
_________District of_________

A B, Plaintiff	)	
	)	
v.	)	
	)	**Civil Action No._____**
C D, Defendant	)	
	)	
v.	)	
	)	
E F, Third-Party Defendant	)	
(Use if needed.)	)	

(Name of Document)

Form 3. Summons.

(Caption – See Form 1.)

To *name the defendant*:

A lawsuit has been filed against you.

Within 21 days after service of this summons on you (not counting the day you received it), you must serve on the plaintiff an answer to the attached complaint or a motion under Rule 12 of the Federal Rules of Civil Procedure. The answer or motion must be served on the plaintiff's attorney,_________, whose address is _________. If you fail to do so, judgment by default will be entered against you for the relief demanded in the complaint. You also must file your answer or motion with the court.

Date _______

____
Clerk of Court

(Court Seal)

(Use 60 days if the defendant is the United States or a United States agency, or is an officer or employee of the United States allowed 60 days by Rule 12(a)(3).)

Form 11. Complaint for Negligence.

(Caption – See Form 1.)

1. (Statement of Jurisdiction – See Form 7.)

2. On _date_, at _place_, the defendant negligently drove a motor vehicle against the plaintiff.

3. As a result, the plaintiff was physically injured, lost wages or income, suffered physical and mental pain, and incurred medical expenses of $________.

Therefore, the plaintiff demands judgment against the defendant for $ ________, plus costs.

(Date and sign – See Form 2).

Form 40. Motion to Dismiss Under Rule 12(b) for Lack of Jurisdiction, Improper Venue, Insufficient Service of Process, or Failure to State a Claim.

(Caption – See Form 1.)

The defendant moves to dismiss the action because:

1. the amount in controversy is less than the sum or value specified by 28 U.S.C. § 1332;

2. the defendant is not subject to the personal jurisdiction of this court;

3. venue is improper (this defendant does not reside in this district and no part of the events or omissions giving rise to the claim occurred in the district);

4. the defendant has not been properly served, as shown by the attached affidavits of ____________; or

5. the complaint fails to state a claim upon which relief can be granted.

(Date and sign – See Form 2.)

Form 70. Judgment on a Jury Verdict.

(Caption – See Form 1.)

This action was tried by a jury with Judge ________ presiding, and the jury has rendered a verdict.

It is ordered that:

[the plaintiff _name_ recover from the defendant _name_ the amount of $_____ with interest at the rate of __%, along with costs.]

[the plaintiff recover nothing, the action be dismissed on the merits, and the defendant _name_ recover costs from the plaintiff _name_.]

Date ________

____
Clerk of Court

Sample Voir Dire

The following are some sample voir dire questions. A full voir dire will generally ask more questions than what are included below. In fact, some voir dire will be very specific. For example, in the O.J. Simpson murder case, jurors were asked about football, knives, domestic abuse, racial matters, what they read and watched on TV, and much more.

- [The parties to the case and the attorneys will be introduced.] Do you know ____________? If yes, what is the nature of your relationship? Will that relationship affect your ability to give a fair trial to all of the parties in this case?
- Does anyone have a medical reason or personal hardship that would make it difficult to serve as a juror in this case?
- Has anyone here previously served as a juror either in a criminal or civil case? If yes, has your previous experience as a juror affected your ability to be fair to all sides in the case?
- Is anyone here a lawyer, married to a lawyer, or in a substantial relationship with a lawyer? Has anyone here studied law or worked in a law office?
- Have you read in the newspapers, read on the Internet, seen on television, or heard on the radio anything about this case, or do you have any knowledge of the facts or events of this case? [If yes, there would be follow-up questions.]
- If you are selected as a juror, do you pledge that you will base your decision on the facts as presented in this trial and not on any past experiences or prior opinions you might have about the subject matter of this case?
- Have you or a close family member ever sued or been sued by someone? [For a criminal case, jurors might be asked if they have ever been victims of a crime.] If so, what was the nature of the lawsuit? [The question might also be more specific. For example, if this was a car accident case, the question might be, "Have you or a close family member ever been involved in a car accident in which there were injuries?" If yes, there would be follow-up questions surrounding the particulars.]
- Do any of you have any religious, philosophical, or other beliefs that prevent you from acting as an impartial juror in this case?
- Do any of you think that you would not be able to follow an instruction of the court if that instruction differed from your own personal views or values?
- Do you know of any reason that you cannot sit in this case with complete fairness and impartiality and decide the case based only on the evidence presented in court and the law as given at the conclusion of the trial? If you or a family member were the defendant, would you be satisfied to have as your juror a person with your frame of mind?

Jurisdiction of the Courts

The following outlines the differences between the federal and state court systems (http://www.uscourts.gov/FederalCourts/UnderstandingtheFederalCourts/Jurisdiction/DifferencebetweenFederalAndStateCourts.aspx).

The U.S. Constitution is the supreme law of the land in the United States. It creates a federal system of government in which power is shared between the federal government and the state governments. Due to federalism, both the federal government and each of the state governments has its own court system.

STRUCTURE	
The Federal Court System	**The State Court System**
• Article III of the Constitution invests the judicial power of the United States in the federal court system. Article III, Section 1 specifically creates the U.S. Supreme Court and gives Congress the authority to create the lower federal courts.	• The Constitution and laws of each state establish the state courts. A court of last resort, often known as a supreme court, is usually the highest court in a state. Some states also have an intermediate court of appeals. Below these appeals courts are the state trial courts. Some are referred to as circuit or district courts.
• Congress has used this power to establish the 13 U.S. courts of appeals, the 94 U.S. district courts, the U.S. Court of Claims, and the U.S. Court of International Trade. U.S. bankruptcy courts handle bankruptcy cases. Magistrate judges handle some district court matters.	• States also usually have courts that handle specific legal matters, e.g., probate court (wills and estates); juvenile court; family court; etc.
• Parties dissatisfied with a decision of a U.S. district court, the U.S. Court of Claims, and/or the U.S. Court of International Trade may appeal to a U.S. court of appeals.	• Parties dissatisfied with the decision of the trial court may take their cases to the intermediate court of appeals.

STRUCTURE	
• A party may ask the U.S. Supreme Court to review a decision of the U.S. Court of Appeals, but the Supreme Court usually is under no obligation to do so. The U.S. Supreme Court is the final arbiter of federal constitutional questions.	• Parties have the option to ask the highest state court to hear the case.
	• Only certain state court cases are eligible for review by the U.S. Supreme Court.

SELECTION OF JUDGES	
The Federal Court System	**The State Court System**
• (Article III, Section 1 of the Constitution) Federal judges are nominated by the President and confirmed by the Senate. They hold office during good behavior, typically, for life. Through congressional impeachment proceedings, federal judges may be removed from office for misbehavior.	• State court judges are selected in a variety of ways, including - election, - appointment for a given number of years, - appointment for life, and - combinations of these methods, e.g., appointment followed by election.

TYPES OF CASES HEARD	
The Federal Court System	**The State Court System**
• Cases that deal with the constitutionality of a law; • Cases involving the laws and treaties of the U.S.; • Cases involving ambassadors and public ministers; • Disputes between two or more states; • Admiralty law; • Bankruptcy; and • Habeas corpus issues.	• Most criminal cases • Probate (involving wills and estates) • Most contract cases • Tort cases (personal injuries) • Family law (marriages, divorces, adoptions), etc. State courts are the final deciders of state laws and constitutions. Their interpretations of federal law or the U.S. Constitution may be appealed to the U.S. Supreme Court. The Supreme Court may choose to hear or not to hear such cases.

ARTICLE I COURTS
Congress has created several Article I or legislative courts that do not have full judicial power. Judicial power is the authority to be the final decider in all questions of Constitutional law, all questions of federal law and to hear claims at the core of habeas corpus issues. Article I courts are U.S. Court of Veterans' Appeals, the U.S. Court of Military Appeals, and the U.S. Tax Court.

One State's Judicial System

The following discusses Maryland's judicial system (http://www.courts.state.md.us/overview.html).

MARYLAND'S JUDICIAL SYSTEM

The Maryland court system has four levels: two trial courts and two appellate courts. The trial courts consider evidence presented in a case and make judgments based on the facts, the law and legal precedent (prior legal decisions from a higher court). Appellate courts review a trial court's actions and decisions and decide whether the trial judge properly followed the law and legal precedent. For jury trials, the appellate court may have to decide whether the jury's decision was proper, given the facts presented and the applicable law. Generally, appellate courts do not decide which party won or lost a trial, nor do they conduct a new trial. Rather, they review the earlier trial and determine whether or not it was fair, according to the law.

TRIAL COURTS

DISTRICT COURT

The District Court of Maryland has 34 locations in 12 districts statewide, with at least one judge presiding in every county and Baltimore City. There are no juries in the District Court; each case is heard and decided by a judge. The District Court hears both civil cases—including claims up to $30,000, domestic violence cases, landlord/tenant disputes, replevin (the recovery of goods claimed to be wrongfully taken or held), and civil cases involving amounts at or less than $5,000—and criminal cases. The District Court hears criminal cases, including motor vehicle/boating violations and other misdemeanors and limited felonies, although the circuit courts share jurisdiction if the penalties authorized are three years or more in prison, a fine of $2,500 or more, or both.

CIRCUIT COURTS

The circuit courts of Maryland, located in all 23 counties and Baltimore City, are the trial courts of general jurisdiction. Circuit courts generally handle the state's major civil cases and more serious criminal matters, along with juvenile cases, family matters, such as divorce, and most appeals from the District Court, orphans' courts and administrative agencies. The circuit courts also can hear, under certain circumstances, civil or criminal cases from the District Court, in which one of the parties has requested a jury trial; cases ordinarily tried in the District Court if the penalty is three or more years in prison, a fine of $2,500 or more, or both; and domestic violence cases.

To obtain information on a specific case in either court, call the clerk's office in the city or county where the case was filed or where the alleged violation occurred.

APPELLATE COURTS

COURT OF SPECIAL APPEALS

The Court of Special Appeals is Maryland's intermediate appellate court. Created in 1966, unless otherwise provided by law, it considers any reviewable judgment, decree, order, or other action of the circuit and orphans' courts. Judges sitting on the Court of Special Appeals generally hear and decide cases in panels of three. In some instances, however, all 13 judges sit *en banc* to hear the case.

COURT OF APPEALS

The Maryland Court of Appeals is the highest court in the state (commonly called the Supreme Court in other states). This Court hears cases almost exclusively by way of certiorari, a process that gives the court the ability to decide which cases to hear. By law, however, the Court of Appeals is required to hear cases involving the death penalty, legislative redistricting, removal of certain state officials, and the certifications of questions of law. The Chief Judge of the Court of Appeals sits on the Court along with six other judges. All seven judges hear oral arguments in each case unless a judge removes him/herself from a case; in this event, a judge from another court, or a retired appellate judge, may be specially assigned to sit in the place of the recused judge.

OTHER BODIES IN MARYLAND

ORPHANS' COURT

Orphans' courts handle wills, estates, and other probate matters. In addition, they have jurisdiction—along with the circuit courts—to appoint guardians of the person, and to protect the estates of unemancipated minors (minors who remain under parental authority). An appeal from an orphans' court generally may be to a circuit court, where the matter is tried de novo or 'as new' before a judge or, if appropriate, a jury, or to the Court of Special Appeals, where the matter is heard 'as is' or on the record.

OFFICE OF ADMINISTRATIVE HEARINGS

Authorized in 1989, the Office of Administrative Hearings listens to contested executive branch administrative law cases, except for those concerning officials or agencies exempted by law. A citizen who disagrees with an action taken by such an agency may appear before an administrative law judge to obtain an impartial review. Administrative law judges are independent of the government agency whose action is being contested. Though based in the Baltimore area, these judges hear cases statewide.

FEDERAL COURTS

Federal courts are authorized by the U.S. Constitution to deal with issues involving laws enacted by Congress, as contrasted with state courts, which apply the laws of their state and local governments. Federal courts handle such diverse matters as bankruptcy, contract disputes, personal injury actions, product liability cases, criminal prosecutions and other matters. There are rules, sometimes complex, governing whether a matter will proceed in a state or federal court. One such rule is that a case in which citizens of more than one state are involved may be brought in a federal court and, if brought in a state court, may be removed by one or more of the parties to federal court. This dual court structure is a distinguishing and innovative feature of the American judicial system.

Chapter 3
Torts

The Administrative Office of the U.S. Courts defines a tort as:

> A civil, not criminal, wrong. A negligent or intentional injury against a person or property, with the exception of breach of contract. (http://www.uscourts.gov/Common/Glossary.aspx)

Torts are defined as either intentional or unintentional. A person who commits a tort is a tortfeasor.

Torts include assault, battery, false imprisonment, defamation (libel and slander), infliction of emotional distress (intentional or negligent), invasion of privacy, conversion, trespass, personal injury cases, tortious interference with contract or business relationships, and wrongful death, among other offenses. As is evident from this list, torts are the subject of many common lawsuits. Some actions, however, can be prosecuted, in separate cases, as both a tort and a crime. For example, a murder suspect can be criminally tried for murder and also be sued in tort under a wrongful death claim. The two actions are not mutually exclusive. A well-known example of this is the O.J. Simpson case, where Simpson was tried criminally for murder and was subsequently sued civilly for wrongful death. Simpson was not convicted criminally, but he was found responsible for the murders in the civil suit and had a judgment of $33.5 million rendered against him. One of the reasons for the different outcomes in the two scenarios is the burden of proof. For a tort, the burden of proof is a preponderance of the evidence. For a criminal case, the burden of proof is beyond a reasonable doubt.

Intentional Torts

For an intentional tort to be proven, the plaintiff must show that there was an act, intent, and harm caused by that intentional act.

The *Cullison* case discusses the intentional torts of trespass, assault, invasion of privacy, and intentional infliction of emotional distress.

CULLISON v. MEDLEY

Supreme Court of Indiana
570 N.E.2d 27 (1991)

KRAHULIK, Justice.

The sole issue presented for review is whether the "impact rule" prohibits Cullison from recovering under any of several legal theories for emotional distress resulting from the Medleys alleged wrongdoings. In his four-count complaint, Cullison alleged trespass, assault, harassment, and intentional infliction of emotional distress and sought to recover damages for his emotional and psychological injury.

In reviewing the propriety of the trial court's entry of summary judgment, we apply the same standard applicable in the trial court. We must construe the pleadings, depositions, answers to interrogatories, and affidavits in the light most favorable to the non-moving party. Only if such evidence shows no genuine issue of material fact and that the moving party is entitled to judgment as a matter of law should the summary judgment be affirmed. Ind.Trial Rule 56; *Ayres v. Indiana Heights Volunteer Fire Dept.* (1986), Ind., 493 N.E.2d 1229, 1234. We conclude that the evidence presented to the trial court construed in favor of the non-moving party, Cullison, establishes questions of fact which require jury resolution on three of the four counts alleged in Cullison's complaint.

According to Cullison's deposition testimony, on February 2, 1986, he encountered Sandy, the 16-year-old daughter of Ernest, in a Linton, Indiana, grocery store parking lot. They exchanged pleasantries and Cullison invited her to have a Coke with him and to come to his home to talk further. A few hours later, someone knocked on the door of his mobile home. Cullison got out of bed and answered the door. He testified that he saw a person standing in the darkness who said that she wanted to talk to him. Cullison answered that he would have to get dressed because he had been in bed. Cullison went back to his bedroom, dressed, and returned to the darkened living room of his trailer. When he entered the living room and turned the lights on, he was confronted by Sandy Medley, as well as by father Ernest, brother Ron, mother Doris, and brother-in-law Terry Simmons. Ernest was on crutches due to knee surgery and had a revolver in a holster strapped to his thigh. Cullison testified that Sandy called him a "pervert" and told him he was "sick," mother Doris berated him while keeping her hand in her pocket, convincing Cullison that she also was carrying a pistol. Ron and Terry said nothing to Cullison, but their presence in his trailer home further intimidated him. Primarily, however, Cullison's attention was riveted to the gun carried by Ernest. Cullison testified that, while Ernest never withdrew the gun from his holster, he "grabbed for the gun a few times and shook the gun" at plaintiff while threatening to "jump astraddle" of Cullison if he did not leave Sandy alone. Cullison testified that Ernest "kept grabbing at it with his hand, like he was going to take it out," and "took it to mean he was going to shoot me" when Ernest threatened to "jump astraddle" of Cullison. Although no one actually touched Cullison, his testimony was that he feared he was about to be shot throughout the episode because Ernest kept moving his hand toward the gun as if to draw the revolver from the holster while threatening Cullison to leave Sandy alone.

As the Medleys were leaving, Cullison suffered chest pains and feared that he was having a heart attack. Approximately two months later, Cullison testified that Ernest glared at him in a menacing manner while again armed with a handgun at a restaurant in Linton. On one of these occasions, Ernest stood next to the booth where Cullison was seated while wearing a pistol and a holster approximately one foot from Cullison's face. Shortly after the incident at his home, Cullison learned that Ernest had previously shot a man. This added greatly to his fear and apprehension of Ernest on the later occasions when Ernest glared at him and stood next to the booth at which he was seated while armed with a handgun in a holster.

Cullison testified that as a result of the incident, he sought psychological counseling and therapy and continued to see a therapist for approximately 18 months. Additionally, Cullison sought psychiatric help and received prescription medication which prevented him from operating power tools or driving an automobile, thus injuring Cullison in his sole proprietorship construction business. Additionally, Cullison testified that he suffered from nervousness, depression, sleeplessness, inability to concentrate and impotency following his run-in with the Medleys.

Trespass

Cullison alleged that the Medleys trespassed when they entered his trailer without his permission after he had gone to the back of the trailer to dress. Every unauthorized entry on the land of another constitutes a trespass. State ex rel. *McPherson v. Beckner* (1892), 132 Ind. 371, 31 N.E. 950; *Evans v. State* (1986) Ind. App. 493 N.E.2d 806. Here, Cullison did not directly or impliedly invite the five members of the Medley family to enter into his trailer home. Clearly, Cullison's complaint properly alleged an actionable count of trespass. The Court of Appeals agreed that a trespass may have occurred and that Cullison may be entitled to receive nominal damages, but relying upon *Indiana Motorcycle Association v. Hudson* (1980), Ind.App., 399 N.E.2d 775, decided that absent a showing of physical injury caused by the defendants or evidence that defendants' behavior was willful, callous or malicious, an action for trespass would not support the emotional distress damages requested by Cullison. The Court of Appeals concluded that because there was no physical injury and the Medleys' actions could not be said to be malicious, callous, or willful, Cullison's claim for mental injuries occasioned by the trespass must fail.

The Court of Appeals accurately stated the rule of law and its justification:

The general rule in Indiana, known as the impact rule, is that damages for mental anguish are recoverable only when accompanied by and resulting from a physical injury. *Charlie Stuart Oldsmobile, Inc. v. Smith* (1976), 171 Ind.App. 315, 357 N.E.2d 247, modified on other grounds, 175 Ind.App. 1, 369 N.E.2d 947. The rationale behind this rule is that absent physical injury, mental anguish is speculative, subject to exaggeration, likely to lead to fictitious claims, and often so unforeseeable that there is no rational basis for awarding damages.

The Court of Appeals applied this rule and rationale to the court in Cullison's complaint alleging trespass.

We now conclude that the rationale for this rule, whatever its historical foundation, is no longer valid and, therefore, the so-called "impact rule" does not apply to prohibit recovery for emotional distress when sustained in the course of a tortious trespass. When one intentionally invades the premises of another in such a way as to provoke a reasonably foreseeable emotional disturbance or trauma of the rightful occupier of the premises, the occupier may, in addition to recovering damages to the realty, if any, recover damages for such emotional injury. The mere fact of a physical injury, however minor, does not make mental distress damages any less speculative, subject to exaggeration, or likely to lead to fictitious claims. In fact, the experience in this state is that juries are equally qualified to judge someone's emotional injury as they are to judge someone's pain and suffering or future pain and suffering, and the presence or absence of some physical injury does nothing to alleviate the jury's burden in deciding whether the elements of mental suffering are present. We note there are those who argue that allowing recovery for mental damages will result in an inundation of the court system with such claims, but we do not believe that the workload occasioned by some possible increase in legitimate claims is any reason to deny or prohibit such claims.

In the present case, the complaint alleges trespass and the testimony of Cullison supports such allegations. It will be for the jury to determine whether the trespass occurred and whether such intentional trespass foreseeably would provoke an emotional disturbance or trauma. Summary judgment was entered inappropriately on count one of Cullison's complaint.

Assault

In count two of his complaint, Cullison alleged an assault. The Court of Appeals decided that, because Ernest never removed his gun from the holster, his threat that he was going to "jump astraddle" of Cullison constituted conditional language which did not express any present intent to harm Cullison and, therefore, was not an assault. Further, the Court of Appeals decided that even if it were to find an assault, summary judgment was still appropriate because Cullison alleged only emotional distress and made no showing that the Medleys' actions were malicious, callous, or willful or that the alleged injuries he suffered were a foreseeable result of the Medleys' conduct. We disagree.

It is axiomatic that assault, unlike battery, is effectuated when one acts intending to cause a harmful or offensive contact with the person of the other or an imminent apprehension of such contact. Restatement (Second) of Torts Sec. 21 (1965). It is the right to be free from the apprehension of a battery which is protected by the tort action which we call an assault. As this Court held approximately 90 years ago in *Kline v. Kline* (1901), 158 Ind. 602, 64 N.E. 9, an assault constitutes "a touching of the mind, if not of the body." Because it is a touching of the mind, as opposed to the body, the damages which are recoverable for an assault are damages for mental trauma and distress. "Any act of such a nature as to excite an apprehension of a battery may constitute an assault. It is an assault to shake a fist under another's nose, to aim or strike at him with a weapon, or to hold it in a threatening position, to rise or advance to strike another, to surround him with a display of force ..." W. Prosser & J. Keaton, *Prosser and Keaton on Torts Sec. 10* (5th ed. 1984). Additionally, the apprehension must be one which would normally be aroused in the mind of a reasonable person. *Id.* Finally, the tort is complete with the invasion of the plaintiff's mental peace.

The facts alleged and testified to by Cullison could, if believed, entitle him to recover for an assault against the Medleys. A jury could reasonably conclude that the Medleys intended to frighten Cullison by surrounding him in his trailer and threatening him with bodily harm while one of them was armed with a revolver, even if that revolver was not removed from the its holster. Cullison testified that Ernest kept grabbing at the pistol as if he were going to take it out, and that Cullison thought Ernest was going to shoot him. It is for the jury to determine whether Cullison's apprehension of being shot or otherwise injured was one which would normally be aroused in the mind of a reasonable person. It was error for the trial court to enter summary judgment on the count two allegation of assault.

Invasion of Privacy

The third count of Cullison's complaint sought to recover damages for "harrassment", but in his brief to the Court of Appeals, Cullison argued that count III more properly alleged the tort of invasion of privacy. Cullison claims that the trial court erred in entering summary judgment against him on this count. The Court of Appeals decided that he had waived this issue by not briefing it at the trial court level but, nevertheless, decided that the facts did not rise to the level of "outrageous wrongful intrusion into one's private activities." 559 N.E.2d at 624. Again, we disagree. The tort of invasion of privacy encompasses four separate forms; viz, appropriation, intrusion, public disclosure of private facts, and false light in the public eye. Prosser and Keaton, *supra* Sec. 117. When the invasion of a plaintiff's right to privacy takes the form of intrusion, it consists of an intrusion upon the plaintiff's physical solitude or seclusion as by invading his home or conducting an illegal search. *Id.* Here, the evidence according to Cullison's testimony, was that he did not invite any of the Medleys into his home and was apprehensive to discover all five of them standing in his darkened living room when he turned on the light. This may constitute an intrusive invasion of Cullison's right of privacy. The allegations that Ernest harrassed Cullison in the Hardee's restaurant or that Sandy and her mother harrassed Cullison by walking past his home in a taunting manner would not constitute an actionable claim for invasion of privacy because plaintiff has no legal right to be left alone on a public street or in a public place. For that reason and because the events which occurred inside the trailer also constitute a trespass, we hold that Cullison cannot simultaneously maintain his action for invasion of privacy and for trespass. For those reasons, we affirm the trial court's entry of summary judgment on this count.

Intentional Infliction of Emotional Distress

Count four alleges an intentional infliction of emotional distress. This tort has not been recognized in this state. The definition of the tort of intentional infliction of emotional distress is that "one who by extreme and outrageous conduct intentionally or recklessly causes severe emotional distress to another is subject to liability for such emotional distress …" Restatement (Second) of Torts Sec. 46 (1965). It is the intent to harm one emotionally that constitutes the basis for the tort of an intentional infliction of emotional distress. We hold that under proper circumstances, liability will attach to a defendant for an intentional infliction of emotional distress, but the facts in this case do not support a finding that the Medleys intended to cause emotional injury to Cullison. Cullison points to evidence that the Medleys knew that he "disliked" guns and, therefore, argues that a jury could infer from this knowledge that Ernest's wearing of a gun was intended to inflict emotional injury on Cullison. We believe that this fact, standing alone, cannot be stretched into such an inference without breaking. The trial court properly entered summary judgment on count four of Cullison's complaint.

CONCLUSION

For all of the reasons stated above, we hereby accept transfer of this cause, vacate the opinion of the Court of Appeals, reverse the entry of summary judgment as to the counts alleging trespass and assault, and affirm the entry of summary judgment on the counts alleging invasion of privacy and intentional infliction of emotional distress, and remand this cause to the trial court.

The following case discusses battery and intentional infliction of emotional distress in a unique situation. The plaintiff's religious beliefs prohibited her from being seen unclothed by a male. Her doctor was made aware of the situation. A male nurse viewed and touched the plaintiff. Does the touching constitute a battery?

COHEN v. SMITH

Appellate Court of Illinois, Fifth District
648 N.E.2d 329 (1995)

Justice CHAPMAN delivered the opinion of the court:

Patricia Cohen was admitted to St. Joseph Memorial Hospital ("Hospital") to deliver her baby. After an examination, Cohen was informed that it would be necessary for her to have a cesarean section. Cohen and her husband allegedly informed her physician, who in turn advised the Hospital staff, that the couple's religious beliefs prohibited Cohen from being seen unclothed by a male. Cohen's doctor assured her husband that their religious convictions would be respected.

During Cohen's cesarean section, Roger Smith, a male nurse on staff at the Hospital, allegedly observed and touched Cohen's naked body. Cohen and her husband filed suit against Nurse Smith and the Hospital. The trial court allowed defendants' motions to dismiss. We reverse.

In reviewing a motion to dismiss for failure to state a cause of action, the court must view all well-pleaded facts in the light most favorable to the plaintiff. (*Business Development Services, Inc. v. Field Container Corp.* (1981), 96 Ill.App.3d 834, 836, 52 Ill.Dec. 405, 408, 422 N.E.2d 86, 89.) A trial court may dismiss a cause of action for failing to state a cause of action, based solely on the pleadings, only if it is clearly apparent that no set of alleged facts can be proven which will entitle a plaintiff to recovery. (*Burdinie v. Village of Glendale Heights* (1990), 139 Ill.2d 501, 504, 152 Ill.Dec. 121, 124, 565 N.E.2d 654, 657.) Therefore, we will consider only the facts alleged by the plaintiffs in their complaints.

This case was originally filed as two separate cases, one against Nurse Smith and the other against the Hospital. The cases were consolidated on appeal. There are strong similarities between the complaints filed, and the arguments made, in each case. Plaintiffs' complaints against both Nurse Smith and the Hospital are stated in three counts: (1) battery, (2) intentional infliction of emotional distress, and (3) violation of the Right of Conscience Act (745 ILCS 70/2 (West 1992)).

* * *

In both the trial court and on appeal, there has been much discussion over various tangential matters, but the two basic issues are: (1) whether the Healing Arts Malpractice Act applies to these cases; and (2) do plaintiffs' complaints state a cause of action for battery, for intentional infliction of emotional distress, and for relief under the Right of Conscience Act.

* * *

The Restatement (Second) of Torts provides that an actor commits a battery if:

"(a) he acts intending to cause a harmful or offensive contact with the person of the other or a third person, or an imminent apprehension of such a contact, and
(b) a harmful contact with the person of the other directly or indirectly results." (Restatement (Second) of Torts, § 13 (1965).)

Liability for battery emphasizes the plaintiff's lack of consent to the touching. (*Cowan v. Insurance Co. of North America* (1974), 22 Ill.App.3d 883, 893, 318 N.E.2d 315, 323.) "Offensive contact" is said to occur when the contact "offends a reasonable sense of personal dignity." Restatement (Second) of Torts § 19 (1965).

Historically, battery was first and foremost a systematic substitution for private retribution. (W. Prosser & Keeton, *Torts* § 9, at 41 (5th ed. 1984) (Prosser).) Protecting personal integrity has always been viewed as an important basis for battery. (Prosser, § 9, at 41.) "Consequently, the defendant is liable not only for contacts which do actual physical harm, but also for those relatively trivial ones which are merely offensive and insulting." (Prosser, § 9, at 41.) This application of battery to remedy offensive and insulting conduct is deeply ingrained in our legal history. As early as 1784, a Pennsylvania defendant was prosecuted for striking the cane of a French ambassador. The court furthered the distinction between harmful offensive batteries and nonharmful offensive batteries:

"As to the assault, this is, perhaps, one of that kind, in which the insult is more to be considered than the actual damage; for, though no great bodily pain is suffered by a blow on the palm of the hand, or the skirt of the coat, yet these are clearly within the definition of assault and battery, and among gentlemen too often induce duelling and terminate in murder." (*Respublica v. De Longchamps* (Pa.1784), 1 Dall. 111, 1 L.Ed. 59, in Gregory, Kalven, & Epstein, *Cases & Materials on Torts* 904–905 (1977).)

Causing actual physical harm is not an element of battery. "A plaintiff is entitled to demand that the defendant refrain from the offensive touching, although the contact results in no visible injury." Prosser, § 9, at 41.

With these definitions in mind, we examine plaintiffs' allegations against Nurse Smith. In count 1, plaintiffs charge defendant with a battery:

"1. That defendant, Roger Smith, on or about December 9, 1990, was acting in his capacity as an agent and employee of St. Joseph Memorial Hospital, Inc., which is located in Jackson County, Illinois;

2. That on or about December 9, 1990, the plaintiff, Patricia K. Cohen, was a patient admitted to St. Joseph Memorial Hospital, Inc. for the purpose of delivery of a baby, and after her admittance it was determined that the baby should be delivered by cesarean section;

3. That based upon information sufficient to form a belief, plaintiff alleges that Roger Smith was made aware that Patricia K. Cohen had strongly held and deeply ingrained moral and religious views which prohibited her from being seen or observed in an unclothed condition by a member of the opposite sex;

4. That Roger Smith is male and was a member of the operating team which was to perform a cesarean section upon Patricia K. Cohen;

5. That Patricia K. Cohen was informed, by and through her husband, Joe Cohen, by the physician who was to perform the cesarean section that Roger Smith's presence in the operating room was necessary for the procedure but the cesarean section could be performed without him seeing Patricia K. Cohen in an unclothed condition;

6. The physician who was to perform the cesarean section instructed Roger Smith that the operation was to be performed without any male seeing Patricia K. Cohen in an unclothed condition;

7. Relying about the assurances provided her by her physician, that no male would observe her in an unclothed condition, Patricia K. Cohen consented to have the cesarean section performed at St. Joseph Memorial Hospital, Inc.;

8. That Roger Smith did act so as to place himself in such a position so as to view and touch Patricia K. Cohen's naked, unclothed, body, and did in fact observe and touch her naked and unclothed body;

9. That based upon information sufficient to form a belief, plaintiff alleges that Roger Smith did intentionally touch and observe Patricia K. Cohen's naked and unclothed body although informed of Patricia K. Cohen's moral and religious beliefs regarding members of the opposite sex observing her in an unclothed condition;

10. That Roger Smith's actions were taken while Patricia K. Cohen was incapacitated, was on the surgical table, and was under the control of Roger Smith."

It is apparent from these quotations, which must be taken as true for purposes of the motion to dismiss, that the plaintiffs in the instant case are not alleging that the cesarean section performed on Cohen violated any medical standard or was performed incorrectly or that any attendant procedure was improper because of any deviation from any appropriate medical standard. The plaintiffs' claim is in no way based upon medical malpractice. Cohen alleges instead that Roger Smith knowingly violated her privacy interests and religious standards and beliefs by touching her without her consent.

The only reason there is some hesitancy over the issue of whether a battery occurred in this case is because the contact took place in a hospital between a medical professional and a patient. If Patricia Cohen had been struck in the nose by Nurse Smith on a public street, everyone would agree that a battery occurred, and under those limited facts, there would be no defense to the battery. In contrast, medical professionals are allowed to touch patients during the course of medical treatment because patients consent, either explicitly or implicitly, to the touching. The violation of a plaintiff's right to bodily and personal integrity by an unconsented-to touching is the essence of a claim for battery. Therefore, it is not the plaintiffs who are seeking damages because of healing act malpractice; it is the defendants who are raising a defense based upon their positions in the healing art fields.

* * *

II. CAUSES OF ACTION

Counts I and II of the plaintiffs' complaint, battery and the intentional infliction of emotional distress, respectively, are based on the same factual basis that Patricia Cohen informed the Hospital and its employees of her religious views that she could not be viewed or touched by a male. Therefore, we will discuss these issues together.

<u>A. Intentional Infliction of Emotional Distress and Battery</u>

Battery has already been defined and discussed. To state a cause of action for intentional infliction of emotional distress, a plaintiff must show:

"(1) extreme and outrageous conduct, (2) intent by the defendant to cause, or reckless disregard of the probability of causing emotional distress, (3) severe or extreme emotional distress suffered by the plaintiff, and (4) an actual proximate causation of emotional distress by the defendant's outrageous conduct." *Tobias v. Winkler* (1987), 156 Ill.App.3d 886, 896, 109 Ill.Dec. 211, 217, 509 N.E.2d 1050, 1056.

The plaintiffs' complaint against Nurse Smith alleges that Smith touched Cohen's naked body after being informed of her moral and religious beliefs against such touching by a male. Similarly, the plaintiffs' complaint against the Hospital alleges that the doctor performing the surgery told Nurse Smith that the operation was to be performed without any male seeing Cohen naked. According to the complaint, despite being informed of Cohen's religious beliefs, Nurse Smith, an agent and employee of the Hospital, intentionally saw and touched Cohen's naked body.

The allegation that both Nurse Smith and the Hospital were informed in advance of plaintiffs' religious beliefs is important in this case, because the religious convictions of plaintiffs might not be those of most people who enter the hospital to give birth. As a matter of fact, plaintiffs' counsel candidly conceded that there would be no cause of action for battery if Patricia Cohen had been placed in Nurse Smith's and the Hospital's care in an emergency situation in which Patricia had been unable to inform the Hospital or its agents of her beliefs. Plaintiffs' attorney acknowledged that his clients' moral and religious views are not widely held in the community and, because of this, plaintiffs could state a claim against defendants only if the plaintiffs plead that the defendants had knowledge of those beliefs. But, he contends, the defendants' knowledge of the plaintiffs' religious beliefs was pleaded in their complaint. Specifically, plaintiffs contend that defendants' knowledge is clearly illustrated by an allegation in the plaintiffs' amended complaint that Nurse Smith requested the presence of the Murphysboro City Police at the Hospital to prevent Mr. Cohen from objecting to Nurse Smith's presence in the operating room while Mrs. Cohen was naked, and to physically restrain Mr. Cohen if necessary.

The fact that the plaintiffs hold deeply ingrained religious beliefs which are not shared by the majority of society does not mean that those beliefs deserve less protection than more mainstream religious beliefs. The plaintiffs were not trying to force their religion on other people; they were only insisting that their beliefs be respected by the Hospital and the Hospital staff.

As we have stated previously, Patricia Cohen was not trying to, and was not entitled to, impose her religious beliefs on others. When she informed the Hospital of her moral and religious beliefs against being viewed and touched by males, the Hospital was free to refuse to accede to those demands. But, according to her complaint, when Cohen made her wishes known to the Hospital, it, at least implicitly, agreed to provide her with treatment within the restrictions placed by her beliefs.

Although most people in modern society have come to accept the necessity of being seen unclothed and being touched by members of the opposite sex during medical treatment, the plaintiffs had not accepted these procedures and, according to their complaint, had informed defendants of their convictions. This case is similar to cases involving Jehovah's Witnesses who were unwilling to accept blood transfusions because of religious convictions. (*In re Estate of Brooks* (1965), 32 Ill.2d 361, 205 N.E.2d 435.) Although most people do not share the Jehovah's Witnesses' beliefs about blood transfusions, our society, and our courts, accept their right to have that belief. Similarly, the courts have consistently recognized individuals' rights to refuse medical treatment even if such a refusal would result in an increased likelihood of the individual's death. ***

* * *

Knowing interference with the right of determination is battery. Our examination of the record reveals that facts charging that interference are pleaded in plaintiffs' complaint against Nurse Smith and against the Hospital. For purposes of a motion on the pleadings, a court must accept these facts as true. (*Business Development Services*, 96 Ill.App.3d at 836, 52 Ill.Dec. at 408, 422 N.E.2d at 89.) Accepting as true the plaintiffs' allegations that they informed defendants of their religious beliefs and that defendants persisted in treating Patricia Cohen as they would have treated a patient without those beliefs, we conclude that the trial court erred in dismissing both the battery and the intentional infliction of emotional distress counts.

* * *

Based on the information found in the Cohens' complaint against Nurse Smith and the Cohens' complaint against the Hospital, we find that the trial court erred in dismissing both complaints.

Find the Tort

The following is testimony from *Snyder v. Turk*, 627 N.E.2d 1053 (1993). Snyder (a scrub nurse) is suing Turk (a surgeon) for actions that occurred during an operation in which they were both involved. Find the tort or torts.

The plaintiff testified that Dr. Turk entered the operating room a little after 5:30 p.m. followed by Dr. Clark:

"[A.] I said good afternoon Dr. Turk and he didn't say anything.

* * *

"Q. Any conversation at this time between you and the defendant?
"A. Dr. Turk looked at Dr. Clark at that point and said, 'She's already made three mistakes.'
"Q. Did you respond?
"A. I said, what have I done Dr. Turk? and he ignored me.
"Q. Does the laparoscopic procedure begin at this point?
"A. Yes.
"Q. And what talk about the, sort of the beginning of the procedure, how does it get going?

"A. Well the beginning of the procedure, I hand off the light cord and the circulating nurse attaches the camera head to the telescope and we start the procedure as planned.
"Q. Was there some problem with trocars or the tubes that will go through the gentleman?
"A. Yes.
"Q. What was the problem?
"A. Dr. Turk had difficulty inserting the trocar through the abdomen. He had to make a couple attempts. He wasn't getting into the peritoneum which allowed him to get into the abdominal cavity which allowed him to blow the CO_2 in, the gas.
"Q. Did Dr. Turk make any comment to you that you had given him the wrong—
"A. He made a comment like, you sabotaged this case again."

At this point, Dr. Turk asked for a longer trocar. It is clear from the evidence that longer trocars were obtained from a supply cupboard.

Dr. Turk then inserted the video camera; however, the picture was a little hazy. The plaintiff attempted to eliminate the hazy picture:

"He said, don't you know how to trouble shoot? Why are you so incompetent? Why would they put somebody in who doesn't know how to use the equipment."

At about this point, the operation was converted to an open incision to do the open cholecystectomy, after Dr. Turk identified a gangrenous gall bladder and Dr. Clark identified it as being friable. The open procedure required a six-inch incision.

After testifying about the conversion, the plaintiff identified plaintiff's exhibit 4 as a regular right-angle clamp, which is used to clamp off blood vessels.

The questioning of the plaintiff then continued:

"Q. Did there come a time when the defendant asked for a right angle?
"A. Yes.
"Q. And what did he say?
"A. Right angle please.
"Q. Did he specify length?
"A. No.
"Q. What did you hand him?
"A. A right angle.
"Q. Did you hand him a tool just like Plaintiff's Exhibit 4?
"A. Yes.

"Q. And when you say you handed it to him, how does that actually happen, you know, what hand are you handing it to, what hand are you using? How is that actually happening across this person's body?
"A. He's standing across from me. I'm right handed, I'd hand it to his right hand. He's reaching his hand out and I put it in his hand.
"Q. You put it in your left hand?
"A. Right, it would be his right hand.
"Q. Where's his left hand?
"A. In the patient's abdomen helping restrict the abdominal cavity.
"Q. When you hand the right angle to the defendant, what happens?
"A. He takes the clamp from me and then he looks at it like he was going to use it and he throws it back at me.
"Q. And what, when you say he threw it back at you, where does the clamp go?
"A. To my mago tray.
"Q. What happens next?
"A. That's when I'm standing there and when he reached up and grabbed my shoulder and my gown and pulled me down from a standing position instantly down to the surgical wound and started screaming, can't you see where I'm working? I'm working in a hole. I need long instruments. I need long right angles now.
"Q. What part of Dr. Turk's body was in contact with yours?
"A. His hand.
"Q. Which hand?
"A. Right hand.
"Q. And I believe you pointed out which shoulder or please show the jury exactly where he makes contact with you?
"A. Right, my left shoulder and down.
"Q. Now immediately before this happened, what, in what position are you? Are you standing, seated, kneeled over; what position are you when he makes contact with your left shoulder?
"A. I'm standing, still on a standing stool.
"Q. And when, you know, right after he makes contact with you, what happens?
"A. I'm pulled from a standing position immediately down to like a 90 degree angle, right down onto the surgical field.
"Q. Did you voluntarily move from wherever you were standing down to the surgical field?
"A. No."

* * *

"Q. Where is your face in the end in relation to the patient there on the table?
"A. Looking right down into the surgical wound.
"Q. And how far is your face from the wound?
"A. Maybe 12 inches.

"Q. Do you remember what you thought and felt at that time?

"A. I was shocked; I was startled. I was scared. I didn't know what was going to happen next, if he was going to hit me—I was just, totally disbelief that this happened.

"Q. How long was your face down by the surgical incision?

"A. Just a very short time.

"Q. So what happens next?

"A. I stand up and try to gain my composure.

"Q. Do you remember what you were thinking or how you were feeling?

"A. I felt like a piece of shit. I had never been humiliated in my whole life. In front of medical students, surgical residents, nursing personnel, professional people, I'm pulled down into this patient's wound. I don't know if I'm going to fall over. He's yelling at me and I'm just shaken.

"Q. What's the next thing that happens?

"A. I turn around and ask Sue to please get me right angles, long right angles.

"Q. Did she?

"A. Yes.

"Q. How long did that take?

"A. Less than a minute.

"Q. When she brought you the long right angles, what did you do with them?

"A. I—I gave them to him.

"Q. What's the next thing that happens with you?

"A. I'm very emotional and I—mean, you know I'm shaken and I ask Sue to please get me relief, I said get Chris, who's the evening supervisor, and please get me some relief.

"Q. Anyone get you relief?

"A. Chris came into the room and I was told that I had to finish the procedure because we have three operating rooms running and there is no one to relieve me.

"Q. Did you stay and finish the procedure?

"A. Yes I did.

"Q. And how much longer did that take?

"A. Probably another half hour.

"Q. Did the defendant make any comments to you or about you during that additional half hour or so?

"A. Yes he did.

"Q. What did he say?

"A. He was talking to Dr. Clark and he kept saying he told him, I don't understand why she's so incompetent, must be passive-aggressive behavior. All she is here to get her paycheck. She's just looking for the time when she can leave.

"Q. Did you respond to any of those comments?

"A. I said, Dr. Turk, I do not appreciate those comments. I have been here many years. I do care about my job, I care about the patient laying [sic] on the table and that's why I'm going to finish this procedure."

The plaintiff also testified that she did not suffer any physical injury from her contact with Dr. Turk.

Unintentional Torts

Unintentional tort cases rely on the proof of four elements—duty (a standard of care or conduct owed by the defendant to the plaintiff), breach (an act or failure to act that is below the applicable standard of care or conduct), causation (the breach of duty is responsible for the harm), and harm (the damage that is caused by the breach). A plaintiff must prove that the defendant owed the plaintiff a specific standard of care or conduct below which the defendant operated, thus resulting in damage or harm to the plaintiff.

The causation element has two additional considerations, proximate cause and foreseeability. Proximate cause is the primary reason that the injury occurred. In other words, the injury would not have occurred "but for" the defendant's conduct. The defendant may not be liable for damages, however, if there are any intervening acts (any independent acts that occurred between the defendant's negligence and the plaintiff's injury) which changed the natural course of events stemming from the original negligence. In *Southall v. Gabel*, 33 Ohio Misc. 194 (1972), the court defined proximate cause as follows:

> Proximate cause is the active and efficient cause that sets in motion a train of events which brings about the result without intervention of any force started and working actively from a new or different and independent source.

The injury must also be within the realm of foreseeability. That is, it must be reasonably anticipated that the defendant's negligence could cause the harm incurred by the plaintiff.

Unintentional torts include the sorts of cases of which most people are aware—the everyday personal injury cases like car accidents and slip and fall cases. Many of these cases grab the attention of the public, the media, politicians, and so on due to the sometimes large monetary judgments awarded to the plaintiffs. Normally for a personal injury case, an attorney agrees to take the case for a contingency fee or percentage of the settlement or judgment. The fees will vary from attorney to attorney, but it is not unusual for an attorney to get a minimum of 33% of the monetary award if the case settles out of court to upwards of 40% if the case goes to trial. This may seem like a great deal of potential money to the attorney, but there is a definite risk–reward element in being a plaintiff's attorney. Most cases do not end with multi-million dollar awards or settlements, and, if there is no monetary award, the plaintiff's attorney will get nothing.

In a suit for recovery in a negligence case, there are two schools of thought: contributory negligence and comparative negligence. Under contributory negligence, if the plaintiff is proven to have contributed at all to the injury or damage, then the plaintiff will be barred from recovery. As of this printing, only Alabama, Maryland, North Carolina, Virginia, and Washington, D.C. still operate under this system. The vast majority of the states rely on some version of comparative negligence. Under comparative negligence, if the plaintiff is found to have some liability for the harm, the plaintiff can recover, but only to the extent that the defendant is liable. For example, if the plaintiff was found to have been liable for the cause of 40% of the injury or damage, then the plaintiff could recover a damage award equal to 60% of the total. (For example, if damages were $100,000, in this case, the plaintiff could receive $60,000.) The types of comparative negligence systems are pure comparative negligence (where the plaintiff can recover something even if the plaintiff is 99% negligent compared to the defendant's 1%) and modified comparative negligence, which most states use. Under modified comparative negligence, there are two systems: 51% and 50% rules. Under the 51% rule, the plaintiff can recover damages only if his/her negligence is 50% or less. Under the 50% rule, the plaintiff can recover damages only if his/her negligence is 49% or less. In a trial, the judge or the jury would assign the level of negligence to each party.

> The *Thoma* case is a classic slip and fall case. Did Cracker Barrel have a duty that it breached which caused harm to Thoma?

THOMA v. CRACKER BARREL OLD COUNTRY STORE, INC.

District Court of Appeal of Florida, First District.
649 So.2d 277 (1995)

KAHN, Judge.

Appellant, Deborah Thoma, claims to have suffered a back injury when she fell in the Tallahassee Cracker Barrel Restaurant on the morning of September 26, 1990. She alleges Cracker Barrel negligently maintained the floor in a particular area of the restaurant either by creating a dangerous condition or by failing to discover a condition that had existed for a sufficient time so that Cracker Barrel knew or should have known about it. We reverse a final summary judgment entered in favor of Cracker Barrel.

* * *

After eating breakfast at the Cracker Barrel, Thoma took three or four steps away from her table when her left foot slid out from under her, causing her to fall. The fall occurred in a common aisle, near the passage from the kitchen to the restaurant. When Thoma got up, she noticed an area 1 foot by 2 feet containing drops of clear liquid. She claims to have slipped on this liquid. Thoma was in the restaurant about thirty minutes before her accident. During that time, she saw no one drop anything on the floor in the area where she fell.

Mr. Leonard McNeal was the only known witness to the fall. He arrived for breakfast about 15 minutes before the accident. His seat was some 12 to 15 feet away from where Thoma fell. McNeal described the area as "a normal area where waitresses would frequently go in and out (the kitchen) door." McNeal felt sure he saw waitresses carrying beverage pitchers in that area. He did not see any Cracker Barrel customers carrying drinks in the area, nor did he see anyone drop or spill anything.

Cracker Barrel's manager, Mr. Charlie Gray, inspected the area of the fall and saw no foreign substance whatever on the floor. According to Mr. Gray, the Cracker Barrel is not a buffet restaurant and he would not expect customers to get up and walk around with food or drinks.

To recover for injuries incurred in a slip and fall accident, the plaintiff must show that the premises owner either created a dangerous condition or had actual or constructive knowledge of a dangerous condition. Notice of a dangerous condition may be established by circumstantial evidence, such as evidence leading to an inference that a substance has been on the floor for a sufficient length of time such that in the exercise of reasonable care the condition should have become known to the premises owner. *Schaap v. Publix Supermarkets, Inc.*, 579 So.2d 831 (Fla. 1st DCA 1991).

We have recently reversed a defense summary judgment in a similar case, *Gonzalez v. Tallahassee Medical Center, Inc.*, 629 So.2d 945 (Fla. 1st DCA 1993). In that case, Gonzalez slipped and fell on a liquid substance that looked like water, but could have been "syrup or Sprite." Her grandson testified that when he came to Gonzalez' aid, he noticed that the liquid "expanded out when pressed upon." He also observed that the fall occurred near a soda drink dispenser set out for customer use and in an area where the cashier had a clear view. The grandson was in the cafeteria ten to fifteen minutes before the accident and did not hear or see anyone spill a liquid in the area of the fall. 629 So.2d at 946. While we declined to speculate on what a jury might do with those facts, we held that inferences arose which "could establish the length of time the dangerous condition had been present on the floor, a critical element in proving that appellee, through the exercise of ordinary care, should have known of the condition."

In the present case, Thoma and McNeal took their breakfast at a location near where Thoma eventually fell. Despite their proximity, neither Thoma nor McNeal saw anyone drop or spill anything. The area of the fall was in clear view of Cracker Barrel employees, since they traversed it regularly on their way in and out of the kitchen. If a jury were to believe Thoma's description of the liquid as covering an area 1 foot by 2 feet, it might also be convinced that Cracker Barrel employees, in the exercise of due diligence, should have noticed the liquid before the accident. No one except Cracker Barrel employees were seen to carry food or beverage in the area of the fall, and the manager of the restaurant would not have expected customers to move around carrying food or drinks.

Cracker Barrel notes that "common sense" suggests "a plethora" of reasonable inferences other than the inferences urged by appellants. We certainly agree with this observation, but take issue with the suggestion that the existence of other possible inferences requires affirmance of the summary judgment in favor of Cracker Barrel. It will be for a jury to determine whether a preponderance of the evidence supports the inferences suggested by Thoma.

REVERSED and REMANDED.

The *Virden* case is another personal injury case with a much different fact pattern from *Thoma*. Again, look for the elements of an unintentional tort, including foreseeability.

VIRDEN v. BETTS AND BEER CONSTRUCTION CO., INC.

Supreme Court of Iowa
656 N.W.2d 805 (2003)

NEUMAN, Justice.

Plaintiff, Ron Virden, worked in the maintenance department of Indianola High School. On the first day of school in 1997, Virden's supervisor asked him to reinstall an angle iron that had fallen from the ceiling of the school's new wrestling room. As Virden was bolting the angle iron into place, he fell from the top of the ten-foot ladder on which he was standing. He sustained severe injuries to his left leg, requiring several surgeries.

Virden sued the contractors, defendants Betts & Beer Construction and Stroh Corporation, who earlier in the year had installed the wrestling room ceiling. Over Virden's objection, the district court granted these defendants summary judgment. It held their negligence, if any, was not the proximate cause of Virden's injuries. Virden appealed and the court of appeals reversed. We granted further review and, now, vacate the court of appeals decision and affirm the judgment of the district court.

I. Scope of Review/Issue on Appeal.

Because this case reaches us on appeal from a summary judgment ruling, our task is to determine whether the record made before the district court demonstrates "no genuine issue as to any material fact and that the moving party is entitled to a judgment as a matter of law." Iowa R. Civ. P. 1.981. We are obliged to "view the evidence in the light most favorable to the plaintiff, giving him the benefit of every legitimate inference the evidence will bear." *Walls v. Jacob North Printing Co.*, 618 N.W.2d 282, 284 (Iowa 2000).

While negligence cases do not ordinarily lend themselves to summary adjudication, *see id.*, summary judgment may be rendered when the material facts fail to show a causal link between the negligence and the injury. See *Ruden v. Jenk*, 543 N.W.2d 605, 612 (Iowa 1996). Issues of proximate cause, like negligence, are generally for the jury to resolve. Iowa R.App. P. 6.14(6)(j); *Hollingsworth v. Schminkey*, 553 N.W.2d 591, 597 (Iowa 1996). They may, however, be decided as a matter of law in an exceptional case. Iowa R.App. P. 6.14(6)(j); *Hollingsworth*, 553 N.W.2d at 597. We have observed that an exceptional case is one in which after construing the evidence in its most favorable light and resolving all doubts in favor of the party seeking to establish proximate cause, the relationship between cause and effect nonetheless is so apparent and so unrelated to defendant's conduct that no reasonable jury could conclude defendant's fault was a proximate cause of plaintiff's injuries. *Johnson v. Junkmann*, 395 N.W.2d 862, 865–66 (Iowa 1986). The question is whether this is such an exceptional case. For the reasons that follow, we think that it is.

II. Analysis.

To sustain his tort claim against these defendants, Virden would have to prove that the defendants owed him a duty of care, they breached that duty, their breach was the actual and proximate cause of Virden's injuries, and he suffered damages. *Walls*, 618 N.W.2d at 285. Virden's petition claimed that defendants' failure to "properly assemble, install and/or inspect the roof system" required Virden to "put himself at risk to re-install the angle iron," leading to his fall from the ladder.

The summary judgment record makes plain that neither Virden nor his employer contacted the defendants about the fallen angle iron before attempting to effect repairs. Virden also concedes that he sought no help in positioning or securing the ladder, even though several pieces of weight-lifting equipment hampered clear access to the repair site. With this record in mind, we turn to the disputed elements of Virden's claim: duty and causation.

A. Duty. Although the defendants argue as a general proposition that they owed no duty of care to Virden, they are unable to defend the district court's ruling on that ground. It is generally held that a building or construction contractor is liable for injuries to, or the death of, third persons occurring after the completion of his work and its acceptance by the contractee, where the work is reasonably certain to endanger third persons if negligently prepared or constructed. *Thompson v. Burke Eng'g Sales Co.*, 252 Iowa 146, 155, 106 N.W.2d 351, 356 (1960). This rule rests on fundamental principles:

[T]he law imposes upon every person who undertakes the performance of an act which, it is apparent, if not done carefully will be dangerous to other persons or the property of other persons the duty to exercise his senses and intelligence to avoid injury, and any such person may be held accountable at law for an injury to person or to property which is directly attributable to a breach of such duty. 57A Am.Jur.2d *Negligence* § 96, at 150 (1989).

The angle iron that fell from the ceiling of the wrestling room was six feet in length and weighed roughly ten pounds. It can hardly be disputed that lack of due care in welding the angle iron in place would put the foreseeable occupants of the room at considerable risk of injury. In other words, the defendants had a duty to Virden, and others using the room, to construct a ceiling that did not fall apart and injure someone. *See Thompson*, 252 Iowa at 149, 106 N.W.2d at 353 (common experience teaches that ceilings do not fall in the absence of negligence).

Virden did not suffer, however, from being hit by the angle iron or tripping over it once it fell from the ceiling. In his words, he was injured when the ladder he stood on to replace the fallen hardware "suddenly kicked out from under [him] and [he] fell." That brings us to the crux of the case.

B. Causation. Defendants' breach of their duty of care only constitutes actionable negligence if it is "also the proximate cause of the injury." *City of Cedar Falls v. Cedar Falls Cmty. Sch. Dist.*, 617 N.W.2d 11, 17 (Iowa 2000). There are two components to the proximate-cause inquiry: "(1) the defendant's conduct must have in fact caused the damages; and (2) the policy of the law must require the defendant to be legally responsible for them." *Id.; see also Gerst v. Marshall,* 549 N.W.2d 810, 815 (Iowa 1996).

With respect to the first component, a plaintiff must at a minimum prove that the damages would not have occurred *but for* the defendant's negligence. *City of Cedar Falls*, 617 N.W.2d at 17; *Gerst*, 549 N.W.2d at 817. Here, viewing the facts in the light most favorable to Virden, we assume that but for the faulty weld in the angle iron he would not have been perched precariously upon a ladder attempting to fix it. So, minimally, the but-for test of causation would survive defendants' motion for summary judgment.

The but-for test is not the end of the inquiry, however. Virden must also tender proof that defendants' negligent welding of the angle iron was a *substantial factor* in bringing about his injury. *City of Cedar Falls*, 617 N.W.2d at 17; *Scoggins v. Wal-Mart Stores, Inc.*, 560 N.W.2d 564, 567 (Iowa 1997). *See generally* Restatement (Second) of Torts § 431 cmt. a (1965) (distinguishing between "substantial cause" and cause "in the so-called philosophic sense, which includes every one of the great number of events without which any happening would not have occurred.") This aspect of the proximate-cause inquiry focuses on the "proximity and forseeablility of the harm flowing from the actor's conduct." *City of Cedar Falls*, 617 N.W.2d at 17.

We have observed that the line between "what is sufficiently proximate and what is too remote is often a thin one." *Hollingsworth*, 553 N.W.2d at 597. We recently drew the line this way:

An injury that is the *natural* and *probable* consequence of an act of negligence is actionable, and such an act is the proximate cause of the injury. But an injury which could not have been foreseen or reasonably anticipated as the *probable* result of an act of negligence is not actionable and such an act is either the remote cause, or no cause whatever, of the injury. *Scoggins*, 560 N.W.2d at 568-69 (quoting *Fly v. Cannon*, 836 S.W.2d 570, 574 (Tenn. Ct.App.1992) (emphasis added)).

Here, the district court assessed defendants' role in Virden's mishap as remote rather than foreseeable. Its conclusion stemmed from the undisputed fact that the instrumentality causing Virden's injury was a tipping or collapsing ladder, not a defective angle iron. We agree. The Re-statement describes this distinction as the difference between the "negligence problem" and the "cause problem":

[W]here the negligence of the act consists in its recognizable tendency to subject another to a particular hazard, the actor cannot be subject to liability for any harm occurring otherwise than by the other's exposure to that hazard. Restatement (Second) of Torts § 430 cmt. a (1965) (citing Restatement (Second) of Torts § 281 cmt. e). Applying this concept to the case before us, we observe that the duty to construct a solid ceiling is not to protect repairmen from perching on tall ladders but to prevent collapsing parts of the ceiling from falling on persons below.

To summarize, the unfortunate outcome of Virden's self-help remedy cannot be said to fall naturally within the scope of the probable risk created by the defendants' failure to properly install the ceiling. Because Virden's fall was not a reasonably foreseeable or probable consequence of *defendants'* negligence, the district court correctly granted judgment in their favor. We therefore vacate the court of appeals' contrary decision and affirm the judgment of the district court.

COURT OF APPEALS DECISION VACATED; DISTRICT COURT JUDGMENT AFFIRMED.

The following case is an unintentional tort case that involves toilet overflow, watering a neighbor's flowers, and electric shock. Were Hebert's injuries foreseeable? Should the defendant be liable for damages?

HEBERT v. ENOS

Appeals Court of Massachusetts, Middlesex.
60 Mass. App. Ct. 817 (2004)

KAFKER, J.

The plaintiff William Hebert (Hebert) brought an action to recover for personal injuries he suffered as a result of receiving a severe electric shock while lawfully on the defendant Carl Enos's property to water the defendant's flowers. Hebert claimed that the defendant's faulty repairs of a second-floor toilet caused the toilet to overflow. The flooding water then reacted with the home's electrical system, creating an electrical current that shocked and injured Hebert when he touched the outside water faucet. Hebert asserted a claim for negligence in his complaint, and his wife sought damages for loss of consortium. The defendant moved for summary judgment on the ground that Hebert's injuries were not a reasonably foreseeable consequence of any negligence on the defendant's part. The judge allowed the defendant's motion for summary judgment, finding that "[t]he injury to [Hebert] was highly extraordinary and 'so remote in everyday life' as to preclude a finding that the alleged negligence was a legal cause of [Hebert's] injuries." We affirm.

Background. The facts and reasonable inferences therefrom, viewed in the light most favorable to the plaintiffs, are as follows. The defendant and the plaintiffs were neighbors in Framingham. The defendant, prior to departing on vacation, asked Hebert to water his flowers while he was away. Hebert agreed and watered the defendant's flowers without incident on the three days leading up to July 4, 2000.

On July 4, 2000, Hebert, while holding the defendant's garden hose in one hand, reached for the outside faucet on the defendant's house. Apparently, upon grabbing the faucet, Hebert received an electric shock that threw him many feet through the air, melted his sneakers and glasses, set his pants on fire, and knocked his dental plate from his mouth. Hebert suffered serious injuries, including burns and exit wounds on his body and damage to his mouth.

* * *

Discussion. When the facts and reasonable inferences therefrom are viewed in the light most favorable to the plaintiffs, we conclude that the plaintiffs submitted sufficient evidence to establish that faulty repairs of the toilet by the defendant resulted in flooding and severe electric shock to Hebert when he touched the faucet. Summary judgment is still appropriate, however, if a plaintiff has no reasonable expectation of proving that "the 821*821 injury to the plaintiff was a foreseeable result of the defendant's negligent conduct." *Kent v. Commonwealth*, 437 Mass. 312, 320 (2002). See *Bergendahl v. Massachusetts Elec. Co.*, 45 Mass. App. Ct. 715, 725 (1998), cert. denied, 528 U.S. 929 (1999) ("While the issue of foreseeability is ordinarily a question of fact for the jury, the court may decide the issue as a matter of law … in the absence of evidence that the risk which resulted in the plaintiff's injury should reasonably have been anticipated by the defendant …" [citation omitted]); *Palsgraf v. Long Island* R.R., 248 N.Y. 339, 345 (1928) ("The range of reasonable apprehension is at times a question for the court, and at times, if varying inferences are possible, a question for the jury").

We say that "[o]ne is bound to anticipate and provide against what usually happens and what is likely to happen, but is not bound in like manner to guard against what is … only remotely and slightly probable." *Falk v. Finkelman*, 268 Mass. 524, 527 (1929). See Restatement (Second) of Torts, § 435(2) (1965) ("The actor's conduct may be held not to be a legal cause of harm to another where … it appears to the court highly extraordinary that it should have brought about the harm"). We look to determine whether the "general character and probability of the injury [were] foreseeable." *Glick v. Prince Italian Foods of Saugus, Inc.*, 25 Mass. App. Ct. 901, 902 (1987). *** We also recognize that "[t]here must be limits to the scope or definition of reasonable foreseeability based on considerations of policy and pragmatic judgment." *Poskus v. Lombardo's of Randolph, Inc.*, 423 Mass. 637, 640 (1996). ***

In the instant case, when we consider the likelihood, character, and location of the harm, we conclude as matter of law that the injuries sustained by Hebert were a "highly extraordinary" consequence of a defective second-floor toilet. See Restatement (Second) of Torts § 435(2). See also *Rae v. Air Speed Inc.*, 386 Mass. 187, 193 (1982); *Bergendahl v. Massachusetts Elec. Co.*, 45 Mass. App. Ct. at 725. Although we can envision a variety of foreseeable injuries arising out of a defective toilet, the electric shock to a neighbor when he touches a faucet outside the house is well beyond the "range of reasonable apprehension" and therefore not foreseeable. *Palsgraf v. Long Island R.R.*, 248 N.Y. at 345. See *Polak v. Whitney*, 21 Mass. App. Ct. 349, 351 (1985) (duty to warn guests extends to "any unreasonable dangers of which [the homeowner] was aware or should reasonably have been aware"). We therefore conclude that Hebert's severe and unfortunate injuries were the consequence of the type of unforeseeable accident for which we do not hold the defendant responsible in tort. The harm Hebert suffered, even when the facts and reasonable inferences that could be drawn therefrom are viewed in the light most favorable to him, was so highly extraordinary that the defendant cannot be required to guard against it.

* * *

Finally, the plaintiffs appear to suggest that so long as the defendant's negligence can be connected in an unbroken causal chain to the resultant harm, and no third party's negligence can be blamed for the injury, the harm is by definition proximate. This is not the law of proximate cause in Massachusetts, nor is it supported by the commentary upon which the plaintiffs rely. Here, the defendant could not have reasonably foreseen the harm that befell Hebert.

Judgment affirmed.

[Footnotes Omitted.]

The following is an excerpt from a California case. The first part is an excerpt from the complaint. The second part is from the plaintiff's trial brief. Are duty, breach, causation, and harm present? If so, was the harm foreseeable? Did the plaintiff have any part in the injury—was there contributory negligence?

STRANGE v. ENTERCOM SACRAMENTO

Superior Court Of California, County Of Sacramento
Case No.: 07AS00377

Plaintiffs complain against Defendants and allege:

FIRST CAUSE OF ACTION

(WRONGFUL DEATH: NEGLIGENCE)

* * *

Complaint for Wrongful Death

4. Leading up to January 12/ 2007/ THE TALENT on The Morning Rave promoted and advertised an on-air radio contest known as "Hold your Wee for a Wii." THE TALENT solicited listeners to apply to participate in this contest. Defendants, and each of them, created, devised, orchestrated, organized, arranged and publicized each element of this contest, including marketing the contest to various sponsors and advertisers. Defendants and each of them determined the rules of the contest, the criteria for contest participants, the duration of the contest, and the contest prizes. Defendants and each of them accepted applications for the contest, and screened and selected the final contestants, including decedent Jennifer Strange.

5. The contestants, including decedent, competed for the right to receive a Nintendo Wii video gaming system that has been in high demand since its release to the public late in 2006. The decedent ardently wished to win the Nintendo Wii system for her children, and applied for the contest. The winner of the contest was selected based on which contestant could consume the most water in a three-hour period without urinating. Defendants provided the location and all facilities (including the drinking water) for the contest, which was conducted on-air and in-studio at KDND 107.9 in Sacramento.

6. At no time before the contest did the decedent sign a release of liability contractually relieving any Defendants of their duty of care in organizing and running the contest.

7. At all times, it was foreseeable to Defendants and each of them that the contestants were at risk for serious illness and/or death as the result of consuming extensive amounts of water in a relatively short period of time. At all relevant times preceding the contest, Defendants were aware that consumption of water to such an extent could result in physical injury or death. Defendants had specific knowledge of a relatively recent fraternity hazing incident in Northern California as a result of which a young man died from over-consumption of water. Defendants had specific knowledge of similar contests at other radio stations in California during which contestants required medical attention as a result of their participation. Defendants were specifically informed before and/or during the contest that the contestants were subject to the risk of serious illness and/or death as a result of their participation.

8. Prior to commencement of the contest, Defendants and each of them failed to conduct a reasonable investigation to determine the relative health risks to prospective contest participants. Defendants negligently failed to consult with appropriate health authorities regarding the relative health risks posed by such an enterprise. Defendants negligently failed to identify specific health risks or inform contest participants, including decedent, of any such risks. Defendants negligently failed to post any health advisories for contest participants, and failed to take any steps to identify prospective participants who might be at risk of injury. Defendants negligently failed to secure any medical professional or paraprofessional services during the contest, even after the contestants begin feeling ill, and similarly failed to require an examination by a competent physician of each contest participant prior to commencement of the contest. Defendants individually and collectively knew or should have known of the health risks of such a contest, but took no reasonable steps to advise, warn, supervise or otherwise protect contest participants including decedent.

9. The decedent complained of feeling ill while in-studio and before claiming her second place prize on-air. Defendants negligently failed to provide any assistance, medical or otherwise, to any of the contestants, including decedent.

10. The negligence of Defendants caused the death of Jennifer Strange. Had the decedent been properly informed of the health risks associated with the contest, she would not have participated. Had medical professional or para-professional services been provided, the decedent would not have consumed the

fatal doses of water, and would have had immediate access to life-saving medical care and treatment as she began to exhibit symptoms consistent with over-consumption of water.

11. Defendants and DOES 31 through 40 otherwise negligently caused or were a substantial factor in causing the death of Jennifer Strange.

12. As a direct result of Defendants' negligence and the death of Jennifer Strange, Plaintiffs have sustained economic damages consisting of (1) the value of lost financial and other support from the decedent, (2) the value of gifts or benefits that the decedent would have provided, (3) the value of funeral and burial expenses, and (4) the reasonable value of household services that the decedent would have provided.

13. As a direct result of Defendants' negligence, and the death of Jennifer Strange, Plaintiffs have also sustained non-economic damages consisting of loss of the decedent's love, companionship, comfort, care, assistance, protection, affection, society, and moral support.

* * *

SECOND CAUSE OF ACTION

(SURVIVOR'S ACTION: NEGLIGENCE)

14. Plaintiffs incorporate herein by reference all allegations of the first cause of action as though fully set forth.

15. Plaintiff WILLIAM A. STRANGE, as the surviving spouse of Jennifer Strange, is her Successor in Interest for purposes of bringing an action under CCP Section 377.30, et. seq. Plaintiff has and/or will comply with CCP Section 377.32.

16. Prior to her death, Jennifer Strange was required to and did employ physicians and surgeons to examine, treat, and care for her as a result of the injuries and Complaint for Wrongful Death illness sustained as a result of participating in Defendants' contest. Plaintiffs and/or the decedent incurred medical and incidental expenses in connection therewith. The exact amount of such expense is unknown to Plaintiffs at this time.

17. Plaintiffs are entitled to punitive damages against Defendants and each of them. By cooperating in the orchestration, direction, promotion and marketing of the contest, THE TALENT, at all relevant times acting in the course and scope of their employment by ENTERCOM, MANAGING AGENTS and DOES 11 through 40/ engaged in conduct that evidenced a willful and knowing disregard of decedent's safety, while ignoring the probable dangerous consequences of such a contest and deliberately failing to avoid those consequences, despite THE TALENTS' individual and collective awareness of the risks of such

conduct. Such conduct was despicable and so vile, base or contemptible that it would be looked down upon and despised by reasonable people. Specifically, Defendants and each of them deliberately failed to undertake sufficient research or investigation to be able to recognize the onset of a medical problem relative to the consumption of vast quantities of water, despite their independent and collective knowledge that such consumption could lead to injury and death. THE TALENT admitted during the broadcast that they should have done more research once various participants, including decedent, began to report medical symptoms. Despite this admission, Defendants, and each of them, failed to act upon clear reports of medical symptoms from decedent that were consistent with the onset of hyponatremia. At no time did Defendants advise decedent to seek medical attention. At no time did Defendants advise decedent to drop out of the contest in response to her symptoms. Instead of offering to provide medical assistance after decedent reported feeling ill, THE TALENT verbally chastised and otherwise coerced her, exhorting her to remain in the contest by threatening that she would be disqualified if she "puked." THE TALENT similarly chastised other contest participants, instructing other personnel to make sure that a participant who appeared to be dead had "signed a release" and emphasizing on numerous occasions those contestants who vomited or urinated would be eliminated.

18. At all relevant times ENTERCOM, MANAGING AGENTS and DOES 11 through 40 were officers, directors or managing agents of said Defendants, empowered to exercise substantial independent authority and judgment in corporate decision capable of determining corporate policy. In that capacity, ENTERCOM, MANAGING AGENTS and DOES 11 through 40 planned, orchestrated, managed, promoted, controlled, supervised, marketed and authorized the despicable conduct of THE TALENT, and otherwise ratified, adopted or approved that conduct, both before and after it occurred.

* * *

PLAINTIFFS' TRIAL BRIEF

Trial Date: August 31, 2009

* * *

III.
FACTUAL BACKGROUND

On January 12, 2007, 28-year old Jennifer Strange died following her participation in a radio contest created, marketed and managed by Defendant ENTERCOM SACRAMENTO, LLC, a subsidiary of Defendant ENTERCOM COMMUNICATIONS CORP. (hereinafter referred to collectively as "ENTERCOM"). Defendant JOHN GEARY (hereinafter referred to as "GEARY") was the Vice President and "Market Manager" (akin to General Manager) of ENTERCOM SACRAMENTO, LLC.

* * *

The "Hold Your Wee for a Wii" contest originated in October, 2006 during a regular meeting of KDND's promotions department and program director with the station's on-air personalities (called the "talent"). Patterned after a similar contest that was the subject of an article in an industry trade publication about events designed to peak listener interest, the Morning Rave adapted it to celebrate the release of Nintendo's new, and really impossible to obtain, gaming system, the "Wii." Contestants would drink water and hold their urine, or "wee", to win a "Wii." Because the Wii was considered a much wanted but hard-to-get item in very short supply around the holidays, the concept was met with enthusiasm by the Defendants' employees. Management approved it on the spot and scheduled the contest to coincide with the upcoming holiday season.

* * *

The most critical written rule ignored by the Morning Rave was that contestants would drink one 8-ounce bottle every 15 minutes. Unfettered by written or broadcast rules, the Morning Rave decided that contestants would drink water every 10 minutes, not every 15. This increased the number of bottles consumed from four to six per hour. Instead of drinking 8-ounces of water per break, the Morning Rave increased this to 76-ounces halfway through the contest. They also imposed a strict time limit to get the water down. These off-the-cuff, ill-considered changes played a substantial role in Jennifer's death.

According to Dr. George Kaysen, Plaintiffs' retained medical expert in the area of kidney function, 4.8 to 5.2 liters of water constituted a lethal dose for Jennifer. Had the Morning Rave followed Pechota's written rules, and had the contest ended at 9:30 a.m. (as it did on January 12, 2007), Jennifer Strange would at most have consumed 104 ounces of water (thirteen 8-ounce bottles) or 3.07 liters, dramatically less than the 4.8 liters threshold that could lead to death, and far from the 208 to 2/6 ounces (6.15 to 6.38 liters) Jennifer ultimately consumed.

Here is the cruelest part of that equation. The rules made up on the spot by the Morning Rave on January 12, 2007 served only one purpose: sheer entertainment value. These actors wanted to create "good radio." To the Morning Rave, "good radio" meant edgy, risky, exciting, even dangerous radio. A contest where adults might soil themselves just to win a video game? Might vomit publicly? Might be embarrassed and humiliated in the most personal and unhygienic of ways? How marvelous! How cutting edge! How captivating! That is why the Morning Rave increased the number of bottles consumed by 150% (from 4 to 6 per hour) and the size of the bottles doubled (from 8 to 16 ounces): to foster humiliation and despair, in the name of entertainment. We know this because at the time, the Morning Rave was famous for these kinds of edgy stunts. They had served KDND well; the Morning Rave was the number one morning show in Sacramento for its target demographic. Cox, Maney, Sweet, Pechota, Diaz—they knew how to create good radio, a fact recognized, condoned and prized by their boss JOHN GEARY, who fostered an environment where they were given free rein to do as they pleased, so long as ratings stayed high. That is why Jennifer Strange died; not because of an oversight, but because ENTERCOM cared about ratings, not risk. The real tragedy is that the Morning Rave had every reason to know the contest was dangerous.

4. ENTERCOM's Morning Rave Aired Two Shows About the Risks of Excessive Water Consumption Before the Contest

In their depositions Adam Cox, Steve Maney and Patricia Sweet insisted that prior to Jennifer's death they had no idea that drinking excessive amounts of water posed a risk of physical harm. Throughout the "Wee" broadcast, these on-air personalities referred repeatedly to the death of Chico State University student Matthew Carrington in February of 2005. Carrington's death from water intoxication during a fraternity hazing was a tragic event that they not only knew about, they made light of it. Yet, each D.J. expressed only vague knowledge of Carrington's death at deposition. There is ample evidence that the Morning Rave appreciated the risk of excessive water consumption well before the contest, and that their testimony to the contrary was duplicitous, at best.

Peter Inzerillo, the show's gag expert was deposed long after Cox, Maney and Sweet. According to Inzerillo (Fester on the show), about a month before the contest the Morning Rave devoted part of a broadcast to the Matt Carrington incident. During that broadcast they made light of Carrington's death and the events leading up to it. They used Carrington's death to segue into a bantering discussion of how much water Fester could drink without getting sick or dying.

A week later, Fester was back in the booth. He was told to drink water from a large glass flower vase formerly used to hold a bouquet of tulips, a gift to Trish from a listener. Fester estimated that he drained the vase four times. Listeners were invited to call in and "bet" on how long he could hold his urine. Soon Fester reported dizziness, nausea and intoxication, all symptoms of hyponatremia, much to the amusement of the on-air talent. In an attempt to find the cause, Trish ran a Google search on one of the many computers available in the booth, limited to the poisonous effects of tulips. The search yielded that while tulips posed no danger to humans, they could adversely affect goats. This generated more banter as the Rave crew compared Fester to goats. Meanwhile, Fester's symptoms worsened. Clearly by the day of the contest the Rave crew knew or should have known that drinking water could cause physical symptoms and in the case of Matt Carrington, death.

* * *

6. ENTERCOM Ignored Repeated Warning Calls from Listeners That the Contest was Dangerous

Shortly after the contest started, listener Eva Brooks phoned the station to report the possibility of water intoxication.

* * *

According to Liz Diaz, the show's producer, who handled all incoming calls to the show, the Brooks call was just the first in a series. Because it was the first call on that topic, she put it through to the "booth" to facilitate a live dialogue between Brooks and the Morning Rave crew. Diaz also testified that she personally took four to five other calls warning about the risk of excessive water consumption after the Brooks call. The only reason she did not pass those calls through to the studio booth was because of a standing rule that precluded "duplicate" calls. At some point she became concerned about the quantity of calls warning that contestants were at risk, and approached Cox, Maney and Sweet. The talent told her to advise listeners that the station was aware of the risk and that all contestants had signed a release. She followed these instructions. These warning calls clearly constitute evidence that despite any alleged lack of prior notice, KDND received actual notice of a risk during the broadcast, in ample time to spare Jennifer's life, yet took not a single step to warn or advise any contestant, or to stop the contest immediately.

Res Ipsa Loquitur

Res ipsa loquitur is a legal concept that literally means "the thing speaks for itself." Each state has its own interpretation of the concept, but two elements must always be present. First, an event must occur that would not occur under normal circumstances unless negligence was involved. Second, the defendant must clearly and solely be in a position of responsibility for the event that caused the damage.

Byrne v. Boadle is the seminal case involving the concept of res ipsa loquitor. It involved Mr. Boadle, who owned a warehouse for his flour business, and Mr. Byrne, who was injured by a barrel of flour that fell from a window as he passed by Mr. Boadle's warehouse. Witnesses saw the barrel fall and hit Byrne. There was no evidence of negligence on Boadle's part.

BYRNE v. BOADLE

2 H. & C. 722 (Exch 1863)

C.B. Pollack stated, "There are certain cases of which it may be said res ipsa loquitur, and this seems one of them. In some cases the Court had held that the mere fact of the accident having occurred is evidence of negligence, as, for instance, in the case of railway collisions."

He further stated, "It is the duty of persons who keep barrels in a warehouse to take care that they do not roll out, and I think that such a case would, beyond all doubt, afford prima facie evidence of negligence. A barrel could not roll out of a warehouse without some negligence, and to say that a plaintiff who is injured by it must call witnesses from the warehouse to prove negligence seems to me preposterous. So in the building or repairing a house, or putting pots on the chimneys, if a person passing along the road is injured by something falling upon him, I think the accident alone would be prima facie evidence of negligence. Or if an article calculated to cause damage is put in a wrong place and does mischief, I think that those whose duty it was to put it in the right place are prima facie responsible, and if there is any state of facts to rebut the presumption of negligence, they must prove them. The present case upon the evidence comes to this, a man is passing in front of the premises of a dealer in flour, and there falls down upon him a barrel of flour. I think it apparent that the barrel was in the custody of the defendant who occupied the premises, and who is responsible for the acts of his servants who had the control of it; and in my opinion the fact of its falling is prima facie evidence of negligence, and the plaintiff who was injured by it is not bound to show that it could not fall without negligence, but if there are any facts inconsistent with negligence it is for the defendant to prove them."

Leikach applies the concept of res ipsa loquitur to a case in which a bottle of soda exploded and injured the plaintiff.

LEIKACH v. ROYAL CROWN BOTTLING COMPANY OF BALTIMORE, INCORPORATED

Court of Appeals of Maryland
261 Md. 541 (1971)

HAMMOND, C.J., delivered the opinion of the Court.

In *Joffre v. Canada Dry, Inc.*, 222 Md. 1, we affirmed the action of the trial judge in directing a verdict for the bottler and the delicatessen store owner in a suit by a claimant who had suffered a severed Achilles tendon when a soda bottle exploded near her in the store. The claimant relied on res ipsa loquitur. In agreeing with the trial judge that the claimant had not shown a greater likelihood that her injury was caused by the negligence of the defendants than by some other cause, we said (at pp. 9–10):

> "The cases from other jurisdictions which have permitted the inference of negligence of the bottler from the exploding of a bottle most often have been those where the probability of an

> intervening cause of the breaking has been excluded by the testimony for the plaintiff. Where that probability is not excluded, the courts usually rule that no liability of the bottler has been shown. For example, where the exploding bottle had been kept in a room to which only the retailer had access and due care was shown after delivery to the retailer until the moment of bursting, res ipsa was held applicable to the bottler in *MacPherson v. Canada Dry Ginger Ale, Inc.* (Sup. Ct. N.J.), 29 A.2d 868. The Court distinguished *Dunn v. Hoffman Beverage Co.* (N.J.), 20 A.2d 352, where the doctrine was held inapplicable because the plaintiff did not exclude other probable causes or show due care in handling after delivery by the bottler. We have noted earlier that the Municipal Court of Appeals for the District of Columbia made the same distinction in the cases of *Canada Dry Ginger Ale Co. v. Jochum* (D.C.) 43 A.2d 42, and *Atwell v. Pepsi-Cola Bottling Co. of Washington (D.C.),* 152 A.2d 196. Compare *Benkendorfer v. Garrett* (Tex. Civ. App.), 143 S.W.2d 1020, in which the exploding bottle had been at the retail store but two days and had not been moved or molested until grasped to be put in the refrigerator when it burst (recovery allowed), with *Kees v. Canada Dry Ginger Ale, Inc.* (Mo. App.), 199 S.W.2d 76, 79, in which the bottle was in the store from January 28 to March 1 and the Court, in denying recovery against the bottler, noted the bottle could have been dropped, mishandled, tampered with and cracked by employees or customers, and the jury could do no more than guess that it had not been subjected to treatment tending to bring about the explosion resulting in injury, after it left the possession of the bottler. Other cases finding a lack of proof of unchanged conditions after the bottle had left the bottler are *Hughs v. Miami Coca Cola Bottling Co.* (Fla.), 19 So.2d 862; and *Monroe v. H.G. Hill Stores, Inc.* (La.), 51 So.2d 645. The cases are collected in an annotation in 4 A.L.R.2d 466.

* * *

In the case now before us the plaintiff below and the appellant here was the owner of a small store who was struck in the eye by part of an exploded soda bottle he had bought from the bottler, the Royal Crown Bottling Company, Inc. (Royal Crown), the defendant below and the appellee here. *** We are of the view that the claimant offered sufficient evidence to permit reasonable men to conclude as jurors that the bottler, and not another, had been negligent and that this negligence resulted in harm to the claimant, and accordingly we will reverse the judgment for the bottler.

The plaintiff, Martin Leikach, and his wife came to this country from Poland. At the times here pertinent they operated a small self-service grocery store at Lexington and Amity Streets in Baltimore, approximately thirty by twenty-five feet. *** There was a display stand for soda bottles located in a recess to the right of the front entrance as one entered. ***

On May 18, 1967, an order of bottled Royal Crown soda products was delivered to the store. The bottles in the order had been inspected, filled, capped and delivered by Royal Crown. Royal Crown's employee handled the entire delivery which consisted in placing much of the order in the refrigerated unit in the store and placing the rest, in six packs, on the display stand. Customarily, the refrigerated unit was replenished by Leikach's employees from the display stand but, because Royal Crown had had a sale on, the order of May 18 was larger than usual and it had not been necessary to move any Royal Crown soda from the stand to the unit between the delivery and the explosion eight days later. Although the warm soda on the stand would have been sold, the neighborhood patrons of the store habitually bought only cold drinks, and no warm soda was sold between May 18 and the morning of the explosion eight days later. The soda products of two other companies shared the stand with those of Royal Crown but there was more of Royal Crown because it outsold the others several times to one.

None of the other companies delivered any bottles to the store between the May 18 delivery of Royal Crown soda and the explosion. The testimony was that if anyone had been near or around the Royal Crown soda on the stand it would have been unusual and have been seen and that no one, including Leikach, tampered with, disturbed or injured any bottle on the stand after May 18 and before the explosion. The bottle that exploded was one of those delivered on May 18.

On the morning of May 26, 1967 Leikach and Judkins arrived together at the store, which had been closed for at least twelve hours, to open up for the day. Leikach unlocked the front door and walked in and Judkins followed. Leikach extended his left hand up to the burglar alarm box high above the soda display stand on the wall that formed the right side of the entrance way as one passed through the door towards the store interior. He turned the key in order to neutralize the alarm system. Both he and Judkins say he did not come in contact with the bottles on the stand in any way and Judkins was not in a position to affect the bottles. Neither the heating system nor the air-conditioning system was on, since the mid-May temperature called for neither, so that there was no sudden change in temperature. As Leikach withdrew his key and turned, one of the bottles on the stand exploded and the neck of the bottle separated from the rest of the bottle and either the cap or the glass, it is not entirely clear which, struck Leikach in the eye. Both Leikach and Judkins testified that the explosion came first and then a six pack fell to the floor with one bottle in pieces and five intact. The eye later had to be removed surgically. Leikach sued Royal Crown, relying on the doctrine of res ipsa loquitur.

Munzert v. American Stores, 232 Md. 97, 104, sets out the three criteria necessary for successful reliance on the doctrine of res ipsa loquitur as:

1. A casualty of a sort which usually does not occur in the absence of negligence.

2. Caused by an instrumentality within the defendant's exclusive control.

3. Under circumstances indicating that the casualty did not result from the act or omission of the plaintiff.

It is apparent and conceded that the first test is satisfied and, although Royal Crown at argument said it believed that Leikach had struck the bottle in the course of turning off the alarm system, the testimony Leikach offered, if believed by the jury, would satisfy the third test. We are here concerned only with the matter of the defendant's "exclusive control" in the context of the stage setting and the actors in the drama before us.

* * *

We are impressed with the reasoning and holding in *Evangelio v. Metropolitan Bottling Co.*, 158 N.E.2d 342, in which the Supreme Judicial Court of Massachusetts retreated from earlier holdings in favor of the bottler and held that the burden of a plaintiff who relies on res ipsa loquitur in an exploding bottle case does not include the exclusion of every possible cause of injury other than that of the bottler's negligence, but does include the proving that there is a greater likelihood that injury was caused by the defendant's negligence than by some other cause, as well as with similar reasoning and holding in *Zarling v. La Salle Coca Cola Bottling Co.* (Wis.), 87 N.W.2d 263.

We think that here the appellant met his burden of showing the greater likelihood that Royal Crown had been negligent and the jury should have been permitted to pass on the issue.

Judgment reversed, with costs, and case remanded for a new trial.

Other Tort Concepts to Consider

Tort Reform

Tort reform is a common point of discussion, particularly around every election period. Trial lawyers are often cited as the cause of rising medical costs and the multiple abuses inherent within the current legal system. While a cap on damages in tort cases may help to diminish some of the problems in society, trial lawyers do help to deliver monetary awards to plaintiffs with legitimate cases. The question is, can the system be improved while still being fair to those who have legitimate cases?

Strict Liability

There are certain courses of conduct (abnormally dangerous activities, keeping wild or dangerous animals, or manufacturing and/or selling a defective product) that are so clearly dangerous to engage in that there is no need to prove any fault on the part of the defendant, unlike with intentional torts and negligence cases. For example, if the plaintiff is injured because the defendant builds a bomb in the defendant's basement which subsequently explodes, or because the defendant's pet lion escapes and terrorizes the neighborhood, or because the defendant manufactures or sells a defective product, then these actions are, in and of themselves, enough to find liability on the part of the defendant for any damages.

Damages

There are two main types of damages that a plaintiff can be awarded—compensatory damages and punitive damages. These are exactly what they sound like. Compensatory damages seek to make the injured party whole or as if the tort never occurred and include such things as reimbursement for medical expenses, property damage, lost wages, etc. Punitive damages are designed to punish the defendant for behavior that may have been reckless, willful, malicious, and so on. Punitive damages serve to not only punish the defendant, but to also put others on notice that the sort of behavior in which the defendant engaged will not be tolerated in society.

Chapter 4
Constitutional Law

The Constitution is the foundation of the American legal system and, as such, touches on most, if not all, areas of society. Its application extends to essentially every field of law, and its discussion cannot be restricted to something called "constitutional law." Cases representing many different issues and fields of law can be and are decided with regard to constitutional issues. Excerpts from constitutional law cases are cited in the discussions of civil procedure, property, intellectual property, family law, and criminal law and procedure within this book. The topic of constitutional law is so vast that it is nearly impossible to confine its discussion to a single chapter. In fact, many law schools dedicate multiple classes to its debate, in addition to the standard first year class.

Discussion of constitutional law can include such topics as the Commerce Clause, the separation of powers, judicial review, the power to regulate, the power to tax, presidential powers, economic interests, and the freedom of association, to name but a few. What come to mind most frequently, however, when one mentions constitutional law are the freedom of religion, the freedom of speech, due process, and equal protection. It is these topics that are covered in this chapter.

Freedom of Speech

The First Amendment rights of an Ohio Ku Klux Klan leader are discussed in *Brandenburg v. Ohio.*

BRANDENBURG v. OHIO

Supreme Court of United States (8–0)
395 U.S. 444 (1969)

PER CURIAM.

The appellant, a leader of a Ku Klux Klan group, was convicted under the Ohio Criminal Syndicalism statute for "advocat[ing] … the duty, necessity, or propriety of crime, sabotage, violence, or unlawful methods of terrorism as a means of accomplishing industrial or political reform" and for "voluntarily assembl[ing] with any society, group, or assemblage of persons formed to teach or advocate the doctrines of criminal syndicalism." Ohio Rev. Code Ann. § 2923.13. He was fined $1,000 and sentenced to one to 10 years' imprisonment. The appellant challenged the constitutionality of the criminal syndicalism statute under the First and Fourteenth Amendments to the United States Constitution, but the intermediate appellate court of Ohio affirmed his conviction without opinion. The Supreme Court of Ohio dismissed his appeal, *sua sponte*, "for the reason that no substantial constitutional question exists herein." It did not file an opinion or explain its conclusions. Appeal was taken to this Court, and we noted probable jurisdiction. 393 U. S. 948 (1968). We reverse.

The record shows that a man, identified at trial as the appellant, telephoned an announcer-reporter on the staff of a Cincinnati television station and invited him to come to a Ku Klux Klan "rally" to be held at a farm in Hamilton County. With the cooperation of the organizers, the reporter and a cameraman attended the meeting and filmed the events. Portions of the films were later broadcast on the local station and on a national network.

The prosecution's case rested on the films and on testimony identifying the appellant as the person who communicated with the reporter and who spoke at the rally. The State also introduced into evidence several articles appearing in the film, including a pistol, a rifle, a shotgun, ammunition, a Bible, and a red hood worn by the speaker in the films.

One film showed 12 hooded figures, some of whom carried firearms. They were gathered around a large wooden cross, which they burned. No one was present other than the participants and the newsmen who made the film. Most of the words uttered during the scene were incomprehensible when the film was projected, but scattered phrases could be understood that were derogatory of Negroes and, in one instance, of Jews. Another scene on the same film showed the appellant, in Klan regalia, making a speech. The speech, in full, was as follows:

"This is an organizers' meeting. We have had quite a few members here today which are—we have hundreds, hundreds of members throughout the State of Ohio. I can quote from a newspaper clipping from the Columbus, Ohio Dispatch, five weeks ago Sunday morning. The Klan has more members in the State of Ohio than does any other organization. We're not a revengent organization, but if our President, our Congress, our Supreme Court, continues to suppress the white, Caucasian race, it's possible that there might have to be some revengeance taken.

We are marching on Congress July the Fourth, four hundred thousand strong. From there we are dividing into two groups, one group to march on St. Augustine, Florida, the other group to march into Mississippi. Thank you."

The second film showed six hooded figures one of whom, later identified as the appellant, repeated a speech very similar to that recorded on the first film. The reference to the possibility of "revengeance" was omitted, and one sentence was added: "Personally, I believe the nigger should be returned to Africa, the Jew returned to Israel." Though some of the figures in the films carried weapons, the speaker did not.

The Ohio Criminal Syndicalism Statute was enacted in 1919. From 1917 to 1920, identical or quite similar laws were adopted by 20 States and two territories. E. Dowell, *A History of Criminal Syndicalism Legislation in the United States 21* (1939). In 1927, this Court sustained the constitutionality of California's Criminal Syndicalism Act, Cal. Penal Code §§ 11400–11402, the text of which is quite similar to that of the laws of Ohio. *Whitney v. California*, 274 U. S. 357 (1927). The Court upheld the statute on the ground that, without more, "advocating" violent means to effect political and economic change involves such danger to the security of the State that the State may outlaw it. Cf. *Fiske v. Kansas*, 274 U. S. 380 (1927). But *Whitney* has been thoroughly discredited by later decisions. See *Dennis v. United States*, 341 U. S. 494, at 507 (1951). These later decisions have fashioned the principle that the constitutional guarantees of free speech and free press do not permit a State to forbid or proscribe advocacy of the use of force or of law violation except where such advocacy is directed to inciting or producing imminent lawless action and is likely to incite or produce such action. As we said in *Noto v. United States*, 367 U. S. 290, 297–298 (1961), "the mere abstract teaching ... of the moral propriety or even moral necessity for a resort to force and violence, is not the same as preparing a group for violent action and steeling it to such action." See also *Herndon v. Lowry*, 301 U. S. 242, 259–261 (1937); *Bond v. Floyd*, 385 U. S. 116, 134 (1966). A statute which fails to draw this distinction impermissibly intrudes upon the freedoms guaranteed by the First and Fourteenth Amendments. It sweeps within its condemnation speech which our Constitution has immunized from governmental control. ***

Measured by this test, Ohio's Criminal Syndicalism Act cannot be sustained. The Act punishes persons who "advocate or teach the duty, necessity, or propriety" of violence "as a means of accomplishing industrial or political reform"; or who publish or circulate or display any book or paper containing such advocacy; or who "justify" the commission of violent acts "with intent to exemplify, spread or advocate the propriety of the doctrines of criminal syndicalism"; or who "voluntarily assemble" with a group formed "to teach or advocate the doctrines of criminal syndicalism." Neither the indictment nor the trial judge's instructions to the jury in any way refined the statute's bald definition of the crime in terms of mere advocacy not distinguished from incitement to imminent lawless action.

Accordingly, we are here confronted with a statute which, by its own words and as applied, purports to punish mere advocacy and to forbid, on pain of criminal punishment, assembly with others merely to advocate the described type of action. Such a statute falls within the condemnation of the First and Fourteenth Amendments. The contrary teaching of *Whitney v. California, supra*, cannot be supported, and that decision is therefore overruled.

Reversed.

[Footnotes Omitted.]

Is pornography protected under the First Amendment? Should it be? *Miller v. California* tackles this issue. Note the close 5–4 vote.

MILLER v. CALIFORNIA

Supreme Court of the United States (5–4)
413 U.S. 15 (1973)

MR. CHIEF JUSTICE BURGER delivered the opinion of the Court.

This is one of a group of "obscenity-pornography" cases being reviewed by the Court in a re-examination of standards enunciated in earlier cases involving what Mr. Justice Harlan called "the intractable obscenity problem." *Interstate Circuit, Inc. v. Dallas*, 390 U. S. 676, 704 (1968) (concurring and dissenting).

Appellant conducted a mass mailing campaign to advertise the sale of illustrated books, euphemistically called "adult" material. After a jury trial, he was convicted of violating California Penal Code § 311.2 (a), a misdemeanor, by knowingly distributing obscene matter, and the Appellate Department, Superior Court of California, County of Orange, summarily affirmed the judgment without opinion. Appellant's conviction was specifically based on his conduct in causing five unsolicited advertising brochures to be sent through the mail in an envelope addressed to a restaurant in Newport Beach, California. The envelope was opened by the manager of the restaurant and his mother. They had not requested the brochures; they complained to the police.

The brochures advertise four books entitled "Intercourse," "Man-Woman," "Sex Orgies Illustrated," and "An Illustrated History of Pornography," and a film entitled "Marital Intercourse." While the brochures contain some descriptive printed material, primarily they consist of pictures and drawings very explicitly depicting men and women in groups of two or more engaging in a variety of sexual activities, with genitals often prominently displayed.

I

This case involves the application of a State's criminal obscenity statute to a situation in which sexually explicit materials have been thrust by aggressive sales action upon unwilling recipients who had in no way indicated any desire to receive such materials. This Court has recognized that the States have a legitimate interest in prohibiting dissemination or exhibition of obscene material when the mode of dissemination carries with it a significant danger of offending the sensibilities of unwilling recipients or of exposure to juveniles. *** It is in this context that we are called on to define the standards which must be used to identify obscene material that a State may regulate without infringing on the First Amendment as applicable to the States through the Fourteenth Amendment.

* * *

II

This much has been categorically settled by the Court, that obscene material is unprotected by the First Amendment. *Kois v. Wisconsin*, 408 U. S. 229 (1972); *United States v. Reidel*, 402 U. S., at 354; *Roth v. United States, supra*, at 485. "The First and Fourteenth Amendments have never been treated as absolutes [footnote omitted]." *** We acknowledge, however, the inherent dangers of undertaking to regulate any form of expression. State statutes designed to regulate obscene materials must be carefully limited. See *Interstate Circuit, Inc. v. Dallas, supra*, at 682–685. As a result, we now confine the permissible scope of such regulation to works which depict or describe sexual conduct. That conduct must be specifically defined by the applicable state law, as written or authoritatively construed. A state offense must also be limited to works which, taken as a whole, appeal to the prurient interest in sex, which portray sexual conduct in a patently offensive way, and which, taken as a whole, do not have serious literary, artistic, political, or scientific value.

The basic guidelines for the trier of fact must be: (a) whether "the average person, applying contemporary community standards" would find that the work, taken as a whole, appeals to the prurient interest, *Kois v. Wisconsin*, *supra*, at 230, quoting *Roth v. United States*, *supra*, at 489; (b) whether the work depicts or describes, in a patently offensive way, sexual conduct specifically defined by the applicable state law; and (c) whether the work, taken as a whole, lacks serious literary, artistic, political, or scientific value. We do not adopt as a constitutional standard the " *utterly* without redeeming social value" test of *Memoirs v. Massachusetts*, 383 U. S., at 419; that concept has never commanded the adherence of more than three Justices at one time. *See supra*, at 21. If a state law that regulates obscene material is thus limited, as written or construed, the First Amendment values applicable to the States through the Fourteenth Amendment are adequately protected by the ultimate power of appellate courts to conduct an independent review of constitutional claims when necessary. ***

We emphasize that it is not our function to propose regulatory schemes for the States. That must await their concrete legislative efforts. It is possible, however, to give a few plain examples of what a state statute could define for regulation under part (b) of the standard announced in this opinion, *supra*:

(a) Patently offensive representations or descriptions of ultimate sexual acts, normal or perverted, actual or simulated.

(b) Patently offensive representations or descriptions of masturbation, excretory functions, and lewd exhibition of the genitals.

Sex and nudity may not be exploited without limit by films or pictures exhibited or sold in places of public accommodation any more than live sex and nudity can be exhibited or sold without limit in such public places. At a minimum, prurient, patently offensive depiction or description of sexual conduct must have serious literary, artistic, political, or scientific value to merit First Amendment protection. *** For example, medical books for the education of physicians and related personnel necessarily use graphic illustrations and descriptions of human anatomy. In resolving the inevitably sensitive questions of fact and law, we must continue to rely on the jury system, accompanied by the safeguards that judges, rules of evidence, presumption of innocence, and other protective features provide, as we do with rape, murder, and a host of other offenses against society and its individual members.

* * *

Under the holdings announced today, no one will be subject to prosecution for the sale or exposure of obscene materials unless these materials depict or describe patently offensive "hard core" sexual conduct specifically defined by the regulating state law, as written or construed. We are satisfied that these specific prerequisites will provide fair notice to a dealer in such materials that his public and commercial activities may bring prosecution.

* * *

It is certainly true that the absence, since *Roth*, of a single majority view of this Court as to proper standards for testing obscenity has placed a strain on both state and federal courts. But today, for the first time since *Roth* was decided in 1957, a majority of this Court has agreed on concrete guidelines to isolate "hard core" pornography from expression protected by the First Amendment. Now we may abandon the casual practice of *Redrup v. New York*, 386 U. S. 767 (1967), and attempt to provide positive guidance to federal and state courts alike.

* * *

III

Under a National Constitution, fundamental First Amendment limitations on the powers of the States do not vary from community to community, but this does not mean that there are, or should or can be, fixed, uniform national standards of precisely what appeals to the "prurient interest" or is "patently offensive."

These are essentially questions of fact, and our Nation is simply too big and too diverse for this Court to reasonably expect that such standards could be articulated for all 50 States in a single formulation, even assuming the prerequisite consensus exists. When triers of fact are asked to decide whether "the average person, applying contemporary community standards" would consider certain materials "prurient," it would be unrealistic to require that the answer be based on some abstract formulation. The adversary system, with lay jurors as the usual ultimate factfinders in criminal prosecutions, has historically permitted triers of fact to draw on the standards of their community, guided always by limiting instructions on the law. To require a State to structure obscenity proceedings around evidence of a *national* "community standard" would be an exercise in futility.

* * *

IV

* * *

In sum, we (a) reaffirm the *Roth* holding that obscene material is not protected by the First Amendment; (b) hold that such material can be regulated by the States, subject to the specific safeguards enunciated above, without a showing that the material is "*utterly* without redeeming social value"; and (c) hold that obscenity is to be determined by applying "contemporary community standards," *see Kois v. Wisconsin*, *supra*, at 230, and *Roth v. United States*, *supra*, at 489, not "national standards." The judgment of the Appellate Department of the Superior Court, Orange County, California, is vacated and the case remanded to that court for further proceedings not inconsistent with the First Amendment standards established by this opinion. *See United States v. 12 200-ft. Reels of Film*, post, at 130 n. 7

Vacated and remanded.

[Footnotes Omitted.]

The Westboro Baptist Church has made news due to its protests at various funerals and its stance that homosexuality is sinful. Some of their familiar protest signs include "Thank God for IEDs," "Thank God for Dead Soldiers," and "God Hates Fags." In this case, the Court examines the Westboro Baptist Church's right to protest and whether that right shields them from tort liability.

SNYDER v. PHELPS

Supreme Court of United States (8–1)
131 S.Ct. 1207 (2011)

Chief Justice ROBERTS delivered the opinion of the Court.

A jury held members of the Westboro Baptist Church liable for millions of dollars in damages for picketing near a soldier's funeral service. The picket signs reflected the church's view that the United States is overly tolerant of sin and that God kills American soldiers as punishment. The question presented is whether the First Amendment shields the church members from tort liability for their speech in this case.

I

A

Fred Phelps founded the Westboro Baptist Church in Topeka, Kansas, in 1955. The church's congregation believes that God hates and punishes the United States for its tolerance of homosexuality, particularly in America's military. The church frequently communicates its views by picketing, often at military funerals. In the more than 20 years that the members of Westboro Baptist have publicized their message, they have picketed nearly 600 funerals. Brief for Rutherford Institute as *Amicus Curiae* 7, n. 14.

Marine Lance Corporal Matthew Snyder was killed in Iraq in the line of duty. Lance Corporal Snyder's father selected the Catholic church in the Snyders' hometown of Westminster, Maryland, as the site for his son's funeral. Local newspapers provided notice of the time and location of the service.

Phelps became aware of Matthew Snyder's funeral and decided to travel to Maryland with six other Westboro Baptist parishioners (two of his daughters and four of his grandchildren) to picket. On the day of the memorial service, the Westboro congregation members picketed on public land adjacent to public streets near the Maryland State House, the United States Naval Academy, and Matthew Snyder's funeral. The Westboro picketers carried signs that were largely the same at all three locations. They stated, for instance: "God Hates the USA/Thank God for 9/11," "America is Doomed," "Don't Pray for the USA," "Thank

God for IEDs," "Thank God for Dead Soldiers," "Pope in Hell," "Priests Rape Boys," "God Hates Fags," "You're Going to Hell," and "God Hates You."

The church had notified the authorities in advance of its intent to picket at the time of the funeral, and the picketers complied with police instructions in staging their demonstration. The picketing took place within a 10-by 25-foot plot of public land adjacent to a public street, behind a temporary fence. App. to Brief for Appellants in No. 08-1026(CA4), pp. 2282–2285 (hereinafter App.). That plot was approximately 1,000 feet from the church where the funeral was held. Several buildings separated the picket site from the church. *Id.*, at 3758. The Westboro picketers displayed their signs for about 30 minutes before the funeral began and sang hymns and recited Bible verses. None of the picketers entered church property or went to the cemetery. They did not yell or use profanity, and there was no violence associated with the picketing. *Id.*, at 2168, 2371, 2286, 2293.

The funeral procession passed within 200 to 300 feet of the picket site. Although Snyder testified that he could see the tops of the picket signs as he drove to the funeral, he did not see what was written on the signs until later that night, while watching a news broadcast covering the event. *Id.*, at 2084–2086.

B

Snyder filed suit against Phelps, Phelps's daughters, and the Westboro Baptist Church (collectively Westboro or the church) in the United States District Court for the District of Maryland under that court's diversity jurisdiction. Snyder alleged five state tort law claims: defamation, publicity given to private life, intentional infliction of emotional distress, intrusion upon seclusion, and civil conspiracy. Westboro moved for summary judgment contending, in part, that the church's speech was insulated from liability by the First Amendment. See 533 F.Supp.2d 567, 570 (Md.2008).

The District Court awarded Westboro summary judgment on Snyder's claims for defamation and publicity given to private life, concluding that Snyder could not prove the necessary elements of those torts. *Id.*, at 572–573. A trial was held on the remaining claims. At trial, Snyder described the severity of his emotional injuries. He testified that he is unable to separate the thought of his dead son from his thoughts of Westboro's picketing, and that he often becomes tearful, angry, and physically ill when he thinks about it. *Id.*, at 588–589. Expert witnesses testified that Snyder's emotional anguish had resulted in severe depression and had exacerbated pre-existing health conditions.

A jury found for Snyder on the intentional infliction of emotional distress, intrusion upon seclusion, and civil conspiracy claims, and held Westboro liable for $2.9 million in compensatory damages and $8 million in punitive damages. ***

In the Court of Appeals, Westboro's primary argument was that the church was entitled to judgment as a matter of law because the First Amendment fully protected Westboro's speech. The Court of Appeals agreed. 580 F.3d 206, 221 (C.A.4 2009). The court reviewed the picket signs and concluded that Westboro's statements were entitled to First Amendment protection because those statements were on matters of public concern, were not provably false, and were expressed solely through hyperbolic rhetoric. *Id.*, at 222–224.

We granted certiorari.

II

To succeed on a claim for intentional infliction of emotional distress in Maryland, a plaintiff must demonstrate that the defendant intentionally or recklessly engaged in extreme and outrageous conduct that caused the plaintiff to suffer severe emotional distress. See *Harris v. Jones*, 281 Md. 560, 565–566, 380 A.2d 611, 614 (1977). The Free Speech Clause of the First Amendment—"Congress shall make no law … abridging the freedom of speech"—can serve as a defense in state tort suits, including suits for intentional infliction of emotional distress. ***

Whether the First Amendment prohibits holding Westboro liable for its speech in this case turns largely on whether that speech is of public or private concern, as determined by all the circumstances of the case. "[S]peech on 'matters of public concern' … is 'at the heart of the First Amendment's protection.'"

* * *

Speech deals with matters of public concern when it can "be fairly considered as relating to any matter of political, social, or other concern to the community," *Connick, supra*, at 146, 103 S.Ct. 1684, or when it "is a subject of legitimate news interest; that is, a subject of general interest and of value and concern to the public," *San Diego, supra*, at 83–84, 125 S.Ct. 521. *** The arguably "inappropriate or controversial character of a statement is irrelevant to the question whether it deals with a matter of public concern." ***

* * *

Deciding whether speech is of public or private concern requires us to examine the "'content, form, and context'" of that speech, "'as revealed by the whole record.'" *Dun & Bradstreet, supra*, at 761, 105 S.Ct. 2939 (quoting *Connick, supra*, at 147–148, 103 S.Ct. 1684). As in other First Amendment cases, the court is obligated "to 'make an independent examination of the whole record' in order to make sure that 'the judgment does not constitute a forbidden intrusion on the field of free expression.'" *Bose Corp. v. Consumers Union of United States, Inc.*, 466 U.S. 485, 499, 104 S.Ct. 1949, 80 L.Ed.2d 502 (1984) (quoting *New York Times, supra*, at 284–286, 84 S.Ct. 710). In considering content, form, and context, no factor is dispositive, and it is necessary to evaluate all the circumstances of the speech, including what was said, where it was said, and how it was said.

The "content" of Westboro's signs plainly relates to broad issues of interest to society at large, rather than matters of "purely private concern." *Dun & Bradstreet, supra*, at 759, 105 S.Ct. 2939. The placards read "God Hates the USA/Thank God for 9/11," "America is Doomed," "Don't Pray for the USA," "Thank God for IEDs," "Fag Troops," "Semper Fi Fags," "God Hates Fags," "Maryland Taliban," "Fags Doom Nations," "Not Blessed Just Cursed," "Thank God for Dead Soldiers," "Pope in Hell," "Priests Rape Boys," "You're Going to Hell," and "God Hates You." App. 3781–3787. While these messages may fall short of refined social or political commentary, the issues they highlight—the political and moral conduct of the United States and its citizens, the fate of our Nation, homosexuality in the military, and scandals involving the Catholic clergy—are matters of public import. The signs certainly convey Westboro's position on those issues, in a manner designed, unlike the private speech in *Dun & Bradstreet*, to reach as broad a public audience as possible. And even if a few of the signs—such as "You're Going to Hell" and "God Hates You"—were viewed as containing messages related to Matthew Snyder or the Snyders specifically, that would not change the fact that the overall thrust and dominant theme of Westboro's demonstration spoke to broader public issues.

Apart from the content of Westboro's signs, Snyder contends that the "context" of the speech—its connection with his son's funeral—makes the speech a matter of private rather than public concern. The fact that Westboro spoke in connection with a funeral, however, cannot by itself transform the nature of Westboro's speech. Westboro's signs, displayed on public land next to a public street, reflect the fact that the church finds much to condemn in modern society. Its speech is "fairly characterized as constituting speech on a matter of public concern," *Connick*, 461 U.S., at 146, 103 S.Ct. 1684, and the funeral setting does not alter that conclusion.

Snyder argues that the church members in fact mounted a personal attack on Snyder and his family, and then attempted to "immunize their conduct by claiming that they were actually protesting the United States' tolerance of homosexuality or the supposed evils of the Catholic Church." Reply Brief for Petitioner 10. We are not concerned in this case that Westboro's speech on public matters was in any way contrived to insulate speech on a private matter from liability. Westboro had been actively engaged in speaking on the subjects addressed in its picketing long before it became aware of Matthew Snyder, and there can be no serious claim that Westboro's picketing did not represent its "honestly believed" views on public issues. *Garrison*, 379 U.S., at 73, 85 S.Ct. 209. There was no pre-existing relationship or conflict between Westboro and Snyder that might suggest Westboro's speech on public matters was intended to mask an attack on Snyder over a private matter. ***

Snyder goes on to argue that Westboro's speech should be afforded less than full First Amendment protection "not only because of the words" but also because the church members exploited the funeral "as a platform to bring their message to a broader audience." *Brief for Petitioner* 44, 40. There is no doubt that Westboro chose to stage its picketing at the Naval Academy, the Maryland State House, and Matthew Snyder's funeral to increase publicity for its views and because of the relation between those sites and its views—in the case of the military funeral, because Westboro believes that God is killing American soldiers as punishment for the Nation's sinful policies.

Westboro's choice to convey its views in conjunction with Matthew Snyder's funeral made the expression of those views particularly hurtful to many, especially to Matthew's father. The record makes clear that the applicable legal term—"emotional distress"—fails to capture fully the anguish Westboro's choice added to Mr. Snyder's already incalculable grief. But Westboro conducted its picketing peacefully on matters of public concern at a public place adjacent to a public street. Such space occupies a "special position in terms of First Amendment protection." *United States v. Grace*, 461 U.S. 171, 180, 103 S.Ct. 1702, 75 L.Ed.2d 736 (1983). "[W]e have repeatedly referred to public streets as the archetype of a traditional public forum," noting that "'[t]ime out of mind' public streets and sidewalks have been used for public assembly and debate." *Frisby v. Schultz*, 487 U.S. 474, 480, 108 S.Ct. 2495, 101 L.Ed.2d 420 (1988).

That said, "[e]ven protected speech is not equally permissible in all places and at all times." *Id.*, at 479, 108 S.Ct. 2495 (quoting *Cornelius v. NAACP Legal Defense & Ed. Fund, Inc.*, 473 U.S. 788, 799, 105 S.Ct. 3439, 87 L.Ed.2d 567 (1985)). Westboro's choice of where and when to conduct its picketing is not beyond the Government's regulatory reach—it is "subject to reasonable time, place, or manner restrictions" that are consistent with the standards announced in this Court's precedents. *Clark v. Community for Creative Non-Violence*, 468 U.S. 288, 293, 104 S.Ct. 3065, 82 L.Ed.2d 221 (1984). Maryland now has a law imposing restrictions on funeral picketing, Md.Crim. Law Code Ann. § 10-205 (Lexis Supp.2010), as do 43 other States and the Federal Government. See Brief for American Legion as *Amicus Curiae* 18–19, n. 2 (listing statutes). To the extent these laws are content neutral, they raise very different questions from the tort verdict at issue in this case. Maryland's law, however, was not in effect at the time of the events at issue here, so we have no occasion to consider how it might apply to facts such as those before us, or whether it or other similar regulations are constitutional.

* * *

Simply put, the church members had the right to be where they were. Westboro alerted local authorities to its funeral protest and fully complied with police guidance on where the picketing could be staged. The picketing was conducted under police supervision some 1,000 feet from the church, out of the sight of those at the church. The protest was not unruly; there was no shouting, profanity, or violence.

The record confirms that any distress occasioned by Westboro's picketing turned on the content and viewpoint of the message conveyed, rather than any interference with the funeral itself. A group of parishioners standing at the very spot where Westboro stood, holding signs that said "God Bless America" and "God Loves You," would not have been subjected to liability. It was what Westboro said that exposed it to tort damages.

Given that Westboro's speech was at a public place on a matter of public concern, that speech is entitled to "special protection" under the First Amendment. Such speech cannot be restricted simply because it is upsetting or arouses contempt. "If there is a bedrock principle underlying the First Amendment, it is that the government may not prohibit the expression of an idea simply because society finds the idea itself offensive or disagreeable." *Texas v. Johnson*, 491 U.S. 397, 414, 109 S.Ct. 2533, 105 L.Ed.2d 342 (1989). Indeed, "the point of all speech protection ... is to shield just those choices of content that in someone's eyes are misguided, or even hurtful." ***

The jury here was instructed that it could hold Westboro liable for intentional infliction of emotional distress based on a finding that Westboro's picketing was "outrageous." "Outrageousness," however, is a highly malleable standard with "an inherent subjectiveness about it which would allow a jury to impose liability on the basis of the jurors' tastes or views, or perhaps on the basis of their dislike of a particular expression." *Hustler*, 485 U.S., at 55, 108 S.Ct. 876 (internal quotation marks omitted). In a case such as this, a jury is "unlikely to be neutral with respect to the content of [the] speech," posing "a real danger of becoming an instrument for the suppression of ... 'vehement, caustic, and sometimes unpleasan[t]'" expression. *Bose Corp.*, 466 U.S., at 510, 104 S.Ct. 1949 (quoting *New York Times*, 376 U.S., at 270, 84 S.Ct. 710). Such a risk is unacceptable; "in public debate [we] must tolerate insulting, and even outrageous, speech in order to provide adequate 'breathing space' to the freedoms protected by the First Amendment." *Boos v. Barry*, 485 U.S. 312, 322, 108 S.Ct. 1157, 99 L.Ed.2d 333 (1988) (some internal quotation marks omitted). What Westboro said, in the whole context of how and where it chose to say it, is entitled to "special protection" under the First Amendment, and that protection cannot be overcome by a jury finding that the picketing was outrageous.

For all these reasons, the jury verdict imposing tort liability on Westboro for intentional infliction of emotional distress must be set aside.

* * *

IV

Our holding today is narrow. We are required in First Amendment cases to carefully review the record, and the reach of our opinion here is limited by the particular facts before us. As we have noted, "the sensitivity and significance of the interests presented in clashes between First Amendment and [state law] rights counsel relying on limited principles that sweep no more broadly than the appropriate context of the instant case." *Florida Star v. B.J. F.*, 491 U.S. 524, 533, 109 S.Ct. 2603, 105 L.Ed.2d 443 (1989).

Westboro believes that America is morally flawed; many Americans might feel the same about Westboro. Westboro's funeral picketing is certainly hurtful and its contribution to public discourse may be negligible. But Westboro addressed matters of public import on public property, in a peaceful manner, in full compliance with the guidance of local officials. The speech was indeed planned to coincide with

Matthew Snyder's funeral, but did not itself disrupt that funeral, and Westboro's choice to conduct its picketing at that time and place did not alter the nature of its speech.

Speech is powerful. It can stir people to action, move them to tears of both joy and sorrow, and—as it did here—inflict great pain. On the facts before us, we cannot react to that pain by punishing the speaker. As a Nation we have chosen a different course—to protect even hurtful speech on public issues to ensure that we do not stifle public debate. That choice requires that we shield Westboro from tort liability for its picketing in this case.

The judgment of the United States Court of Appeals for the Fourth Circuit is affirmed.

It is so ordered.

[Footnotes Omitted.]

It may not be commonly known that video games are protected under the First Amendment. This case examines whether a California law restricting the sale of violent video games to minors meets Constitutional standards.

BROWN v. ENTERTAINMENT MERCHANTS ASSOCIATION

Supreme Court of United States (7–2)

564 U.S.___ (2011)

Justice SCALIA delivered the opinion of the Court.

We consider whether a California law imposing restrictions on violent video games comports with the First Amendment.

I

California Assembly Bill 1179 (2005), Cal. Civ. Code Ann. §§1746–1746.5 (West 2009) (Act), prohibits the sale or rental of "violent video games" to minors, and requires their packaging to be labeled "18." The Act covers games "in which the range of options available to a player includes killing, maiming, dismembering, or sexually assaulting an image of a human being, if those acts are depicted" in a manner that "[a] reasonable person, considering the game as a whole, would find appeals to a deviant or morbid interest of minors," that is "patently offensive to prevailing standards in the community as to what is suitable for minors," and that "causes the game, as a whole, to lack serious literary, artistic, political, or scientific value for minors." §1746(d)(1)(A). Violation of the Act is punishable by a civil fine of up to $1,000. §1746.3.

* * *

II

California correctly acknowledges that video games qualify for First Amendment protection. The Free Speech Clause exists principally to protect discourse on public matters, but we have long recognized that it is difficult to distinguish politics from entertainment, and dangerous to try. "Everyone is familiar with instances of propaganda through fiction. What is one man's amusement, teaches another's doctrine." *Winters v. New York*, 333 U. S. 507, 510 (1948). Like the protected books, plays, and movies that preceded them, video games communicate ideas—and even social messages—through many familiar literary devices (such as characters, dialogue, plot, and music) and through features distinctive to the medium (such as the player's interaction with the virtual world). That suffices to confer First Amendment protection. Under our Constitution, "esthetic and moral judgments about art and literature ... are for the individual to make, not for the Government to decree, even with the mandate or approval of a majority." *United States v. Playboy Entertainment Group, Inc.*, 529 U. S. 803, 818 (2000). And whatever the challenges of applying the Constitution to ever-advancing technology, "the basic principles of freedom of speech and the press, like the First Amendment's command, do not vary" when a new and different medium for communication appears. *Joseph Burstyn, Inc. v. Wilson*, 343 U. S. 495, 503 (1952).

The most basic of those principles is this: "[A]s a general matter, ... government has no power to restrict expression because of its message, its ideas, its subject matter, or its content." *Ashcroft v. American Civil Liberties Union*, 535 U. S. 564, 573 (2002) (internal quotation marks omitted). There are of course exceptions. " 'From 1791 to the present,' ... the First Amendment has 'permitted restrictions upon the content of speech in a few limited areas,' and has never 'include[d] a freedom to disregard these traditional limitations.' " *United States v. Stevens*, 559 U. S. ___, ___ (2010) (slip op., at 5) (quoting *R. A. V. v. St. Paul*, 505 U. S. 377, 382–383 (1992)). These limited areas—such as obscenity, *Roth v. United States*, 354 U. S. 476, 483 (1957), incitement, *Brandenburg v. Ohio*, 395 U. S. 444, 447–449 (1969) (*per curiam*), and fighting words, *Chaplinsky v. New Hampshire*, 315 U. S. 568, 572 (1942)—represent "well-defined and narrowly limited classes of speech, the prevention and punishment of which have never been thought to raise any Constitutional problem," *id.*, at 571–572.

Last Term, in *Stevens,* we held that new categories of unprotected speech may not be added to the list by a legislature that concludes certain speech is too harmful to be tolerated. *Stevens* concerned a federal statute purporting to criminalize the creation, sale, or possession of certain depictions of animal cruelty. See 18 U. S. C. §48 (amended 2010). The statute covered depictions "in which a living animal is intentionally maimed, mutilated, tortured, wounded, or killed" if that harm to the animal was illegal where the "the creation, sale, or possession t[ook] place," §48(c)(1). A saving clause largely borrowed from our obscenity jurisprudence, see *Miller v. California*, 413 U. S. 15, 24 (1973), exempted depictions with "serious religious, political, scientific, educational, journalistic, historical, or artistic value," §48(b). We held that statute to be an impermissible content-based restriction on speech. There was no American tradition of forbidding the *depiction* of animal cruelty—though States have long had laws against *committing* it.

The Government argued in *Stevens* that lack of a historical warrant did not matter; that it could create new categories of unprotected speech by applying a "simple balancing test" that weighs the value of a particular category of speech against its social costs and then punishes that category of speech if it fails the test. *Stevens*, 559 U. S., at ___ (slip op., at 7). We emphatically rejected that "startling and dangerous" proposition. *Ibid*. "Maybe there are some categories of speech that have been historically unprotected, but have not yet been specifically identified or discussed as such in our case law." *Id.*, at ___ (slip op., at 9). But without persuasive evidence that a novel restriction on content is part of a long (if heretofore unrecognized) tradition of proscription, a legislature may not revise the "judgment [of] the American people," embodied in the First Amendment, "that the benefits of its restrictions on the Government outweigh the costs." *Id.*, at ___ (slip op., at 7).

That holding controls this case. As in *Stevens*, California has tried to make violent-speech regulation look like obscenity regulation by appending a saving clause required for the latter. That does not suffice. Our cases have been clear that the obscenity exception to the First Amendment does not cover whatever a legislature finds shocking, but only depictions of "sexual conduct," *Miller, supra*, at 24. See also *Cohen v. California*, 403 U. S. 15, 20 (1971); *Roth, supra*, at 487, and n. 20.

Stevens was not the first time we have encountered and rejected a State's attempt to shoehorn speech about violence into obscenity. In *Winters*, we considered a New York criminal statute "forbid[ding] the massing of stories of bloodshed and lust in such a way as to incite to crime against the person," 333 U.S., at 514. The New York Court of Appeals upheld the provision as a law against obscenity. "[T]here can be no more precise test of written indecency or obscenity," it said, "than the continuing and changeable experience of the community as to what types of books are likely to bring about the corruption of public morals or other analogous injury to the public order." *Id.*, at 514 (internal quotation marks omitted). That is of course the same expansive view of governmental power to abridge the freedom of speech based on interest-balancing that we rejected in *Stevens*. Our opinion in *Winters*, which concluded that the New York statute failed a heightened vagueness standard applicable to restrictions upon speech entitled to First Amendment protection, 333 U.S., at 517–519, made clear that violence is not part of the obscenity that the Constitution permits to be regulated. The speech reached by the statute contained "no indecency or obscenity in any sense heretofore known to the law." *Id.*, at 519.

Because speech about violence is not obscene, it is of no consequence that California's statute mimics the New York statute regulating obscenity-for-minors that we upheld in *Ginsberg v. New York*, 390 U.S. 629 (1968). That case approved a prohibition on the sale to minors of *sexual* material that would be obscene from the perspective of a child. We held that the legislature could "adjus[t] the definition of obscenity 'to social realities by permitting the appeal of this type of material to be assessed in terms of the sexual interests …' of … minors." *Id.*, at 638 (quoting *Mishkin v. New York*, 383 U.S. 502, 509 (1966)). And because "obscenity is not protected expression," the New York statute could be sustained so long as the legislature's judgment that the proscribed materials were harmful to children "was not irrational." 390 U.S., at 641.

The California Act is something else entirely. It does not adjust the boundaries of an existing category of unprotected speech to ensure that a definition designed for adults is not uncritically applied to children. California does not argue that it is empowered to prohibit selling offensively violent works *to adults*—and it is wise not to, since that is but a hair's breadth from the argument rejected in *Stevens*. Instead, it wishes to create a wholly new category of content-based regulation that is permissible only for speech directed at children.

That is unprecedented and mistaken. "[M]inors are entitled to a significant measure of First Amendment protection, and only in relatively narrow and well-defined circumstances may government bar public dissemination of protected materials to them." *Erznoznik v. Jacksonville*, 422 U.S. 205, 212–213 (1975) (citation omitted). No doubt a State possesses legitimate power to protect children from harm, *Ginsberg, supra*, at 640–641; *Prince v. Massachusetts*, 321 U.S. 158, 165 (1944), but that does not include a free-floating power to restrict the ideas to which children may be exposed. "Speech that is neither obscene as to youths nor subject to some other legitimate proscription cannot be suppressed solely to protect the young from ideas or images that a legislative body thinks unsuitable for them." *Erznoznik*, *supra*, at 213–214.

California's argument would fare better if there were a longstanding tradition in this country of specially restricting children's access to depictions of violence, but there is none. Certainly the *books* we give children to read—or read to them when they are younger—contain no shortage of gore. *Grimm's Fairy Tales*, for example, are grim indeed. As her just deserts for trying to poison Snow White, the wicked queen is made to dance in red hot slippers "till she fell dead on the floor, a sad example of envy and jealousy." *The Complete Brothers Grimm Fairy Tales* 198 (2006 ed.). Cinderella's evil stepsisters have their eyes pecked out by doves. *Id.*, at 95. And Hansel and Gretel (children!) kill their captor by baking her in an oven. *Id.*, at 54.

High-school reading lists are full of similar fare. Homer's Odysseus blinds Polyphemus the Cyclops by grinding out his eye with a heated stake. *The Odyssey of Homer*, Book IX, p. 125 (S. Butcher & A. Lang transls. 1909) ("Even so did we seize the fiery-pointed brand and whirled it round in his eye, and the blood flowed about the heated bar. And the breath of the flame singed his eyelids and brows all about, as the ball of the eye burnt away, and the roots thereof crackled in the flame"). In the Inferno, Dante and Virgil watch corrupt politicians struggle to stay submerged beneath a lake of boiling pitch, lest they be skewered by devils above the surface. *Canto XXI*, pp. 187–189 (A. Mandelbaum transl. Bantam Classic ed. 1982). And Golding's *Lord of the Flies* recounts how a schoolboy called Piggy is savagely murdered *by other children* while marooned on an island. W. Golding, *Lord of the Flies* 208–209 (1997 ed.).

This is not to say that minors' consumption of violent entertainment has never encountered resistance. In the 1800's, dime novels depicting crime and "penny dreadfuls" (named for their price and content) were blamed in some quarters for juvenile delinquency. See Brief for Cato Institute as *Amicus Curiae* 6–7. When motion pictures came along, they became the villains instead. "The days when the police looked upon dime novels as the most dangerous of textbooks in the school for crime are drawing to a close.... They say that the moving picture machine ... tends even more than did the dime novel to turn the thoughts of the easily influenced to paths which sometimes lead to prison." Moving Pictures as Helps to Crime, N.Y. Times, Feb. 21, 1909, quoted in Brief for Cato Institute, at 8. For a time, our Court did permit broad censorship of movies because of their capacity to be "used for evil," see *Mutual Film Corp. v. Industrial Comm'n of Ohio*, 236 U.S. 230, 242 (1915) , but we eventually reversed course, *Joseph Burstyn, Inc.*, 343 U.S., at 502; see also *Erznoznik, supra*, at 212–214 (invalidating a drive-in movies restriction designed to protect children). Radio dramas were next, and then came comic books. Brief for Cato Institute, at 10–11. Many in the late 1940's and early 1950's blamed comic books for fostering a "preoccupation with violence and horror" among the young, leading to a rising juvenile crime rate. See Note, Regulation of Comic Books, 68 Harv. L.Rev. 489, 490 (1955). But efforts to convince Congress to restrict comic books failed. Brief for Comic Book Legal Defense Fund as *Amicus Curiae* 11–15. And, of course, after comic books came television and music lyrics.

California claims that video games present special problems because they are "interactive," in that the player participates in the violent action on screen and determines its outcome. The latter feature is nothing new: Since at least the publication of The Adventures of You: Sugarcane Island in 1969, young readers of choose-your-own-adventure stories have been able to make decisions that determine the plot by following instructions about which page to turn to. Cf. *Interactive Digital Software Assn. v. St.Louis County*, 329 F.3d 954, 957–958 (CA8 2003). As for the argument that video games enable participation in the violent action, that seems to us more a matter of degree than of kind. As Judge Posner has observed, all literature is interactive. "[T]he better it is, the more interactive. Literature when it is successful draws the reader into the story, makes him identify with the characters, invites him to judge them and quarrel with them, to experience their joys and sufferings as the reader's own." *American Amusement Machine Assn. v. Kendrick*, 244 F.3d 572, 577 (CA7 2001) (striking down a similar restriction on violent video games).

Justice Alito has done considerable independent re-search to identify, see *post,* at 14–15, nn. 13–18, video games in which "the violence is astounding," post, at 14. "Victims are dismembered, decapitated, disemboweled, set on fire, and chopped into little pieces … Blood gushes, splatters, and pools." *Ibid.* Justice Alito recounts all these disgusting video games in order to disgust us—but disgust is not a valid basis for restricting expression. And the same is true of Justice Alito's description, *post,* at 14–15, of those video games he has discovered that have a racial or ethnic motive for their violence—"'ethnic cleansing' [of] … African Americans, Latinos, or Jews." To what end does he relate this? Does it somehow increase the "aggressiveness" that California wishes to suppress? Who knows? But it does arouse the reader's ire, and the reader's desire to put an end to this horrible message. Thus, ironically, JUSTICE ALITO 's argument highlights the precise danger posed by the California Act: that the *ideas* expressed by speech—whether it be violence, or gore, or racism—and not its objective effects, may be the real reason for governmental proscription.

III

Because the Act imposes a restriction on the content of protected speech, it is invalid unless California can demonstrate that it passes strict scrutiny—that is, unless it is justified by a compelling government interest and is narrowly drawn to serve that interest. *R.A.V.*, 505 U.S., at 395. The State must specifically identify an "actual problem" in need of solving, *Playboy*, 529 U.S., at 822–823, and the curtailment of free speech must be actually necessary to the solution, see *R. A. V., supra*, at 395. That is a demanding standard. "It is rare that a regulation restricting speech because of its content will ever be permissible." *Playboy, supra*, at 818.

California cannot meet that standard. At the outset, it acknowledges that it cannot show a direct causal link between violent video games and harm to minors. Rather, relying upon our decision in *Turner Broadcasting System, Inc. v. FCC*, 512 U.S. 622 (1994), the State claims that it need not produce such proof because the legislature can make a predictive judgment that such a link exists, based on competing psychological studies. But reliance on Turner Broadcasting is misplaced. That decision applied *intermediate scrutiny* to a content-neutral regulation. *Id.*, at 661–662. California's burden is much higher, and because it bears the risk of uncertainty, see *Playboy, supra*, at 816–817, ambiguous proof will not suffice.

The State's evidence is not compelling. California relies primarily on the research of Dr. Craig Anderson and a few other research psychologists whose studies purport to show a connection between exposure to violent video games and harmful effects on children. These studies have been rejected by every court to consider them, and with good reason: They do not prove that violent video games *cause* minors to *act* aggressively (which would at least be a beginning). Instead, "[n]early all of the research is based on correlation, not evidence of causation, and most of the studies suffer from significant, admitted flaws in methodology." *Video Software Dealers Assn*. 556 F.3d, at 964. They show at best some correlation between exposure to violent entertainment and minuscule real-world effects, such as children's feeling more aggressive or making louder noises in the few minutes after playing a violent game than after playing a nonviolent game.

Even taking for granted Dr. Anderson's conclusions that violent video games produce some effect on children's feelings of aggression, those effects are both small and indistinguishable from effects produced by other media. In his testimony in a similar lawsuit, Dr. Anderson admitted that the "effect sizes" of children's exposure to violent video games are "about the same" as that produced by their exposure to violence on television. App. 1263. And he admits that the *same* effects have been found when children watch cartoons starring Bugs Bunny or the Road Runner, *id.*, at 1304, or when they play video games like Sonic the Hedgehog that are rated "E" (appropriate for all ages), *id.*, at 1270, or even when they "vie[w] a picture of a gun," *id.*, at 1315–1316.

Of course, California has (wisely) declined to restrict Saturday morning cartoons, the sale of games rated for young children, or the distribution of pictures of guns. The consequence is that its regulation is wildly underinclusive when judged against its asserted justification, which in our view is alone enough to defeat it. Underinclusiveness raises serious doubts about whether the government is in fact pursuing the interest it invokes, rather than disfavoring a particular speaker or viewpoint. See *City of Ladue v. Gilleo*, 512 U.S. 43, 51 (1994); *Florida Star v. B.J.F.*, 491 U.S. 524, 540 (1989). Here, California has singled out the purveyors of video games for disfavored treatment—at least when compared to booksellers, cartoonists, and movie producers—and has given no persuasive reason why.

The Act is also seriously underinclusive in another respect—and a respect that renders irrelevant the contentions of the concurrence and the dissents that video games are qualitatively different from other portrayals of violence. The California Legislature is perfectly willing to leave this dangerous, mind-altering material in the hands of children so long as one parent (or even an aunt or uncle) says it's OK. And there are not even any requirements as to how this parental or avuncular relationship is to be verified; apparently the child's or putative parent's, aunt's, or uncle's say-so suffices. That is not how one addresses a serious social problem.

California claims that the Act is justified in aid of parental authority: By requiring that the purchase of violent video games can be made only by adults, the Act ensures that parents can decide what games are appropriate. At the outset, we note our doubts that punishing third parties for conveying protected speech to children *just in case* their parents disapprove of that speech is a proper governmental means of aiding parental authority. Accepting that position would largely vitiate the rule that "only in relatively narrow and well-defined circumstances may government bar public dissemination of protected materials to [minors]." *Erznoznik*, 422 U.S., at 212–213.

But leaving that aside, California cannot show that the Act's restrictions meet a substantial need of parents who wish to restrict their children's access to violent video games but cannot do so. The video-game industry has in place a voluntary rating system designed to inform consumers about the content of games. The system, implemented by the Entertainment Software Rating Board (ESRB), assigns age-specific ratings to each video game submitted: EC (Early Childhood); E (Everyone); E10+ (Everyone 10 and older); T (Teens); M (17 and older); and AO (Adults Only—18 and older). App. 86. The Video Software

Dealers Association encourages retailers to prominently display information about the ESRB system in their stores; to refrain from renting or selling adults-only games to minors; and to rent or sell "M" rated games to minors only with parental consent. *Id.*, at 47. In 2009, the Federal Trade Commission (FTC) found that, as a result of this system, "the video game industry outpaces the movie and music industries" in "(1) restricting target-marketing of mature-rated products to children; (2) clearly and prominently disclosing rating information; and (3) restricting children's access to mature-rated products at retail." FTC, Report to Congress, Marketing Violent Entertainment to Children 30 (Dec. 2009), online at http://www.ftc.gov/os/2009/12/P994511violententertainment.pdf (as visited June 24, 2011, and available in Clerk of Court's case file) (FTC Report). This system does much to ensure that minors cannot purchase seriously violent games on their own, and that parents who care about the matter can readily evaluate the games their children bring home. Filling the remaining modest gap in concerned-parents' control can hardly be a compelling state interest.

And finally, the Act's purported aid to parental authority is vastly overinclusive. Not all of the children who are forbidden to purchase violent video games on their own have parents who *care* whether they purchase violent video games. While some of the legislation's effect may indeed be in support of what some parents of the restricted children actually want, its entire effect is only in support of what the State thinks parents *ought* to want. This is not the narrow tailoring to "assisting parents" that restriction of First Amendment rights requires.

* * *

California's effort to regulate violent video games is the latest episode in a long series of failed attempts to censor violent entertainment for minors. While we have pointed out above that some of the evidence brought forward to support the harmfulness of video games is unpersuasive, we do not mean to demean or disparage the concerns that underlie the attempt to regulate them—concerns that may and doubtless do prompt a good deal of parental oversight. We have no business passing judgment on the view of the California Legislature that violent video games (or, for that matter, any other forms of speech) corrupt the young or harm their moral development. Our task is only to say whether or not such works constitute a "well-defined and narrowly limited clas[s] of speech, the prevention and punishment of which have never been thought to raise any Constitutional problem," *Chaplinsky*, 315 U.S., at 571–572 (the answer plainly is no); and if not, whether the regulation of such works is justified by that high degree of necessity we have described as a compelling state interest (it is not). Even where the protection of children is the object, the constitutional limits on governmental action apply.

California's legislation straddles the fence between (1) addressing a serious social problem and (2) helping concerned parents control their children. Both ends are legitimate, but when they affect First Amendment rights they must be pursued by means that are neither seriously underinclusive nor seriously overinclusive. See *Church of Lukumi Babalu Aye, Inc. v. Hialeah*, 508 U.S. 520, 546 (1993). As a means of protecting children from portrayals of violence, the legislation is seriously underinclusive, not only because it excludes portrayals other than video games, but also because it permits a parental or avuncular veto. And as a means of assisting concerned parents it is seriously overinclusive because it abridges the First Amendment rights of young people whose parents (and aunts and uncles) think violent video games are a harmless pastime. And the overbreadth in achieving one goal is not cured by the underbreadth in achieving the other. Legislation such as this, which is neither fish nor fowl, cannot survive strict scrutiny.

We affirm the judgment below.

It is so ordered.

Freedom of Religion

The *Lemon* case crystallizes the three-part test that is used to determine whether a law violates the Establishment clause of the First Amendment.

LEMON v. KURTZMAN

Supreme Court of United States (8–0)
403 U.S. 602 (1971)

MR. CHIEF JUSTICE BURGER delivered the opinion of the Court.

These two appeals raise questions as to Pennsylvania and Rhode Island statutes providing state aid to church-related elementary and secondary schools. Both statutes are challenged as violative of the Establishment and Free Exercise Clauses of the First Amendment and the Due Process Clause of the Fourteenth Amendment.

Pennsylvania has adopted a statutory program that provides financial support to nonpublic elementary and secondary schools by way of reimbursement for the cost of teachers' salaries, textbooks, and instructional materials in specified secular subjects. Rhode Island has adopted a statute under which the State pays directly to teachers in nonpublic elementary schools a supplement of 15% of their annual salary. Under each statute state aid has been given to church-related educational institutions. We hold that both statutes are unconstitutional.

* * *

II

In *Everson v. Board of Education*, 330 U. S. 1 (1947), this Court upheld a state statute that reimbursed the parents of parochial school children for bus transportation expenses. There MR. JUSTICE BLACK, writing for the majority, suggested that the decision carried to "the verge" of forbidden territory under the Religion Clauses. *Id.*, at 16. Candor compels acknowledgment, moreover, that we can only dimly perceive the lines of demarcation in this extraordinarily sensitive area of constitutional law.

The language of the Religion Clauses of the First Amendment is at best opaque, particularly when compared with other portions of the Amendment. Its authors did not simply prohibit the establishment of a state church or a state religion, an area history shows they regarded as very important and fraught with great dangers. Instead they commanded that there should be "no law *respecting* an establishment of religion." A law may be one "respecting" the forbidden objective while falling short of its total realization. A law "respecting" the proscribed result, that is, the establishment of religion, is not always easily identifiable as one violative of the Clause. A given law might not *establish* a state religion but nevertheless be one "respecting" that end in the sense of being a step that could lead to such establishment and hence offend the First Amendment.

In the absence of precisely stated constitutional prohibitions, we must draw lines with reference to the three main evils against which the Establishment Clause was intended to afford protection: "sponsorship, financial support, and active involvement of the sovereign in religious activity." *Walz v. Tax Commission*, 397 U. S. 664, 668 (1970).

Every analysis in this area must begin with consideration of the cumulative criteria developed by the Court over many years. Three such tests may be gleaned from our cases. First, the statute must have a secular legislative purpose; second, its principal or primary effect must be one that neither advances nor inhibits religion, *Board of Education v. Allen*, 392 U. S. 236, 243 (1968); finally, the statute must not foster "an excessive government entanglement with religion." *Walz*, *supra*, at 674.

Inquiry into the legislative purposes of the Pennsylvania and Rhode Island statutes affords no basis for a conclusion that the legislative intent was to advance religion. On the contrary, the statutes themselves clearly state that they are intended to enhance the quality of the secular education in all schools covered by the compulsory attendance laws. There is no reason to believe the legislatures meant anything else. A State always has a legitimate concern for maintaining minimum standards in all schools it allows to operate. As in *Allen*, we find nothing here that undermines the stated legislative intent; it must therefore be accorded appropriate deference.

In *Allen* the Court acknowledged that secular and religious teachings were not necessarily so intertwined that secular textbooks furnished to students by the State were in fact instrumental in the teaching of religion. 392 U. S., at 248. The legislatures of Rhode Island and Pennsylvania have concluded that secular and religious education are identifiable and separable. In the abstract we have no quarrel with this conclusion.

The two legislatures, however, have also recognized that church-related elementary and secondary schools have a significant religious mission and that a substantial portion of their activities is religiously oriented. They have therefore sought to create statutory restrictions designed to guarantee the separation between secular and religious educational functions and to ensure that State financial aid supports only the former. All these provisions are precautions taken in candid recognition that these programs approached, even if they did not intrude upon, the forbidden areas under the Religion Clauses. We need not decide whether these legislative precautions restrict the principal or primary effect of the programs to the point where they do not offend the Religion Clauses, for we conclude that the cumulative impact of the entire relationship arising under the statutes in each State involves excessive entanglement between government and religion.

III

* * *

Our prior holdings do not call for total separation between church and state; total separation is not possible in an absolute sense. Some relationship between government and religious organizations is inevitable. *Zorach v. Clauson*, 343 U. S. 306, 312 (1952); *Sherbert v. Verner*, 374 U. S. 398, 422 (1963) (HARLAN, J., dissenting). Fire inspections, building and zoning regulations, and state requirements under compulsory school-attendance laws are examples of necessary and permissible contacts. ***

* * *

In order to determine whether the government entanglement with religion is excessive, we must examine the character and purposes of the institutions that are benefited, the nature of the aid that the State provides, and the resulting relationship between the government and the religious authority. MR. JUSTICE HARLAN, in a separate opinion in *Walz, supra*, echoed the classic warning as to "programs, whose very nature is apt to entangle the state in details of administration ..." *Id.*, at 695. Here we find that both statutes foster an impermissible degree of entanglement.

* * *

(a) Rhode Island program

We do not assume, however, that parochial school teachers will be unsuccessful in their attempts to segregate their religious beliefs from their secular educational responsibilities. But the potential for impermissible fostering of religion is present. The Rhode Island Legislature has not, and could not, provide state aid on the basis of a mere assumption that secular teachers under religious discipline can avoid conflicts. The State must be certain, given the Religion Clauses, that subsidized teachers do not inculcate religion—indeed the State here has undertaken to do so. To ensure that no trespass occurs, the State has therefore carefully conditioned its aid with pervasive restrictions. An eligible recipient must teach only those courses that are offered in the public schools and use only those texts and materials that are found in the public schools. In addition the teacher must not engage in teaching any course in religion.

A comprehensive, discriminating, and continuing state surveillance will inevitably be required to ensure that these restrictions are obeyed and the First Amendment otherwise respected. Unlike a book, a teacher cannot be inspected once so as to determine the extent and intent of his or her personal beliefs and subjective acceptance of the limitations imposed by the First Amendment. These prophylactic contacts will involve excessive and enduring entanglement between state and church.

There is another area of entanglement in the Rhode Island program that gives concern. The statute excludes teachers employed by nonpublic schools whose average per-pupil expenditures on secular education equal or exceed the comparable figures for public schools. In the event that the total expenditures of an otherwise eligible school exceed this norm, the program requires the government to examine the school's records in order to determine how much of the total expenditures is attributable to secular education and how much to religious activity. This kind of state inspection and evaluation of the religious content of a religious organization is fraught with the sort of entanglement that the Constitution forbids. It is a relationship pregnant with dangers of excessive government direction of church schools and hence of churches. The Court noted "the hazards of government supporting churches" in *Walz v. Tax Commission*, *supra*, at 675, and we cannot ignore here the danger that pervasive modern governmental power will ultimately intrude on religion and thus conflict with the Religion Clauses.

(b) Pennsylvania program

* * *

As we noted earlier, the very restrictions and surveillance necessary to ensure that teachers play a strictly nonideological role give rise to entanglements between church and state. The Pennsylvania statute, like that of Rhode Island, fosters this kind of relationship. Reimbursement is not only limited to courses offered in the public schools and materials approved by state officials, but the statute excludes "any subject matter expressing religious teaching, or the morals or forms of worship of any sect." In addition, schools seeking reimbursement must maintain accounting procedures that require the State to establish the cost of the secular as distinguished from the religious instruction.

The Pennsylvania statute, moreover, has the further defect of providing state financial aid directly to the church-related school. This factor distinguishes both *Everson* and *Allen*, for in both those cases the

Court was careful to point out that state aid was provided to the student and his parents—not to the church-related school. *Board of Education v. Allen, supra*, at 243–244; *Everson v. Board of Education, supra*, at 18. In *Walz v. Tax Commission, supra*, at 675, the Court warned of the dangers of direct payments to religious organizations:

"Obviously a direct money subsidy would be a relationship pregnant with involvement and, as with most governmental grant programs, could encompass sustained and detailed administrative relationships for enforcement of statutory or administrative standards ..."

The history of government grants of a continuing cash subsidy indicates that such programs have almost always been accompanied by varying measures of control and surveillance. The government cash grants before us now provide no basis for predicting that comprehensive measures of surveillance and controls will not follow. In particular the government's post-audit power to inspect and evaluate a church-related school's financial records and to determine which expenditures are religious and which are secular creates an intimate and continuing relationship between church and state.

IV

A broader base of entanglement of yet a different character is presented by the divisive political potential of these state programs. In a community where such a large number of pupils are served by church-related schools, it can be assumed that state assistance will entail considerable political activity. Partisans of parochial schools, understandably concerned with rising costs and sincerely dedicated to both the religious and secular educational missions of their schools, will inevitably champion this cause and promote political action to achieve their goals. Those who oppose state aid, whether for constitutional, religious, or fiscal reasons, will inevitably respond and employ all of the usual political campaign techniques to prevail. Candidates will be forced to declare and voters to choose. It would be unrealistic to ignore the fact that many people confronted with issues of this kind will find their votes aligned with their faith.

Ordinarily political debate and division, however vigorous or even partisan, are normal and healthy manifestations of our democratic system of government, but political division along religious lines was one of the principal evils against which the First Amendment was intended to protect. Freund, Comment, Public Aid to Parochial Schools, 82 Harv. L. Rev. 1680, 1692 (1969). The potential divisiveness of such conflict is a threat to the normal political process. *Walz v. Tax Commission, supra*, at 695 (separate opinion of HARLAN, J.). See also *Board of Education v. Allen*, 392 U. S., at 249 (HARLAN, J., concurring); *Abington School District v. Schempp*, 374 U. S. 203, 307 (1963) (Goldberg, J., concurring). To have States or communities divide on the issues presented by state aid to parochial schools would tend to confuse and obscure other issues of great urgency. We have an expanding array of vexing issues, local and national, domestic and international, to debate and divide on. It conflicts with our whole history and tradition to permit questions of the Religion Clauses to assume such importance in our legislatures and in our elections that they could divert attention from the myriad issues and problems that confront every level of government. The highways of church and state relationships are not likely to be one-way streets, and the Constitution's authors sought to protect religious worship from the pervasive power of government. The history of many countries attests to the hazards of religion's intruding into the political arena or of political power intruding into the legitimate and free exercise of religious belief.

* * *

V

* * *

The merit and benefits of these schools, however, are not the issue before us in these cases. The sole question is whether state aid to these schools can be squared with the dictates of the Religion Clauses. Under our system the choice has been made that government is to be entirely excluded from the area of religious instruction and churches excluded from the affairs of government. The Constitution decrees that religion must be a private matter for the individual, the family, and the institutions of private choice, and that while some involvement and entanglement are inevitable, lines must be drawn.

The judgment of the Rhode Island District Court in No. 569 and No. 570 is affirmed. The judgment of the Pennsylvania District Court in No. 89 is reversed, and the case is remanded for further proceedings consistent with this opinion.

> The following case examines the free exercise of religion. Specifically, does an Oregon law that prohibits the religious use of peyote (an hallucinogen) violate the Free Exercise clause of the First Amendment?

EMPLOYMENT DIVISION, DEPARTMENT OF HUMAN RESOURCES OF OREGON v. SMITH

Supreme Court of the United States (6–3)

494 U.S. 872 (1990)

Justice SCALIA delivered the opinion of the Court.

This case requires us to decide whether the Free Exercise Clause of the First Amendment permits the State of Oregon to include religiously inspired peyote use within the reach of its general criminal prohibition on use of that drug, and thus permits the State to deny unemployment benefits to persons dismissed from their jobs because of such religiously inspired use.

I

Oregon law prohibits the knowing or intentional possession of a "controlled substance" unless the substance has been prescribed by a medical practitioner. Ore.Rev.Stat. § 475.992(4) (1987). The law defines "controlled substance" as a drug classified in Schedules I through V of the Federal Controlled Substances Act, 21 U.S.C. §§ 811–812 (1982 ed. and Supp. V), as modified by the State Board of Pharmacy. Ore.Rev. Stat. § 475.005(6) (1987). Persons who violate this provision by possessing a controlled substance listed on Schedule I are "guilty of a Class B felony." § 475.992(4)(a). As compiled by the State Board of Pharmacy under its statutory authority, *see* Ore.Rev.Stat. § 475.035 (1987), Schedule I contains the drug peyote, a hallucinogen derived from the plant Lophophorawilliamsii Lemaire. Ore.Admin. Rule 855-80-021(3)(s) (1988).

Respondents Alfred Smith and Galen Black were fired from their jobs with a private drug rehabilitation organization because they ingested peyote for sacramental purposes at a ceremony of the Native American Church, of which both are members. When respondents applied to petitioner Employment Division for unemployment compensation, they were determined to be ineligible for benefits because they had been discharged for work-related "misconduct". The Oregon Court of Appeals reversed that determination, holding that the denial of benefits violated respondents' free exercise rights under the First Amendment.

* * *

Before this Court in 1987, petitioner continued to maintain that the illegality of respondents' peyote consumption was relevant to their constitutional claim. We agreed, concluding that if a State has prohibited through its criminal laws certain kinds of religiously motivated conduct without violating the First Amendment, it certainly follows that it may impose the lesser burden of denying unemployment compensation benefits to persons who engage in that conduct. *Employment Div., Dept. of Human Resources of Oregon v. Smith*, 485 U.S. 660, 670 (1988) (*Smith I*). We noted, however, that the Oregon Supreme Court had not decided whether respondents' sacramental use of peyote was in fact proscribed by Oregon's controlled substance law, and that this issue was a matter of dispute between the parties. Being "uncertain about the legality of the religious use of peyote in Oregon," we determined that it would not be "appropriate for us to decide whether the practice is protected by the Federal Constitution." *Id.* at 673. Accordingly, we [p876] vacated the judgment of the Oregon Supreme Court and remanded for further proceedings. *Id.* at 674.

On remand, the Oregon Supreme Court held that respondents' religiously inspired use of peyote fell within the prohibition of the Oregon statute, which "makes no exception for the sacramental use" of the drug. 307 Or. 68, 72–73, 763 P.2d 146, 148 (1988). It then considered whether that prohibition was valid under the Free Exercise Clause, and concluded that it was not. The court therefore reaffirmed its previous ruling that the State could not deny unemployment benefits to respondents for having engaged in that practice.

We again granted certiorari. 489 U.S. 1077 (1989).

II

Respondents' claim for relief rests on our decisions in *Sherbert v. Verner, supra, Thomas v. Review Board, Indiana Employment Security Div., supra,* and *Hobbie v. Unemployment Appeals Comm'n of Florida,* 480 U.S. 136 (1987), in which we held that a State could not condition the availability of unemployment insurance on an individual's willingness to forgo conduct required by his religion. As we observed in *Smith I,* however, the conduct at issue in those cases was not prohibited by law. We held that distinction to be critical, for if Oregon does prohibit the religious use of peyote, and if that prohibition is consistent with the Federal Constitution, there is no federal right to engage in that conduct in Oregon, and the State is free to withhold unemployment compensation from respondents for engaging in work-related misconduct, despite its religious motivation. 485 U.S. at 672. Now that the Oregon Supreme Court has confirmed that Oregon does prohibit the religious use of peyote, we proceed to consider whether that prohibition is permissible under the Free Exercise Clause.

A

The Free Exercise Clause of the First Amendment, which has been made applicable to the States by incorporation into the Fourteenth Amendment, *see Cantwell v. Connecticut,* 310 U.S. 296, 303 (1940), provides that "Congress shall make no law respecting an establishment of religion, or prohibiting the free exercise thereof ..." U.S. Const. Am. I (emphasis added). The free exercise of religion means, first and foremost, the right to believe and profess whatever religious doctrine one desires. Thus, the First Amendment obviously excludes all "governmental regulation of religious beliefs as such." *Sherbert v. Verner, supra,* 374 U.S. at 402. The government may not compel affirmation of religious belief, *see Torcaso v. Watkins,* 367 U.S. 488 (1961), punish the expression of religious doctrines it believes to be false, *United States v. Ballard,* 322 U.S. 78, 86-88 (1944), impose special disabilities on the basis of religious views or religious status, *see McDaniel v. Paty,* 435 U.S. 618 (1978); *Fowler v. Rhode Island,* 345 U.S. 67, 69 (1953); *cf. Larson v. Valente,* 456 U.S. 228, 245 (1982), or lend its power to one or the other side in controversies over religious authority or dogma, *see Presbyterian Church v. Hull Church,* 393 U.S. 440, 445–452 (1969); *Kedroff v. St. Nicholas Cathedral,* 344 U.S. 94, 95–119 (1952); *Serbian Eastern Orthodox Diocese v. Milivojevich,* 426 U.S. 696, 708–725 (1976).

But the "exercise of religion" often involves not only belief and profession but the performance of (or abstention from) physical acts: assembling with others for a worship service, participating in sacramental use of bread and wine, proselytizing, abstaining from certain foods or certain modes of transportation. It would be true, we think (though no case of ours has involved the point), that a state would be "prohibiting the free exercise [of religion]" if it sought to ban such acts or abstentions only when they are engaged in for religious reasons, or only because of the religious belief that they display. It would doubtless be unconstitutional, for example, to ban the casting of "statues that are to be used [p878] for worship purposes," or to prohibit bowing down before a golden calf.

Respondents in the present case, however, seek to carry the meaning of "prohibiting the free exercise [of religion]" one large step further. They contend that their religious motivation for using peyote places them beyond the reach of a criminal law that is not specifically directed at their religious practice, and that is concededly constitutional as applied to those who use the drug for other reasons. They assert, in other words, that "prohibiting the free exercise [of religion]" includes requiring any individual to observe a generally applicable law that requires (or forbids) the performance of an act that his religious belief forbids (or requires). As a textual matter, we do not think the words must be given that meaning. It is no more necessary to regard the collection of a general tax, for example, as "prohibiting the free exercise [of religion]" by those citizens who believe support of organized government to be sinful than it is to regard the same tax as "abridging the freedom ... of the press" of those publishing companies that must pay the tax as a condition of staying in business. It is a permissible reading of the text, in the one case as in the other, to say that, if prohibiting the exercise of religion (or burdening the activity of printing) is not the object of the tax, but merely the incidental effect of a generally applicable and otherwise valid provision, the First Amendment has not been offended. Compare *Citizen Publishing Co. v. United States*, 394 U.S. 131, 139 (1969) (upholding application of antitrust laws to press), with *Grosjean v. American Press Co.*, 297 U.S. 233, 250–251 (1936) (striking down license tax applied only to newspapers with weekly circulation above a specified level); see generally *Minneapolis Star & Tribune Co. v. Minnesota Commissioner of Revenue*, 460 U.S. 575, 581 (1983).

Our decisions reveal that the latter reading is the correct one. We have never held that an individual's religious beliefs [p879] excuse him from compliance with an otherwise valid law prohibiting conduct that the State is free to regulate. On the contrary, the record of more than a century of our free exercise jurisprudence contradicts that proposition. As described succinctly by Justice Frankfurter in *Minersville School Dist. Bd. of Educ. v. Gobitis*, 310 U.S. 586, 594–595 (1940):

> Conscientious scruples have not, in the course of the long struggle for religious toleration, relieved the individual from obedience to a general law not aimed at the promotion or restriction of religious beliefs. The mere possession of religious convictions which contradict the relevant concerns of a political society does not relieve the citizen from the discharge of political responsibilities. (Footnote omitted.)

We first had occasion to assert that principle in *Reynolds v. United States*, 98 U.S. 145 (1879), where we rejected the claim that criminal laws against polygamy could not be constitutionally applied to those whose religion commanded the practice. "Laws," we said,

> are made for the government of actions, and while they cannot interfere with mere religious belief and opinions, they may with practices … Can a man excuse his practices to the contrary because of his religious belief? To permit this would be to make the professed doctrines of religious belief superior to the law of the land, and in effect to permit every citizen to become a law unto himself. *Id.* at 166–167.

Subsequent decisions have consistently held that the right of free exercise does not relieve an individual of the obligation to comply with a valid and neutral law of general applicability on the ground that the law proscribes (or prescribes) conduct that his religion prescribes (or proscribes).

* * *

If the "compelling interest" test is to be applied at all, then, it must be applied across the board, to all actions thought to be religiously commanded. Moreover, if "compelling interest" really means what it says (and watering it down here would subvert its rigor in the other fields where it is applied), many laws will not meet the test. Any society adopting such a system would be courting anarchy, but that danger increases in direct proportion to the society's diversity of religious beliefs, and its determination to coerce or suppress none of them. Precisely because "we are a cosmopolitan nation made up of people of almost every conceivable religious preference," *Braunfeld v. Brown*, 366 U.S. at 606, and precisely because we value and protect that religious divergence, we cannot afford the luxury of deeming *presumptively invalid*, as applied to the religious objector, every regulation of conduct that does not protect an interest of the highest order. The rule respondents favor would open the prospect of constitutionally required religious exemptions from civic obligations of almost every conceivable kind—ranging from compulsory military service, *see, e.g., Gillette v. United States*, 401 U.S. 437 (1971), to the payment of taxes, see, e.g., *United States v. Lee, supra*; to health and safety regulation such as manslaughter and child neglect laws, *see, e.g., Funkhouser v. State*, 763 P.2d 695 (Okla.Crim.App.1988), compulsory vaccination laws, *see, e.g., Cude v. State*, 237 Ark. 927, 377 S.W.2d 816 (1964), drug laws, *see, e.g., Olsen v. Drug Enforcement Administration*, 279 U.S.App.D.C. 1, 878 F.2d 1458 (1989), and traffic laws, *see Cox v. New Hampshire*, 312 U.S. 569 (1941); to social welfare legislation such as minimum wage laws, see *Susan and Tony Alamo Foundation v. Secretary of Labor*, 471 U.S. 290 (1985), child labor laws, *see Prince v. Massachusetts*, 321 U.S. 158 (1944), animal cruelty laws, *see, e.g., Church of the Lukumi Babalu Aye Inc. v. City of Hialeah*, 723 F.Supp. 1467 (S.D.Fla.1989), *cf. State v. Massey*, 229 N.C. 734, 51 S.E.2d 179, *appeal dism'd*, 336 U.S. 942 (1949), environmental protection laws, *see United States v. Little*, 638 F.Supp. 337 (Mont.1986), and laws providing for equality of opportunity for the races, *see, e.g., Bob Jones University v. United States*, 461 U.S. 574, 603–604 (1983). The First Amendment's protection of religious liberty does not require this.

* * *

Because respondents' ingestion of peyote was prohibited under Oregon law, and because that prohibition is constitutional, Oregon may, consistent with the Free Exercise Clause, deny respondents unemployment compensation when their dismissal results from use of the drug. The decision of the Oregon Supreme Court is accordingly reversed.

It is so ordered.

[Footnotes Omitted.]

Due Process and Equal Protection

Due process issues arise when a law affects the rights of all citizens; for example, a law that restricts free speech or privacy rights. Equal protection issues arise if a law treats certain people differently from others; for example, a law that restricts a particular race from enjoying free speech or privacy rights when all other races are not similarly restricted. In the Family Law chapter, *Griswold v. Connecticut* and *Eisenstadt v. Baird* are discussed. Both cases cover the right to contraception, but *Griswold* is based on due process (privacy rights) and *Eisenstadt* is based on equal protection (the different treatment of married and unmarried persons). *Kelo v. City of New London* from the Property Law chapter is another example of a due process case, while *Loving v. Virginia* from the Family Law chapter is another example of an equal protection case.

The table below outlines the three levels of scrutiny or tests that all laws challenged as being unconstitutional must meet in order to be deemed constitutional. The level of scrutiny applied is different depending on what the law addresses (i.e., race versus gender or a First Amendment right versus the right to own a sandwich shop).

	Strict Scrutiny	Intermediate/ Heightened Scrutiny	Rational Basis
Due Process	1st Amendment rights, privacy, interstate travel, voting Test: Is the law or governmental action necessary to serve a compelling governmental interest?	There is no intermediate/ heightened scrutiny test that the courts have applied to due process.	Everything else Test: Is the law or governmental action rationally related to a legitimate governmental interest?
Equal Protection	Race, national origin, religion Test: Is the law or governmental action necessary to serve a compelling governmental interest?	Gender, illegitimacy Test: Is the law or governmental action substantially related to an important governmental interest?	Sexual orientation, age, disability, or anything not listed in the first two boxes Test: Is the law or governmental action rationally related to a legitimate governmental interest?

People have the right to refuse medical treatment, and, in so doing, they know that the refusal will often lead to their deaths. But, do people have the right to decide when and how to end their lives through assisted suicide or euthanasia? Is that a Constitutionally-protected privacy right? *Washington v. Glucksberg* examines the right to die under Due Process of the Fourteenth Amendment.

WASHINGTON v. GLUCKSBERG

United States Supreme Court (9–0)

521 U.S. 702 (1997)

Chief Justice Rehnquist delivered the opinion of the Court.

The question presented in this case is whether Washington's prohibition against "caus[ing]" or "aid[ing]" a suicide offends the Fourteenth Amendment to the United States Constitution. We hold that it does not.

It has always been a crime to assist a suicide in the State of Washington. In 1854, Washington's first Territorial Legislature outlawed "assisting another in the commission of self-murder." Today, Washington law provides: "A person is guilty of promoting a suicide attempt when he knowingly causes or aids another person to attempt suicide." Wash. Rev. Code § 9A.36.060(1) (1994). "Promoting a suicide attempt" is a felony, punishable by up to five years' imprisonment and up to a $10,000 fine. §§ 9A.36.060(2) and 9A.20.021(1)(c). At the same time, Washington's Natural Death Act, enacted in 1979, states that the "withholding or withdrawal of life-sustaining treatment" at a patient's direction "shall not, for any purpose, constitute a suicide." Wash. Rev. Code § 70.122.070(1).

Petitioners in this case are the State of Washington and its Attorney General. Respondents Harold Glucksberg, M. D., Abigail Halperin, M. D., Thomas A. Preston, M. D., and Peter Shalit, M. D., are physicians who practice in Washington. These doctors occasionally treat terminally ill, suffering patients, and declare that they would assist these patients in ending their lives if not for Washington's assisted-suicide ban. In January 1994, respondents, along with three gravely ill, pseudonymous plaintiffs who have since died and Compassion in Dying, a nonprofit organization that counsels people considering physician-assisted suicide, sued in the United States District Court, seeking a declaration that Wash. Rev. Code § 9A.36.060(1) (1994) is, on its face, unconstitutional. *Compassion in Dying v. Washington*, 850 F. Supp. 1454, 1459 (WD Wash. 1994).

The plaintiffs asserted "the existence of a liberty interest protected by the Fourteenth Amendment which extends to a personal choice by a mentally competent, terminally ill adult to commit physician-assisted suicide." *Ibid.* Relying primarily on *Planned Parenthood of Southeastern Pa. v. Casey*, 505 U. S. 833 (1992), and *Cruzan v. Director,* Mo. Dept. of Health, 497 U. S. 261 (1990), the District Court agreed, 850 F. Supp., at 1459–1462, and concluded that Washington's assisted-suicide ban is unconstitutional because it "places an undue burden on the exercise of [that] constitutionally protected liberty interest." *Id.*, at 1465. The District Court also decided that the Washington statute violated the Equal Protection Clause's requirement that " 'all persons similarly situated … be treated alike.' " *Id.*, at 1466 (quoting *Cleburne v. Cleburne Living Center, Inc.*, 473 U. S. 432, 439 (1985)).

A panel of the Court of Appeals for the Ninth Circuit reversed, emphasizing that "[i]n the two hundred and five years of our existence no constitutional right to aid in killing oneself has ever been asserted and upheld by a court of final jurisdiction." *Compassion in Dying v. Washington*, 49 F. 3d 586, 591 (1995). The Ninth Circuit reheard the case *en banc*, reversed the panel's decision, and affirmed the District Court. *Compassion in Dying v. Washington*, 79 F. 3d 790, 798 (1996). Like the District Court, the *en banc* Court of Appeals emphasized our *Casey* and *Cruzan* decisions. 79 F. 3d, at 813–816. The court also discussed what it described as "historical" and "current societal attitudes" toward suicide and assisted suicide, *id.*, at 806–812, and concluded that "the Constitution encompasses a due process liberty interest in controlling the time and manner of one's death—that there is, in short, a constitutionally-recognized 'right to die.' " *Id.*, at 816. After "[w]eighing and then balancing" this interest against Washington's various interests, the court held that the State's assisted-suicide ban was unconstitutional "as applied to terminally ill competent adults who wish to hasten their deaths with medication prescribed by their physicians." *Id.*, at 836, 837. The court did not reach the District Court's equal protection holding. *Id.*, at 838. We granted certiorari, 518 U. S. 1057 (1996), and now reverse.

I

We begin, as we do in all due process cases, by examining our Nation's history, legal traditions, and practices. [*Author's note: The Court included a detailed discussion on suicide going back to English law.*]

* * *

II

The Due Process Clause guarantees more than fair process, and the "liberty" it protects includes more than the absence of physical restraint. *Collins v. Harker Heights*, 503 U. S. 115, 125 (1992) (Due Process Clause "protects individual liberty against 'certain government actions regardless of the fairness of the procedures used to implement them'") (quoting *Daniels v. Williams*, 474 U. S. 327, 331 (1986)). The Clause also provides heightened protection against government interference with certain fundamental rights and liberty interests. *Reno v. Flores*, 507 U. S. 292, 301–302 (1993); *Casey*, 505 U. S., at 851. In a long line of cases, we have held that, in addition to the specific freedoms protected by the Bill of Rights, the "liberty" specially protected by the Due Process Clause includes the rights to marry, *Loving v. Virginia*, 388 U. S. 1 (1967); to have children, *Skinner v. Oklahoma ex rel. Williamson*, 316 U. S. 535 (1942); to direct the education and upbringing of one's children, *Meyer v. Nebraska*, 262 U. S. 390 (1923); *Pierce v. Society* of Sisters, 268 U. S. 510 (1925); to marital privacy, *Griswold v. Connecticut*, 381 U. S. 479 (1965); to use contraception, *ibid.*; Eisenstadt v. Baird, 405 U. S. 438 (1972); to bodily integrity, *Rochin v. California*, 342 U. S. 165 (1952), and to abortion, *Casey, supra*. We have also assumed, and strongly suggested, that the Due Process Clause protects the traditional right to refuse unwanted life saving medical treatment. *Cruzan*, 497 U. S., at 278–279.

But we "ha[ve] always been reluctant to expand the concept of substantive due process because guide posts for responsible decision making in this unchartered area are scarce and open-ended." *Collins*, 503 U. S., at 125. By extending constitutional protection to an asserted right or liberty interest, we, to a great extent, place the matter outside the arena of public debate and legislative action. We must therefore "exercise the utmost care whenever we are asked to break new ground in this field," *ibid.*, lest the liberty protected by the Due Process Clause be subtly transformed into the policy preferences of the Members of this Court, *Moore*, 431 U. S., at 502 (plurality opinion).

Our established method of substantive-due-process analysis has two primary features: First, we have regularly observed that the Due Process Clause specially protects those fundamental rights and liberties which are, objectively, "deeply rooted in this Nation's history and tradition," *id.*, at 503 (plurality opinion); *Snyder v. Massachusetts*, 291 U. S. 97, 105 (1934) ("so rooted in the traditions and conscience of our people as to be ranked as fundamental"), and "implicit in the concept of ordered liberty," such that "neither liberty nor justice would exist if they were sacrificed," *Palko v. Connecticut*, 302 U. S. 319, 325, 326 (1937). Second, we have required in substantive-due-process cases a "careful description" of the asserted fundamental liberty interest. *Flores, supra*, at 302; *Collins, supra*, at 125; *Cruzan, supra*, at 277–278. Our Nation's history, legal traditions, and practices thus provide the crucial "guide posts for responsible decision making,"

Collins, *supra*, at 125, that direct and restrain our exposition of the Due Process Clause. As we stated recently in *Flores,* the Fourteenth Amendment "forbids the government to infringe ... 'fundamental' liberty interests at all, no matter what process is provided, unless the infringement is narrowly tailored to serve a compelling state interest." 507 U. S., at 302.

* * *

Turning to the claim at issue here, the Court of Appeals stated that "[p]roperly analyzed, the first issue to be resolved is whether there is a liberty interest in determining the time and manner of one's death," 79 F. 3d, at 801, or, in other words, "[i]s there a right to die?," *id.*, at 799. Similarly, respondents assert a "liberty to choose how to die" and a right to "control of one's final days," Brief for Respondents 7, and describe the asserted liberty as "the right to choose a humane, dignified death," *id.*, at 15, and "the liberty to shape death," *id.*, at 18. As noted above, we have a tradition of carefully formulating the interest at stake in substantive due-process cases. For example, although *Cruzan* is often described as a "right to die" case, see 79 F. 3d, at 799; *post*, at 745 (Stevens, J., concurring in judgments) (*Cruzan* recognized "the more specific interest in making decisions about how to confront an imminent death"), we were, in fact, more precise: We assumed that the Constitution granted competent persons a "constitutionally protected right to refuse lifesaving hydration and nutrition." *Cruzan*, 497 U. S., at 279; *id.*, at 287 (O'Connor, J., concurring) ("[A] liberty interest in refusing unwanted medical treatment may be inferred from our prior decisions"). The Washington statute at issue in this case prohibits "aid[ing] another person to attempt suicide," Wash. Rev. Code § 9A.36.060(1) (1994), and, thus, the question before us is whether the "liberty" specially protected by the Due Process Clause includes a right to commit suicide which itself includes a right to assistance in doing so.

We now inquire whether this asserted right has any place in our Nation's traditions. Here, as discussed *supra*, at 710–719, we are confronted with a consistent and almost universal tradition that has long rejected the asserted right, and continues explicitly to reject it today, even for terminally ill, mentally competent adults. To hold for respondents, we would have to reverse centuries of legal doctrine and practice, and strike down the considered policy choice of almost every State. See *Jackman v. Rosenbaum Co.*, 260 U. S. 22, 31 (1922) ("If a thing has been practised for two hundred years by common consent, it will need a strong case for the Fourteenth Amendment to affect it"); *Flores*, 507 U. S., at 303 ("The mere novelty of such a claim is reason enough to doubt that 'substantive due process' sustains it").

Respondents contend, however, that the liberty interest they assert *is* consistent with this Court's substantive-due-process line of cases, if not with this Nation's history and practice. Pointing to *Casey* and *Cruzan*, respondents read our jurisprudence in this area as reflecting a general tradition of "self-sovereignty," Brief for Respondents 12, and as teaching that the "liberty" protected by the Due Process Clause includes "basic and intimate exercises of personal autonomy," *id.*, at 10; see *Casey*, 505 U. S., at 847 ("It is a promise of the Constitution that there is a realm of personal liberty which the government may not enter"). According to respondents, our liberty jurisprudence, and the broad, individualistic principles it reflects, protects the "liberty of competent, terminally ill adults to make end-of-life decisions free of undue government interference." Brief for Respondents 10. The question presented in this case, however, is whether the protections of the Due Process Clause include a right to commit suicide with another's assistance. With this "careful description" of respondents' claim in mind, we turn to *Casey* and *Cruzan*.

In *Cruzan*, we considered whether Nancy Beth Cruzan, who had been severely injured in an automobile accident and was in a persistive vegetative state, "ha[d] a right under the United States Constitution which would require the hospital to withdraw life-sustaining treatment" at her parents' request. 497 U. S., at 269. We began with the observation that "[a]t common law, even the touching of one person by another without consent and without legal justification was a battery." *Ibid*. We then discussed the related rule that "informed consent is generally required for medical treatment." *Ibid*. After reviewing a long line of relevant state cases, we concluded that "the common-law doctrine of informed consent is viewed as generally encompassing the right of a competent individual to refuse medical treatment." *Id*., at 277. Next, we reviewed our own cases on the subject, and stated that "[t]he principle that a competent person has a constitutionally protected liberty interest in refusing unwanted medical treatment may be inferred from our prior decisions." *Id*., at 278. Therefore, "for purposes of [that] case, we assume[d] that the United States Constitution would grant a competent person a constitutionally protected right to refuse life saving hydration and nutrition." *Id*., at 279; see *id*., at 287 (O'Connor, J., concurring). We concluded that, notwithstanding this right, the Constitution permitted Missouri to require clear and convincing evidence of an incompetent patient's wishes concerning the withdrawal of life-sustaining treatment. *Id*., at 280–281.

Respondents contend that in *Cruzan* we "acknowledged that competent, dying persons have the right to direct the removal of life-sustaining medical treatment and thus hasten death," Brief for Respondents 23, and that "the constitutional principle behind recognizing the patient's liberty to direct the withdrawal of artificial life support applies at least as strongly to the choice to hasten impending death by consuming lethal medication," *id*., at 26. Similarly, the Court of Appeals concluded that "Cruzan, by recognizing a liberty interest that includes the refusal of artificial provision of life-sustaining food and water, necessarily recognize[d] a liberty interest in hastening one's own death." 79 F. 3d, at 816.

The right assumed in *Cruzan*, however, was not simply deduced from abstract concepts of personal autonomy. Given the common-law rule that forced medication was a battery, and the long legal tradition protecting the decision to refuse unwanted medical treatment, our assumption was entirely consistent with this Nation's history and constitutional traditions. The decision to commit suicide with the assistance of another may be just as personal and profound as the decision to refuse unwanted medical treatment, but it has never enjoyed similar legal protection. Indeed, the two acts are widely and reasonably regarded as quite distinct. See *Quill v. Vacco*, *post*, at 800–808. In *Cruzan* itself, we recognized that most States outlawed assisted suicide—and even more do today—and we certainly gave no intimation that the right to refuse unwanted medical treatment could be somehow transmuted into a right to assistance in committing suicide. 497 U. S., at 280.

Respondents also rely on *Casey*. There, the Court's opinion concluded that "the essential holding of *Roe v. Wade* [, 410 U. S. 113 (1973),] should be retained and once again reaffirmed." 505 U. S., at 846. We held, first, that a woman has a right, before her fetus is viable, to an abortion "without undue interference from the State"; second, that States may restrict postviability abortions, so long as exceptions are made to protect a woman's life and health; and third, that the State has legitimate interests throughout a pregnancy in protecting the health of the woman and the life of the unborn child. *Ibid*. In reaching this conclusion, the opinion discussed in some detail this Court's substantive-due-process tradition of interpreting the Due Process Clause to protect certain fundamental rights and "personal decisions relating to marriage, procreation, contraception, family relationships, child rearing, and education," and noted that many of those rights and liberties "involv[e] the most intimate and personal choices a person may make in a lifetime." *Id*., at 851.

The Court of Appeals, like the District Court, found *Casey* "'highly instructive'" and "'almost prescriptive'" for determining "'what liberty interest may inhere in a terminally ill person's choice to commit suicide'":

> "Like the decision of whether or not to have an abortion, the decision how and when to die is one of 'the most intimate and personal choices a person may make in a lifetime,' a choice 'central to personal dignity and autonomy.'" 79 F. 3d, at 813–814.

Similarly, respondents emphasize the statement in *Casey* that:

> "At the heart of liberty is the right to define one's own concept of existence, of meaning, of the universe, and of the mystery of human life. Beliefs about these matters could not define the attributes of personhood were they formed under compulsion of the State." 505 U. S., at 851.

Brief for Respondents 12. By choosing this language, the Court's opinion in *Casey* described, in a general way and in light of our prior cases, those personal activities and decisions that this Court has identified as so deeply rooted in our history and traditions, or so fundamental to our concept of constitutionally ordered liberty, that they are protected by the Fourteenth Amendment. The opinion moved from the recognition that liberty necessarily includes freedom of conscience and belief about ultimate considerations to the observation that "though the abortion decision may originate within the zone of conscience and belief, it is *more than a philosophic exercise*." *Casey*, 505 U. S., at 852 (emphasis added). That many of the rights and liberties protected by the Due Process Clause sound in personal autonomy does not warrant the sweeping conclusion that any and all important, intimate, and personal decisions are so protected, *San Antonio Independent School Dist. v. Rodriguez*, 411 U. S. 1, 33–35 (1973), and *Casey* did not suggest otherwise.

The history of the law's treatment of assisted suicide in this country has been and continues to be one of the rejection of nearly all efforts to permit it. That being the case, our decisions lead us to conclude that the asserted "right" to assistance in committing suicide is not a fundamental liberty interest protected by the Due Process Clause. The Constitution also requires, however, that Washington's assisted suicide ban be rationally related to legitimate government interests. See *Heller v. Doe*, 509 U. S. 312, 319–320 (1993); *Flores*, 507 U. S., at 305. This requirement is unquestionably met here. As the court below recognized, 79 F. 3d, at 816–817, Washington's assisted-suicide ban implicates a number of state interests. See 49 F. 3d, at 592-593; Brief for State of California et al. as *Amici Curiae* 26–29; Brief for United States as *Amicus Curiae* 16–27.

First, Washington has an "unqualified interest in the preservation of human life." *Cruzan*, 497 U. S., at 282. The State's prohibition on assisted suicide, like all homicide laws, both reflects and advances its commitment to this interest.

* * *

The State also has an interest in protecting the integrity and ethics of the medical profession.

* * *

Next, the State has an interest in protecting vulnerable groups—including the poor, the elderly, and disabled persons—from abuse, neglect, and mistakes.

* * *

The State's interest here goes beyond protecting the vulnerable from coercion; it extends to protecting disabled and terminally ill people from prejudice, negative and inaccurate stereotypes, and "societal indifference." 49 F. 3d, at 592. The State's assisted-suicide ban reflects and reinforces its policy that the lives of terminally ill, disabled, and elderly people must be no less valued than the lives of the young and healthy, and that a seriously disabled person's suicidal impulses should be interpreted and treated the same way as anyone else's. ***

Finally, the State may fear that permitting assisted suicide will start it down the path to voluntary and perhaps even involuntary euthanasia.

* * *

We need not weigh exactingly the relative strengths of these various interests. They are unquestionably important and legitimate, and Washington's ban on assisted suicide is at least reasonably related to their promotion and protection. We therefore hold that Wash. Rev. Code § 9A.36.060(1) (1994) does not violate the Fourteenth Amendment, either on its face or "as applied to competent, terminally ill adults who wish to hasten their deaths by obtaining medication prescribed by their doctors." 79 F. 3d, at 838.

* * *

Throughout the Nation, Americans are engaged in an earnest and profound debate about the morality, legality, and practicality of physician-assisted suicide. Our holding permits this debate to continue, as it should in a democratic society. The decision of the *en banc* Court of Appeals is reversed, and the case is remanded for further proceedings consistent with this opinion.

It is so ordered.

[Footnotes Omitted.]

Craig v. Boren is an equal protection case that examines an Oklahoma statute that had different drinking ages for men and women.

CRAIG v. BOREN

Supreme Court of United States

429 U.S. 190 (1976)

MR. JUSTICE BRENNAN delivered the opinion of the Court.

The interaction of two sections of an Oklahoma statute, Okla. Stat., Tit. 37, §§ 241 and 245 (1958 and Supp. 1976), prohibits the sale of "nonintoxicating" 3.2% beer to males under the age of 21 and to females under the age of 18. The question to be decided is whether such a gender-based differential constitutes a denial to males 18–20 years of age of the equal protection of the laws in violation of the Fourteenth Amendment.

This action was brought in the District Court for the Western District of Oklahoma on December 20, 1972, by appellant Craig, a male then between 18 and 21 years of age, and by appellant Whitener, a licensed vendor of 3.2% beer. The complaint sought declaratory and injunctive relief against enforcement of the gender-based differential on the ground that it constituted invidious discrimination against males 18–20 years of age. A three-judge court convened under 28 U. S. C. § 2281 sustained the constitutionality of the statutory differential and dismissed the action. 399 F. Supp. 1304 (1975). We noted probable jurisdiction of appellants' appeal, 423 U. S. 1047 (1976). We reverse.

* * *

II

A

Before 1972, Oklahoma defined the commencement of civil majority at age 18 for females and age 21 for males. Okla. Stat., Tit. 15, § 13 (1972 and Supp. 1976). In contrast, females were held criminally responsible as adults at age 18 and males at age 16. Okla. Stat., Tit. 10, § 1101 (a) (Supp. 1976). After the Court of Appeals for the Tenth Circuit held in 1972, on the authority of *Reed v. Reed*, 404 U. S. 71 (1971), that the age distinction was unconstitutional for purposes of establishing criminal responsibility as adults, *Lamb v. Brown*, 456 F. 2d 18, the Oklahoma Legislature fixed age 18 as applicable to both males and females. Okla. Stat., Tit. 10, § 1101 (a) (Supp. 1976). In 1972, 18 also was established as the age of majority for males and females in civil matters, Okla. Stat., Tit. 15, § 13 (1972 and Supp. 1976), except that §§ 241 and 245 of the 3.2% beer statute were simultaneously codified to create an exception to the gender-free rule.

Analysis may appropriately begin with the reminder that *Reed* emphasized that statutory classifications that distinguish between males and females are "subject to scrutiny under the Equal Protection Clause." 404 U. S., at 75. To withstand constitutional challenge, previous cases establish that classifications by gender must serve important governmental objectives and must be substantially related to achievement of those objectives. Thus, in *Reed*, the objectives of "reducing the workload on probate courts," *id.*, at 76, and "avoiding intrafamily controversy," *id.*, at 77, were deemed of insufficient importance to sustain use of an overt gender criterion in the appointment of administrators of intestate decedents' estates. Decisions following *Reed* similarly have rejected administrative ease and convenience as sufficiently important objectives to justify gender-based classifications. *** And only two Terms ago, *Stanton v. Stanton*, 421 U. S. 7 (1975), expressly stating that *Reed v. Reed* was "controlling," 421 U. S., at 13, held that *Reed* required invalidation of a Utah differential age-of-majority statute, notwithstanding the statute's coincidence with and furtherance of the State's purpose of fostering "old notions" of role typing and preparing boys for their expected performance in the economic and political worlds. 421 U. S., at 14–15.

Reed v. Reed has also provided the underpinning for decisions that have invalidated statutes employing gender as an inaccurate proxy for other, more germane bases of classification. Hence, "archaic and overbroad" generalizations, *Schlesinger v. Ballard*, *supra*, at 508, concerning the financial position of servicewomen, *Frontiero v. Richardson*, *supra*, at 689 n. 23, and working women, *Weinberger v. Wiesenfeld*, 420 U. S. 636, 643 (1975), could not justify use of a gender line in determining eligibility for certain governmental entitlements. Similarly, increasingly outdated misconceptions concerning the role of females in the home rather than in the "marketplace and world of ideas" were rejected as loose-fitting characterizations incapable of supporting state statutory schemes that were premised upon their accuracy. *Stanton v. Stanton*, *supra*; *Taylor v. Louisiana*, 419 U. S. 522, 535 n. 17 (1975). In light of the weak congruence between gender and the characteristic or trait that gender purported to represent, it was necessary that the legislatures choose either to realign their substantive laws in a gender-neutral fashion, or to adopt procedures for identifying those instances where the sex-centered generalization actually comported with fact. *See, e. g., Stanley v. Illinois, supra.*, at 658; cf. *Cleveland Board of Education v. LaFleur*, 414 U. S. 632, 650 (1974).

In this case, too, "*Reed*, we feel, is controlling ...," *Stanton v. Stanton, supra*, at 13. We turn then to the question whether, under *Reed*, the difference between males and females with respect to the purchase of 3.2% beer warrants the differential in age drawn by the Oklahoma statute. We conclude that it does not.

B

The District Court recognized that *Reed v. Reed* was controlling. In applying the teachings of that case, the court found the requisite important governmental objective in the traffic-safety goal proffered by the Oklahoma Attorney General. It then concluded that the statistics introduced by the appellees established that the gender-based distinction was substantially related to achievement of that goal.

C

We accept for purposes of discussion the District Court's identification of the objective underlying §§ 241 and 245 as the enhancement of traffic safety. Clearly, the protection of public health and safety represents an important function of state and local governments. However, appellees' statistics in our view cannot support the conclusion that the gender-based distinction closely serves to achieve that objective and therefore the distinction cannot under *Reed* withstand equal protection challenge.

The appellees introduced a variety of statistical surveys. First, an analysis of arrest statistics for 1973 demonstrated that 18–20-year-old male arrests for "driving under the influence" and "drunkenness" substantially exceeded female arrests for that same age period. Similarly, youths aged 17–21 were found to be overrepresented among those killed or injured in traffic accidents, with males again numerically exceeding females in this regard. Third, a random roadside survey in Oklahoma City revealed that young males were more inclined to drive and drink beer than were their female counterparts. Fourth, Federal Bureau of Investigation nationwide statistics exhibited a notable increase in arrests for "driving under the influence." Finally, statistical evidence gathered in other jurisdictions, particularly Minnesota and Michigan, was offered to corroborate Oklahoma's experience by indicating the pervasiveness of youthful participation in motor vehicle accidents following the imbibing of alcohol. Conceding that "the case is not free from doubt," 399 F. Supp., at 1314, the District Court nonetheless concluded that this statistical showing substantiated "a rational basis for the legislative judgment underlying the challenged classification." *Id.*, at 1307.

Even were this statistical evidence accepted as accurate, it nevertheless offers only a weak answer to the equal protection question presented here. The most focused and relevant of the statistical surveys, arrests of 18–20-year-olds for alcohol-related driving offenses, exemplifies the ultimate unpersuasiveness of this evidentiary record. Viewed in terms of the correlation between sex and the actual activity that Oklahoma seeks to regulate—driving while under the influence of alcohol—the statistics broadly establish that .18% of females and 2% of males in that age group were arrested for that offense. While such a disparity is not trivial in a statistical sense, it hardly can form the basis for employment of a gender line as a classifying device. Certainly if maleness is to serve as a proxy for drinking and driving, a correlation of 2% must be considered an unduly tenuous "fit." Indeed, prior cases have consistently rejected the use of sex as a decisionmaking factor even though the statutes in question certainly rested on far more predictive empirical relationships than this.

* * *

There is no reason to belabor this line of analysis. It is unrealistic to expect either members of the judiciary or state officials to be well versed in the rigors of experimental or statistical technique. But this merely illustrates that proving broad sociological propositions by statistics is a dubious business, and one that inevitably is in tension with the normative philosophy that underlies the Equal Protection Clause. Suffice to say that the showing offered by the appellees does not satisfy us that sex represents a legitimate, accurate proxy for the regulation of drinking and driving. In fact, when it is further recognized that Oklahoma's statute prohibits only the selling of 3.2% beer to young males and not their drinking the beverage once acquired (even after purchase by their 18–20-year-old female companions), the relationship between gender and traffic safety becomes far too tenuous to satisfy *Reed*'s requirement that the gender-based difference be substantially related to achievement of the statutory objective.

We hold, therefore, that under *Reed*, Oklahoma's 3.2% beer statute invidiously discriminates against males 18–20 years of age.

* * *

We conclude that the gender-based differential contained in Okla. Stat., Tit. 37, § 245 (1976 Supp.) constitutes a denial of the equal protection of the laws to males aged 18–20 and reverse the judgment of the District Court.

It is so ordered.

[Footnotes Omitted.]

Chapter 5
Property

One of the first things children learn is the concept of property. "Mine" is a constant refrain of children—"my ball," "my crayons," etc. As children get older and become adults, rules are needed to define who has rights to property. Very simply, that is what property law is. Property law can be described as the field of law that covers people and their things. Who has ownership rights, how those rights are transferred, who can use the property regardless of ownership rights, and what rights an individual has in the property s/he owns are some of the issues addressed in the field of property law.

There are three categories of property. Personal property consists of the items that an individual typically considers to be his/her stuff—cars, books, jewelry, stocks, cash, bank accounts, etc. Real property refers to land and buildings, otherwise known as real estate. The bulk of this chapter deals with issues relating to real property. Intellectual property is the third type of property and will be discussed in Chapter 6.

> The following law review excerpt is provided to give the reader a different perspective on property. People generally think that they have a good concept of what property is, as does Mr. Black below, but after his discussion, is Black any clearer as to what property actually is?

Felix S. Cohen, Dialogue on Private Property, 9 Rutgers L.Rev. 357–361 (1954)

DOES PRIVATE PROPERTY EXIST?

Now, let us see if we can get a clearer notion of the kind of facts that we are dealing with when we talk about property. We have all agreed that there is such a thing as private property in the United States, but suppose we run into a skeptic who refuses to accept our agreement. What evidence, Mr. Black, can you produce to show that private property really exists?

B. Well, here is a book that is my property. You can see it, feel it, weigh it. What better proof could there be of the existence of private property?

C. I can see the shape and color of the book very well, but I don't see its propertiness. What sort of evidence can you put forward to show that the book is your property?

B. Well, I paid for it.

C. Did you pay for your last haircut?

B. Yes.

C. And did you pay for last year's tuition, and last month's board, and your last railroad trip?

B. Yes.

C. But these things are not your property just because you paid for them, are they?

B. No, I suppose not, but now you are talking about past events and I am talking about a material object, a book, that I bought and paid for, which is something quite different from last year's tuition, or last night's dinner.

C. You could cite in support of that distinction, the definition of property given by Aigler, Bigelow and Powell: "Human beings … have various needs and desires. Many of these relate to external objects with which they are in some way associated … The law of property may be looked at as an attempt upon the part of the state, acting through its courts and administrative officers, to give a systematized recognition of and protection of these attitudes and desires on the part of individuals towards things."

B. Yes, I think that clarifies our idea of property.

C. But is the copyright to a song a material, external object?

B. No, I suppose not.

C. And what about a mortgage or a patent on a chemical process or a future interest? These things can be property without being material objects, can't they?

B. Yes, I suppose they can.

C. Then what makes something property may be something intangible, invisible, unweighable, without shape or color?

B. I suppose that may be true in some cases, at least with respect to certain forms of intangible property.

C. Well, let's take the simplest case of tangible property, a piece of real estate, an acre of land on the outskirts of New Haven that you, let us assume, own in fee simple absolute. Would you say that the soil and the rock and the trees are tangible?

B. Yes, they certainly are.

C. But if you cut down the trees and sell them for firewood, the real property is still there on the outskirts of New Haven?

B. Yes.

C. And if you cut the sod and sell that, and dig up the top soil and sand and gravel and rock and sell that, the real property is still there on the outskirts of New Haven and you still have your fee simple absolute?

B. Yes.

C. Then a fee simple absolute is a sector of space in time and no more tangible than a song or a patent?

B. I see no way of avoiding that conclusion.

C. But you are not happy with this conclusion?

B. No, your questions seem to make property vanish into empty space.

C. Perhaps that is because you are assuming that reality always has a position in space. It seems to me that you and Aigler, Bigelow and Powell, are all prisoners of common sense, which is usually the metaphysics of 500 years back. In this case the current common sense is the metaphysical doctrine of Duns Scotus, William of Occam, and other 14th and 15th century scholastics, who held that all reality is tangible and exists in space. That idea runs through a great deal of common-law doctrine. Take, for example, the ceremony of *livery of seizin*, by which in transferring a possessory estate in land you actually pick up a piece of the sod and soil and hand to the grantee; or take the old common-law rule that a mortgage consists of a piece of paper, and if this piece of paper is destroyed, the mortgage disappears. Why should we assume that all reality exists in space? Do our differences of opinion exist in space? Why not recognize that spatial existence is only one of many realms of reality and that in dealing with the law we cannot limit ourselves entirely to the realm of spatial or physical existence?

Personal Property

One of the issues affecting personal property is what happens with found property. The *Paset* case below deals with the issue of lost and found.

PASET v. OLD ORCHARD BANK AND TRUST COMPANY

Illinois Appellate Court — First District (3rd Division) (1978)

378 N.E.2d 1264 (1978)

Reversed and remanded.

Mr. JUSTICE SIMON delivered the opinion of the court:

On May 8, 1974, the plaintiff, Bernice Paset, a safety deposit box subscriber at the defendant Old Orchard Bank (the bank), found $6,325 in currency on the seat of a chair in an examination booth in the safety deposit vault. The chair was partially under a table. The plaintiff notified officers of the bank and turned the money over to them. She then was told by bank officials that the bank would try to locate the owner, and that she could have the money if the owner was not located within 1 year.

The bank wrote to everyone who had been in the safety deposit vault area either on the day of, or on the day preceding, the discovery, stating that some property had been found and inviting the customers to describe any property they might have lost. No one reported the loss of currency, and the money remained unclaimed a year after it had been found. However, when the plaintiff requested the money, the bank refused to deliver it to her, explaining that it was obligated to hold the currency for the owner.

The safety deposit vault area of the bank was located on a lower floor of the bank. This area was separated from a lobby by a gate, and, according to an affidavit filed by the bank, entrance to the safety deposit vault area was restricted to bank employees and customers maintaining safety deposit boxes in the vault. The affidavit stated that no customer could enter this vault without the consent of a bank guard or employee stationed at the gate, and that customers were allowed to enter only after their signatures were verified. When a customer entered, a bank employee would accompany the customer to the safety deposit vault to obtain the box and then escort him to one of the 16 examination booths maintained in the area.

* * *

This appeal, then, requires a determination of whether a finder of cash in an examining booth in a safety deposit vault may be a keeper under the Illinois estray statute and an analysis of the extent to which the common law concepts of lost and mislaid property apply to the statute.

The estray statute provides in sections 27 and 28:

"If any person or persons find any lost goods, money, bank notes, or other choses in action, of any description whatever, such person or persons shall inform the owner thereof, if known, *** If the owner is unknown and if such property found is of the value of $15 or upwards, the finder or finders shall, within 5 days after such finding as aforesaid, appear before some circuit judge residing in the county, and make affidavit of the description thereof, the time and place when and where the same was found, that no alteration has been made in the appearance thereof since the finding of the same, that the owner thereof is unknown to him and that he has not secreted, withheld or disposed of any part thereof. The judge shall enter an order stating the value of the property found as near as he can ascertain. A certified copy of such order and the affidavit of the finder shall, within 10 days after the order has been entered, be transmitted to the county clerk to be recorded in his estray book, and filed in his office." Ill. Rev. Stat. 1975, ch. 50, par. 27.

"If the value thereof exceeds the sum of $15, the county clerk, within 20 days after receiving the certified copy of the judge's order shall cause an advertisement to be set up on the court house door, and in 3 other of the most public places in the county, and also a notice thereof to be published for 3 weeks successively in some public newspaper printed in this state and if the owner of such goods, money, bank notes, or other choses in action does not appear and claim the same *** within one year after the advertisement thereof as aforesaid, the ownership of such property shall vest in the finder." (Ill. Rev. Stat. 1975, ch. 50, par. 28.)

The Illinois estray statute's principal purposes are to encourage and facilitate the return of property to the true owner, and then to reward a finder for his honesty if the property remains unclaimed. The statute provides an incentive for finders to report their discoveries by making it possible for them, after the passage of the requisite time, to acquire legal title to the property they have found. (*See* Comment, *Lost, Mislaid, and Abandoned Property*, 8 Fordham L. Rev. 222, 234–235 (1939).) By directing the county clerk to publicize and advertise the property, the statute further enhances the opportunity of the owner to recover what he has lost.

• 1, 2 Traditionally, the common law has treated lost and mislaid property differently for the purposes of determining ownership of property someone has found. Mislaid property is that which is intentionally put in a certain place and later forgotten; at common law a finder acquires no rights to mislaid property. The element of intentional deposit present in the case of mislaid property is absent in the case of lost property, for property is deemed lost when it is unintentionally separated from the dominion of its owner. The general rule is that the finder is entitled to possession of lost property against everyone except the true owner. We are not concerned in this case with abandoned property where the owner, intending to relinquish all rights to his property, leaves it free to be appropriated by any other person. Although at common law the finder is entitled to keep abandoned property, the plaintiff has not taken the position that the money here was abandoned. *Jackson v. Steinberg* (1948), 186 Ore. 129, 200 P.2d 376, 377; 1 Am. Jr. 2d *Abandoned, Lost, and Unclaimed Property* §§ 1, 2 (1962).

* * *

Thus, we do not accept the bank's initial argument that the money was mislaid rather than lost. It is complete speculation to infer, as the bank urges, that the money was deliberately placed by its owner on the chair located partially under a table in the examining booth, and then forgotten. If the money was intentionally placed on the chair by someone who forgot where he left it, the bank's notice to safety deposit box subscribers should have alerted the owner. The failure of an owner to appear to claim the money in the interval since its discovery is affirmative evidence that the property was not mislaid. *Toledo*

Trust Co. v. Simmons (1935), 52 Ohio App. 373, 3 N.E.2d 661; *Burnley v. First National Bank* (1953), 87 Pa. D. & C. 433.

• 3 Because the evidence, though ambiguous, tends to indicate that the money probably was not mislaid, and because neither party contends that the money was abandoned, we conclude that the ambiguity should, as a matter of public policy, be resolved in favor of the presumption that the money was lost. This conclusion is in harmony with the above mentioned purposes of the estray statute, for it construes the statute liberally rather than technically, with the result that the statute is brought into play rather than rejected. Such an application of the statute better effectuates the legislature's goal of restoring property to a true owner; it provides incentive for a finder to report his discovery by rewarding him if the true owner does not appear within the statutorily determined time limit. Accordingly, we reject the bank's first contention that the money was mislaid and the estray statute irrelevant, and conclude that the money was "lost," and so encompassed by the Illinois estray statute.

* * *

Therefore, looking at both the common law and estray statute, we accept the *Pyle* conclusion that where property is found in a bank safety deposit vault area, the bank as owner of the premises should hold the property on a temporary basis as custodian until ownership is determined. This is a just result not inconsistent with the purposes of the estray statute, for the return of property to its true owner is best promoted by requiring the finder to leave the property temporarily with the owner of the premises where it was found. (See Comment, Lost, Mislaid and Abandoned Property, 8 Fordham L. Rev. 222, 234–35 (1939); Morton, Public Policy and the Finders Cases, 1 Wyo. L.J. 101 (1946).) We merely amplify the holding in *Pyle* by ruling that the estray statute provides the proper method for resolving the eventual question of ownership of the property if the true owner does not claim it, a problem which the *Pyle* court expressly stated it was not reaching. Therefore, we conclude that the estray statute vested ownership in the finder of the property in this case when the owner did not appear after the legislatively designated time of 1 year—at which point the bank's temporary custody and possession was terminated.

* * *

The alternative to the conclusion we reach is impractical. It would, as the court in *Dolitsky* suggested, label the bank a gratuitous bailee for an unknown owner, with the requirement that the bank hold the property indefinitely—despite the probability that after 4 years, the owner will never appear. The bank's record of its safety deposit box subscribers who visited the vault on the day of or the day preceding the plaintiff's discovery gave the bank the opportunity to search for the owner among this limited group. The bank also had sufficient time to contact any subscriber who had not been in his box since the date the plaintiff discovered the money. Consequently, in view of the opportunities the bank had to search out the owner of the money among this limited group, of the notice the bank gave to that group, and of the plaintiff's undisputed compliance with the estray statute, vesting the ownership of the money in the finder is a more pragmatic and sensible solution than having the bank continue to hold the money indefinitely.

Accordingly, the judgment of the circuit court is reversed and the case is remanded, directions to enter judgment in favor of the plaintiff finder.

Judgment reversed and remanded with directions.

[Footnotes Omitted.]

Suppose that someone undergoes an operation with the subsequent removal of cells from his/her body. Then, suppose that scientists create something of value from those cells. Should the patient share in any profits derived from the value of the use of his/her cells? The *Moore* case deals with property rights to one's own cells.

MOORE v. REGENTS OF THE UNIVERSITY OF CALIFORNIA

Supreme Court of California, En Banc

793 P.2d 479 (1990)

I. INTRODUCTION

PANELLI, Justice.

We granted review in this case to determine whether plaintiff has stated a cause of action against his physician and other defendants for using his cells [51 Cal.3d 125] in potentially lucrative medical research without his permission. Plaintiff alleges that his physician failed to disclose preexisting research and economic interests in the cells before obtaining consent to the medical procedures by which they were extracted. The superior court sustained all defendants' demurrers to the third amended complaint, and the Court of Appeal reversed. We hold that the complaint states a cause of action for breach of the physician's disclosure obligations, but not for conversion.

II. FACTS

* * *

Moore first visited UCLA Medical Center on October 5, 1976, shortly after he learned that he had hairy-cell leukemia. After hospitalizing Moore and "withdr[awing] extensive amounts of blood, bone marrow aspirate, and other bodily substances," Golde confirmed that diagnosis. At this time all [51 Cal.3d 126] defendants, including Golde, were aware that "certain blood products and blood components were of great value in a number of commercial and scientific efforts" and that access to a patient whose blood contained these substances would provide "competitive, commercial, and scientific advantages."

On October 8, 1976, Golde recommended that Moore's spleen be removed. Golde informed Moore "that he had reason to fear for his life, and that the proposed splenectomy operation ... was necessary to slow down the progress of his disease." Based upon Golde's representations, Moore signed a written consent form authorizing the splenectomy.

Before the operation, Golde and Quan "formed the intent and made arrangements to obtain portions of [Moore's] spleen following its removal" and to take them to a separate research unit. Golde gave written instructions to this effect on October 18 and 19, 1976. These research activities "were not intended to have ... any relation to [Moore's] medical ... care." However, neither Golde nor Quan informed Moore of their plans to conduct this research or requested his permission. Surgeons at UCLA Medical Center, whom the complaint does not name as defendants, removed Moore's spleen on October 20, 1976.

Moore returned to the UCLA Medical Center several times between November 1976 and September 1983. He did so at Golde's direction and based upon representations "that such visits were necessary and required for his health and well-being, and based upon the trust inherent in and by virtue of the physician-patient relationship ..." On each of these visits Golde withdrew additional samples of "blood, blood serum, skin, bone marrow aspirate, and sperm." On each occasion Moore travelled to the UCLA Medical Center from his home in Seattle because he had been told that the procedures were to be performed only there and only under Golde's direction.

"In fact, [however,] throughout the period of time that [Moore] was under [Golde's] care and treatment, ... the defendants were actively involved in a number of activities which they concealed from [Moore] ..." Specifically, defendants were conducting research on Moore's cells and planned to "benefit financially and competitively ... [by exploiting the cells] and [their] exclusive access to [the cells] by virtue of [Golde's] on-going physician–patient relationship ..."

Sometime before August 1979, Golde established a cell line from Moore's T-lymphocytes. On January 30, 1981, the Regents applied for a patent on the cell line, listing Golde and Quan as inventors. "[B]y virtue of an established policy ..., [the] Regents, Golde, and Quan would share in any royalties or profits ... arising out of [the] patent." The patent issued on March 20, 1984, naming Golde and Quan as the inventors of the cell line and the Regents as the assignee of the patent. (U.S. Patent No. 4,438,032 (Mar. 20, 1984).)

The Regents' patent also covers various methods for using the cell line to produce lymphokines. Moore admits in his complaint that "the true clinical potential of each of the lymphokines ... [is] difficult to predict, [but] ... competing commercial firms in these relevant fields have published reports in biotechnology industry periodicals predicting a potential market of approximately $3.01 Billion Dollars by the year 1990 for a whole range of [such lymphokines] ..."

With the Regents' assistance, Golde negotiated agreements for commercial development of the cell line and products to be derived from it. Under an agreement with Genetics Institute, Golde "became a paid consultant" and "acquired the rights to 75,000 shares of common stock." Genetics Institute also agreed to pay Golde and the Regents "at least $330,000 over three years, including a pro-rata share of [Golde's] salary and fringe benefits, in exchange for ... exclusive access to the materials and research performed" on the cell line and products derived from it. On June 4, 1982, [51 Cal.3d 128] Sandoz "was added to the agreement," and compensation payable to Golde and the Regents was increased by $110,000. "[T]hroughout this period, ... Quan spent as much as 70 [percent] of her time working for [the] Regents on research" related to the cell line.

* * *

III. DISCUSSION

* * *

B. Conversion

Moore also attempts to characterize the invasion of his rights as a conversion—a tort that protects against interference with possessory and ownership interests in personal property. He theorizes that he continued to own his cells following their removal from his body, at least for the purpose of directing their use, and that he never consented to their use in potentially [51 Cal.3d 135] lucrative medical research. Thus, to complete Moore's argument, defendants' unauthorized use of his cells constitutes a conversion. As a result of the alleged conversion, Moore claims a proprietary interest in each of the products that any of the defendants might ever create from his cells or the patented cell line.

No court, however, has ever in a reported decision imposed conversion liability for the use of human cells in medical research. While that fact does not end our inquiry, it raises a flag of caution. In effect, what Moore is asking us to do is to impose a tort duty on scientists to investigate the consensual pedigree of each human cell sample used in research. To impose such a duty, which would affect medical research of importance to all of society, implicates policy concerns far removed from the traditional, two-party ownership disputes in which the law of conversion arose. Invoking a tort theory originally used to determine whether the loser or the finder of a horse had the better title, Moore claims ownership of the results of socially important medical research, including the genetic code for chemicals that regulate the functions of every human being's immune system.

* * *

1. Moore's Claim Under Existing Law

"To establish a conversion, plaintiff must establish an actual interference with his ownership or right of possession ... Where plaintiff neither has title to the property alleged to have been converted, nor possession thereof, he cannot maintain an action for conversion." (*Del E. Webb Corp. v. Structural Materials Co.* (1981) 123 Cal.App.3d 593, 610–611, 176 Cal.Rptr. 824, emphasis added. *See also General Motors A. Corp. v. Dallas* (1926) 198 Cal. 365, 370, 245 P. 184.)

Since Moore clearly did not expect to retain possession of his cells following their removal, to sue for their conversion he must have retained [51 Cal.3d 137] an ownership interest in them. But there are several reasons to doubt that he did retain any such interest. First, no reported judicial decision supports Moore's claim, either directly or by close analogy. Second, California statutory law drastically limits any continuing interest of a patient in excised cells. Third, the subject matters of the Regents' patent—the patented cell line and the products derived from it—cannot be Moore's property.

* * *

The extension of conversion law into this area will hinder research by restricting access to the necessary raw materials. Thousands of human cell lines already exist in tissue repositories, such as the American Type Culture Collection and those operated by the National Institutes of Health and the American Cancer Society. These repositories respond to tens of thousands [51 Cal.3d 145] of requests for samples annually. Since the patent office requires the holders of patents on cell lines to make samples available to anyone, many patent holders place their cell lines in repositories to avoid the administrative burden of responding to requests. (OTA Rep., *supra*, at p. 53.) At present, human cell lines are routinely copied and distributed to other researchers for experimental purposes, usually free of charge. This exchange of scientific materials, which still is relatively free and efficient, will surely be compromised if each cell sample becomes the potential subject matter of a lawsuit. (OTA Rep., *supra*, at p. 52.)

* * *

For these reasons, we hold that the allegations of Moore's third amended complaint state a cause of action for breach of fiduciary duty or lack of informed consent, but not conversion.

[Footnotes omitted.]

Restrictive Covenants

Restrictive covenants are requirements in a deed that restrict a landowner's ability to do "something" with a property at issue. That "something" is defined within the covenant.

Shelley v. Kraemer addresses the constitutionality of restrictive covenants based on race.

SHELLEY v. KRAEMER

Supreme Court of the United States (6–0)

331 U.S. 1 (1948)

Mr. Chief Justice VINSON delivered the opinion of the Court.

These cases present for our consideration questions relating to the validity of court enforcement of private agreements, generally described as restrictive covenants, which have as their purpose the exclusion of persons of designated race or color from the Basic constitutional issues of obvious importance have been raised.

The first of these cases comes to this Court on certiorari to the Supreme Court of Missouri. On February 16, 1911, thirty out of a total of thirty-nine owners of property fronting both sides of Labadie Avenue between Taylor Avenue and Cora Avenue in the city of St. Louis, signed an agreement, which was subsequently recorded, providing in part:

' *** the said property is hereby restricted to the use and occupancy for the term of Fifty (50) years from this date, so that it shall be a condition all the time and whether recited and referred to as (sic) not in subsequent conveyances and shall attach to the land, as a condition precedent to the sale of the same, that hereafter no part of said property or any portion thereof shall be, for said term of Fifty-years, occupied by any person not of the Caucasian race, it being intended hereby to restrict the use of said property for said period of time against the occupancy as owners or tenants of any portion of said property for resident or other purpose by people of the Negro or Mongolian Race.'

* * *

On August 11, 1945, pursuant to a contract of sale, petitioners Shelley, who are Negroes, for valuable consideration received from one Fitzgerald a warranty deed to the parcel in question. The trial court found that petitioners had no actual knowledge of the restrictive agreement at the time of the purchase.

On October 9, 1945, respondents, as owners of other property subject to the terms of the restrictive covenant, brought suit in Circuit Court of the city of St. Louis praying that petitioners Shelley be restrained from taking possession of the property and that judgment be entered divesting title out of petitioners Shelley and revesting title in the immediate grantor or in such other person as the court should direct. The trial court denied the requested relief on the ground that the restrictive agreement, upon which respondents based their action, had never become final and complete because it was the intention of the parties to that agreement that it was not to become effective until signed by all property owners in the district, and signatures of all the owners had never been obtained.

The Supreme Court of Missouri sitting *en banc* reversed and directed the trial court to grant the relief for which respondents had prayed. That court held the agreement effective and concluded that enforcement of its provisions violated no rights guaranteed to petitioners by the Federal Constitution. At the time the court rendered its decision, petitioners were occupying the property in question.

The second of the cases under consideration comes to this Court from the Supreme Court of Michigan. The circumstances presented do not differ materially from the Missouri case. In June, 1934, one Ferguson and his wife, who then owned the property located in the city of Detroit which is involved in this case, executed a contract providing in part:

'This property shall not be used or occupied by any person or persons except those of the Caucasian race.

'It is further agreed that this restriction shall not be effective unless at least eighty percent of the property fronting on both sides of the street in the block where our land is located is subjected to this or a similar restriction.'

The agreement provided that the restrictions were to remain in effect until January 1, 1960. The contract was subsequently recorded; and similar agreements were executed with respect to eighty percent of the lots in the block in which the property in question is situated.

By deed dated November 30, 1944, petitioners, who were found by the trial court to be Negroes, acquired title to the property and thereupon entered into its occupancy. On January 30, 1945, respondents, as owners of property subject to the terms of the restrictive agreement, brought suit against petitioners in the Circuit Court of Wayne County. After a hearing, the court entered a decree directing petitioners to move from the property within ninety days. Petitioners were further enjoined and restrained from using or occupying the premises in the future. On appeal, the Supreme Court of Michigan affirmed, deciding adversely to petitioners' contentions that they had been denied rights protected by the Fourteenth Amendment.

Petitioners have placed primary reliance on their contentions, first raised in the state courts, that judicial enforcement of the restrictive agreements in these cases has violated rights guaranteed to petitioners by the Fourteenth Amendment of the Federal Constitution and Acts of Congress passed pursuant to that Amendment. Specifically, petitioners urge that they have been denied the equal protection of the laws, deprived of property without due process of law, and have been denied privileges and immunities of citizens of the United States. We pass to a consideration of those issues.

* * *

It should be observed that these covenants do not seek to proscribe any particular use of the affected properties. Use of the properties for residential occupancy, as such, is not forbidden. The restrictions of these agreements, rather, are directed toward a designated class of persons and seek to determine who may and who may not own or make use of the properties for residential purposes. The excluded class is defined wholly in terms of race or color; 'simply that and nothing more.'

It cannot be doubted that among the civil rights intended to be protected from discriminatory state action by the Fourteenth Amendment are the rights to acquire, enjoy, own and dispose of property. Equality in the enjoyment of property rights was regarded by the framers of that Amendment as an essential pre-condition to the realization of other basic civil rights and liberties which the Amendment was intended to guarantee.

* * *

Here the particular patterns of discrimination and the areas in which the restrictions are to operate, are determined, in the first instance, by the terms of agreements among private individuals. Participation of the State consists in the enforcement of the restrictions so defined. The crucial issue with which we are here confronted is whether this distinction removes these cases from the operation of the prohibitory provisions of the Fourteenth Amendment.

Since the decision of this Court in *the Civil Rights Cases*, 1883, 109 U.S. 3, 3 S.Ct. 18, 27 L.Ed. 835, the principle has become firmly embedded in our constitutional law that the action inhibited by the first section of the Fourteenth Amendment is only such action as may fairly be said to be that of the States. That Amendment erects no shield against merely private conduct, however discriminatory or wrongful.

We conclude, therefore, that the restrictive agreements standing alone cannot be regarded as a violation of any rights guaranteed to petitioners by the Fourteenth Amendment. So long as the purposes of those agreements are effectuated by voluntary adherence to their terms, it would appear clear that there has been no action by the State and the provisions of the Amendment have not been violated. *Cf. Corrigan v. Buckley, supra.*

But here there was more. These are cases in which the purposes of the agreements were secured only by judicial enforcement by state courts of the restrictive terms of the agreements. The respondents urge that judicial enforcement of private agreements does not amount to state action; or, in any event, the participation of the State is so attenuated in character as not to amount to state action within the meaning of the Fourteenth Amendment. Finally, it is suggested, even if the States in these cases may be deemed to have acted in the constitutional sense, their action did not deprive petitioners of rights guaranteed by the Fourteenth Amendment. We move to a consideration of these matters.

II.

That the action of state courts and of judicial officers in their official capacities is to be regarded as action of the State within the meaning of the Fourteenth Amendment, is a proposition which has long been established by decisions of this Court. That principle was given expression in the earliest cases involving the construction of the terms of the Fourteenth Amendment. Thus, in *Commonwealth of Virginia v. Rives,* 1880, 100 U.S. 313, 318, 25 L.Ed. 667, this Court stated: 'It is doubtless true that a State may act through different agencies,—either by its legislative, its executive, or its judicial authorities; and the prohibitions of the amendment extend to all action of the State denying equal protection of the laws, whether it be action by one of these agencies or by another.' In *Ex parte Commonwealth of Virginia*, 1880, 100 U.S. 339, 347, 25 L.Ed. 676, the Court observed: 'A State acts by its legislative, its executive, or its judicial authorities. It can act in no other way.' In *the Civil Rights Cases*, 1883, 109 U.S. 3, 11, 17, 3 S.Ct. 18, 21, 27 L.Ed. 835, this Court pointed out that the Amendment makes void 'state action of every kind' which is inconsistent with the guaranties therein contained, and extends to manifestations of 'state authority in the shape of laws, customs, or judicial or executive proceedings.' Language to like effect is employed no less than eighteen times during the course of that opinion.

Similar expressions, giving specific recognition to the fact that judicial action is to be regarded as action on the State for the purposes of the Fourteenth Amendment, are to be found in numerous cases which have been more recently decided. In *Twining v. New Jersey*, 1908, 211 U.S. 78, 90, 91, 29 S.Ct. 14, 16, 53 L.Ed. 97, the Court said: 'The judicial act of the highest court of the state, in authoritatively construing and enforcing its laws, is the act of the state.' In *Brinkerhoff-Faris Trust & Savings Co. v. Hill*, 1930, 281 U.S. 673, 680, 50 S.Ct. 451, 454, 74 L.Ed. 1107, the Court, through Mr. Justice Brandeis, stated: 'The federal guaranty of due process extends to state action through its judicial as well as through its legislative, executive, or administrative branch of government.' Further examples of such declarations in the opinions of this Court are not lacking.

* * *

The short of the matter is that from the time of the adoption of the Fourteenth Amendment until the present, it has been the consistent ruling of this Court that the action of the States to which the Amendment has reference, includes action of state courts and state judicial officials. Although, in construing the terms of the Fourteenth Amendment, differences have from time to time been expressed as to whether particular types of state action may be said to offend the Amendment's prohibitory provisions, it has never been suggested that state court action is immunized from the operation of those provisions simply because the act is that of the judicial branch of the state government.

III.

Against this background of judicial construction, extending over a period of some three-quarters of a century, we are called upon to consider whether enforcement by state courts of the restrictive agreements in these cases may be deemed to be the acts of those States; and, if so, whether that action has denied these petitioners the equal protection of the laws which the Amendment was intended to insure.

We have no doubt that there has been state action in these cases in the full and complete sense of the phrase. The undisputed facts disclose that petitioners were willing purchasers of properties upon which they desired to establish homes. The owners of the properties were willing sellers; and contracts of sale were accordingly consummated. It is clear that but for the active intervention of the state courts, supported by the full panoply of state power, petitioners would have been free to occupy the properties in question without restraint.

These are not cases, as has been suggested, in which the States have merely abstained from action, leaving private individuals free to impose such discriminations as they see fit. Rather, these are cases in which the States have made available to such individuals the full coercive power of government to deny to petitioners, on the grounds of race or color, the enjoyment of property rights in premises which petitioners are willing and financially able to acquire and which the grantors are willing to sell. The difference between judicial enforcement and nonenforcement of the restrictive covenants is the difference to petitioners between being denied rights of property available to other members of the community and being accorded full enjoyment of those rights on an equal footing.

The enforcement of the restrictive agreements by the state courts in these cases was directed pursuant to the common-law policy of the States as formulated by those courts in earlier decisions. In the Missouri case, enforcement of the covenant was directed in the first instance by the highest court of the State after the trial court had determined the agreement to be invalid for want of the requisite number of signatures. In the Michigan case, the order of enforcement by the trial court was affirmed by the highest state court. The judicial action in each case bears the clear and unmistakable imprimatur of the State. We have noted that previous decisions of this Court have established the proposition that judicial action is not immunized from the operation of the Fourteenth Amendment simply because it is taken pursuant to the state's common-law policy. Nor is the Amendment ineffective simply because the particular pattern of discrimination, which the State has enforced, was defined initially by the terms of a private agreement. State action, as that phrase is understood for the purposes of the Fourteenth Amendment, refers to exertions of state power in all forms. And when the effect of that action is to deny rights subject to the protection of the Fourteenth Amendment, it is the obligation of this Court to enforce the constitutional commands.

We hold that in granting judicial enforcement of the restrictive agreements in these cases, the States have denied petitioners the equal protection of the laws and that, therefore, the action of the state courts cannot stand. We have noted that freedom from discrimination by the States in the enjoyment of property rights was among the basic objectives sought to be effectuated by the framers of the Fourteenth Amendment. That such discrimination has occurred in these cases is clear. Because of the race or color of these petitioners they have been denied rights of ownership or occupancy enjoyed as a matter of course by other citizens of different race or color. The Fourteenth Amendment declares 'that all persons, whether colored or white, shall stand equal before the laws of the States, and, in regard to the colored race, for whose protection the amendment was primarily designed, that no discrimination shall be made against them by law because of their color.' *Strauder v. West Virginia, supra*, 100 U.S. at 307, 25 L.Ed. 664. Only recently this Court has had occasion to declare that a state law which denied equal enjoyment of property rights to a designated class of citizens of specified race and ancestry, was not a legitimate exercise of the state's police power but violated the guaranty of the equal protection of the laws. *Oyama v. California*, 1948, 332 U.S. 633, 68 S.Ct. 269. Nor may the discriminations imposed by the state courts in these cases be justified as proper exertions of state police power. *Cf. Buchanan v. Warley, supra.*

* * *

The problem of defining the scope of the restrictions which the Federal Constitution imposes upon exertions of power by the States has given rise to many of the most persistent and fundamental issues which this Court has been called upon to consider. That problem was foremost in the minds of the framers of the Constitution, and since that early day, has arisen in a multitude of forms. The task of determining whether the action of a State offends constitutional provisions is one which may not be undertaken lightly. Where, however, it is clear that the action of the State violates the terms of the fundamental charter, it is the obligation of this Court so to declare.

The historical context in which the Fourteenth Amendment became a part of the Constitution should not be forgotten. Whatever else the framers sought to achieve, it is clear that the matter of primary concern was the establishment of equality in the enjoyment of basic civil and political rights and the preservation of those rights from discriminatory action on the part of the States based on considerations of race or color. Seventy-five years ago this Court announced that the provisions of the Amendment are to be construed with this fundamental purpose in mind. Upon full consideration, we have concluded that in these cases the States have acted to deny petitioners the equal protection of the laws guaranteed by the Fourteenth Amendment. Having so decided, we find it unnecessary to consider whether petitioners have also been deprived of property without due process of law or denied privileges and immunities of citizens of the United States.

For the reasons stated, the judgment of the Supreme Court of Missouri and the judgment of the Supreme Court of Michigan must be reversed.

Reversed.

[Footnotes omitted.]

The *Blevins* case takes a look at the use of property in a residential neighborhood as a group home for developmentally disabled citizens.

BLEVINS v. BARRY-LAWRENCE COUNTY ASSOCIATION FOR RETARDED CITIZENS

Supreme Court of Missouri, En Banc
707 S.W.2d 407 (1986)

WELLIVER, Judge.

This is an appeal from a circuit court judgment enjoining appellant, Barry-Lawrence County Association for Retarded Citizens, from using its property as a group home for retarded individuals. Respondents, Jess and Nedra Blevins, brought this equitable action alleging that said use violates a restrictive covenant on the lot. We transferred the cause prior to opinion of the court of appeals. Rule 83.06. We reverse.

Appellant owns Lot 23 and the residence thereon in the Wildwood Estates Subdivision of Cassville, Missouri, and it plans on establishing a group home for eight unrelated mentally retarded persons.

Respondents own Lot 24, which is across the street from appellant's property. The subdivision is protected by restrictive covenants, which provide in relevant part:

> 1. The aforesaid real property shall be used for residential purposes only. No buildings shall be erected, altered, placed or permitted to remain on said real property other than single or double family dwellings not to exceed two and one-half stories in height and private garages for not more than two cars. No detached structures shall be permitted.

Respondents argue that appellant's intended use of its property will contravene this covenant. Appellant responds by alleging (1) that its intended use does not violate the covenant; (2) that awarding an equitable injunction would violate public policy, as illustrated by the recently enacted § 89.020, RSMo Supp. 1985 which forbids either zoning ordinances or restrictive covenants from excluding group homes for mentally retarded individuals; and (3) that § 89.020 must be given retroactive effect and, therefore, the provision of the restrictive covenant is void.

At the outset, this Court shares the observation of the trial court that the briefing and argument in this case were "excellent," and we greatly appreciate the thorough manner in which counsel have presented this Court with an exhaustive analysis of the case law in other jurisdictions.

It is a well-established rule that restrictive covenants are not favorites of the law, and when interpreting such covenants, courts should give effect to the intent of the parties as expressed in the plain language of the covenant; but, when there is any ambiguity or substantial doubt as to the meaning, restrictive covenants will be read narrowly in favor of the free use of property. *Shepherd v. State*, 427 S.W.2d 382, 386–87 (Mo.1968); *St. Louis Union Trust Co. v. Tipton Electric*, 636 S.W.2d 357, 359 (Mo.App.1982); *Udo Siebel-Spath v. Construction Enterprises*, 633 S.W.2d 86, 88 (Mo.App.1982). See generally 20 Am.Jur.2d Covenants § 185–187 (1965). It might be noted that respondent attempted to establish the intent of the parties to the covenant by offering the testimony of one of the original developers. Such evidence, however, is neither binding as a matter of law nor usually admissible. See *Shepherd v. State, supra*, at 386–87. See also 20 Am.Jur.2d Covenants § 322–24 (1965).

The initial question is whether the group home for eight unrelated persons and two house parents violates the restriction against any use other than for "residential purposes only." In *Shepherd v. State*, 427 S.W.2d 382 (Mo.1968), this Court interpreted the phrase "residential purposes" in a restrictive covenant. This Court quoted with approval the following definition of "residential purposes":

> Giving the words their plain and ordinary meaning, we would say that … it is, one in which people reside or dwell, or which they make their homes, as distinguished from one which is used for commercial or business purposes.

* * *

It is beyond doubt that the operation of the group home in question has all the characteristics of a residential as opposed to a commercial use. The home is owned and run by a non-profit organization, and the underlying theory behind establishing such a home is that it serves as a surrogate family arrangement. There is no commercial enterprise, and the home is neither a boarding house nor an institutional facility. The trial court found the following facts relative to the operation of the home:

> [Appellant] operates a number of "group homes" in which mentally retarded adults live in a residential setting with "house parents", often a husband and wife, who provide supervision and care for the retarded adults.

* * *

The group home as contemplated to be operated in Wildwood Estates by defendant is designed to allow the residents to develop their social, emotional and intellectual skills by living in a stable family-type environment. The house parents and residents function in an integrated family-style unit instead of as independent individuals who share only a place to sleep and eat. Residents are involved in performing simpl[e] household duties and participate in discussing, and if possible, resolving problems existing in the home and in making decisions as to the nature of group activities. Although ultimate decisions are left to house parents and/or the defendants board. The entire group often attends church, goes shopping and travels about the community in a body.

... [F]ormal training for the retarded residents does not take place in the group home, but rather is conducted at an activity center or sheltered workshop during the workweek. Within the group home, the house parents encourage the development of social skills and simple homemaking skills by the individual living there. The primary purpose of a residential group home is to provide a living situation as normal as possible for developmentally disabled residents of the community and is ordinarily not a temporary living arrangement but, depending upon the individual, a resident may remain in the group home months, years or for their entire lifetime.

The trial court also found that prospective occupants of group homes are carefully screened and are admitted, at first, only on a trial basis. We believe that these findings of fact clearly indicate that appellant's intended use of Lot 23 as a group home is a residential purpose under the restrictive covenant.

Faced with a similar factual situation, a substantial number of courts have held that the operation of a group home is a residential purpose within the meaning of a covenant with such a restriction. ***

* * *

*** The court held that the covenant established both a use and structural restriction. "The first sentence ... requires the lots to be residential; the rest of the covenant requires that any structure be a single-family dwelling." *Id.* at 1021. Next, the court gave the following explanation for its holding that the group home is a residential use:

> It is the purpose and method of operation which serves to distinguish the proposed residential use of the home from that normally incident to a purely commercial operation. Financial gain is clearly not the motivation of the Association in the operation of the home.

The five women are to function as a single housekeeping unit by sharing in the preparation of meals, performing housekeeping duties and planning recreational activities. Most of the women have outside employment. The housekeeper will provide supervision and guidance similar to that of the head of any household. The day-to-day activities occurring at the home, as viewed from the outside, will not make it appear unlike the rest of the neighborhood. The essential purpose of the group home is to create a normal family atmosphere dissimilar from that found in traditional institutional care for the mentally handicapped. The operation of a group home is thus distinguishable from a use that is commercial—i.e., a boarding house that provides food and lodging only—or is institutional in character. Furthermore, no educational training would be provided at the home nor would there be medical or nursing care administered to the residents. In virtually all respects, save for the mental capacity of those who would live in the home, the on-the-premises operations would be much like a typical suburban household. *Jackson v. Williams, supra,* at 1022.

The remaining question is whether appellant's intended use of the property violates the second sentence of the restrictive covenant, which prohibits erecting, altering, placing or permitting any building "other than single or double family dwellings not to exceed two and one-half stories in height and private garages for not more than two cars." Respondents argue that this restriction is a restriction on the use of the property; and, if a restriction on use, appellant's group home is neither a single nor a double family dwelling.

By its plain terms, however, this restriction applies only to structures and not to the use of the property. The language, therefore, is substantially different than the covenant being construed in *London v. Handicapped Facilities Board of St. Charles County,* 637 S.W.2d 212, 214 (Mo.App.1982), where the court enjoined a group home under a restriction prohibiting "[n]o more than one family shall live in any residence ..." The restriction more closely resembles the covenant in *Jackson v. Williams,* where the court held that the group home did not violate the second sentence of the restriction which permitted only single-family dwellings:

> The term "family" was, in fact, used without a definition and hence did not necessarily exclude from its meaning a group of unrelated persons living together in a home. This phrase was intended to describe the character of the structure rather than limit the use of the property to single-family residence. When, as here, the restrictive covenant under consideration prohibits occupancy of more than one family unit but does not address itself to the composition of the

> family, a court is loathe to restrict a family unit to that composed of persons who are related, one to another, by consanguinity or affinity.

Jackson v. Williams, *supra*, at 1023. Similarly, in *J.T. Hobby & Son, Inc. v. Family Homes*, etc., 302 N.C. 64, 274 S.E.2d 174, 181 (1981), the court held that a "provision in a restrictive covenant as to the character of the structure which may be located upon a lot does not by itself constitute a restriction of the premises to a particular use." A number of other jurisdictions have reached a similar conclusion.

* * *

The record indicates that appellant does not intend to alter the structure of the residence on its lot. We hold, therefore, that appellant's intended use of its property does not violate the terms of the restrictive covenant. The trial court judgment granting the injunction is reversed.

[Footnotes omitted.]

Eminent Domain

The 5th Amendment of the U.S. Constitution protects citizens against governmental taking of their property. It says in part "… nor shall private property be taken for public use without just compensation." Eminent domain is the process by which the government is allowed to take private property for public use as long as the property owner is justly compensated.

> The *Kelo* case examines the issue of what a "public use" is.

KELO v. CITY OF NEW LONDON

Supreme Court of United States (5–4)
545 U.S. 469 (2005)

JUSTICE STEVENS delivered the opinion of the Court.

In 2000, the city of New London approved a development plan that, in the words of the Supreme Court of Connecticut, was "projected to create in excess of 1,000 jobs, to increase tax and other revenues, and to revitalize an economically distressed city, including its downtown and waterfront areas." 268 Conn. 1, 5, 843 A. 2d 500, 507 (2004). In assembling the land needed for this project, the city's development agent has purchased property from willing sellers and proposes to use the power of eminent domain to acquire the remainder of the property from unwilling owners in exchange for just compensation. The question presented is whether the city's proposed disposition of this property qualifies as a "public use" within the meaning of the Takings Clause of the Fifth Amendment to the Constitution.

I

The city of New London (hereinafter City) sits at the junction of the Thames River and the Long Island Sound in southeastern Connecticut. Decades of economic decline led a state agency in 1990 to designate the City a "distressed municipality." In 1996, the Federal Government closed the Naval Undersea Warfare Center, which had been located in the Fort Trumbull area of the City and had employed over 1,500 people. In 1998, the City's unemployment rate was nearly double that of the State, and its population of just under 24,000 residents was at its lowest since 1920.

These conditions prompted state and local officials to target New London, and particularly its Fort Trumbull area, for economic revitalization. To this end, respondent New London Development Corporation (NLDC), a private nonprofit entity established some years earlier to assist the City in planning economic development, was reactivated. In January 1998, the State authorized a $5.35 million bond issue to support the NLDC's planning activities and a $10 million bond issue toward the creation of a Fort Trumbull State Park. In February, the pharmaceutical company Pfizer Inc. announced that it would build a $300 million research facility on a site immediately adjacent to Fort Trumbull; local planners hoped that Pfizer would draw new business to the area, thereby serving as a catalyst to the area's rejuvenation. After receiving initial approval from the city council, the NLDC continued its planning activities and held a series of neighborhood meetings to educate the public about the process. In May, the city council authorized the NLDC to formally submit its plans to the relevant state agencies for review. Upon obtaining state-level approval, the NLDC finalized an integrated development plan focused on 90 acres of the Fort Trumbull area.

The Fort Trumbull area is situated on a peninsula that juts into the Thames River. The area comprises approximately 115 privately owned properties, as well as the 32 acres of land formerly occupied by the naval facility (Trumbull State Park now occupies 18 of those 32 acres). The development plan encompasses seven parcels. Parcel 1 is designated for a waterfront conference hotel at the center of a "small urban village" that will include restaurants and shopping. This parcel will also have marinas for both recreational and commercial uses. A pedestrian "riverwalk" will originate here and continue down the coast, connecting the waterfront areas of the development. Parcel 2 will be the site of approximately 80 new residences organized into an urban neighborhood and linked by public walkway to the remainder of the development, including the state park. This parcel also includes space reserved for a new U. S. Coast Guard Museum. Parcel 3, which is located immediately north of the Pfizer facility, will contain at least 90,000 square feet of research and development office space. Parcel 4A is a 2.4-acre site that will be used either to support the adjacent state park, by providing parking or retail services for visitors, or to support the nearby marina. Parcel 4B will include a renovated marina, as well as the final stretch of the riverwalk. Parcels 5, 6, and 7 will provide land for office and retail space, parking, and water-dependent commercial uses. App. 109–113.

The NLDC intended the development plan to capitalize on the arrival of the Pfizer facility and the new commerce it was expected to attract. In addition to creating jobs, generating tax revenue, and helping to "build momentum for the revitalization of downtown New London," *id.*, at 92, the plan was also designed to make the City more attractive and to create leisure and recreational opportunities on the waterfront and in the park.

The city council approved the plan in January 2000, and designated the NLDC as its development agent in charge of implementation. See Conn. Gen. Stat. § 8-188 (2005). The city council also authorized the NLDC to purchase property or to acquire property by exercising eminent domain in the City's name. § 8-193. The NLDC successfully negotiated the purchase of most of the real estate in the 90-acre area, but its negotiations with petitioners failed. As a consequence, in November 2000, the NLDC initiated the condemnation proceedings that gave rise to this case.

II

Petitioner Susette Kelo has lived in the Fort Trumbull area since 1997. She has made extensive improvements to her house, which she prizes for its water view. Petitioner Wilhelmina Dery was born in her Fort Trumbull house in 1918 and has lived there her entire life. Her husband Charles (also a petitioner) has lived in the house since they married some 60 years ago. In all, the nine petitioners own 15 properties in Fort Trumbull—4 in parcel 3 of the development plan and 11 in parcel 4A. Ten of the parcels are occupied by the owner or a family member; the other five are held as investment properties. There is no allegation that any of these properties is blighted or otherwise in poor condition; rather, they were condemned only because they happen to be located in the development area.

In December 2000, petitioners brought this action in the New London Superior Court. They claimed, among other things, that the taking of their properties would violate the "public use" restriction in the Fifth Amendment. After a 7-day bench trial, the Superior Court granted a permanent restraining order prohibiting the taking of the properties located in parcel 4A (park or marina support). It, however, denied petitioners relief as to the properties located in parcel 3 (office space). App. to Pet. for Cert. 343–350.

After the Superior Court ruled, both sides took appeals to the Supreme Court of Connecticut. That court held, over a dissent, that all of the City's proposed takings were valid. It began by upholding the lower court's determination that the takings were authorized by chapter 132, the State's municipal development statute. See Conn. Gen. Stat. § 8-186 et seq. (2005). That statute expresses a legislative determination that the taking of land, even developed land, as part of an economic development project is a "public use" and in the "public interest." 268 Conn., at 18–28, 843 A. 2d, at 515–521. Next, relying on cases such as *Hawaii Housing Authority v. Midkiff*, 467 U. S. 229 (1984), and *Berman v. Parker*, 348 U. S. 26 (1954), the court held that such economic development qualified as a valid public use under both the Federal and State Constitutions. 268 Conn., at 40, 843 A. 2d, at 527.

* * *

We granted certiorari to determine whether a city's decision to take property for the purpose of economic development satisfies the "public use" requirement of the Fifth Amendment. 542 U. S. 965 (2004).

III

Two polar propositions are perfectly clear. On the one hand, it has long been accepted that the sovereign may not take the property of A for the sole purpose of transferring it to another private party B, even though A is paid just compensation. On the other hand, it is equally clear that a State may transfer property from one private party to another if future "use by the public" is the purpose of the taking; the condemnation of land for a railroad with common-carrier duties is a familiar example. Neither of these propositions, however, determines the disposition of this case.

As for the first proposition, the City would no doubt be forbidden from taking petitioners' land for the purpose of conferring a private benefit on a particular private party. See *Midkiff*, 467 U. S., at 245 ("A purely private taking could not withstand the scrutiny of the public use requirement; it would serve no legitimate purpose of government and would thus be void"); *Missouri Pacific R. Co. v. Nebraska*, 164 U. S. 403 (1896). Nor would the City be allowed to take property under the mere pretext of a public purpose, when its actual purpose was to bestow a private benefit. The takings before us, however, would be executed pursuant to a "carefully considered" development plan. 268 Conn., at 54, 843 A. 2d, at 536. The trial judge and all the members of the Supreme Court of Connecticut agreed that there was no evidence of an illegitimate purpose in this case. Therefore, as was true of the statute challenged in *Midkiff*, 467 U. S., at 245, the City's development plan was not adopted "to benefit a particular class of identifiable individuals."

On the other hand, this is not a case in which the City is planning to open the condemned land—at least not in its entirety—to use by the general public. Nor will the private lessees of the land in any sense be required to operate like common carriers, making their services available to all comers.

* * *

The disposition of this case therefore turns on the question whether the City's development plan serves a "public purpose." Without exception, our cases have defined that concept broadly, reflecting our longstanding policy of deference to legislative judgments in this field.

In *Berman v. Parker*, 348 U. S. 26 (1954), this Court upheld a redevelopment plan targeting a blighted area of Washington, D. C., in which most of the housing for the area's 5,000 inhabitants was beyond repair. Under the plan, the area would be condemned and part of it utilized for the construction of streets, schools, and other public facilities. The remainder of the land would be leased or sold to private parties for the purpose of redevelopment, including the construction of low-cost housing.

The owner of a department store located in the area challenged the condemnation, pointing out that his store was not itself blighted and arguing that the creation of a "better balanced, more attractive community" was not a valid public use. *Id.*, at 31. Writing for a unanimous Court, Justice Douglas refused to evaluate this claim in isolation, deferring instead to the legislative and agency judgment that the area "must be planned as a whole" for the plan to be successful. *Id.*, at 34. The Court explained that "community redevelopment programs need not, by force of the Constitution, be on a piecemeal basis—lot by lot, building by building." *Id.*, at 35. The public use underlying the taking was unequivocally affirmed:

"We do not sit to determine whether a particular housing project is or is not desirable. The concept of the public welfare is broad and inclusive … The values it represents are spiritual as well as physical, aesthetic as well as monetary. It is within the power of the legislature to determine that the community should be beautiful as well as healthy, spacious as well as clean, well-balanced as well as carefully patrolled. In the present case, the Congress and its authorized agencies have made determinations that take into account a wide variety of values. It is not for us to reappraise them. If those who govern the District of Columbia decide that the Nation's Capital should be beautiful as well as sanitary, there is nothing in the Fifth Amendment that stands in the way." *Id.*, at 33.

* * *

IV

Those who govern the City were not confronted with the need to remove blight in the Fort Trumbull area, but their determination that the area was sufficiently distressed to justify a program of economic rejuvenation is entitled to our deference. The City has carefully formulated an economic development plan that it believes will provide appreciable benefits to the community, including—but by no means limited to—new jobs and increased tax revenue. As with other exercises in urban planning and development, the City is endeavoring to coordinate a variety of commercial, residential, and recreational uses of land, with the hope that they will form a whole greater than the sum of its parts. To effectuate this plan, the City has invoked a state statute that specifically authorizes the use of eminent domain to promote economic development. Given the comprehensive character of the plan, the thorough deliberation that preceded its adoption, and the limited scope of our review, it is appropriate for us, as it was in *Berman*, to resolve the challenges of the individual owners, not on a piecemeal basis, but rather in light of the entire plan. Because that plan unquestionably serves a public purpose, the takings challenged here satisfy the public use requirement of the Fifth Amendment.

To avoid this result, petitioners urge us to adopt a new bright-line rule that economic development does not qualify as a public use. Putting aside the unpersuasive suggestion that the City's plan will provide only purely economic benefits, neither precedent nor logic supports petitioners' proposal. Promoting economic development is a traditional and long-accepted function of government. There is, moreover, no principled way of distinguishing economic development from the other public purposes that we have recognized. In our cases upholding takings that facilitated agriculture and mining, for example, we emphasized the importance of those industries to the welfare of the States in question, *see, e. g., Strickley,* 200 U. S. 527; in *Berman*, we endorsed the purpose of transforming a blighted area into a "well-balanced" community through redevelopment, 348 U. S., at 33; in *Midkiff*, we upheld the interest in breaking up a land oligopoly that "created artificial deterrents to the normal functioning of the State's residential land market," 467 U. S., at 242; and in *Monsanto*, we accepted Congress' purpose of eliminating a "significant barrier to entry in the pesticide market," 467 U. S., at 1014–1015. It would be incongruous to hold that the City's interest in the economic benefits to be derived from the development of the Fort Trumbull area has less of a public character than any of those other interests. Clearly, there is no basis for exempting economic development from our traditionally broad understanding of public purpose.

Petitioners contend that using eminent domain for economic development impermissibly blurs the boundary between public and private takings. Again, our cases foreclose this objection. Quite simply, the government's pursuit of a public purpose will often benefit individual private parties. For example, in *Midkiff*, the forced transfer of property conferred a direct and significant benefit on those lessees who were previously unable to purchase their homes. In *Monsanto*, we recognized that the "most direct beneficiaries" of the data-sharing provisions were the subsequent pesticide applicants, but benefiting them in this way was necessary to promoting competition in the pesticide market. 467 U. S., at 1014. The owner of the department store in *Berman* objected to "taking from one businessman for the benefit of another businessman," 348 U. S., at 33, referring to the fact that under the redevelopment plan land would be leased or sold to private developers for redevelopment. Our rejection of that contention has particular relevance to the instant case: "The public end may be as well or better served through an agency of private enterprise than through a department of government—or so the Congress might conclude. We cannot say that public ownership is the sole method of promoting the public purposes of community redevelopment projects." *Id.*, at 33–34.

It is further argued that without a bright-line rule nothing would stop a city from transferring citizen A's property to citizen B for the sole reason that citizen B will put the property to a more productive use and thus pay more taxes. Such a one-to-one transfer of property, executed outside the confines of an integrated development plan, is not presented in this case. While such an unusual exercise of government power would certainly raise a suspicion that a private purpose was afoot, the hypothetical cases posited by petitioners can be confronted if and when they arise. They do not warrant the crafting of an artificial restriction on the concept of public use.

* * *

Just as we decline to second-guess the City's considered judgments about the efficacy of its development plan, we also decline to second-guess the City's determinations as to what lands it needs to acquire in order to effectuate the project. "It is not for the courts to oversee the choice of the boundary line nor to sit in review on the size of a particular project area. Once the question of the public purpose has been decided, the amount and character of land to be taken for the project and the need for a particular tract to complete the integrated plan rests in the discretion of the legislative branch." *Berman*, 348 U. S., at 35–36.

In affirming the City's authority to take petitioners' properties, we do not minimize the hardship that condemnations may entail, notwithstanding the payment of just compensation. We emphasize that nothing in our opinion precludes any State from placing further restrictions on its exercise of the takings power. Indeed, many States already impose "public use" requirements that are stricter than the federal baseline. Some of these requirements have been established as a matter of state constitutional law, while others are expressed in state eminent domain statutes that carefully limit the grounds upon which takings may be exercised. As the submissions of the parties and their amici make clear, the necessity and wisdom of using eminent domain to promote economic development are certainly matters of legitimate public debate. This Court's authority, however, extends only to determining whether the City's proposed condemnations are for a "public use" within the meaning of the Fifth Amendment to the Federal Constitution. Because over a century of our case law interpreting that provision dictates an affirmative answer to that question, we may not grant petitioners the relief that they seek.

The judgment of the Supreme Court of Connecticut is affirmed.

It is so ordered.

[Footnotes omitted.]

JUSTICE O'CONNOR, with whom THE CHIEF JUSTICE, JUSTICE SCALIA, and JUSTICE THOMAS join, dissenting.

Over two centuries ago, just after the Bill of Rights was ratified, Justice Chase wrote:

"An ACT of the Legislature (for I cannot call it a law) contrary to the great first principles of the social compact, cannot be considered a rightful exercise of legislative authority … A few instances will suffice to explain what I mean … [A] law that takes property from A and gives it to B: It is against all reason and justice, for a people to entrust a Legislature with SUCH powers; and, therefore, it cannot be presumed that they have done it." *Calder v. Bull*, 3 Dall. 386, 388 (1798) (emphasis deleted).

Today the Court abandons this long-held, basic limitation on government power. Under the banner of economic development, all private property is now vulnerable to being taken and transferred to another private owner, so long as it might be upgraded—i. e., given to an owner who will use it in a way that the legislature deems more beneficial to the public—in the process. To reason, as the Court does, that the incidental public benefits resulting from the subsequent ordinary use of private property render economic development takings "for public use" is to wash out any distinction between private and public use of property—and thereby effectively to delete the words "for public use" from the Takings Clause of the Fifth Amendment. Accordingly I respectfully dissent.

I

Petitioners are nine resident or investment owners of 15 homes in the Fort Trumbull neighborhood of New London, Connecticut. Petitioner Wilhelmina Dery, for example, lives in a house on Walbach Street that has been in her family for over 100 years. She was born in the house in 1918; her husband, petitioner Charles Dery, moved into the house when they married in 1946. Their son lives next door with his family in the house he received as a wedding gift, and joins his parents in this suit. Two petitioners keep rental properties in the neighborhood.

In February 1998, Pfizer Inc., the pharmaceuticals manufacturer, announced that it would build a global research facility near the Fort Trumbull neighborhood. Two months later, New London's city council gave initial approval for the New London Development Corporation (NLDC) to prepare the development plan at issue here. The NLDC is a private, nonprofit corporation whose mission is to assist the city council in economic development planning. It is not elected by popular vote, and its directors and employees are privately appointed. Consistent with its mandate, the NLDC generated an ambitious plan for redeveloping 90 acres of Fort Trumbull in order to "complement the facility that Pfizer was planning to build, create jobs, increase tax and other revenues, encourage public access to and use of the city's waterfront, and eventually 'build momentum' for the revitalization of the rest of the city." App. to Pet. for Cert. 5.

Petitioners own properties in two of the plan's seven parcels—Parcel 3 and Parcel 4A. Under the plan, Parcel 3 is slated for the construction of research and office space as a market develops for such space. It will also retain the existing Italian Dramatic Club (a private cultural organization) though the homes of three plaintiffs in that parcel are to be demolished. Parcel 4A is slated, mysteriously, for "'park support.'" *Id.*, at 345–346. At oral argument, counsel for respondents conceded the vagueness of this proposed use, and offered that the parcel might eventually be used for parking. Tr. of Oral Arg. 36.

To save their homes, petitioners sued New London and the NLDC, to whom New London has delegated eminent domain power. Petitioners maintain that the Fifth Amendment prohibits the NLDC from condemning their properties for the sake of an economic development plan. Petitioners are not hold-outs; they do not seek increased compensation, and none is opposed to new development in the area. Theirs is an objection in principle: They claim that the NLDC's proposed use for their confiscated property is not a "public" one for purposes of the Fifth Amendment. While the government may take their homes to build a road or a railroad or to eliminate a property use that harms the public, say petitioners, it cannot take their property for the private use of other owners simply because the new owners may make more productive use of the property.

II

The Fifth Amendment to the Constitution, made applicable to the States by the Fourteenth Amendment, provides that "private property [shall not] be taken for public use, without just compensation." When interpreting the Constitution, we begin with the unremarkable presumption that every word in the document has independent meaning, "that no word was unnecessarily used, or needlessly added." *Wright v. United States*, 302 U. S. 583, 588 (1938). In keeping with that presumption, we have read the Fifth Amendment's language to impose two distinct conditions on the exercise of eminent domain: "[T]he taking must be for a 'public use' and 'just compensation' must be paid to the owner." *Brown v. Legal Foundation of Wash.*, 538 U. S. 216, 231–232 (2003).

These two limitations serve to protect "the security of Property," which Alexander Hamilton described to the Philadelphia Convention as one of the "great obj[ects] of Gov[ernment]." 1 Records of the Federal Convention of 1787, p. 302 (M. Farrand ed. 1911). Together they ensure stable property ownership by providing safeguards against excessive, unpredictable, or unfair use of the government's eminent domain power—particularly against those owners who, for whatever reasons, may be unable to protect themselves in the political process against the majority's will.

While the Takings Clause presupposes that government can take private property without the owner's consent, the just compensation requirement spreads the cost of condemnations and thus "prevents the public from loading upon one individual more than his just share of the burdens of government." *Monongahela Nav. Co. v. United States*, 148 U. S. 312, 325 (1893); see also *Armstrong v. United States*, 364 U. S. 40, 49 (1960). The public use requirement, in turn, imposes a more basic limitation, circumscribing the very scope of the eminent domain power: Government may compel an individual to forfeit her property for the public's use, but not for the benefit of another private person. This requirement promotes fairness as well as security. Cf. *Tahoe-Sierra Preservation Council, Inc. v. Tahoe Regional Planning Agency*, 535 U. S. 302, 336 (2002) ("The concepts of 'fairness and justice' … underlie the Takings Clause").

Where is the line between "public" and "private" property use? We give considerable deference to legislatures' determinations about what governmental activities will advantage the public. But were the political branches the sole arbiters of the public-private distinction, the Public Use Clause would amount to little more than hortatory fluff. An external, judicial check on how the public use requirement is interpreted, however limited, is necessary if this constraint on government power is to retain any meaning. See *Cincinnati v. Vester*, 281 U. S. 439, 446 (1930) ("It is well established that … the question [of] what is a public use is a judicial one").

Our cases have generally identified three categories of takings that comply with the public use requirement, though it is in the nature of things that the boundaries between these categories are not always firm. Two are relatively straightforward and uncontroversial. First, the sovereign may transfer private property to public ownership—such as for a road, a hospital, or a military base. *See, e. g., Old Dominion Land Co. v. United States*, 269 U. S. 55 (1925); *Rindge Co. v. County of Los Angeles*, 262 U. S. 700 (1923). Second, the sovereign may transfer private property to private parties, often common carriers, who make the property available for the public's use—such as with a railroad, a public utility, or a stadium. *See, e. g., National Railroad Passenger Corporation v. Boston & Maine Corp.*, 503 U. S. 407 (1992); *Mt. Vernon-Woodberry Cotton Duck Co. v. Alabama Interstate Power Co.*, 240 U. S. 30 (1916). But "public ownership" and "use-by-the-public" are sometimes too constricting and impractical ways to define the scope of the Public Use Clause. Thus we have allowed that, in certain circumstances and to meet certain exigencies, takings that serve a public purpose also satisfy the Constitution even if the property is destined for subsequent private use. *See, e. g., Berman v. Parker*, 348 U. S. 26 (1954); *Hawaii Housing Authority v. Midkiff*, 467 U. S. 229 (1984).

This case returns us for the first time in over 20 years to the hard question of when a purportedly "public purpose" taking meets the public use requirement. It presents an issue of first impression: Are economic development takings constitutional? I would hold that they are not. We are guided by two precedents about the taking of real property by eminent domain. In *Berman*, we upheld takings within a blighted neighborhood of Washington, D. C. The neighborhood had so deteriorated that, for example, 64.3% of its dwellings were beyond repair. 348 U. S., at 30. It had become burdened with "overcrowding of dwellings," "lack of adequate streets and alleys," and "lack of light and air." *Id.*, at 34. Congress had determined that the neighborhood had become "injurious to the public health, safety, morals, and welfare" and that it was necessary to "eliminat[e] all such injurious conditions by employing all means necessary and appropriate for the purpose," including eminent domain. *Id.*, at 28 (internal quotation marks omitted). Mr. Berman's department store was not itself blighted. Having approved of Congress' decision to eliminate the harm to the public emanating from the blighted neighborhood, however, we did not second-guess its decision to treat the neighborhood as a whole rather than lot-by-lot. *Id.*, at 34–35; see also *Midkiff*, 467 U. S., at 244 ("[I]t is only the taking's purpose, and not its mechanics, that must pass scrutiny").

In *Midkiff*, we upheld a land condemnation scheme in Hawaii whereby title in real property was taken from lessors and transferred to lessees. At that time, the State and Federal Governments owned nearly 49% of the State's land, and another 47% was in the hands of only 72 private landowners. Concentration of land ownership was so dramatic that on the State's most urbanized island, Oahu, 22 landowners owned 72.5% of the fee simple titles. *Id.*, at 232. The Hawaii Legislature had concluded that the oligopoly in land ownership was "skewing the State's residential fee simple market, inflating land prices, and injuring the public tranquility and welfare," and therefore enacted a condemnation scheme for redistributing title. *Ibid.*

In those decisions, we emphasized the importance of deferring to legislative judgments about public purpose. Because courts are ill equipped to evaluate the efficacy of proposed legislative initiatives, we rejected as unworkable the idea of courts' "'deciding on what is and is not a governmental function and ... invalidating legislation on the basis of their view on that question at the moment of decision, a practice which has proved impracticable in other fields.'" *Id.*, at 240–241 (quoting United States ex rel. *TVA v. Welch*, 327 U. S. 546, 552 (1946)); see *Berman, supra*, at 32 ("[T]he legislature, not the judiciary, is the main guardian of the public needs to be served by social legislation"); see also *Lingle v. Chevron U. S. A. Inc.*, 544 U. S. 528 (2005). Likewise, we recognized our inability to evaluate whether, in a given case, eminent domain is a necessary means by which to pursue the legislature's ends. *Midkiff, supra*, at 242; *Berman, supra*, at 33.

Yet for all the emphasis on deference, *Berman* and *Midkiff* hewed to a bedrock principle without which our public use jurisprudence would collapse: "A purely private taking could not withstand the scrutiny of the public use requirement; it would serve no legitimate purpose of government and would thus be void." *Midkiff*, 467 U. S., at 245; *id.*, at 241 ("[T]he Court's cases have repeatedly stated that 'one person's property may not be taken for the benefit of another private person without a justifying public purpose, even though compensation be paid'" (quoting *Thompson v. Consolidated Gas Util. Corp.*, 300 U. S. 55, 80 (1937))); see also *Missouri Pacific R. Co. v. Nebraska,* 164 U. S. 403, 417 (1896). To protect that principle, those decisions reserved "a role for courts to play in reviewing a legislature's judgment of what constitutes a public use ... [though] the Court in *Berman* made clear that it is 'an extremely narrow' one." *Midkiff, supra*, at 240 (quoting *Berman, supra*, at 32).

The Court's holdings in *Berman* and *Midkiff* were true to the principle underlying the Public Use Clause. In both those cases, the extraordinary, precondemnation use of the targeted property inflicted affirmative harm on society—in *Berman* through blight resulting from extreme poverty and in *Midkiff* through oligopoly resulting from extreme wealth. And in both cases, the relevant legislative body had found that eliminating the existing property use was necessary to remedy the harm. *Berman, supra*, at 28–29; *Midkiff, supra*, at 232. Thus a public purpose was realized when the harmful use was eliminated. Because each taking directly achieved a public benefit, it did not matter that the property was turned over to private use. Here, in contrast, New London does not claim that Susette Kelo's and Wilhelmina Dery's well-maintained homes are the source of any social harm. Indeed, it could not so claim without adopting the absurd argument that any single-family home that might be razed to make way for an apartment building, or any church that might be replaced with a retail store, or any small business that might be more lucrative if it were instead part of a national franchise, is inherently harmful to society and thus within the government's power to condemn.

In moving away from our decisions sanctioning the condemnation of harmful property use, the Court today significantly expands the meaning of public use. It holds that the sovereign may take private property currently put to ordinary private use, and give it over for new, ordinary private use, so long as the new use is predicted to generate some secondary benefit for the public—such as increased tax revenue, more jobs, maybe even esthetic pleasure. But nearly any lawful use of real private property can be said to generate some incidental benefit to the public. Thus, if predicted (or even guaranteed) positive side effects are enough to render transfer from one private party to another constitutional, then the words "for public use" do not realistically exclude any takings, and thus do not exert any constraint on the eminent domain power.

* * *

The Court also puts special emphasis on facts peculiar to this case: The NLDC's plan is the product of a relatively careful deliberative process; it proposes to use eminent domain for a multipart, integrated plan rather than for isolated property transfer; it promises an array of incidental benefits (even esthetic ones), not just increased tax revenue; it comes on the heels of a legislative determination that New London is a depressed municipality. *See, e.g., ante*, at 487 ("[A] one-to-one transfer of property, executed outside the confines of an integrated development plan, is not presented in this case"). JUSTICE KENNEDY, too, takes great comfort in these facts. *Ante*, at 493 (concurring opinion). But none has legal significance to blunt the force of today's holding. If legislative prognostications about the secondary public benefits of a new use can legitimate a taking, there is nothing in the Court's rule or in JUSTICE KENNEDY's gloss on that rule to prohibit property transfers generated with less care, that are less comprehensive, that happen to result from less elaborate process, whose only projected advantage is the incidence of higher taxes, or that hope to transform an already prosperous city into an even more prosperous one.

* * *

It was possible after *Berman* and *Midkiff* to imagine unconstitutional transfers from A to B. Those decisions endorsed government intervention when private property use had veered to such an extreme that the public was suffering as a consequence. Today nearly all real property is susceptible to condemnation on the Court's theory. In the prescient words of a dissenter from the infamous decision in *Poletown*, "[n]ow that we have authorized local legislative bodies to decide that a different commercial or industrial use of property will produce greater public benefits than its present use, no homeowner's, merchant's or manufacturer's property, however productive or valuable to its owner, is immune from condemnation for the benefit of other private interests that will put it to a 'higher' use." 410 Mich., at 644–645, 304 N. W. 2d, at 464 (opinion of Fitzgerald, J.). This is why economic development takings "seriously jeopardiz[e] the security of all private property ownership." *Id.*, at 645, 304 N. W. 2d, at 465 (Ryan, J., dissenting).

Any property may now be taken for the benefit of another private party, but the fallout from this decision will not be random. The beneficiaries are likely to be those citizens with disproportionate influence and power in the political process, including large corporations and development firms. As for the victims, the government now has license to transfer property from those with fewer resources to those with more. The Founders cannot have intended this perverse result. "[T]hat alone is a just government," wrote James Madison, "which impartially secures to every man, whatever is his own." For the *National Gazette, Property* (Mar. 27, 1792), reprinted in *14 Papers of James Madison* 266 (R. Rutland et al. eds. 1983).

I would hold that the takings in both Parcel 3 and Parcel 4A are unconstitutional, reverse the judgment of the Supreme Court of Connecticut, and remand for further proceedings.

The *Causby* case examines what constitutes a "taking" under the doctrine of eminent domain.

UNITED STATES v. CAUSBY

Supreme Court of United States (5–2)
328 U.S. 256 (1946)

MR. JUSTICE DOUGLAS delivered the opinion of the Court.

This is a case of first impression. The problem presented is whether respondents' property was taken, within the meaning of the Fifth Amendment, by frequent and regular flights of army and navy aircraft over respondents' land at low altitudes. The Court of Claims held that there was a taking and entered judgment for respondents, one judge dissenting. 104 Ct. Cls. 342, 60 F. Supp. 751. The case is here on a petition for a writ of certiorari which we granted because of the importance of the question presented.

Respondents own 2.8 acres near an airport outside of Greensboro, North Carolina. It has on it a dwelling house, and also various outbuildings which were mainly used for raising chickens. The end of the airport's northwest-southeast runway is 2,220 feet from respondents' barn and 2,275 feet from their house. The path of glide to this runway passes directly over the property—which is 100 feet wide and 1,200 feet long. The 30 to 1 safe glide angle approved by the Civil Aeronautics Authority passes over this property at 83 feet, which is 67 feet above the house, 63 feet above the barn and 18 feet above the highest tree. The use by the United States of this airport is pursuant to a lease executed in May, 1942, for a term commencing June 1, 1942, and ending June 30, 1942, with a provision for renewals until June 30, 1967, or six months after the end of the national emergency, whichever is the earlier.

Various aircraft of the United States use this airport—bombers, transports and fighters. The direction of the prevailing wind determines when a particular runway is used. The northwest-southeast runway in question is used about four per cent of the time in taking off and about seven per cent of the time in landing. Since the United States began operations in May, 1942, its four-motored heavy bombers, other planes of the heavier type, and its fighter planes have frequently passed over respondents' land and buildings in considerable numbers and rather close together. They come close enough at times to appear barely to miss the tops of the trees and at times so close to the tops of the trees as to blow the old leaves off. The noise is startling. And at night the glare from the planes brightly lights up the place. As a result of the noise, respondents had to give up their chicken business. As many as six to ten of their chickens were killed in one day by flying into the walls from fright. The total chickens lost in that manner was about 150. Production also fell off. The result was the destruction of the use of the property as a commercial chicken farm. Respondents are frequently deprived of their sleep and the family has become nervous and frightened. Although there have been no airplane accidents on respondents' property, there have been several accidents near the airport and close to respondents' place. These are the essential facts found by the Court of Claims. On the basis of these facts, it found that respondents' property had depreciated in value. It held that the United States had taken an easement over the property on June 1, 1942, and that the value of the property destroyed and the easement taken was $2,000.

I. The United States relies on the Air Commerce Act of 1926, 44 Stat. 568, 49 U.S.C. § 171, as amended by the Civil Aeronautics Act of 1938, 52 Stat. 973, 49 U.S.C. § 401. Under those statutes the United States has "complete and exclusive national sovereignty in the air space" over this country. 49 U.S.C. § 176 (a). They grant any citizen of the United States "a public right of freedom of transit in air commerce through the navigable air space of the United States." 49 U.S.C. § 403. And "navigable air space" is defined as "airspace above the minimum safe altitudes of flight prescribed by the Civil Aeronautics Authority." 49 U.S.C. § 180. And it is provided that "such navigable airspace shall be subject to a public right of freedom of interstate and foreign air navigation." *Id.* It is, therefore, argued that since these flights were within the minimum safe altitudes of flight which had been prescribed, they were an exercise of the declared right of travel through the airspace. The United States concludes that when flights are made within the navigable airspace without any physical invasion of the property of the landowners, there has been no taking of property. It says that at most there was merely incidental damage occurring as a consequence of authorized air navigation. It also argues that the landowner does not own superadjacent airspace which he has not subjected to possession by the erection of structures or other occupancy. Moreover, it is argued that even if the United States took airspace owned by respondents, no compensable damage was shown. Any damages are said to be merely consequential for which no compensation may be obtained under the Fifth Amendment.

It is ancient doctrine that at common law ownership of the land extended to the periphery of the universe—*Cujusest solum ejus est usque ad coelum*. But that doctrine has no place in the modern world. The air is a public highway, as Congress has declared. Were that not true, every transcontinental flight would subject the operator to countless trespass suits. Common sense revolts at the idea. To recognize such private claims to the airspace would clog these highways, seriously interfere with their control and development in the public interest, and transfer into private ownership that to which only the public has a just claim.

But that general principle does not control the present case. For the United States conceded on oral argument that if the flights over respondents' property rendered it uninhabitable, there would be a taking compensable under the Fifth Amendment. It is the owner's loss, not the taker's gain, which is the measure of the value of the property taken. *United States v. Miller*, 317 U.S. 369. Market value fairly determined is the normal measure of the recovery. *Id.* And that value may reflect the use to which the land could readily be converted, as well as the existing use. *United States v. Powelson*, 319 U.S. 266, 275, and cases cited. If, by reason of the frequency and altitude of the flights, respondents could not use this land for any purpose, their loss would be complete. It would be as complete as if the United States had entered upon the surface of the land and taken exclusive possession of it.

We agree that in those circumstances there would be a taking. Though it would be only an easement of flight which was taken, that easement, if permanent and not merely temporary, normally would be the equivalent of a fee interest. It would be a definite exercise of complete dominion and control over the surface of the land.

* * *

We have said that the airspace is a public highway. Yet it is obvious that if the landowner is to have full enjoyment of the land, he must have exclusive control of the immediate reaches of the enveloping atmosphere. Otherwise buildings could not be erected, trees could not be planted, and even fences could not be run. The principle is recognized when the law gives a remedy in case overhanging structures are erected on adjoining land. The landowner owns at least as much of the space above the ground as he can occupy or use in connection with the land. See *Hinman v. Pacific Air Transport*, 84 F.2d 755. The fact that he does not occupy it in a physical sense—by the erection of buildings and the like—is not material. As we have said, the flight of airplanes, which skim the surface but do not touch it, is as much an appropriation of the use of the land as a more conventional entry upon it. We would not doubt that, if the United States erected an elevated railway over respondents' land at the precise altitude where its planes now fly, there would be a partial taking, even though none of the supports of the structure rested on the land. The reason is that there would be an intrusion so immediate and direct as to subtract from the owner's full enjoyment of the property and to limit his exploitation of it. While the owner does not in any physical manner occupy that stratum of airspace or make use of it in the conventional sense, he does use it in somewhat the same sense that space left between buildings for the purpose of light and air is used. The superadjacent airspace at this low altitude is so close to the land that continuous invasions of it affect the use of the surface of the land itself. We think that the landowner, as an incident to his ownership, has a claim to it and that invasions of it are in the same category as invasions of the surface.

In this case, as in *Portsmouth Co. v. United States, supra,* the damages were not merely consequential. They were the product of a direct invasion of respondents' domain. As stated in *United States v. Cress,* 243 U.S. 316, 328, " ... it is the character of the invasion, not the amount of damage resulting from it, so long as the damage is substantial, that determines the question whether it is a taking."

* * *

The airplane is part of the modern environment of life, and the inconveniences which it causes are normally not compensable under the Fifth Amendment. The airspace, apart from the immediate reaches above the land, is part of the public domain. We need not determine at this time what those precise limits are. Flights over private land are not a taking, unless they are so low and so frequent as to be a direct and immediate interference with the enjoyment and use of the land. We need not speculate on that phase of the present case. For the findings of the Court of Claims plainly establish that there was a diminution in value of the property and that the frequent, low-level flights were the direct and immediate cause. We agree with the Court of Claims that a servitude has been imposed upon the land.

* * *

Since on this record it is not clear whether the easement taken is a permanent or a temporary one, it would be premature for us to consider whether the amount of the award made by the Court of Claims was proper.

The judgment is reversed and the cause is remanded to the Court of Claims so that it may make the necessary findings in conformity with this opinion.

Reversed.

Zoning

Zoning laws allow governments to decide how land will be used.

In *Euclid*, the Supreme Court renders an opinion on the constitutionality of zoning laws.

VILLAGE OF EUCLID, OHIO v. AMBLER REALTY CO.

Supreme Court of the United States
272 U.S. 365 (1926)

Mr. Justice SUTHERLAND delivered the opinion of the Court.

* * *

The enforcement of the ordinance is intrusted to the inspector of buildings, under rules and regulations of the board of zoning appeals. Meetings of the board are public, and minutes of its proceedings are kept. It is authorized to adopt rules and regulations to carry into effect provisions of the ordinance. Decisions of the inspector of buildings may be appealed to the board by any person claiming to be adversely affected by any such decision. The board is given power in specific cases of practical difficulty or unnecessary hardship to interpret the ordinance in harmony with its general purpose and intent, so that the public health, safety and general welfare may be secure and substantial justice done. Penalties are prescribed for violations, and it is provided that the various provisions are to be regarded as independent and the holding of any provision to be unconstitutional, void or ineffective shall not affect any of the others.

The ordinance is assailed on the grounds that it is in derogation of section 1 of the Fourteenth Amendment to the federal Constitution in that it deprives appellee of liberty and property without due process of law and denies it the equal protection of the law, and that it offends against certain provisions of the Constitution of the state of Ohio. The prayer of the bill is for an injunction restraining the enforcement of the ordinance and all attempts to impose or maintain as to appellee's property any of the restrictions, limitations or conditions. The court below held the ordinance to be unconstitutional and void, and enjoined its enforcement, 297 F. 307.

Before proceeding to a consideration of the case, it is necessary to determine the scope of the inquiry. The bill alleges that the tract of land in question is vacant and has been held for years for the purpose of selling and developing it for industrial uses, for which it is especially adapted, being immediately in the path or progressive industrial development; that for such uses it has a market value of about $10,000 per acre, but if the use be limited to residential purposes the market value is not in excess of $2,500 per acre; that the first 200 feet of the parcel back from Euclid avenue, if unrestricted in respect of use, has a value of $150 per front foot, but if limited to residential uses, and ordinary mercantile business be excluded therefrom, its value is not in excess of $50 per front foot.

It is specifically averred that the ordinance attempts to restrict and control the lawful uses of appellee's land, so as to confiscate and destroy a great part of its value; that it is being enforced in accordance with its terms; that prospective buyers of land for industrial, commercial, and residential uses in the metropolitan district of Cleveland are deterred from buying any part of this land because of the existence of the ordinance and the necessity thereby entailed of conducting burdensome and expensive litigation in order to vindicate the right to use the land for lawful and legitimate purposes; that the ordinance constitutes a cloud upon the land, reduces and destroys its value, and has the effect of diverting the normal industrial, commercial, and residential development thereof to other and less favorable locations.

The record goes no farther than to show, as the lower court found, that the normal and reasonably to be expected use and development of that part of appellee's land adjoining Euclid avenue is for general trade and commercial purposes, particularly retail stores and like establishments, and that the normal and reasonably to be expected use and development of the residue of the land is for industrial and trade purposes. Whatever injury is inflicted by the mere existence and threatened enforcement of the ordinance is due to restrictions in respect of these and similar uses, to which perhaps should be added—if not included in the foregoing—restrictions in respect of apartment houses. Specifically there is nothing in the record to suggest that any damage results from the presence in the ordinance of those restrictions relating to churches, schools, libraries, and other public and semipublic buildings. It is neither alleged nor proved that there is or may be a demand for any part of appellee's land for any of the last-named uses, and we cannot assume the existence of facts which would justify an injunction upon this record in respect to this class of restrictions. For present purposes the provisions of the ordinance in respect of these uses may therefore be put aside as unnecessary to be considered. It is also unnecessary to consider the effect of the restrictions in respect of U-1 districts, since none of appellee's land falls within that class. We proceed, then, to a consideration of those provisions of the ordinance to which the case as it is made relates, first disposing of a preliminary matter.

* * *

Building zone laws are of modern origin. They began in this country about 25 years ago. Until recent years, urban life was comparatively simple; but, with the great increase and concentration of population, problems have developed, and constantly are developing, which require, and will continue to require, additional restrictions in respect of the use and occupation of private lands in urban communities. Regulations, the wisdom, necessity, and validity of which, as applied to existing conditions, are so apparent that they are now uniformly sustained, a century ago, or even half a century ago, probably would have been rejected as arbitrary and oppressive. Such regulations are sustained, under the complex conditions of our day, for reasons analogous to those which justify traffic regulations, which, before the advent of automobiles and rapid transit street railways, would have been condemned as fatally arbitrary and unreasonable. And in this there is no inconsistency, for, while the meaning of constitutional guaranties never varies, the scope of their application must expand or contract to meet the new and different conditions which are constantly coming within the field of their operation. In a changing world it is impossible that it should be otherwise. But although a degree of elasticity is thus imparted, not to the meaning, but to the application of constitutional principles, statutes and ordinances, which, after giving due weight to the new conditions, are found clearly not to conform to the Constitution, of course, must fall.

The ordinance now under review, and all similar laws and regulations, must find their justification in some aspect of the police power, asserted for the public welfare. The line which in this field separates the legitimate from the illegitimate assumption of power is not capable of precise delimitation. It varies with circumstances and conditions. A regulatory zoning ordinance, which would be clearly valid as applied to the great cities, might be clearly invalid as applied to rural communities. In solving doubts, the maxim '*sic utere tuo ut alienum non laedas*,' which lies at the foundation of so much of the common low of nuisances, ordinarily will furnish a fairly helpful clew. And the law of nuisances, likewise, may be consulted, not for the purpose of controlling, but for the helpful aid of its analogies in the process of ascertaining the scope of, the power. Thus the question whether the power exists to forbid the erection of a building of a particular kind or for a particular use, like the question whether a particular thing is a nuisance, is to be determined, not by an abstract consideration of the building or of the thing considered apart, but by considering it in connection with the circumstances and the locality. *Sturgis v. Bridgeman*, L. R. 11 Ch. 852, 865. A nuisance may be merely a right thing in the wrong place, like a pig in the parlor instead of the barnyard. If the validity of the legislative classification for zoning purposes be fairly debatable, the legislative judgment must be allowed to control. *Radice v. New York*, 264 U.S. 292, 294, 44 S. Ct. 325.

There is no serious difference of opinion in respect of the validity of laws and regulations fixing the height of buildings within reasonable limits, the character of materials and methods of construction, and the adjoining area which must be left open, in order to minimize the danger of fire or collapse, the evils of overcrowding and the like, and excluding from residential sections offensive trades, industries and structures likely to create nuisances. ***.

Here, however, the exclusion is in general terms of all industrial establishments, and it may thereby happen that not only offensive or dangerous industries will be excluded, but those which are neither offensive nor dangerous will share the same fate. But this is no more than happens in respect of many practice-forbidding laws which this court has upheld, although drawn in general terms so as to include individual cases that may turn out to be innocuous in themselves. *Hebe Co. v. Shaw*, 248 U.S. 297, 303, 39 S. Ct. 125; *Pierce Oil Corp. v. City of Hope*, 248 U.S. 498, 500, 39 S. Ct. 172. The inclusion of a reasonable margin, to insure effective enforcement, will not put upon a law, otherwise valid, the stamp of invalidity. Such laws may also find their justification in the fact that, in some fields, the bad fades into the good by such insensible degrees that the two are not capable of being readily distinguished and separated in terms of legislation. In the light of these considerations, we are not prepared to say that the end in view was not sufficient to justify the general rule of the ordinance, although some industries of an innocent character might fall within the proscribed class. It cannot be said that the ordinance in this respect 'passes the bounds of reason and assumes the character of a merely arbitrary fiat.' *Purity Extract Co. v. Lynch*, 226 U.S. 192, 204, 33 S. Ct. 44, 47 (57 L. Ed. 184). Moreover, the restrictive provisions of the ordinance in this particular may be sustained upon the principles applicable to the broader exclusion from residential districts of all business and trade structures, presently to be discussed.

It is said that the village of Euclid is a mere suburb of the city of Cleveland; that the industrial development of that city has now reached and in some degree extended into the village, and in the obvious course of things will soon absorb the entire area for industrial enterprises; that the effect of the ordinance is to divert this natural development elsewhere, with the consequent loss of increased values to the owners of the lands within the village borders. But the village, though physically a suburb of Cleveland, is politically a separate municipality, with powers of its own and authority to govern itself as it sees fit, within the limits of the organic law of its creation and the state and federal Constitutions. Its governing authorities, presumably representing a majority of its inhabitants and voicing their will, have determined, not that industrial development shall cease at its boundaries, but that the course of such development shall proceed within definitely fixed lines. If it be a proper exercise of the police power to relegate industrial establishments to localities separated from residential sections, it is not easy to find a sufficient reason for denying the power because the effect of its exercise is to divert an industrial flow from the course which it would follow, to the injury of the residential public, if left alone, to another course where such injury will be obviated. It is not meant by this, however, to exclude the possibility of cases where the general public interest would so far outweigh the interest of the municipality that the municipality would not be allowed to stand in the way.

We find no difficulty in sustaining restrictions of the kind thus far reviewed. The serious question in the case arises over the provisions of the ordinance excluding from residential districts apartment houses, business houses, retail stores and shops, and other like establishments. This question involves the validity of what is really the crux of the more recent zoning legislation, namely, the creation and maintenance of residential districts, from which business and trade of every sort, including hotels and apartment houses, are excluded. Upon that question this court has not thus far spoken. The decisions of the state courts are numerous and conflicting; but those which broadly sustain the power greatly outnumber those which deny it altogether or narrowly limit it, and it is very apparent that there is a constantly increasing tendency in the direction of the broader view. We shall not attempt to review these decisions at length, but content ourselves with citing a few as illustrative of all.

* * *

The relief sought here is of the same character, namely, an injunction against the enforcement of any of the restrictions, limitations, or conditions of the ordinance. And the gravamen of the complaint is that a portion of the land of the appellee cannot be sold for certain enumerated uses because of the general and broad restraints of the ordinance. What would be the effect of a restraint imposed by one or more or the innumerable provisions of the ordinance, considered apart, upon the value or marketability of the lands, is neither disclosed by the bill nor by the evidence, and we are afforded no basis, apart from mere speculation, upon which to rest a conclusion that it or they would have any appreciable effect upon those matters. Under these circumstances, therefore, it is enough for us to determine, as we do, that the ordinance in its general scope and dominant features, so far as its provisions are here involved, is a valid exercise of authority, leaving other provisions to be dealt with as cases arise directly involving them.

And this is in accordance with the traditional policy of this court. In the realm of constitutional law, especially, this court has perceived the embarrassment which is likely to result from an attempt to formulate rules or decide questions beyond the necessities of the immediate issue. It has preferred to follow the method of a gradual approach to the general by a systematically guarded application and extension of constitutional principles to particular cases as they arise, rather than by out of hand attempts to establish general rules to which future cases must be fitted. This process applies with peculiar force to the solution of questions arising under the due process clause of the Constitution as applied to the exercise of the flexible powers of police, with which we are here concerned.

Decree reversed.

Regulatory Taking

Regulatory taking is neither eminent domain nor zoning, but it has similarities to both. In a regulatory taking case, a statute or regulation determines how a piece of property may or may not be used. Examples of legislation that may involve regulatory taking are landmark preservation and environmental protection laws. Because the law defines how the property can be used or what can be done with it, it is possible that the property's value may not only be lessened, but that the income derived from the property may be decreased as well. Given this, should the government be forced to compensate the property owner under the 5th Amendment for the lost value, even though the property owner still maintains ownership? Or, should the government be required to purchase the property outright as in an eminent domain taking?

It is well known that governments often designate certain structures or properties as historical landmarks. Such a designation may impact what the owner can do with the property. The *Penn Central* case considers the issue of regulatory taking as applied to the preservation of historical landmarks.

PENN CENTRAL TRANSPORTATION COMPANY v. CITY OF NEW YORK

Supreme Court of the United States (6–3)
438 U.S. 104 (1978)

Mr. Justice BRENNAN delivered the opinion of the Court.

The question presented is whether a city may, as part of a comprehensive program to preserve historic landmarks and historic districts, place restrictions on the development of individual historic landmarks—in addition to those imposed by applicable zoning ordinances—without effecting a "taking" requiring the payment of "just compensation." Specifically, we must decide whether the application of New York City's Landmarks Preservation Law to the parcel of land occupied by Grand Central Terminal has "taken" its owners' property in violation of the Fifth and Fourteenth Amendments.

I

A

Over the past 50 years, all 50 States and over 500 municipalities have enacted laws to encourage or require the preservation of buildings and areas with historic or aesthetic importance. These nationwide legislative efforts have been precipitated by two concerns. The first is recognition that, in recent years, large numbers of historic structures, landmarks, and areas have been destroyed without adequate consideration of either the values represented therein or the possibility of preserving the destroyed properties for use in economically productive ways. The second is a widely shared belief that structures with special historic, cultural, or architectural significance enhance the quality of life for all. Not only do these buildings and their workmanship represent the lessons of the past and embody precious features of our heritage, they serve as examples of quality for today. "[H]istoric conservation is but one aspect of the much larger problem, basically an environmental one, of enhancing—or perhaps developing for the first time—the quality of life for people."

* * *

The New York City law is typical of many urban landmark laws in that its primary method of achieving its goals is not by acquisitions of historic properties, but rather by involving public entities in land-use decisions affecting these properties and providing services, standards, controls, and incentives that will encourage preservation by private owners and users. While the law does place special restrictions on landmark properties as a necessary feature to the attainment of its larger objectives, the major theme of the law is to ensure the owners of any such properties both a "reasonable return" on their investments and maximum latitude to use their parcels for purposes not inconsistent with the preservation goals.

* * *

Although the designation of a landmark and landmark site restricts the owner's control over the parcel, designation also enhances the economic position of the landmark owner in one significant respect. Under New York City's zoning laws, owners of real property who have not developed their property to the full extent permitted by the applicable zoning laws are allowed to transfer development rights to contiguous parcels on the same city block. See New York City, Zoning Resolution Art. I, ch. 2, § 12-10 (1978) (definition of "zoning lot"). A 1968 ordinance gave the owners of landmark sites additional opportunities to transfer development rights to other parcels. Subject to a restriction that the floor area of the transferee lot may not be increased by more than 20% above its authorized level, the ordinance permitted transfers from a landmark parcel to property across the street or across a street intersection. In 1969, the law governing the conditions under which transfers from landmark parcels could occur was liberalized, see New York City Zoning Resolutions 74-79 to 74-793, apparently to ensure that the Landmarks Law would not unduly restrict the development options of the owners of Grand Central Terminal. See Marcus, Air Rights Transfers in New York City, 36 Law & Contemp. Prob. 372, 375 (1971). The class of recipient lots was expanded to include lots "across a street and opposite to another lot or lots which except for the intervention of streets or street intersections f[or]m a series extending to the lot occupied by the landmark building[, provided that] all lots [are] in the same ownership." New York City Zoning Resolution 74-79 (emphasis deleted). In addition, the 1969 amendment permits, in highly commercialized areas like midtown Manhattan, the transfer of all unused development rights to a single parcel. *Ibid.*

* * *

II

The issues presented by appellants are (1) whether the restrictions imposed by New York City's law upon appellants' exploitation of the Terminal site effect a "taking" of appellants' property for a public use within the meaning of the Fifth Amendment, which of course is made applicable to the States through the Fourteenth Amendment, see *Chicago, B. & Q. R. Co. v. Chicago*, 166 U.S. 226, 239, 17 S.Ct. 581, 585, 41 L.Ed. 979 (1897), and, (2), if so, whether the transferable development rights afforded appellants constitute "just compensation" within the meaning of the Fifth Amendment. We need only address the question whether a "taking" has occurred.

* * *

More importantly for the present case, in instances in which a state tribunal reasonably concluded that "the health, safety, morals, or general welfare" would be promoted by prohibiting particular contemplated uses of land, this Court has upheld land-use regulations that destroyed or adversely affected recognized real property interests.

* * *

B

In contending that the New York City law has "taken" their property in violation of the Fifth and Fourteenth Amendments, appellants make a series of arguments, which, while tailored to the facts of this case, essentially urge that any substantial restriction imposed pursuant to a landmark law must be accompanied by just compensation if it is to be constitutional. Before considering these, we emphasize what is not in dispute. Because this Court has recognized, in a number of settings, that States and cities may enact land-use restrictions or controls to enhance the quality of life by preserving the character and desirable aesthetic features of a city, *** appellants do not contest that New York City's objective of preserving structures and areas with special historic, architectural, or cultural significance is an entirely permissible governmental goal. They also do not dispute that the restrictions imposed on its parcel are appropriate means of securing the purposes of the New York City law. Finally, appellants do not challenge any of the specific factual premises of the decision below. They accept for present purposes both that the parcel of land occupied by Grand Central Terminal must, in its present state, be regarded as capable of earning a reasonable return, and that the transferable development rights afforded appellants by virtue of the Terminal's designation as a landmark are valuable, even if not as valuable as the rights to construct above the Terminal. In appellants' view none of these factors derogate from their claim that New York City's law has effected a "taking."

They first observe that the airspace above the Terminal is a valuable property interest, citing *United States v. Causby, supra*. They urge that the Landmarks Law has deprived them of any gainful use of their "air rights" above the Terminal and that, irrespective of the value of the remainder of their parcel, the city has "taken" their right to this superadjacent airspace, thus entitling them to "just compensation" measured by the fair market value of these air rights.

Apart from our own disagreement with appellants' characterization of the effect of the New York City law, see *infra*, at 134–135, the submission that appellants may establish a "taking" simply by showing that they have been denied the ability to exploit a property interest that they heretofore had believed was available for development is quite simply untenable. Were this the rule, this Court would have erred not only in upholding laws restricting the development of air rights, see *Welch v. Swasey, supra*, but also in approving those prohibiting both the subjacent, *see Goldblatt v. Hempstead*, 369 U.S. 590, 82 S.Ct. 987, 8 L.Ed.2d 130 (1962), and the lateral, *see Gorieb v. Fox*, 274 U.S. 603, 47 S.Ct. 675, 71 L.Ed. 1228 (1927), development of particular parcels. "Taking" jurisprudence does not divide a single parcel into discrete segments and attempt to determine whether rights in a particular segment have been entirely abrogated. In deciding whether a particular governmental action has effected a taking, this Court focuses rather both on the character of the action and on the nature and extent of the interference with rights in the parcel as a whole—here, the city tax block designated as the "landmark site."

Secondly, appellants, focusing on the character and impact of the New York City law, argue that it effects a "taking" because its operation has significantly diminished the value of the Terminal site. Appellants concede that the decisions sustaining other land-use regulations, which, like the New York City law, are reasonably related to the promotion of the general welfare, uniformly reject the proposition that diminution in property value, standing alone, can establish a "taking," *** and that the "taking" issue in these contexts is resolved by focusing on the uses the regulations permit. See also *Goldblatt v. Hempstead, supra*. Appellants, moreover, also do not dispute that a showing of diminution in property value would not establish a taking if the restriction had been imposed as a result of historic-district legislation, see generally *Maher v. New Orleans*, 516 F.2d 1051 (CA5 1975), but appellants argue that New York City's regulation of individual landmarks is fundamentally different from zoning or from historic-district legislation because the controls imposed by New York City's law apply only to individuals who own selected properties.

Stated baldly, appellants' position appears to be that the only means of ensuring that selected owners are not singled out to endure financial hardship for no reason is to hold that any restriction imposed on individual landmarks pursuant to the New York City scheme is a "taking" requiring the payment of "just compensation." Agreement with this argument would, of course, invalidate not just New York City's law, but all comparable landmark legislation in the Nation. We find no merit in it.

* * *

C

Rejection of appellants' broad arguments is not, however, the end of our inquiry, for all we thus far have established is that the New York City law is not rendered invalid by its failure to provide "just compensation" whenever a landmark owner is restricted in the exploitation of property interests, such as air rights, to a greater extent than provided for under applicable zoning laws. We now must consider whether the interference with appellants' property is of such a magnitude that "there must be an exercise of eminent domain and compensation to sustain [it]." *Pennsylvania Coal Co. v. Mahon*, 260 U.S., at 413, 43 S.Ct., at 159. That inquiry may be narrowed to the question of the severity of the impact of the law on appellants' parcel, and its resolution in turn requires a careful assessment of the impact of the regulation on the Terminal site.

Unlike the governmental acts in *Goldblatt, Miller, Causby, Griggs*, and *Hadacheck*, the New York City law does not interfere in any way with the present uses of the Terminal. Its designation as a landmark not only permits but contemplates that appellants may continue to use the property precisely as it has been used for the past 65 years: as a railroad terminal containing office space and concessions. So the law does not interfere with what must be regarded as Penn Central's primary expectation concerning the use of the parcel. More importantly, on this record, we must regard the New York City law as permitting Penn Central not only to profit from the Terminal but also to obtain a "reasonable return" on its investment.

Appellants, moreover, exaggerate the effect of the law on their ability to make use of the air rights above the Terminal in two respects. First, it simply cannot be maintained, on this record, that appellants have been prohibited from occupying *any* portion of the airspace above the Terminal. While the Commission's actions in denying applications to construct an office building in excess of 50 stories above the Terminal may indicate that it will refuse to issue a certificate of appropriateness for any comparably sized structure, nothing the Commission has said or done suggests an intention to prohibit any construction above the Terminal. The Commission's report emphasized that whether any construction would be allowed depended upon whether the proposed addition "would harmonize in scale, material and character with [the Terminal]." Record 2251. Since appellants have not sought approval for the construction of a smaller structure, we do not know that appellants will be denied any use of any portion of the airspace above the Terminal.

Second, to the extent appellants have been denied the right to build above the Terminal, it is not literally accurate to say that they have been denied *all* use of even those pre-existing air rights. Their ability to use these rights has not been abrogated; they are made transferable to at least eight parcels in the vicinity of the Terminal, one or two of which have been found suitable for the construction of new office buildings. Although appellants and others have argued that New York City's transferable development-rights program is far from ideal, the New York courts here supportably found that, at least in the case of the Terminal, the rights afforded are valuable. While these rights may well not have constituted "just compensation" if a "taking" had occurred, the rights nevertheless undoubtedly mitigate whatever financial burdens the law has imposed on appellants and, for that reason, are to be taken into account in considering the impact of regulation. Cf. *Goldblatt v. Hempstead*, 369 U.S., at 594 n. 3, 82 S.Ct., at 990 n. 3.

On this record, we conclude that the application of New York City's Landmarks Law has not effected a "taking" of appellants' property. The restrictions imposed are substantially related to the promotion of the general welfare and not only permit reasonable beneficial use of the landmark site but also afford appellants opportunities further to enhance not only the Terminal site proper but also other properties.

The *Lucas* case considers the issue of regulatory taking as applied to a beachfront management statute and the restrictions imposed on an owner of beachfront lots.

LUCAS v. SOUTH CAROLINA COASTAL COUNCIL

Supreme Court of the United States (6–2)
505 U.S. 1003 (1992)

Justice SCALIA delivered the opinion of the Court.

In 1986, petitioner David H. Lucas paid $975,000 for two residential lots on the Isle of Palms in Charleston County, South Carolina, on which he intended to build single-family homes. In 1988, however, the South Carolina Legislature enacted the Beachfront Management Act, S.C.Code § 48-39-250 *et seq*. (Supp.1990) (Act), which had the direct effect of barring petitioner from erecting any permanent habitable structures on his two parcels. See § 48-39-290(A). A state trial court found that this prohibition rendered Lucas's parcels "valueless." App. to Pet. for Cert. 37. This case requires us to decide whether the Act's dramatic effect on the economic value of Lucas's lots accomplished a taking of private property under the Fifth and Fourteenth Amendments requiring the payment of "just compensation." U.S. Const., Amdt. 5.

* * *

We granted certiorari.

* * *

III

A.

Prior to Justice Holmes' exposition in *Pennsylvania Coal Co. v. Mahon*, 260 U.S. 393, 43 S.Ct. 158, 67 L.Ed. 322 (1922), it was generally thought that the Takings Clause reached only a "direct appropriation" of property, *Legal Tender Cases*, 12 Wall. 457, 551, 20 L.Ed. 287 (1871), or the functional equivalent of a "practical ouster of [the owner's] possession." *** Justice Holmes recognized in *Mahon*, however, that if the protection against physical appropriations of private property was to be meaningfully enforced, the government's power to redefine the range of interests included in the ownership of property was necessarily constrained by constitutional limits. 260 U.S., at 414–415, 43 S.Ct., at 160. If, instead, the uses of private property were subject to unbridled, uncompensated qualification under the police power, "the natural tendency of human nature [would be] to extend the qualification more and more until at last private property disappear[ed]." *Id.*, at 415, 43 S.Ct., at 160. These considerations gave birth in that case to the oft-cited maxim that, "while property may be regulated to a certain extent, if regulation goes too far it will be recognized as a taking." *Ibid.*

Nevertheless, our decision in *Mahon* offered little insight into when, and under what circumstances, a given regulation would be seen as going "too far" for purposes of the Fifth Amendment. In 70-odd years of succeeding "regulatory takings" jurisprudence, we have generally eschewed any " 'set formula' " for determining how far is too far, preferring to "engag[e] in … essentially *ad hoc*, factual inquiries," *Penn Central Transportation Co. v. New York City*, 438 U.S. 104, 124, 98 S.Ct. 2646, 2659, 57 L.Ed.2d 631 (1978) (quoting *Goldblatt v. Hempstead*, 369 U.S. 590, 594, 82 S.Ct. 987, 990, 8 L.Ed.2d 130 (1962)). See Epstein, *Takings: Descent and Resurrection*, 1987 Sup.Ct. Rev. 1, 4. We have, however, described at least two discrete categories of regulatory action as compensable without case-specific inquiry into the public interest advanced in support of the restraint. The first encompasses regulations that compel the property owner to suffer a physical "invasion" of his property. In general (at least with regard to permanent invasions), no matter how minute the intrusion, and no matter how weighty the public purpose behind it, we have required compensation. For example, in *Loretto v. Teleprompter Manhattan CATV Corp.*, 458 U.S. 419, 102 S.Ct. 3164, 73 L.Ed.2d 868 (1982), we determined that New York's law requiring landlords to allow television cable companies to emplace cable facilities in their apartment buildings constituted a taking, *id.*, at 435–440, 102 S.Ct., at 3175–3178, even though the facilities occupied at most only 11/2 cubic feet of the landlords' property, see *id.*, at 438, n. 16, 102 S.Ct., at 3177. See also *United States v. Causby*, 328 U.S. 256, 265, and n. 10, 66 S.Ct. 1062, 1067, and n. 10, 90 L.Ed. 1206 (1946) (physical invasions of airspace); cf. *Kaiser Aetna v. United States*, 444 U.S. 164, 100 S.Ct. 383, 62 L.Ed.2d 332 (1979) (imposition of navigational servitude upon private marina).

The second situation in which we have found categorical treatment appropriate is where regulation denies all economically beneficial or productive use of land. *** As we have said on numerous occasions, the Fifth Amendment is violated when land-use regulation "does not substantially advance legitimate state interests *or denies an owner economically viable use of his land.*" *Agins, supra*, 447 U.S., at 260, 100 S.Ct., at 2141 (citations omitted) (emphasis added).

We have never set forth the justification for this rule. Perhaps it is simply, as Justice Brennan suggested, that total deprivation of beneficial use is, from the landowner's point of view, the equivalent of a physical appropriation. See *San Diego Gas & Electric Co. v. San Diego*, 450 U.S., at 652, 101 S.Ct., at 1304 (Brennan, J., dissenting). "[F]or what is the land but the profits thereof[?]" 1 E. Coke, Institutes ch. 1, § 1 (1st Am. ed. 1812). Surely, at least, in the extraordinary circumstance when *no* productive or economically beneficial use of land is permitted, it is less realistic to indulge our usual assumption that the legislature is simply "adjusting the benefits and burdens of economic life," *Penn Central Transportation Co.*, 438 U.S., at 124, 98 S.Ct., at 2659, in a manner that secures an "average reciprocity of advantage" to everyone concerned. *Pennsylvania Coal Co. v. Mahon*, 260 U.S., at 415, 43 S.Ct., at 160. And the *functional* basis for permitting the government, by regulation, to affect property values without compensation—that "Government hardly could go on if to some extent values incident to property could not be diminished without paying for every such change in the general law," *id.*, at 413, 43 S.Ct., at 159—does not apply to the relatively rare situations where the government has deprived a landowner of all economically beneficial uses.

On the other side of the balance, affirmatively supporting a compensation requirement, is the fact that regulations that leave the owner of land without economically beneficial or productive options for its use—typically, as here, by requiring land to be left substantially in its natural state—carry with them a heightened risk that private property is being pressed into some form of public service under the guise of mitigating serious public harm. *See, e.g., Annicelli v. South Kingstown*, 463 A.2d 133, 140–141 (R.I.1983) (prohibition on construction adjacent to beach justified on twin grounds of safety and "conservation of open space"); *Morris County Land Improvement Co. v. Parsippany-Troy Hills Township*, 40 N.J. 539, 552–553, 193 A.2d 232, 240 (1963) (prohibition on filling marshlands imposed in order to preserve region as water detention basin and create wildlife refuge). As Justice Brennan explained: "From the government's point of view, the benefits flowing to the public from preservation of open space through regulation may be equally great as from creating a wildlife refuge through formal condemnation or increasing electricity production through a dam project that floods private property." *San Diego Gas & Elec. Co., supra*, 450 U.S., at 652, 101 S.Ct., at 1304 (Brennan, J., dissenting). The many statutes on the books, both state and federal, that provide for the use of eminent domain to impose servitudes on private scenic lands preventing developmental uses, or to acquire such lands altogether, suggest the practical equivalence in this setting of negative regulation and appropriation. *See, e.g.*, 16 U.S.C. § 410ff-1(a) (authorizing acquisition of "lands, waters, or interests [within Channel Islands National Park] (including but not limited to scenic easements)"); § 460aa-2(a) (authorizing acquisition of "any lands, or lesser interests therein, including mineral interests and scenic easements" within Sawtooth National Recreation Area); §§ 3921–3923 (authorizing acquisition of wetlands); N.C. Gen.Stat. § 113A-38 (1990) (authorizing acquisition of, *inter alia*, "'scenic easements'" within the North Carolina natural and scenic rivers system); Tenn.Code Ann. §§ 11-15-101–11-15-108 (1987) (authorizing acquisition of "protective easements" and other rights in real property adjacent to State's historic, architectural, archaeological, or cultural resources).

We think, in short, that there are good reasons for our frequently expressed belief that when the owner of real property has been called upon to sacrifice *all* economically beneficial uses in the name of the common good, that is, to leave his property economically idle, he has suffered a taking.

* * *

Where the State seeks to sustain regulation that deprives land of all economically beneficial use, we think it may resist compensation only if the logically antecedent inquiry into the nature of the owner's estate shows that the proscribed use interests were not part of his title to begin with. This accords, we think, with our "takings" jurisprudence, which has traditionally been guided by the understandings of our citizens regarding the content of, and the State's power over, the "bundle of rights" that they acquire when they obtain title to property. It seems to us that the property owner necessarily expects the uses of his property to be restricted, from time to time, by various measures newly enacted by the State in legitimate exercise of its police powers; "[a]s long recognized, some values are enjoyed under an implied limitation and must yield to the police power." *Pennsylvania Coal Co. v. Mahon*, 260 U.S., at 413, 43 S.Ct., at 159. And in the case of personal property, by reason of the State's traditionally high degree of control over commercial dealings, he ought to be aware of the possibility that new regulation might even render his property economically worthless (at least if the property's only economically productive use is sale or manufacture for sale), see *Andrus v. Allard*, 444 U.S. 51, 66–67, 100 S.Ct. 318, 327, 62 L.Ed.2d 210 (1979) (prohibition on sale of eagle feathers). In the case of land, however, we think the notion pressed by the Council that title is somehow held subject to the "implied limitation" that the State may subsequently eliminate all economically valuable use is inconsistent with the historical compact recorded in the Takings Clause that has become part of our constitutional culture.

Where "permanent physical occupation" of land is concerned, we have refused to allow the government to decree it anew (without compensation), no matter how weighty the asserted "public interests" involved, *Loretto v. Teleprompter Manhattan CATV Corp.*, 458 U.S., at 426, 102 S.Ct., at 3171—though we assuredly *would* permit the government to assert a permanent easement that was a pre-existing limitation upon the landowner's title. Compare *Scranton v. Wheeler*, 179 U.S. 141, 163, 21 S.Ct. 48, 57, 45 L.Ed. 126 (1900) (interests of "riparian owner in the submerged lands ... bordering on a public navigable water" held subject to Government's navigational servitude), with *Kaiser Aetna v. United States*, 444 U.S., at 178–180, 100 S.Ct., at 392–393 (imposition of navigational servitude on marina created and rendered navigable at private expense held to constitute a taking). We believe similar treatment must be accorded confiscatory regulations, *i.e.*, regulations that prohibit all economically beneficial use of land: Any limitation so severe cannot be newly legislated or decreed (without compensation), but must inhere in the title itself, in the restrictions that background principles of the State's law of property and nuisance already place upon land ownership. A law or decree with such an effect must, in other words, do no more than duplicate the result that could have been achieved in the courts by adjacent landowners (or other uniquely affected persons) under the State's law of private nuisance, or by the State under its complementary power to abate nuisances that affect the public generally, or otherwise.

On this analysis, the owner of a lake bed, for example, would not be entitled to compensation when he is denied the requisite permit to engage in a landfilling operation that would have the effect of flooding others' land. Nor the corporate owner of a nuclear generating plant, when it is directed to remove all improvements from its land upon discovery that the plant sits astride an earthquake fault. Such regulatory action may well have the effect of eliminating the land's only economically productive use, but it does not proscribe a productive use that was previously permissible under relevant property and nuisance principles. The use of these properties for what are now expressly prohibited purposes was *always* unlawful, and (subject to other constitutional limitations) it was open to the State at any point to make the implication of those background principles of nuisance and property law explicit. *See Michelman, Property, Utility, and Fairness, Comments on the Ethical Foundations of "Just Compensation" Law*, 80 *Harv.L.Rev.* 1165, 1239–1241 (1967). In light of our traditional resort to "existing rules or understandings that stem from an independent source such as state law" to define the range of interests that qualify for protection as "property" under the Fifth (and Fourteenth) amendments, *** this recognition that the Takings Clause does not require compensation when an owner is barred from putting land to a use that is proscribed by those "existing rules or understandings" is surely unexceptional. When, however, a regulation that declares "off-limits" all economically productive or beneficial uses of land goes beyond what the relevant background principles would dictate, compensation must be paid to sustain it.

The "total taking" inquiry we require today will ordinarily entail (as the application of state nuisance law ordinarily entails) analysis of, among other things, the degree of harm to public lands and resources, or adjacent private property, posed by the claimant's proposed activities, see, *e.g.*, Restatement (Second) of Torts §§ 826, 827, the social value of the claimant's activities and their suitability to the locality in question, *see, e.g., id.*, §§ 828(a) and (b), 831, and the relative ease with which the alleged harm can be avoided through measures taken by the claimant and the government (or adjacent private landowners) alike, *see, e.g., id.*, §§ 827(e), 828(c), 830. The fact that a particular use has long been engaged in by similarly situated owners ordinarily imports a lack of any common-law prohibition (though changed circumstances or new knowledge may make what was previously permissible no longer so, see Restatement (Second) of Torts, *supra*, § 827, comment *g*. So also does the fact that other landowners, similarly situated, are permitted to continue the use denied to the claimant.

It seems unlikely that common-law principles would have prevented the erection of any habitable or productive improvements on petitioner's land; they rarely support prohibition of the "essential use" of land, *Curtin v. Benson*, 222 U.S. 78, 86, 32 S.Ct. 31, 33, 56 L.Ed. 102 (1911). The question, however, is one of state law to be dealt with on remand. We emphasize that to win its case South Carolina must do more than proffer the legislature's declaration that the uses Lucas desires are inconsistent with the public interest, or the conclusory assertion that they violate a common-law maxim such as *sic utere tuo ut alienum non laedas*. As we have said, a "State, by *ipse dixit*, may not transform private property into public property without compensation …" *Webb's Fabulous Pharmacies, Inc. v. Beckwith*, 449 U.S. 155, 164, 101 S.Ct. 446, 452, 66 L.Ed.2d 358 (1980). Instead, as it would be required to do if it sought to restrain Lucas in a common-law action for public nuisance, South Carolina must identify background principles of nuisance and property law that prohibit the uses he now intends in the circumstances in which the property is presently found. Only on this showing can the State fairly claim that, in proscribing all such beneficial uses, the Beachfront Management Act is taking nothing.

The judgment is reversed and the cause remanded for proceedings not inconsistent with this opinion.

Other Property Concepts

Deeds and Tenancies

Warranty Deed

A person transferring property (the grantor) via a warranty deed assures that there is good and clear title to the property. Warranties include that the grantor has the legal ability to convey the property, that the property is free of encumbrances (i.e., any liens or easements), and that no other parties have a superior (or pre-existing) claim to the title to the property.

Quitclaim Deed

A quitclaim deed contains no warranties. A person transferring a property via a quitclaim deed transfers only the rights in the property that s/he has. There is no guarantee that the transferor's title to the property is good.

Joint Tenancy

Joint tenancy is the ownership of property by two or more people with the right of survivorship. Each tenant owns an undivided interest in the property. The right of survivorship means that if a joint tenant dies, the surviving party or parties maintain ownership of the property as a whole. For example, if Jim and Phil own a property as joint tenants and Jim dies, Phil will own the entire property upon Jim's death.

Tenancy by the Entirety

This is essentially the same as a joint tenancy, but it only applies to married couples.

Tenancy in Common

A tenancy in common is the ownership of property by two or more people whereby each person owns a specific share of the property. Each owner, however, has equal rights to possess the property. There is no right of survivorship as in a joint tenancy.

Easement

Easements establish the rights of individuals other than the land owner to use a piece of land. Easements allow for land use in a wide variety of situations. For example, easements allow utility companies to install gas or electrical lines under or over someone's property. Easements also allow individuals without access to a main road from their property to drive across another person's property to access that main road.

The Purchase of Real Property

An important activity in society is the purchase of property, particularly that of residential homes. The following are some of the terms applicable to this transaction.

Deed of Trust

The deed of trust documents that the loan used to purchase the property is secured by the property. It explains the rights and obligations of the borrower, the lender, and the trustee (an individual or company that the lender chooses to represent its interests should it become necessary to foreclose). The foreclosure process is easier with a deed of trust than with a mortgage, since the lender does not need to file suit in court. The trustee can simply sell the property pursuant to the requirements of the deed of trust. The deed of trust will be recorded in the land records in the local courthouse along with the deed. A small majority of states use deeds of trust.

Mortgage

As with a deed of trust, a mortgage documents that the loan used to purchase a property is secured by the property. There are no trustees involved, however. The mortgage is just between the purchaser and the lender. In order to foreclose under a mortgage, the lender will need to file suit in court. Like deeds of trust, mortgages are also filed in the land records with the deed to the property.

Real Estate Settlement Procedures Act (RESPA)

RESPA is the federal statute that is designed to protect homebuyers. It covers loans on one- to four-family residences, including most purchase loans, refinances, assumed loans, property improvement loans, home equity loans, and reverse mortgages. RESPA does not cover cash sales for property, rental and other business properties, and transactions where the home seller instead of a lender holds the mortgage. As stated on the HUD (Department of Housing and Urban Development) website, "RESPA is about closing costs and settlement procedures. RESPA requires that consumers receive disclosures at various times in the transaction and outlaws kickbacks that increase the cost of settlement services."

Title Search and Title Examination

Prior to a purchase of real property, a title search is conducted by reviewing the land records at the local courthouse. The title search is performed by an abstractor who will summarize his/her findings in a title abstract or report. The information that the abstractor finds will then be sent to the settlement attorney or settlement company for review. This review constitutes the title exam. Its purpose is to detect any possible issues with the title to the property; for example, whether the seller has good title to the property and can in fact sell it to the purchaser or if there are any unpaid or outstanding liens on the property.

Title Insurance

Title insurance protects lenders and owners from any issues affecting title to the property that were not discovered in either the title search or title exam. If, for example, there was a mistake in the land records and a previous deed was not properly recorded on the property purchased, a major issue for both the lender and the owner of the property could occur. Title insurance covers losses that might arise from such an issue.

Warranty of Habitability

The warranty of habitability requires landlords to ensure that a residential property is fit for people to occupy. It does not require the property to be in perfect condition, but rather to be free of issues that would negatively affect the safety and/or health of the residents.

Wills & Trusts

Wills and trusts are legal specialties unto themselves. Both wills and trusts allow individuals to direct what happens to their property upon their death. Additionally, trusts can help people to manage their assets while they are still living. A recent development in trust law is the creation of pet trusts. According to the ASPCA (The American Society for the Prevention of Cruelty to Animals), as of 2011, 44 states had passed pet trust legislation. A pet trust puts a legally enforceable plan in place to care for one's pets in the event the owner can no longer care for them.

Chapter 6 Intellectual Property

The World Intellectual Property Organization (WIPO), an agency of the United Nations, defines intellectual property (IP) as:

> creations of the mind: inventions, literary and artistic works, and symbols, names, images, and designs used in commerce.
>
> IP is divided into two categories: Industrial property, which includes inventions (patents), trademarks, industrial designs, and geographic indications of source; and Copyright, which includes literary and artistic works such as novels, poems and plays, films, musical works, artistic works such as drawings, paintings, photographs and sculptures, and architectural designs. Rights related to copyright include those of performing artists in their performances, producers of phonograms in their recordings, and those of broadcasters in their radio and television programs. (http://www.wipo.int/about-ip/en/)

The concept of intellectual property is not a new one. In fact, it has been of such importance throughout history that the writers of the U.S. Constitution specifically granted powers to Congress to effectuate laws that address it. Article I, Section 8, which defines the powers of Congress, includes "Congress shall have power … to promote the progress of science and useful arts, by securing for limited times to authors and inventors the exclusive right to their respective writings and discoveries."

This concept provides individuals with the ability to not only create and invent, but to also have the right to exclusively earn money from those creations and inventions. By protecting "the exclusive right to their respective writings and discoveries," people and businesses have the incentive to invest their time, effort, and capital in the creative process. This process ultimately benefits society through the advancement of the arts, sciences, technology, and so on. According to the United States Patent and Trademark Office, there are four ways to protect intellectual property: patents, trade secrets, trademarks, and copyrights.

Patents

The following information is from the United States Patent and Trademark Office's brochure, *General Information Concerning Patents*, January 2010 (http://www.uspto.gov/patents/resources/general_info_concerning_patents.pdf).

Functions of the United States Patent and Trademark Office

The United States Patent and Trademark Office (USPTO or Office) is an agency of the U.S. Department of Commerce. The role of the USPTO is to grant patents for the protection of inventions and to register trademarks. It serves the interest of inventors and businesses with respect to their inventions and corporate products, and service identifications. It also advises and assists the President of the United States, the Secretary of Commerce, the bureaus and offices of the Department of Commerce and other agencies of the government in matters involving all domestic and global aspects of "intellectual property." Through the preservation, classification, and dissemination of patent information, the Office promotes the industrial and technological progress of the nation and strengthens the economy.

In discharging its patent related duties, the USPTO examines applications and grants patents on inventions when applicants are entitled to them; it publishes and disseminates patent information, records assignments of patents, maintains search files of U.S. and foreign patents, and maintains a search room for public use in examining issued patents and records. The Office supplies copies of patents and official records to the public. It provides training to practitioners as to requirements of the patent statutes and regulations, and it publishes the Manual of Patent Examining Procedure to elucidate these. Similar functions are performed relating to trademarks. By protecting intellectual endeavors and encouraging technological progress, the USPTO seeks to preserve the United States' technological edge, which is key to our current and future competitiveness. The USPTO also disseminates patent and trademark information that promotes an understanding of intellectual property protection and facilitates the development and sharing of new technologies worldwide.

* * *

What Is a Patent?

A patent for an invention is the grant of a property right to the inventor, issued by the United States Patent and Trademark Office. Generally, the term of a new patent is 20 years from the date on which the application for the patent was filed in the United States or, in special cases, from the date an earlier related application was filed, subject to the payment of maintenance fees. U.S. patent grants are effective only within the United States, U.S. territories, and U.S. possessions. Under certain circumstances, patent term extensions or adjustments may be available.

The right conferred by the patent grant is, in the language of the statute and of the grant itself, "the right to exclude others from making, using, offering for sale, or selling" the invention in the United States or "importing" the invention into the United States. What is granted is not the right to make, use, offer for sale, sell or import, but the right to exclude others from making, using, offering for sale, selling or importing the invention. Once a patent is issued, the patentee must enforce the patent without aid of the USPTO.

There are three types of patents:

1. **Utility patents** may be granted to anyone who invents or discovers any new and useful process, machine, article of manufacture, or composition of matter, or any new and useful improvement thereof;

2. **Design patents** may be granted to anyone who invents a new, original, and ornamental design for an article of manufacture; and

3. **Plant patents** may be granted to anyone who invents or discovers and asexually reproduces any distinct and new variety of plant.

* * *

What Can Be Patented

The patent law specifies the general field of subject matter that can be patented and the conditions under which a patent may be obtained.

In the language of the statute, any person who "invents or discovers any new and useful process, machine, manufacture, or composition of matter, or any new and useful improvement thereof, may obtain a patent," subject to the conditions and requirements of the law. The word "process" is defined by law as a process, act or method, and primarily includes industrial or technical processes. The term "machine" used in the statute needs no explanation. The term "manufacture" refers to articles that are made, and includes all manufactured articles. The term "composition of matter" relates to chemical compositions and may include mixtures of ingredients as well as new chemical compounds. These classes of subject matter taken together include practically everything that is made by man and the processes for making the products.

The Atomic Energy Act of 1954 excludes the patenting of inventions useful solely in the utilization of special nuclear material or atomic energy in an atomic weapon. See 42 U.S.C. 2181(a).

The patent law specifies that the subject matter must be "useful." The term "useful" in this connection refers to the condition that the subject matter has a useful purpose and also includes operativeness, that is, a machine which will not operate to perform the intended purpose would not be called useful, and therefore would not be granted a patent.

Interpretations of the statute by the courts have defined the limits of the field of subject matter that can be patented, thus it has been held that the laws of nature, physical phenomena, and abstract ideas are not patentable subject matter.

A patent cannot be obtained upon a mere idea or suggestion. The patent is granted upon the new machine, manufacture, etc., as has been said, and not upon the idea or suggestion of the new machine. A complete description of the actual machine or other subject matter for which a patent is sought is required.

Novelty and Non-Obviousness, Conditions For Obtaining A Patent

In order for an invention to be patentable it must be new as defined in the patent law, which provides that an invention cannot be patented if: "(a) the invention was known or used by others in this country, or patented or described in a printed publication in this or a foreign country, before the invention thereof by the applicant for patent," or "(b) the invention was patented or described in a printed publication in this or a foreign country or in public use or on sale in this country more than one year prior to the application for patent in the United States …"

If the invention has been described in a printed publication anywhere in the world, or if it was known or used by others in this country before the date that the applicant made his/her invention, a patent cannot be obtained. If the invention has been described in a printed publication anywhere, or has been in public use or on sale in this country more than one year before the date on which an application for patent is filed in this country, a patent cannot be obtained. In this connection it is immaterial when the invention was made, or whether the printed publication or public use was by the inventor himself/herself or by someone else. If the inventor describes the invention in a printed publication or uses the invention publicly, or places it on sale, he/she must apply for a patent before one year has gone by, otherwise any right to a patent will be lost. The inventor must file on the date of public use or disclosure, however, in order to preserve patent rights in many foreign countries.

Even if the subject matter sought to be patented is not exactly shown by the prior art, and involves one or more differences over the most nearly similar thing already known, a patent may still be refused if the differences would be obvious. The subject matter sought to be patented must be sufficiently different from what has been used or described before that it may be said to be nonobvious to a person having ordinary skill in the area of technology related to the invention. For example, the substitution of one color for another, or changes in size, are ordinarily not patentable.

The United States Patent and Trademark Office

Congress established the United States Patent and Trademark Office (USPTO or Office) to issue patents on behalf of the government. The Patent Office as a distinct bureau dates from the year 1802 when a separate official in the Department of State who became known as "Superintendent of Patents" was placed in charge of patents. The revision of the patent laws enacted in 1836 reorganized the Patent Office and designated the official in charge as Commissioner of Patents. The Patent Office remained in the Department of State until 1849 when it was transferred to the Department of Interior. In 1925 it was transferred to the Department of Commerce where it is today. The name of the Patent Office was changed to the Patent and Trademark Office in 1975 and changed to the United States Patent and Trademark Office in 2000.

The USPTO administers the patent laws as they relate to the granting of patents for inventions, and performs other duties relating to patents. Applications for patents are examined to determine if the applicants are entitled to patents under the law and patents are granted when applicants are so entitled. The USPTO publishes issued patents and most patent applications 18 months from the earliest effective application filing date, and makes various other publications concerning patents. The USPTO also records assignments of patents, maintains a search room for the use of the public to examine issued patents and records, and supplies copies of records and other papers, and the like. Similar functions are performed with respect to the registration of trademarks. The USPTO has no jurisdiction over questions of infringement and the enforcement of patents.

The head of the Office is the Under Secretary of Commerce for Intellectual Property and Director of the United States Patent and Trademark Office (Director). The Director's staff includes the Deputy Under Secretary of Commerce and Deputy Director of the USPTO, the Commissioner for Patents, the Commissioner for Trademarks, and other officials. As head of the Office, the Director superintends or performs all duties respecting the granting and issuing of patents and the registration of trademarks; exercises general supervision over the entire work of the USPTO; prescribes the rules, subject to the approval of the Secretary of Commerce, for the conduct of proceedings in the USPTO, and for recognition of attorneys and agents; decides various questions brought before the Office by petition as prescribed by the rules; and performs other duties necessary and required for the administration of the United States Patent and Trademark Office.

The work of examining applications for patents is divided among a number of examining technology centers (TC), each TC having jurisdiction over certain assigned fields of technology. Each TC is headed by group directors and staffed by examiners and support staff. The examiners review applications for patents and determine whether patents can be granted. An appeal can be taken to the Board of Patent Appeals and Interferences from their decisions refusing to grant a patent, and a review by the Director of the USPTO may be had on other matters by petition. The examiners also identify applications that claim the same invention and may initiate proceedings, known as interferences, to determine who was the first inventor.

In addition to the examining TCs, other offices perform various services, such as receiving and distributing mail, receiving new applications, handling sales of printed copies of patents, making copies of records, inspecting drawings, and recording assignments.

At present, the USPTO has over 6,500 employees, of whom about half are examiners and others with technical and legal training. Patent applications are received at the rate of over 450,000 per year. The Office receives over five million pieces of mail each year.

* * *

Nature of Patent and Patent Rights

The patent is issued in the name of the United States under the seal of the United States Patent and Trademark Office, and is either signed by the Director of the USPTO or is electronically written thereon and attested by an Office official. The patent contains a grant to the patentee, and a printed copy of the specification and drawing is annexed to the patent and forms a part of it. The grant confers "the right to exclude others from making, using, offering for sale, or selling the invention throughout the United States or importing the invention into the United States" and its territories and possessions for which the term of the patent shall be generally 20 years from the date on which the application for the patent was filed in the United States or, if the application contains a specific reference to an earlier filed application under 35 U.S.C. 120, 121 or 365(c), from the date of the earliest such application was filed, and subject to the payment of maintenance fees as provided by law.

The exact nature of the right conferred must be carefully distinguished, and the key is in the words "right to exclude" in the phrase just quoted. The patent does not grant the right to make, use, offer for sale or sell or import the invention but only grants the exclusive nature of the right. Any person is ordinarily free to make, use, offer for sale or sell or import anything he/she pleases, and a grant from the government is not necessary. The patent only grants the right to exclude others from making, using, offering for sale or selling or importing the invention. Since the patent does not grant the right to make, use, offer for sale, or sell, or import the invention, the patentee's own right to do so is dependent upon the rights of others and whatever general laws might be applicable. A patentee, merely because he/she has received a patent for an invention, is not thereby authorized to make, use, offer for sale, or sell, or import the invention if doing so would violate any law.

* * *

The term of the patent shall be generally 20 years from the date on which the application for the patent was filed in the United States or, if the application contains a specific reference to an earlier filed application under 35 U.S.C. 120, 121 or 365(c), from the date of the earliest such application was filed, and subject to the payment of maintenance fees as provided by law. A maintenance fee is due 3 1/2, 7 1/2 and 11 1/2 years after the original grant for all patents issuing from the applications filed on and after

December 12, 1980. The maintenance fee must be paid at the stipulated times to maintain the patent in force. After the patent has expired anyone may make, use, offer for sale, or sell or import the invention without permission of the patentee, provided that matter covered by other unexpired patents is not used. The terms may be extended for certain pharmaceuticals and for certain circumstances as provided by law.

Maintenance Fees

All utility patents that issue from applications filed on or after December 12, 1980 are subject to the payment of maintenance fees which must be paid to maintain the patent in force. These fees are due at 3 1/2, 7 1/2 and 11 1/2 years from the date the patent is granted and can be paid without a surcharge during the "window period" which is the six-month period preceding each due date, e.g., three years to three years and six months. (See fee schedule for a list of maintenance fees.) In submitting maintenance fees and any necessary surcharges, identification of the patents for which maintenance fees are being paid must include the patent number, and the application number of the U.S. application for the patent on which the maintenance fee is being paid. If the payment includes identification of only the patent number, the Office may apply payment to the patent identified by patent number in the payment or the Office may return the payment. (See 37, Code of Federal Regulations, section 1.366(c).)

Failure to pay the current maintenance fee on time may result in expiration of the patent. A six-month grace period is provided when the maintenance fee may be paid with a surcharge. The grace period is the six-month period immediately following the due date. The USPTO does not mail notices to patent owners that maintenance fees are due. If, however, the maintenance fee is not paid on time, efforts are made to remind the responsible party that the maintenance fee may be paid during the grace period with a surcharge. If the maintenance fee is not paid on time and the maintenance fee and surcharge are not paid during the grace period, the patent expires on the date the grace period ends.

Assignments and Licenses

A patent is personal property and may be sold to others or mortgaged; it may be bequeathed by a will; and it may pass to the heirs of a deceased patentee. The patent law provides for the transfer or sale of a patent, or of an application for patent, by an instrument in writing. Such an instrument is referred to as an assignment and may transfer the entire interest in the patent. The assignee, when the patent is assigned to him or her, becomes the owner of the patent and has the same rights that the original patentee had.

The statute also provides for the assignment of a part interest, that is, a half interest, a fourth interest, etc., in a patent. There may also be a grant that conveys the same character of interest as an assignment but only for a particularly specified part of the United States. A mortgage of patent property passes ownership thereof to the mortgagee or lender until the mortgage has been satisfied and a retransfer from the mortgagee back to the mortgagor, the borrower, is made. A conditional assignment also passes ownership of the patent and is regarded as absolute until canceled by the parties or by the decree of a competent court.

An assignment, grant, or conveyance of any patent or application for patent should be acknowledged before a notary public or officer authorized to administer oaths or perform notarial acts. The certificate of such acknowledgment constitutes prima facie evidence of the execution of the assignment, grant, or conveyance.

* * *

Infringement of Patents

Infringement of a patent consists of the unauthorized making, using, offering for sale, or selling any patented invention within the United States or U.S. Territories, or importing into the United States of any patented invention during the term of the patent. If a patent is infringed, the patentee may sue for relief in the appropriate federal court. The patentee may ask the court for an injunction to prevent the continuation of the infringement and may also ask the court for an award of damages because of the infringement. In such an infringement suit, the defendant may raise the question of the validity of the patent, which is then decided by the court. The defendant may also aver that what is being done does not constitute infringement. Infringement is determined primarily by the language of the claims of the patent and, if what the defendant is making does not fall within the language of any of the claims of the patent, there is no literal infringement.

Suits for infringement of patents follow the rules of procedure of the federal courts. From the decision of the district court, there is an appeal to the Court of Appeals for the Federal Circuit. The Supreme Court may thereafter take a case by writ of certiorari. If the United States Government infringes a patent, the patentee has a remedy for damages in the United States Court of Federal Claims. The government may use any patented invention without permission of the patentee, but the patentee is entitled to obtain compensation for the use by or for the government. The Office has no jurisdiction over questions relating to infringement of patents. In examining applications for patent, no determination is made as to whether the invention sought to be patented infringes any prior patent. An improvement invention may be patentable, but it might infringe a prior unexpired patent for the invention improved upon, if there is one.

Patent Marking and Patent Pending

A patentee who makes or sells patented articles, or a person who does so for or under the patentee is required to mark the articles with the word "Patent" and the number of the patent. The penalty for failure to mark is that the patentee may not recover damages from an infringer unless the infringer was duly notified of the infringement and continued to infringe after the notice.

The marking of an article as patented when it is not in fact patented is against the law and subjects the offender to a penalty. Some persons mark articles sold with the terms "Patent Applied For" or "Patent Pending." These phrases have no legal effect, but only give information that an application for patent has been filed in the USPTO. The protection afforded by a patent does not start until the actual grant of the patent. False use of these phrases or their equivalent is prohibited.

Design Patents

The patent laws provide for the granting of design patents to any person who has invented any new and nonobvious ornamental design for an article of manufacture. The design patent protects only the appearance of an article, but not its structural or functional features. The proceedings relating to granting of design patents are the same as those relating to other patents with a few differences. See current fee schedule for the filing fee for a design application. A design patent has a term of 14 years from grant, and no fees are necessary to maintain a design patent in force. If on examination it is determined that an applicant is entitled to a design patent under the law, a notice of allowance will be sent to the applicant or applicant's attorney, or agent, calling for the payment of an issue fee. The drawing of the design patent conforms to the same rules as other drawings, but no reference characters are allowed and the drawing should clearly depict the appearance, since the drawing defines the scope of patent protection.

* * *

Plant Patents

The law also provides for the granting of a patent to anyone who has invented or discovered and asexually reproduced any distinct and new variety of plant, including cultivated sports, mutants, hybrids, and newly found seedlings, other than a tuber-propagated plant or a plant found in an uncultivated state.

Asexually propagated plants are those that are reproduced by means other than from seeds, such as by the rooting of cuttings, by layering, budding, grafting, inarching, etc.

With reference to tuber-propagated plants, for which a plant patent cannot be obtained, the term "tuber" is used in its narrow horticultural sense as meaning a short, thickened portion of an underground branch. Such plants covered by the term "tuber-propagated" are the Irish potato and the Jerusalem artichoke.

An application for a plant patent consists of the same parts as other applications. The term of a plant patent shall be 20 years from the date on which the application for the patent was filed in the United States or, if the application contains a specific reference to an earlier filed application under 35 U.S.C. 120, 121 or 365(c), from the date the earliest such application was filed.

The specification should include a complete detailed description of the plant and the characteristics thereof that distinguish the same over related known varieties, and its antecedents, expressed in botanical terms in the general form followed in standard botanical text books or publications dealing with the varieties of the kind of plant involved (evergreen tree, dahlia plant, rose plant, apple tree, etc.), rather than a mere broad non-botanical characterization such as commonly found in nursery or seed catalogs. The specification should also include the origin or parentage of the plant variety sought to be patented and must particularly point out where and in what manner the variety of plant has been asexually reproduced. The Latin name of the genus and species of the plant should be stated. Where color is a distinctive feature of the plant, the color should be positively identified in the specification by reference to a designated color as given by a recognized color dictionary. Where the plant variety originated as a newly found seedling, the specification must fully describe the conditions (cultivation, environment, etc.) under which the seedling was found growing to establish that it was not found in an uncultivated state.

A plant patent is granted on the entire plant. It therefore follows that only one claim is necessary and only one is permitted. The oath or declaration required of the applicant in addition to the statements required for other applications must include the statement that the applicant has asexually reproduced the new plant variety. If the plant is a newly found plant, the oath or declaration must also state that the plant was found in a cultivated area.

Plant patent drawings are not mechanical drawings and should be artistically and competently executed. The drawing must disclose all the distinctive characteristics of the plant capable of visual representation. When color is a distinguishing characteristic of the new variety, the drawing must be in color. Two duplicate copies of color drawings must be submitted. All color drawings should include a one-inch margin at the top for Office markings when the patent is printed.

Specimens of the plant variety, its flower or fruit, should not be submitted unless specifically called for by the examiner. The filing fee on each plant application and the issue fee can be found in the fee schedule. For a qualifying small entity most fees are reduced by half. 35 U.S.C. 41(h)(1). Plant patent applications may be published pursuant to Title 35, United States Code, Section 122(b), but the publication fee is not reduced for small entities.

All inquiries relating to plant patents and pending plant patent applications should be directed to the United States Patent and Trademark Office and not to the Department of Agriculture.

The Plant Variety Protection Act (Public Law 91577), approved December 24, 1970, provides for a system of protection for sexually reproduced varieties, for which protection was not previously provided, under the administration of a Plant Variety Protection Office within the Department of Agriculture. Requests for information regarding the protection of sexually reproduced varieties should be addressed to Commissioner, Plant Variety Protection Office, Agricultural Marketing Service, National Agricultural Library Bldg., Room 0, 10301 Baltimore Blvd., Beltsville, Md. 20705-2351.

Treaties and Foreign Patents

Since the rights granted by a U.S. patent extend only throughout the territory of the United States and have no effect in a foreign country, an inventor who wishes patent protection in other countries must apply for a patent in each of the other countries or in regional patent offices. Almost every country has its own patent law, and a person desiring a patent in a particular country must make an application for patent in that country, in accordance with the requirements of that country.

The laws of many countries differ in various respects from the patent law of the United States. In most foreign countries, publication of the invention before the date of the application will bar the right to a patent. Most foreign countries require that the patented invention must be manufactured in that country after a certain period, usually three years. If there is no manufacture within this period, the patent may be void in some countries, although in most countries the patent may be subject to the grant of compulsory licenses to any person who may apply for a license.

There is a treaty relating to patents which is adhered to by 169 countries, including the United States, and is known as the Paris Convention for the Protection of Industrial Property. It provides that each country guarantees to the citizens of the other countries the same rights in patent and trademark matters that it gives to its own citizens. The treaty also provides for the right of priority in the case of patents, trademarks and industrial designs (design patents). This right means that, on the basis of a regular first application filed in one of the member countries, the applicant may, within a certain period of time, apply for protection in all the other member countries. These later applications will then be regarded as if they had been filed on the same day as the first application. Thus, these later applicants will have priority over applications for the same invention that may have been filed during the same period of time by other persons. Moreover, these later applications, being based on the first application, will not be invalidated by any acts accomplished in the interval, such as, for example, publication or exploitation of the invention, the sale of copies of the design, or use of the trademark. The period of time mentioned above, within which the subsequent applications may be filed in the other countries, is 12 months in the case of first applications for patent and six months in the case of industrial designs and trademarks.

Another treaty, known as the Patent Cooperation Treaty, was negotiated at a diplomatic conference in Washington, D.C., in June of 1970. The treaty came into force on January 24, 1978, and is presently (as of March 29, 2005) adhered to by over 126 countries, including the United States. The treaty facilitates the filing of applications for patent on the same invention in member countries by providing, among other things, for centralized filing procedures and a standardized application format.

The timely filing of an international application affords applicants an international filing date in each country which is designated in the international application and provides (1) a search of the invention and (2) a later time period within which the national applications for patent must be filed. A number of patent attorneys specialize in obtaining patents in foreign countries.

Under U.S. law it is necessary, in the case of inventions made in the United States, to obtain a license from the Director of the USPTO before applying for a patent in a foreign country. Such a license is required if the foreign application is to be filed before an application is filed in the United States or before the expiration of six months from the filing of an application in the United States unless a filing receipt with a license grant issued earlier. The filing of an application for a U.S. patent constitutes the request for a license and the granting or denial of such request is indicated in the filing receipt mailed to each applicant. After six months from the U.S. filing, a license is not required unless the invention has been ordered to be kept secret. If the invention has been ordered to be kept secret, the consent to the filing abroad must be obtained from the Director of the USPTO during the period the order of secrecy is in effect.

* * *

Design Patents

(http://www.uspto.gov/patents/resources/types/designapp.jsp#differ)

Definition of a Design

A design consists of the visual ornamental characteristics embodied in, or applied to, an article of manufacture. Since a design is manifested in appearance, the subject matter of a design patent application may relate to the configuration or shape of an article, to the surface ornamentation applied to an article, or to the combination of configuration and surface ornamentation. A design for surface ornamentation is inseparable from the article to which it is applied and cannot exist alone. It must be a definite pattern of surface ornamentation, applied to an article of manufacture.

In discharging its patent-related duties, the United States Patent and Trademark Office (USPTO or Office) examines applications and grants patents on inventions when applicants are entitled to them. The patent law provides for the granting of design patents to any person who has invented any new, original and ornamental design for an article of manufacture. A design patent protects only the appearance of the article and not structural or utilitarian features.

Types of Designs and Modified Forms

An ornamental design may be embodied in an entire article or only a portion of an article, or may be ornamentation applied to an article. If a design is directed to just surface ornamentation, it must be shown applied to an article in the drawings, and the article must be shown in broken lines, as it forms no part of the claimed design.

A design patent application may only have a single claim (37 CFR § 1.153). Designs that are independent and distinct must be filed in separate applications since they cannot be supported by a single claim. Designs are independent if there is no apparent relationship between two or more articles.

For example, a pair of eyeglasses and a door handle are independent articles and must be claimed in separate applications. Designs are considered distinct if they have different shapes and appearances even though they are related articles. For example, two vases having different surface ornamentation creating distinct appearances must be claimed in separate applications. However, modified forms, or embodiments of a single design concept may be filed in one application. For example, vases with only minimal configuration differences may be considered a single design concept and both embodiments may be included in a single application.

The Difference Between Design and Utility Patents

In general terms, a "utility patent" protects the way an article is used and works (35 U.S.C. 101), while a "design patent" protects the way an article looks (35 U.S.C. 171). Both design and utility patents may be obtained on an article if invention resides both in its utility and ornamental appearance. While utility and design patents afford legally separate protection, the utility and ornamentality of an article are not easily separable. Articles of manufacture may possess both functional and ornamental characteristics.

Diamond v. Chakrabarty examines whether genetically-engineered life forms can be patented.

DIAMOND v. CHAKRABARTY

Supreme Court of the United States (5–4)
447 U.S. 303 (1980)

Syllabus

Title 35 U.S.C. § 101 provides for the issuance of a patent to a person who invents or discovers "any" new and useful "manufacture" or "composition of matter." Respondent filed a patent application relating to his invention of a human-made, genetically engineered bacterium capable of breaking down crude oil, a property which is possessed by no naturally occurring bacteria. A patent examiner's rejection of the patent application's claims for the new bacteria was affirmed by the Patent Office Board of Appeals on the ground that living things are not patentable subject matter under § 101. The Court of Customs and Patent Appeals reversed, concluding that the fact that micro-organisms are alive is without legal significance for purposes of the patent law.

Held: A live, human-made micro-organism is patentable subject matter under § 101. Respondent's micro-organism constitutes a "manufacture" or "composition of matter" within that statute. Pp. 308–318.

(a) In choosing such expansive terms as "manufacture" and "composition of matter," modified by the comprehensive "any," Congress contemplated that the patent laws should be given wide scope, and the relevant legislative history also supports a broad construction. While laws of nature, physical phenomena, and abstract ideas are not patentable, respondent's claim is not to a hitherto unknown natural phenomenon, but to a nonnaturally occurring manufacture or composition of matter—a product of human ingenuity "having a distinctive name, character [and] use." *Hartranft v. Wiegmann*, 121 U.S. 609, 615, 7 S.Ct. 1240, 1243, 30 L.Ed. 1012; *Funk Brothers Seed Co. v. Kalo Inoculant Co.*, 333 U.S. 127, 68 S.Ct. 440, 92 L.Ed. 588, distinguished. Pp. 308–310.

(b) The passage of the 1930 Plant Patent Act, which afforded patent protection to certain asexually reproduced plants, and the 1970 Plant Variety Protection Act, which authorized protection for certain sexually reproduced plants but excluded bacteria from its protection, does not evidence congressional understanding that the terms "manufacture" or "composition of matter" in § 101 do not include living things. Pp. 310–314.

(c) Nor does the fact that genetic technology was unforeseen when Congress enacted § 101 require the conclusion that micro-organisms cannot qualify as patentable subject matter until Congress expressly authorizes such protection. The unambiguous language of § 101 fairly embraces respondent's invention. Arguments against patentability under § 101, based on potential hazards that may be generated by genetic research, should be addressed to the Congress and the Executive, not to the Judiciary. Pp. 314–318.

596 F.2d 952, affirmed.

The *State Street* case considers if and/or when a mathematical algorithm can be patented.

STATE STREET BANK & TRUST CO. v. SIGNATURE FINANCIAL GROUP, INC.

United States Court of Appeals, Federal Circuit

149 F.3d 1368 (1998)

RICH, Circuit Judge.

Signature Financial Group, Inc. (Signature) appeals from the decision of the United States District Court for the District of Massachusetts granting a motion for summary judgment in favor of State Street Bank & Trust Co. (State Street), finding U.S. Patent No. 5,193,056 (the '056 patent) invalid on the ground that the claimed subject matter is not encompassed by 35 U.S.C. § 101 (1994). See *State Street Bank & Trust Co. v. Signature Financial Group, Inc.*, 927 F.Supp. 502, 38 USPQ2d 1530 (D.Mass.1996). We reverse and remand because we conclude that the patent claims are directed to statutory subject matter.

BACKGROUND

Signature is the assignee of the '056 patent which is entitled "Data Processing System for Hub and Spoke Financial Services Configuration." The '056 patent issued to Signature on 9 March 1993, naming R. Todd Boes as the inventor. The '056 patent is generally directed to a data processing system (the system) for implementing an investment structure which was developed for use in Signature's business as an administrator and accounting agent for mutual funds. In essence, the system, identified by the proprietary name Hub and Spoke TM, facilitates a structure whereby mutual funds (Spokes) pool their assets in an investment portfolio (Hub) organized as a partnership. This investment configuration provides the administrator of a mutual fund with the advantageous combination of economies of scale in administering investments coupled with the tax advantages of a partnership.

State Street and Signature are both in the business of acting as custodians and accounting agents for multi-tiered partnership fund financial services. State Street negotiated with Signature for a license to use its patented data processing system described and claimed in the '056 patent. When negotiations broke down, State Street brought a declaratory judgment action asserting invalidity, unenforceability, and noninfringement in Massachusetts district court, and then filed a motion for partial summary judgment of patent invalidity for failure to claim statutory subject matter under § 101. The motion was granted and this appeal followed.

DISCUSSION

* * *

The following facts pertinent to the statutory subject matter issue are either undisputed or represent the version alleged by the nonmovant. *See Anderson v. Liberty Lobby, Inc.*, 477 U.S. 242, 255, 106 S.Ct. 2505, 91 L.Ed.2d 202 (1986). The patented invention relates generally to a system that allows an administrator to monitor and record the financial information flow and make all calculations necessary for maintaining a partner fund financial services configuration. As previously mentioned, a partner fund financial services configuration essentially allows several mutual funds, or "Spokes," to pool their investment funds into a single portfolio, or "Hub," allowing for consolidation of, *inter alia*, the costs of administering the fund combined with the tax advantages of a partnership. In particular, this system provides means for a daily allocation of assets for two or more Spokes that are invested in the same Hub. The system determines the percentage share that each Spoke maintains in the Hub, while taking into consideration daily changes both in the value of the Hub's investment securities and in the concomitant amount of each Spoke's assets.

In determining daily changes, the system also allows for the allocation among the Spokes of the Hub's daily income, expenses, and net realized and unrealized gain or loss, calculating each day's total investments based on the concept of a book capital account. This enables the determination of a true asset value of each Spoke and accurate calculation of allocation ratios between or among the Spokes. The system additionally tracks all the relevant data determined on a daily basis for the Hub and each Spoke, so that aggregate year end income, expenses, and capital gain or loss can be determined for accounting and for tax purposes for the Hub and, as a result, for each publicly traded Spoke.

It is essential that these calculations are quickly and accurately performed. In large part this is required because each Spoke sells shares to the public and the price of those shares is substantially based on the Spoke's percentage interest in the portfolio. In some instances, a mutual fund administrator is required to calculate the value of the shares to the nearest penny within as little as an hour and a half after the market closes. Given the complexity of the calculations, a computer or equivalent device is a virtual necessity to perform the task.

The '056 patent application was filed 11 March 1991. It initially contained six "machine" claims, which incorporated means-plus-function clauses, and six method claims. According to Signature, during prosecution the examiner contemplated a § 101 rejection for failure to claim statutory subject matter. However, upon cancellation of the six method claims, the examiner issued a notice of allowance for the remaining present six claims on appeal. Only claim 1 is an independent claim.

* * *

*** Section 101 reads:

> Whoever invents or discovers any new and useful process, machine, manufacture, or composition of matter, or any new and useful improvement thereof, may obtain a patent therefor, subject to the conditions and requirements of this title.

The plain and unambiguous meaning of § 101 is that any invention falling within one of the four stated categories of statutory subject matter may be patented, provided it meets the other requirements for patentability set forth in Title 35, i.e., those found in §§ 102, 103, and 112, p 2.

The repetitive use of the expansive term "any" in § 101 shows Congress's intent not to place any restrictions on the subject matter for which a patent may be obtained beyond those specifically recited in § 101. Indeed, the Supreme Court has acknowledged that Congress intended § 101 to extend to "anything under the sun that is made by man." *Diamond v. Chakrabarty*, 447 U.S. 303, 309, 100 S.Ct. 2204, 65 L.Ed.2d

144 (1980); see also *Diamond v. Diehr*, 450 U.S. 175, 182, 101 S.Ct. 1048, 67 L.Ed.2d 155 (1981). Thus, it is improper to read limitations into § 101 on the subject matter that may be patented where the legislative history indicates that Congress clearly did not intend such limitations. See *Chakrabarty*, 447 U.S. at 308, 100 S.Ct. 2204 ("We have also cautioned that courts 'should not read into the patent laws limitations and conditions which the legislature has not expressed.'" (citations omitted)).

The "Mathematical Algorithm" Exception

The Supreme Court has identified three categories of subject matter that are unpatentable, namely "laws of nature, natural phenomena, and abstract ideas." *Diehr*, 450 U.S. at 185, 101 S.Ct. 1048. Of particular relevance to this case, the Court has held that mathematical algorithms are not patentable subject matter to the extent that they are merely abstract ideas. *** In *Diehr*, the Court explained that certain types of mathematical subject matter, standing alone, represent nothing more than abstract ideas until reduced to some type of practical application, i.e., "a useful, concrete and tangible result." *Alappat*, 33 F.3d at 1544, 31 USPQ2d at 1557.

Unpatentable mathematical algorithms are identifiable by showing they are merely abstract ideas constituting disembodied concepts or truths that are not "useful." From a practical standpoint, this means that to be patentable an algorithm must be applied in a "useful" way. In *Alappat*, we held that data, transformed by a machine through a series of mathematical calculations to produce a smooth waveform display on a rasterizer monitor, constituted a practical application of an abstract idea (a mathematical algorithm, formula, or calculation), because it produced "a useful, concrete and tangible result"—the smooth waveform.

Similarly, in *Arrhythmia Research Technology Inc. v. Corazonix Corp.*, 958 F.2d 1053, 22 USPQ2d 1033 (Fed. Cir.1992), we held that the transformation of electrocardiograph signals from a patient's heartbeat by a machine through a series of mathematical calculations constituted a practical application of an abstract idea (a mathematical algorithm, formula, or calculation), because it corresponded to a useful, concrete or tangible thing—the condition of a patient's heart.

Today, we hold that the transformation of data, representing discrete dollar amounts, by a machine through a series of mathematical calculations into a final share price, constitutes a practical application of a mathematical algorithm, formula, or calculation, because it produces "a useful, concrete and tangible result"—a final share price momentarily fixed for recording and reporting purposes and even accepted and relied upon by regulatory authorities and in subsequent trades.

* * *

CONCLUSION

The appealed decision is reversed and the case is remanded to the district court for further proceedings consistent with this opinion.

REVERSED and REMANDED.

[Footnotes Omitted.]

Trade Secrets

Most states have enacted a version of the Uniform Trade Secrets Act. A trade secret is proprietary information that is of such value to a company that it takes great efforts to keep that information secret. Unlike a patent, a trade secret will never expire, assuming it can be kept secret. Examples of valuable trade secrets include the secret recipes for Kentucky Fried Chicken and Coca-Cola. A drawback for using trade secret laws to protect proprietary information is that once the product is available on the market, it can be reverse engineered, and what was once secret will no longer be veiled from the public.

The essential difference between patents and trade secrets is as follows. Patents are expensive to acquire in terms of application fees, drawing or design fees, and legal fees, and they also take a long time to be issued. The benefit, however, is that the information contained therein is proprietary by law for 20 years. Trade secrets, on the other hand, cost nothing to create and take only so long to establish as it takes to develop the product or information. The financial issues for trade secrets revolve around the protection of the proprietary information and the legal prosecution of those committing theft or unauthorized use of that information.

Bond v. Polycycle applies Maryland's trade secret statute to technology designed to separate "adherent foreign matter from solid materials."

BOND v. POLYCYCLE, INC.

Court of Special Appeals of Maryland
732 A.2d 970 (1999)

ADKINS, Judge.

This case is an appeal from an order of the Circuit Court for Baltimore County issued by the Honorable Norris Byrnes against Martin Bond, appellant, in favor of PolyCycle Corporation (PolyCycle), appellee. The trial court found that Bond misappropriated a trade secret and issued an injunction restricting him from disclosing or making use of the technology he developed on behalf of PolyCycle. PolyCycle was also awarded attorneys' fees. Appellant timely noted this appeal.

Appellant asks us to determine whether the trial court erred in: 1) finding that he violated the Maryland Uniform Trade Secrets Act; 2) concluding, without the appropriate finding of fact, that he usurped a corporate opportunity; 3) ordering him to pay appellee's counsel fees; and 4) placing an unreasonable restraint on his right to free speech.

For the reasons that follow, we perceive no error and affirm the judgment of the circuit court.

FACTS

Prior to July 1995, George Brown and Marvin Marks were involved in discussions concerning a potential investment in Antaeus Group, Inc. (Antaeus). Later, Brown and Marks approached appellant, an engineer, and asked him to review a technology patented by Antaeus, which separated toxins from medical waste. It was Brown and Marks's idea that the same technology could be used to remove paint and other adherents from plastic in a way that would be non-destructive to the plastic. In essence, the process broke the plastic into small pieces and applied a combination of heat and agitation to break the bond between the paint adherent and the plastic, without changing the physical or chemical properties of the plastic. In exchange for Bond's review of the technology, Brown and Marks offered him a share of a proposed joint venture to license and commercialize the technology.

Appellant reviewed the technology and concluded that it had great economic potential. As a result, Bond, Brown, and Marks formed PolyCycle in 1995 "[t]o engage in the business of designing and manufacturing equipment for use in the separation of adherent foreign matter from solid materials, including the separation of paint from plastic resins and providing the use of such equipment as a service to others …" In exchange for a license to use the Antaeus process and common stock in Antaeus, PolyCycle paid Antaeus $700,000 and agreed to pay it future royalties.

Bond was named the president of PolyCycle and was responsible for the daily operations of the company. Brown was responsible for accounting, while Marks performed marketing and consulting services. It was agreed that no one would receive compensation for his work. Bond estimated that the development of the technology would take up to six months and cost approximately $75,000 to $100,000.

Bond began to undertake the development and improvement of the Antaeus technology. After renting space for the business, and purchasing equipment and supplies, Bond determined that the Antaeus technology was not suitable for PolyCycle's needs without modification. One problem with the existing apparatus was that it did not recycle the water used in the process. Therefore, Bond added a hydrocyclone to the machine to recycle the water. Secondly, to improve the process, Bond replaced the Vaughan chopping pump with a Dicon mixing pump. Lastly, Bond modified the pressure vessels on the equipment to further aid the process.

In addition to modifying the equipment, Bond sought customers for PolyCycle. Specifically, Bond targeted the automobile industry. When Bond discussed the technology with potential customers, he required that they sign a confidentiality agreement, which stated that the technology belonged to PolyCycle.

As a result of a delay of more than two years and costs of approximately $500,000, meetings were held to review PolyCycle's progress. At one of these meetings, Bond requested a salary for his efforts, but Brown and Marks declined the request, citing PolyCycle's failure to generate a profit. Bond then consulted with an attorney and sought assistance in negotiating a compensation package. Bond's subsequent compensation demand upon PolyCycle merely resulted in further estrangement of the parties.

Bond also sought legal advice on whether his improvements to the technology were patentable. After conferring with his attorney, Bond believed that his modified process was not sufficiently different from the existing technology to warrant a patent. He testified, however, that he believed based on his attorneys' advice, that he was entitled to use any modifications of the Antaeus technology for which he was responsible, but that PolyCycle might have the right to use his modifications.

On September 23, 1997, Bond, through counsel, wrote to Marks and Brown and informed them that he had determined that the Antaeus technology was not commercially viable, but that he had developed an alternative technology that he believed was economically viable. Bond further stated that this alternative technology did not belong to PolyCycle, and contended that it belonged to him. The next day, on September 24, 1997, Bond resigned from PolyCycle as a director and officer. When Bond left, he took all of the technology with him, including computer files, papers, and records pertaining to the technology.

In addition to taking the computer files, he deleted the files from PolyCycle's computers. In response, PolyCycle brought this suit, seeking to compel the return of, and restrict the use of, such information.

DISCUSSION

I.

Maryland Trade Secrets Act

The Maryland Uniform Trade Secrets Act (MUTSA) defines a trade secret as:

[I]nformation, including a formula, pattern, compilation, program, device, method, technique, or process, that:

(1) Derives independent economic value, actual or potential, from not being generally known to, and not being readily ascertainable by proper means by, other persons who can obtain economic value from its disclosure or use; and

(2) Is the subject of efforts that are reasonable under the circumstances to maintain its secrecy.

Md.Code (1975, 1990 Repl.Vol.), § 11-1201 of the Commercial Law Article. The subject matter of a trade secret:

> 'may be an industrial secret like a secret machine, process, or formula, or it may be industrial know-how (an increasingly important ancillary of patented inventions); it may be information of any sort; it may be an idea of a scientific nature, or of a literary nature … or it may be a slogan or suggestion for a method of advertising; lastly, the subject-matter may be the product of work, or expenditure of money, or of trial and error, or the expenditure of time.'

Space Aero Prods. Co. v. R.E. Darling Co., 238 Md. 93, 105, 208 A.2d 74, cert. denied, 382 U.S. 843, 86 S.Ct. 77, 15 L.Ed.2d 83 (1965) (quoting Amedee E. Turner, *The Law of Trade Secrets* 4 (1962)).

* * *

Appellant contends that the trial court erred in finding this process to be a trade secret. His argument has two prongs: 1) the components of the machine are all available on the open market; and 2) the fundamental concept of breaking plastics into pieces and applying heated water and agitation is "widely known in the plastics industry." We find his argument flawed.

The availability of components in the open market is not dispositive. In *Coca-Cola Bottling Co. of Shreveport, Inc. v. Coca-Cola Co.*, 107 F.R.D. 288 (D.Del. 1985), the United States District Court for the District of Delaware analyzed "one of the best-kept trade secrets in the world": the complete formula for Coca-Cola. *Id.* at 289. The court explained that "although most of the ingredients are public knowledge, the ingredient that gives Coca-Cola its distinctive taste is a secret combination of flavoring oils and ingredients known as 'Merchandise 7X.'" *Id.* (citation omitted). The court further explained that it is the formula for Merchandise 7X that is tightly guarded. The formula for Merchandise 7X is only known by two persons within the Coca-Cola Company and the only written record of the formula is kept in a security vault at the Trust Company Bank in Atlanta, Georgia, which can only be opened via a resolution from the Board of Directors of Coca-Cola. See *id.*

Although the formula for the PolyCycle technology may not have been kept in a locked vault, only Bond knows the "secret formula" of how small to make the pieces of plastic, how much water to use, the appropriate temperature of the water, the proper level of agitation to apply, and the length of the agitation process. As appellee correctly points out, "[I]t is those elements, mixed and processed precisely in a certain manner, that define the PolyCycle process, just as much as the specific blend of … available ingredients defines Coca-Cola." Thus, we reject the first prong of appellant's argument.

Head Ski Co. v. Kam Ski Co., 158 F.Supp. 919 (D.Md.1958), is helpful in addressing the second prong of appellant's argument that the concept of applying heated water and agitation to pieces of broken plastic is widely known. Although *Head Ski* predates the enactment of MUTSA, it is persuasive authority. In this federal case, Head Ski Co. sought an injunction prohibiting Kam Ski Co. from using a certain manufacturing process for metal skis that the owners of Kam Ski Co. learned while employed at Head Ski Co.

Like appellant, Kam Ski Co. argued that the process it used to manufacture its skis was not Head Ski's trade secret because the process, methods, and materials it used were known and used on the open market. The court rejected that argument and explained that Kam Ski Co. "overlooks the fact that a knowledge of the particular process, method or material which is most appropriate to achieve the desired result may itself be a trade secret. So may a knowledge of the best combination of processes, methods, tools and materials." *Id.* at 923. The court further reasoned:

> Similarly, although the materials used are available for purchase by anyone, the choice of a particular material was dictated by years of experimenting. Tests of a ski purchased on the open market would have disclosed many of the secrets, if one knew which tests were important. But the qualities for which one should test the materials are an important part of the secrets learned over the years. Defendants did not buy a Head ski on the open market and test the materials. They had learned while working for Head what materials he used, and where a test was necessary they tested material on which they had been working for Head … 'It matters not that the defendants could have gained their knowledge from a study of the expired patent and the plaintiffs' publicly marketed product. The fact is that they did not. Instead they gained

> it from the plaintiffs via the confidential relationship, and in so doing incurred a duty not to use it to the plaintiffs' detriment.' *Id.* at 922–23 (quoting *Franke v. Wiltschek*, 209 F.2d 493, 495 (2d Cir.1953)).

For the same reasons enunciated in *Head Ski*, we reject appellant's contention that the PolyCycle technology is not a trade secret just because there are other technologies that utilize the application of heated water and agitation to broken pieces of plastic. Appellant's knowledge was not acquired by a general study of technologies available in the market place. Appellant acquired his knowledge when Marks and Brown offered him the opportunity to participate in the joint venture, and later, when acting as an agent for PolyCycle, he utilized PolyCycle's funds in the development process.

After considering all of the appropriate factors identified in the Restatement, the trial court properly determined that the PolyCycle technology constituted a trade secret.

II.

Misappropriation of Trade Secret

Bond's second contention revolves around the timing of his resignation from PolyCycle. Appellant argues that, because he resigned from his position as a director and president of PolyCycle on September 24, 1997, his subsequent appropriation of the computer files, drawings, etc., could not be enjoined because he no longer owed a duty to the corporation. Appellant is mistaken. It is undisputed that appellant embarked on the development of the recycling technology for the benefit of PolyCycle. As the trial judge stated:

> The only corporate opportunity that Polycycle has is the commercialization of this process … When negotiations broke down in September of 1997, Mr. Bond decided that he had had enough … On the evening of September the 23rd, prior to resigning, he took all the work product that he had done in the preceding two years on improving this process from the computer, placed it on a floppy disc, [sic] then erased it from the company computers. He then took the disc [sic] and it appears every other piece of paper within the corporation and went down the road with it … Whether he did it on the 23rd or the 25th, I don't find of any moment in this case, and that is because what he was appropriating was the trade secret that I find belonged to the company.

* * *

The trial judge was correct in finding that the date of appellant's resignation from his position as an officer was immaterial, because the recycling technology is the property of PolyCycle. *See Homer v. Crown*

Cork & Seal Co., 155 Md. 66, 78, 141 A. 425 (1928) (characterizing a trade secret as property of a corporation). The property of the corporation could not be appropriated by Bond simply because he resigned from his position as a director and officer a day earlier.

Trade secret law governs "the owner's entitlement to relief [from] harm, or potential harm, caused when his trade secret is taken by misappropriation." George J. Alexander, *Commercial Torts* 85 (2d ed.1988) (footnote omitted). As the Supreme Court explained:

> The law … protects the holder of a trade secret against disclosure or use when the knowledge is gained, not by the owner's volition, but by some 'improper means,' Restatement of Torts § 757(a), which may include theft, wiretapping, or even aerial reconnaissance. A trade secret law, however, does not offer protection against discovery by fair and honest means, such as by independent invention, accidental disclosure, or by so-called reverse engineering, that is by starting with the known product and working backward to divine the process which aided in its development or manufacture.

Kewanee Oil Co. v. Bicron Corp., 416 U.S. 470, 475-76, 94 S.Ct. 1879, 1883, 40 L.Ed.2d 315 (1974).

Under the MUTSA, misappropriation of a trade secret includes:

> (1) Acquisition of a trade secret of another by a person who knows or has reason to know that the trade secret was acquired by improper means; or
> (2) Disclosure or use of a trade secret of another without express or implied consent by a person who:
> (i) used improper means to acquire knowledge of the trade secret; …

See CL § 11-1201(c); *see also Diamond v. T. Rowe Price Assocs.*, 852 F.Supp. 372, 412 (D.Md.1994) (holding that, "In order to qualify as misappropriation under MUTSA, one must either acquire the trade secret by improper means or disclose the trade secret without express or implied consent."). Appellant did not have either express or implied consent to disclose PolyCycle's process, or authority to abscond with PolyCycle's trade secret and use it for his own benefit after he resigned. A trade secret "constitute[s] a part of the assets …" of a corporation and as "property of the … Corporation, … [no] unauthorized person, firm, or corporation has any right to make use of them." Homer, 155 Md. at 78–79, 141 A. 425. Without authority from PolyCycle, appellant's taking of its computer files relating to the process constituted a theft, and therefore a misappropriation under CL § 11-1201. See CL § 11-1201(b).

Moreover, "[a]s a general rule, a former employee is obligated not to disclose or use the confidential information acquired during his employment." *Alexander, supra*, at 102–03; *see also Maryland Metals, Inc. v. Metzner*, 282 Md. 31, 38, 382 A.2d 564 (1978); *Inflight Newspapers, Inc. v. Magazines In-Flight* LLC, 990 F.Supp. 119, 137 (E.D.N.Y.1997); Restatement (Second) of Agency § 396(b) (1994).

Accordingly, the trial court did not err in failing to find a specific date of resignation. In light of the trial court's determination that the technology was a trade secret, knowledge of which Bond acquired while employed at PolyCycle, his date of resignation is not material.

[Footnotes Omitted.]

* * *

JUDGMENT AFFIRMED; CASE REMANDED TO THE CIRCUIT COURT FOR BALTIMORE COUNTY FOR FURTHER PROCEEDINGS CONSISTENT WITH THIS OPINION; COSTS TO BE PAID BY APPELLANT.

> *LeJeune* is another trade secrets case that applies the Maryland Uniform Trade Secrets Act. In this case, the trade secrets consist of a company's pricing and cost information, strategic plan, and product specifications.

LeJEUNE v. COIN ACCEPTORS, INC.

Court of Appeals of Maryland

849 A.2d 451 (2004)

BATTAGLIA, Judge.

This case of first impression involves the provisions of the Maryland Uniform Trade Secrets Act, codified under Maryland Code, Sections 11-1201 through 11-1209 of the Commercial Law Article (1975, 2000 Repl.Vol.). William LeJeune appeals from a preliminary injunction issued by the Circuit Court for Anne Arundel County, enjoining him from working for Mars Electronics, Inc. (hereinafter "Mars") in a number of specified industries. The Circuit Court found that, if LeJeune were permitted to work in those industries, his former employer and Mars' principal competitor, Coin Acceptors, Inc. (hereinafter "Coinco"), would suffer irreparable injury because LeJeune had misappropriated trade secrets that would give Mars an unfair competitive advantage. We conclude that the evidence supports a finding of trade secret misappropriation. We also conclude, however, that the Circuit Court erred in relying on the theory of "inevitable disclosure" when ruling on the preliminary injunction. Therefore, we vacate the injunction and remand this case to the Circuit Court for further proceedings consistent with this Opinion.

I. Background

A. Facts

Coinco is a Missouri corporation in the business of designing, manufacturing, and servicing coin acceptors, coin changers, bill validators, and similar machines. Coinco divides its efforts to market and sell these machines into three separate "channels": "Vending," which includes beverage bottlers such as Coke and Pepsi; "Amusement," which includes video game manufacturers and distributors; and "Specialty Markets," which includes transit or transportation companies or companies that offer "self-check-out" services.

* * *

While employed with Coinco, LeJeune never entered into a non-compete or confidentiality agreement with Coinco. He worked in sales and was not involved in manufacturing or research and development. He did, however, develop an extensive understanding of Coinco's products through his service and sales experience. He also learned of Coinco's pricing, pricing strategies, marketing and business initiatives, and selling strategies but was not privy to all information relating to Coinco's contracts with customers. LeJeune worked from his home in Annapolis, where he regularly received company documents.

* * *

In addition to the computer files, LeJeune also retained hard copies of a number of other Coinco documents. Included among those documents were Coinco's price and cost information, Coinco's service pricing, a list of Coinco's preferred distributors, and detailed technical specifications relating to a Coinco's amusement product, the MC2600, and a Coinco vending product, the Bill Pro Validator. The pricing and cost information is sensitive because Coinco uses a tiered-pricing system.

Coinco's efforts to maintain the confidentiality of company information included limiting access to company documents to only personnel who needed to know the information. To this end, Coinco guarded the computer files on its mainframe computer with a password system, which allowed Coinco to control the employees' access to company information. Coinco also negotiates "non-disclosure" agreements with many of its clients to ensure that those clients do not share pricing information with other Coinco customers or Coinco competitors. In addition, Coinco's "Employee Handbook" states that its business methods are "proprietary," and employees should protect such information as confidential. Many of Coinco's pricing documents and other strategic information, including information at issue in this case (i.e., the Specialty Markets Strategic Plan, pricing and cost documents, and Bill Pro Validator specifications), were marked "confidential."

LeJeune stated that he did not discuss proprietary Coinco information, such as Coinco's price list, customer list, or strategic plan, with anyone at Mars. According to LeJeune, he did not know that Coinco was concerned about his knowledge of confidential information until he learned of Coinco's suit against him, at which time he returned all of the alleged confidential Coinco documents and files.

* * *

III. Discussion

A. Maryland Uniform Trade Secrets Act

* * *

Long before the enactment of the Maryland Uniform Trade Secrets Act in 1989, Maryland and other jurisdictions within and outside the United States had regulated the protection of trade secrets. *See* MILTON E. BABIRAK, JR., *The Maryland Uniform Trade Secrets Act: A Critical Summary of the Act and Case Law*, 31 U. BALT. L.REV. 181, 183 (2002) (hereinafter "Babirak"). One scholar has submitted that, even under Roman law, a businessperson had a cause of action against a competitor who enticed the businessperson's slave to divulge confidential business information. *Id.* (citing A. ARTHUR SCHILLER, *Trade Secrets and the Roman Law: The Actio Servi Corrupti*, 30 COLUM. L.REV. 837, 838 n. 5 (1930)). At least since 1837, when the court in *Vickery v. Welch*, 36 Mass. 523 (1837) ordered the seller of a chocolate mill not to disclose his secret chocolate-making formula to anyone other than the buyer of the mill, courts in the United States have taken action to protect the secrecy of a type of confidential business information called "trade secrets." *See Babirak* at 184.

* * *

1. Coinco's Trade Secrets

We begin by examining whether the alleged trade secrets in this case qualify as such under the Maryland Uniform Trade Secrets Act (hereinafter "MUTSA"). LeJeune posits that Coinco failed to make reasonable efforts to protect the secrecy of its information; therefore, according to LeJeune, the documents and information that he retained do not qualify as trade secrets. On the other hand, Coinco alleges that numerous computer files and documents that LeJeune had in his possession were confidential, proprietary items that meet the definition of "trade secrets." In particular, Coinco complains that, of the computer files taken by LeJeune, the Executable Budgeting Software and Special Markets Strategic Marketing Plan were trade secrets. Coinco also claims that LeJeune retained trade secrets in hard-copy form, including pricing and cost information, service pricing information, a list of preferred distributors, and specifications of the MC2600 and Bill Pro Validator.

Section 11-1201(e) of MUTSA defines the term "trade secret" to mean:

information, including a formula, pattern, compilation, program, device, method, technique, or process that:

(1) Derives independent economic value, actual or potential, from not being generally known to, and not being readily ascertainable by proper means by, other persons who can obtain economic value from its disclosure or use; and

(2) Is the subject of efforts that are reasonable under the circumstances to maintain its secrecy.

Section 11-1201(e) of MUTSA.

* * *

*** Therefore, Coinco's cost and profit information, if available to Mars, could allow Mars to undercut all of Coinco's prices, giving Mars an easy economic advantage. Because of the unique, competitive nature of the currency acceptor industry, the detailed specifications of the MC2600 and Bill Pro Validator also had economic value to Mars. Should Mars learn the technology used in those machines, it could apply that technology to improve the commercial value of its own products.

We have identified no evidence suggesting that Mars, without spending a great deal of resources, could obtain all of this information from the marketplace. Indeed, Coinco is a privately held company and does not release its profit information in public filings with the Securities and Exchange Commission. The evidence supports a finding that the information contained in the computer files and hard-copy documents (i.e., the budgeting software, Specialty Markets Strategic Plan, pricing and cost documents, and MC2600 and Bill Pro Validator specifications) had economic value to Mars and was not "readily ascertainable."

Furthermore, it is apparent from the record that Coinco took reasonable measures to maintain the secrecy of the pricing and cost information, Specialty Markets Strategic Plan, and machine specifications. Because of its tiered pricing scheme, Coinco negotiated non-disclosure agreements with its customers to prevent them from discussing prices with other customers. In addition, Coinco marked "confidential" on the specifications for the Bill Pro Validator as well as the Specialty Markets Strategic Plan and other pricing documents that LeJeune either burned or kept in hard copy form. In the company's employee handbook, Coinco communicated the secret nature of its manufacturing processes and business methods by requiring employees to protect such information as confidential. In light of these efforts, we hold that the trial court appropriately determined that the specifications of the MC2600 and Bill Pro Validator as well as the pricing and cost data contained on the Specialty Markets Strategic Plan, Executable Budgeting Software, and other hardcopy pricing documents qualify as trade secrets under MUTSA.

* * *

PRELIMINARY INJUNCTION VACATED; CASE REMANDED TO THE CIRCUIT COURT FOR ANNE ARUNDEL COUNTY FOR FURTHER PROCEEDINGS CONSISTENT WITH THIS OPINION; COSTS TO BE PAID BY APPELLEE.

[Footnotes Omitted.]

Sample Clause from a Non-Disclosure Agreement

Non-disclosure agreements (NDA) are signed by companies or individuals interested in sharing confidential information with each other, often as the precursor to doing business with each other. The agreements generally define what the confidential information is, what the parties to the NDA can and cannot do with that information, how long the confidential information must be protected, and what the remedies for any breach of the NDA are. The following is a sample clause from an NDA referencing trade secrets.

"The duty to protect all Confidential Information disclosed hereunder will continue for five (5) years or until the Confidential Information becomes publicly known or is made generally available through no action of Receiving Party or its employees, whichever comes sooner. Notwithstanding the foregoing, to the extent that the Disclosing Party has disclosed information that constitutes a trade secret, the Receiving Party agrees to keep confidential such trade secret for as long as the information qualifies as a trade secret under law."

Trademarks

The following Q & A excerpts are from the U.S. Patent and Trademark Office's Trademark FAQ webpage (http://www.uspto.gov/faq/trademarks.jsp). Note that each state has its own trademark registration policies and procedures for people only interested in protecting a trademark on the state level (http://www.uspto.gov/trademarks/process/State_Trademark_Links.jsp). A discussion on the protection of a trademark is included in Chapter 11 under the section entitled "Fashion and Trademark Protection."

What is a trademark?

A trademark is a word, phrase, symbol or design, or a combination thereof, that identifies and distinguishes the source of the goods of one party from those of others.

What is a service mark?

A service mark is a word, phrase, symbol or design, or a combination thereof, that identifies and distinguishes the source of a service rather than goods. The term "trademark" is often used to refer to both trademarks and service marks.

What is a certification mark?

A certification mark is any word, phrase, symbol or design, or a combination thereof owned by one party who certifies the goods and services of others when they meet certain standards. The owner of the mark exercises control over the use of the mark; however, because the sole purpose of a certification mark is to indicate that certain standards have been met, use of the mark is by others.

Must I register my trademark?

No. You can establish rights in a mark based on use of the mark in commerce, without a registration. However, owning a federal trademark registration on the Principal Register provides several important benefits.

What are the benefits of federal trademark registration?

Owning a federal trademark registration on the Principal Register provides several advantages, including:

- Public notice of your claim of ownership of the mark;
- A legal presumption of your ownership of the mark and your exclusive right to use the mark nationwide on or in connection with the goods/services listed in the registration;
- The ability to bring an action concerning the mark in federal court;
- The use of the U.S. registration as a basis to obtain registration in foreign countries;
- The ability to record the U.S. registration with the U.S. Customs and Border Protection (CBP) Service to prevent importation of infringing foreign goods;
- The right to use the federal registration symbol ® and
- Listing in the United States Patent and Trademark Office's online databases.

Do federal regulations govern the use of the designations "TM" or "SM" or the ® symbol?

If you claim rights to use a mark, you may use the "TM" (trademark) or "SM" (service mark) designation to alert the public to your claim of ownership of the mark, regardless of whether you have filed an application with the United States Patent and Trademark Office (USPTO). However, you may only use the federal registration symbol "®" after the USPTO actually *registers a mark*, and not while an application is pending.

Can you register the name of a musical group or band?

A band name may function as a service mark for "entertainment services in the nature of performances by a musical group" if it is used to identify live performances.

Is registration of my mark guaranteed?

No. The examining attorney will review the application and may issue refusals based on the Trademark Act of 1946, 15 U.S.C. §1051 *et seq.*, or the *Trademark Rules of Practice*, 37 C.F.R. Part 2. The most common reasons for refusing registration are because the mark is:

- Likely to cause confusion with a mark in a registration or prior application;
- Descriptive for the goods/services;
- A geographic term;
- A surname;
- Ornamental as applied to the goods.

* * *

How long does a trademark registration last?

The registration is valid as long as you timely file all post registration maintenance documents. You must file a "Declaration of Use under Section 8" between the fifth and sixth year following registration. In addition, you must file a combined "Declaration of Use and Application for Renewal under Sections 8 and 9" between the ninth and tenth year after registration, and every 10 years thereafter.

Is a federal registration valid outside of the United States?

No. However, certain countries recognize a United States registration as a basis for filing an application to register a mark in those countries under international treaties.

Disparagement

Trademarks that are disparaging are not allowed to be registered with the USPTO.

The Lanham Act, Section 2(a), states that an applicant will not be refused registration of a trademark unless it "… [c]onsists of or comprises immoral, deceptive, or scandalous matter; or matter which may disparage or falsely suggest a connection with persons, living or dead, institutions, beliefs, or national symbols, or bring them into contempt, or disrepute …"

In 1992, a group of Native Americans filed a petition to invalidate the trademarks of the Washington Redskins under Section 2(a). As outlined in *Harjo v. Pro-Football, Inc.* below, the Native American petitioners claimed that both the word "redskin(s)" and the team logos were "pejorative, derogatory, denigrating, offensive, scandalous, contemptuous, disreputable, disparaging and racist …"

In a 145-page decision issued in 1998 (http://des.uspto.gov/Foia/ReterivePdf?flNm=92021069-04-02-1999&system=TTABIS) by the Trademark Trial and Appeal Board (TTAB), the trademarks of the Washington Redskins were cancelled. In their deliberations, the TTAB discussed the tests of disparagement and scandalousness as follows:

Disparagement Test: "Then, to determine whether matter may be disparaging, we undertake a two step process of considering, first, the likely meaning of the matter in question and, second, whether that meaning may be disparaging."

Scandalousness Test: "First, the Court or Board determines the likely meaning of the matter in question and, second, whether, in view of the likely meaning, the matter is scandalous to a substantial composite of the general public."

Furthermore, regarding contempt and disrepute, the TTAB referred to the Disparagement Test. "We incorporate by reference our preceding analysis, discussion of the facts, and conclusions with respect to disparagement. As we have indicated, *supra*, the guidelines for determining whether matter in the marks in the challenged registrations may be disparaging to Native Americans are equally applicable to determining whether such matter brings Native Americans into contempt or disrepute."

Pro-Football, Inc., the owner of the Redskins' trademarks, appealed. Ultimately, a decision by the U.S. Court of Appeals, 565 F.3d 880 (D.C. Cir. 2009), allowed Pro-Football, Inc. to maintain its trademarks due to an issue with the timing of the filing of the case, known as laches.

U.S. DEPARTMENT OF COMMERCE PATENT AND TRADEMARK OFFICE

Trademark Trial and Appeal Board

HARJO v. PRO-FOOTBALL, INC.

Cancellation No. 21,069 to Registration Nos. 1,606,810;
1,085,092; 987,127; 986,668; 978,824; and 836,122
Before Sams, Cissel and Walters, Administrative Trademark Judges

* * *

Introduction

Suzan Shown Harjo, Raymond D. Apodaca, Vine Deloria, Jr., Norbert S. Hill, Jr., Mateo Romero, William A. Means, and Manley A. Begay, Jr. filed their petition to cancel the registrations of the marks identified below, all owned by Pro-Football, Inc.:

> THE WASHINGTON REDSKINS and REDSKINS for
> "entertainment services—namely, presentations
> of professional football contests";

REDSKINETTES for "entertainment services, namely, cheerleaders who perform dance routines at professional football games and exhibitions and other personal appearances";

The Redskins

for "entertainment services—namely, football exhibitions rendered live in stadia and through the media of radio and television broadcasts";

and the following two marks for "entertainment services—namely, presentations of professional football contests":

WASHINGTON

REDSKINS

and

The Redskins

Petitioners allege that they are Native American persons and enrolled members of federally recognized Indian tribes. As grounds for cancellation, petitioners assert that the word "redskin(s)" or a form of that word appears in the mark in each of the registrations sought to be canceled; that the word "redskin(s)" "was and is a pejorative, derogatory, denigrating, offensive, scandalous, contemptuous, disreputable, disparaging and racist designation for a Native American person"; that the marks in Registration Nos. 986,668 and 987,127 "also include additional matter that, in the context used by registrant, is offensive, disparaging and scandalous"; and that registrant's use of the marks in the identified registrations "offends" petitioners and other Native Americans. Petitioners assert, further, that the marks in the identified registrations "consist of or comprise matter which disparages Native American persons, and brings them into contempt, ridicule, and disrepute" and "consist of or comprise scandalous matter"; and that, therefore, under Section 2(a) of the Trademark Act, 15 U.S.C. 1052(a), the identified registrations should be canceled.

Respondent, in its answer, denies the salient allegations of the petition to cancel and asserts that "through long, substantial and widespread use, advertising and promotion in support thereof and media coverage, said marks have acquired a strong secondary meaning identifying the entertainment services provided by respondent in the form of professional games in the National Football League"; and that "the marks sought to be canceled herein cannot reasonably be understood to refer to the Petitioners or to any of the groups or organizations to which they belong [as] the marks refer to the Washington Redskins football team which is owned by Respondent and thus cannot be interpreted as disparaging any of the Petitioners or as bringing them into contempt or disrepute."

* * *

Decision: As to each of the registrations subject to the petition to cancel herein, the petition to cancel under Section 2(a) of the Act is granted on the grounds that the subject marks may disparage Native Americans and may bring them into contempt or disrepute. As to each of the registrations subject to the petition to cancel herein, the petition to cancel under Section 2(a) of the Act is denied on the ground that the subject marks consist of or comprise scandalous matter. The registrations will be canceled in due course.

[Footnotes Omitted.]

Author's note: Another group of Native Americans has filed a petition that is currently before the TTAB, based on essentially the same claims as *Harjo*. The case is *Blackhorse v. Pro-Football, Inc.* and the petition can be found at http://64.38.12.138/docs/blackhorse081106.pdf.

Copyrights

The following excerpts are from *Copyright Basics*, a publication of the U.S. Copyright Office (http://www.copyright.gov/circs/circ01.pdf).

What Is Copyright?

Copyright is a form of protection provided by the laws of the United States (title 17, *U. S. Code*) to the authors of "original works of authorship," including literary, dramatic, musical, artistic, and certain other intellectual works. This protection is available to both published and unpublished works. Section 106 of the 1976 Copyright Act generally gives the owner of copyright the exclusive right to do and to authorize others to do the following:

- reproduce the work in copies or phonorecords
- prepare derivative works based upon the work
- distribute copies or phonorecords of the work to the public by sale or other transfer of ownership, or by rental, lease, or lending
- perform the work publicly, in the case of literary, musical, dramatic, and choreographic works, pantomimes, and motion pictures and other audiovisual works
- display the work publicly, in the case of literary, musical, dramatic, and choreographic works, pantomimes, and pictorial, graphic, or sculptural works, including the individual images of a motion picture or other audiovisual work
- perform the work publicly (in the case of sound recordings*) by means of a digital audio transmission

In addition, certain authors of works of visual art have the rights of attribution and integrity as described in section 106A of the 1976 Copyright Act. For further information, see Circular 40, *Copyright Registration for Works of the Visual Arts*.

It is illegal for anyone to violate any of the rights provided by the copyright law to the owner of copyright. These rights, however, are not unlimited in scope. Sections 107 through 122 of the 1976 Copyright Act establish limitations on these rights. In some cases, these limitations are specified exemptions from copyright liability. One major limitation is the doctrine of "fair use," which is given a statutory basis in section 107 of the 1976 Copyright Act. In other instances, the limitation takes the form of a "compulsory license" under which certain limited uses of copyrighted works are permitted upon payment of specified royalties and compliance with statutory conditions. For further information about the limitations of any of these rights, consult the copyright law or write to the Copyright Office.

***Note: Sound recordings are defined in the law as "works that result from the fixation of a series of musical, spoken, or other sounds, but not including the sounds accompanying a motion picture or other audiovisual work." Common examples include recordings of music, drama, or lectures. A sound recording is not the same as a phonorecord. A phonorecord is the physical object in which works of authorship are embodied. The word "phonorecord" includes cassette tapes, CDs, and vinyl disks as well as other formats.**

Who Can Claim Copyright?

Copyright protection subsists from the time the work is created in fixed form. The copyright in the work of authorship immediately becomes the property of the author who created the work. Only the author or those deriving their rights through the author can rightfully claim copyright.

In the case of works made for hire, the employer and not the employee is considered to be the author. Section 101 of the copyright law defines a "work made for hire" as:

1. a work prepared by an employee within the scope of his or her employment; or
2. a work specially ordered or commissioned for use as:
   - a contribution to a collective work
   - a part of a motion picture or other audiovisual work
   - a translation
   - a supplementary work
   - a compilation
   - an instructional text
   - a test
   - answer material for a test
   - an atlas

if the parties expressly agree in a written instrument signed by them that the work shall be considered a work made for hire.

The authors of a joint work are co-owners of the copyright in the work, unless there is an agreement to the contrary.

Copyright in each separate contribution to a periodical or other collective work is distinct from copyright in the collective work as a whole and vests initially with the author of the contribution.

Two General Principles

- Mere ownership of a book, manuscript, painting, or any other copy or phonorecord does not give the possessor the copyright. The law provides that transfer of ownership of any material object that embodies a protected work does not of itself convey any rights in the copyright.

- Minors may claim copyright, but state laws may regulate the business dealings involving copyrights owned by minors. For information on relevant state laws, consult an attorney.

* * *

What Works Are Protected?

Copyright protects "original works of authorship" that are fixed in a tangible form of expression. The fixation need not be directly perceptible so long as it may be communicated with the aid of a machine or device. Copyrightable works include the following categories:

1. literary works
2. musical works, including any accompanying words
3. dramatic works, including any accompanying music
4. pantomimes and choreographic works
5. pictorial, graphic, and sculptural works
6. motion pictures and other audiovisual works
7. sound recordings
8. architectural works

These categories should be viewed broadly. For example, computer programs and most "compilations" may be registered as "literary works"; maps and architectural plans may be registered as "pictorial, graphic, and sculptural works."

What Is Not Protected by Copyright?

Several categories of material are generally not eligible for federal copyright protection. These include among others:

- Works that have not been fixed in a tangible form of expression (for example, choreographic works that have not been notated or recorded, or improvisational speeches or performances that have not been written or recorded)
- Titles, names, short phrases, and slogans; familiar symbols or designs; mere variations of typographic ornamentation, lettering, or coloring; mere listings of ingredients or contents
- Ideas, procedures, methods, systems, processes, concepts, principles, discoveries, or devices, as distinguished from a description, explanation, or illustration
- Works consisting entirely of information that is common property and containing no original authorship (for example: standard calendars, height and weight charts, tape measures and rulers, and lists or tables taken from public documents or other common sources)

How to Secure a Copyright

Copyright Secured Automatically upon Creation

The way in which copyright protection is secured is frequently misunderstood. No publication or registration or other action in the Copyright Office is required to secure copyright. See the following note. There are, however, certain definite advantages to registration.

Copyright is secured automatically when the work is created, and a work is "created" when it is fixed in a copy or phonorecord for the first time. "Copies" are material objects from which a work can be read or visually perceived either directly or with the aid of a machine or device, such as books, manuscripts, sheet music, film, videotape, or microfilm. "Phonorecords" are material objects embodying fixations of sounds (excluding, by statutory definition, motion picture soundtracks), such as cassette tapes, CDs, or vinyl disks. Thus, for example, a song (the "work") can be fixed in sheet music ("copies") or in phonograph disks ("phonorecords"), or both. If a work is prepared over a period of time, the part of the work that is fixed on a particular date constitutes the created work as of that date.

* * *

Notice of Copyright

The use of a copyright notice is no longer required under U. S. law, although it is often beneficial. Because prior law did contain such a requirement, however, the use of notice is still relevant to the copyright status of older works.

Notice was required under the 1976 Copyright Act. This requirement was eliminated when the United States adhered to the Berne Convention, effective March 1, 1989. Although works published without notice before that date could have entered the public domain in the United States, the Uruguay Round Agreements Act (URAA) restores copyright in certain foreign works originally published without notice. For further information about copyright amendments in the URAA, see Circular 38b.

The Copyright Office does not take a position on whether copies of works first published with notice before March 1, 1989, which are distributed on or after March 1, 1989, must bear the copyright notice.

Use of the notice may be important because it informs the public that the work is protected by copyright, identifies the copyright owner, and shows the year of first publication. Furthermore, in the event that a work is infringed, if a proper notice of copyright appears on the published copy or copies to which a defendant in a copyright infringement suit had access, then no weight shall be given to such a defendant's interposition of a defense based on innocent infringement in mitigation of actual or statutory damages, except as provided in section 504(c)(2) of the copyright law. Innocent infringement occurs when the infringer did not realize that the work was protected.

The use of the copyright notice is the responsibility of the copyright owner and does not require advance permission from, or registration with, the Copyright Office.

Form of Notice for Visually Perceptible Copies

The notice for visually perceptible copies should contain all the following three elements:

1. The symbol © (the letter C in a circle), or the word "Copyright," or the abbreviation "Copr."; *and*
2. The year of first publication of the work. In the case of compilations or derivative works incorporating previously published material, the year date of first publication of the compilation or derivative work is sufficient. The year date may be omitted where a pictorial, graphic, or sculptural work, with accompanying textual matter, if any, is reproduced in or on greeting cards, postcards, stationery, jewelry, dolls, toys, or any useful article; *and*
3. The name of the owner of copyright in the work, or an abbreviation by which the name can be recognized, or a generally known alternative designation of the owner.

Example: © *2010 John Doe*

The "C in a circle" notice is used only on "visually perceptible copies." Certain kinds of works—for example, musical, dramatic, and literary works—may be fixed not in "copies" but by means of sound in an audio recording. Since audio recordings such as audio tapes and phonograph disks are "phonorecords" and not "copies," the "C in a circle" notice is not used to indicate protection of the underlying musical, dramatic, or literary work that is recorded.

Form of Notice for Phonorecords of Sound Recordings

The notice for phonorecords embodying a sound recording should contain all the following three elements:

1. The symbol ℗ (the letter P in a circle); *and*

2. The year of first publication of the sound recording; *and*

3. The name of the owner of copyright in the sound recording, or an abbreviation by which the name can be recognized, or a generally known alternative designation of the owner. If the producer of the sound recording is named on the phonorecord label or container and if no other name appears in conjunction with the notice, the producer's name shall be considered a part of the notice.

Example: ℗ *2010 A.B.C. Records Inc.*

* * *

Position of Notice

The copyright notice should be affixed to copies or phonorecords in such a way as to "give reasonable notice of the claim of copyright." The three elements of the notice should ordinarily appear together on the copies or phonorecords or on the phonorecord label or container. The Copyright Office has issued regulations concerning the form and position of the copyright notice in the *Code of Federal Regulations* (37 *CFR* 201.20). For more information, see Circular 3, *Copyright Notice*.

* * *

How Long Copyright Protection Endures

Works Originally Created on or after January 1, 1978

A work that was created (fixed in tangible form for the first time) on or after January 1, 1978, is automatically protected from the moment of its creation and is ordinarily given a term enduring for the author's life plus an additional 70 years after the author's death. In the case of "a joint work prepared by two or more authors who did not work for hire," the term lasts for 70 years after the last surviving author's death. For works made for hire, and for anonymous and pseudonymous works (unless the author's identity is revealed in Copyright Office records), the duration of copyright will be 95 years from publication or 120 years from creation, whichever is shorter.

Works Originally Created Before January 1, 1978, But Not Published or Registered by That Date

These works have been automatically brought under the statute and are now given federal copyright protection. The duration of copyright in these works is generally computed in the same way as for works created on or after January 1, 1978:

the life-plus-70 or 95/120-year terms apply to them as well. The law provides that in no case would the term of copyright for works in this category expire before December 31, 2002, and for works published on or before December 31, 2002, the term of copyright will not expire before December 31, 2047.

Works Originally Created and Published or Registered before January 1, 1978

Under the law in effect before 1978, copyright was secured either on the date a work was published with a copyright notice or on the date of registration if the work was registered in unpublished form. In either case, the copyright endured for a first term of 28 years from the date it was secured. During the last (28th) year of the first term, the copyright was eligible for renewal. The Copyright Act of 1976 extended the renewal term from 28 to 47 years for copyrights that were subsisting on January 1, 1978, or for pre-1978 copyrights restored under the Uruguay Round Agreements Act (URAA), making these works eligible for a total term of protection of 75 years. Public Law 105-298, enacted on October 27, 1998, further extended the renewal term of copyrights still subsisting on that date by an additional 20 years, providing for a renewal term of 67 years and a total term of protection of 95 years.

Public Law 102-307, enacted on June 26, 1992, amended the 1976 Copyright Act to provide for automatic renewal of the term of copyrights secured between January 1, 1964, and December 31, 1977. Although the renewal term is automatically provided, the Copyright Office does not issue a renewal certificate for these works unless a renewal application and fee are received and registered in the Copyright Office.

Public Law 102-307 makes renewal registration optional. Thus, filing for renewal registration is no longer required to extend the original 28-year copyright term to the full 95 years. However, some benefits accrue to renewal registrations that were made during the 28th year.

For more detailed information on renewal of copyright and the copyright term, see Circular 15, *Renewal of Copyright*; Circular 15a, *Duration of Copyright*; and Circular 15t, *Extension of Copyright Terms.*

* * *

International Copyright Protection

There is no such thing as an "international copyright" that will automatically protect an author's writings throughout the entire world. Protection against unauthorized use in a particular country depends, basically, on the national laws of that country. However, most countries do offer protection to foreign works under certain conditions, and these conditions have been greatly simplified by international copyright treaties and conventions. For further information and a list of countries that maintain copyright relations with the United States, see Circular 38a, *International Copyright Relations of the United States.*

Copyright Registration

In general, copyright registration is a legal formality intended to make a public record of the basic facts of a particular copyright. However, registration is not a condition of copyright protection. Even though registration is not a requirement for protection, the copyright law provides several inducements or advantages to encourage copyright owners to make registration. Among these advantages are the following:

- Registration establishes a public record of the copyright claim.
- Before an infringement suit may be filed in court, registration is necessary for works of U. S. origin.

- If made before or within five years of publication, registration will establish prima facie evidence in court of the validity of the copyright and of the facts stated in the certificate.
- If registration is made within three months after publication of the work or prior to an infringement of the work, statutory damages and attorney's fees will be available to the copyright owner in court actions. Otherwise, only an award of actual damages and profits is available to the copyright owner.
- Registration allows the owner of the copyright to record the registration with the U. S. Customs Service for protection against the importation of infringing copies. For additional information, go to the U. S. Customs and Border Protection website at *www.cbp.gov/*.

Registration may be made at any time within the life of the copyright. Unlike the law before 1978, when a work has been registered in unpublished form, it is not necessary to make another registration when the work becomes published, although the copyright owner may register the published edition, if desired.

Selle v. Gibb provides a good overview of the issues involved in a copyright infringement case. In this case, the Bee Gees were sued for copyright infringement for their song "How Deep Is Your Love."

SELLE v. GIBB

United States Court of Appeals, Seventh Circuit
741 F.2d 896 (1984)

CUDAHY, Circuit Judge.

The plaintiff, Ronald H. Selle, brought a suit against three brothers, Maurice, Robin and Barry Gibb, known collectively as the popular singing group, the Bee Gees, alleging that the Bee Gees, in their hit tune, "How Deep Is Your Love," had infringed the copyright of his song, "Let It End." The jury returned a verdict in plaintiff's favor on the issue of liability in a bifurcated trial. The district court, Judge George N. Leighton, granted the defendants' motion for judgment notwithstanding the verdict and, in the alternative, for a new trial. *Selle v. Gibb*, 567 F.Supp. 1173 (N.D.Ill.1983). We affirm the grant of the motion for judgment notwithstanding the verdict.

I

Selle composed his song, "Let It End," in one day in the fall of 1975 and obtained a copyright for it on November 17, 1975. He played his song with his small band two or three times in the Chicago area and sent a tape and lead sheet of the music to eleven music recording and publishing companies. Eight of the companies returned the materials to Selle; three did not respond. This was the extent of the public dissemination of Selle's song. Selle first became aware of the Bee Gees' song, "How Deep Is Your Love," in May 1978 and thought that he recognized the music as his own, although the lyrics were different. He also saw the movie, "Saturday Night Fever," the sound track of which features the song "How Deep Is Your Love," and again recognized the music. He subsequently sued the three Gibb brothers; Paramount Pictures Corporation, which made and distributed the movie; and Phonodisc, Inc., now known as Polygram Distribution, Inc., which made and distributed the cassette tape of "How Deep Is Your Love."

The Bee Gees are internationally known performers and creators of popular music. They have composed more than 160 songs; their sheet music, records and tapes have been distributed worldwide, some of the albums selling more than 30 million copies. The Bee Gees, however, do not themselves read or write music. In composing a song, their practice was to tape a tune, which members of their staff would later transcribe and reduce to a form suitable for copyrighting, sale and performance by both the Bee Gees and others.

In addition to their own testimony at trial, the Bee Gees presented testimony by their manager, Dick Ashby, and two musicians, Albhy Galuten and Blue Weaver, who were on the Bee Gees' staff at the time "How Deep Is Your Love" was composed. These witnesses described in detail how, in January 1977, the Bee Gees and several members of their staff went to a recording studio in the Chateau d'Herouville about 25 miles northwest of Paris. There the group composed at least six new songs and mixed a live album. Barry Gibb's testimony included a detailed explanation of a work tape which was introduced into evidence and played in court. This tape preserves the actual process of creation during which the brothers, and particularly Barry, created the tune of the accused song while Weaver, a keyboard player, played the tune which was hummed or sung by the brothers. Although the tape does not seem to preserve the very beginning of the process of creation, it does depict the process by which ideas, notes, lyrics and bits of the tune were gradually put together.

Following completion of this work tape, a demo tape was made. The work tape, demo tape and a vocal-piano version taken from the demo tape are all in the key of E flat. Lead sheet music, dated March 6, 1977, is in the key of E. On March 7, 1977, a lead sheet of "How Deep Is Your Love" was filed for issuance of a United States copyright, and in November 1977, a piano-vocal arrangement was filed in the Copyright Office.

The only expert witness to testify at trial was Arrand Parsons, a professor of music at Northwestern University who has had extensive professional experience primarily in classical music. He has been a program annotator for the Chicago Symphony Orchestra and the New Orleans Symphony Orchestra and has authored works about musical theory. Prior to this case, however, he had never made a comparative analysis of two popular songs. Dr. Parsons testified on the basis of several charts comparing the musical notes of each song and a comparative recording prepared under his direction.

According to Dr. Parsons' testimony, the first eight bars of each song (Theme A) have twenty-four of thirty-four notes in plaintiff's composition and twenty-four of forty notes in defendants' composition which are identical in pitch and symmetrical position. Of thirty-five rhythmic impulses in plaintiff's composition and forty in defendants', thirty are identical. In the last four bars of both songs (Theme B), fourteen notes in each are identical in pitch, and eleven of the fourteen rhythmic impulses are identical. Both Theme A and Theme B appear in the same position in each song but with different intervening material.

Dr. Parsons testified that, in his opinion, "the two songs had such striking similarities that they could not have been written independent of one another." Tr. 202. He also testified that he did not know of two songs by different composers "that contain as many striking similarities" as do the two songs at issue here. However, on several occasions, he declined to say that the similarities could only have resulted from copying.

Following presentation of the case, the jury returned a verdict for the plaintiff on the issue of liability, the only question presented to the jury. Judge Leighton, however, granted the defendants' motion for judgment notwithstanding the verdict and, in the alternative, for a new trial. He relied primarily on the plaintiff's inability to demonstrate that the defendants had access to the plaintiff's song, without which a claim of copyright infringement could not prevail regardless how similar the two compositions are. Further, the plaintiff failed to contradict or refute the testimony of the defendants and their witnesses describing the independent creation process of "How Deep Is Your Love." Finally, Judge Leighton concluded that "the inferences on which plaintiff relies is not a logical, permissible deduction from proof of 'striking similarity' or substantial similarity; it is 'at war with the undisputed facts,' and it is inconsistent with the proof of nonaccess to plaintiff's song by the Bee Gees at the time in question." 567 F.Supp. at 1183 (citations omitted).

II

Both we and the district court must be reluctant to remove an issue from the purview of the jury on either a directed verdict or a judgment notwithstanding the verdict. Nonetheless, we have a duty to determine whether there is sufficient evidence to support the position of the nonmoving party, in this case, the plaintiff. The standards applicable to a motion for judgment notwithstanding the verdict and to a directed verdict are, of course, the same. All the evidence, taken as a whole, must be viewed in the light most favorable to the nonmoving party. This evidence must provide a sufficient basis from which the jury could have reasonably reached a verdict without speculation or drawing unreasonable inferences which conflict with the undisputed facts.

* * *

III

Selle's primary contention on this appeal is that the district court misunderstood the theory of proof of copyright infringement on which he based his claim. Under this theory, copyright infringement can be demonstrated when, even in the absence of any direct evidence of access, the two pieces in question are so strikingly similar that access can be inferred from such similarity alone. Selle argues that the testimony of his expert witness, Dr. Parsons, was sufficient evidence of such striking similarity that it was permissible for the jury, even in the absence of any other evidence concerning access, to infer that the Bee Gees had access to plaintiff's song and indeed copied it.

In establishing a claim of copyright infringement of a musical composition, the plaintiff must prove (1) ownership of the copyright in the complaining work; (2) originality of the work; (3) copying of the work by the defendant, and (4) a substantial degree of similarity between the two works. *See* Sherman, *Musical Copyright Infringement: The Requirement of Substantial Similarity. Copyright Law Symposium*, Number 92, American Society of Composers, Authors and Publishers 81–82. Columbia University Press (1977) [hereinafter "Sherman, Musical Copyright Infringement"]. The only element which is at issue in this appeal is proof of copying; the first two elements are essentially conceded, while the fourth (substantial similarity) is, at least in these circumstances, closely related to the third element under plaintiff's theory of the case.

Proof of copying is crucial to any claim of copyright infringement because no matter how similar the two works may be (even to the point of identity), if the defendant did not copy the accused work, there is no infringement. *Arnstein v. Edward B. Marks Music Corp.*, 82 F.2d 275 (2d Cir.), motion to set aside decree denied, 86 F.2d 715 (2d Cir.1936). However, because direct evidence of copying is rarely available, the plaintiff can rely upon circumstantial evidence to prove this essential element, and the most important component of this sort of circumstantial evidence is proof of access. *See generally* 3 Nimmer, *Copyright* Sec. 13.02 at 13-9 (1983) [hereinafter "Nimmer, *Copyright*"]. The plaintiff may be able to introduce direct evidence of access when, for example, the work was sent directly to the defendant (whether a musician or a publishing company) or a close associate of the defendant. On the other hand, the plaintiff may be able to establish a reasonable possibility of access when, for example, the complaining work has been widely disseminated to the public. *See, e.g., Abkco Music, Inc. v. Harrisongs Music, Ltd.*, 722 F.2d 988, 998 (2d Cir.1983) (finding of access based on wide dissemination); Sherman, Musical Copyright Infringement, at 82.

If, however, the plaintiff does not have direct evidence of access, then an inference of access may still be established circumstantially by proof of similarity which is so striking that the possibilities of independent creation, coincidence and prior common source are, as a practical matter, precluded. If the plaintiff presents evidence of striking similarity sufficient to raise an inference of access, then copying is presumably proved simultaneously, although the fourth element (substantial similarity) still requires proof that the defendant copied a substantial amount of the complaining work. The theory which Selle attempts to apply to this case is based on proof of copying by circumstantial proof of access established by striking similarity between the two works.

One difficulty with plaintiff's theory is that no matter how great the similarity between the two works, it is not their similarity per se which establishes access; rather, their similarity tends to prove access in light of the nature of the works, the particular musical genre involved and other circumstantial evidence of access. In other words, striking similarity is just one piece of circumstantial evidence tending to show access and must not be considered in isolation; it must be considered together with other types of circumstantial evidence relating to access.

As a threshold matter, therefore, it would appear that there must be at least some other evidence which would establish a reasonable possibility that the complaining work was available to the alleged infringer. As noted, two works may be identical in every detail, but, if the alleged infringer created the accused work independently or both works were copied from a common source in the public domain, then there is no infringement. Therefore, if the plaintiff admits to having kept his or her creation under lock and key, it would seem logically impossible to infer access through striking similarity. Thus, although it has frequently been written that striking similarity alone can establish access, the decided cases suggest that this circumstance would be most unusual. The plaintiff must always present sufficient evidence to support a reasonable possibility of access because the jury cannot draw an inference of access based upon speculation and conjecture alone.

For example, in *Twentieth Century-Fox Film Corp. v. Dieckhaus*, 153 F.2d 893 (8th Cir.), cert. denied, 329 U.S. 716, 67 S.Ct. 46, 91 L.Ed. 621 (1946), the court reversed a finding of infringement based solely on the similarities between plaintiff's book and defendant's film. The court stated that the plaintiff herself presented no evidence that the defendant had had access to her book, and the only people to whom the plaintiff had given a copy of her book testified that they had not given it to the defendant. While the court also concluded that the similarities between the book and the film were not that significant, the result turned on the fact that "[t]he oral and documentary evidence in the record ... establishes the fact that the defendant had no access to plaintiff's book unless the law of plagiarism permits the court to draw an inference contrary to such proof from its finding of similarities on comparison of the book with the picture." *Id.* at 897. Thus, although proof of striking similarity may permit an inference of access, the plaintiff must still meet some minimum threshold of proof which demonstrates that the inference of access is reasonable.

The greatest difficulty perhaps arises when the plaintiff cannot demonstrate any direct link between the complaining work and the defendant but the work has been so widely disseminated that it is not unreasonable to infer that the defendant might have had access to it. In *Cholvin v. B. & F. Music Co.*, 253 F.2d 102 (7th Cir.1958), the plaintiffs' work had been distributed in 2000 professional copies of sheet music and four recordings, of which 200,000 records were sold, and it had been performed on several nationwide broadcasts. The court held that, in light of this circumstantial evidence, it was reasonable to infer, in combination with similarities between the two pieces, that there had been an infringement. In *Abkco Music, Inc. v. Harrisongs Music, Ltd.*, 722 F.2d 988, 997–99 (2d Cir.1983), the court found that there had been a copyright infringement based on a theory of subconscious copying. The complaining work, "He's So Fine," had been the most popular song in the United States for five weeks and among the thirty top hits in England for seven weeks during the year in which George Harrison composed "My Sweet Lord," the infringing song. This evidence, in addition to Harrison's own admission that the two songs were "strikingly similar," supported the finding of infringement. On the other hand, in *Jewel Music Publishing Co. v. Leo Feist, Inc.*, 62 F.Supp. 596, 598 (S.D.N.Y.1945), almost 10,000 copies of the complaining song had been distributed or sold and the music had also been broadcast on national performances. The court still concluded that the showing of access was insufficient, in combination with the other evidence, to support a reasonable inference of access.

The possibility of access in the present case is not as remote as that in *Dieckhaus* because neither side elicited testimony from the individuals (primarily employees of the publishing companies) to whom the plaintiff had distributed copies of his song. Such evidence might have conclusively disproved access. On the other hand, Selle's song certainly did not achieve the extent of public dissemination existing in *Cholvin*, *Jewel Music Publishing Co.*, or *Harrisongs Music*, and there was also no evidence that any of the defendants or their associates were in Chicago on the two or three occasions when the plaintiff played his song publicly. It is not necessary for us, given the facts of this case, to determine the number of copies which must be publicly distributed to raise a reasonable inference of access. Nevertheless, in this case, the availability of Selle's song, as shown by the evidence, was virtually de minimis.

In granting the defendants' motion for judgment notwithstanding the verdict, Judge Leighton relied primarily on the plaintiff's failure to adduce any evidence of access and stated that an inference of access may not be based on mere conjecture, speculation or a bare possibility of access. 567 F.Supp. at 1181. Thus, in *Testa v. Janssen*, 492 F.Supp. 198, 202–03 (W.D.Pa.1980), the court stated that "[t]o support a finding of access, plaintiffs' evidence must extend beyond mere speculation or conjecture. And, while circumstantial evidence is sufficient to establish access, a defendant's opportunity to view the copyrighted work must exist by a reasonable possibility—not a bare possibility" (citation omitted).

* * *

Judge Leighton thus based his decision on what he characterized as the plaintiff's inability to raise more than speculation that the Bee Gees had access to his song. The extensive testimony of the defendants and their witnesses describing the creation process went essentially uncontradicted, and there was no attempt even to impeach their credibility. Judge Leighton further relied on the principle that the testimony of credible witnesses concerning a matter within their knowledge cannot be rejected without some impeachment, contradiction or inconsistency with other evidence on the particular point at issue. *Dieckhaus, supra*, 153 F.2d at 899–900. *See also Chesapeake and Ohio Railroad Co. v. Martin*, 283 U.S. 209, 216, 51 S.Ct. 453, 456, 75 L.Ed. 983 (1931). Judge Leighton's conclusions that there was no more than a bare possibility that the defendants could have had access to Selle's song and that this was an insufficient basis from which the jury could have reasonably inferred the existence of access seem correct. The plaintiff has failed to meet even the minimum threshold of proof of the possibility of access and, as Judge Leighton has stated, an inference of access would thus seem to be "at war with the undisputed facts." 567 F.Supp. at 1183.

IV

The grant of the motion for judgment notwithstanding the verdict might, if we were so minded, be affirmed on the basis of the preceding analysis of the plaintiff's inability to establish a reasonable inference of access. This decision is also supported by a more traditional analysis of proof of access based only on the proof of "striking similarity" between the two compositions. The plaintiff relies almost exclusively on the testimony of his expert witness, Dr. Parsons, that the two pieces were, in fact, "strikingly similar." Yet formulating a meaningful definition of "striking similarity" is no simple task, and the term is often used in a conclusory or circular fashion.

Sherman defines "striking similarity" as a term of art signifying "that degree of similarity as will permit an inference of copying even in the absence of proof of access ..." Sherman, Musical Copyright Infringement, at 84 n. 15. Nimmer states that, absent proof of access, "the similarities must be so striking as to preclude the possibility that the defendant independently arrived at the same result." Nimmer, *Copyright*, at 13–14.

"Striking similarity" is not merely a function of the number of identical notes that appear in both compositions. Cf. *Wilkie v. Santly Brothers, Inc.*, 13 F.Supp. 136 (S.D.N.Y.1935), aff'd, 91 F.2d 978 (2d Cir.), cert. denied, 302 U.S. 735, 58 S.Ct. 120, 82 L.Ed. 568 (1937), aff'd on reargument, 94 F.2d 1023 (2d Cir.1938) (comparison of note structure demonstrates striking similarity), and *Jewel Music Publishing Co. v. Leo Feist, Inc.*, 62 F.Supp. 596 (S.D.N.Y.1945) (in light of plaintiff's inability to establish access, degree of similarity despite identity or near identity of several bars was not striking). An important factor in analyzing the degree of similarity of two compositions is the uniqueness of the sections which are asserted to be similar.

If the complaining work contains an unexpected departure from the normal metric structure or if the complaining work includes what appears to be an error and the accused work repeats the unexpected element or the error, then it is more likely that there is some connection between the pieces. *See, e.g., Nordstrom v. Radio Corporation of America*, 251 F.Supp. 41, 42 (D.Colo.1965). If the similar sections are particularly intricate, then again it would seem more likely that the compositions are related. Finally, some dissimilarities may be particularly suspicious. *See, e.g., Meier Co. v. Albany Novelty Manufacturing Co.*, 236 F.2d 144, 146 (2d Cir.1956) (inversion and substitution of certain words in a catalogue in a "crude effort to give the appearance of dissimilarity" are themselves evidence of copying); *Blume v. Spear*, 30 F. 629, 631 (S.D.N.Y.1887) (variations in infringing song were placed so as to indicate deliberate copying); Sherman, *Musical Copyright Infringement*, at 84–88. While some of these concepts are borrowed from literary copyright analysis, they would seem equally applicable to an analysis of music.

The judicially formulated definition of "striking similarity" states that "plaintiffs must demonstrate that 'such similarities are of a kind that can only be explained by copying, rather than by coincidence, independent creation, or prior common source.'" *Testa v. Janssen*, 492 F.Supp. 198, 203 (W.D.Pa.1980) (quoting *Stratchborneo v. Arc Music Corp.*, 357 F.Supp. 1393, 1403 (S.D.N.Y.1973)). See also *Scott v. WKJG, Inc.*, 376 F.2d 467, 469 (7th Cir.1967) (the similarities must be "so striking and of such nature as to preclude the possibility of coincidence, accident or independent creation."); *Arnstein v. Porter*, 154 F.2d 464, 468 (2d Cir.1946) (same); *Scott v. Paramount Pictures Corp.*, 449 F.Supp. 518, 520 (D.D.C.1978) (same). Sherman adds:

> To prove that certain similarities are "striking," plaintiff must show that they are the sort of similarities that cannot satisfactorily be accounted for by a theory of coincidence, independent creation, prior common source, or any theory other than that of copying. Striking similarity is an extremely technical issue—one with which, understandably, experts are best equipped to deal. Sherman, *Musical Copyright Infringement*, at 96.

Finally, the similarities should appear in a sufficiently unique or complex context as to make it unlikely that both pieces were copied from a prior common source, *Sheldon v. Metro-Goldwyn Pictures Corp.*, 81 F.2d 49, 54 (2d Cir.), cert. denied, 298 U.S. 669, 56 S.Ct. 835, 80 L.Ed. 1392 (1936), or that the defendant was able to compose the accused work as a matter of independent creation, *Nichols v. Universal Pictures Corp.*, 45 F.2d 119, 122 (2d Cir.1930), cert. denied, 282 U.S. 902, 51 S.Ct. 216, 75 L.Ed. 795 (1931). See also *Darrell v. Joe Morris Music Co.*, 113 F.2d 80 (2d Cir.1940) ("simple, trite themes ... are likely to recur spontaneously ... and [only few] ... suit the infantile demands of the popular ear"); *Arnstein v. Edward B. Marks Music Corp.*, 82 F.2d 275, 277 (2d Cir.1936). Cf. *Abkco Music, Inc. v. Harrisongs Music, Ltd.*, 722 F.2d 988, 998 (2d Cir.1983) (finding of a "highly unique pattern" makes copying more likely). With these principles in mind, we turn now to an analysis of the evidence of "striking similarity" presented by the plaintiff.

As noted, the plaintiff relies almost entirely on the testimony of his expert witness, Dr. Arrand Parsons. The defendants did not introduce any expert testimony, apparently because they did not think Parsons' testimony needed to be refuted. Defendants are perhaps to some degree correct in asserting that Parsons, although eminently qualified in the field of classical music theory, was not equally qualified to analyze popular music tunes.

More significantly, however, although Parsons used the magic formula, "striking similarity," he only ruled out the possibility of independent creation; he did not state that the similarities could only be the result of copying. In order for proof of "striking similarity" to establish a reasonable inference of access, especially in a case such as this one in which the direct proof of access is so minimal, the plaintiff must show that the similarity is of a type which will preclude any explanation other than that of copying.

In addition, to bolster the expert's conclusion that independent creation was not possible, there should be some testimony or other evidence of the relative complexity or uniqueness of the two compositions. Dr. Parsons' testimony did not refer to this aspect of the compositions and, in a field such as that of popular music in which all songs are relatively short and tend to build on or repeat a basic theme, such testimony would seem to be particularly necessary. We agree with the Sixth Circuit which explained that "we do not think the affidavit of [the expert witness], stating in conclusory terms that 'it is extremely unlikely that one set [of architectural plans] could have been prepared without access to the other set,' can fill the gap which is created by the absence of any direct evidence of access." *Scholz Homes, Inc. v. Maddox*, 379 F.2d 84, 86 (6th Cir.1967).

To illustrate this deficiency more concretely, we refer to a cassette tape, Plaintiff's Exhibit 27, and the accompanying chart, Plaintiff's Exhibit 26. These exhibits were prepared by the defendants but introduced into evidence by the plaintiff. The tape has recorded on it segments of both themes from both the Selle and the Gibb songs interspersed with segments of other compositions as diverse as "Footsteps," "From Me To You" (a Lennon-McCartney piece), Beethoven's 5th Symphony, "Funny Talk," "Play Down," and "I'd Like To Leave If I May" (the last two being earlier compositions by Barry Gibb). There are at least superficial similarities among these segments, when played on the same musical instrument, and the plaintiff failed to elicit any testimony from his expert witness about this exhibit which compared the Selle and the Gibb songs to other pieces of contemporary, popular music. These circumstances indicate that the plaintiff failed to sustain his burden of proof on the issue of "striking similarity" in its legal sense—that is, similarity which reasonably precludes the possibility of any explanation other than that of copying.

The plaintiff's expert witness does not seem to have addressed any issues relating to the possibility of prior common source in both widely disseminated popular songs and the defendants' own compositions. At oral argument, plaintiff's attorney stated that the burden of proving common source should be on the defendant; however, the burden of proving "striking similarity," which, by definition, includes taking steps to minimize the possibility of common source, is on the plaintiff. In essence, the plaintiff failed to prove to the requisite degree that the similarities identified by the expert witness—although perhaps "striking" in a non-legal sense—were of a type which would eliminate any explanation of coincidence, independent creation or common source, including, in this case, the possibility of common source in earlier compositions created by the Bee Gees themselves or by others. In sum, the evidence of striking similarity is not sufficiently compelling to make the case when the proof of access must otherwise depend largely upon speculation and conjecture.

Therefore, because the plaintiff failed both to establish a basis from which the jury could reasonably infer that the Bee Gees had access to his song and to meet his burden of proving "striking similarity" between the two compositions, the grant by the district court of the defendants' motion for judgment notwithstanding the verdict is affirmed. Because of our doubts concerning the defendants' cross-appeal on the denial of the summary judgment, we order that, under Fed.R.App.P. 38, each party shall bear its own costs.

[Footnotes Omitted.]

Sampling

Recording artists often sample ("taking portions of earlier musical compositions and sound recordings and transforming, adapting, or piecing them together to create new works") other artists' recordings to use in their own music. The following article discusses the legal issues surrounding sampling. For additional information on compulsory licenses and license rates visit http://www.copyright.gov/circs/circ73.pdf and http://www.copyright.gov/carp/m200a.pdf, respectively.

An Introduction to the Law of Sampling

by Charles E. Colman, Esq.[1]

Summary

"Sampling" is the practice of taking portions of earlier musical compositions and sound recordings and transforming, adapting, or piecing them together to create new works. It is sometimes considered a subcategory of so-called "appropriation art." Significant skill is required to sample effectively, whether one uses either digital or analog technology. Further, the new works created through sampling often reignite interest in older sampled works. Nevertheless, sampling currently exists in a legal grey area, with little guidance from the courts on the boundaries between permissible reinvention of prior works and actionable copyright infringement. The uncertainty surrounding the legality of sampling has accelerated the creation of a "clearance culture," in which artists and record labels are often forced to choose between paying large sums of money to obtain licenses to sample copyrighted works, abstaining from sampling altogether, or proceeding with sampling at the risk of a lawsuit. Because the legality of sampling cannot be understood without a foundation in the basic principles of copyright law, it is necessary to review those principles before moving on to the specific topic at hand.

1 Charles E. Colman is the founder of Charles Colman Law, PLLC (http://charlescolmanlaw.com), where he litigates intellectual property disputes and otherwise counsels clients in creative fields like fashion, music, film, and visual art Charles graduated from Yale College with a B.A. in Linguistics (cum laude, Distinction in Major) and received his J.D. from Columbia Law School (James Kent Scholar, Harlan Fiske Stone Scholar.) At Columbia, he served as an Articles Editor for the Columbia Journal of Law & the Arts and provided research assistance to leading copyright scholar Professor Jane Ginsburg Immediately after law school, Charles worked as a litigation associate at Patterson Belknap Webb & Tyler LLP.

In addition to representing clients, Charles serves as Co-Vice Chair of the American Bar Association's Special Committee on Copyrights and New Technologies, and as Co-Chair of the ABA's Fashion Design Legislation Subcommittee. He was recently appointed a lecturer in fashion law at Parsons, The New School for Design. Charles also blogs about legal issues in fashion at http://lawoffashion.com and contributes a regular column on fashion law to Styleite.com. He can be reached at cc@ charlescolmanlaw.com.

1. Sources of Copyright Law and a Copyright Owner's "Exclusive Rights"

Federal copyright law is codified in statute (beginning at 17 U.S.C. § 101) and elaborated upon in a substantial body of "case law"—that is, judicial opinions resulting from past disputes. The U.S. Copyright Act confers certain "exclusive rights" on those who fix "original works of authorship" in tangible form. These exclusive rights are laid out in 17 U.S.C. § 106, and can be summed up, for present purposes, as follows:

- To reproduce a copyrighted work
- To create "derivative works"[2] based upon the copyrighted work
- To distribute copies of the copyrighted work to the public
- For works other than sound recordings, to "perform the copyrighted work publicly"
- For works other than sound recordings, to "display the copyrighted work publicly"
- For sound recordings, to "perform the copyrighted work publicly by means of a digital audio transmission"

It is important to understand that copyright can (and often does) exist in both a musical composition *and* a particular recording of that composition; in other words, for most songs, there are at least two potential copyrights at issue. Furthermore, a particular copyright may be jointly owned or split up into pieces among "licensees"—sometimes by the particular right granted (reproduction versus distribution), sometimes by geography, etc. A "license," which simply means a grant of some right that is less *than* full ownership, may be exclusive (for example, "you are the only distributor of this album in Japan") or non-exclusive (for example, "you are entitled, along with anyone else I allow in the future, to use my song in a commercial.")

Copyright may exist in "compilation and derivative works," but *no protection is granted to portions of such a work in which "preexisting material ... has been used unlawfully."* 17 U.S.C. § 103(a) (emphasis mine). In other words, if a new work is based entirely on a previous copyrighted work without adequate permission, the new work may not be entitled to copyright at all.

2. Limitations on a Copyright Owner's "Exclusive Rights"

One important threshold requirement for a copyright infringement plaintiff, especially in the context of sampling, is a showing of "substantial similarity" between the original copyrighted work and the new, allegedly infringing work. The traditional test for evaluating substantial similarity between two works is whether "the ordinary observer, unless he set out to detect the disparities [between the two works], would be disposed to overlook them, and regard their aesthetic appeal as the same."[3] However, courts

2 A "derivative work" is "a work based upon one or more preexisting works, such as a translation, musical arrangement, dramatization, fictionalization, motion picture version, sound recording, art reproduction, abridgment, condensation, or any other form in which a work may be recast, transformed, or adapted. A work consisting of editorial revisions, annotations, elaborations, or other modifications which, as a whole, represent an original work of authorship, is a 'derivative work.'" 17 U.S.C. § 101 (emphasis mine).

3 *Peter Pan Fabrics v. Martin Weiner Corp.*, 274 F.2d 487, 489 (2d Cir. 1960).

have sometimes focused instead on the amount of the original work used,[4] or examined whether the new work has imported the original work's "overall essence or structure."[5] Regardless of the test employed, if there is no "substantial similarity" between the two works at issue, there is no copyright infringement, and that is the end of the inquiry.

However, even in situations where two works *are* "substantially similar," copyright infringement has not necessarily occurred. Beginning in Section 107 of Title 17 of the U.S. Code, the Copyright Act provides a series of "limitations" on the copyright owner's exclusive rights under Section 106. The most important of these limitations, for the purposes of liability for sampling, is Section 107's creation of a defense to copyright infringement known as "fair use." Section 107 provides four factors that are intended to guide the fair use analysis:

1. the purpose and character of the use, including whether such use is of a commercial nature or is for nonprofit educational purposes;
2. the nature of the copyrighted work;
3. the amount and substantiality of the portion used in relation to the copyrighted work as a whole; and
4. the effect of the use upon the potential market for or value of the copyrighted work.

While these factors provide useful guideposts for predicting the outcomes of fair use disputes, it is also crucial to consult judicial opinions to see how past disputes with similar factual situations were resolved.

Many have observed that courts tasked with making fair use determinations have placed significant emphasis on whether one's use of another's copyrighted material was "transformative."[6] According to the conventional wisdom, if a new use is not transformative, it will only rarely be considered a "fair use." With that said, the fact that one's use of another's copyright material *is* transformative—as is often true in the sampling context—does not necessarily guarantee that a court will deem the use to be "fair," requiring no permission or compensation. Rather, the court will examine the other fair use factors and prior case law ("precedent") in order to make this determination.

As legal conclusions go, fair use determinations are among the more difficult to draw. This is especially true in the area of musical sampling, because there are relatively few published decisions applying the fair use factors to sampling (and even fewer "important" decisions providing meaningful guidance in this area); 2) the published decisions that do exist on sampling are in tension to some degree, as explained below; and 3) fair use determinations tend to be very fact-specific, often hinging on a judge's intuitive sense of who has the moral high ground in a particular case.

4 See *Ringgold v. Black Entertainment Television*, 126 F.3d 70, 75 (2d Cir. 1997).

5 *Newton v. Diamond*, 349 F.3d 591, 596 (9th Cir. 2003).

6 See, e.g., *Campbell v. Acuff-Rose Music*, 510 U.S. 569, 579 (1994).

3. State Law Protection for Pre-1972 Sound Recordings

A troublesome, but important, wrinkle in the copyright scheme is that until the year 2067,[7] sound recordings made before February 15, 1972, are governed by *state copyright law*—also known as "common-law copyright"—and not by federal copyright law. This system will persist until 2067, unless current proposals to "federalize" common-law copyright in sound recordings gain traction.[8] In 2005, the highest state court in New York, the Court of Appeals, ruled that pre-1972 sound recordings are indeed entitled to state-law protection until the federal Copyright Act takes over in 2067. *See Capitol Records v. Naxos of America*, 4 N.Y.3d 540, 560 (2005). There is very little case law addressing the application of the fair use defense to *state-law* copyright infringement claims, but a 2008 New York Supreme Court (as the trial-level court is called in New York) opinion essentially applied the federal statutory fair use factors and case law as if they were part of New York law.[9] While it is likely other courts will adopt a similar approach in the future, the issue of fair use remains unsettled as of this writing.

4. The Unsettled Legal Landscape in the Sampling Context

Unless one obtains licenses (or colloquially, "clears" the rights) to any musical compositions and sound recordings sampled used in new works distributed publicly—whether for profit *or not*—the copyright-law doctrines of "substantial similarity" and "fair use" will determine whether the user has engaged in copyright infringement.

As noted above, fair use determinations are made, in broad strokes, by the four factors laid out in 17 U.S.C. § 107, but are also guided by factually similar precedent. While appellate cases from a district court's own circuit are controlling, opinions from other circuits are merely "persuasive" precedent that can be adopted or rejected. Naturally, the decisions of the U.S. Supreme Court bind the entire federal judiciary. Unfortunately, the Supreme Court has not decided any "substantial similarity" or "fair use" cases centered on sampling, and there are very few published federal circuit court decisions on point.[10] Probably the most significant Supreme Court opinion in this general area is:

---

7 17 U.S.C. § 301(c)

8 See Avonne Bell, Public Knowledge, "Federalization of Pre-1972 Sound Recordings: A Debate about Uncertainty and Public Access," Jun. 22, 2011, at http://www.publicknowledge.org/blog/federalization-pre-1972-sound-recordings-deba.

9 See *EMI Records Ltd. v. Capitol Records*, 601209/08, 2008 N.Y. Misc. LEXIS 8213, at **17 (Sup. Ct. N.Y. Cty. Aug. 8, 2008) ("Although New York cases have not applied the doctrine of fair use, New York case law has shown that factors such as the purpose and character of the copyrighted work, nature, amount, and market effect have been discussed and comport with the federal statutory fair use regime.")

10 Technically, no federal opinion is binding in the interpretation of state copyright law (which, as noted above, covers pre-1972 sound recordings), though as mentioned above, state courts adjudicating disputes over pre-1972 recordings will likely follow federal decisions whose reasoning is persuasive.

Campbell v. Acuff-Rose Music, 510 U.S. 569 (1994)

In this case, 2 Live Crew had parodied Roy Orbison's ballad "Oh, Pretty Woman," whose copyright in the musical composition was owned by Acuff-Rose Music.[11] The original *sound recording* was not at issue here, only the musical composition, which had been so altered as to fall outside the scope of the Copyright Act's "cover song" compulsory license provision. The Sixth Circuit had ruled that the commercial nature of 2 Live Crew's parody weighed against a finding of fair use.

The U.S. Supreme Court reversed the appellate court, stating that the most important consideration for the first fair use factor ("the purpose and character of the use") is whether the use of another's copyrighted material is "transformative," and *not* whether it was commercial or not-for-profit. The Court affirmed the principle that a parody may be a fair use, as it "it can provide social benefit, by shedding light on an earlier work, and, in the process, creating a new one."[12] However, because the Court was focused on the parodic nature of the 2 Live Crew song, the import of its decision for *non*-parodic sampling is unclear.

Probably the most significant federal circuit court opinions on sampling are:

Newton v. Diamond, 349 F.3d 591 (9th Cir. 2003)

Here, the Beastie Boys had obtained a license from ECM Records to use a sound recording of composer/flutist James Newton's musical composition "Choir," but were either unable or unwilling to clear rights to the underlying composition (to which Newton had retained the copyright.) The Beastie Boys nevertheless sampled a three-note, six-second segment of the "Choir" track, which they looped in the background of their song "Pass the Mic." Newton sued for copyright infringement of the underlying musical composition.

The Ninth Circuit (whose jurisdiction includes many of the Western states, including California) observed: "The practice of music sampling will often present cases where the degree of similarity is high. Indeed, unless the sample has been altered or digitally manipulated, it will be identical to the original. [But if] the similarity is only as to nonessential matters, then a finding of no substantial similarity should result."[13] Here, "the sampled portion [was] neither quantitatively nor qualitatively significant" relative to the original composition, so "[t]he works [were] not substantially similar" and "Beastie Boys' use of the 'Choir' composition was *de minimis*."[14] As a result, Newton's copyright infringement claim was dismissed.

This case shows that, as least where the *musical composition* is concerned, a defendant might not have to invoke fair use where the portion of the original song used is trivial. Compare this result with the ruling in the following case.

---

11 Copyrights in musical compositions are often owned by publishing companies like Acuff-Rose. Copyrights in sound recordings are typically owned by record labels. It can be difficult to track down the copyright owners of a musical composition or sound recording, as companies may have gone out of business, merged, etc.

12 *Id.* at 579.

13 *Id.* at 597.

14 *Id.* at 598. The term "de minimis" means an alleged wrong is too trivial for a court to grant relief.

Bridgeport Music v. Dimension Films, 410 F.3d 792 (6th Cir. 2005)

This action arose from a sample of the track "Get Off Your Ass and Jam" in the hip-hop song "100 Miles and Runnin," the latter of which was included in the soundtrack of the movie *I Got the Hook Up*. The owner of the sampled material sued the filmmakers for including a portion of their sound recording in the soundtrack. Here, the trial-level court ruled—as the Ninth Circuit had ruled in the *Newton* case—that the filmmakers' use of the sample was *de minimis*.

However, the Sixth Circuit Court of Appeals (whose jurisdiction covers four states, including the relatively important "music states" of Michigan and Tennessee) rejected the *de minimis* rationale and created what the court admitted was a "new rule": that sampling a sound recording is *prima facie* copyright infringement, regardless of how small or unrecognizable the sample may be. In other words, where sound recordings are concerned, courts need not apply the "substantial similarity" test at all—apparently a first in copyright law. In a now-infamous passage, the Court wrote: "Get a license or do not sample."[15]

After a fairly vociferous reaction by certain groups, the Sixth Circuit amended its opinion to make clear that it had addressed only the "substantial similarity" component of copyright infringement, and had not ruled out the possible defense of fair use in sampling situations.[16] Nevertheless, the Court's absolutist language does not bode well for would-be samplers in the Sixth Circuit.

What the Case Law Means for Sampling

The *Bridgeport* case has been rejected by at least one federal district court[17] and one state court,[18] as well as numerous commentators (including the influential legal treatise *Nimmer on Copyright*.[19]) However, it remains controlling law in federal-court proceedings in Michigan, Ohio, Kentucky, and Tennessee. By contrast, the Ninth Circuit in *Newton* employed reasoning that is more favorable to those who use samples in their work, but the case technically concerned only the sampling of musical compositions and not of sound recordings. The reasoning of the Supreme Court in *Campbell* was favorable to transformative use. The Second Circuit Court of Appeals, whose jurisdiction covers the important "music state" of New York, has not issued a definitive pronouncement on sampling as of this writing.

The *Bridgeport* issue may ultimately go to the Supreme Court. In the meantime, however, the risk of a sampler being sued in one of the Sixth Circuit states, or in a jurisdiction without its own sampling case law that decides to adopt the harsh *Bridgeport* rule, has prompted those with the funds to clear samples whenever possible. This relatively new industry practice, referred to (often pejoratively) as a "clearance culture," is described in the next section.

---

15 *Id.* at 801.
16 *Id.* at 805.
17 See *Saregama India Ltd. v. Mosley*, 687 F. Supp. 2d 1325, 1341 (S.D. Fla. 2009).
18 See *EMI Records Ltd. v. Capitol Records*, 601209/08, 2008 N.Y. Misc. LEXIS 8213, at **8 (Sup. Ct. N.Y. Cty. Aug. 8, 2008)
19 Nimmer on Copyright §13.03[2][b].

5. Our Modern "Clearance Culture"

The lack of definitive guidance on the legality of sampling has led to a cautious "clearance culture" in which entities that can afford to do so often pay to obtain a license of any necessary rights to even small portions of sound recordings and the underlying musical compositions.

Unlike the use of entire musical compositions for the purpose of a song "cover," the use of compositions and sound recordings is *not* governed by a so-called "compulsory license" regime. This means that while a copyright owner cannot stop someone from covering his or her composition, provided the covering artist complies with the procedures and pays the statutory royalty rate laid out in 17 U.S.C. § 115 (and accompanying regulations), a copyright owner *can* potentially use the court system to stop someone from making a new work that incorporates a sample of her copyrighted work—*unless* that use is not "substantially similar" to the portion of the original work used (as in the *Newton* case) or qualifies as a "fair use" under 17 U.S.C. § 107.

Because of the unpredictability of fair use determinations, the harsh precedent of *Bridgeport* and the lack of more recent circuit-court precedent on sampling, the cost of litigation (even if a defendant is ultimately successful), the possibility of a judge awarding "statutory" damages (which range as high as $150,000 per work for acts of "willful" infringement) and/or attorneys' fees, many no longer view the use of unlicensed samples as a viable option. Thus, a complicated framework has evolved in which copyright owners, including individuals, publishers, and record labels, license works at whatever rate that owner (who is often no longer the original songwriter/recording artist) decides to set. This framework first began to coalesce in the mid-1990s, but has been institutionalized to an even greater degree since the *Bridgeport* decision. In this "brave new world" of sampling regulation, the identity of the would-be sampler (or his record label) often matters just as much—if not more so—than the amount he can pay.

This is not to say that the cost of sampling is a trivial concern, even for major recording artists. The cost of clearing rights to samples begins at roughly $500 per sample (for a sample clearance company to search for and conduct preliminary negotiations with a copyright owner, not including the actual licensing fee) and can range as high as $100,000 per sample, in extreme cases.[20] The average cost of clearing a single sample is reportedly $5,000 to $15,000. Some copyright owners have a reputation for turning down all requests to license their works; others are notoriously litigious when uncleared samples come to their attention. These economic and legal considerations have necessarily had an impact on the creative process of musicians, especially in the sampling-oriented genre of hip hop. Some artists report that their record labels essentially "cap" the number of samples they can use on a particular song or album. Artists without record labels to advance the funds to license samples, or who record on their own and lack the funds for sample clearance, often have no choice but to avoid sampling altogether or use uncleared samples—at the risk of being sued.

---

20 Kembrew McLeod & Peter DiCola, Creative License: The Law and Culture of Digital Sampling (Duke 2011), at 153. The remainder of this paragraph is likewise corroborated by McLeod and DiCola's book.

Many consider this state of affairs to be less than ideal. As a result, attorneys, artists, non-profit organizations, and others have proposed various legislative overhauls of the current sampling regime, for reasons of efficiency, artistic freedom, fairness, or a combination of these concerns. Proposals have included the creation of a new compulsory license for samples, akin to the Copyright Act's "cover song" license provision; a codification of sampling in or around the Copyright Act's provision on fair use; industry-created standards that would provide guidance but lack the force of law; and at the opposite end of the ideological spectrum, uniform adoption of the *Bridgeport* rule: "Get a license or do not sample." These proposals notwithstanding, the issue of sampling has thus far been low on lawmakers' list of priorities; this may be due, in part, to the small number of centralized lobbying interests representing actual or would-be "samplers" and perhaps no central funnel to harness the interests of a diffuse public that would likely enjoy greater availability of music incorporating samples, but does not have a significant stake in the debate.

Campaigns and the Use of Music

One issue that arises almost every election cycle is the use of music in political campaigns. Politicians use music to excite the crowds and to send a message regarding the type of candidate s/he is, the type of campaign s/he is running, or the vision that s/he has for America. What happens, however, when an artist does not want to have a candidate use her/his music, because s/he either does not support that particular candidate or because s/he simply does not want to be associated with any political campaign? What rights does an artist have to control her/his music with regards to political campaigns? The following article discusses this issue.

Copyright and Political Campaigns

by Randolph Frazier, Esq.[21]

Music is a powerful medium for conveying emotions and ideas. As such, American political campaigns have used music for two centuries to promote particular parties, candidates, and platforms. But singers and songwriters ("artists") have not always welcomed campaign uses of their music, particularly when a campaign has not sought the artist's permission and when its party, candidate, or viewpoint is not supported by the artist.

In 1984, Bruce Springsteen became one of the first artists to contest a politician's unauthorized use of a song, when President Ronald Reagan played "Born in the U.S.A."[22] during his reelection campaign.[23] Ignoring the objections of Springsteen and others, campaigns continued to engage in unauthorized use of popular songs over the years. Recently, artists have become increasingly vocal over such non-permissive uses. Indeed, during the 2008 presidential election, Democrats and Republicans drew heat for their respective unauthorized uses of copyrighted songs. The Barack Obama campaign received a request from singer Samuel Moore to cease and desist from playing "Hold On, I'm Comin'"[24] at rallies,

21 Randolph Frazier is a lawyer, philanthropist, and filmmaker living in New York City. His practice focuses on the transactional needs of artists and social entrepreneurs. He is a founding member of UNICEF's Next Generation, a group of young professionals raising money and awareness on behalf of children in developing nations. Frazier graduated magna cum laude from Yale with a B.A. in Film Studies and Theater Studies, and received his law degree from Harvard, where he was an Editor of the Harvard Law Review. He recently produced his first film, which is on the festival circuit, and is shopping his first screenplay.

22 Bruce Springsteen, Born in the U.S.A., on Born in the U.S.A. (Columbia Records 1984).

23 Kurt Loder, The Rolling Stone Interview: Bruce Springsteen, Rolling Stone, Dec. 6 1984.

24 Sam & Dave, Soul Man, on Soul Men (Stax/Atlantic Records 1967).

while John McCain's campaign received cease and desist demands from numerous artists including ABBA, Bon Jovi, the Foo Fighters, Heart, John Mellencamp, and Van Halen.[25]

It is apparent that disputes between campaigns and artists over unauthorized song uses are a growing concern, and copyright law may not protect artists from contested campaign uses. The extent to which artists are protected may vary based on the manner in which a campaign uses their music. Playing a song at a rally, for example, may afford a lesser degree of protection than incorporating a song in a commercial or on a website. And changing a song's lyrics to comment on opponents or issues may yet again alter the degree of protection.

Unauthorized Song Use at Public Events

Rallies and similar public events are essential tools of political campaigns. At these events, music plays a critical role, creating atmosphere, energizing crowds, and driving home candidates' messages. The use of a song at a campaign event constitutes a "public performance" and, as such, requires a performing rights license.

The American Society of Composers, Authors, and Publishers (ASCAP), Broadcast Music, Inc. (BMI), and the Society of European Stage Authors and Composers (SESAC) are the performing rights organizations (PROs) responsible for licensing artists' songs. Some venues have "blanket licenses" from the PROs, which permit them to publicly perform any of millions of songs from their music catalogs. A campaign's use of a particular song during an event at the venue would be legally permissible if the song appears in one of the licensed catalogs. In other instances, campaigns must purchase public performance licenses from the PROs, not the artists, to comply with copyright law. Artists are generally unaware of these purchases and, thus, respond only after a public performance of their song has taken place.

While properly secured licenses may protect campaigns from copyright infringement claims, aggrieved artists have nonetheless protested candidates' use of their songs, and at times advanced causes of action other than copyright infringement. In 2008, Ann and Nancy Wilson of the musical group Heart sent a cease and desist letter to the McCain-Palin campaign, which had played their song "Barracuda"[26] twice at the Republican National Convention. Although the Wilson sisters did not wish to be associated with the RNC, copyright law did not provide them a remedy for their song's unauthorized use, in part due to the nature of copyright in music.

Under the Copyright Act, a songwriter possesses a property right in the musical composition that is distinct from the singer's property right in the song's performance. Section 106 of the Act grants the owner of the copyright in the musical composition the exclusive right to reproduce the song, make derivative

25 David C. Johnston, Recent Development, The Singer Did Not Approve This Message: Analyzing the Unauthorized Use of Copyrighted Music in Political Advertisements in *Jackson Browne v. John McCain*, 27 Cardozo Arts & Ent. L.J. 687, 689.
26 Heart, Barracuda, on Little Queen (Portrait Records 1977).

versions, distribute phonorecords to the public, perform the song publicly, and "in the case of sound recordings, to perform the copyrighted work publicly by means of a digital audio transmission."[27] The owner of the copyright in the sound recording possesses fewer rights. Indeed, § 114 of the Copyright Act does not provide a public performance right in sound recordings.[28] Therefore, the public performance of a song at a campaign event requires only the purchase of a license from the owner of the copyright in the underlying composition, *not* the artist who performed the composition.

With respect to "Barracuda," the RNC purchased a "blanket license" from ASCAP, allowing the McCain campaign to play the song at the convention center. Although the Wilson sisters were two of the song's composers as well as its performers, they were nevertheless without a remedy under the Copyright Act.[29] They did not have a public performance right in their sound recording and, like most songwriters, they did not have an exemption for political use under their PRO licensing agreement.[30]

Licensed public performances of songs at rallies may, however, be actionable under the Lanham Act, if a campaign falsely implies an endorsement by the artist.[31] For example, a campaign's repeated use of a particular song during the entrance of a candidate might falsely imply the artist's endorsement of the candidate, the party, or both. Rooted in trademark law and principles of false advertising, a Lanham Act claim in this context would likely require the plaintiff to establish that, as a result of the song's repeated use, reasonable people would assume that the plaintiff endorsed or was associated with the campaign. But no court has addressed a Lanham Act claim vis-à-vis the public performance of a song at a campaign event.

Unauthorized Song Use in Campaign Commercials and Videos

In addition to rallies and events, campaigns use music on candidates' websites and in commercials and videos. In these instances, copyright infringement claims by artists may be more successful, since the purchase of the PROs' licenses does not permit the making of recordings of songs for videos or advertisements.

In 2008, singer-songwriter Jackson Browne sued Senator John McCain, the RNC, and the Ohio Republican Party (ORP)[32] over McCain's unauthorized use of the song "Running on Empty"[33] in a campaign video produced by the ORP. The video, which was posted on YouTube, broadcast on television, and published

27 17 U.S.C. § 106 (2006).

28 See 17 U.S.C. § 114 (2006).

29 Sarah Schacter, The Barracuda Lacuna: Music, Political Campaigns, and the First Amendment, 99 Geo. L.J. 571, 576–77.

30 See *ibid* at 603.

31 Robert W. Clarida and Andrew P. Sparkler, Singing the Campaign Blues: Politicians Often Tone Deaf to Songwriters' Rights, Landslide, November/December 2010, available at http://www.americanbar.org/content/Dam/aba/migrated/intelprop/magazine/LandslideNovDec2010_Clarida.authcheckdam.pdf.

32 *Browne v. McCain*, 611 F. Supp. 2d 1073 (C.D. Cal. 2009).

33 Jackson Browne, Running on Empty, on Running on Empty (Asylum Records 1978).

on several websites, used Browne's song without a license of any kind as background music for a commercial criticizing Barack Obama's position on gasoline conservation.

Browne filed suit in a California federal district court, asserting a cause of action for copyright infringement based on the video's unlicensed use of his song on its soundtrack, as well as a Lanham Act claim based on the video's suggestion that he endorsed McCain and the Republican party. It also alleged a state law claim for violation of Browne's right of publicity based on the video's unauthorized use of his voice.

The McCain legal team put forth an affirmative defense of fair use, moving to dismiss for failure to state a claim upon which relief can be granted under Federal Rule of Civil Procedure 12(b)(6). As codified in § 107 of the Copyright Act, fair use permits the unauthorized use of copyrighted works for limited purposes, such as commentary, criticism, news reporting, and scholarship.[34] Pursuant to the statute, courts employ a four-factor balancing test to ascertain whether the use made of the copyrighted work is a fair use, weighing

> (1) the purpose and character of the use, including whether such use is of a commercial nature or is for nonprofit educational purposes;
> (2) the nature of the copyrighted work;
> (3) the amount and substantiality of the portion used in relation to the copyrighted work as a whole; and
> (4) the effect of the use upon the potential market for or value of the copyrighted work.[35]

In addition to these factors, a number of courts have incorporated into their analysis a "transformative use" factor, looking at whether the unauthorized use is "productive" and "employ[s] the quoted matter in a different manner or for a different purpose from the original."[36] Transformative uses of copyrighted works cohere with the policy goal of the Copyright Act—to "promote the Progress of Science and useful Arts"[37]—because they endow earlier works with new insights and understandings.[38]

The court in *Browne v. McCain* rejected the defendants' fair use argument, and declined to undertake a fair use analysis.[39] Such an analysis would have been unlikely to favor McCain: (1) the use of the contested song likely qualified as "commercial" in nature, because the McCain campaign stood to profit (from campaign donations) as a result of the video; (2) the copyrighted work was creative in nature rather than factual; (3) the video used a substantial amount of Browne's work (approximately 20 seconds); and (4)

34 17 U.S.C. § 107 (2006).
35 *Ibid.*
36 Pierre N. Leval, Toward a Fair Use Standard, 103 *Harv. L. Rev.* 1105, 1111 (1990).
37 U.S. Const. art. I, § 8, cl. 8.
38 See Leval, *supra* note 36, at 1111.
39 Browne, 611 F. Supp. 2d at 1078.

there was actual market harm to Browne, since he could have licensed the song himself and thereby profited financially.[40]

Rewriting Lyrics to Popular Songs

Occasionally, campaigns rewrite the lyrics of popular songs in order to advance political messages. The new lyrics, typically recorded atop instrumental versions of copyrighted songs, may mock opponents or call attention to issues, causes, or platforms. In these instances, campaign-defendants may argue that their unauthorized use constitutes parody and, as such, is protected by the fair use doctrine.

Recently, in *Henley v. DeVore*,[41] a California federal district court addressed the issue of parody and fair use in this context. Don Henley, the lead singer of the musical group The Eagles, and songwriter Mike Campbell filed suit against a Republican candidate for the U.S. Senate, Chuck DeVore, over campaign videos that used Henley's songs "The Boys of Summer"[42] and "All She Wants to Do Is Dance."[43] The campaign wrote new lyrics for both songs, criticizing the actions of President Barack Obama in "The Hope of November" (a rewrite of "The Boys of Summer") and attacking DeVore's opponent, Senator Barbara Boxer, in "All She Wants to Do Is Tax" (a rewrite of "All She Wants to Do Is Dance"). The campaign posted these videos on YouTube and other Internet sites.

Henley's complaint alleged copyright infringement, as well as false association or endorsement under the Lanham Act and a state law claim based on unfair business practices. With respect to the infringement claim, the defendants asserted a fair use defense, arguing that their works were parody and therefore noninfringing. Courts typically grant a high degree of fair use deference to parody. While true parody is self-referential, criticizing the copyrighted work or its artist, satire uses a copyrighted work to criticize something exogenous to the work itself or its artist.[44] Under this logic, courts have extended greater deference to parody than satire.

In *Henley*, the court applied the four-factor balancing test discussed above, determining that neither song satisfied the defendants' burden of establishing the affirmative defense of fair use. While "The Hope of November" hewed closer to parody, "All She Wants to Do Is Tax" was found to be highly satirical in nature. Using the four factors, the court concluded that (1) the campaign used both songs for commercial purposes; (2) the original works were creative rather than factual; (3) the campaign borrowed a substantial amount (lyrically and musically) from the original songs; and (4) the campaign's use of the entire musical composition adversely impacted the market for the original version.

---

40 Clarida, *supra* note 31.

41 No. 09-481, 2010 U.S. Dist. LEXIS 67987 (C.D. Cal. June 10, 2010).

42 Don Henley, The Boys of Summer, on Building the Perfect Beast (Geffen Records 1984).

43 Don Henley, All She Wants To Do Is Dance, on Building the Perfect Beast (Geffen Records 1984).

44 *Campbell v. Acuff-Rose Music, Inc.*, 510 U.S. 569, 580–81 ("Parody needs to mimic an original to make its point, and so has some claim to use the creation of its victim's (or collective victims') imagination, whereas satire can stand on its own two feet and so requires justification for the very act of borrowing.").

With respect to the Lanham Act claim for false endorsement, the *Henley* court found for the defendants. The court stated that there was no precedent supporting the notion that a performer holds a trademark on his performance of a song. Moreover, a reasonable listener would not believe that Henley performed the campaign songs himself, due to objective differences between Henley's voice and that of the singer of the contested version.

Conclusion

Music is likely to remain an integral part of the campaign trail, making unauthorized use of artists' songs an ongoing issue. In June of 2011, GOP Representative Michele Bachman drew attention for her unauthorized use of singer-songwriter Tom Petty's "American Girl"[45] when she announced her candidacy for U.S. President.[46] Bachmann is the first candidate in the 2012 election cycle to come under fire, but will almost certainly not be the last. At present, no case on a contested song use has gone to trial and, thus, unauthorized song use continues, checked only by the protests of the artists themselves.

45 Tom Petty & the Heartbreakers, American Girl, on Tom Petty & the Heartbreakers (Shelter Records 1977).

46 Eriq Gardner, Tom Petty Takes on Bachmann Over American Girl, Reuters.com, June 28, 2011, available at http://www.reuters.com/article/2011/06/29/us-tompetty-idUSTRE75S00F20110629.

Chapter 7
Corporate Law

Before reviewing some of the concepts in corporate law, it is important to know some of the various entities that businesses can organize as. The following chart will be fully discussed in class. If this particular class is not attended (or if this book is being read for fun), just a little bit of Internet research will help in the completion of the chart.

	General Partnership	Limited Partnership	C Corporation	S Corporation	Limited Liability Company (LLC)	Sole Proprietorship
Limited Liability						
Number of Owners						
Pass-through Profit & Loss (P&L)						
Annual Meeting						
Perpetual Existence						
Other						

Benefit Corporation

A recent development in corporate law is the creation of the benefit corporation. In 2010, Maryland became the first state to pass legislation authorizing benefit corporations. Virginia, Vermont, Hawaii, and New Jersey followed thereafter. In 2011, Maryland became the first, and thus far only state, to pass similar legislation authorizing the creation of benefit LLCs.

Vermont defines a benefit corporation as follows:

> (A) providing low income or underserved individuals or communities with beneficial products or services; (B) promoting economic opportunity for individuals or communities beyond the creation of jobs in the normal course of business; (C) preserving or improving the environment; (D) improving human health; (E) promoting the arts or sciences or the advancement of knowledge; (F) increasing the flow of capital to entities with a public benefit purpose; and (G) the accomplishment of any other identifiable benefit for society or the environment. (http://www.sec.state.vt.us/corps/)

Benefit corporations are unique entities in that they allow businesses to look beyond just making a profit. Benefit corporations allow businesses to include a focus on a public benefit as part of their corporate decision-making process. Furthermore, a benefit corporation will protect directors of the company from shareholder suits for breach of fiduciary duty for any decisions that do not maximize profit.

Non-Profits

A non-profit corporation is simply a corporation that is organized for a purpose other than earning profit for shareholders. That does not mean that a non-profit corporation cannot make a profit. Any profit earned, however, must be kept in-house for the furtherance of its purpose.

Piercing the Corporate Veil

Incorporating a business protects its individual owners and directors from personal liability. However, in order to maintain that corporate protection, businesses must maintain corporate formalities, such as meetings of the board of directors with documented minutes, non-personal use of corporate funds, and timely filing of annual reports. If a court finds that a corporation has failed to maintain corporate formalities, it can "pierce the corporate veil" and attach personal liability directly to the individual corporate owners or directors.

The following case applies the principles of piercing the corporate veil to the Flemming Fruit Company.

DeWITT TRUCK BROKERS v. FLEMMING FRUIT COMPANY

United States Court of Appeals, Fourth Circuit
540 F.2d 681 (1976)

DONALD RUSSELL, Circuit Judge:

In this action on debt, the plaintiff seeks, by piercing the corporate veil under the law of South Carolina, to impose individual liability on the president of the indebted corporation individually. The District Court, making findings of fact which may be overturned only if clearly erroneous, pierced the corporate veil and imposed individual liability. The individual defendant appeals. We affirm.

At the outset, it is recognized that a corporation is an entity, separate and distinct from its officers and stockholders, and that its debts are not the individual indebtedness of its stockholders. This is expressed in the presumption that the corporation and its stockholders are separate and distinct. *Fishman v. State* (1973), 128 Ga.App. 505, 197 S.E.2d 467, 473. And this oft-stated principle is equally applicable, whether the corporation has many or only one stockholder. But this concept of separate entity is merely a legal theory, "introduced for purposes of convenience and to subserve the ends of justice," and the courts "decline to recognize (it) whenever recognition of the corporate form would extend the principle of incorporation 'beyond its legitimate purposes and (would) produce injustices or inequitable consequences.'" *** Accordingly, "in an appropriate case and in furtherance of the ends of justice," the corporate veil will be pierced and the corporation and its stockholders "will be treated as identical." 18 Am.Juris.2d at 559.

This power to pierce the corporate veil, though, is to be exercised "reluctantly" and "cautiously" and the burden of establishing a basis for the disregard of the corporate fiction rests on the party asserting such claim.

* * *

But, in applying the "instrumentality" or "alter ego" doctrine, the courts are concerned with reality and not form, with how the corporation operated and the individual defendant's relationship to that operation. *Collins v. United States* (S.D.Ga.1974), 386 F.Supp. 17, 20, aff'd, 5 Cir.,514 F.2d 1282. One court has suggested that courts should abjure "the mere incantation of the term 'instrumentality'" in this context and, since the issue is one of fact, should take pains to spell out the specific factual basis for its conclusion. *Kirvo Industrial Supp. Co. v. National Distill. & Chem. Corp., supra*, 483 F.2d at 1103. And the authorities have indicated certain facts which are to be given substantial weight in this connection. One fact which all the authorities consider significant in the inquiry, and particularly so in the case of the one-man or closely-held corporation, is whether the corporation was grossly undercapitalized for the purposes of the corporate undertaking. *** And, "(t)he obligation to provide adequate capital begins with incorporation and is a continuing obligation thereafter * * * during the corporation's operations." See *Gillespie, supra*; Dix, *Adequate Risk Capital*, 52 Nw.U.L.Rev. 478, 494 (1958). Other factors that are emphasized in the application of the doctrine are failure to observe corporate formalities, non-payment of dividends, the insolvency of the debtor corporation at the time, siphoning of funds of the corporation by the dominant stockholder, non-functioning of other officers or directors, absence of corporate records, and the fact that the corporation is merely a facade for the operations of the dominant stockholder or stockholders. The conclusion to disregard the corporate entity may not, however, rest on a single factor, whether undercapitalization, disregard of corporation's formalities, or what-not, but must involve a number of such factors; in addition, it must present an element of injustice or fundamental unfairness. But undercapitalization, coupled with disregard of corporate formalities, lack of participation on the part of the other stockholders, and the failure to pay dividends while paying substantial sums, whether by way of salary or otherwise, to the dominant stockholder, all fitting into a picture of basic unfairness, has been regarded fairly uniformly to constitute a basis for an imposition of individual liability under the doctrine.

A recent case illustrative of the application of some of those factors in finding warrant to disregard the corporate shield is *G. M. Leasing Corp. v. United States, supra*, 514 F.2d at 935. There, the District Court found as a fact that the corporation was not the "alter ego" of the defendant. On appeal, this finding was held to be "clearly erroneous" and individual liability was imposed. In reaching this conclusion, the Court found that the defendant had "substantial, if not exclusive, control over appellee; " that the other directors "were nothing more than figureheads" who "attended no directors meetings, and were paid no salaries," and that there were no "minutes of stockholders' meetings."

If these factors, which were deemed significant in other cases concerned with this same issue, are given consideration here, the finding of the District Court that the corporate entity should be disregarded was not clearly erroneous. Certainly the corporation was, in practice at least, a close, one-man corporation from the very beginning. Its incorporators were the defendant Flemming, his wife and his attorney. It began in 1962 with a capitalization of 5,000 shares, issued for a consideration of one dollar each. In some manner which Flemming never made entirely clear, approximately 2,000 shares were retired. At the times involved here Flemming owned approximately 90% of the corporation's outstanding stock, according to his own testimony, though this was not verified by any stock records. Flemming was obscure on who the other stockholders were and how much stock these other stockholders owned, giving at different times conflicting statements as to who owned stock and how much. His testimony on who were the officers and directors was hardly more direct. He testified that the corporation did have one other director, Ed Bernstein, a resident of New York. It is significant, however, that, whether Bernstein was nominally a director or not, there were no corporate records of a real directors' meeting in all the years of the corporation's existence and Flemming conceded this to be true. Flemming countered this by testifying that Bernstein traveled a great deal and that his contacts with Bernstein were generally by telephone. The evidence indicates rather clearly that Bernstein was, like the directors in G. M. Leasing, "nothing more than (a) figurehead(s)," who had "attended no directors meeting," and even more crucial, never received any fee or reimbursement of expenses or salary of any kind from the corporation.

The District Court found, also, that the corporation never had a stockholders' meeting. This accorded with Flemming's own testimony when originally deposed. Later, it is true, he sought to disown this admission and produce minutes of five stockholders' meetings, which incidentally were identical in form. He would explain his earlier admission by saying he had misunderstood a simple question such as whether the corporation had ever had a stockholders' meeting. The trial judge, who observed the witnesses and their demeanor on the stand, found the defendant's disavowal of his earlier testimony in this regard unconvincing and concluded that his earlier admission was correct. It is thus clear that corporate formalities, even rudimentary formalities, were not observed by the defendant.

Beyond the absence of any observance of corporate formalities is the purely personal matter in which the corporation was operated. No stockholder or officer of the corporation other than Flemming ever received any salary, dividend, or fee from the corporation, or, for that matter, apparently exercised any voice in its operation or decisions. In all the years of the corporation's existence, Flemming was the sole beneficiary of its operations and its continued existence was for his exclusive benefit. During these years he was receiving from $15,000 to $25,000 each year from a corporation, which, during most of the time, was showing no profit and apparently had no working capital. Moreover, the payments to Flemming were authorized under no resolution of the board of directors of the corporation, as recorded in any minutes of a board meeting. Actually, it would seem that Flemming's withdrawals varied with what could be taken out of the corporation at the moment: If this amount were $15,000 that was Flemming's withdrawal; if it were $25,000 that was his withdrawal.

To summarize: The District Court found, and there was evidence to sustain the findings, that there was here a complete disregard of "corporate formalities" in the operation of the corporation, which functioned, not for the benefit of all stockholders, but only for the financial advantage of Flemming, who was the sole stockholder to receive one penny of profit from the corporation in the decade or more that it operated, and who made during that period all the corporate decisions and dominated the corporation's operations.

That the corporation was undercapitalized, if indeed it were not without any real capital, seems obvious. Its original stated "risk capital" had long since been reduced to approximately $3,000 by a reduction in the outstanding capital, or at least this would seem to be inferable from the record, and even this, it seems fair to conclude, had been seemingly exhausted by a long succession of years when the corporation operated at no profit. The inability of the corporation to pay a dividend is persuasive proof of this want of capital. In fact, the defendant Flemming makes no effort to refute the evidence of want of any capital reserves on the part of the corporation. It appears patent that the corporation was actually operating at all times involved here on someone else's capital. This conclusion follows from a consideration of the manner in which Flemming operated in the name of the corporation during the year when plaintiff's indebtedness was incurred.

The corporation was engaged in the business of a commission agent, selling fruit produce for the account of growers of farm products such as peaches and watermelons in the Edgefield, South Carolina, area. It never purported to own such products; to repeat, it (always acting through Flemming) sold the products as agent for the growers. Under the arrangement with the growers, it was to remit to the grower the full sale price, less any transportation costs incurred in transporting the products from the growers' farm or warehouse to the purchaser and its sales commission. An integral part of these collections was, as stated, represented by the plaintiff's transportation charges. Accordingly, during the period involved here, the corporation had as operating funds seemingly only its commissions and the amount of the plaintiff's transportation charges, for which the corporation had claimed credit in its settlement with its growers. At the time, however, Flemming was withdrawing funds from the corporation at the rate of at least $15,000 per year; and doing this, even though he must have known that the corporation could only do this by withholding payment of the transportation charges due the plaintiff, which in the accounting with the growers Flemming represented had been paid the plaintiff. And, it is of some interest that the amount due the plaintiff for transportation costs was approximately the same as the $15,000 minimum annual salary the defendant testified he was paid by the corporation. Were the opinion of the District Court herein to be reversed, Flemming would be permitted to retain substantial sums from the operations of the corporation without having any real capital in the undertaking, risking nothing of his own and using as operating capital what he had collected as due the plaintiff. Certainly, equity and fundamental justice support individual liability of Flemming for plaintiff's charges, payment for which he asserted in his accounting with the growers that he had paid and for which he took credit on such accounting. This case patently presents a blending of the very factors which courts have regarded as justifying a disregard of the corporate entity in furtherance of basic and fundamental fairness.

Finally, it should not be overlooked that at some point during the period when this indebtedness was being incurred whether at the beginning or at a short time later is not clear in the record the plaintiff became concerned about former delays in receipt of payment for its charges and, to allay that concern, Flemming stated to the plaintiff, according to the latter's testimony as credited by the District Court, that "he (i.e., Flemming) would take care of (the charges) personally, if the corporation failed to do so ***." On this assurance, the plaintiff contended that it continued to haul for the defendant. The existence of this promise by Flemming is not disputed. Flemming simply would absolve himself of any obligation thereunder because the plaintiff has sued him individually instead of waiting patiently for the defendant to pay it at the latter's pleasure, if ever a rather lame excuse, since it was obvious that a legal action was the only recourse the plaintiff had to make Flemming abide by his promise. This assurance was given for the obvious purpose of promoting the individual advantage of Flemming. This follows because the only person who could profit from the continued operation of the corporation was Flemming. When one, who is the sole beneficiary of a corporation's operations and who dominates it, as did Flemming in this case, induces a creditor to extend credit to the corporation on such an assurance as given here, that fact has been considered by many authorities sufficient basis for piercing the corporate veil.

* * *

For the reasons stated, we conclude that the findings of the District Court herein are not clearly erroneous and the judgment of the District Court is

AFFIRMED.

[Footnotes omitted.]

In *Baatz v. Arrow Bar*, the court reviews the plaintiff's request to pierce the corporate veil of Arrow Bar. Unlike the previous case, however, the court decides in *Baatz* that the corporate veil should remain intact.

BAATZ v. ARROW BAR

Supreme Court of South Dakota

452 N.W.2d 138 (1990)

SABERS, Justice.

Facts

Kenny and Peggy were seriously injured in 1982 when Roland McBride crossed the center line of a Sioux Falls street with his automobile and struck them while they were riding on a motorcycle. McBride was uninsured at the time of the accident and apparently is judgment proof.

Baatz alleges that Arrow Bar served alcoholic beverages to McBride prior to the accident while he was already intoxicated. Baatz commenced this action in 1984, claiming that Arrow Bar's negligence in serving alcoholic beverages to McBride contributed to the injuries they sustained in the accident. Edmond and LaVella Neuroth formed the Arrow Bar, Inc. in May 1980. During the next two years they contributed $50,000 to the corporation pursuant to a stock subscription agreement. The corporation purchased the Arrow Bar business in June 1980 for $155,000 with a $5,000 down payment. Edmond and

LaVella executed a promissory note personally guaranteeing payment of the $150,000 balance. In 1983 the corporation obtained bank financing in the amount of $145,000 to pay off the purchase agreement. Edmond and LaVella again personally guaranteed payment of the corporate debt. Edmond is the president of the corporation, and Jacquette Neuroth serves as the manager of the business.In 1987 the trial court entered summary judgment in favor of Arrow Bar and the individual defendants. Baatz appealed that judgment and we reversed and remanded to the trial court for trial. *Baatz, supra*. Shortly before the trial date, Edmond, LaVella, and Jacquette moved for and obtained summary judgment dismissing them as individual defendants. Baatz appeals. We affirm.

* * *

2. Individual Liability by Piercing the Corporate Veil.

Baatz claims that even if Arrow Bar, Inc. is the licensee, the corporate veil should be pierced, leaving the Neuroths, as the shareholders of the corporation, individually liable. A corporation shall be considered a separate legal entity until there is sufficient reason to the contrary. *** When continued recognition of a corporation as a separate legal entity would "produce injustices and inequitable consequences," then a court has sufficient reason to pierce the corporate veil. *Farmers Feed & Seed, Inc. v. Magnum Enter., Inc.*, 344 N.W.2d 699, 701 (S.D.1984). Factors that indicate injustices and inequitable consequences and allow a court to pierce the corporate veil are:

1. fraudulent representation by corporation directors;
2. undercapitalization;
3. failure to observe corporate formalities;
4. absence of corporate records;
5. payment by the corporation of individual obligations; or
6. use of the corporation to promote fraud, injustice, or illegalities.

Id. When the court deems it appropriate to pierce the corporate veil, the corporation and its stockholders will be treated identically. *Mobridge, supra.*

Baatz advances several arguments to support his claim that the corporate veil of Arrow Bar, Inc. should be pierced, but fails to support them with facts, or misconstrues the facts.

First, Baatz claims that since Edmond and LaVella personally guaranteed corporate obligations, they should also be personally liable to Baatz. However, the personal guarantee of a loan is a contractual agreement and cannot be enlarged to impose tort liability. Moreover, the personal guarantee creates individual liability for a corporate obligation, the opposite of factor 5), above. As such, it supports, rather than detracts from, recognition of the corporate entity.

Baatz also argues that the corporation is simply the alter ego of the Neuroths, and, in accord with *Loving Saviour Church v. United States,* 556 F.Supp. 688 (D.S.D.1983), aff'd, 728 F.2d 1085 (8th Cir.1984), the corporate veil should be pierced. Baatz' discussion of the law is adequate, but he fails to present evidence that would support a decision in his favor in accordance with that law. When an individual treats a corporation "as an instrumentality through which he [is] conducting his personal business," a court may disregard the corporate entity. *Larson v. Western Underwriters, Inc.*, 77 S.D. 157, 163, 87 N.W.2d 883, 886 (1958). Baatz fails to demonstrate how the Neuroths were transacting personal business through the corporation. In fact, the evidence indicates the Neuroths treated the corporation separately from their individual affairs.

Baatz next argues that the corporation is undercapitalized. Shareholders must equip a corporation with a reasonable amount of capital for the nature of the business involved. See *Curtis v. Feurhelm*, 335 N.W.2d 575 (S.D.1983). Baatz claims the corporation was started with only $5,000 in borrowed capital, but does not explain how that amount failed to equip the corporation with a reasonable amount of capital. In addition, Baatz fails to consider the personal guarantees to pay off the purchase contract in the amount of $150,000, and the $50,000 stock subscription agreement. There simply is no evidence that the corporation's capital in whatever amount was inadequate for the operation of the business. Normally questions relating to individual shareholder liability resulting from corporate undercapitalization should not be reached until the primary question of corporate liability is determined. Questions depending in part upon other determinations are not normally ready for summary judgment. However, simply asserting that the corporation is undercapitalized does not make it so. Without some evidence of the inadequacy of the capital, Baatz fails to present specific facts demonstrating a genuine issue of material fact. *Ruane, supra.*

Finally, Baatz argues that Arrow Bar, Inc. failed to observe corporate formalities because none of the business' signs or advertising indicated that the business was a corporation. Baatz cites SDCL 47-2-36 as requiring the name of any corporation to contain the word corporation, company, incorporated, or limited, or an abbreviation for such a word. In spite of Baatz' contentions, the corporation is in compliance with the statute because its corporate name—Arrow Bar, Inc.—includes the abbreviation of the word incorporated. Furthermore, the "mere failure upon occasion to follow all the forms prescribed by law for the conduct of corporate activities will not justify" disregarding the corporate entity. Even if the corporation is improperly using its name, that alone is not a sufficient reason to pierce the corporate veil. This is especially so where, as here, there is no relationship between the claimed defect and the resulting harm.

In addition, the record is void of any evidence which would support imposition of individual liability by piercing the corporate veil under any of the other factors listed above in 1), 4) or 6).

In summary, Baatz fails to present specific facts that would allow the trial court to find the existence of a genuine issue of material fact. There is no indication that any of the Neuroths personally served an alcoholic beverage to McBride on the day of the accident. Nor is there any evidence indicating that the

Neuroths treated the corporation in any way that would produce the injustices and inequitable consequences necessary to justify piercing the corporate veil. In fact, the only evidence offered is otherwise. Therefore, we affirm summary judgment dismissing the Neuroths as individual defendants.

Business Judgment Rule

Courts will seek to refrain from second guessing the directors of a company for their business decisions, assuming those decisions are made with the appropriate fiduciary care, that is honestly, with reasonable care, and in good faith. In other words, corporate executives are allowed to make bad business decisions without being subject to liability, as long as those decisions are made without disregard for and abandonment of their fiduciary responsibilities.

The following short excerpt provides a good explanation of the business judgment rule. The court finds that, although some of the decisions made by the DeHarts may not have been smart, their decisions were appropriate under the business judgment rule.

NURSING HOME BUILDING CORPORATION v. DeHART

Court of Appeals of Washington, Division 1
535 P.2d 137 (1975)

SWANSON, Judge.

* * *

Nursing Home Building corporation, doing business as Arden Nursing Home (hereinafter referred to as 'the corporation'), appeals from a judgment which awarded it only $9,914.85 of its $121,865 claim based upon alleged fraudulent misappropriation of corporate funds by Richard L. and Phoebe DeHart, the former sole shareholders of the corporation.

* * *

Directing our attention to the second category of alleged 'fraudulent misappropriation,' the corporation asserts that such expenditures as management fees to the DeHarts, leased automobiles, and miscellaneous fringe benefits amounted to a waste of corporate assets and that the DeHarts failed to sustain the burden of proving that the expenditures were made in good faith. We disagree. Courts are reluctant to interfere with the internal management of corporations and generally refuse to substitute their judgment for that of the directors. See *Sanders v. E-Z Park, Inc.*, 57 Wash.2d 474, 358 P.2d 138 (1960). The 'business judgment rule' immunizes management from liability in a corporate transaction undertaken within both the power of the corporation and the authority of management where there is a reasonable basis to indicate that the transaction was made in good faith. An excellent statement of the 'business judgment rule' is found in W. Fletcher § 1039 at pages 621–25:

> It is too well settled to admit of controversy that ordinarily neither the directors [535 P.2d 144] nor the other officers of a corporation are liable for mere mistake or errors of judgment, either of law or fact. In other words, directors of a commercial corporation may take chances, the same kind of chances that a man would take in his own business. Because they are given this wide latitude, the law will not hold directors liable for honest errors, for mistakes of judgment, when they act without corrupt motive and in good faith, that is, for mistakes which may properly be classified under the head of honest mistakes. And that is true even though the errors may be so gross that they may demonstrate the unfitness of the directors to manage the corporate affairs. This rule is commonly referred to as the 'business judgment rule.'(Footnotes omitted.) See also H. Henn, Law of Corporations § 242 (1970).

In this connection, the trial court entered detailed findings of fact which are not disputed and state as follows:

> Mr. and Mrs. DeHart were experienced in the operation of businesses of various types, including nursing home. Both were involved in the day-to-day management of Arden Nursing Home on a full-time or greater than full-time basis; most of the time they were in possession of Arden Nursing Home. Each was licensed by the State of Washington as nursing home administrators. Each performed a variety of duties and responsibilities in addition to the day-to-day management.

Finding of Fact No. 5.

Mr. and Mrs. DeHart each received a management fee of $1,000.00 a month, plus certain fringe benefits such as a leased car, car operation expenses and key man life insurance. The cars were used predominantly for corporate purposes. The DeHarts used credit cards for such items as lunch conferences with staff, for entertainment of doctors and nurses who might refer patients to Arden. While some of these expenses may not have been necessary or wise in retrospect, all of these expenses were reasonable expenditures for proper business purposes.

* * *

Smith v. Van Gorkom provides another good discussion of the business judgment rule. In contrast to the previous case, the court in this case finds that the Board of Directors did violate the business judgment rule.

SMITH v. VAN GORKOM

Supreme Court of Delaware

488 A.2d 858 (1985)

* * *

Under Delaware law, the business judgment rule is the offspring of the fundamental principle, codified in 8 Del.C. § 141(a), that the business and affairs of a Delaware corporation are managed by or under its board of directors. *** In carrying out their managerial roles, directors are charged with an unyielding fiduciary duty to the corporation and its shareholders. *Loft, Inc. v. Guth*, Del.Ch., 2 A.2d 225 (1938), aff'd, Del.Supr., 5 A.2d 503 (1939). The business judgment rule exists to protect and promote the full and free exercise of the managerial power granted to Delaware directors. *Zapata Corp. v. Maldonado, supra* at 782. The rule itself "is a presumption that in making a business decision, the directors of a corporation acted on an informed basis, in good faith and in the honest belief that the action taken was in the best interests of the company." *Aronson, supra* at 812. Thus, the party attacking a board decision as uninformed must rebut the presumption that its business judgment was an informed one. *Id.*

The determination of whether a business judgment is an informed one turns on whether the directors have informed themselves "prior to making a business decision, of all material information reasonably available to them." *Id.*

Under the business judgment rule there is no protection for directors who have made "an unintelligent or unadvised judgment." *Mitchell v. Highland-Western Glass*, Del.Ch., 167 A. 831, 833 (1933). A director's duty to inform himself in preparation for a decision derives from the fiduciary capacity in which he serves the corporation and its stockholders. *Lutz v. Boas*, Del.Ch., 171 A.2d 381 (1961). *See Weinberger v. UOP, Inc., supra; Guth v. Loft, supra*. Since a director is vested with the responsibility for the management of the affairs of the corporation, he must execute that duty with the recognition that he acts on behalf of others. Such obligation does not tolerate faithlessness or self-dealing. But fulfillment of the fiduciary function requires more than the mere absence of bad faith or fraud. Representation of the financial interests of others imposes on a director an affirmative duty to protect those interests and to proceed with a critical eye in assessing information of the type and under the circumstances present here. See *Lutz v. Boas, supra*; *Guth v. Loft, supra* at 510. Compare *Donovan v. Cunningham*, 5th Cir., 716 F.2d 1455, 1467 (1983); *Doyle v. Union Insurance Company*, Neb.Supr., 277 N.W.2d 36 (1979); *Continental Securities Co. v. Belmont*, N.Y.App., 99 N.E. 138, 141 (1912).

Thus, a director's duty to exercise an informed business judgment is in the nature of a duty of care, as distinguished from a duty of loyalty.

* * *

On the record before us, we must conclude that the Board of Directors did not reach an informed business judgment on September 20, 1980 in voting to "sell" the Company for $55 per share pursuant to the Pritzker cash-out merger proposal. Our reasons, in summary, are as follows:

> The directors (1) did not adequately inform themselves as to Van Gorkom's role in forcing the "sale" of the Company and in establishing the per share purchase price; (2) were uninformed as to the intrinsic value of the Company; and (3) given these circumstances, at a minimum, were grossly negligent in approving the "sale" of the Company upon two hours' consideration, without prior notice, and without the exigency of a crisis or emergency.

As has been noted, the Board based its September 20 decision to approve the cash-out merger primarily on Van Gorkom's representations. None of the directors, other than Van Gorkom and Chelberg, had any prior knowledge that the purpose of the meeting was to propose a cash-out merger of Trans Union. No members of Senior Management were present, other than Chelberg, Romans and Peterson; and the latter two had only learned of the proposed sale an hour earlier. Both general counsel Moore and former general counsel Browder attended the meeting, but were equally uninformed as to the purpose of the meeting and the documents to be acted upon.

Without any documents before them concerning the proposed transaction, the members of the Board were required to rely entirely upon Van Gorkom's 20-minute oral presentation of the proposal. No written summary of the terms of the merger was presented; the directors were given no documentation to support the adequacy of $55 price per share for sale of the Company; and the Board had before it nothing more than Van Gorkom's statement of his understanding of the substance of an agreement which he admittedly had never read, nor which any member of the Board had ever seen.

* * *

To summarize: we hold that the directors of Trans Union breached their fiduciary duty to their stockholders (1) by their failure to inform themselves of all information reasonably available to them and relevant to their decision to recommend the Pritzker merger; and (2) by their failure to disclose all material information such as a reasonable stockholder would consider important in deciding whether to approve the Pritzker offer.

We hold, therefore, that the Trial Court committed reversible error in applying the business judgment rule in favor of the director defendants in this case.

On remand, the Court of Chancery shall conduct an evidentiary hearing to determine the fair value of the shares represented by the plaintiffs' class, based on the intrinsic value of Trans Union on September 20, 1980. Such valuation shall be made in accordance with *Weinberger v. UOP, Inc., supra* at 712–715. Thereafter, an award of damages may be entered to the extent that the fair value of Trans Union exceeds $55 per share.

Self-Dealing

Part of a director's fiduciary duty is the requirement that s/he not "self deal." That is, a director cannot take advantage of an opportunity that s/he becomes aware of in his/her corporate capacity without first advising the company of that opportunity. If, after full disclosure, the company chooses not to pursue the opportunity, the director may then take advantage of it.

> In *Northeast Harbor Golf Club, Inc. v. Harris*, the court examines whether or not the president of the golf club violated her fiduciary duty by engaging in self-dealing when she purchased land adjacent to the golf club.

NORTHEAST HARBOR GOLF CLUB, INC. v. HARRIS

Supreme Judicial Court of Maine

661 A.2d 1146 (1995)

ROBERTS, Justice.

Northeast Harbor Golf Club, Inc., appeals from a judgment entered in the Superior Court (Hancock County, Atwood, J.) following a nonjury trial. The Club maintains that the trial court erred in finding that Nancy Harris did not breach her fiduciary duty as president of the Club by purchasing and developing property abutting the golf course. Because we today adopt principles different from those applied by the trial court in determining that Harris's activities did not constitute a breach of the corporate opportunity doctrine, we vacate the judgment.

I.

The Facts

Nancy Harris was the president of the Northeast Harbor Golf Club, a Maine corporation, from 1971 until she was asked to resign in 1990. The Club also had a board of directors that was responsible for making or approving significant policy decisions. The Club's only major asset was a golf course in Mount Desert. During Harris's tenure as president, the board occasionally discussed the possibility of developing some of the Club's real estate in order to raise money. Although Harris was generally in favor of tasteful development, the board always "shied away" from that type of activity.

In 1979, Robert Suminsby informed Harris that he was the listing broker for the Gilpin property, which comprised three noncontiguous parcels located among the fairways of the golf course. The property included an unused right-of-way on which the Club's parking lot and clubhouse were located. It was also encumbered by an easement in favor of the Club allowing foot traffic from the green of one hole to the next tee. Suminsby testified that he contacted Harris because she was the president of the Club and he believed that the Club would be interested in buying the property in order to prevent development.

Harris immediately agreed to purchase the Gilpin property in her own name for the asking price of $45,000. She did not disclose her plans to purchase the property to the Club's board prior to the purchase. She informed the board at its annual August meeting that she had purchased the property, that she intended to hold it in her own name, and that the Club would be "protected." The board took no action in response to the Harris purchase. She testified that at the time of the purchase she had no plans to develop the property and that no such plans took shape until 1988.

In 1984, while playing golf with the postmaster of Northeast Harbor, Harris learned that a parcel of land owned by the heirs of the Smallidge family might be available for purchase. The Smallidge parcel was surrounded on three sides by the golf course and on the fourth side by a house lot. It had no access to the road. With the ultimate goal of acquiring the property, Harris instructed her lawyer to locate the Smallidge heirs. Harris testified that she told a number of individual board members about her attempt to acquire the Smallidge parcel. At a board meeting in August 1985, Harris formally disclosed to the board that she had purchased the Smallidge property. The minutes of that meeting show that she told the board she had no present plans to develop the Smallidge parcel. Harris testified that at the time of the purchase of the Smallidge property she nonetheless thought it might be nice to have some houses there. Again, the board took no formal action as a result of Harris's purchase. Harris acquired the Smallidge property from ten heirs, paying a total of $60,000. In 1990, Harris paid $275,000 for the lot and building separating the Smallidge parcel from the road in order to gain access to the otherwise landlocked parcel.

The trial court expressly found that the Club would have been unable to purchase either the Gilpin or Smallidge properties for itself, relying on testimony that the Club continually experienced financial difficulties, operated annually at a deficit, and depended on contributions from the directors to pay its bills. On the other hand, there was evidence that the Club had occasionally engaged in successful fund-raising, including a two-year period shortly after the Gilpin purchase during which the Club raised $115,000. The Club had $90,000 in a capital investment fund at the time of the Smallidge purchase.

In 1987 or 1988, Harris divided the real estate into 41 small lots, 14 on the Smallidge property and 27 on the Gilpin property. Apparently as part of her estate plan, Harris conveyed noncontiguous lots among the 41 to her children and retained others for herself. In 1991, Harris and her children exchanged deeds to reassemble the small lots into larger parcels. At the time the Club filed this suit, the property was divided into 11 lots, some owned by Harris and others by her children who are also defendants in this case. Harris estimated the value of all the real estate at the time of the trial to be $1,550,000.

In 1988, Harris, who was still president of the Club, and her children began the process of obtaining approval for a five-lot subdivision known as Bushwood on the lower Gilpin property. Even when the board learned of the proposed subdivision, a majority failed to take any action. A group of directors formed a separate organization in order to oppose the subdivision on the basis that it violated the local zoning ordinance. After Harris's resignation as president, the Club also sought unsuccessfully to challenge the subdivision. See *Northeast Harbor Golf Club, Inc. v. Town of Mount Desert*, 618 A.2d 225 (Me.1992). Plans of Harris and her family for development of the other parcels are unclear, but the local zoning ordinance would permit construction of up to 11 houses on the land as currently divided.

After Harris's plans to develop Bushwood became apparent, the board grew increasingly divided concerning the propriety of development near the golf course. At least two directors, Henri Agnese and Nick Ludington, testified that they trusted Harris to act in the best interests of the Club and that they had no problem with the development plans for Bushwood. Other directors disagreed.

In particular, John Schafer, a Washington, D.C., lawyer and long-time member of the board, took issue with Harris's conduct. He testified that he had relied on Harris's representations at the time she acquired the properties that she would not develop them. According to Schafer, matters came to a head in August 1990 when a number of directors concluded that Harris's development plans irreconcilably conflicted with the Club's interests. As a result, Schafer and two other directors asked Harris to resign as president. In April 1991, after a substantial change in the board's membership, the board authorized the instant lawsuit against Harris for the breach of her fiduciary duty to act in the best interests of the corporation.

The board simultaneously resolved that the proposed housing development was contrary to the best interests of the corporation.

The Club filed a complaint against Harris, her sons John and Shepard, and her daughter-in-law Melissa Harris. As amended, the complaint alleged that during her term as president Harris breached her fiduciary duty by purchasing the lots without providing notice and an opportunity for the Club to purchase the property and by subdividing the lots for future development. The Club sought an injunction to prevent development and also sought to impose a constructive trust on the property in question for the benefit of the Club.

The trial court found that Harris had not usurped a corporate opportunity because the acquisition of real estate was not in the Club's line of business. Moreover, it found that the corporation lacked the financial ability to purchase the real estate at issue. Finally, the court placed great emphasis on Harris's good faith. It noted her long and dedicated history of service to the Club, her personal oversight of the Club's growth, and her frequent financial contributions to the Club. The court found that her development activities were "generally ... compatible with the corporation's business." This appeal followed.

II.

The Corporate Opportunity Doctrine

Corporate officers and directors bear a duty of loyalty to the corporations they serve. As Justice Cardozo explained the fiduciary duty in *Meinhard v. Salmon*, 249 N.Y. 458, 164 N.E. 545, 546 (1928):

> A trustee is held to something stricter than the morals of the marketplace. Not honesty alone, but the punctilio of an honor the most sensitive, is then the standard of behavior. As to this there has developed a tradition that is unbending and inveterate.

Maine has embraced this "unbending and inveterate" tradition. Corporate fiduciaries in Maine must discharge their duties in good faith with a view toward furthering the interests of the corporation. They must disclose and not withhold relevant information concerning any potential conflict of interest with the corporation, and they must refrain from using their position, influence, or knowledge of the affairs of the corporation to gain personal advantage. *See Rosenthal v. Rosenthal*, 543 A.2d 348, 352 (Me.1988); 13-A M.R.S.A. § 716 (Supp.1994).

Despite the general acceptance of the proposition that corporate fiduciaries owe a duty of loyalty to their corporations, there has been much confusion about the specific extent of that duty when, as here, it is contended that a fiduciary takes for herself a corporate opportunity. *See, e.g.*, Victor Brudney & Robert C. Clark, *A New Look at Corporate Opportunities*, 94 HARV.L.REV. 998, 998 (1981) ("Not only are the common formulations vague, but the courts have articulated no theory that would serve as a blueprint for constructing meaningful rules."). This case requires us for the first time to define the scope of the corporate opportunity doctrine in Maine.

Various courts have embraced different versions of the corporate opportunity doctrine. The test applied by the trial court and embraced by Harris is generally known as the "line of business" test. The seminal case applying the line of business test is *Guth v. Loft, Inc.*, 5 A.2d 503 (Del.1939). In *Guth*, the Delaware Supreme Court adopted an intensely factual test stated in general terms as follows:

> [I]f there is presented to a corporate officer or director a business opportunity which the corporation is financially able to undertake, is, from its nature, in the line of the corporation's business and is of practical advantage to it, is one in which the corporation has an interest or a reasonable expectancy, and, by embracing the opportunity, the self-interest of the officer or director will be brought into conflict with that of his corporation, the law will not permit him to seize the opportunity for himself.

Id. at 511. The "real issue" under this test is whether the opportunity "was so closely associated with the existing business activities ... as to bring the transaction within that class of cases where the acquisition of the property would throw the corporate officer purchasing it into competition with his company." *Id.* at 513. The Delaware court described that inquiry as "a factual question to be decided by reasonable inferences from objective facts." *Id.*

The line of business test suffers from some significant weaknesses. First, the question whether a particular activity is within a corporation's line of business is conceptually difficult to answer. The facts of the instant case demonstrate that difficulty. The Club is in the business of running a golf course. It is not in the business of developing real estate. In the traditional sense, therefore, the trial court correctly observed that the opportunity in this case was not a corporate opportunity within the meaning of the *Guth* test. Nevertheless, the record would support a finding that the Club had made the policy judgment that development of surrounding real estate was detrimental to the best interests of the Club. The acquisition of land adjacent to the golf course for the purpose of preventing future development would have enhanced the ability of the Club to implement that policy. The record also shows that the Club had occasionally considered reversing that policy and expanding its operations to include the development of surrounding real estate. Harris's activities effectively foreclosed the Club from pursuing that option with respect to prime locations adjacent to the golf course.

Second, the *Guth* test includes as an element the financial ability of the corporation to take advantage of the opportunity. The court in this case relied on the Club's supposed financial incapacity as a basis for excusing Harris's conduct. Often, the injection of financial ability into the equation will unduly favor the inside director or executive who has command of the facts relating to the finances of the corporation. Reliance on financial ability will also act as a disincentive to corporate executives to solve corporate financing and other problems. In addition, the Club could have prevented development without spending $275,000 to acquire the property Harris needed to obtain access to the road.

The Massachusetts Supreme Judicial Court adopted a different test in *Durfee v. Durfee & Canning, Inc.*, 323 Mass. 187, 80 N.E.2d 522 (1948). The *Durfee* test has since come to be known as the "fairness test." According to *Durfee*, the true basis of governing doctrine rests on the unfairness in the particular circumstances of a director, whose relation to the corporation is fiduciary, taking advantage of an opportunity [for her personal profit] when the interest of the corporation justly call[s] for protection. This calls for application of ethical standards of what is fair and equitable … in particular sets of facts.

Id. at 529 (quoting Ballantine on Corporations 204-05 (rev. ed. 1946)). As with the *Guth* test, the Durfee test calls for a broad-ranging, intensely factual inquiry. The *Durfee* test suffers even more than the *Guth* test from a lack of principled content. It provides little or no practical guidance to the corporate officer or director seeking to measure her obligations.

The Minnesota Supreme Court elected "to combine the 'line of business' test with the 'fairness' test." *Miller v. Miller*, 301 Minn. 207, 222 N.W.2d 71, 81 (1974). It engaged in a two-step analysis, first determining whether a particular opportunity was within the corporation's line of business, then scrutinizing "the equitable considerations existing prior to, at the time of, and following the officer's acquisition." *Id.* The *Miller* court hoped by adopting this approach "to ameliorate the often-expressed criticism that the [corporate opportunity] doctrine is vague and subjects today's corporate management to the danger of unpredictable liability." *Id.* In fact, the test adopted in *Miller* merely piles the uncertainty and vagueness of the fairness test on top of the weaknesses in the line of business test.

Despite the weaknesses of each of these approaches to the corporate opportunity doctrine, they nonetheless rest on a single fundamental policy. At bottom, the corporate opportunity doctrine recognizes that a corporate fiduciary should not serve both corporate and personal interests at the same time. As we observed in *Camden Land Co. v. Lewis*, 101 Me. 78, 97, 63 A. 523, 531 (1905), corporate fiduciaries "owe their whole duty to the corporation, and they are not to be permitted to act when duty conflicts with interest. They cannot serve themselves and the corporation at the same time." The various formulations of the test are merely attempts to moderate the potentially harsh consequences of strict adherence to that policy. It is important to preserve some ability for corporate fiduciaries to pursue personal business interests that present no real threat to their duty of loyalty.

III.
The American Law Institute Approach

In an attempt to protect the duty of loyalty while at the same time providing long-needed clarity and guidance for corporate decisionmakers, the American Law Institute has offered the most recently developed version of the corporate opportunity doctrine. PRINCIPLES OF CORPORATE GOVERNANCE § 5.05 (May 13, 1992), provides as follows:

§ 505 Taking of Corporate Opportunities by Directors or Senior Executives

(a) General Rule. A director [§ 1.13] or senior executive [§ 1.33] may not take advantage of a corporate opportunity unless:

(1) The director or senior executive first offers the corporate opportunity to the corporation and makes disclosure concerning the conflict of interest [§ 1.14(a)] and the corporate opportunity [§ 1.14(b)];
(2) The corporate opportunity is rejected by the corporation; and
(3) Either:

(A) The rejection of the opportunity is fair to the corporation;

(B) The opportunity is rejected in advance, following such disclosure, by disinterested directors [§ 1.15], or, in the case of a senior executive who is not a director, by a disinterested superior, in a manner that satisfies the standards of the business judgment rule [§ 4.01(c)]; or

(C) The rejection is authorized in advance or ratified, following such disclosure, by disinterested shareholders [§ 1.16], and the rejection is not equivalent to a waste of corporate assets [§ 1.42].

(b) Definition of a Corporate Opportunity. For purposes of this Section, a corporate opportunity means:

(1) Any opportunity to engage in a business activity of which a director or senior executive becomes aware, either:

(A) In connection with the performance of functions as a director or senior executive, or under circumstances that should reasonably lead the director or senior executive to believe that the person offering the opportunity expects it to be offered to the corporation; or

(B) Through the use of corporate information or property, if the resulting opportunity is one that the director or senior executive should reasonably be expected to believe would be of interest to the corporation; or

(2) Any opportunity to engage in a business activity of which a senior executive becomes aware and knows is closely related to a business in which the corporation is engaged or expects to engage.

(c) Burden of Proof. A party who challenges the taking of a corporate opportunity has the burden of proof, except that if such party establishes that the requirements of Subsection (a)(3)(B) or (C) are not met, the director or the senior executive has the burden of proving that the rejection and the taking of the opportunity were fair to the corporation.

(d) Ratification of Defective Disclosure. A good faith but defective disclosure of the facts concerning the corporate opportunity may be cured if at any time (but no later than a reasonable time after suit is filed challenging the taking of the corporate opportunity) the original rejection of the corporate opportunity is ratified, following the required disclosure, by the board, the shareholders, or the corporate decisionmaker who initially approved the rejection of the corporate opportunity, or such decisionmaker's successor.

(e) Special Rule Concerning Delayed Offering of Corporate Opportunities. Relief based solely on failure to first offer an opportunity to the corporation under Subsection (a)(1) is not available if: (1) such failure resulted from a good faith belief that the business activity did not constitute a corporate opportunity, and (2) not later than a reasonable time after suit is filed challenging the taking of the corporate opportunity, the corporate opportunity is to the extent possible offered to the corporation and rejected in a manner that satisfies the standards of Subsection (a).

The central feature of the ALI test is the strict requirement of full disclosure prior to taking advantage of any corporate opportunity. *Id.*, § 5.05(a)(1). "If the opportunity is not offered to the corporation, the director or senior executive will not have satisfied § 5.05(a)." *Id.*, cmt. to § 5.05(a). The corporation must then formally reject the opportunity. *Id.*, § 505(a)(2). The ALI test is discussed at length and ultimately applied by the Oregon Supreme Court in *Klinicki v. Lundgren*, 298 Or. 662, 695 P.2d 906 (1985). As *Klinicki* describes the test, "full disclosure to the appropriate corporate body is … an absolute condition precedent to the validity of any forthcoming rejection as well as to the availability to the director or principal senior executive of the defense of fairness." *Id.* at 920. A "good faith but defective disclosure" by the corporate officer may be ratified after the fact only by an affirmative vote of the disinterested directors or shareholders. PRINCIPLES OF CORPORATE GOVERNANCE § 5.05(d).

The ALI test defines "corporate opportunity" broadly. It includes opportunities "closely related to a business in which the corporation is engaged." *Id.*, § 5.05(b). It also encompasses any opportunities that accrue to the fiduciary as a result of her position within the corporation. *Id.* This concept is most clearly illustrated by the testimony of Suminsby, the listing broker for the Gilpin property, which, if believed by the factfinder, would support a finding that the Gilpin property was offered to Harris specifically in her capacity as president of the Club. If the factfinder reached that conclusion, then at least the opportunity to acquire the Gilpin property would be a corporate opportunity. The state of the record concerning the Smallidge purchase precludes us from intimating any opinion whether that too would be a corporate opportunity.

Under the ALI standard, once the Club shows that the opportunity is a corporate opportunity, it must show either that Harris did not offer the opportunity to the Club or that the Club did not reject it properly.

If the Club shows that the board did not reject the opportunity by a vote of the disinterested directors after full disclosure, then Harris may defend her actions on the basis that the taking of the opportunity was fair to the corporation. *Id.*, § 5.05(c). If Harris failed to offer the opportunity at all, however, then she may not defend on the basis that the failure to offer the opportunity was fair. *Id.*, cmt. to § 5.05(c).

The *Klinicki* court viewed the ALI test as an opportunity to bring some clarity to a murky area of the law. *Klinicki*, 695 P.2d at 915. We agree, and today we follow the ALI test. The disclosure-oriented approach provides a clear procedure whereby a corporate officer may insulate herself through prompt and complete disclosure from the possibility of a legal challenge. The requirement of disclosure recognizes the paramount importance of the corporate fiduciary's duty of loyalty. At the same time it protects the fiduciary's ability pursuant to the proper procedure to pursue her own business ventures free from the possibility of a lawsuit.

The importance of disclosure is familiar to the law of corporations in Maine. Pursuant to 13-A M.R.S.A. § 717 (1981), a corporate officer or director may enter into a transaction with the corporation in which she has a personal or adverse interest only if she discloses her interest in the transaction and secures ratification by a majority of the disinterested directors or shareholders. Section 717 is part of the Model Business Corporations Act, adopted in Maine in 1971. P.L.1971, ch. 439, § 1. Like the ALI rule, section 717 was designed to "eliminate the inequities and uncertainties caused by the existing rules." MODEL BUSINESS CORP. ACT § 41, p 2, at 844 (1971).

IV.
Conclusion

The question remains how our adoption of the rule affects the result in the instant case. The trial court made a number of factual findings based on an extensive record. The court made those findings, however, in the light of legal principles that are different from the principles that we today announce. Similarly, the parties did not have the opportunity to develop the record in this case with knowledge of the applicable legal standard. In these circumstances, fairness requires that we remand the case for further proceedings. Those further proceedings may include, at the trial court's discretion, the taking of further evidence.

Judgment vacated.

Remanded for further proceedings consistent with the opinion herein.

All concurring.

[Footnotes omitted.]

Sample Form for Incorporation

The following is a sample form for incorporation (http://www.scc.virginia.gov/clk/dom_corp.aspx).

COMMONWEALTH OF VIRGINIA
STATE CORPORATION COMMISSION

ARTICLES OF INCORPORATION
OF A VIRGINIA STOCK CORPORATION

SCC619
(07/05)

The undersigned, pursuant to Chapter 9 of Title 13.1 of the Code of Virginia, state(s) as follows:

1. The name of the corporation is

____.

2. The number of shares authorized to be issued by the corporation is ____________.

3. A. The name of the corporation's initial registered agent is

____.

B. The initial registered agent is (mark appropriate box):

(1) an individual who is a resident of Virginia and
☐ an initial director of the corporation.

☐ a member of the Virginia State Bar.

OR

(2) ☐ a domestic or foreign stock or nonstock corporation, limited liability company or registered limited liability partnership authorized to transact business in Virginia.

4. A. The corporation's initial registered office address, including the street and number, if any, which is identical to the business office of the initial registered agent, is

______________________________________, VA __________.
(number/street) (city or town) (zip)

B. The registered office is physically located in the ☐ county or ☐ city of ________________.

5. The initial directors are:

NAME(S)	ADDRESS(ES)
____________________	____________________
	____________________
____________________	____________________
	____________________

6. INCORPORATOR(S):

SIGNATURE(S)	PRINTED NAME(S)
____________________	____________________
____________________	____________________

Telephone number (optional): ____________________

See instructions on the reverse.

NOTES

The articles must be in the English language, typewritten or printed in black, legible and reproducible.

This form contains the minimum number of provisions required by Virginia law to be set forth in the articles of incorporation of a Virginia stock corporation. If additional provisions are desired, then the complete articles of incorporation, including the additional provisions, must be typewritten on white, opaque paper 8 1/2" by 11" in size, using only one side of a page, and free of visible watermarks and background logos. A minimum of a 1" margin must be provided on the left, top and bottom margins of a page and 1/2" at the right margin. This form **may not** be submitted with an attachment.

You can download this form from our website at **www.scc.virginia.gov/clk/formfee.aspx**

INSTRUCTIONS

1. **Name**: The corporate name must contain the word "corporation," "incorporated," "company" or "limited"; or the abbreviation "corp.," "inc.," "co." or "ltd." The name of the corporation may not contain any word or phrase which indicates or implies that it is organized for the purpose of conducting any business other than a business which it is authorized to conduct. The proposed name must be distinguishable upon the records of the Commission. See § 13.1-630 of the Code of Virginia. To check

the availability of a corporate name, please contact the Clerk's Office Call Center at (804) 371-9733 or toll-free in Virginia at (866) 722-2551.

2. **Shares**: List the total number of shares the corporation is authorized to issue (note: the charter fee and annual registration fee are based on the number of authorized shares). If more than one class or series of shares is to be authorized, the articles must set forth the number of authorized shares of each class or series and a distinguishing designation for each class or series (e.g., common, preferred, etc.) and set forth the preferences, rights and limitations of each class or series. See §§ 13.1-619 and 13.1-638 of the Code of Virginia.

3. **Registered agent**: A. Provide the name of the registered agent. The corporation may not serve as its own registered agent. See §§ 13.1-619 and 13.1-634 of the Code of Virginia.
B. Check one of the boxes to indicate the qualification of the registered agent. The registered agent must be one of the options listed. No other person or entity may serve as the registered agent.

4. **Registered office**: A. The location of the registered office must be identical to the business office of the registered agent. See § 13.1-634 of the Code of Virginia. The address of the registered office must include a street address. A rural route and box number may only be used if no street address is associated with the registered office's location. A post office box is only acceptable for towns/cities that have a population of 2,000 or less if no street address or rural route and box number is associated with the registered office's location.
B. Provide the name of the county or independent city where the registered office is physically located. Counties and independent cities in Virginia are separate local jurisdictions. See §§ 13.1-619 and 13.1-634 of the Code of Virginia.

5. **Directors**: If the registered agent's qualification in 3.B is that of an initial director, then the names and addresses of all the initial directors must be included in the articles of incorporation. A corporation can have directors immediately upon formation only if they are named in the articles.

6. **Incorporator(s)**: One or more persons must sign the articles of incorporation in this capacity. See § 13.1-604 of the Code of Virginia.

It is a Class 1 misdemeanor for any person to sign a document he or she knows is false in any material respect with intent that the document be delivered to the Commission for filing.

[*Author's note: Instructions on how to submit deleted.*]

Charter fee: 1,000,000 or fewer authorized shares—$50 for each 25,000 shares or fraction thereof; more than 1 million shares—$2,500.

Filing fee: $25.

Chapter 8 Contracts

Simply stated, a contract is a promise or a set of promises to do or not to do "something," whether that be for a service to be performed, the purchase of an item, nondisclosure of information, employment, or a myriad of other possibilities.

For a contract to be enforceable, three elements must be present—an offer, an acceptance, and consideration.

Offer. The American Law Institute (ALI) defines an offer as being "the manifestation of willingness to enter into a bargain, so made as to justify another person in understanding that his assent to that bargain is invited and will conclude it." In other words, an offer is an invitation to participate in some exchange between parties, where the party that receives the offer can make the contract binding through his/her acceptance.

Acceptance. The ALI further states that "[a]cceptance of an offer is a manifestation of assent to the terms thereof made by the offeree in a manner invited or required by the offer." Generally speaking, acceptance may occur by agreeing to the contract terms, for example by signing a contract, or by performing some act pursuant to the offer, for example by the transfer of funds.

Consideration. Consideration can be defined simply as some exchange of value. This exchange can be in the form of money for a product, the trade of specific items, the performance of services, the receipt of something of value if a party agrees to not do something, etc. Consideration does not necessarily require the exchange to be for things of equal value.

There are restrictions on who can be legally bound by a contract. According to the American Law Institute, minors, the mentally disabled, intoxicated individuals, and individuals who have been placed under a guardianship cannot be bound by a contract that they sign. If an individual falling under one of these categories does sign a contract, that contract will be considered a voidable contract. Voidable contracts have proper offer, acceptance, and consideration. But, since the contract is entered into by an individual who does not have the legal capacity to undertake the required contractual duties, the contract is voidable. For example, a contract is not void outright in the case of a minor, because the minor can still go through with the contract if s/he wants. However, if s/he does not, the court could void the contract, since s/he was a minor when agreement to the contract was made.

Mailbox Rule—A Form of Acceptance

An important issue in a contract dispute can be the determination of when an offer is accepted. The "mailbox rule" states that a contract is formed once the acceptance is mailed. In contrast, a rejection of a contract is not effective until it is received by the offeror. The mailbox rule is discussed in the following case. Interestingly, if someone sends a rejection, changes his/her mind, and then sends an acceptance, the mailbox rule would not apply. Whichever letter the offeror received first would be in effect.

CANTU v. CENTRAL EDUCATION AGENCY

Court of Appeals of Texas, Austin

884 S.W.2d 565 (1994)

BEA ANN SMITH, Justice.

* * *

BACKGROUND

The facts in this cause are undisputed. Cantu was hired as a special-education teacher by the San Benito Consolidated Independent School District under a one-year contract for the 1990-91 school year. On Saturday, August 18, 1990, shortly before the start of the school year, Cantu hand-delivered to her supervisor a letter of resignation, effective August 17, 1990. In this letter, Cantu requested that her final paycheck be forwarded to an address in McAllen, Texas, some fifty miles from the San Benito office where she tendered the resignation. The San Benito superintendent of schools, the only official authorized to accept resignations on behalf of the school district, received Cantu's resignation on Monday, August 20. The superintendent wrote a letter accepting Cantu's resignation the same day and deposited the letter, properly stamped and addressed, in the mail at approximately 5:15 p.m. that afternoon. At about 8:00 a.m. the next morning, August 21, Cantu hand-delivered to the superintendent's office a letter withdrawing her resignation. This letter contained a San Benito return address. In response, the superintendent hand-delivered that same day a copy of his letter mailed the previous day to inform Cantu that her resignation had been accepted and could not be withdrawn.

The State Commissioner of Education concluded that, because the school district's acceptance of Cantu's resignation was effective when mailed, an agreement to rescind Cantu's employment contract was in force when she attempted to withdraw her offer of resignation and the school district's refusal to honor her contract was not unlawful.

DISCUSSION

The sole legal question presented for our review is the proper scope of the "mailbox rule"[1] under Texas law and whether the rule was correctly applied by the Commissioner and district court. None of the parties to this appeal disputes that an agreement to rescind Cantu's employment contract requires the elements of an offer, acceptance, and consideration. *See Texas Gas Util. Co. v. Barrett*, 460 S.W.2d 409, 414 (Tex.1970). Rather, Cantu contends in a single point of error that the trial court erred in ruling that the agreement to rescind her contract of employment became effective when the superintendent deposited his letter accepting Cantu's resignation in the mail. Cantu argues that, under Texas law, an acceptance binds the parties in contract on mailing only if the offeror has sent the offer by mail or has expressly authorized acceptance by mail. There was no express authorization for the school district to accept Cantu's offer by mail. The question presented is whether authorization to accept by mail may be implied only when the offer is delivered by mail or also when the existing circumstances make it reasonable for the offeree to so accept.

The aphorism "the offeror is the master of his offer" reflects the power of the offeror to impose conditions on acceptance of an offer, specify the manner of acceptance, or withdraw the offer before the offeree has effectively exercised the power of acceptance. However, more often than not, an offeror does not expressly authorize a particular mode, medium, or manner of acceptance. Consequently, particularly with parties communicating at a distance, a rule of law is needed to establish the point of contract formation and allocate the risk of loss and inconvenience that inevitably falls to one of the parties between the time that the offeree exercises, and the offeror receives, the acceptance. *See* 1 Arthur L. Corbin, *Contracts* § 78 (1963).

As Professor Corbin notes, courts could adopt a rule that no acceptance is effective until received, absent express authorization by the offeror; however, the mailbox rule, which makes acceptance effective on dispatch, closes the deal and enables performance more promptly, and places the risk of inconvenience on the party who originally has power to control the manner of acceptance. *Id.* Moreover, "the mailing of a letter has long been a customary and expected way of accepting [an] offer." *Id.* Therefore, "[e]ven though the offer was not made by mail and there was no [express] authorization, the existing circumstances may be such as to make it reasonable for the offeree to accept by mail and to give the offeror reason to know that the acceptance will be so made." *Id.* In short, acceptance by mail is impliedly authorized if reasonable under the circumstances.

The Restatement approves and adopts this approach: an acceptance by any medium reasonable under the circumstances is effective on dispatch, absent a contrary indication in the offer. Restatement (Second) of Contracts §§ 30(2), 63(a), 65, 66 (1979). In addition, the Restatement specifically recognizes that acceptance by mail is ordinarily reasonable if the parties are negotiating at a distance or *even if a written offer is delivered in person to an offeree in the same city. Id.* § 65 cmt. c (emphasis added). The same standard, *viz.*, whether the manner of acceptance is reasonable under the circumstances, governs offer and acceptance in commercial transactions under the Texas Business and Commerce Code. *See* Tex.Bus. & Com.Code Ann. § 2.206 (West 1968).

* * *

A more recent opinion of the supreme court, *McKinney v. Croan*, 144 Tex. 9, 188 S.W.2d 144 (1945), suggests that circumstances indicating the reasonableness of an acceptance be considered in determining whether an acceptance by mail is impliedly authorized and effective on mailing. In holding that a reply to a request for admissions was effective when mailed, the *McKinney* court specifically noted that the "parties resided about 350 miles apart," in addition to noting that the request was sent by mail. *Id.* 188 S.W.2d at 145. The court also cited to 17 C.J.S. *Contracts* § 52, which reads in part:

The request or authorization to communicate the acceptance by mail is implied in two cases, namely: (1) Where the post is used to make the offer ... (2) *Where the circumstances are such that it must have been within the contemplation of the parties that according to the ordinary usages of mankind the post might be used as a means of communicating the acceptance.* (Emphasis added).

The *McKinney* court's express mention of the distance between the parties as a circumstance making acceptance by mail reasonable and its affirmation of an authority following the modern trend that *either* mail delivery of the offer *or* reasonable circumstances might impliedly authorize communication by mail convince us that Texas law is not frozen into the rigid 1903 position urged by appellant. As we noted earlier, Texas courts are directed by statute to consider whether acceptance by mail is reasonable under the circumstances in commercial transactions. *Tex.Bus. & Com.Code Ann.* § 2.206 (West 1968). We hold that it is proper to consider whether acceptance by mail is reasonably implied under the circumstances, whether or not the offer was delivered by mail.

Looking at the circumstances presented for our review, we agree with the Commissioner and the trial court that it was reasonable for the superintendent to accept Cantu's offer of resignation by mail. Cantu tendered her resignation shortly before the start of the school year—at a time when both parties could not fail to appreciate the need for immediate action by the district to locate a replacement. In fact, she delivered the letter on a Saturday, when the Superintendent could neither receive nor respond to her offer, further delaying matters by two days. Finally, Cantu's request that her final paycheck be forwarded to an address some fifty miles away indicated that she could no longer be reached in San Benito and that she did not intend to return to the school premises or school-district offices. The Commissioner of

Education and district court properly concluded that it was reasonable for the school district to accept Cantu's offer by mail. We overrule appellant's point of error.

CONCLUSION

We affirm the trial-court judgment that the Commission correctly determined that the school district accepted Cantu's resignation, rescinding her employment contract, before Cantu attempted to withdraw her offer of resignation.

[1] The mailbox rule provides that the properly addressed acceptance of an offer is effective when deposited in the mail, unless otherwise agreed or provided by law. *Black's Law Dictionary* 952 (6th ed. 1990).

[Other Footnotes Omitted.]

Adequacy of Consideration

Hamer v. Sidway is a well known case that discusses the adequacy of consideration. This case is about an uncle, William E. Story, who offered his nephew, William E. Story, 2d, $5000 if he would refrain from smoking, drinking, swearing, and gambling. Hamer became involved in this case as the owner of the rights to the $5000 when Story, 2d sold and assigned his rights to his wife Libbie, who then sold and assigned her rights to Hamer. As the executor of the uncle's estate, Sidway refused to pay the sum to Hamer due to what Sidway considered to be a lack of consideration.

HAMER v. SIDWAY

Court of Appeals of New York

124 NY 538 (1891)

PARKER, J.

The question which provoked the most discussion by counsel on this appeal, and which lies at the foundation of plaintiff's asserted right of recovery, is whether by virtue of a contract defendant's testator William E. Story became indebted to his nephew William E. Story, 2d, on his twenty-first birthday in the sum of five thousand dollars. The trial court found as a fact that 'on the 20th day of March, 1869, William E.

Story agreed to and with William E. Story, 2d, that if he would refrain from drinking liquor, using tobacco, swearing, and playing cards or billiards for money until he should become 21 years of age then he, the said William E. Story, would at that time pay him, the said William E. Story, 2d, the sum of $5,000 for such refraining, to which the said William E. Story, 2d, agreed,' and that he 'in all things fully performed his part of said agreement.'

The defendant contends that the contract was without consideration to support it, and, therefore, invalid. He asserts that the promisee by refraining from the use of liquor and tobacco was not harmed but benefited; that that which he did was best for him to do independently of his uncle's promise, and insists that it follows that unless the promisor was benefited, the contract was without consideration. A contention, which if well founded, would seem to leave open for controversy in many cases whether that which the promisee did or omitted to do was, in fact, of such benefit to him as to leave no consideration to support the enforcement of the promisor's agreement. Such a rule could not be tolerated, and is without foundation in the law. The Exchequer Chamber, in 1875, defined consideration as follows: 'A valuable consideration in the sense of the law may consist either in some right, interest, profit or benefit accruing to the one party, or some forbearance, detriment, loss or responsibility given, suffered or undertaken by the other.' Courts 'will not ask whether the thing which forms the consideration does in fact benefit the promisee or a third party, or is of any substantial value to anyone. It is enough that something is promised, done, forborne or suffered by the party to whom the promise is made as consideration for the promise made to him.' (*Anson's Prin. of Con.* 63.)

'In general a waiver of any legal right at the request of another party is a sufficient consideration for a promise.' (*Parsons on Contracts*, 444.)

'Any damage, or suspension, or forbearance of a right will be sufficient to sustain a promise.' (*Kent*, vol. 2, 465, 12th ed.)

Pollock, in his work on contracts, page 166, after citing the definition given by the Exchequer Chamber already quoted, says: 'The second branch of this judicial description is really the most important one. Consideration means not so much that one party is profiting as that the other abandons some legal right in the present or limits his legal freedom of action in the future as an inducement for the promise of the first.'

Now, applying this rule to the facts before us, the promisee used tobacco, occasionally drank liquor, and he had a legal right to do so. That right he abandoned for a period of years upon the strength of the promise of the testator that for such forbearance he would give him $5,000. We need not speculate on the effort which may have been required to give up the use of those stimulants. It is sufficient that he restricted his lawful freedom of action within certain prescribed limits upon the faith of his uncle's agreement, and now having fully performed the conditions imposed, it is of no moment whether such performance actually proved a benefit to the promisor, and the court will not inquire into it, but were it a proper subject of inquiry, we see nothing in this record that would permit a determination that the uncle was not benefited in a legal sense. Few cases have been found which may be said to be precisely in point, but such as have been support the position we have taken.

* * *

In *Lakota v. Newton*, an unreported case in the Superior Court of Worcester, Mass., the complaint averred defendant's promise that 'if you (meaning plaintiff) will leave off drinking for a year I will give you $100,' plaintiff's assent thereto, performance of the condition by him, and demanded judgment therefor. Defendant demurred on the ground, among others, that the plaintiff's declaration did not allege a valid and sufficient consideration for the agreement of the defendant. The demurrer was overruled.

In *Talbott v. Stemmons* (a Kentucky case not yet reported), the step- grandmother of the plaintiff made with him the following agreement: 'I do promise and bind myself to give my grandson, Albert R. Talbott, $500 at my death, if he will never take another chew of tobacco or smoke another cigar during my life from this date up to my death, and if he breaks this pledge he is to refund double the amount to his mother.' The executor of Mrs. Stemmons demurred to the complaint on the ground that the agreement was not based on a sufficient consideration. The demurrer was sustained and an appeal taken therefrom to the Court of Appeals, where the decision of the court below was reversed. In the opinion of the court it is said that 'the right to use and enjoy the use of tobacco was a right that belonged to the plaintiff and not forbidden by law. The abandonment of its use may have saved him money or contributed to his health, nevertheless, the surrender of that right caused the promise, and having the right to contract with reference to the subject-matter, the abandonment of the use was a sufficient consideration to uphold the promise.' Abstinence from the use of intoxicating liquors was held to furnish a good consideration for a promissory note in *Lindell v. Rokes* (60 Mo. 249).

* * *

Does the following offer to Mike "The Situation" Sorrentino constitute adequate consideration?

News Release

ABERCROMBIE & FITCH PROPOSES A WIN-WIN SITUATION

New Albany, Ohio, August 12, 2011: Abercrombie & Fitch Co. (NYSE: ANF) today reported that it has offered compensation to Michael 'The Situation' Sorrentino, a character in MTV's TV show *The Jersey Shore* to cease wearing A&F products.

A spokesperson for Abercrombie & Fitch commented:

"We are deeply concerned that Mr. Sorrentino's association with our brand could cause significant damage to our image. We understand that the show is for entertainment purposes, but believe this association is contrary to the aspirational nature of our brand, and may be distressing to many of our fans. We have therefore offered a substantial payment to Michael 'The Situation' Sorrentino and the producers of MTV's *The Jersey Shore* to have the character wear an alternate brand. We have also extended this offer to other members of the cast, and are urgently waiting a response."

Abercrombie & Fitch
Brand Senses Department
(614) 283-6500

At the end of the second quarter, the Company operated a total of 1,073 stores. The Company operated 316 Abercrombie & Fitch stores, 179 abercrombie kids stores, 501 Hollister Co. stores and 18 Gilly Hicks stores in the United States. The Company operated 10 Abercrombie & Fitch stores, four abercrombie kids stores, 44 Hollister Co. stores and one Gilly Hicks store internationally. The Company operates e-commerce websites at www.abercrombie.com, www.abercrombiekids.com, www.hollisterco.com and www.gillyhicks.com.

Quasi-Contract

Falling under the realm of contract law are concepts that do not rely on an actual agreed upon contract, but rather upon contracts that are implied by law. Quasi-contracts seek to enforce justice and equity in situations where damage occurs to the plaintiff because the defendant fails to fulfill promises made to the plaintiff or because a defendant obtains unjust enrichment at the expense of the plaintiff. These concepts are known as promissory estoppel and quantum meruit, respectively.

Promissory Estoppel

The basic elements for a claim based on promissory estoppel are: 1) a party makes a promise, 2) a second party relies on that promise, and 3) the party that relied on the promise suffered some injury. (It is important to note that the promise need not be supported by consideration.) In such a case, in order to avoid an injustice, the court may award damages to the injured party. This concept will be detailed in the cases that follow.

In the *Cohen* case, Cohen provided information to reporters with the promise that his identity would be kept secret. The newspapers published his identity as the source. The day the stories were published, Cohen was fired. Under promissory estoppel, can Cohen recover damages?

COHEN v. COWLES MEDIA COMPANY

Supreme Court of Minnesota

479 N.W.2d 387 (1992)

SIMONETT, Justice.

This case comes to us on remand from the United States Supreme Court. We previously held that plaintiff's verdict of $200,000 could not be sustained on a theory of breach of contract. On remand, we now conclude the verdict is sustainable on the theory of promissory estoppel and affirm the jury's award of damages.

* * *

On October 28, 1982, the *Minneapolis Star and Tribune* (now the *Star Tribune*) and the *St. Paul Pioneer Press* each published a story on the gubernatorial election campaign, reporting that Marlene Johnson, the DFL nominee for lieutenant governor, had been charged in 1969 for three counts of unlawful assembly and in 1970 had been convicted of shoplifting. Both newspapers revealed that Dan Cohen had supplied this information to them. The Star Tribune identified Cohen as a political associate of the Independent-Republican gubernatorial candidate and named the advertising firm where Cohen was employed.

Cohen then commenced this lawsuit against defendants Cowles Media Company, publisher of the *Minneapolis Star Tribune*, and Northwest Publications, Inc., publisher of the *St. Paul Pioneer Press Dispatch*. It was undisputed that Cohen had given the information about Marlene Johnson's arrests and conviction to a reporter for each of the newspapers in return for the reporters' promises that Cohen's identity be kept confidential. The newspapers' editors overruled these promises. The disparaging information about the candidate leaked in the closing days of the election campaign was such, decided the editors, that the identity of the source of the information was as important, as newsworthy, as the information itself. Put another way, the real news story was one of political intrigue, and the information about the particular candidate was only a part, an incomplete part, of that story. Moreover, not to reveal the source, felt the editors, would be misleading, as it would cast suspicion on others; and, in any event, it was likely only a matter of time before competing news media would uncover Cohen's identity. Finally, the *Star Tribune* had endorsed the Perpich-Johnson ticket in its opinion section, and thus to withhold Cohen's identity might be construed as an effort by the newspaper to protect its favored candidates. On the same day as the newspaper stories were published, Cohen was fired.

* * *

III.

What, then, should be the appropriate disposition of this case? We conclude a retrial is unnecessary.

Under promissory estoppel, a promise which is expected to induce definite action by the promisee, and does induce the action, is binding if injustice can be avoided only by enforcing the promise. *Cohen I*, 457 N.W.2d at 204; Restatement (Second) of Contracts § 90(1) (1981). First of all, the promise must be clear and definite. As a matter of law, such a promise was given here. *Cohen I*, 457 N.W.2d at 204 ("[W]e have, without dispute, the reporters' unambiguous promise to treat Cohen as an anonymous source."). Secondly, the promisor must have intended to induce reliance on the part of the promisee, and such reliance must have occurred to the promisee's detriment. Here again, these facts appear as a matter of law. In reliance on the promise of anonymity, Cohen turned over the court records and, when the promises to keep his name confidential were broken, he lost his job. *Id.*

This leads to the third step in a promissory estoppel analysis: Must the promise be enforced to prevent an injustice? As the Wisconsin Supreme Court has held, this is a legal question for the court, as it involves a policy decision. *Hoffman v. Red Owl Stores, Inc.*, 26 Wis.2d 683, 698, 133 N.W.2d 267, 275 (1965); see also *Kramer v. Alpine Valley Resort, Inc.*, 108 Wis.2d 417, 422, 321 N.W.2d 293, 296 (1982) (third element is a question of law); *Grouse v. Group Health Plan, Inc.*, 306 N.W.2d 114, 116 (Minn.1981) (this court on appeal found all three elements of promissory estoppel were present).

It Is perhaps worth noting that the test is not whether the promise should be enforced to do justice, but whether enforcement is required to prevent an injustice. As has been observed elsewhere, it is easier to recognize an unjust result than a just one, particularly in a morally ambiguous situation. Cf. Edmond Cahn, *The Sense of Injustice* (1964). The newspapers argue it is unjust to be penalized for publishing the whole truth, but it is not clear this would result in an injustice in this case. For example, it would seem veiling Cohen's identity by publishing the source as someone close to the opposing gubernatorial ticket would have sufficed as a sufficient reporting of the "whole truth."

Cohen, on the other hand, argues that it would be unjust for the law to countenance, at least in this instance, the breaking of a promise. We agree that denying Cohen any recourse would be unjust. What is significant in this case is that the record shows the defendant newspapers themselves believed that they generally must keep promises of confidentiality given a news source. The reporters who actually gave the promises adamantly testified that their promises should have been honored. The editors who countermanded the promises conceded that never before or since have they reneged on a promise of confidentiality. A former *Minneapolis Star* managing editor testified that the newspapers had "hung Mr. Cohen out to dry because they didn't regard him very highly as a source." The *Pioneer Press Dispatch* editor stated nothing like this had happened in her 27 years in journalism. The *Star Tribune*'s editor testified that protection of sources was "extremely important." Other experts, too, stressed the ethical importance, except on rare occasions, of keeping promises of confidentiality. It was this long-standing journalistic tradition that Cohen, who has worked in journalism, relied upon in asking for and receiving a promise of anonymity.

Neither side in this case clearly holds the higher moral ground, but in view of the defendants' concurrence in the importance of honoring promises of confidentiality, and absent the showing of any compelling need in this case to break that promise, we conclude that the resultant harm to Cohen requires a remedy here to avoid an injustice. In short, defendants are liable in damages to plaintiff for their broken promise.

This leaves, then, the issue of damages. For promissory estoppel, "[t]he remedy granted for breach may be limited as justice requires." Restatement (Second) of Contracts § 90(1) (1981). *See generally Midamar Corp. v. National-Ben Franklin Ins. Co.*, 898 F.2d 1333, 1338–39 (8th Cir.1990); *Hoffman v. Red Owl Stores*, Inc., 26 Wis.2d at 701, 133 N.W.2d at 276. In this case the jury was instructed:

A party is entitled to recover for a breach of contract only those damages which: (a) arise directly and naturally in the usual course of things from the breach itself; or (b) are the consequences of special circumstances known to or reasonably supposed to have been contemplated by the parties when the contract was made.

This instruction, we think, provided an appropriate damages remedy for the defendants' broken promise, whether considered under a breach of contract or a promissory estoppel theory. There was evidence to support the jury's award of $200,000, and we see no reason to remand this case for a new trial on damages alone.

Our prior reversal of the verdict having been vacated, we now affirm the court of appeals' decision, but on promissory estoppel grounds. We affirm, therefore, plaintiff's verdict and judgment for $200,000 compensatory damages.

Affirmed on remand on different grounds.

> *Shoemaker* provides another good discussion on the concept of promissory estoppel. The issue in this case is a promise to purchase insurance for the Shoemakers' home.

SHOEMAKER v. COMMONWEALTH BANK

Superior Court of Pennsylvania
700 A.2d 1003 (1997)

JOHNSON, Judge:

We are asked to determine whether a mortgagor who is obligated by a mortgage to maintain insurance on the mortgaged property can establish a cause of action in promissory estoppel based upon an oral promise made by the mortgagee to obtain insurance. We find no merit in those portions of the instant case sounding in fraud and breach of contract. We conclude, nevertheless, that a mortgagee's promise to obtain insurance can be actionable on a theory of promissory estoppel. Accordingly, on this appeal from the order granting summary judgment to the mortgagee, we affirm in part, reverse in part and remand for further proceedings.

Lorraine and Robert S. Shoemaker obtained a $25,000 mortgage on their home from Commonwealth Bank (Commonwealth). The mortgage agreement provided that the Shoemakers were required to "carry insurance" on the property. By January 1994, the Shoemakers had allowed the home-owners' insurance policy covering their home to expire. In 1995, the Shoemakers' home, still uninsured, was destroyed by fire. The parties disagree as to the series of events that occurred after the insurance had lapsed.

The Shoemakers allege that Commonwealth sent a letter to them, dated January 20, 1994, that informed them that their insurance had been cancelled and that if they did not purchase a new insurance policy, Commonwealth might "be forced to purchase [insurance] and add the premium to [their] loan balance." The Shoemakers further allege that Mrs. Shoemaker received a telephone call from a representative of Commonwealth in which the representative informed her that if the Shoemakers did not obtain insurance, Commonwealth would do so and would add the cost of the premium to the balance of the mortgage. The Shoemakers assert that they assumed, based on the letter and phone conversation, that Commonwealth had obtained insurance on their home. They also contend that they received no further contact from Commonwealth regarding the insurance and that they continued to pay premiums as a part of their loan payments. Only after the house burned, the Shoemakers allege, did they learn that the house was uninsured.

Commonwealth, on the other hand, admits that it sent the letter of January 20, but denies the Shoemakers' allegations regarding the contents of the alleged conversation between its representative and Mrs. Shoemaker. Commonwealth further claims that it obtained insurance coverage for the Shoemakers' home and notified them of this fact by a letter dated February 4, 1994. Commonwealth also asserts that it elected to allow this coverage to expire on December 1, 1994, and that, by the letter dated October 25, 1994, it informed the Shoemakers of this fact and reminded them of their obligation under the mortgage to carry insurance on the property. The Shoemakers deny receiving any letter from Commonwealth regarding the insurance other than the letter dated January 20, 1994, that informed them that their policy had expired.

* * *

We must next determine whether the Shoemakers' allegations and the evidence that they have presented are sufficient to create genuine issues of material fact with regard to each element of a promissory estoppel cause of action and thus survive Commonwealth's motion for summary judgment. The first element of a promissory estoppel cause of action is that the promisor made a promise that he should reasonably have expected to induce action or forbearance on the part of the promisee. *Holewinski, supra*, at 178, 649 A.2d at 714. The Shoemakers have alleged that the bank promised to obtain insurance on their behalf and that it would add this cost to their mortgage payment. Mrs. Shoemaker testified in her deposition and swore in an affidavit that a representative from Commonwealth stated that the bank would acquire insurance if she did not and that she instructed the representative to take that action. Because the Shoemakers claim that Commonwealth's promise to obtain insurance was, essentially, conditioned upon the Shoemakers course of conduct, i.e., that Commonwealth would obtain insurance if they did not, we conclude that this evidence, if believed, would be sufficient to allow a jury to find that Commonwealth made a promise upon which it reasonably should have expected the Shoemakers to rely. See *Holewinski, supra*.

The second element of a promissory estoppel cause of action is that the promisee actually relied upon the promise. *Id.* at 178, 649 A.2d at 714. The Shoemakers allege that they actually relied upon Commonwealth's promise and, thus, failed to obtain insurance. In support of this allegation, Mrs. Shoemaker testified in her deposition and swore in her affidavit that she instructed Commonwealth's representative to acquire insurance on her behalf. We conclude that this evidence, if believed, would be sufficient to allow a jury to find that the Shoemakers relied upon Commonwealth's promise to obtain insurance. See *Holewinski, supra*.

The final element of a promissory estoppel cause of action is that injustice can be avoided only by enforcement of the promise. *Id.* at 178, 649 A.2d at 714. One of the factors that a court may consider in determining whether a promisee has satisfied this element is "'the reasonableness of the promisee's reliance.'" Thatcher's Drug Store, *supra*, at 477, 636 A.2d at 160, quoting Restatement (Second) of Contracts § 90, cmt. b. Mrs. Shoemaker testified that she and her husband received no communication from Commonwealth regarding their insurance after her conversation with a Commonwealth representative in early 1994. Commonwealth, on the other hand, asserts that it sent the Shoemakers letters informing them that their house would be uninsured after December 1, 1994. We conclude that this evidence is sufficient to create a genuine issue of material fact regarding the reasonableness of the Shoemakers' reliance. Accordingly, we hold that the trial court erred by granting summary judgment on the Shoemakers' promissory estoppel claim.

Quantum Meruit

Quantum meruit, which means "as much as he deserves," allows a plaintiff to be compensated for any services and/or materials that s/he provided to the defendant, if the defendant accepted those services and/or materials and knew that the plaintiff expected to be paid for them.

The concept of quantum meruit is discussed in the *Montes* case below.

MONTES v. NAISMITH AND TREVINO AND CONSTRUCTION COMPANY

Court of Civil Appeals of Texas, Corpus Christi
459 S.W.2d 691 (1970)

SHARPE, Justice.

This suit was brought by appellee, Naismith and Trevino, a corporation, to recover $3835.36 for labor performed and materials furnished on the homestead of appellant Abraham Montes (sometimes referred to as Abe Montes), for attorney's fees and foreclosure of lien. After nonjury trial, judgment was rendered for appellee in the amount of $1760.00 expressly based upon quantum meruit plus attorney's fees of $550.00. Appellee waived its claim for foreclosure of lien because it was undisputed that no written contract had been entered into prior to furnishing of the labor and materials in question. The trial court filed findings of fact and conclusions of law.

* * *

The background facts may be briefly stated as follows. Appellant, Montes, and one Abdon Perez, during or about the month of August, 1968, conducted oral negotiations for Perez to furnish labor and material and make certain improvements on the home of Montes for the amount of $3560.00. A written agreement was never executed by the parties, and in such connection Montes testified as follows:

* * *

Perez arranged for appellee Naismith and Trevino to do the work on the job. After being paid $1800.00 by Montes, Perez withdrew from the transaction. Appellee furnished labor and materials to Montes of the reasonable value of $3835.36, for which amount demand was made and suit thereafter brought against him. The judgment of the trial court in favor of appellee for $1760.00 represents the difference between $3560.00, the price orally agreed upon by Montes and Perez for the work to be done, and the amount of $1800.00 paid by Montes to Perez.

The twenty-one findings of fact and two conclusions of law made by the trial court read as follows:

I. Findings of Fact

1. At all relevant times, Naismith and Trevino Construction Company, is a Texas Corporation engaged in general contracting business in and around Corpus Christi, Texas.
2. Abdon Perez was an individual doing business as Perez Construction and Re-modeling Company who orally agreed to perform certain home improvements for the Defendant, Abe Montes.
3. That Perez and Montes agreed upon a price for the work of $3,560.00.
4. Montes paid Perez the sum of $1,800.00 only during the course of the work.
5. Perez contacted the Plaintiff, Naismith and Trevino, and arranged for it to furnish all of the labor and materials in the prosecution of the job which Naismith and Trevino did.
6. That prior to Naismith and Trevino's completion of the job Perez withdrew from any further contact with the job.
7. That Perez did not pay Plaintiff, Naismith and Trevino, any money for their labor and materials.
8. That Plaintiff, Naismith and Trevino, furnished labor and materials to Defendant, Montes at and on his residence of the reasonable value in Nueces County, Texas, of $3,835.36.
9. That Plaintiff, Naismith and Trevino, substantially completed the work assigned them.
10. That Plaintiff, Naismith and Trevino, satisfactorily completed the work assigned them.
11. That materials and labor furnished by Naismith and Trevino to and on the residence of Defendant Montes were used and enjoyed and are presently used and enjoyed by Montes.
12. That the improvements and labor furnished by Naismith and Trevino enhanced the Defendants residence in at least the sum of $3,835.36.
13. That labor and materials furnished by Naismith and Trevino to and on Defendants residence were accepted by the Defendant.
14. That of the price of $3,560.00 Montes owed a balance of $1,760.00 which he was aware of.
15. That Montes accepted the labor and materials of Naismith and Trevino knowing that their value exceeded what he had paid Perez by at least the sum of $1,760.00.
16. That Montes knew Naismith and Trevino had not been paid any money by Perez.
17. That Montes knew, or reasonably should have known that Naismith and Trevino expected to be paid for their services by Montes in light of the abandonment by Perez.
18. That Naismith and Trevino continued working with the full knowledge and consent of Montes after Perez had left the job.
19. That Naismith and Trevino looked to Montes for payment, if not of their total bill, for at least the sum of $1,760.00.
20. That Naismith and Trevino were reasonable in their expectations of payment by Montes.
21. Naismith and Trevino invoiced Montes on the termination of their work, 11-29-68.

* * *

Recovery was granted to appellee in this case under the theory of quantum meruit. In this Court no question has been raised concerning the sufficiency of appellee's pleadings to support a recovery on that theory. The pleadings herein are similar to those in *Bratcher v. Moore*, 219 S.W.2d 527 (Tex.Civ. App., Amarillo, 1949, n.w.h.). The essential elements of recovery under quantum meruit are: (1) Valuable services were rendered or materials furnished, (2) for the person sought to be charged, (3) which services and materials were accepted by the person sought to be charged, used and enjoyed by him, (4) under such circumstances as reasonably notified the person sought to be charged that the plaintiff, in performing such services was expecting to be paid by the person sought to be charged. ***

* * *

The judgment of the court below must be considered in the light of the sixteen unchallenged findings of fact and the conclusions of law made by the trial judge. Under findings numbers 3, 8–14, and 19–20 it is established that appellee furnished labor and materials to Montes of the reasonable value of $3835.36, which enhanced the value of Montes' residence in at least that amount; that the labor and materials were accepted, used and enjoyed by Montes; that appellee substantially and satisfactorily completed the work assigned to it; that Montes owed a balance of $1760.00 of the $3560.00 price orally agreed on by Perez and Montes; and that Naismith and Trevino reasonably looked to Montes for payment, if not for their total bill, for at least the sum of $1760.00.

We believe that the unchallenged findings of fact along with facts established by undisputed evidence were sufficient to authorize the trial court to find and conclude that each of the essential elements of quantum meruit were present. We further believe that appellant has not demonstrated that the evidence is legally or factually insufficient to support the five findings of fact complained of in his brief. Under these conditions we agree with the two conclusions of law made by the trial court.

Appellant's argument includes a number of other contentions which are not specifically assigned as error and which we are not required to pass upon under the circumstances.

The judgment of the trial court is affirmed.

Other Things to Know in Contracts

Mitigation of Damages

The non-breaching party (or plaintiff in a lawsuit) has to take reasonable steps to limit the loss incurred from a breach of contract. For example, if a lessee breaks his/her lease and the landlord makes no attempt to find a new tenant, the landlord may not receive as much in damages, as s/he possibly would have, had s/he tried to mitigate his/her losses by finding a new tenant.

Liquidated Damages

These are damages previously agreed upon in a contract that will be paid by the breaching party to the non-breaching party. For example, a builder promises to pay a museum $15,000 in the event that the builder is unable to finish an annex to the museum in 3 months time. If by the end of the 3 months the annex is incomplete, the builder must pay the museum the $15,000 as agreed upon within the contract.

Void Contract

A void contract is a contract that may have offer, acceptance, and consideration, but it is, nonetheless, not enforceable. An example of a void contract is a contract to commit an illegal activity, such as the purchase of drugs or murder for hire. Clearly, these are activities that no one would want to document in a contract. But, if they did, a court would not enforce the contract, since it would be void.

Unenforceable Contract

An unenforceable contract is a contract that has proper offer, acceptance, and consideration, but it will not be enforced by a court for various reasons, one of which being impossibility. For example, two parties agree on the sale of a car. The car is subsequently stolen by a third party. The person wanting to purchase the car sues the seller, because the seller, in the purchaser's opinion, failed to abide by the contract. The court would not enforce the contract against the seller, since there is no way for the seller to sell a car that he no longer has in his possession.

Specific Performance

Specific performance refers to cases where a contract is for something rare or unique—a painting, land, a rare baseball card, etc. For example, specific performance can force a defendant to sell a rare rookie Babe Ruth baseball card to the plaintiff as agreed to within a contract, because the item to be sold is unique and cannot be purchased elsewhere by the plaintiff. Specific performance, however, cannot be invoked for services. An individual cannot force someone (i.e., Rihanna) to either work for or provide services (i.e. sing in a concert) to him/her. An individual can, however, keep someone from providing his or her unique services (i.e. performing at an alternative venue) to someone else through an injunction for the length of the original contract.

Sokoloff reviews whether architectural plans qualify for the remedy of specific performance.

SOKOLOFF v. HARRIMAN ESTATES DEVELOPMENT CORP.

Court of Appeals of the State of New York

754 N.E.2d 184 (2001)

LEVINE, J.

* * *

In March 1998, plaintiffs purchased land in the Village of Sands Point, Nassau County, in contemplation of building a new home on the property. For a total of $65,000, defendant Harriman Estates Development Corp., a residential contractor, offered to provide plaintiffs with certain pre-construction services, including furnishing an "architectural and site plan/landscape design" and assisting them in obtaining a building permit. The offer was set forth by Harriman in a March 12, 1998 letter, which established a payment schedule and requested payment of a $10,000 retainer fee. Plaintiffs accepted the offer by paying Harriman the retainer fee. Thereafter, following several meetings between plaintiffs, Harriman and defendant Frederick Ercolino, an architect, the architectural plans were finalized, filed with the Village and approved.

Although plaintiffs paid Harriman a total of $55,000 for the architectural plans and other services, and tendered the remaining balance due under the terms of their agreement with Harriman, Harriman and Ercolino refused to allow plaintiffs to use these plans to build their home. After plaintiffs rejected Harriman's offer to build the home for an estimated cost of $1,895,000 (a sum significantly greater than Harriman's earlier estimates), Harriman for the first time informed plaintiffs that the architectural plans could not be used to construct the house unless it was hired as the builder. ***

* * *

By contrast, in the *first* cause of action—the only cause of action at issue at the Appellate Division and before this Court—plaintiffs seek specific performance of their contract with Harriman and allege that Harriman was acting as their agent in procuring architectural drawings and plans from Ercolino.

* * *

We also reject Harriman's assertion that specific performance is an inappropriate remedy because the architectural plans are not unique and a dollar value can be placed on the purchase of replacement plans. In general, specific performance will not be ordered where money damages "would be adequate to protect the expectation interest of the injured party" (Restatement [Second] of Contracts § 359; *see* also, *Van Wagner Adv. Corp. v. S & M Enters.*, 67 NY2d 186, 191–194). Specific performance is a proper remedy, however, where "the subject matter of the particular contract is unique and has no established market value" (*Van Wagner Adv. Corp. v. S & M Enters., supra*, at 193).

The decision whether or not to award specific performance is one that rests in the sound discretion of the trial court. In determining whether money damages would be an adequate remedy, a trial court must consider, among other factors, the difficulty of proving damages with reasonable certainty and of procuring a suitable substitute performance with a damages award (see, Restatement [Second] of Contracts § 360). Specific performance is an appropriate remedy for a breach of contract concerning goods that "are unique in kind, quality or personal association" where suitable substitutes are unobtainable or unreasonably difficult or inconvenient to procure (*see, id.*, comment *c*).

In this case, plaintiffs have alleged that "[t]he architectural plans and drawings are unique in that they are based upon a design conceived by the plaintiffs," and that without specific performance they "would have to change their requirements" as to the design of their new home. These allegations are sufficient to withstand a motion to dismiss for failure to state a cause of action. Whether money damages would adequately compensate plaintiffs for loss of these allegedly unique architectural plans is a matter to be resolved at a later stage, not on a motion to dismiss the complaint.

* * *

Accordingly, the order of the Appellate Division should be reversed, with costs, and the motion of defendant Harriman Estates Development Corp. to dismiss the first cause of action of the complaint against it denied.

Order reversed, etc.

Some Common Contract Clauses

There are contracts for everything—sales contracts, employment contracts, services contracts, leases, etc. Each contract will obviously include the specific details concerning the transaction being negotiated. However, there are many common clauses that are included in contracts, regardless of the specifics of the transaction. A small sampling of these common clauses is discussed below.

Definitions. It is important to define the terms of the contract—who is the "customer," what is the "product," what are the "services," and so on. If there are any terms specific to the transaction, those terms should also be defined. Some contracts define the terms within the text of the agreement. Others contain a section exclusively for defining the terms of the agreement. Some contracts do both. For example, a contract might say in sentence form, "Customer agrees to purchase 5 (five) blue widgets, 18 (eighteen) green widgets, and 7 (seven) yellow widgets (collectively "Product")." From thereon out, when the capitalized term "Product" is written in the contract, it is clear that the term is defined as the three types of widgets mentioned above. If the contract has a definition section, the definition may look like this: "Product" means 5 (five) blue widgets, 18 (eighteen) green widgets, and 7 (seven) yellow widgets."

Force Majeure. This clause expresses the parties' intent that any major incident beyond the control of a given party will not cause the affected party to be in breach of the contract or be liable for any delays that ensue. Force Majeure includes events, such as floods, earthquakes, riots, war, strikes, etc.

Term. How long is the agreement for?

Termination. Can the parties get out of the contract before the term is over? If so, how?

Governing Law/Jurisdiction. Under what state law will the contract be viewed? If there is a need to bring a legal action, in what courts will the action be brought?

Notice. How, where, and to whom should notice be sent if the parties need to communicate with each other? This can be an important clause. If notice is not properly sent, it could affect a party's rights under the contract. For example, if a party wishes to terminate the contract according to the termination clause, but they send notice of termination to the wrong address or wrong person, that party may have lost their ability to terminate the contract because of its failure to send proper notice.

Entire Agreement. This clause basically states that everything that was meant to be in the agreement is in the agreement. Any other discussions, memos, emails, etc. are irrelevant—the contract being signed is the controlling document and supercedes anything previous.

Chapter 9
Family Law

In a law and society context, family law is an area of utmost importance. Nothing touches society more than issues involving and challenging the family unit. The news is constantly full of stories that raise the questions of what rights families have, what rights individuals in a family relationship have, and what control government has over the family unit. Family law encompasses a wide variety of potential legal issues, including issues on marriage, divorce, custody, alimony, abortion, procreation (including non-procreative sexual activities), contraception, adoption, surrogacy, senior citizens (elder law), children (juvenile law), domestic abuse, guardianships, assisted suicide, grandparents rights, partners rights, and more. People are legitimately very passionate over these issues. This chapter will highlight but a few of these areas.

Privacy Rights

A Connecticut contraception ban was the impetus for *Griswold v. Connecticut.* In this decision, the Court establishes a Constitutional zone of privacy "created by several fundamental constitutional guarantees."

GRISWOLD v. CONNECTICUT

Supreme Court of United States (7–2)
381 U.S. 479 (1965)

MR. JUSTICE DOUGLAS delivered the opinion of the Court.

Appellant Griswold is Executive Director of the Planned Parenthood League of Connecticut. Appellant Buxton is a licensed physician and a professor at the Yale Medical School who served as Medical Director for the League at its Center in New Haven—a center open and operating from November 1 to November 10, 1961, when appellants were arrested.

They gave information, instruction, and medical advice to *married persons* as to the means of preventing conception. They examined the wife and prescribed the best contraceptive device or material for her use. Fees were usually charged, although some couples were serviced free.

The statutes whose constitutionality is involved in this appeal are §§ 53-32 and 54-196 of the General Statutes of Connecticut (1958 rev.). The former provides:

> "Any person who uses any drug, medicinal article or instrument for the purpose of preventing conception shall be fined not less than fifty dollars or imprisoned not less than sixty days nor more than one year or be both fined and imprisoned."

Section 54-196 provides:

> "Any person who assists, abets, counsels, causes, hires or commands another to commit any offense may be prosecuted and punished as if he were the principal offender."

The appellants were found guilty as accessories and fined $100 each, against the claim that the accessory statute as so applied violated the Fourteenth Amendment. The Appellate Division of the Circuit Court affirmed. The Supreme Court of Errors affirmed that judgment. 151 Conn. 544, 200 A. 2d 479. We noted probable jurisdiction. 379 U. S. 926.

* * *

The association of people is not mentioned in the Constitution nor in the Bill of Rights. The right to educate a child in a school of the parents' choice—whether public or private or parochial—is also not mentioned. Nor is the right to study any particular subject or any foreign language. Yet the First Amendment has been construed to include certain of those rights.

By *Pierce v. Society of Sisters, supra*, the right to educate one's children as one chooses is made applicable to the States by the force of the First and Fourteenth Amendments. By *Meyer v. Nebraska, supra*, the same dignity is given the right to study the German language in a private school. In other words, the State may not, consistently with the spirit of the First Amendment, contract the spectrum of available knowledge. The right of freedom of speech and press includes not only the right to utter or to print, but the right to distribute, the right to receive, the right to read (*Martin v. Struthers*, 319 U. S. 141, 143) and freedom of inquiry, freedom of thought, and freedom to teach (see *Wieman v. Updegraff*, 344 U. S. 183, 195)—indeed the freedom of the entire university community. *Sweezy v. New Hampshire*, 354 U. S. 234, 249–250, 261–263; *Barenblatt v. United States*, 360 U. S. 109, 112; *Baggett v. Bullitt*, 377 U. S. 360, 369. Without those peripheral rights the specific rights would be less secure. And so we reaffirm the principle of the Pierce and the Meyer cases.

In *NAACP v. Alabama*, 357 U. S. 449, 462, we protected the "freedom to associate and privacy in one's associations," noting that freedom of association was a peripheral First Amendment right. Disclosure of membership lists of a constitutionally valid association, we held, was invalid "as entailing the likelihood of a substantial restraint upon the exercise by petitioner's members of their right to freedom of association." *Ibid.* In other words, the First Amendment has a penumbra where privacy is protected from governmental intrusion. In like context, we have protected forms of "association" that are not political in the customary sense but pertain to the social, legal, and economic benefit of the members. *NAACP v. Button*, 371 U. S. 415, 430–431. In *Schware v. Board of Bar Examiners*, 353 U. S. 232, we held it not permissible to bar a lawyer from practice, because he had once been a member of the Communist Party. The man's "association with that Party" was not shown to be "anything more than a political faith in a political party" (*id.*, at 244) and was not action of a kind proving bad moral character. *Id.*, at 245–246.

Those cases involved more than the "right of assembly" —a right that extends to all irrespective of their race or ideology. *De Jonge v. Oregon*, 299 U. S. 353. The right of "association," like the right of belief (*Board of Education v. Barnette*, 319 U. S. 624), is more than the right to attend a meeting; it includes the right to express one's attitudes or philosophies by membership in a group or by affiliation with it or by other lawful means. Association in that context is a form of expression of opinion; and while it is not expressly included in the First Amendment its existence is necessary in making the express guarantees fully meaningful.

The foregoing cases suggest that specific guarantees in the Bill of Rights have penumbras, formed by emanations from those guarantees that help give them life and substance. See *Poe v. Ullman*, 367 U. S. 497, 516–522 (dissenting opinion). Various guarantees create zones of privacy. The right of association contained in the penumbra of the First Amendment is one, as we have seen. The Third Amendment in its prohibition against the quartering of soldiers "in any house" in time of peace without the consent of the owner is another facet of that privacy. The Fourth Amendment explicitly affirms the "right of the people to be secure in their persons, houses, papers, and effects, against unreasonable searches and seizures." The Fifth Amendment in its Self-Incrimination Clause enables the citizen to create a zone of privacy which government may not force him to surrender to his detriment. The Ninth Amendment provides: "The enumeration in the Constitution, of certain rights, shall not be construed to deny or disparage others retained by the people."

The Fourth and Fifth Amendments were described in *Boyd v. United States*, 116 U. S. 616, 630, as protection against all governmental invasions "of the sanctity of a man's home and the privacies of life." We recently referred in *Mapp v. Ohio*, 367 U. S. 643, 656, to the Fourth Amendment as creating a "right to privacy, no less important than any other right carefully and particularly reserved to the people." ***

We have had many controversies over these penumbral rights of "privacy and repose." *** These cases bear witness that the right of privacy which presses for recognition here is a legitimate one.

The present case, then, concerns a relationship lying within the zone of privacy created by several fundamental constitutional guarantees. And it concerns a law which, in forbidding the *use* of contraceptives rather than regulating their manufacture or sale, seeks to achieve its goals by means having a maximum destructive impact upon that relationship. Such a law cannot stand in light of the familiar principle, so often applied by this Court, that a "governmental purpose to control or prevent activities constitutionally subject to state regulation may not be achieved by means which sweep unnecessarily broadly and thereby invade the area of protected freedoms." *NAACP v. Alabama*, 377 U. S. 288, 307. Would we allow the police to search the sacred precincts of marital bedrooms for telltale signs of the use of contraceptives? The very idea is repulsive to the notions of privacy surrounding the marriage relationship.

We deal with a right of privacy older than the Bill of Rights—older than our political parties, older than our school system. Marriage is a coming together for better or for worse, hopefully enduring, and intimate to the degree of being sacred. It is an association that promotes a way of life, not causes; a harmony in living, not political faiths; a bilateral loyalty, not commercial or social projects. Yet it is an association for as noble a purpose as any involved in our prior decisions.

Reversed.

The *Eisenstadt* case applies the holding in *Griswold* to a Massachusetts statute that banned contraceptives for single individuals. Under the Equal Protection Clause, the court holds that married and non-married individuals could not be treated differently when it came to the use of contraceptives.

EISENSTADT v. BAIRD

Supreme Court of the United States (6–1)

405 U.S. 438 (1972)

MR. JUSTICE BRENNAN delivered the opinion of the Court.

Appellee William Baird was convicted at a bench trial in the Massachusetts Superior Court under Massachusetts General Laws Ann., c. 272, § 21, first, for exhibiting contraceptive articles in the course of delivering a lecture on contraception to a group of students at Boston University and, second, for giving a young woman a package of Emko vaginal foam at the close of his address. The Massachusetts Supreme Judicial Court unanimously set aside the conviction for exhibiting contraceptives on the ground that it violated Baird's First Amendment rights, but by a four-to-three vote sustained the conviction for giving away the foam. *Commonwealth v. Baird*, 355 Mass. 746, 247 N. E. 2d 574 (1969). Baird subsequently filed a petition for a federal writ of habeas corpus, which the District Court dismissed. 310 F. Supp. 951 (1970). On appeal, however, the Court of Appeals for the First Circuit vacated the dismissal and remanded the action with directions to grant the writ discharging Baird. 429 F. 2d 1398 (1970). This appeal by the Sheriff of Suffolk County, Massachusetts, followed, and we noted probable jurisdiction. 401 U. S. 934 (1971). We affirm.

Massachusetts General Laws Ann., c. 272, § 21, under which Baird was convicted, provides a maximum five-year term of imprisonment for "whoever … gives away … any drug, medicine, instrument or article whatever for the prevention of conception," except as authorized in § 21A. Under § 21A, "[a] registered physician may administer to or prescribe for any married person drugs or articles intended for the prevention of pregnancy or conception. [And a] registered pharmacist actually engaged in the business of pharmacy may furnish such drugs or articles to any married person presenting a prescription from a registered physician." As interpreted by the State Supreme Judicial Court, these provisions make it a felony for anyone, other than a registered physician or pharmacist acting in accordance with the terms of § 21A, to dispense any article with the intention that it be used for the prevention of conception. The statutory scheme distinguishes among three distinct classes of distributees—*first*, married persons may obtain contraceptives to prevent pregnancy, but only from doctors or druggists on prescription; *second*, single persons may not obtain contraceptives from anyone to prevent pregnancy; and, *third*, married or single persons may obtain contraceptives from anyone to prevent, not pregnancy, but the spread of disease. This construction of state law is, of course, binding on us. *E. g., Groppi v. Wisconsin*, 400 U. S. 505, 507 (1971).

* * *

We agree that the goals of deterring premarital sex and regulating the distribution of potentially harmful articles cannot reasonably be regarded as legislative aims of §§ 21 and 21A. And we hold that the statute, viewed as a prohibition on contraception *per se*, violates the rights of single persons under the Equal Protection Clause of the Fourteenth Amendment.

* * *

The basic principles governing application of the Equal Protection Clause of the Fourteenth Amendment are familiar. AS THE CHIEF JUSTICE only recently explained in *Reed v. Reed*, 404 U. S. 71, 75–76 (1971):

> "In applying that clause, this Court has consistently recognized that the Fourteenth Amendment does not deny to States the power to treat different classes of persons in different ways. *** The Equal Protection Clause of that amendment does, however, deny to States the power to legislate that different treatment be accorded to persons placed by a statute into different classes on the basis of criteria wholly unrelated to the objective of that statute. A classification 'must

> be reasonable, not arbitrary, and must rest upon some ground of difference having a fair and substantial relation to the object of the legislation, so that all persons similarly circumstanced shall be treated alike.' *Royster Guano Co. v. Virginia*, 253 U. S. 412, 415 (1920)."

The question for our determination in this case is whether there is some ground of difference that rationally explains the different treatment accorded married and unmarried persons under Massachusetts General Laws Ann., c. 272, §§ 21 and 21A. For the reasons that follow, we conclude that no such ground exists.

* * *

If under *Griswold* the distribution of contraceptives to married persons cannot be prohibited, a ban on distribution to unmarried persons would be equally impermissible. It is true that in *Griswold* the right of privacy in question inhered in the marital relationship. Yet the marital couple is not an independent entity with a mind and heart of its own, but an association of two individuals each with a separate intellectual and emotional makeup. If the right of privacy means anything, it is the right of the *individual,* married or single, to be free from unwarranted governmental intrusion into matters so fundamentally affecting a person as the decision whether to bear or beget a child. ***

On the other hand, if *Griswold* is no bar to a prohibition on the distribution of contraceptives, the State could not, consistently with the Equal Protection Clause, outlaw distribution to unmarried but not to married persons. In each case the evil, as perceived by the State, would be identical, and the underinclusion would be invidious. Mr. Justice Jackson, concurring in *Railway Express Agency v. New York*, 336 U. S. 106, 112–113 (1949), made the point:

> "The framers of the Constitution knew, and we should not forget today, that there is no more effective practical guaranty against arbitrary and unreasonable government than to require that the principles of law which officials would impose upon a minority must be imposed generally. Conversely, nothing opens the door to arbitrary action so effectively as to allow those officials to pick and choose only a few to whom they will apply legislation and thus to escape the political retribution that might be visited upon them if larger numbers were affected. Courts can take no better measure to assure that laws will be just than to require that laws be equal in operation."

Although Mr. Justice Jackson's comments had reference to administrative regulations, the principle he affirmed has equal application to the legislation here. We hold that by providing dissimilar treatment for married and unmarried persons who are similarly situated, Massachusetts General Laws Ann., c. 272, §§ 21 and 21A, violate the Equal Protection Clause. The judgment of the Court of Appeals is

Affirmed.

[Footnotes Omitted.]

Lawrence v. Texas examines the constitutionality of a Texas anti-sodomy statute.

LAWRENCE v. TEXAS

Supreme Court of United States (6–3)
539 U.S. 558 (2003)

JUSTICE KENNEDY delivered the opinion of the Court.

Liberty protects the person from unwarranted government intrusions into a dwelling or other private places. In our tradition the State is not omnipresent in the home. And there are other spheres of our lives and existence, outside the home, where the State should not be a dominant presence. Freedom extends beyond spatial bounds. Liberty presumes an autonomy of self that includes freedom of thought, belief, expression, and certain intimate conduct. The instant case involves liberty of the person both in its spatial and in its more transcendent dimensions.

I

The question before the Court is the validity of a Texas statute making it a crime for two persons of the same sex to engage in certain intimate sexual conduct.

In Houston, Texas, officers of the Harris County Police Department were dispatched to a private residence in response to a reported weapons disturbance. They entered an apartment where one of the petitioners, John Geddes Lawrence, resided. The right of the police to enter does not seem to have been questioned. The officers observed Lawrence and another man, Tyron Garner, engaging in a sexual act. The two petitioners were arrested, held in custody overnight, and charged and convicted before a Justice of the Peace.

The complaints described their crime as "deviate sexual intercourse, namely anal sex, with a member of the same sex (man)." App. to Pet. for Cert. 127a, 139a. The applicable state law is Tex. Penal Code Ann.

§ 21.06(a) (2003). It provides: "A person commits an offense if he engages in deviate sexual intercourse with another individual of the same sex." The statute defines "[d]eviate sexual intercourse" as follows:

> "(A) any contact between any part of the genitals of one person and the mouth or anus of another person; or
> "(B) the penetration of the genitals or the anus of another person with an object." § 21.01(1).

The petitioners exercised their right to a trial *de novo* in Harris County Criminal Court. They challenged the statute as a violation of the Equal Protection Clause of the Fourteenth Amendment and of a like provision of the Texas Constitution. Tex. Const., Art. 1, § 3a. Those contentions were rejected. The petitioners, having entered a plea of *nolo contendere*, were each fined $200 and assessed court costs of $141.25. App. to Pet. for Cert. 107a–110a.

The Court of Appeals for the Texas Fourteenth District considered the petitioners' federal constitutional arguments under both the Equal Protection and Due Process Clauses of the Fourteenth Amendment. After hearing the case *en banc* the court, in a divided opinion, rejected the constitutional arguments and affirmed the convictions. 41 S. W. 3d 349 (2001). The majority opinion indicates that the Court of Appeals considered our decision in *Bowers v. Hardwick*, 478 U. S. 186 (1986), to be controlling on the federal due process aspect of the case. *Bowers* then being authoritative, this was proper.

We granted certiorari, 537 U. S. 1044 (2002), to consider three questions:

1. Whether petitioners' criminal convictions under the Texas "Homosexual Conduct" law—which criminalizes sexual intimacy by same-sex couples, but not identical behavior by different-sex couples—violate the Fourteenth Amendment guarantee of equal protection of the laws.

2. Whether petitioners' criminal convictions for adult consensual sexual intimacy in the home violate their vital interests in liberty and privacy protected by the Due Process Clause of the Fourteenth Amendment.

3. Whether *Bowers v. Hardwick, supra*, should be overruled? See Pet. for Cert. i. The petitioners were adults at the time of the alleged offense. Their conduct was in private and consensual.

II

We conclude the case should be resolved by determining whether the petitioners were free as adults to engage in the private conduct in the exercise of their liberty under the Due Process Clause of the Fourteenth Amendment to the Constitution. For this inquiry we deem it necessary to reconsider the Court's holding in *Bowers*.

There are broad statements of the substantive reach of liberty under the Due Process Clause in earlier cases, including *Pierce v. Society of Sisters*, 268 U. S. 510 (1925), and *Meyer v. Nebraska*, 262 U. S. 390 (1923); but the most pertinent beginning point is our decision in *Griswold v. Connecticut*, 381 U. S. 479 (1965).

In *Griswold* the Court invalidated a state law prohibiting the use of drugs or devices of contraception and counseling or aiding and abetting the use of contraceptives. The Court described the protected interest as a right to privacy and placed emphasis on the marriage relation and the protected space of the marital bedroom. *Id.*, at 485.

After *Griswold* it was established that the right to make certain decisions regarding sexual conduct extends beyond the marital relationship. In *Eisenstadt v. Baird*, 405 U. S. 438 (1972), the Court invalidated a law prohibiting the distribution of contraceptives to unmarried persons. The case was decided under the Equal Protection Clause, *id.*, at 454; but with respect to unmarried persons, the Court went on to state the fundamental proposition that the law impaired the exercise of their personal rights, *ibid.* It quoted from the statement of the Court of Appeals finding the law to be in conflict with fundamental human rights, and it followed with this statement of its own:

> "It is true that in *Griswold* the right of privacy in question inhered in the marital relationship … If the right of privacy means anything, it is the right of the individual, married or single, to be free from unwarranted governmental intrusion into matters so fundamentally affecting a person as the decision whether to bear or beget a child." *Id.*, at 453.

The opinions in *Griswold* and *Eisenstadt* were part of the background for the decision in *Roe v. Wade*, 410 U. S. 113 (1973). As is well known, the case involved a challenge to the Texas law prohibiting abortions, but the laws of other States were affected as well. Although the Court held the woman's rights were not absolute, her right to elect an abortion did have real and substantial protection as an exercise of her liberty under the Due Process Clause. The Court cited cases that protect spatial freedom and cases that go well beyond it. *Roe* recognized the right of a woman to make certain fundamental decisions affecting her destiny and confirmed once more that the protection of liberty under the Due Process Clause has a substantive dimension of fundamental significance in defining the rights of the person.

In *Carey v. Population Services Int'l*, 431 U. S. 678 (1977), the Court confronted a New York law forbidding sale or distribution of contraceptive devices to persons under 16 years of age. Although there was no single opinion for the Court, the law was invalidated. Both *Eisenstadt* and *Carey*, as well as the holding and rationale in *Roe*, confirmed that the reasoning of *Griswold* could not be confined to the protection of rights of married adults. This was the state of the law with respect to some of the most relevant cases when the Court considered *Bowers v. Hardwick*.

The facts in *Bowers* had some similarities to the instant case. A police officer, whose right to enter seems not to have been in question, observed Hardwick, in his own bedroom, engaging in intimate sexual conduct with another adult male. The conduct was in violation of a Georgia statute making it a criminal offense to engage in sodomy. One difference between the two cases is that the Georgia statute prohibited the conduct whether or not the participants were of the same sex, while the Texas statute, as we have seen, applies only to participants of the same sex. Hardwick was not prosecuted, but he brought an action in federal court to declare the state statute invalid. He alleged he was a practicing homosexual and that the criminal prohibition violated rights guaranteed to him by the Constitution. The Court, in an opinion by Justice White, sustained the Georgia law. Chief Justice Burger and Justice Powell joined the opinion of the Court and filed separate, concurring opinions. Four Justices dissented. 478 U. S., at 199 (opinion of Blackmun, J., joined by Brennan, Marshall, and Stevens, JJ.); *id.*, at 214 (opinion of Stevens, J., joined by Brennan and Marshall, JJ.).

The Court began its substantive discussion in *Bowers* as follows: "The issue presented is whether the Federal Constitution confers a fundamental right upon homosexuals to engage in sodomy and hence invalidates the laws of the many States that still make such conduct illegal and have done so for a very long time." *Id.*, at 190. That statement, we now conclude, discloses the Court's own failure to appreciate the extent of the liberty at stake. To say that the issue in *Bowers* was simply the right to engage in certain sexual conduct demeans the claim the individual put forward, just as it would demean a married couple were it to be said marriage is simply about the right to have sexual intercourse. The laws involved in *Bowers* and here are, to be sure, statutes that purport to do no more than prohibit a particular sexual act. Their penalties and purposes, though, have more far-reaching consequences, touching upon the most private human conduct, sexual behavior, and in the most private of places, the home. The statutes do seek to control a personal relationship that, whether or not entitled to formal recognition in the law, is within the liberty of persons to choose without being punished as criminals.

This, as a general rule, should counsel against attempts by the State, or a court, to define the meaning of the relationship or to set its boundaries absent injury to a person or abuse of an institution the law protects. It suffices for us to acknowledge that adults may choose to enter upon this relationship in the confines of their homes and their own private lives and still retain their dignity as free persons. When sexuality finds overt expression in intimate conduct with another person, the conduct can be but one element in a personal bond that is more enduring. The liberty protected by the Constitution allows homosexual persons the right to make this choice.

* * *

[Author's note: The Court includes an interesting discussion on the history of laws against sodomy and homosexual conduct which is not included here due to space limitations.]

It must be acknowledged, of course, that the Court in *Bowers* was making the broader point that for centuries there have been powerful voices to condemn homosexual conduct as immoral. The condemnation has been shaped by religious beliefs, conceptions of right and acceptable behavior, and respect for the traditional family. For many persons these are not trivial concerns but profound and deep convictions accepted as ethical and moral principles to which they aspire and which thus determine the course of their lives. These considerations do not answer the question before us, however. The issue is whether the majority may use the power of the State to enforce these views on the whole society through operation of the criminal law. "Our obligation is to define the liberty of all, not to mandate our own moral code." *Planned Parenthood of Southeastern Pa. v. Casey*, 505 U. S. 833, 850 (1992).

Chief Justice Burger joined the opinion for the Court in *Bowers* and further explained his views as follows: "Decisions of individuals relating to homosexual conduct have been subject to state intervention throughout the history of Western civilization. Condemnation of those practices is firmly rooted in Judeao-Christian moral and ethical standards." 478 U. S., at 196. As with Justice White's assumptions about history, scholarship casts some doubt on the sweeping nature of the statement by Chief Justice Burger as it pertains to private homosexual conduct between consenting adults. ***.

* * *

In *Bowers* the Court referred to the fact that before 1961 all 50 States had outlawed sodomy, and that at the time of the Court's decision 24 States and the District of Columbia had sodomy laws. 478 U. S., at 192–193. Justice Powell pointed out that these prohibitions often were being ignored, however. Georgia, for instance, had not sought to enforce its law for decades. *Id.*, at 197–198, n. 2 ("The history of nonenforcement suggests the moribund character today of laws criminalizing this type of private, consensual conduct").

* * *

Of even more importance, almost five years before *Bowers* was decided the European Court of Human Rights considered a case with parallels to *Bowers* and to today's case. An adult male resident in Northern Ireland alleged he was a practicing homosexual who desired to engage in consensual homosexual conduct. The laws of Northern Ireland forbade him that right. He alleged that he had been questioned, his home had been searched, and he feared criminal prosecution. The court held that the laws proscribing the conduct were invalid under the European Convention on Human Rights. *Dudgeon v. United Kingdom,* 45 Eur. Ct. H. R. (1981) ¶ 52. Authoritative in all countries that are members of the Council of Europe (21 nations then, 45 nations now), the decision is at odds with the premise in *Bowers* that the claim put forward was insubstantial in our Western civilization.

In our own constitutional system the deficiencies in *Bowers* became even more apparent in the years following its announcement. The 25 States with laws prohibiting the relevant conduct referenced in the

Bowers decision are reduced now to 13, of which 4 enforce their laws only against homosexual conduct. In those States where sodomy is still proscribed, whether for same-sex or heterosexual conduct, there is a pattern of nonenforcement with respect to consenting adults acting in private. The State of Texas admitted in 1994 that as of that date it had not prosecuted anyone under those circumstances. *State v. Morales*, 869 S. W. 2d 941, 943.

* * *

Equality of treatment and the due process right to demand respect for conduct protected by the substantive guarantee of liberty are linked in important respects, and a decision on the latter point advances both interests. If protected conduct is made criminal and the law which does so remains unexamined for its substantive validity, its stigma might remain even if it were not enforceable as drawn for equal protection reasons. When homosexual conduct is made criminal by the law of the State, that declaration in and of itself is an invitation to subject homosexual persons to discrimination both in the public and in the private spheres. The central holding of *Bowers* has been brought in question by this case, and it should be addressed. Its continuance as precedent demeans the lives of homosexual persons.

The stigma this criminal statute imposes, moreover, is not trivial. The offense, to be sure, is but a class C misdemeanor, a minor offense in the Texas legal system. Still, it remains a criminal offense with all that imports for the dignity of the persons charged. The petitioners will bear on their record the history of their criminal convictions. Just this Term we rejected various challenges to state laws requiring the registration of sex offenders. *Smith v. Doe*, 538 U. S. 84 (2003); *Connecticut Dept. of Public Safety v. Doe*, 538 U. S. 1 (2003). We are advised that if Texas convicted an adult for private, consensual homosexual conduct under the statute here in question the convicted person would come within the registration laws of at least four States were he or she to be subject to their jurisdiction. Pet. for Cert. 13, and n. 12 (citing Idaho Code §§ 18-8301 to 18-8326 (Cum. Supp. 2002); La. Code Crim. Proc. Ann. §§ 15:540–15:549 (West 2003); Miss. Code Ann. §§ 45-33-21 to 45-33-57 (Lexis 2003); S. C. Code Ann. §§ 23-3-400 to 23-3-490 (West 2002)). This underscores the consequential nature of the punishment and the state-sponsored condemnation attendant to the criminal prohibition. Furthermore, the Texas criminal conviction carries with it the other collateral consequences always following a conviction, such as notations on job application forms, to mention but one example.

The foundations of *Bowers* have sustained serious erosion from our recent decisions in *Casey* and *Romer*. When our precedent has been thus weakened, criticism from other sources is of greater significance. In the United States criticism of *Bowers* has been substantial and continuing, disapproving of its reasoning in all respects, not just as to its historical assumptions. See, *e. g.*, C. Fried, *Order and Law: Arguing the Reagan Revolution—A Firsthand Account* 81–84 (1991); R. Posner, *Sex and Reason* 341–350 (1992). The courts of five different States have declined to follow it in interpreting provisions in their own state constitutions parallel to the Due Process Clause of the Fourteenth Amendment ***.

To the extent *Bowers* relied on values we share with a wider civilization, it should be noted that the reasoning and holding in *Bowers* have been rejected elsewhere. The European Court of Human Rights has followed not *Bowers* but its own decision in *Dudgeon v. United Kingdom*. See *P. G. & J. H. v. United Kingdom*, App. No. 00044787/98, ¶ 56 (Eur. Ct. H. R., Sept. 25, 2001); *Modinos v. Cyprus*, 259 Eur. Ct. H. R. (1993); *Norris v. Ireland*, 142 Eur. Ct. H. R. (1988). Other nations, too, have taken action consistent with an affirmation of the protected right of homosexual adults to engage in intimate, consensual conduct. See Brief for Mary Robinson et al. as *Amici Curiae* 11–12. The right the petitioners seek in this case has been accepted as an integral part of human freedom in many other countries. There has been no showing that in this country the governmental interest in circumscribing personal choice is somehow more legitimate or urgent.

The doctrine of *stare decisis* is essential to the respect accorded to the judgments of the Court and to the stability of the law. It is not, however, an inexorable command. *Payne v. Tennessee,* 501 U. S. 808, 828 (1991) ("*Stare decisis* is not an inexorable command; rather, it `is a principle of policy and not a mechanical formula of adherence to the latest decision'" (quoting *Helvering v. Hallock*, 309 U. S. 106, 119 (1940))). In *Casey* we noted that when a court is asked to overrule a precedent recognizing a constitutional liberty interest, individual or societal reliance on the existence of that liberty cautions with particular strength against reversing course. 505 U. S., at 855–856; see also *id.*, at 844 ("Liberty finds no refuge in a jurisprudence of doubt"). The holding in *Bowers*, however, has not induced detrimental reliance comparable to some instances where recognized individual rights are involved. Indeed, there has been no individual or societal reliance on *Bowers* of the sort that could counsel against overturning its holding once there are compelling reasons to do so. *Bowers* itself causes uncertainty, for the precedents before and after its issuance contradict its central holding.

The rationale of *Bowers* does not withstand careful analysis. In his dissenting opinion in *Bowers* Justice Stevens came to these conclusions:

> "Our prior cases make two propositions abundantly clear. First, the fact that the governing majority in a State has traditionally viewed a particular practice as immoral is not a sufficient reason for upholding a law prohibiting the practice; neither history nor tradition could save a law prohibiting miscegenation from constitutional attack. Second, individual decisions by married persons, concerning the intimacies of their physical relationship, even when not intended to produce offspring, are a form of `liberty' protected by the Due Process Clause of the Fourteenth Amendment. Moreover, this protection extends to intimate choices by unmarried as well as married persons." 478 U. S., at 216 (footnotes and citations omitted).

JUSTICE STEVENS' analysis, in our view, should have been controlling in *Bowers* and should control here.

Bowers was not correct when it was decided, and it is not correct today. It ought not to remain binding precedent. *Bowers v. Hardwick* should be and now is overruled.

The present case does not involve minors. It does not involve persons who might be injured or coerced or who are situated in relationships where consent might not easily be refused. It does not involve public conduct or prostitution. It does not involve whether the government must give formal recognition to any relationship that homosexual persons seek to enter. The case does involve two adults who, with full and mutual consent from each other, engaged in sexual practices common to a homosexual lifestyle. The petitioners are entitled to respect for their private lives. The State cannot demean their existence or control their destiny by making their private sexual conduct a crime. Their right to liberty under the Due Process Clause gives them the full right to engage in their conduct without intervention of the government. "It is a promise of the Constitution that there is a realm of personal liberty which the government may not enter." *Casey, supra*, at 847. The Texas statute furthers no legitimate state interest which can justify its intrusion into the personal and private life of the individual.

Had those who drew and ratified the Due Process Clauses of the Fifth Amendment or the Fourteenth Amendment known the components of liberty in its manifold possibilities, they might have been more specific. They did not presume to have this insight. They knew times can blind us to certain truths and later generations can see that laws once thought necessary and proper in fact serve only to oppress. As the Constitution endures, persons in every generation can invoke its principles in their own search for greater freedom.

The judgment of the Court of Appeals for the Texas Fourteenth District is reversed, and the case is remanded for further proceedings not inconsistent with this opinion.

The Right to Marry

Virginia Jeter and Richard Loving, an African-American woman and a white man, were married in Washington, DC. The couple, however, lived in Virginia where interracial marriages were banned. This case examines the constitutionality of such a ban. Are there any parallels between the ban on interracial marriage and the ban that most states currently still have on gay marriage? Can the analysis from this case be applied when considering the issues surrounding gay marriage?

LOVING v. COMMONWEALTH OF VIRGINIA

Supreme Court of the United States (9–0)

388 U.S. 1 (1967)

Mr. Chief Justice WARREN delivered the opinion of the Court.

This case presents a constitutional question never addressed by this Court: whether a statutory scheme adopted by the State of Virginia to prevent marriages between persons solely on the basis of racial classifications violates the Equal Protection and Due Process Clauses of the Fourteenth Amendment. For reasons which seem to us to reflect the central meaning of those constitutional commands, we conclude that these statutes cannot stand consistently with the Fourteenth Amendment.

In June 1958, two residents of Virginia, Mildred Jeter, a Negro woman, and Richard Loving, a white man, were married in the District of Columbia pursuant to its laws. Shortly after their marriage, the Lovings returned to Virginia and established their marital abode in Caroline County. At the October Term, 1958, of the Circuit Court of Caroline County, a grand jury issued an indictment charging the Lovings with violating Virginia's ban on interracial marriages. On January 6, 1959, the Lovings pleaded guilty to the charge and were sentenced to one year in jail; however, the trial judge suspended the sentence for a period of 25 years on the condition that the Lovings leave the State and not return to Virginia together for 25 years. He stated in an opinion that:

'Almighty God created the races white, black, yellow, malay and red, and he placed them on separate continents. And but for the interference with his arrangement there would be no cause for such marriages. The fact that he separated the races shows that he did not intend for the races to mix.'

After their convictions, the Lovings took up residence in the District of Columbia.

* * *

The two statutes under which appellants were convicted and sentenced are part of a comprehensive statutory scheme aimed at prohibiting and punishing interracial marriages. The Lovings were convicted of violating § 20-58 of the Virginia Code:

'Leaving State to evade law.—If any white person and colored person shall go out of this State, for the purpose of being married, and with the intention of returning, and be married out of it, and afterwards return to and reside in it, cohabiting as man and wife, they shall be punished as provided in § 20-59, and the marriage shall be governed by the same law as if it had been solemnized in this State. The fact of their cohabitation here as man and wife shall be evidence of their marriage.'

Section 20-59, which defines the penalty for miscegenation, provides:

'Punishment for marriage.—If any white person intermarry with a colored person, or any colored person intermarry with a white person, he shall be guilty of a felony and shall be punished by confinement in the penitentiary for not less than one nor more than five years.'

Other central provisions in the Virginia statutory scheme are § 20-57, which automatically voids all marriages between 'a white person and a colored person' without any judicial proceeding, and §§ 20-54 and 1-14 which, respectively, define 'white persons' and 'colored persons and Indians' for purposes of the statutory prohibitions. The Lovings have never disputed in the course of this litigation that Mrs. Loving is a 'colored person' or that Mr. Loving is a 'white person' within the meanings given those terms by the Virginia statutes.

Virginia is now one of 16 States which prohibit and punish marriages on the basis of racial classifications. Penalties for miscegenation arose as an incident to slavery and have been common in Virginia since the colonial period. The present statutory scheme dates from the adoption of the Racial Integrity Act of 1924, passed during the period of extreme nativism which followed the end of the First World War. The central features of this Act, and current Virginia law, are the absolute prohibition of a 'white person' marrying other than another 'white person,' a prohibition against issuing marriage licenses until the issuing official is satisfied that the applicants' statements as to their race are correct, certificates of 'racial composition' to be kept by both local and state registrars, and the carrying forward of earlier prohibitions against racial intermarriage.

I.

In upholding the constitutionality of these provisions in the decision below, the Supreme Court of Appeals of Virginia referred to its 1955 decision in *Naim v. Naim*, 197 Va. 80, 87 S.E.2d 749, as stating the reasons supporting the validity of these laws. In *Naim*, the state court concluded that the State's legitimate purposes were 'to preserve the racial integrity of its citizens,' and to prevent 'the corruption of blood,' 'a mongrel breed of citizens,' and 'the obliteration of racial pride,' obviously an endorsement of the doctrine of White Supremacy. *Id.*, at 90, 87 S.E.2d, at 756. The court also reasoned that marriage has traditionally been subject to state regulation without federal intervention, and, consequently, the regulation of marriage should be left to exclusive state control by the Tenth Amendment.

While the state court is no doubt correct in asserting that marriage is a social relation subject to the State's police power, *Maynard v. Hill*, 125 U.S. 190, 8 S.Ct. 723, 31 L.Ed. 654 (1888), the State does not contend in its argument before this Court that its powers to regulate marriage are unlimited notwithstanding the commands of the Fourteenth Amendment. Nor could it do so in light of *Meyer v. State of Nebraska,* 262 U.S. 390, 43 S.Ct. 625, 67 L.Ed. 1042 (1923), and *Skinner v. State of Oklahoma*, 316 U.S. 535, 62 S.Ct. 1110, 86 L.Ed. 1655 (1942). Instead, the State argues that the meaning of the Equal Protection Clause, as illuminated by the statements of the Framers, is only that state penal laws containing an interracial element as part of the definition of the offense must apply equally to whites and Negroes in the sense that members of each race are punished to the same degree. Thus, the State contends that, because its miscegenation statutes punish equally both the white and the Negro participants in an interracial marriage, these statutes, despite their reliance on racial classifications do not constitute an invidious discrimination based upon race. The second argument advanced by the State assumes the validity of its equal application theory. The argument is that, if the Equal Protection Clause does not outlaw miscegenation statutes because of their reliance on racial classifications, the question of constitutionality would thus become whether there was any rational basis for a State to treat interracial marriages differently from other marriages. On this question, the State argues, the scientific evidence is substantially in doubt and, consequently, this Court should defer to the wisdom of the state legislature in adopting its policy of discouraging interracial marriages.

Because we reject the notion that the mere 'equal application' of a statute containing racial classifications is enough to remove the classifications from the Fourteenth Amendment's proscription of all invidious racial discriminations, we do not accept the State's contention that these statutes should be upheld if there is any possible basis for concluding that they serve a rational purpose. The mere fact of equal application does not mean that our analysis of these statutes should follow the approach we have taken in cases involving no racial discrimination where the Equal Protection Clause has been arrayed against a statute discriminating between the kinds of advertising which may be displayed on trucks in *New York City, Railway Express Agency, Inc. v. People of State of New York*, 336 U.S. 106, 6 § .Ct. 463, 93 L.Ed. 533 (1949), or an exemption in Ohio's *ad valorem* tax for merchandise owned by a non-resident in a storage warehouse, *Allied Stores of Ohio, Inc. v. Bowers*, 358 U.S. 522, 79 S.Ct. 437, 3 L.Ed.2d 480 (1959). In these cases, involving distinctions not drawn according to race, the Court has merely asked whether there is any rational foundation for the discriminations, and has deferred to the wisdom of the state legislatures. In the case at bar, however, we deal with statutes containing racial classifications, and the fact of equal application does not immunize the statute from the very heavy burden of justification which the Fourteenth Amendment has traditionally required of state statutes drawn according to race.

* * *

The State finds support for its 'equal application' theory in the decision of the Court in *Pace v. State of Alabama*, 106 U.S. 583, 1 S.Ct. 637, 27 L.Ed. 207 (1883). In that case, the Court upheld a conviction under an Alabama statute forbidding adultery or fornication between a white person and a Negro which imposed a greater penalty than that of a statute proscribing similar conduct by members of the same race. The Court reasoned that the statute could not be said to discriminate against Negroes because the punishment for each participant in the offense was the same. However, as recently as the 1964 Term, in rejecting the reasoning of that case, we stated 'Pace represents a limited view of the Equal Protection Clause which has not withstood analysis in the subsequent decisions of this Court.' *McLaughlin v. Florida, supra*, 379 U.S. at 188, 85 S.Ct. at 286. As we there demonstrated, the Equal Protection Clause requires the consideration of whether the classifications drawn by any statute constitute an arbitrary and invidious discrimination. The clear and central purpose of the Fourteenth Amendment was to eliminate all official state sources of invidious racial discrimination in the States. ***

There can be no question but that Virginia's miscegenation statutes rest solely upon distinctions drawn according to race. The statutes proscribe generally accepted conduct if engaged in by members of different races. Over the years, this Court has consistently repudiated '(d)istinctions between citizens solely because of their ancestry' as being 'odious to a free people whose institutions are founded upon the doctrine of equality.' *Hirabayashi v. United States*, 320 U.S. 81, 100, 63 S.Ct. 1375, 1385, 87 L.Ed. 1774 (1943). At the very least, the Equal Protection Clause demands that racial classifications, especially suspect in criminal statutes, be subjected to the 'most rigid scrutiny,' *Korematsu v. United States*, 323 U.S. 214, 216, 65 S.Ct. 193, 194, 89 L.Ed. 194 (1944), and, if they are ever to be upheld, they must be shown to be necessary to the accomplishment of some permissible state objective, independent of the racial discrimination which it was the object of the Fourteenth Amendment to eliminate. Indeed, two members of this Court have already stated that they 'cannot conceive of a valid legislative purpose *** which makes the color of a person's skin the test of whether his conduct is a criminal offense.' *McLaughlin v. Florida, supra*, 379 U.S. at 198, 85 S.Ct. at 292, (Stewart, J., joined by Douglas, J., concurring).

There is patently no legitimate overriding purpose independent of invidious racial discrimination which justifies this classification. The fact that Virginia prohibits only interracial marriages involving white persons demonstrates that the racial classifications must stand on their own justification, as measures designed to maintain White Supremacy. We have consistently denied the constitutionality of measures which restrict the rights of citizens on account of race. There can be no doubt that restricting the freedom to marry solely because of racial classifications violates the central meaning of the Equal Protection Clause.

II.

These statutes also deprive the Lovings of liberty without due process of law in violation of the Due Process Clause of the Fourteenth Amendment. The freedom to marry has long been recognized as one of the vital personal rights essential to the orderly pursuit of happiness by free men.

Marriage is one of the 'basic civil rights of man,' fundamental to our very existence and survival. *Skinner v. State of Oklahoma*, 316 U.S. 535, 541, 62 S.Ct. 1110, 1113, 86 L.Ed. 1655 (1942). See also *Maynard v. Hill,* 125 U.S. 190, 8 S.Ct. 723, 31 L.Ed. 654 (1888). To deny this fundamental freedom on so unsupportable a basis as the racial classifications embodied in these statutes, classifications so directly subversive of the principle of equality at the heart of the Fourteenth Amendment, is surely to deprive all the State's citizens of liberty without due process of law. The Fourteenth Amendment requires that the freedom of choice to marry not be restricted by invidious racial discriminations. Under our Constitution, the freedom to marry or not marry, a person of another race resides with the individual and cannot be infringed by the State.

These convictions must be reversed. It is so ordered.

Reversed.

[Footnotes Omitted.]

The Supreme Judicial Court of Massachusetts examines the issues concerning gay marriage under the Massachusetts Constitution in the *Goodridge* case.

GOODRIDGE v. DEPARTMENT OF PUBLIC HEALTH

Supreme Judicial Court of Massachusetts, Suffolk
798 NE 2d 941 (2003)

MARSHALL, C.J.

Marriage is a vital social institution. The exclusive commitment of two individuals to each other nurtures love and mutual support; it brings stability to our society. For those who choose to marry, and for their children, marriage provides an abundance of legal, financial, and social benefits. In return it imposes weighty legal, financial, and social obligations. The question before us is whether, consistent with the Massachusetts Constitution, the Commonwealth may deny the protections, benefits, and obligations conferred by civil marriage to two individuals of the same sex who wish to marry. We conclude that it may not. The Massachusetts Constitution affirms the dignity and equality of all individuals. It forbids the creation of second-class citizens. In reaching our conclusion we have given full deference to the arguments made by the Commonwealth. But it has failed to identify any constitutionally adequate reason for denying civil marriage to same-sex couples.

We are mindful that our decision marks a change in the history of our marriage law. Many people hold deep-seated religious, moral, and ethical convictions that marriage should be limited to the union of one man and one woman, and that homosexual conduct is immoral. Many hold equally strong religious, moral, and ethical convictions that same-sex couples are entitled to be married, and that homosexual persons should be treated no differently than their heterosexual neighbors. Neither view answers the question before us. Our concern is with the Massachusetts Constitution as a charter of governance for every person properly within its reach. "Our obligation is to define the liberty of all, not to mandate our own moral code." *Lawrence v. Texas*, 123 S. Ct. 2472, 2480 (2003) (Lawrence), quoting *Planned Parenthood of Southeastern Pa. v. Casey*, 505 U.S. 833, 850 (1992).

Whether the Commonwealth may use its formidable regulatory authority to bar same-sex couples from civil marriage is a question not previously addressed by a Massachusetts appellate court. It is a question the United States Supreme Court left open as a matter of Federal law in *Lawrence*, *supra* at 2484, where it was not an issue. There, the Court affirmed that the core concept of common human dignity protected by the Fourteenth Amendment to the United States Constitution precludes government intrusion into the deeply personal realms of consensual adult expressions of intimacy and one's choice of an intimate partner. The Court also reaffirmed the central role that decisions whether to marry or have children bear in shaping one's identity. *Id.* at 2481. The Massachusetts Constitution is, if anything, more protective of individual liberty and equality than the Federal Constitution; it may demand broader protection for fundamental rights; and it is less tolerant of government intrusion into the protected spheres of private life.

Barred access to the protections, benefits, and obligations of civil marriage, a person who enters into an intimate, exclusive union with another of the same sex is arbitrarily deprived of membership in one of our community's most rewarding and cherished institutions. That exclusion is incompatible with the constitutional principles of respect for individual autonomy and equality under law.

* * *

III

A

The larger question is whether, as the department claims, government action that bars same-sex couples from civil marriage constitutes a legitimate exercise of the State's authority to regulate conduct, or whether, as the plaintiffs claim, this categorical marriage exclusion violates the Massachusetts Constitution. We have recognized the long-standing statutory understanding, derived from the common law, that "marriage" means the lawful union of a woman and a man. But that history cannot and does not foreclose the constitutional question.

The plaintiffs' claim that the marriage restriction violates the Massachusetts Constitution can be analyzed in two ways. Does it offend the Constitution's guarantees of equality before the law? Or do the liberty and due process provisions of the Massachusetts Constitution secure the plaintiffs' right to marry their chosen partner? In matters implicating marriage, family life, and the upbringing of children, the two constitutional concepts frequently overlap, as they do here. *** Much of what we say concerning one standard applies to the other.

We begin by considering the nature of civil marriage itself. Simply put, the government creates civil marriage. In Massachusetts, civil marriage is, and since pre-Colonial days has been, precisely what its name implies: a wholly secular institution. *** No religious ceremony has ever been required to validate a Massachusetts marriage. *Id.*

In a real sense, there are three partners to every civil marriage: two willing spouses and an approving State. See *DeMatteo v. DeMatteo*, 436 Mass. 18, 31 (2002) ("Marriage is not a mere contract between two parties but a legal status from which certain rights and obligations arise"); *Smith v. Smith*, 171 Mass. 404, 409 (1898) (on marriage, the parties "assume[] new relations to each other and to the State"). *** While only the parties can mutually assent to marriage, the terms of the marriage—who may marry and what obligations, benefits, and liabilities attach to civil marriage—are set by the Commonwealth. Conversely, while only the parties can agree to end the marriage (absent the death of one of them or a marriage void *ab initio*), the Commonwealth defines the exit terms. *See* G. L. c. 208.

Civil marriage is created and regulated through exercise of the police power. *See Commonwealth v. Stowell*, 389 Mass. 171, 175 (1983) (regulation of marriage is properly within the scope of the police power). "Police power" (now more commonly termed the State's regulatory authority) is an old-fashioned term for the Commonwealth's lawmaking authority, as bounded by the liberty and equality guarantees of the Massachusetts Constitution and its express delegation of power from the people to their government. In broad terms, it is the Legislature's power to enact rules to regulate conduct, to the extent that such laws are "necessary to secure the health, safety, good order, comfort, or general welfare of the community" (citations omitted). *Opinion of the Justices*, 341 Mass. 760, 785 (1960). See *Commonwealth v. Alger*, 7 Cush. 53, 85 (1851).

Without question, civil marriage enhances the "welfare of the community." It is a "social institution of the highest importance." *French v. McAnarney, supra*. Civil marriage anchors an ordered society by encouraging stable relationships over transient ones. It is central to the way the Commonwealth identifies individuals, provides for the orderly distribution of property, ensures that children and adults are cared for and supported whenever possible from private rather than public funds, and tracks important epidemiological and demographic data.

Marriage also bestows enormous private and social advantages on those who choose to marry. Civil marriage is at once a deeply personal commitment to another human being and a highly public celebration of the ideals of mutuality, companionship, intimacy, fidelity, and family. "It is an association that promotes a way of life, not causes; a harmony in living, not political faiths; a bilateral loyalty, not commercial or social projects." *Griswold v. Connecticut*, 381 U.S. 479, 486 (1965). Because it fulfils yearnings for security, safe haven, and connection that express our common humanity, civil marriage is an esteemed institution, and the decision whether and whom to marry is among life's momentous acts of self-definition.

Tangible as well as intangible benefits flow from marriage. The marriage license grants valuable property rights to those who meet the entry requirements, and who agree to what might otherwise be a burdensome degree of government regulation of their activities. See *Leduc v. Commonwealth*, 421 Mass. 433, 435 (1995), cert. denied, 519 U.S. 827 (1996) ("The historical aim of licensure generally is preservation of public health, safety, and welfare by extending the public trust only to those with proven qualifications"). The Legislature has conferred on "each party [in a civil marriage] substantial rights concerning the assets of the other which unmarried cohabitants do not have." *Wilcox v. Trautz*, 427 Mass. 326, 334 (1998). See *Collins v. Guggenheim*, 417 Mass. 615, 618 (1994) (rejecting claim for equitable distribution of property where plaintiff cohabited with but did not marry defendant); *Feliciano v. Rosemar Silver Co.*, 401 Mass. 141, 142 (1987) (government interest in promoting marriage would be "subverted" by recognition of "a right to recover for loss of consortium by a person who has not accepted the correlative responsibilities of marriage"); *Davis v. Misiano*, 373 Mass. 261, 263 (1977) (unmarried partners not entitled to rights of separate support or alimony). *See generally Attorney Gen. v. Desilets*, 418 Mass. 316, 327–328 & nn. 10, 11 (1994).

The benefits accessible only by way of a marriage license are enormous, touching nearly every aspect of life and death. The department states that "hundreds of statutes" are related to marriage and to marital benefits. With no attempt to be comprehensive, we note that some of the statutory benefits conferred by the Legislature on those who enter into civil marriage include, as to property: joint Massachusetts income tax filing (G. L. c. 62C, § 6); tenancy by the entirety (a form of ownership that provides certain protections against creditors and allows for the automatic descent of property to the surviving spouse without probate) (G. L. c. 184, § 7); extension of the benefit of the homestead protection (securing up to $300,000 in equity from creditors) to one's spouse and children (G. L. c. 188, § 1); automatic rights to inherit the property of a deceased spouse who does not leave a will (G. L. c. 190, § 1); the rights of elective share and of dower (which allow surviving spouses certain property rights where the decedent spouse has not made adequate provision for the survivor in a will) (G. L. c. 191, § 15, and G. L. c. 189); entitlement to wages owed to a deceased employee (G. L. c. 149, § 178A [general] and G. L. c. 149, § 178C [public employees]); eligibility to continue certain businesses of a deceased spouse (e.g., G. L. c. 112, § 53 [dentist]); the right to share the medical policy of one's spouse (e.g., G. L. c. 175, § 108, Second [a] [3] [defining insured's "dependent" to include one's spouse), *see Connors v. Boston*, 430 Mass. 31, 43 (1999) [domestic partners of city employees not included within term "dependent" as used in G. L. c. 32B, § 2]); thirty-nine week continuation of health coverage for the spouse of a person who is laid off or dies (e.g., G. L. c. 175, § 110G); preferential options under the Commonwealth's pension system (see G. L. c. 32, § 12 [2] ["Joint and Last Survivor Allowance"]); preferential benefits in the Commonwealth's medical program,

MassHealth (e.g., 130 Code Mass. Regs. § 515.012 [A], prohibiting placing lien on long-term care patient's former home if spouse still lives there); access to veterans' spousal benefits and preferences (e.g., G. L. c. 115, § 1 [defining "dependents"] and G. L. c. 31, § 26 [State employment] and § 28 [municipal employees]); financial protections for spouses of certain Commonwealth employees (fire fighters, police officers, and prosecutors, among others) killed in the performance of duty (e.g., G. L. c. 32, §§ 100-103); the equitable division of marital property on divorce (G. L. c. 208, § 34); temporary and permanent alimony rights (G. L. c. 208, §§ 17 and 34); the right to separate support on separation of the parties that does not result in divorce (G. L. c. 209, § 32); and the right to bring claims for wrongful death and loss of consortium, and for funeral and burial expenses and punitive damages resulting from tort actions (G. L. c. 229, §§ 1 and 2; G. L. c. 228, § 1. *See Feliciano v. Rosemar Silver Co., supra*).

Exclusive marital benefits that are not directly tied to property rights include the presumptions of legitimacy and parentage of children born to a married couple (G. L. c. 209C, § 6, and G. L. c. 46, § 4B); and evidentiary rights, such as the prohibition against spouses testifying against one another about their private conversations, applicable in both civil and criminal cases (G. L. c. 233, § 20). Other statutory benefits of a personal nature available only to married individuals include qualification for bereavement or medical leave to care for individuals related by blood or marriage (G. L. c. 149, § 52D); an automatic "family member" preference to make medical decisions for an incompetent or disabled spouse who does not have a contrary health care proxy, see *Shine v. Vega*, 429 Mass. 456, 466 (1999); the application of predictable rules of child custody, visitation, support, and removal out-of-State when married parents divorce (e.g., G. L. c. 208, § 19 [temporary custody], § 20 [temporary support], § 28 [custody and support on judgment of divorce], § 30 [removal from Commonwealth], and § 31 [shared custody plan]; priority rights to administer the estate of a deceased spouse who dies without a will, and the requirement that a surviving spouse must consent to the appointment of any other person as administrator (G. L. c. 38, § 13 [disposition of body], and G. L. c. 113, § 8 [anatomical gifts]); and the right to interment in the lot or tomb owned by one's deceased spouse (G. L. c. 114, §§ 29–33).

Where a married couple has children, their children are also directly or indirectly, but no less auspiciously, the recipients of the special legal and economic protections obtained by civil marriage. Notwithstanding the Commonwealth's strong public policy to abolish legal distinctions between marital and nonmarital children in providing for the support and care of minors, see *Department of Revenue v. Mason M.*, 439 Mass. 665 (2003); *Woodward v. Commissioner of Social Sec.*, 435 Mass. 536, 546 (2002), the fact remains that marital children reap a measure of family stability and economic security based on their parents' legally privileged status that is largely inaccessible, or not as readily accessible, to nonmarital children. Some of these benefits are social, such as the enhanced approval that still attends the status of being a marital child. Others are material, such as the greater ease of access to family-based State and Federal benefits that attend the presumptions of one's parentage.

It is undoubtedly for these concrete reasons, as well as for its intimately personal significance, that civil marriage has long been termed a "civil right." See, e.g., *Loving v. Virginia*, 388 U.S. 1, 12 (1967) ("Marriage is one of the 'basic civil rights of man,' fundamental to our very existence and survival"), quoting *Skinner v. Oklahoma*, 316 U.S. 535, 541 (1942); ***. The United States Supreme Court has described the right to marry as "of fundamental importance for all individuals" and as "part of the fundamental 'right of privacy' implicit in the Fourteenth Amendment's Due Process Clause." *Zablocki v. Redhail*, 434 U.S. 374, 384 (1978). See *Loving v. Virginia, supra* ("The freedom to marry has long been recognized as one of the vital personal rights essential to the orderly pursuit of happiness by free men").

Without the right to marry—or more properly, the right to choose to marry—one is excluded from the full range of human experience and denied full protection of the laws for one's "avowed commitment to an intimate and lasting human relationship." *Baker v. State, supra* at 229. Because civil marriage is central to the lives of individuals and the welfare of the community, our laws assiduously protect the individual's right to marry against undue government incursion. Laws may not "interfere directly and substantially with the right to marry." *Zablocki v. Redhail, supra* at 387. *See Perez v. Sharp*, 32 Cal. 2d 711, 714 (1948) ("There can be no prohibition of marriage except for an important social objective and reasonable means").

* * *

B

For decades, indeed centuries, in much of this country (including Massachusetts) no lawful marriage was possible between white and black Americans. That long history availed not when the Supreme Court of California held in 1948 that a legislative prohibition against interracial marriage violated the due process and equality guarantees of the Fourteenth Amendment, *Perez v. Sharp*, 32 Cal. 2d 711, 728 (1948), or when, nineteen years later, the United States Supreme Court also held that a statutory bar to interracial marriage violated the Fourteenth Amendment, *Loving v. Virginia*, 388 U.S. 1 (1967). As both Perez and Loving make clear, the right to marry means little if it does not include the right to marry the person of one's choice, subject to appropriate government restrictions in the interests of public health, safety, and welfare. *See Perez v. Sharp, supra* at 717 ("the essence of the right to marry is freedom to join in marriage with the person of one's choice"). See also *Loving v. Virginia, supra* at 12. In this case, as in *Perez* and *Loving*, a statute deprives individuals of access to an institution of fundamental legal, personal, and social significance—the institution of marriage—because of a single trait: skin color in *Perez* and *Loving*, sexual orientation here. As it did in *Perez* and *Loving*, history must yield to a more fully developed understanding of the invidious quality of the discrimination.

* * *

The department posits three legislative rationales for prohibiting same-sex couples from marrying: (1) providing a "favorable setting for procreation"; (2) ensuring the optimal setting for child rearing, which the department defines as "a two-parent family with one parent of each sex"; and (3) preserving scarce State and private financial resources. We consider each in turn.

The judge in the Superior Court endorsed the first rationale, holding that "the state's interest in regulating marriage is based on the traditional concept that marriage's primary purpose is procreation." This is incorrect. Our laws of civil marriage do not privilege procreative heterosexual intercourse between married people above every other form of adult intimacy and every other means of creating a family. General Laws c. 207 contains no requirement that the applicants for a marriage license attest to their ability or intention to conceive children by coitus. Fertility is not a condition of marriage, nor is it grounds for divorce. People who have never consummated their marriage, and never plan to, may be and stay married. *See Franklin v. Franklin*, 154 Mass. 515, 516 (1891) ("The consummation of a marriage by coition is not necessary to its validity"). People who cannot stir from their deathbed may marry. *See* G. L. c. 207, § 28A. While it is certainly true that many, perhaps most, married couples have children together (assisted or unassisted), it is the exclusive and permanent commitment of the marriage partners to one another, not the begetting of children, that is the *sine qua non* of civil marriage.

* * *

The department's first stated rationale, equating marriage with unassisted heterosexual procreation, shades imperceptibly into its second: that confining marriage to opposite-sex couples ensures that children are raised in the "optimal" setting. Protecting the welfare of children is a paramount State policy. Restricting marriage to opposite-sex couples, however, cannot plausibly further this policy.

* * *

The department has offered no evidence that forbidding marriage to people of the same sex will increase the number of couples choosing to enter into opposite-sex marriages in order to have and raise children. There is thus no rational relationship between the marriage statute and the Commonwealth's proffered goal of protecting the "optimal" child rearing unit. Moreover, the department readily concedes that people in same-sex couples may be "excellent" parents. These couples (including four of the plaintiff couples) have children for the reasons others do—to love them, to care for them, to nurture them. But the task of child rearing for same-sex couples is made infinitely harder by their status as outliers to the marriage laws.

* * *

In this case, we are confronted with an entire, sizeable class of parents raising children who have absolutely no access to civil marriage and its protections because they are forbidden from procuring a marriage license. It cannot be rational under our laws, and indeed it is not permitted, to penalize children by depriving them of State benefits because the State disapproves of their parents' sexual orientation.

The third rationale advanced by the department is that limiting marriage to opposite-sex couples furthers the Legislature's interest in conserving scarce State and private financial resources. The marriage restriction is rational, it argues, because the General Court logically could assume that same-sex couples are more financially independent than married couples and thus less needy of public marital benefits, such as tax advantages, or private marital benefits, such as employer-financed health plans that include spouses in their coverage.

An absolute statutory ban on same-sex marriage bears no rational relationship to the goal of economy. First, the department's conclusory generalization—that same-sex couples are less financially dependent on each other than opposite-sex couples—ignores that many same-sex couples, such as many of the plaintiffs in this case, have children and other dependents (here, aged parents) in their care. The department does not contend, nor could it, that these dependents are less needy or deserving than the dependents of married couples. Second, Massachusetts marriage laws do not condition receipt of public and private financial benefits to married individuals on a demonstration of financial dependence on each other; the benefits are available to married couples regardless of whether they mingle their finances or actually depend on each other for support.

The department suggests additional rationales for prohibiting same-sex couples from marrying, which are developed by some amici. It argues that broadening civil marriage to include same-sex couples will trivialize or destroy the institution of marriage as it has historically been fashioned. Certainly our decision today marks a significant change in the definition of marriage as it has been inherited from the common law, and understood by many societies for centuries. But it does not disturb the fundamental value of marriage in our society.

Here, the plaintiffs seek only to be married, not to undermine the institution of civil marriage. They do not want marriage abolished. They do not attack the binary nature of marriage, the consanguinity provisions, or any of the other gate-keeping provisions of the marriage licensing law. Recognizing the right of an individual to marry a person of the same sex will not diminish the validity or dignity of opposite-sex marriage, any more than recognizing the right of an individual to marry a person of a different race devalues the marriage of a person who marries someone of her own race. If anything, extending civil marriage to same-sex couples reinforces the importance of marriage to individuals and communities. That same-sex couples are willing to embrace marriage's solemn obligations of exclusivity, mutual support, and commitment to one another is a testament to the enduring place of marriage in our laws and in the human spirit.

* * *

The history of constitutional law "is the story of the extension of constitutional rights and protections to people once ignored or excluded." *United States v. Virginia*, 518 U.S. 515, 557 (1996) (construing equal protection clause of Fourteenth Amendment to prohibit categorical exclusion of women from public military institute). This statement is as true in the area of civil marriage as in any other area of civil rights. See, e.g., *Turner v. Safley*, 482 U.S. 78 (1987); *Loving v. Virginia*, 388 U.S. 1 (1967); *Perez v. Sharp*, 32 Cal.2d

711 (1948). As a public institution and a right of fundamental importance, civil marriage is an evolving paradigm. ***

* * *

The marriage ban works a deep and scarring hardship on a very real segment of the community for no rational reason. The absence of any reasonable relationship between, on the one hand, an absolute disqualification of same-sex couples who wish to enter into civil marriage and, on the other, protection of public health, safety, or general welfare, suggests that the marriage restriction is rooted in persistent prejudices against persons who are (or who are believed to be) homosexual. "The Constitution cannot control such prejudices but neither can it tolerate them. Private biases may be outside the reach of the law, but the law cannot, directly or indirectly, give them effect." *Palmore v. Sidoti*, 466 U.S. 429, 433 (1984) (construing Fourteenth Amendment). Limiting the protections, benefits, and obligations of civil marriage to opposite-sex couples violates the basic premises of individual liberty and equality under law protected by the Massachusetts Constitution.

IV

We consider next the plaintiffs' request for relief. ***

Here, no one argues that striking down the marriage laws is an appropriate form of relief. Eliminating civil marriage would be wholly inconsistent with the Legislature's deep commitment to fostering stable families and would dismantle a vital organizing principle of our society. We face a problem similar to one that recently confronted the Court of Appeal for Ontario, the highest court of that Canadian province, when it considered the constitutionality of the same-sex marriage ban under the Canadian Charter of Rights and Freedoms (Charter), part of Canada's Federal Constitution. See *Halpern v. Toronto* (City), 172 O.A.C. 276 (2003). Canada, like the United States, adopted the common law of England that civil marriage is "the voluntary union for life of one man and one woman, to the exclusion of all others." *Id.* at par. (36), quoting *Hyde v. Hyde*, [1861–1873] All E.R. 175 (1866). In holding that the limitation of civil marriage to opposite-sex couples violated the Charter, the Court of Appeal refined the common-law meaning of marriage. We concur with this remedy, which is entirely consonant with established principles of jurisprudence empowering a court to refine a common-law principle in light of evolving constitutional standards. *See Powers v. Wilkinson*, 399 Mass. 650, 661–662 (1987) (reforming common-law rule of construction of "issue"); *Lewis v. Lewis*, 370 Mass. 619, 629 (1976) (abolishing common-law rule of certain interspousal immunity).

We construe civil marriage to mean the voluntary union of two persons as spouses, to the exclusion of all others. This reformulation redresses the plaintiffs' constitutional injury and furthers the aim of marriage to promote stable, exclusive relationships. It advances the two legitimate State interests the department has identified: providing a stable setting for child rearing and conserving State resources. It leaves intact the Legislature's broad discretion to regulate marriage. *See Commonwealth v. Stowell*, 389 Mass. 171, 175 (1983).

In their complaint the plaintiffs request only a declaration that their exclusion and the exclusion of other qualified same-sex couples from access to civil marriage violates Massachusetts law. We declare that barring an individual from the protections, benefits, and obligations of civil marriage solely because that person would marry a person of the same sex violates the Massachusetts Constitution. We vacate the summary judgment for the department. We remand this case to the Superior Court for entry of judgment consistent with this opinion. Entry of judgment shall be stayed for 180 days to permit the Legislature to take such action as it may deem appropriate in light of this opinion. See, e.g., *Michaud v. Sheriff of Essex County*, 390 Mass. 523, 535–536 (1983).

So ordered.

[Footnotes Omitted.]

Abortion

No law and society book would be complete without a mention of abortion rights. People are either for or against abortion for a plethora of reasons, including but not limited to individual liberties, religious beliefs, philosophical concerns, and human rights issues. In *Roe v. Wade*, the Supreme Court found that the right to abortion was a privacy issue and was thus protected under the Constitution.

Much of the controversy and ultimately the legal right to abortions under the Constitution revolve around the issue of when life begins. If there were ever to be a definitive determination that life began at conception, the right to abortion would obviously not exist. There would be no exceptions to allow for abortions in cases to protect the health or save the life of the mother, in cases of rape or incest, or in cases where a child would be born with devastating birth defects.

This determination would cause ripple effects in society that could grow to tsunami-like proportions, as areas such as in vitro fertilization and medical research would necessarily become involved. If human life begins at conception, then the embryonic cells that result from the union of egg and sperm would hold the same rights as a human. Would in vitro fertilization, therefore, become illegal? How can one justify freezing an embryo for sometimes years on end if it is considered to be a human life? Can one simply throw away any unused and/or unwanted embryos? Can one sell the embryos or even put them up for adoption? Are embryos property? Can one utilize stem cells derived from any part of the developmental process for research or to help cure disease, neurological disorders, or paralysis? Each of these issues comes down to this … when is a human a human?

The following are short excerpts from the *Roe v. Wade* oral re-arguments. Ms. Weddington represents Roe. Mr. Flowers represents Texas. The full transcript and audio recordings can be found at The Oyez Project, *Roe v. Wade*, 410 U.S. 113 (1973) available at: (http://oyez.org/cases/1970-1979/1971/1971_70_18) (last visited Saturday, August 27, 2011).

Justice Harry A. Blackmun: Well, do I get from this then that your case depends primarily on the proposition that the fetus has no constitutional rights?

Ms. Sarah Weddington: It depends on saying that the woman has a fundament constitutional right and that the state has not proved any compelling interest for regulation in the area.

Even if the Court, at some point, determined the fetus to be entitled to constitutional protection, you would still get back into the weighing of one life against another.

Justice Byron R. White: And that's what's involved in this case, weighing one's life against another?

Ms. Sarah Weddington: No, Your Honor.

I said that would be what would be involved if the facts were different and the state could prove that there was a person for the constitutional right.

Justice Potter Stewart: Well, if it were established that an unborn fetus is a person within the protection of the Fourteenth Amendment, you would have almost an impossible case here, would you not?

Ms. Sarah Weddington: I would have a very difficult case. [Laughter]

Justice Potter Stewart: You certainly would because you'd have the same kind of thing you'd have to say that this would be the equivalent to after the child was born.

Ms. Sarah Weddington: That's right.

Justice Potter Stewart: If the mother thought that it bothered her health having the child around, she could have it killed.

Isn't that correct?

Ms. Sarah Weddington: That's correct.

* * *

Mr. Robert C. Flowers: Your Honor, it's our position that your definition of a person is so basic.

It's so fundamental that it is—the framers of the constitution had not even set out to define.

We can only go to what the teachings at the time that the constitution was framed.

We have numerous listings in the brief by Mr. Joe Witherspoon, a professor at the University of Texas, that tries to trace back what was in their mind when they had the person concept when they drew up the constitution.

He quoted Blackstone in 1765 and he observed in his commentaries that life, this right is inherent by nature in every individual and exists even before the child is born.

I submit to you that the Declaration of Independence, we hold, is—

Justice Harry A. Blackmun: When you quote Blackstone, is it not true that in Blackstone's time abortion was not a felony?

Mr. Robert C. Flowers: That's true, Your Honor, but what my point there was to see the thinking of the framers of the constitution from the people they've learned from and the general attitude of the time.

Justice Harry A. Blackmun: Well, I think—I'm just wondering if there's a basic consistency there and let me go back to something else that you said.

Is it not true or is it true that the medical profession itself is not in agreement as to when life begins?

Mr. Robert C. Flowers: I think that's true, sir.

But from a layman's stand point, medically speaking, we would say that at the moment of conception from the chromosomes, every potential that anybody in this room has is present from the moment of conception.

Justice Harry A. Blackmun: Then you're speaking of potential of life.

Mr. Robert C. Flowers: Yes, sir.

Justice Harry A. Blackmun: With which everyone can agree perhaps.

Mr. Robert C. Flowers: On the 7th day, I think that the heart, in some form, starts beating.

On the 20th day, practically all the facilities are there that you and I have, Your Honor.

I think—

Justice Byron R. White: If you're correct that the fetus is a person, then I don't suppose you'd have a—the state would have great trouble permitting an abortion, wouldn't it?

Mr. Robert C. Flowers: Yes, sir.

Justice Byron R. White: In any circumstance.

Mr. Robert C. Flowers: It would, yes, sir.

Justice Byron R. White: To save the life of the mother or her health or anything else?

Mr. Robert C. Flowers: Well, there would be the balancing of the two lives and I think that—

Justice Byron R. White: What would you choose?

Would you choose to kill the innocent one or what?

Mr. Robert C. Flowers: Well, in this—in our statutes, the state did choose that way, Your Honor.

Well, in the protection of the mother.

Justice Thurgood Marshall: Well, could the State of Texas say that if it's for the benefit of the health of the wife, they can kill the husband?

Mr. Robert C. Flowers: I'm sorry, I didn't understand.

Justice Thurgood Marshall: Could Texas say, if it comes to a situation for the benefit and the health of the wife that the husband has to die, could they kill him?

Mr. Robert C. Flowers: I wouldn't think so.

Justice Thurgood Marshall: That's right.

* * *

Justice Potter Stewart: It's an offense to kill a child in the process of childbirth.

Mr. Robert C. Flowers: Yes.

Justice Potter Stewart: Isn't it?

Mr. Robert C. Flowers: It would be immediately before childbirth or right in the proximity of the child being born.

Justice Thurgood Marshall: Which, is not an abortion.

Mr. Robert C. Flowers: Which is not—would not be an abortion, yes, you're correct.

It would be homicide.

And we feel that the concept of fetus being in the—within the concept of a person within the framework of the United States Constitution and the Texas Constitution is an extremely fundamental thing.

Justice Potter Stewart: Of course, if you're right about that, you can sit down.

You've won your case.

Mr. Robert C. Flowers: Your Honor—

Justice Potter Stewart: That acceptance of ours may be the Texas abortion law presently goes too far in allowing abortion.

Mr. Robert C. Flowers: Yes, sir.

That's exactly right.

We feel that this is the only question really that this Court has to answer.

We have—

Justice Byron R. White: Do you think the case is over for you?

You've lost your case if the fetus or the embryo is not a person, is that it?

Mr. Robert C. Flowers: Yes, sir.

I would say so.

* * *

Justice Potter Stewart: If you're right that an unborn is a person, then you can't leave it to the legislature to play fast and loose without dealing with that person.

In other words, if you're correct in your basic submission that an unborn fetus is a person, then abortion law such as that which New York has is grossly unconstitutional, isn't it?

Mr. Robert C. Flowers: That's right.

Yes, sir.

Justice Potter Stewart: Allowing the killing of people.

Mr. Robert C. Flowers: Yes, sir.

Justice Potter Stewart: Of persons.

Mr. Robert C. Flowers: Your Honor, the Massachusetts, I might point out—

Justice Potter Stewart: So you can't leave this up to the legislature.

There's a constitutional problem, isn't there?

Mr. Robert C. Flowers: Well, if there would be exceptions within this—

Justice Potter Stewart: And the basic constitutional question initially is whether or not an unborn fetus is a person, isn't it?

Mr. Robert C. Flowers: Yes, and entirely to the constitutional perspective.

Justice Potter Stewart: It's critical to this case, is it not?

Mr. Robert C. Flowers: Yes, sir, it is …

Frozen Embryos

A divorced couple had a disagreement over their frozen pre-embryos. The court in *J.B. v. M.B.* discusses the disposition of those pre-embryos.

J.B. v. M.B.

Supreme Court of New Jersey
783 A.2d 707 (2001)

The opinion of the Court was delivered by PORITZ, C.J.

In this case, a divorced couple disagree about the disposition of seven preembryos that remain in storage after the couple, during their marriage, undertook in vitro fertilization procedures. We must first decide whether the husband and wife have entered into an enforceable contract that is now determinative on the disposition issue. If not, we must consider how such conflicts should be resolved by our courts.

Although the reproductive technology to accomplish in vitro fertilization has existed since the 1970s, there is little caselaw to guide us in our inquiry.

I

A

J.B. and M.B. were married in February 1992. After J.B. suffered a miscarriage early in the marriage, the couple encountered difficulty conceiving a child and sought medical advice from the Jefferson Center for Women's Specialties. Although M.B. did not have infertility problems, J.B. learned that she had a condition that prevented her from becoming pregnant. On that diagnosis, the couple decided to attempt in vitro fertilization at the Cooper Center for In Vitro Fertilization, P.C. (the Cooper Center).

* * *

The Cooper Center's consent form describes the procedure:

> IVF [or in vitro fertilization] will be accomplished in a routine fashion: that is, ovulation induction followed by egg recovery, insemination, fertilization, embryo development and embryo transfer of up to three or four embryos in the stimulated cycle. With the couple's consent, any "extra" embryos beyond three or four will be cryopreserved according to our freezing protocol and stored at -196C. Extra embryos, upon thawing, must meet certain criteria for viability before being considered eligible for transfer. These criteria require that a certain minimum number of cells composing the embryo survive the freeze-thaw process. These extra embryos will be transferred into the woman's uterus in one or more future menstrual cycles for the purpose of establishing a normal pregnancy. The physicians and embryologists on the IVF team will be responsible for determining the appropriate biological conditions and the timing for transfers of cryopreserved embryos.

The consent form also contains language discussing the control and disposition of the preembryos:

> The control and disposition of the embryos belongs to the Patient and her Partner. You will be asked to execute the attached legal statement regarding control and disposition of cryopreserved embryos. The IVF team will not be obligated to proceed with the transfer of any cryopreserved embryos if experience indicates the risks outweigh the benefits.

Before undertaking in vitro fertilization in March 1995, the Cooper Center gave J.B. and M.B. the consent form with an attached agreement for their signatures. The agreement states, in relevant part:

> I, J.B. (patient), and M.B. (partner), agree that all control, direction, and ownership of our tissues will be relinquished to the IVF Program under the following circumstances:

> 1. A dissolution of our marriage by court order, unless the court specifies who takes control and direction of the tissues …

B

* * *

The couple's final judgment of divorce, entered in September 1998, resolved all issues except disposition of the preembryos. Shortly thereafter, the trial court granted J.B.'s motion for summary judgment on that issue. The court found that the reason for the parties' decision to attempt in vitro fertilization—to create a family as a married couple—no longer existed. J.B. and M.B. had become parents and were now divorced. Moreover, M.B. was not infertile and could achieve parenthood in the future through natural means. The court did not accept M.B.'s argument that the parties undertook the in vitro fertilization procedure to "create life," and found no need for further fact finding on the existence of an agreement between them, noting that there was no written contract memorializing the parties' intentions. Because the husband was "fully able to father a child," and because he sought control of the preembryos "merely to donate them to another couple," the court concluded that the wife had "the greater interest and should prevail."

The Appellate Division affirmed. *J.B. v. M.B.*, 331 N.J.Super. 223, 751 A.2d 613 (2000). The court noted the inconsistency between the trial court's finding that "the parties engaged in IVF to create their child within the context of their marriage" and M.B.'s claim that the couple had entered into an agreement to donate or use, and not to destroy, the preembryos. *Id.* at 228, 751 A.2d 613. Before the Appellate Division, the husband argued that his constitutional right to procreate had been violated by the ruling of the trial court and sought a remand to establish the parties' understanding regarding the disposition of the preembryos. *Ibid.*

The Appellate Division understood this case to "involv[e] an attempt to enforce an alleged agreement to use embryos to create a child." *Id.* at 231, 751 A.2d 613. It initially examined that "attempt" in the context of two fundamental rights, "the right to procreate and the right not to procreate," citing *Skinner v. Oklahoma*, 316 U.S. 535, 541, 62 S.Ct. 1110, 1113, 86 L.Ed. 1655, 1660 (1942), and *Roe v. Wade*, 410 U.S. 113, 152–53, 93 S.Ct. 705, 726, 35 L.Ed.2d 147, 176–77 (1973), among other cases. *J.B., supra*, 331 N.J.Super. at 231–32, 751 A.2d 613. The court found that, on the facts presented, the conflict between those rights was "more apparent than real." *Id.* at 232, 751 A.2d 613. It observed that destruction of the preembryos would not seriously impair M.B.'s constitutional right to procreate since "he retains the capacity to father children." *Ibid.* In contrast, allowing donation or use of the preembryos would impair J.B.'s right not to procreate "[e]ven if [she was] relieved of the financial and custodial responsibility for her child" because she would then have been forced to allow strangers to raise that child. *Ibid.* In those circumstances, and assuming "that the Fourteenth Amendment applies," the court found no impairment of the husband's constitutional rights. *Ibid.*

Nonetheless, the court chose not to decide this case on constitutional grounds. *Id.* at 233, 751 A.2d 613. In its view, whether court enforcement of the alleged agreement would constitute state action under the Fourteenth Amendment was unclear, and resolution of the constitutional issue was not necessary to dispose of the litigation. *Id.* at 233–34, 751 A.2d 613. The court concluded "that a contract to procreate is contrary to New Jersey public policy and is unenforceable." *Id.* at 234, 751 A.2d 613. In affirming the judgment of the trial court in favor of J.B., the panel considered the parties' views and the trial court's opinion, and determined that destruction of the preembryos was required. *Id.* at 235, 751 A.2d 613.

We granted certification, 165 N.J. 530, 760 A.2d 783 (2000), and now modify and affirm the judgment of the Appellate Division.

* * *

III

In essence, J.B. and M.B. have agreed only that on their divorce the decision in respect of control, and therefore disposition, of their cryopreserved preembryos will be directed by the court. In this area, however, there are few guideposts for decision-making. Advances in medical technology have far outstripped the development of legal principles to resolve the inevitable disputes arising out of the new reproductive opportunities now available. For infertile couples, those opportunities may present the only way to have a biological family. Yet, at the point when a husband and wife decide to begin the in vitro fertilization process, they are unlikely to anticipate divorce or to be concerned about the disposition of preembryos on divorce. As they are both contributors of the genetic material comprising the preembryos, the decision should be theirs to make. ***

But what if, as here, the parties disagree. Without guidance from the Legislature, we must consider a means by which courts can engage in a principled review of the issues presented in such cases in order to achieve a just result. Because the claims before us derive, in part, from concepts found in the Federal Constitution and the Constitution of this State, we begin with those concepts.

A

Both parties and the ACLU Amici invoke the right to privacy in support of their respective positions. More specifically, they claim procreational autonomy as a fundamental attribute of the privacy rights guaranteed by both the Federal and New Jersey Constitutions. Their arguments are based on various opinions of the United States Supreme Court that discuss the right to be free from governmental interference with procreational decisions. ***

In *Skinner v. Oklahoma*, *supra*, the Court spoke of that most "basic liberty[ ]" when rejecting, on equal protection grounds, an Oklahoma statute that required sterilization of certain repeat criminal offenders. 316 U.S. at 541, 62 S.Ct. at 1113, 86 L.Ed. at 1660. "Marriage and procreation," said Justice Douglas, "are fundamental to the very existence and survival of the race." *Ibid.* Later, in Griswold, *supra*, and Eisenstadt, *supra*, the Court invalidated statutes restricting use of and access to contraceptives by both married and unmarried couples, stating in *Griswold* that prohibitions on the use of contraceptives unconstitutionally infringe on the sanctity and privacy of the marital relationship, 381 U.S. at 485–86, 85 S.Ct. at 1682, 14 L.Ed.2d at 515–16, and, in Eisenstadt, that "[i]f the right of privacy means anything, it is the right of the individual, married or single, to be free from unwarranted governmental intrusion into matters so fundamentally affecting a person as the decision whether to bear or beget a child," 405 U.S. at 453, 92 S.Ct. at 1038, 31 L. Ed.2d at 362.

This Court also has recognized the fundamental nature of procreational rights. In *In re Baby M*, we considered a custody dispute between a father and a surrogate mother. 10,9 N.J. 396, 537 A.2d 1227 (1988). Although the case involved the enforceability of a surrogacy contract, the father asserted that his right to procreate supported his claim for custody of Baby M. *Id.* at 447–48, 537 A.2d 1227. We held that the right to procreate was not implicated by the custody battle, which dealt with parental rights after birth. *Ibid.* We observed, however, that "the rights of personal intimacy, of marriage, of sex, of family, of procreation ... are fundamental rights protected by both the federal and state Constitutions." *Id.* at 447, 537 A.2d 1227; see also *In re Grady,* 8,5 N.J. 235, 426 A.2d 467 (1981) (recognizing that decisions in *Griswold* and *Eisenstadt* ended "any doubt about a personal right to prevent conception," and holding that "an individual's constitutional right of privacy includes the right to undergo sterilization voluntarily"); cf. *Schroeder v. Perkel,* 87 N.J. 53, 66, 432 A.2d 834 (1981) (allowing recovery against defendants whose negligent diagnosis deprived mother of right to choose not to conceive child with genetic defect).

Those decisions provide a framework within which disputes over the disposition of preembryos can be resolved. In *Davis, supra*, for example, a divorced couple could not agree on the disposition of their unused, cryopreserved preembryos. 842 S.W.2d at 589. The Tennessee Supreme Court balanced the right to procreate of the party seeking to donate the preembryos (the wife), against the right not to procreate of the party seeking destruction of the preembryos (the husband). *Id.* at 603. The court concluded that the husband's right would be significantly affected by unwanted parenthood "with all of its possible financial and psychological consequences." *Ibid.* In his case, that burden was the greater because, as a child, he had been separated from his parents after they divorced and his mother suffered a nervous breakdown. *Id.* at 603–04. Because of his personal experiences, the husband was "vehemently opposed to fathering a child that would not live with both parents." *Id.* at 604.

Against that interest, the court weighed the wife's "burden of knowing that the lengthy IVF procedures she underwent were futile, and that the preembryos to which she contributed genetic material would never become children." *Ibid.* Although that burden was not insignificant, the court found that it did not outweigh the father's interest in avoiding procreation. *Ibid.* The court held that the scales "[o]rdinarily" would tip in favor of the right not to procreate if the opposing party could become a parent through other reasonable means. *Ibid.*

B

We agree with the Tennessee Supreme Court that "[o]rdinarily, the party wishing to avoid procreation should prevail." *Ibid*. Here, the Appellate Division succinctly described the "apparent" conflict between J.B. and M.B.:

In the present case, the wife's right not to become a parent seemingly conflicts with the husband's right to procreate. The conflict, however, is more apparent than real. Recognition and enforcement of the wife's right would not seriously impair the husband's right to procreate. Though his right to procreate using the wife's egg would be terminated, he retains the capacity to father children. ***

In other words, M.B.'s right to procreate is not lost if he is denied an opportunity to use or donate the preembryos. M.B. is already a father and is able to become a father to additional children, whether through natural procreation or further in vitro fertilization. In contrast, J.B.'s right not to procreate may be lost through attempted use or through donation of the preembryos. Implantation, if successful, would result in the birth of her biological child and could have life-long emotional and psychological repercussions. *** Her fundamental right not to procreate is irrevocably extinguished if a surrogate mother bears J.B.'s child. We will not force J.B. to become a biological parent against her will.

C

The court below "conclude[d] that a contract to procreate is contrary to New Jersey public policy and is unenforceable." 331 N.J.Super. at 234, 751 A.2d 613. That determination follows the reasoning of the Massachusetts Supreme Judicial Court in *A.Z. v. B.Z.*, wherein an agreement to compel biological parenthood was deemed unenforceable as a matter of public policy. 431 Mass. 150, 725 N.E.2d 1051, 1057–58 (2000). The Massachusetts court likened enforcement of a contract permitting implantation of preembryos to other contracts to enter into familial relationships that were unenforceable under the laws of Massachusetts, i.e., contracts to marry or to give up a child for adoption prior to the fourth day after birth. *Id.*, 431 Mass. 150, 725 N.E.2d at 1058. In a similar vein, the court previously had refused to enforce a surrogacy contract without a reasonable waiting period during which the surrogate mother could revoke her consent, and a contract to abandon or to prevent marriage. *Id.*, 431 Mass. 150, 725 N.E.2d at 1059. Likewise, the court declined to enforce a contract that required an individual to become a parent. *Id.*, 431 Mass. 150, 725 N.E.2d at 1058.

* * *

That public policy also led this Court to conclude in *Baby M, supra*, that a surrogacy contract was unenforceable. 109 N.J. at 433-34, 537 A.2d 1227. We held that public policy prohibited a binding agreement to require a surrogate, there the biological mother, to surrender her parental rights. *Id.* at 411, 537 A.2d 1227. The contract in *Baby M* provided for a $10,000 payment to the surrogate for her to be artificially inseminated, carry the child to term, and then, after the child's birth, relinquish parental rights to the father and his wife. *Id.* at 411–12, 537 A.2d 1227. The surrogate mother initially surrendered the child to the father, but subsequently reconsidered her decision and fled with *Baby M. Id.* at 414–15, 537 A.2d 1227. In an action by the father to enforce the surrogacy contract, we held that the contract conflicted with "(1) laws prohibiting the use of money in connection with adoptions; (2) laws requiring proof of parental unfitness or abandonment before termination of parental rights is ordered or an adoption is granted; and (3) laws that make surrender of custody and consent to adoption revocable in private placement adoptions." *Id.* at 423, 537 A.2d 1227. Our decision was consistent with the policy expressed earlier in *Sees, supra*, that consent to terminate parental rights was revocable in all but statutorily approved circumstances. 74 N.J. at 212, 377 A.2d 628.

Enforcement of a contract that would allow the implantation of preembryos at some future date in a case where one party has reconsidered his or her earlier acquiescence raises similar issues. If implantation is successful, that party will have been forced to become a biological parent against his or her will. We note disagreement on the issue both among legal commentators and in the limited caselaw on the subject.

* * *

The public policy concerns that underlie limitations on contracts involving family relationships are protected by permitting either party to object at a later date to provisions specifying a disposition of preembryos that that party no longer accepts. Moreover, despite the conditional nature of the disposition provisions, in the large majority of cases the agreements will control, permitting fertility clinics and other like facilities to rely on their terms. Only when a party affirmatively notifies a clinic in writing of a change in intention should the disposition issue be reopened. Principles of fairness dictate that agreements provided by a clinic should be written in plain language, and that a qualified clinic representative should review the terms with the parties prior to execution. Agreements should not be signed in blank, as in A.Z., *supra*, 725 N.E.2d at 1057, or in a manner suggesting that the parties have not given due consideration to the disposition question. Those and other reasonable safeguards should serve to limit later disputes.

Finally, if there is disagreement as to disposition because one party has reconsidered his or her earlier decision, the interests of both parties must be evaluated. See *supra* at 716–17. Because ordinarily the party choosing not to become a biological parent will prevail, we do not anticipate increased litigation as a result of our decision. In this case, after having considered that M.B. is a father and is capable of fathering additional children, we have affirmed J.B.'s right to prevent implantation of the preembryos. We express no opinion in respect of a case in which a party who has become infertile seeks use of stored preembryos against the wishes of his or her partner, noting only that the possibility of adoption also may be a consideration, among others, in the court's assessment.

IV

Under the judgment of the Appellate Division, the seven remaining preembryos are to be destroyed. It was represented to us at oral argument, however, that J.B. does not object to their continued storage if M.B. wishes to pay any fees associated with that storage. M.B. must inform the trial court forthwith whether he will do so; otherwise, the preembryos are to be destroyed.

The judgment of the Appellate Division is affirmed as modified.

[Footnotes Omitted.]

Family Leave

In the *Knussman* case, the court decides whether there was a violation of a male state trooper's Constitutional rights, under the Equal Protection Clause, when he was denied leave under the Family and Medical Leave Act.

KNUSSMAN v. STATE OF MARYLAND

United States Court Of Appeals for the Fourth Circuit

272 F.3d 625 (4th Cir. 2001)

TRAXLER, Circuit Judge:

Howard Kevin Knussman, a trooper in the Maryland State Police, brought an action alleging that the State of Maryland and several individual employees of the Maryland State Police (collectively "the defendants") unlawfully discriminated against him on the basis of his gender, for which he sought recourse under 42 U.S.C.A. § 1983 (West Supp. 2000); and that the defendants violated his rights under the Family and Medical Leave Act of 1993 (FMLA), see 29 U.S.C.A. §§ 2601–2654 (West 1999), for which he sought recourse under § 1983 and directly under the FMLA. Following a jury trial and various post-trial motions, judgment in the amount of $375,000 was entered against only one of the defendants—Jill Mullineaux, a civilian employee of the Maryland State Police.

On appeal, Mullineaux contends that she was entitled to qualified immunity. Alternatively, she challenges the verdict on several grounds. We conclude that Mullineaux was not entitled to qualified immunity; however, we find that the award of damages was excessive. Accordingly, we set aside the jury's award of damages and remand for further proceedings on that issue.

I.

In 1994, Knussman learned that his wife Kimberly was pregnant. At the time, Knussman held the rank of trooper first class and served as a paramedic on medevac helicopters in the Aviation Division of the Maryland State Police ("MSP"). Unfortunately, Kim's pregnancy was difficult and ultimately resulted in her confinement to bed rest in the latter stages prior to delivery. In October 1994, Knussman submitted a written request to his supervisor asking that Knussman be permitted to take four to eight weeks of paid "family sick leave" to care for his wife and spend time with his family following the birth of his child. J.A. 121. Eventually, Knussman was informed by the MSP Director of Flight Operations, First Sergeant Ronnie P. Creel, that there was "no way" that he would be allowed more than two weeks. Creel testified that, at the time of Knussman's request, the Aviation Division was understaffed. According to Knussman, Creel misinformed him that if he wanted more leave, he would be forced to take unpaid leave because the FMLA did not entitle him to further paid leave. Knussman testified that he was unfamiliar with the FMLA because the MSP had failed to provide proper notice to its employees about their rights under the FMLA.

In early December, shortly before the Knussmans' daughter was born, Jill Mullineaux, manager of the medical leave and benefit section of the MSP Personnel Management Division, notified all MSP employees of a new Maryland statutory provision that allowed the use of paid sick leave by a state employee to care for a newborn. See Md. Code Ann., State Pers. & Pens. §§ 7-502(b)(3), 7-508 (1994). The statute permitted "[p]rimary care givers" to "use, without certification of illness or disability, up to 30 days of accrued sick leave to care for [a] child ... immediately following: ... the birth of the employee's child." Md. Code Ann., State Pers. & Pens. § 7-508(a)(1). A "[p]rimary care giver" was defined as "an employee who is primarily responsible for the care and nurturing of a child." Md. Code Ann., State Pers. & Pens. § 7-508(a)(1). By contrast, a "[s]econdary care giver," i.e., "an employee who is secondarily responsible for the care and nurturing of a child," might use up to 10 days of accrued sick leave without providing proof of illness or disability. Md. Code Ann., State Pers. & Pens. § 7-508(b)(1). In contrast to "family sick leave," which required an employee to provide verification of a family member's illness, the new "nurturing leave" provision permitted an employee to use paid sick leave without providing any medical documentation, since this type of leave was not actually related to the illness or disability of the employee or the employee's family.

* * *

The Knussmans' daughter was born on December 9, 1994. Kimberly Knussman, however, continued to experience health problems. Before his authorized 10-day leave expired, Knussman contacted Sergeant

J.C. Collins, one of his supervisors, and inquired whether his status could be changed to that of primary care giver and his paid sick leave extended to 30 days under section 7-508(a). Knussman explained to Collins that he was the primary care giver for the child because, given his wife's condition following delivery, he was performing the majority of the essential functions such as diaper changing, feeding, bathing and taking the child to the doctor.

* * *

On the day before Knussman was scheduled to return to work, Knussman made a final attempt at obtaining additional sick leave. Sergeant Carl Lee, one of Knussman's immediate superiors, had earlier informed Knussman that although nurturing leave as a primary care giver was probably not an option, Knussman might be eligible for additional paid leave under the family sick leave provision, see Md. Code Ann., State Pers. & Pens. § 7-502(b)(2), as long as he could demonstrate that it was medically necessary for him to care for his wife. Knussman contacted Mullineaux to find out what information he needed to supply for family sick leave. During this conversation, Knussman again discussed his eligibility for nurturing leave as a primary care provider under section 7-508(a) with Mullineaux, who explained that "God made women to have babies and, unless [he] could have a baby, there is no way [he] could be primary care [giver]," J.A. 153, and that his wife had to be "in a coma or dead," J.A. 154, for Knussman to qualify as the primary care giver.

* * *

II.

A.

We first consider the issue of whether the evidence adduced at trial is sufficient to establish that Mullineaux committed a constitutional violation under the law as it currently stands. In a nutshell, Knussman's contention is that Mullineaux applied a facially neutral statute unequally solely on the basis of a gender stereotype in violation of the Equal Protection Clause of the Fourteenth Amendment. The only distinction created by the statute was between "primary care givers" and "secondary care givers," the former being entitled to 30 days of accrued sick leave to care for a newborn and the latter being entitled to 10 days of accrued sick leave. See Md. Code Ann., State Pers. & Pens. § 7-508. The statute made no reference to gender. Rather, the gender classification was created in the application of § 7-508. Viewed in the light most favorable to Knussman, Mullineaux, based on the comments of an administrative assistant to the DOP's Director of Legislation, took the position that only mothers could qualify for additional paid leave as primary care givers under § 7-508(a). Essentially, Mullineaux applied an irrebutable presumption that the mother is the primary care giver, and therefore entitled to greater employment benefits.

We agree with Knussman that Mullineaux's conduct violated his rights under the Equal Protection Clause. Government classifications drawn on the basis of gender have been viewed with suspicion for three decades, beginning with the Supreme Court's decision in *Reed v. Reed*, 404 U.S. 71, 77 (1971), in which the Court condemned "dissimilar treatment for men and women who are … similarly situated." As its equal protection jurisprudence developed in subsequent cases, the Court did not view gender classifications as "benign":

> [S]ince sex, like race and national origin, is an immutable characteristic determined solely by the accident of birth, the imposition of special disabilities upon the members of a particular sex because of their sex would seem to violate "the basic concept of our system that legal burdens should bear some relationship to individual responsibility …" And what differentiates sex from such nonsuspect [classifications] as intelligence or physical disability … is that the sex characteristics frequently bears no relation to ability to perform or contribute to society.

* * *

Thus, a gender classification is subject to heightened scrutiny and will fail unless it "serve[s] important governmental objectives and [is] substantially related to achievement of those objectives."

* * *

In particular, justifications for gender-based distinctions that are rooted in "overbroad generalizations about the different talents, capacities, or preferences of males and females" will not suffice. *VMI*, 518 U.S. at 533. "Legislative classifications which distribute benefits and burdens on the basis of gender carry the inherent risk of reinforcing stereotypes about the 'proper place' of women and their need for special protection." *Orr v. Orr*, 440 U.S. 268, 283 (1979). Thus, gender classifications that appear to rest on nothing more than conventional notions about the proper station in society for males and females have been declared invalid time and again by the Supreme Court. For example, in *Frontiero*, the Supreme Court invalidated a federal statute that permitted a male member of the uniformed services automatically to claim his wife, for purposes of obtaining additional benefits, as a dependent, but precluded a female member from so claiming her husband unless she could demonstrate that he was, in fact, dependent upon her for more than half of his support. See 411 U.S. at 678–79. The Court concluded that the purported reason for the different treatment of males and females, administrative convenience, was premised on the impermissibly broad assumption that wives are dependent upon their husbands for support. *See id.* at 689 (rejecting the Government's argument "that Congress might reasonably have concluded that it would be both cheaper and easier simply conclusively to presume that wives of male members are financially dependent upon their husbands"). In Wengler, the Supreme Court struck down a Missouri workers' compensation provision that automatically paid death benefits to a widow but required a widower to demonstrate that he was actually dependent on his wife's earnings or that he was mentally or physically incapacitated. The Wengler Court again rejected the stereotypical justification offered for treating males and females differently—"that most women are dependent on male wage earners and that it is more efficient to presume dependency in the case of women than to engage in case-to-case determination[s]."

446 U.S. at 151. And, in *Weinberger v. Wiesenfeld*, 420 U.S. 636 (1975), the Supreme Court invalidated a provision of the Social Security Act that paid benefits to a widow and her minor children based on her deceased husband's earnings but, in the case of a deceased wife, provided benefits only to the minor children and not the widower. See *id.* at 637–39. The section of the Social Security Act at issue there was premised upon "the notion that men are more likely than women to be the primary supporters of their spouses and children." *Id.* at 645; see also *Califano v. Goldfarb*, 430 U.S. 199, 201–02 (1977) (invalidating Social Security provision requiring a widower, but not a widow, to prove dependency); *Orr*, 440 U.S. at 280–83 (holding unconstitutional an Alabama statute making alimony available to wives only).

Gender classifications based upon generalizations about typical gender roles in the raising and nurturing of children have met a similar fate. In *Stanley v. Illinois*, 405 U.S. 645 (1972), the Court determined that an Illinois statute was infirm under equal protection principles where unmarried fathers were presumed to be unfit to raise their children but married mothers (as well as married fathers) were presumed fit, meaning that "the children of unwed fathers [became] wards of the State upon the death of the mother." *Id.* at 646. The Court determined that "all Illinois parents are constitutionally entitled to a hearing on their fitness before their children are removed from their custody" and that denying a hearing to unwed fathers while granting it to unwed mothers (and married fathers) "is inescapably contrary to the Equal Protection Clause." *Id.* at 658; see also Weinberger, 420 U.S. at 652 (observing that "a father, no less than a mother, has a constitutionally protected right to the companionship, care, custody, and management of the children" (internal quotation marks omitted)).

In *Caban v. Mohammed*, 441 U.S. 380 (1979), the Court specifically rejected the argument that a state can classify based solely upon the idea that the maternal child-raising role is necessarily primary. There, a New York law gave unwed mothers the power to block the adoption of their children, in the majority of cases, by withholding consent; unwed fathers—even those with a substantial relationship with their children—did not enjoy the same power. Thus, the statute in Caban treated unmarried parents differently based on their gender. In holding that the statute did not bear a substantial relation to an important governmental interest, the Court rejected the argument that "the distinction is justified by a fundamental difference between maternal and paternal relations—that 'a natural mother, absent special circumstances, bears a closer relationship with her child … than a father does.'" *Id.* at 388 (ellipsis in original). The Caban Court observed that "[c]ontrary to appellees' argument and to the apparent presumption underlying [the New York statute], maternal and paternal roles are not invariably different in importance" and thus "reject[ed] … the claim that the broad, gender-based distinction of [the statute] is required by any universal difference between maternal and paternal relations at every phase of a child's development." *Id.* at 389.

The defendants have not even attempted to explain how an irrebuttable presumption in favor of the mother under § 7-508 relates to an important state interest. We conclude that the presumption employed by Mullineaux here was not substantially related to an important governmental interest and, therefore, was not permissible under the Equal Protection Clause.

* * *

AFFIRMED IN PART, VACATED IN PART, AND REMANDED

Wrongful Birth/Wrongful Life

The crux of a wrongful birth suit rests in the contention that parents are deprived of the opportunity to end a pregnancy or to not conceive in the first place due to negligence on the part of the doctor. In other words, but for the doctor's negligence, the parents would have made the choice to not have the child, most likely due to some birth defect or abnormality. Wrongful birth is a generally accepted cause of action (a tort). A wrongful life case is similar, but this action is brought by the child him or herself (or by a guardian on behalf of the child).

> As will be seen in the following case, wrongful life suits are not widely accepted.

KASSAMA v. MAGAT

Court of Special Appeals of Maryland

767 A.2d 348 (2001)

SALMON, Judge.

In this "wrongful life" case, an infant plaintiff asserts that she would have been better off if she had never been born and that she should have been aborted. This presents a question of first impression in Maryland, *viz*:

> May a doctor whose negligence caused a mother not to abort her pregnancy be successfully sued for "wrongful life" by a genetically defective child born as a consequence of the doctor's negligence?

We hold that Maryland does not recognize a cause of action for wrongful life and, accordingly, answer that question in the negative.

Other issues that arose out of a companion "wrongful birth" claim must also be decided.

I. PROCEDURAL AND FACTUAL BACKGROUND

On September 19, 1995, a daughter, Ibrion Fatuo Kassama, was born to Millicent Kassama. The delivery was uneventful; unfortunately, however, Ibrion was born with Down's Syndrome. During her pregnancy, Mrs. Kassama was treated by Dr. Aaron H. Magat, a board-certified obstetrician and gynecologist.

* * *

III. MEDICAL BACKGROUND

An alpha fetoprotein ("AFP") blood test is used to detect genetic defects. Ideally, the blood sample for the AFP test is drawn when a woman is fifteen to sixteen weeks pregnant, but it is acceptable to obtain a blood sample as late as nineteen weeks. An abnormally high AFP test score indicates that the fetus may have spina bifida, open spinal cord congenital abnormalities, or certain other serious potential problems. An abnormally low score is associated with Down's Syndrome.

Even if an AFP test shows an increased risk of Down's Syndrome or other serious potential problems, the test is not definitive—it merely shows a potential problem. To find out for certain whether a fetus is afflicted with certain genetic problems, the mother must undergo an amniocentesis, a test whereby a physician, with the assistance of an ultrasound machine, extracts genetic material from the fluid in the sac surrounding the fetus. The material extracted is sent to a laboratory that grows the cells contained in the fluid in order to obtain a genetic profile. Once the results of an amniocentesis is known, the mother must consider the test results and, assuming there is still time for an abortion, decide whether she wants to abort the pregnancy. The parties agreed at trial that if an amniocentesis had been performed in this case it would have shown that the fetus Mrs. Kassama was carrying had Down's Syndrome.

In *Roe v. Wade*, 410 U.S. 113, 125, 93 S.Ct. 705, 35 L.Ed.2d 147 (1973), Judge Blackman noted that the normal term of human pregnancy is 266 days (38 weeks). When *Roe* was decided, it was believed that a fetus was viable "at about seven [767 A.2d 353] months (28 weeks) but [that viability] may occur earlier, even at 24 weeks." *Id.* at 160, 93 S.Ct. 705. (Citing L. Hellman & J. Pritchard, *Williams Obstetrics* 493 (14th ed.1971)). More recently, in *Planned Parenthood v. Casey*, 505 U.S. 833, 112 S.Ct. 2791, 120 L.Ed.2d 674 (1992), Justice O'Connor observed that viability sometimes occurs as early as twenty-three weeks. *Id.* at 860, 112 S.Ct. 2791.

IV. MARYLAND'S ABORTION LAWS

There is no statutory time limitation in Maryland after which a genetically defective fetus or one suffering from a "serious deformity or abnormality" may not be terminated. In this regard, section 20-209(b) of the Health General article of the Annotated Code of Maryland (2000 Repl.Vol.) reads:

> (b) State Intervention. Except as otherwise provided in this subtitle, the State may not interfere with the decision of a woman to terminate a pregnancy:

1. Before the fetus is viable; or

2. At any time during the woman's pregnancy, if:
   (i) The termination procedure is necessary to protect the life or health of the woman; or
   (ii) The fetus is affected by genetic defect or serious deformity or abnormality.

As will be seen, however, the fact that Maryland's abortion law is extremely liberal does not mean that a woman can find a Maryland doctor who will perform an abortion at any time merely because the mother is carrying a genetically defective fetus.

* * *

IX. ISSUE 3

As a result of being afflicted with Down's Syndrome, Ibrion is moderately retarded and has a congenital heart defect. In her wrongful-life claim, Ibrion seeks to recover for emotional pain and suffering, as well as recompense for the medical and educational expenses incurred (and to be incurred) as a consequence of being afflicted with Down's Syndrome.

Maryland, along with most other states, has recognized wrongful-birth suits like the one brought by Mrs. Kassama. *Reed v. Campagnolo*, 332 Md. 226, 630 A.2d 1145 (1993). As will be seen, however, the vast majority of courts that have considered the matter have rejected wrongful-life claims.

A wrongful-birth claim differs from a wrongful-life claim in that the latter is brought by or on behalf of the disabled child, and the damages claimed are different. *** Using traditional negligence analysis, as has been used in other birth-related claims, a wrongful-life action asserts that the defendant/doctor owed a duty—directly or derivatively—to the infant plaintiff. See Hutton Brown et al., *Special Project: Legal Rights and Issues Surrounding Conception, Pregnancy, and Birth*, 39 Vand. L.Rev. 597, 750–55, 767 (1986). The gravamen of a wrongful-life action is the assertion that but for the physician's negligence the mother would have had an abortion and the child would never have had to experience the pain and expenses occasioned by injuries and/or diseases that the physician could have foreseen. *Id.* at 750. Because it was not the doctor who caused the defect, this amounts to an assertion on the part of the infant plaintiff, "not that [he or she] should not have been born without defects, but that [he or she] should not have been born at all." *Procanik v. Cillo*, 97 N.J. 339, 478 A.2d 755, 760 (1984). The injury complained of in a wrongful-life lawsuit is life itself.

The Supreme Court of Pennsylvania, in *Ellis v. Sherman*, 512 Pa. 14, 515 A.2d 1327, 1329 (1986), took the view that wrongful-life claims should be rejected because the plaintiff could not prove a "legal injury." The Court explained:

> Thus an "injury" is a harm that is inflicted upon one person or entity by another. The condition about which the plaintiff complains, a diseased life, was inflicted upon the plaintiff not by any

> person, but by the plaintiff's genetic constitution. Thus, it may not be said that the plaintiff has suffered a legal injury, for even though his physical and mental condition is unfortunate, and even though this condition presumably would constitute a legal injury if it had been inflicted by some negligent or intentional act of another, in this case, the condition was caused not by another, but by natural processes. It is not, therefore, a legal injury.

Id.

The New York Court of Appeals articulated a different reason for rejecting wrongful-life claims when it ruled that such claims should not be allowed because of the impossibility of calculating damages. *Becker v. Schwartz*, 46 N.Y.2d 401, 413 N.Y.S.2d 895, 386 N.E.2d 807 (1978). The Becker Court said:

> Whether it is better never to have been born at all than to have been born with even gross deficiencies is a mystery more properly to be left to the philosophers and the theologians. Surely the law can assert no competence to resolve the issue, particularly in view of the very nearly uniform high value which the law and mankind has placed on human life, rather than its absence. Not only is there to be found no predicate at common law or in statutory enactment for judicial recognition of the birth of a defective child as an injury to the child; the implications of any such proposition are staggering. Would claims be honored, assuming the breach of an identifiable duty, for less than a perfect birth? And by what standards or by whom would perfection be defined?***
>
> Simply put, a cause of action brought on behalf of an infant seeking recovery for wrongful life demands a calculation of damages dependent upon a comparison between the [child's] choice of life in an impaired state and nonexistence. This comparison the law is not equipped to make. Recognition of so novel a cause of action requiring, as it must, creation of a hypothetical formula for the measurement of an infant's damages is best reserved for legislative, rather than judicial, attention.

Id. at 812 (citations omitted) ***.

The impossibility of calculating damages is, of course, determinative, because it is a fundamental goal of tort law to put the victim, insofar as it is possible to do so by compensatory damages, in the position that he/she would have been in if the defendant had not been negligent. *Tucker v. Calmar S.S. Corp.*, 356 F.Supp. 709, 711 (D.Md.1973). Twenty-three states have rejected wrongful-life claims based on the belief that it would be an impossible task to calculate damages based on a comparison between life in an impaired state and non-existence. ***.

The West Virginia Supreme Court, in *James G. v. Caserta*, 175 W.Va. 406, 332 S.E.2d 872 (1985), held that even if the child was injured, his injury was not caused by the physician's negligence and for that reason rejected a wrongful-life claim. *Id.* at 881.

In *Phillips v. United States*, 508 F.Supp. 537 (D.S.C.1980), the Court held that the public policy of South Carolina barred a wrongful-life claim, notwithstanding the Court's finding that neither the speculative nature of the plaintiff's damages or the difficulty of identifying the child's injury would bar the child's recovery. *Id.* at 543–44. In reaching its decision, the Phillips Court focused on the "'preciousness of human life.'" *Id.* at 543. Other states have adopted the "preciousness of human life" premise as an alternative ground to reject wrongful-life claims. ***.

In eight states, the Legislature has acted affirmatively to prohibit wrongful-life claims by statute. See Idaho Code § 5-334 (2000); Ind.Code Ann. § 34-12-1-1 (Michie 2000); Minn.Stat. § 145.424 (2000); Mo.Rev. Stat. § 188.130 (1999); N.D. Cent.Code § 32-03-43 (2000); 42 Pa. Cons.Stat. § 8305 (2000); S.D. Codified Laws § 21-55-1 (Michie 2000); Utah Code Ann. § 78-11-24 (2000).

The seminal case recognizing a child's right to recover at least some damages in a wrongful-life action is *Turpin v. Sortini*, 31 Cal.3d 220, 182 Cal.Rptr. 337, 643 P.2d 954 (1982). In the *Turpin* case, Dr. Adam Sortini examined James and Donna Turpin's daughter (Hope) and advised the parents that Hope's hearing was within normal limits. *Id.* at 956. Approximately one year later, the child was correctly diagnosed as being "stone deaf" as a result of a hereditary ailment. *Id.* In their complaint, the Turpins alleged that if they had known that Hope was deaf they would not have conceived their second child (Joy), who suffered from the same total deafness as did her sister. *Id.* The Turpins, on behalf of Joy, brought a wrongful-life action in which they sought:

> (1) general damages for being "deprived of the fundamental right of a child to be born as a whole, functional human being without total deafness" and (2) special damages for the "extraordinary expenses for specialized teaching, training and hearing equipment" which she will incur during her lifetime as a result of her hearing impairment.

Id.

The trial court sustained a demurrer to the Turpins' wrongful-life action. *Id.* On appeal, the defendants/ appellees took the position that Joy had suffered "no legally cognizable injury or rationally ascertainable damages as a result of their alleged negligence." *Id.* at 960.

In *Turpin*, the California Supreme Court recognized that there was a "critical difference between wrongful-life actions and the ordinary prenatal injury cases." *Id.* at 961. In the ordinary prenatal injury case, where some negligent act on the part of the defendant injures the fetus, the child would have been born healthy but for the defendant's negligence; however, in a wrongful-birth case, the obvious tragic fact is that plaintiff never had a chance "to be born as a whole, functional human being without total deafness"; if defendants have performed their job properly, [the plaintiff] would not have been born with hearing intact, but—according to the complaint—would not have been at all.

Id.

The *Turpin* Court observed:

> Because nothing defendants could have done would have given plaintiff an unimpaired life, it appears inconsistent with basic tort principle to view the injury for which defendants are legally responsible solely by reference to plaintiff's present condition without taking into consideration the fact that if defendants had not been negligent she would have not been born at all.

Id. (citations omitted).

The Court rejected the proposition that impaired life is always preferable to non-life, saying:

> While it thus seems doubtful that a child's claim for general damages should properly be denied on the rationale that the value of impaired life, as a matter of law, always exceeds the value of non-life, we believe that the out-of-state decisions are on sounder ground in holding that—with respect to the child's claim for pain and suffering or other general damages—recovery should be denied because (1) it is simply impossible to determine in any rational or reasonable fashion whether the plaintiff has in fact suffered an injury in being born impaired rather than not being born, and (2) even if it were possible to overcome the first hurdle, it would be impossible to assess general damages in any fair, nonspeculative manner.

Id. at 963.

In reaching this decision, the Court quoted from Justice Weintraub's separate opinion in *Gleitman v. Cosgrove*, 49 N.J. 22, 227 A.2d 689, 711 (1967):

> Ultimately, the infant's complaint is that he would be better off not to have been. Man, who knows nothing of death or nothingness, cannot possibly know whether that is so.
> We must remember that the choice is not being born with health or being born without it ... Rather the choice is between a worldly existence and none at all ... To recognize a right not to be born is to enter an area in which no one can find his way.

Turpin, 182 Cal.Rptr. 337, 643 P.2d at 963.

After rejecting the infant plaintiff's claim for general damages, the *Turpin* Court held that a plaintiff in a wrongful-life cause of action was entitled to recover damages for "'extraordinary expenses for specialized teaching, training and hearing equipment'" that she would incur during her lifetime because of her deafness. *Id.* at 965. According to the Court, these types of extraordinary expenses stood on a "different footing" than general damages. *Id.* After observing that parents, in wrongful-birth actions, were permitted to recover medical expenses incurred on behalf of a child born with disability, the Court said:

> Although the parent and child cannot, of course, both recover for the same medical expenses, we believe it would be illogical and anomalous to permit only parents, and not the child, to recover for the cost of the child's own medical care. If such a distinction were established, the afflicted child's receipt of necessary medical expenses might well depend on the wholly fortuitous circumstances of whether the parents are available to sue and recover such damages or whether the medical expenses are incurred at a time when the parents remain legally responsible for providing such care.
>
> *Id.* at 965. The distinction between general damages and "extraordinary expense" that the Court made was that the latter expenses were "both certain and readily measurable … [and] in many instances … vital not only to the child's well being but to his or her very survival." *Id.*

In *Siemieniec v. Lutheran Gen. Hosp.*, 117 Ill.2d 230, 111 Ill.Dec. 302, 512 N.E.2d 691 (1987), the Supreme Court of Illinois puts its finger on the essential flaw in the rationale of the *Turpin* opinion. The Court said:

> In awarding special damages, … the *Turpin* court ignored the reasoning that prevented an award of general damages. The problem of establishing the fact of injury was simply passed over, and all discussion focused on the nonspeculative nature of a recovery for extraordinary medical expenses.

Id. at 700.

The reasoning of the *Turpin* Court has been criticized by many other commentators. As an example, the California Law Review published a case note shortly after *Turpin* was decided that criticized the Turpins' court decision. See Kurtis J. Kearl, note, *Turpin v. Sortini*: Recognizing the Unsupportable Cause of Action for Wrongful Life, 71 Cal.L.Rev. 1278 (1983). We are in accord with the views expressed by the author of that note, who said:

The court's recognition of the wrongful life cause of action is unjustified by traditional legal principles or sound public policy. The *Turpin* court failed to account fully and consistently for the fundamental flaw of the wrongful life claim—the inability to make the required comparison between the plaintiff's actual condition and nonexistence. Without this comparison, a plaintiff can never establish that she has suffered any detriment which would entitle her to recovery. While the court acknowledged this flaw, it nevertheless granted special damages to a plaintiff who could not demonstrate that she had suffered harm in being born. The policy considerations that led the court to contravene established legal principles do not require creation of a new cause of action. The same result could have been achieved through existing law without doing violence to traditional tort principles.

Attempts by the *Turpin* court and others to circumvent this fundamental obstacle to recovery have not adequately dealt with the inherent conceptual difficulties of the wrongful life claim. In view of the peculiar nature of this cause of action, the supreme court should have followed the unanimous consensus of the other jurisdictions that had considered the question and refused to allow any recovery in a wrongful life claim. *Id.* at 1296–97.

Despite criticism such as those just mentioned, the Washington Supreme Court, in *Harbeson v. Parke-Davis, Inc.*, 98 Wash.2d 460, 656 P.2d 483 (1983), followed, with no deviation, the reasoning of the *Turpin* Court and disallowed general damages but allowed the plaintiff in a wrongful-life suit to recover damages covering the medical and educational needs of the child. *Id.* at 493.

Likewise, the Supreme Court of New Jersey, in *Procanik v. Cillo*, 97 N.J. 339, 478 A.2d 755 (1984), also followed the lead of the *Turpin* Court and recognized a wrongful-life action but restricted monies recoverable to special damages for extraordinary medical expenses. *Id.* at 762.

* * *

We adopt the view accepted by the highest courts of twenty-three of our sister states that have refused to recognize a cause of action for wrongful life because it is an impossible task to calculate damages based on a comparison between life in an impaired state and no life at all. Attempts by the highest courts in California, Washington, and New Jersey to circumvent this problem are unpersuasive.

For the foregoing reasons we hold that the trial judge did not err when he granted the defense motion for judgment as to Ibrion's wrongful-life claim.

JUDGMENT AFFIRMED; COSTS TO BE PAID BY APPELLANTS.

[Footnotes Omitted.]

Chapter 10
Criminal Law & Procedure

As with civil procedure, there are distinct rules that determine how a criminal case will move through the legal system. And, as with civil procedure, there are federal rules (http://www.uscourts.gov/uscourts/RulesAndPolicies/rules/2010%20Rules/Criminal%20Procedure.pdf), as well as each state's own rules.

To provide a sense of what is covered in the Federal Rules of Criminal Procedure, the nine titles (or parts) are included below.

Title I. Applicability
Title II. Preliminary Proceedings
Title III. The Grand Jury, the Indictment, and the Information
Title IV. Arraignment and Preparation For Trial
Title V. Venue
Title VI. Trial
Title VII. Post-Conviction Procedures
Title VIII. Supplementary and Special Proceedings
Title IX. General Provisions

Some particular examples of criminal procedure rules include:

- Rule 11, under Title IV, which discusses the rules concerning pleas and plea agreements.
- Rule 12.2, under Title IV, which discusses the insanity defense.
- Rules 15 and 16, under Title IV, which discuss depositions, discovery, and inspection.
- Rule 24, under Title VI, which discusses jurors, including voir dire and the number of peremptory challenges; the number of peremptory challenges differ depending on the type of case (capital, other felony, or misdemeanor).
- Rule 32, under Title VII, which discusses sentencing and judgment.
- Rule 44, under Title IX, which discusses the appointment of counsel for a defendant.
- Rule 60, under Title IX, which discusses victim's rights.

Discussions of criminal law typically include examination of cases that highlight the seminal issues of criminal law. Cases such as *Miranda v. Arizona* and *Mapp v. Ohio* embody the pillars upon which criminal law has been built. A short and annotated list of these important cases is included at the end of the chapter.

An alternative way to view the system of criminal procedure, however, is to explore how the U.S. government explains the criminal justice system to different audiences. Included in this chapter is an excerpt from a document in which the Administrative Office of the U.S. Courts describes to judges and court administrators from other countries how the U.S. system works. A second excerpt is from a document in which the Administrative Office of the U.S. Courts explains the process to journalists and discusses how they can best perform their role as journalists. Both of these documents provide a good overview of the U.S. system of criminal procedure through a uniquely different set of eyes.

The Federal Court System in the United States: An Introduction for Judges and Judicial Administrators in Other Countries

The following is an excerpt from *The Federal Court System in the United States, An Introduction for Judges and Judicial Administrators in Other Countries*, published by The Administrative Office of the U.S. Courts (http://www.uscourts.gov/uscourts/FederalCourts/Publications/English.pdf).

The judicial process in a criminal case differs from a civil case in several important ways. The parties in the case are the United States attorney (the prosecutor representing the Department of Justice) and the defendant or defendants. Criminal investigations are conducted by the Department of Justice and other law enforcement agencies, which are both part of the executive branch. The court plays no role in criminal investigations. Its role in the criminal justice process is to apply the law and make legal and factual decisions.

Three main levels of federal criminal offenses have been defined by Congress. Felony offenses are the most serious crimes and may be punished by more than one year in prison. Misdemeanor offenses are less serious and may be punished by up to one year in prison. The least serious offenses, known as petty offenses, may be punished by up to six months imprisonment. Most petty offenses are addressed through fines rather than a prison sentence.

After a person is arrested, a pretrial services officer or probation officer of the court immediately interviews the defendant and conducts an investigation of the defendant's background. The information obtained by the pretrial services officer or probation officer will be used to help a judge decide whether to release the defendant into the community before trial and whether to impose conditions of release.

At an initial appearance, a judge (normally a magistrate judge) advises the defendant of the charges filed, considers whether the defendant should be held in custody until trial, and determines whether there is "probable cause" to believe that an offense has been committed and the defendant has committed it. Defendants who are unable to hire their own attorney are advised of their right to a court-appointed attorney. Each district court, by statute, is required to have in place a plan for providing competent attorneys to represent defendants who cannot afford their own attorneys. The court may appoint a federal public defender (a full-time federal official appointed by the court of appeals), a community public defender (a member of a community-based legal aid organization funded by a grant from the judiciary), or a private attorney who has agreed to accept such appointments from the court. In all these types of appointments, the attorney who represents the defendant is paid by the court from funds appropriated to the judiciary by Congress. Defendants released into the community before trial may be required to obey certain restrictions, such as home confinement or drug testing, and to make periodic reports to a pretrial services officer to ensure appearance at trial.

Under the Constitution, a felony criminal case may only proceed beyond the initial stages if the defendant is indicted by a grand jury. The grand jury reviews evidence presented to it by the United States attorney and decides whether there is sufficient evidence to require a defendant to stand trial.

The defendant enters a plea to the charges brought by the United States attorney at a hearing known as an arraignment. Most defendants—more than 90%—plead guilty rather than go to trial. If a defendant pleads guilty in return for the government agreeing to drop certain charges or to recommend a less severe sentence, the agreement often is called a "plea bargain." If the defendant pleads guilty, the judge may impose a sentence at that time, but more commonly will schedule a hearing to determine the sentence at a later date. If the defendant pleads not guilty, the judge will proceed to schedule a trial.

Criminal cases include a limited amount of pretrial discovery proceedings similar to those in civil cases, with substantial restrictions to protect the identity of government informants and to prevent intimidation of witnesses. The attorneys also may file motions, which are requests for rulings by the court before the trial. For example, defense attorneys often file a motion to suppress evidence, which asks the court to exclude from the trial evidence that the defendant believes was obtained by the government in violation of the defendant's constitutional rights.

In a criminal trial, the burden of proof is on the government. Defendants do not have to prove their innocence. Instead, the government must provide evidence to convince the jury of the defendant's guilt. The standard of proof in a criminal trial is much higher than in a civil case. It must be "beyond a reasonable doubt," which means the evidence must be so strong that there is no reasonable doubt that the defendant committed the crime. The judge instructs the jury on the law and the decisions that the jury must make.

If a defendant is found not guilty, the defendant is released and the government may not appeal. Nor can the person be charged again with the same crime in a federal court. The Constitution prohibits "double jeopardy," or being tried twice for the same offense.

In determining the defendant's sentence, the judge must consult special federal sentencing guidelines issued by the United States Sentencing Commission, an organization within the judicial branch. The sentencing guidelines are designed to:

- incorporate the purposes of sentencing (i.e., just punishment, deterrence, incapacitation, and rehabilitation);
- provide certainty and fairness in sentencing by avoiding unwarranted disparity among offenders with similar characteristics convicted of similar criminal conduct, while permitting some judicial flexibility to take into account relevant aggravating and mitigating factors;
- reflect, to the extent practicable, advancement in the knowledge of human behavior as it relates to the criminal justice process.

The sentencing guidelines provide federal judges with consistent sentencing ranges that take into account both the seriousness of the criminal conduct and the defendant's criminal record. Based on the severity of the offense, the guidelines assign most federal crimes to one of 43 "offense levels." Each offender is also assigned to one of six "criminal history categories" based upon the extent and recency of his or her past misconduct. The point at which the offense level and criminal history category intersect on the Commission's sentencing table determines an offender's guideline range. In order to provide flexibility, the top of each guideline range exceeds the bottom by six months or 25 percent (whichever is greater).

Ordinarily, the judge is advised to choose a sentence from within the guideline range unless the court identifies a factor that the Sentencing Commission failed to consider that should result in a different sentence. However, the judge must in all cases provide the reasons for the sentence. Sentences outside the guideline range are subject to review by the courts of appeals for "unreasonableness," and all sentences can be reviewed for incorrect application of the relevant guidelines or law.

In most felony cases the judge waits for the results of a presentence investigation report, prepared by the court's probation office, before imposing a sentence. The presentence investigation report summarizes for the court the background information needed to determine the appropriate sentence, including a thorough exploration of the circumstances of the offense and the defendant's criminal background and characteristics. The report applies the sentencing guidelines to the individual defendant and the crimes for which he or she has been found guilty. During sentencing, the court may consider not only the evidence produced at trial, but all relevant information that may be provided by the pretrial services officer, the United States attorney, and the defense attorney. In unusual circumstances, the court may depart from the sentence calculated according to the sentencing guidelines.

A sentence may include time in prison, a fine to be paid to the government, community service, and restitution to be paid to crime victims. If the convicted defendant Is released, the court's probation officers assist the court in enforcing any conditions that are imposed as part of a criminal sentence. The supervision of offenders also may involve services such as substance abuse testing and treatment programs, job counseling, and alternative detention options.

A Journalist's Guide to the Federal Courts

The following is an excerpt from *A Journalist's Guide to the Federal Courts*, published by The Administrative Office of the U.S. Courts (http://www.uscourts.gov/News/Viewer.aspx?doc=/uscourts/News/docs/JournalistGuide2008.pdf).

The Investigation

A defendant may be arrested in the course of allegedly committing a crime. But the criminal cases that attract media attention most often involve a protracted investigation prior to a defendant's arrest. The investigation will generally be conducted by the FBI, but other federal agencies may be involved depending on the nature of the alleged crime (DEA for drug investigations, SEC for securities investigations, etc.).

To obtain a search warrant or arrest warrant, the law enforcement agent and an assistant U.S. attorney will have to make an application to a magistrate judge or district court judge. The applications will be accompanied by an affidavit filed by the lead law enforcement agent, which is meant to provide the judge with evidence of probable cause. Both documents can be valuable for reporters. The application itself—a one-page form—will include information about the defendant, and the affidavit will include an overview of the facts of the case.

To avoid public disclosure of the investigation, search warrant applications generally are sealed, at least until the search is conducted and sometimes until after the arrest is made. While they are sealed, the warrant application will typically show up on the court's docket under a title that gives away nothing about the substance of the case, such as "*In re search warrant application.*"

But if a search warrant application is unsealed before an arrest, that provides a valuable lead that an investigation is underway. Courthouse beat reporters should review unsealed warrants on a regular basis. The ways that clerk's offices file search warrant applications vary greatly from office to office; you'll have to ask at your courthouse about the easiest way to routinely review the documents.

Prosecutors use three terms to describe people involved in investigations, and it is critical that you distinguish among them. A "witness" is someone who merely has information useful to the investigation. A "subject" of an investigation is a person whose conduct is within the scope of a criminal probe, although they themselves may not be suspected of breaking the law. A "target" is someone who is likely to be indicted. A subject of an investigation can become a target.

Indictment

Before the target of an investigation is arrested, prosecutors generally will take the evidence they have gathered to a grand jury. Grand juries are composed of 16 to 23 citizens. Agreement by a bare majority is required to find probable cause exists that a crime was committed.

Grand juries are formally supervised by a district judge, often the chief judge, but for all practical purposes they function day-to-day under the auspices of the U.S. Attorney's Office. Only prosecutors present evidence before a grand jury, and a finding of probable cause—necessary to issue an indictment—is a relatively low standard of proof.

The indictment lists the crimes the defendant allegedly committed and describes the facts the government believes support those allegations. It is a roadmap to what the prosecution intends to prove at trial. Grand jury indictments are returned to the district court—usually to a magistrate judge—in a sealed court hearing. Indictments generally are unsealed after a defendant is arrested.

A criminal case also can begin without an indictment. In these cases, the lead investigator swears out a criminal complaint, called an "information," setting forth the same kinds of allegations and facts that would be contained in an indictment. Absent an indictment, the prosecution must convince a judge that there is probable cause to proceed with the case. These hearings are held in open court after the defendant has been arrested in a felony case. A defendant can agree to waive indictment and proceed with the case based on the criminal complaint, or can demand that the prosecutor seek an indictment.

Defendant Appears in Court

Within hours of the defendant's arrest, he or she will make an initial appearance in court. Defendants are typically not represented by counsel at this hearing. They are advised of the charges they face, their rights are explained to them by the judge, and counsel is appointed if defendants cannot afford to hire their own lawyer. Defendants will be remanded to the custody of the U.S. Marshals Service at the conclusion of this hearing unless they are released, in which case conditions of release will be set.

Defendants are provided with the services of a court interpreter in all courtroom appearances when language is a barrier to the effective administration of justice.

If no indictment has been issued, the defendant will next have a preliminary examination hearing, at which the government will present its evidence. If the judge finds there is probable cause (or if an indictment has already been returned), there will then be a detention hearing, where it will be determined whether the defendant needs to be held in jail until trial. Both sides may present evidence at this hearing, as well as cross-examine the other side's witnesses.

The decision whether to release the defendant is governed by the Bail Reform Act of 1984 and subsequent amendments to it. The law presumes that defendants should be released on personal recognizance or unsecured personal bond (that is, without putting up any money or other asset as security) unless the judge determines "that such release will not reasonably assure the appearance of the person as required or will endanger the safety of any other person or the community."

> The likelihood the defendant will flee and the danger they pose to the community are the only two factors a judge may consider in a detention hearing.

The judge can put restrictions on defendants—such as requiring a secured bond, forfeiture of a passport, electronic monitoring of defendants' location, requiring they remain in their home, etc. But the judge must choose "the least restrictive ... condition, or combination of conditions, that ... will reasonably assure the appearance of the person as required and the safety of any other person and the community."

There are exceptions to the presumption that defendants should be released pending trial. The Act creates a rebuttable presumption that defendants should not be released under the following circumstances:

- The defendant is accused of one of a list of crimes listed in the statute, and was previously convicted of committing one of the specified crimes while free on bail.
- The judge finds there is probable cause the defendant committed a federal drug offense that carries a penalty of 10 years or more in prison.
- The judge finds there is probable cause the defendant used a firearm to commit a felony.

To rebut the presumption and release a defendant, the judge must find that some condition or combination of conditions of release will assure defendants' appearance at trial and safeguard the community.

Prior to the detention hearing, a member of the court's Pretrial Services office will speak to the defendant and as many family members as possible. The officer will file a report with the judge, prosecutor, and defense counsel that makes a recommendation whether the defendant can be released and, if so, under what conditions. This is a recommendation only, and it is not binding on the judge.

> Pretrial reports are always filed under seal, but they often are discussed at length during the detention hearing.

A decision to release or detain a defendant that is made by a magistrate judge may be reviewed by a district judge on the motion of either party. (This is a kind of appeal, though the word "appeal" is not used to describe it.) Detention orders may also be appealed to the court of appeals after a district judge rules on them.

The last of the early hearings in a criminal case is the arraignment. The defendant's counsel is asked three questions:

- Does the defendant waive a formal arraignment, at which the indictment would be read in its entirety?
- How does the defendant plead, guilty or not guilty?
- Does the defendant request a trial by jury? (If not, the case will be decided by the judge in what is known as a bench trial.)

If a formal arraignment is waived—as it almost always is—the hearing can be over in five minutes.

At the arraignment, some judges also schedule the trial date and dates for motion hearings. Under the Speedy Trial Act, criminal defendants are entitled to a trial that begins no later than 70 days from the date the indictment or information was filed, or from the date the defendant appears before a judge, whichever is later. The defendant can waive the right to a speedy trial, or the judge can waive the requirements of the Act by finding that the interests of justice require it.

These four hearings can be held at a single time under certain circumstances. In some courts magistrate judges hold all of these hearings; in other courts, some are held by magistrate judges while others are held by District Court judges. In most courts, the District Court judge who will handle the trial is assigned to the case after the initial appearance; check with the clerk's office for that judge's name. Judges are assigned to cases at random, to avoid the possibility that prosecutors might "judge shop" their case to a jurist considered friendly to prosecution arguments.

Pretrial Motions and Hearings

A wide variety of motions may be made prior to trial. Among the most common that are filed by the defense are:

- Motions to relocate the trial through a change of venue, claiming pretrial publicity will make it impossible to select an impartial jury.
- Motions challenging the admissibility of certain pieces of evidence.
- Motions seeking access to evidence in the possession of the prosecution. This phase of the case, known as motion practice, occurs primarily on paper. Only if a judge feels that oral argument of the issues or evidence from witnesses would aid in a decision will a hearing be held.

During the pretrial phase, you also may encounter efforts to seal what hearings there are. Most pretrial hearings must be open to the public, but there are a complicated set of exceptions. Media organizations may decide to oppose the sealing of court records.

Plea Bargains and Sentencing

More than 90 percent of federal defendants plead guilty. Some do so during the pretrial phase as part of a plea bargain, in exchange for the prosecutors' dropping some charges or recommending a more lenient sentence.

Two documents are filed with the court at the plea hearing: the plea agreement, which outlines what charges are being pleaded to and which are being dropped; and a statement of facts describing what the defendant admits to doing. Both generally are available only after the hearing has ended.

During the hearing, the judge will conduct what is known as the plea colloquy, in which defendants are informed of the rights they are giving up and the crimes they are admitting. At some point, the judge will ask the defendants to, in their words, describe what they did.

Sentencing is generally scheduled for a month or more after the plea hearing, to allow time for the staff of the court's Probation Office to prepare a presentence investigation report. The probation officer will speak to the defendant, family members, friends, and others as part of the investigation. The report is always filed with the judge, prosecutor, and defense counsel under seal. Starting in 1987, sentencing in federal court was governed by the U.S. Sentencing Guidelines. They are set by the U.S. Sentencing Commission (http://www.ussc.gov), a judicial branch agency created by Congress to make sentencing more determinate and lessen sentencing disparities. In January 2005, the U.S. Supreme Court ruled that the guidelines are merely advisory. Judges are urged to consider the guidelines but now can depart from the guideline ranges, so long as the sentence is reasonable and does not exceed the maximum term set by statute for a particular crime.

The presentence report makes a recommendation as to how the guidelines rate the seriousness of the offense and the defendant's criminal history. Prosecutors and defense counsel will have made a similar estimate when they agreed to the plea bargain. The judge is not required to follow the recommendations of the Probation Office or the parties. During the sentencing hearing, defendants are given a chance to tell the court anything they believe the judge should consider before imposing sentence.

The Trial

Jury Selection

During jury selection, which is also known as voir dire, the lawyers, the judge or both will question prospective jurors about their backgrounds and their ability to be impartial. Prospective jurors may be struck from the panel in two ways. Lawyers may exercise a "challenge for cause," claiming the juror could not be impartial. If the judge agrees, the potential juror is excused. "Peremptory challenges" allow lawyers to remove a juror without stating a reason. Both sides are given a limited number of these peremptory challenges.

Jury selection in death penalty and other complex cases can take several weeks. In some courts, judges handling a high-profile trial will call in 200 or more jurors to fill out an extensive questionnaire, and then call in 20 or more a day to be questioned individually and challenged for cause. On the final day of jury selection in such cases, the qualified pool of jurors is called in, both sides exercise their peremptory challenges, and the jury is seated.

> Federal criminal juries typically have 12 members, plus up to six alternate jurors. To insure everyone pays attention to the testimony, no juror knows which of them are alternates until they are excused after closing arguments.

You should never contact a prospective juror or his or her family or close friends, nor should you speak about the case if you know you are in the presence of a juror while a case is active. This is considered jury tampering—a crime.

In cases in which judges are concerned about the safety of jurors, the jury may be anonymous, identified only by numbers. No one, other than the person in the clerk's office who arranges their payment (jurors are paid $40 per day), will know their names in such a case. A judge may decide that a need exists to sequester a jury—keep all jurors in the court's custody until a trial concludes.

Opening Statements

It is opening *statements* and closing *arguments*. At the beginning of a trial, lawyers are limited to telling the jury what they believe the evidence will show. Only at the end can they marshal those facts to make an argument the defendant did or did not commit the crime.

Prosecutors go first because they bear the burden of proving beyond a reasonable doubt that the defendant committed the crime. Defense counsel are not obligated to make an opening statement or present any may choose to make an opening statement at the conclusion of the initial set of prosecution witnesses, known as the prosecution's case-in-chief.

Testimony, Exhibits, and Transcripts

Some individual judges or local rules of court require the prosecution to file a list of potential witnesses prior to trial, along with a list of exhibits that may be entered into evidence. These lists can provide a handy reference for reporters. Check the case file about a week before trial begins.

Prosecution witnesses take the stand first. Each can be cross-examined by the defense. If a witness is cross-examined, the prosecution is permitted a "redirect," asking the witness only questions related to the topics discussed during cross-examination. You are free to speak to witnesses after they are excused by the court, unless the judge indicates the witness is subject to recall to the stand later in the trial. The witness, however, is not obligated to respond to your questions, and often may be advised by counsel not to do so.

> The defendant has the choice whether to testify. No inference of guilt may be drawn by the jurors if the defendant chooses not to testify.

At the end of the prosecution's case-in-chief, the defense likely will make what is known as a Rule 29 motion.

Named after Federal Rule of Criminal Procedure 29, the motion asks the judge to acquit the defendant because the prosecution's evidence is insufficient to sustain a conviction. This motion may also be made after the conclusion of testimony by the defense witnesses. These motions are almost always denied because the prosecution's case is rarely that weak. But if the motion is granted, the defendant goes free; the prosecution cannot appeal such a ruling and the defendant cannot be tried again in federal court on the same charges because of the constitutional protection against double jeopardy. If, however, the judge waits to rule on the motion until after the jury reaches a verdict, and that verdict is guilty, prosecutors can then appeal the judge's acquittal.

During testimony, both sides will seek to introduce pieces of evidence. If the judge allows an item to be admitted, it becomes part of the public record of the case and should be available for members of the media to inspect and copy. However, your interest in seeing the item sometimes conflicts with the court's interest in insuring none of the evidence is tampered with. This is another of those issues you'll want to broach with your contact person in the clerk's office. Getting a copy of the exhibit from the party that introduced it is another option you can pursue.

Transcripts of courtroom proceedings are provided to the court and litigants by a court reporter. Many court reporters are trained in what is called real-time court reporting, which makes a daily copy of a transcript available, for a fee.

Closing Arguments

The prosecution goes first, followed by the defense and a rebuttal by the prosecution. Because the prosecution has the burden of proof, it gets the final word.

Jury Instructions, Deliberations, and the Verdict

After the closing arguments, the judge will give the jury its final instructions. Both sides may contest the content of those instructions because they can have an enormous effect on the jury's verdict.

During deliberations, the jurors may have questions about the evidence or the instructions. They will give a note to the Deputy Marshal or some court employee, who will take it to the judge. The judge will then call the lawyers back into court, discuss what the answer to the note should be, call the jurors back into the courtroom, and give them the answer.

Criminal juries must reach a unanimous verdict of guilty or not guilty. The jury may say at some point that it is hopelessly deadlocked. At this point, judges typically give the jury what's known as an Allen charge. Named after a 1896 U.S. Supreme Court case, the Allen charge urges jurors to reconsider their opinions and try again to reach a verdict. If they attempt to do so but still report they are deadlocked, the judge may declare a mistrial.

> After a mistrial, prosecutors may retry the defendant on the same charges without violating the Constitution's ban on double jeopardy.

In most federal courthouses, once a jury has reached a verdict, it is announced as soon as all the lawyers can get to the courtroom. You may have as little as 15 minutes warning.

Once a jury's members have been dismissed by the judge, you are free to speak to them. (The clerk's office may be willing to provide the names and addresses of the jurors, unless the jury is anonymous.) Still, no juror is obligated to speak with you.

In high-profile cases, the crush of media attention can be overwhelming for some jurors. In such cases judges will sometimes have court security personnel escort the jurors out a back door of the courthouse. You may want to suggest to your contact person in the clerk's office that the judge ask any jurors who would be willing to speak to the media to remain in the jury room or convene at a specific location inside or outside the courthouse. That gives journalists the access they want, while providing a controlled environment in which the jurors can feel comfortable.

Death Penalty Cases

Federal judges, following the U.S. Sentencing Guidelines, determine and impose sentences in all cases except death penalty cases. If a defendant facing the death penalty is found guilty, the same jury that convicted him will determine his sentence. It has only two choices: execution or life in prison. A second phase of the trial, referred to as the penalty phase, then takes place. Both sides can present witnesses who will testify about the seriousness of the crime and any mitigating factors, such as the defendant's life experiences and lack of a prior criminal history.

Covering Federal Appellate Court

The nation's 94 federal judicial districts are organized into 12 regional circuits, each of which has a United States court of appeals. A court of appeals hears appeals from the district courts located within its circuit, as well as appeals from decisions of federal administrative agencies and some original proceedings filed directly with the courts of appeals.

A list of the 12 regional circuits and of the judicial districts they encompass is in the appendix. The Court of Appeals for the Federal Circuit is based in Washington, D.C., and has nationwide jurisdiction to hear appeals in specialized cases. The court hears appeals from the U.S. Court of International Trade, the U.S. Court of Federal Claims, and the U.S. Patent and Trademark Office. It also exclusively hears certain types of cases appealed from the district courts, primarily those involving patent laws.

The Appeals Process

The losing party in a decision by a federal trial court usually has the right to appeal the final decision to a federal court of appeals. Similarly, a litigant not satisfied with a decision made by a federal administrative agency usually may seek review by a court of appeals. Parties who contest decisions made in certain federal agencies—for example, disputes over Social Security benefits—may be required to seek review first in a district court rather than go directly to an appeals court.

In a civil case, either side may appeal the judgment based on a jury verdict or bench trial. In a criminal case, the defendant may appeal a conviction based on a guilty verdict, but the government may not appeal if a defendant is found not guilty. Either side in a criminal case may appeal a sentence that is imposed after a guilty verdict if it departs from the sentencing guidelines.

If the dissatisfied party in the district court plans an appeal, the first step usually is to file a notice of appeal in the district court, which informs the court of appeals and other parties.

A litigant who files an appeal from a district court decision is known as an appellant. The term "petitioner" is used for a litigant who files an appeal from an administrative agency or who appeals an original proceeding. The appellant (petitioner) bears the burden of showing that the trial court or administrative agency made a legal error that affected the decision in the case. The court of appeals makes its decision based on the record of the case established by the trial court or agency. The court of appeals does not receive additional evidence or hear witnesses. The court of appeals also may review the factual findings made by the trial court or agency, but typically may overturn a decision on factual grounds only if the findings were "clearly erroneous."

Three-Judge Panels

Appeals normally are decided by panels of three judges working together. A panel may include a senior circuit or district judge, a district judge from a district court within the particular circuit, or a visiting circuit or district judge from another circuit. In general, judges are assigned to panels randomly. The judges may play no role in determining who will sit on which panel or in the assignment of cases to a particular panel. Indeed, the creation of the panels and the assignment of cases to individual panels are separate functions often performed by different court units.

Additionally, judges do not participate in cases in which their participation would constitute a conflict of interest or create an appearance of impropriety. In such circumstances, the judge should recuse himself or herself from the case.

The appellant presents legal arguments to the panel in a written brief, seeking to persuade the judges that the trial court committed substantial error, and that the trial court's decision should therefore be reversed. The party who prevailed in the trial court, known as the appellee (or respondent for administrative agency appeals), argues in a reply brief that the trial court was correct, or that any error made was not significant enough to affect the outcome of the case.

In the majority of circuits, most appeals are decided solely on the basis of briefs submitted to the court. In other circuits, the court more often renders its decision after oral argument, which is a structured discussion in which both sides present arguments on the legal principles in the dispute. Each side is given a short time, typically 15 minutes, to present its case, but the judges may interrupt to ask any questions they have.

Oral arguments traditionally are open to the public.

Judicial Conference policy leaves it to the individual appellate courts to decide whether electronic and photographic coverage of oral arguments will be allowed. The Second and Ninth Circuits will consider requests for such coverage in civil cases. The Seventh, Eighth and Ninth Circuits make available on the Internet digital recordings of oral arguments.

Some time after the submission of briefs or after oral argument, the court of appeals will issue a decision, usually accompanied by an opinion explaining its rationale. A decision may be reached by a 3–0 or 2–1 vote. A decision will take into account and apply any relevant precedents, similar cases already decided by that court, or by the Supreme Court.

This decision will be controlling unless: (1) the judges send the case back to the trial court for additional proceedings (i.e. remand the case); (2) the court determines on its own that the matter should be reheard because of a potential conflict with a prior decision; (3) the parties seek a rehearing before the panel; (4) the parties seek review before the full appeals court (called an *en banc* session); or (5) the parties seek review in the U.S. Supreme Court.

Federal courts of appeals issue tens of thousands of decisions each year, and only a small percentage of them are taken to the Supreme Court, which grants review only to a fraction of the cases it receives. Opinions issued by the courts of appeals and by the Supreme Court are posted on the respective court web sites.

Important Cases and Concepts

GIDEON v. WAINWRIGHT, 372 U.S. 335 (1963): The 6th Amendment's right to counsel is applied to the states through the 14th Amendment for defendants facing felony charges.

MIRANDA v. ARIZONA, 384 U.S. 436 (1966): Upon arrest or upon being taken into custody, defendants have the right to be informed that they can remain silent and that they have the right to an attorney. Movies and TV have familiarized everyone with the following typical Miranda warning: "You have the right to remain silent. Anything you say can and will be used against you in a court of law. You have the right to speak to an attorney and to have an attorney present during any questioning. If you cannot afford a lawyer, one will be provided for you at government expense." Some states, such as Maryland, go a little bit further in their clarification of the defendant's rights. The following is from the Maryland Office of the Public Defender (http://www.opd.state.md.us/mirandarights.html).

> Before a law enforcement officer may question you regarding the possible commission of a crime, he or she must read you your Miranda Rights and ask if you understand these rights.

1. You have the right to remain silent and refuse to answer questions. Do you understand?
2. Anything you do say may be used against you in a court of law. Do you understand?
3. You have the right to consult an attorney before speaking to the police and to have an attorney present during questioning now or in the future. Do you understand?
4. If you cannot afford an attorney, one will be appointed for you before any questioning if you wish. Do you understand?

5. If you decide to answer questions now without an attorney present you will still have the right to stop answering at any time until you talk to an attorney. Do you understand?
6. Knowing and understanding your rights as I have explained them to you, are you willing to answer my questions without an attorney present?

MAPP v. OHIO, 367 U.S. 643 (1961): Evidence gained from unreasonable search and seizures is subject to the exclusionary rule in both federal and state cases under the 4th Amendment.

DUNCAN v. LOUISIANA, 391 U.S. 145 (1968): Defendants in criminal cases for non-petty offenses have the right to a jury trial under the 6th Amendment.

BOARD OF EDUCATION v. EARLS, 536 U.S. 822 (2002): Drug testing of students involved in competitive extra-curricular activities was found to be constitutional. There was no violation of the 4th Amendment.

KYLLO v. UNITED STATES, 533 U.S. 27 (2001): The use of a thermal imaging device to "see" into a home was found to constitute a search and thus, without a warrant, violated the 4th Amendment.

GPS and the Fourth Amendment

Does the placing of a GPS tracking device on someone's car by the police without a warrant violate that person's Fourth Amendment rights to be free from an unreasonable search?

UNITED STATES v. JONES

Supreme Court Of The United States (9-0)

565 U. S.____ (2012)

JUSTICE SCALIA delivered the opinion of the Court.

We decide whether the attachment of a Global Positioning-System (GPS) tracking device to an individual's vehicle, and subsequent use of that device to monitor the vehicle's movements on public streets, constitutes a search or seizure within the meaning of the Fourth Amendment.

I

In 2004 respondent Antoine Jones, owner and operator of a nightclub in the District of Columbia, came under suspicion of trafficking in narcotics and was made the target of an investigation by a joint FBI and Metropolitan Police Department task force. Officers employed various investigative techniques, including visual surveillance of the nightclub, installation of a camera focused on the front door of the club, and a pen register and wiretap covering Jones's cellular phone.

Based in part on information gathered from these sources, in 2005 the Government applied to the United States District Court for the District of Columbia for a warrant authorizing the use of an electronic tracking device on the Jeep Grand Cherokee registered to Jones's wife. A warrant issued, authorizing installation of the device in the District of Columbia and within 10 days.

On the 11th day, and not in the District of Columbia but in Maryland, agents installed a GPS tracking device on the undercarriage of the Jeep while it was parked in a public parking lot. Over the next 28 days, the Government used the device to track the vehicle's movements, and once had to replace the device's battery when the vehicle was parked in a different public lot in Maryland. By means of signals from multiple satellites, the device established the vehicle's location within 50 to 100 feet, and communicated that location by cellular phone to a Government computer. It relayed more than 2,000 pages of data over the 4-week period.

The Government ultimately obtained a multiple-count indictment charging Jones and several alleged coconspirators with, as relevant here, conspiracy to distribute and possess with intent to distribute five kilograms or more of cocaine and 50 grams or more of cocaine base, in violation of 21 U. S. C. §§841 and 846. Before trial, Jones filed a motion to suppress evidence obtained through the GPS device. The District Court granted the motion only in part, suppressing the data obtained while the vehicle was parked in the garage adjoining Jones's residence. 451 F. Supp. 2d 71, 88 (2006). It held the remaining data admissible, because "'[a] person traveling in an automobile on public thoroughfares has no reasonable expectation of privacy in his movements from one place to another.'" *Ibid.* (quoting *United States* v. *Knotts*, 460 U. S. 276, 281 (1983)). Jones's trial in October 2006 produced a hung jury on the conspiracy count.

In March 2007, a grand jury returned another indictment, charging Jones and others with the same conspiracy. The Government introduced at trial the same GPS derived locational data admitted in the first trial, which connected Jones to the alleged conspirators' stash house that contained $850,000 in cash, 97 kilograms of cocaine, and 1 kilogram of cocaine base. The jury returned a guilty verdict, and the District Court sentenced Jones to life imprisonment.

The United States Court of Appeals for the District of Columbia Circuit reversed the conviction because of admission of the evidence obtained by warrantless use of the GPS device which, it said, violated the Fourth Amendment. *United States v. Maynard*, 615 F. 3d 544 (2010).The D. C. Circuit denied the Government's petition for rehearing en banc, with four judges dissenting. 625 F. 3d 766 (2010). We granted certiorari, 564 U. S. ___ (2011).

II

A

The Fourth Amendment provides in relevant part that "[t]he right of the people to be secure in their persons, houses, papers, and effects, against unreasonable searches and seizures, shall not be violated." It is beyond dispute that a vehicle is an "effect" as that term is used in the Amendment. *United States* v. *Chadwick*, 433 U. S. 1, 12 (1977). We hold that the Government's installation of a GPS device on a target's vehicle, and its use of that device to monitor the vehicle's movements, constitutes a "search."

It is important to be clear about what occurred in this case: The Government physically occupied private property for the purpose of obtaining information. We have no doubt that such a physical intrusion would have been considered a "search" within the meaning of the Fourth Amendment when it was adopted. *Entick* v. *Carrington*, 95 Eng. Rep. 807 (C. P. 1765), is a "case we have described as a 'monument of English freedom' 'undoubtedly familiar' to 'every American statesman' at the time the Constitution was adopted, and considered to be 'the true and ultimate expression of constitutional law'" with regard to search and seizure. *Brower* v. *County of Inyo*, 489 U. S. 593, 596 (1989) (quoting *Boyd* v. *United States*, 116 U. S. 616, 626 (1886)). In that case, Lord Camden expressed in plain terms the significance of property rights in search-and-seizure analysis:

> "[O]ur law holds the property of every man so sacred, that no man can set his foot upon his neighbour's close without his leave; if he does he is a trespasser, though he does no damage at all; if he will tread upon his neighbour's ground, he must justify it by law." *Entick, supra*, at 817.

The text of the Fourth Amendment reflects its close connection to property, since otherwise it would have referred simply to "the right of the people to be secure against unreasonable searches and seizures"; the phrase "in their persons, houses, papers, and effects" would have been superfluous.

Consistent with this understanding, our Fourth Amendment jurisprudence was tied to common-law trespass, at least until the latter half of the 20th century. *Kyllo* v. *United States*, 533 U. S. 27, 31 (2001); Kerr, The Fourth Amendment and New Technologies: Constitutional Myths and the Case for Caution, 102 Mich. L. Rev. 801, 816 (2004). Thus, in *Olmstead* v. *United States*, 277 U. S. 438 (1928), we held that wire-taps attached to telephone wires on the public streets did not constitute a Fourth Amendment search because "[t]here was no entry of the houses or offices of the defendants," *id.*, at 464.

Our later cases, of course, have deviated from that exclusively property-based approach. In *Katz* v. *United States*, 389 U. S. 347, 351 (1967), we said that "the Fourth Amendment protects people, not places," and found a violation in attachment of an eavesdropping device to a public telephone booth. Our later cases have applied the analysis of Justice Harlan's concurrence in that case, which said that a violation occurs when government officers violate a person's "reasonable expectation of privacy," *id.*, at 360. See, *e.g.*, *Bond* v. *United States*, 529 U. S. 334 (2000); *California* v. *Ciraolo*, 476 U. S. 207 (1986); *Smith* v. *Maryland*, 442 U. S. 735 (1979).

The Government contends that the Harlan standard shows that no search occurred here, since Jones had no "reasonable expectation of privacy" in the area of the Jeep accessed by Government agents (its underbody) and in the locations of the Jeep on the public roads, which were visible to all. But we need not address the Government's contentions, because Jones's Fourth Amendment rights do not rise or fall with the *Katz* formulation. At bottom, we must "assur[e] preservation of that degree of privacy against government that existed when the Fourth Amendment was adopted." *Kyllo, supra*, at 34. As explained, for most of our history the Fourth Amendment was understood to embody a particular concern for government trespass upon the areas ("persons, houses, papers, and effects") it enumerates. *Katz* did not repudiate that understanding. Less than two years later the Court upheld defendants' contention that the Government could not introduce against them conversations between other people obtained by warrantless placement of electronic surveillance devices in their homes. The opinion rejected the dissent's contention that there was no Fourth Amendment violation "unless the conversational privacy of the homeowner himself is invaded." *Alderman* v. *United States*, 394 U. S. 165, 176 (1969). "[W]e [do not] believe that *Katz*, by holding that the Fourth Amendment protects persons and their private conversations, was intended to withdraw any of the protection which the Amendment extends to the home . . . ." *Id.*, at 180.

* * *

B

The concurrence begins by accusing us of applying "18th-century tort law." *Post*, at 1. That is a distortion. What we apply is an 18th-century guarantee against unreasonable searches, which we believe must provide *at a minimum* the degree of protection it afforded when it was adopted. The concurrence does not share that belief. It would apply *exclusively Katz's* reasonable-expectation of-privacy test, even when that eliminates rights that previously existed.

The concurrence faults our approach for "present[ing] particularly vexing problems" in cases that do not involve physical contact, such as those that involve the transmission of electronic signals. *Post*, at 9. We entirely fail to understand that point. For unlike the concurrence, which would make *Katz* the *exclusive* test, we do not make trespass the exclusive test. Situations involving merely the transmission of electronic signals without trespass would *remain* subject to *Katz* analysis.

In fact, it is the concurrence's insistence on the exclusivity of the *Katz* test that needlessly leads us into "particularly vexing problems" in the present case. This Court has to date not deviated from the understanding that mere visual observation does not constitute a search. See *Kyllo*, 533 U. S., at 31–32. We accordingly held in *Knotts* that "[a] person traveling in an automobile on public thoroughfares has no reasonable expectation of privacy in his movements from one place to another." 460 U. S., at 281. Thus, even assuming that the concurrence is correct to say that "[t]raditional surveillance" of Jones for a 4-week period "would have required a large team of agents, multiple vehicles, and perhaps aerial assistance," *post*, at 12, our cases suggest that such visual observation is constitutionally permissible. It may be that achieving the same result through electronic means, without an accompanying trespass, is an unconstitutional invasion of privacy, but the present case does not require us to answer that question.

And answering it affirmatively leads us needlessly into additional thorny problems. The concurrence posits that "relatively short-term monitoring of a person's movements on public streets" is okay, but that "the use of longer term GPS monitoring in investigations of *most offenses*" is no good. *Post*, at 13 (emphasis added). That introduces yet another novelty into our jurisprudence. There is no precedent for the proposition that whether a search has occurred depends on the nature of the crime being investigated. And even accepting that novelty, it remains unexplained why a 4-week investigation is "surely" too long and why a drug-trafficking conspiracy involving substantial amounts of cash and narcotics is not an "extraordinary offens[e]" which may permit longer observation. See post, at 13–14. What of a 2-day monitoring of a suspected purveyor of stolen electronics? Or of a 6-month monitoring of a suspected terrorist? We may have to grapple with these "vexing problems" in some future case where a classic trespassory search is not involved and resort must be had to *Katz* analysis; but there is no reason for rushing forward to resolve them here.

* * *

The judgment of the Court of Appeals for the D. C. Circuit is affirmed.

It is so ordered.

[Footnotes Omitted.]

Chapter 11
Fashion Law

Why include a chapter on fashion law? Because it is relatively new, it is unique, and it demonstrates the law's reach into all areas of American society.

> The following article provides a good review of intellectual property issues as applied to a specific industry—fashion law.

An Introduction to Fashion Law

by Charles E. Colman, Esq.

What is "Fashion Law"?

There are different ways to characterize a practitioner's particular niche within the law. Some attorneys focus primarily on the litigation/transactional divide, calling themselves a "litigator" or a "corporate lawyer." Some attorneys proclaim a narrower focus, especially in areas of the law that are considered highly specialized—for example, bankruptcy and tax law. For these attorneys, the focus is on a particular body of law, and the client's industry is secondary. Recently, more and more practitioners have begun to market themselves based on the specific industries they serve. Thus, a few decades ago, some attorneys became "entertainment lawyers," and they were followed by "art lawyers," "sports lawyers," and most recently, "fashion lawyers."

Of course, there were always fashion companies in need of legal services, and many of those companies continue to patronize law firms without a self-proclaimed "Fashion Law Group." But starting in roughly 2005,[1] attorneys serving primarily fashion clients began employing the term "fashion lawyer," and the term is beginning to catch on. While the American Bar Association still does not have a dedicated Fashion Law Committee (it does have a Fashion Design Legislation Subcommittee), the last two years have seen the formation of fashion law committees at both the New York State and New York City Bar Associations.

1 Staci Riordan, "Fashion Law 101: How To Create A Movement," Fox Rothschild LLP Fashion Law Blog, Jul. 13, 2011, at http://fashionlaw.foxrothschild.com/2011/07/articles/fashion-law/fashion-law-101-how-to-create-a-movement/.

What exactly does a "fashion lawyer" do? Most attorneys working in this area would likely agree that intellectual property ("IP") protection—specifically, trademark protection—is at the heart of their practice. (Counterfeiting, a central concern for the fashion industry, is one type of trademark infringement.) Other issues encountered by fashion lawyers range from relatively straightforward contract disputes to arcane rules governing the importation and taxation of garments and textiles; and from regulatory restrictions on advertising and labeling to fashion industry-specific quirks in real estate and employment. Outside counsel will typically practice in one or two of these areas; few attorneys will be able to effectively litigate a trademark lawsuit and carry out a merger between two companies. Thus, perhaps the only true "fashion lawyers" are in-house attorneys at fashion companies who oversee all of these issues, either directly or by supervising the work of outside specialists. This chapter focuses on IP, the core of "fashion law."

Copyright in Fashion

The fashion industry is an unusual animal. In many industries, the scarcity of the products sold has a fairly direct effect on the price charged. In the fashion industry, however, a typical design will not be "scarce," because most—though not all—products sold by the fashion industry are ineligible for copyright protection. This leaves most designs vulnerable to "knockoff" artists who quickly make lower-cost versions of popular outfits available soon after the "original" or "authentic" version of the garment has been revealed to the public. The retail chain Forever 21 is particularly infamous for making low-cost versions of high-end garments; as a result, it has been sued over 50 times under copyright and trademark theories, virtually always settling with plaintiffs before trial and leading some to believe that this practice is simply part of the company's business model.[2]

Why are most fashion designs unprotected by copyright? The answer is clear, if unsatisfying. Under federal law, "pictorial, graphic, and sculptural works" are generally eligible for copyright protection, and in fact, automatically receive such protection immediately upon fixation in a tangible medium. Thus, the moment one creates an *illustration* of a garment, that illustration is protected by copyright. However, if/when that illustration is turned into a three-dimensional garment, the legal picture changes. The U.S. federal courts (which have exclusive jurisdiction over cases arising under the U.S. Copyright Act) have unanimously concluded that most garments and accessories are "useful articles,"[3] which the Copyright Act excludes from copyright-eligible subject matter. *See* 17 U.S.C. § 101. As a result, fashion generally receives no protection under federal copyright law, with some exceptions—most notably, original fabric patterns, jewelry, and elements of fashion design that are "physical or conceptually separable" as independent works of work.[4]

2 Jenna Sauers, "How Forever 21 Keeps Getting Away With Designer Knockoffs," *Jezebel*, Jul. 20, 2011, at http://jezebel.com/5822762/ (in which Professor Susan Scafidi of the Fordham Fashion Law Institute speculates: "[T]his is just part of their business strategy. They go ahead and they take what they want, and when they get caught, they pay up. It's probably cheaper than licensing it in the first place.")

3 See 17 U.S.C. § 101; *Chosun Int'l v. Chrisha Creations*, 413 F.3d 324, 328 (2d Cir. 2005).

4 *See Kieselstein-Cord v. Accessories by Pearl*, 632 F.2d 989 (2d Cir. 1980) (sculptural belt buckle found eligible for copyright protection).

This state of affairs is, quite naturally, frustrating for many designers. Thus, repeatedly over the years, and in each of the past five Congressional sessions, bills have been introduced that would create quasi-copyright protection for certain fashion articles. The current legislation on the issue, the "Innovative Design Protection and Piracy Prevention Act" ("IDPPPA"), would create a special three-year term of protection for designs featuring "a unique, distinguishable, non-trivial and non-utilitarian variation over prior designs." However, even with this rather stringent test for protection, the IDPPPA remains controversial and may not become law in the near future.[5]

In the meantime, "design patent" protection is the closest thing the U.S. has to a system that reliably protects the ornamental aspects of useful goods. Under 35 U.S.C. § 171, "[w]hoever invents any new, original, and ornamental design for an article of manufacture may obtain a patent thereof, subject to the conditions and requirements of [the Patent Act]." While this might sound promising for fashion designers, in practice it does little good. Patent registrations are very expensive and time-consuming to obtain, so this form of IP protection will typically make sense only for segments of the fashion industry whose products vary little from season to season, like footwear, undergarments, and certain accessories.

Trademarks in Fashion

Without copyright or patent protection, most designs are vulnerable to lower-cost knockoffs. With the proliferation of such knockoffs, the consumer has a choice where to purchase, and how much to spend on, similar (if not identical) goods. Partly for this reason, higher-end fashion companies put on runway shows and spend millions of dollars on advertising to create a certain "magic" or "exclusivity" surrounding their brands, to which consumers are drawn for reasons of fantasy, status, and perhaps even quality. This is where trademark law steps in, attempting to ensure that no third party "free-rides" on that hard-earned "magic."

The key question in trademark law is whether use of a given mark (or sometimes, distinctive design) would create a "likelihood of confusion" among consumers as to the origin, sponsorship, or affiliation of the good. Courts and policymakers have reasoned that consumers should be able to rely on indicators of source (like brand names and logos) and that companies should be able to reap the benefit of their investment in a brand without fear of free-riders.

Generally, this plays out in a straightforward manner. But the analysis in fashion has several quirks. There is a debate raging in the courts and among the public regarding the extent to which colors may serve as trademarks in the fashion industry. Second, it may come as some surprise to learn that one can engage in trademark infringement simply by using his or her own name to sell fashion articles.

---

5 L.J. Jackson, "Some Designers Say Their Work Deserves Copyright Protection; Others Say It Would Harm the Industry," ABA Journal (Jul. 1, 2011), available at http://www.abajournal.com/magazine/article/the_genuine_article/.

In *JA Apparel v. Abboud*, 568 F.3d 390 (2d Cir. 2009), for example, designer Joseph Abboud had sold the right to use his name in connection with apparel, but began a new line marketed as "jaz by Joseph Abboud." The company that had purchased the rights to his name sued, and the district court ultimately held that Abboud was entitled to use his name going forward only under very narrow circumstances. In the earlier case of *Gucci v. Gucci Shops, Inc.*, 688 F.Supp. 916, 928 (S.D.N.Y. 1988), designer Paolo Gucci attempted to sell clothes under his own name after a falling-out with the family company. Although the court was sympathetic, Gucci, like Abboud, was enjoined from using his name in connection with clothing, except under narrow circumstances. What were these circumstances? In both cases, the courts forbade the designers from using their names *as trademarks*; the judges permitted use of the designers' names as part of a description, provided that description appeared in a smaller font than the trademark *and* consumers were informed that the designers had no affiliation with their namesake companies.

The Rise of Licensing

Perhaps the most significant trademark-related development in the past fifty years of the fashion industry is the rise of the licensing agreement. A "license" is, at its essence, a promise not to sue another for using one's intellectual property. Trademark licenses are very common in the fashion industry—indeed, they have become practically ubiquitous—because they allow a brand owner to expand and further monetize its trademark by handing over the right to market products under the brand name in a particular region or in connection with particular products.

For example, a lucky company might successfully negotiate for the right to be Chanel's exclusive licensee in Turkey, meaning no one else (perhaps not even the brand owner) can sell goods under the Chanel brand name in that region. Another licensee might negotiate for the right to manufacture "Chanel" watches, a technologically complex product whose manufacture is beyond the expertise of most fashion houses. From an economic standpoint, it often makes sense to "farm out" these responsibilities to companies who specialize in a certain geographic region or category of good. (Indeed, a single licensee may manufacture a product (say, sunglasses) for dozens of brands ranging from low-end to luxury. When the manufacturer does nothing more than produce the good, a license may not be necessary; often, however, they do a great deal more.) With relatively little additional effort, the brand owner (the "licensor") receives a royalty from the licensee, which is typically calculated based on a percentage of net sales, and usually subject to a minimum dollar amount that the licensee will pay each year regardless of its actual sales. Sometimes, the licensor must promise that a certain percentage of the royalties it receives will be reinvested into the brand. For a luxury brand, one common arrangement is a "six-two" licensing deal, whereby the brand owner gets 8% of the licensee's net sales, but must invest a quarter of that revenue into advertising and product promotion.

Licensing agreements are often lengthy, as they are the end result of negotiation between the parties, each of which wants to protect itself. However, the desire to negotiate favorable terms must be counterbalanced against the desire to preserve a positive relationship with the licensee; after all, the execution of the license is only the first step toward what both parties hope will be a profitable collaboration. Nevertheless, certain provisions are practically mandatory, from the licensor's point of view. For example, a licensor must both include *and* exercise quality-control provisions in order to protect its trademark; brand owners who failed to do so have been punished by the court under the so-called "naked licensing" doctrine.[6] Further, the licensor must ensure that the licensee will not accrue any rights *of its own* in the trademark. (This second principle may apply even in the absence of a provision to that effect, but of course, lawyers are known for their "one can never be too careful" attitude, so licensors may insist on this.)

These days, some companies are little more than licensors of trademarks they have acquired from other companies. Some do not engage in any manufacturing or sales at all, handling only marketing and brand management—and some, not even that. Other companies are "hybrids," manufacturing goods under certain brand names or product lines while "licensing out" others.[7]

Infringement and Counterfeiting

Unauthorized use of another's protected design or brand name, except in certain circumstances, will constitute infringement of the owner's intellectual property rights. The precise circumstances in which no license is necessary are complex, and have been the subject of thousand-page treatises. To oversimplify, however, unauthorized use of a copyrighted design without a license is permissible where the third party's work is not "substantially similar" to the copyright owner's work, or where the third party's use constitutes "fair use" of the original material under 17 U.S.C. § 107. (See discussion at "An Introduction to the Law of Sampling," at p. 248.) In trademark law, unauthorized use of another's brand name is permissible where that use is not likely to cause confusion about the origin or sponsorship of goods and is not likely to "dilute" a famous brand; referring to a brand in a newspaper article, for example, is unlikely to do either. Trademark law has other exceptions to liability for infringement, including statutory and nominative "fair use" (which differ from the identically-named doctrine in copyright law), the primary purpose of which is to allow a third party to use another's mark in a descriptive—i.e., "non-source-identifying"—sense.

Where the exceptions to infringement do not apply, and the IP owner can prove all of the elements of an infringement (or dilution) claim, he will often be entitled to an injunction from the court ordering the infringer to stop using the IP in question, and/or monetary damages. The most severe form of trademark infringement, trademark counterfeiting (which occurs when one knowingly uses a "spurious mark which is identical with, or substantially indistinguishable from [plaintiff's] registered mark"[8]), carries with it a potential for higher damages and even criminal penalties.

---

6 As the U.S. Court of Appeals for the Seventh Circuit explained in *Gorenstein Enterprises, Inc. v. Quality Care-USA, Inc.*, 874 F.2d 431, 435 (7th Cir. 1989), "[t]he owner of a trademark has a duty to ensure the consistency of the trademarked good or service. If he does not fulfill this duty, he forfeits the trademark."

7 Although we have not discussed copyright or patent licenses here, many of the same principles apply; in those instances, however, it is not the brand name that is licensed for third-party use, but rather a particular pattern, design, or technology.

8 See 15 U.S.C. § 1127.

Once considered a fairly low priority for law enforcement officials and policymakers, fashion-related counterfeiting has attracted increased attention in recent years, as reports by various organizations have purported to show a connection between counterfeiting and child labor, organized crime, and even terrorist activities. Further, as the U.S. economy continues to evolve into an "information-based" (as opposed to manufacturing-based) economy, many policymakers have come to recognize that the protection of intellectual property has serious ramifications for the country's general economic well-being.

Recent Developments in Secondary Liability

Recognizing infringement as a problem, however, does not resolve the question of what to do about it. Whereas it was once relatively easy to make "busts" on warehouses or cargo containers chock-full of infringing goods, the distribution channels for such goods have, largely due to widespread Internet access, become more numerous and decentralized. In a recent, high-profile lawsuit, for example, Chanel sued 399 different websites for trafficking and/or facilitating the sale of counterfeit goods.[9]

The U.S. federal courts are still in the process of developing the standards to guide determinations of liability for "intermediaries" like ISPs or auction sites, when those intermediaries' services facilitated (or even encouraged) infringement by "end users." While copyright owners and practitioners have the guidance of the "Digital Millenium Copyright Act" (1998), which establishes certain "safe harbors" for intermediaries and enumerates the steps necessary to qualify for those safe harbors, the DMCA does not apply to trademark infringement. Thus, at this point, the contours of "secondary liability" in the trademark realm remain almost entirely up to the courts. Fortunately, one recent case went a long way toward delineating these contours. In *Tiffany (NJ) Inc. v. eBay Inc.*, 600 F. 3d 93, 105 (2d Cir. 2010), the U.S. Court of Appeals for the Second Circuit ruled, among other things, that a service provider like eBay can only be held liable for infringement by its users *if* it continues to provide its services to a specific individual who it knows, or has reason to know, is selling counterfeit goods. Note, however, that this standard raises questions of its own; furthermore, many other circuit courts have not adopted a test akin to that announced in *Tiffany*.

Unsurprisingly, brand owners have attempted to speed up this process through legislative action. Many lobbying groups representing the interests of brand owners support the "PROTECT IP" Act,[10] which would provide brand owners with a variety of additional tools to stop infringement on "rogue" websites, especially when they are located abroad and litigation is thus not feasible. As in many areas of intellectual property (and the law generally), the bill has fierce opponents, including those intermediaries who would face increased burdens under the proposed law.[11]

---

9 See Ken Ritter (Associated Press), "Chanel files Internet trademark lawsuit in Las Vegas," Bloomberg/BusinessWeek, Sept. 21, 2011, available at http://www.businessweek.com/ap/financialnews/D9PT3SI00.htm (last visited Oct. 11, 2011).

10 "Preventing Real Online Threats to Economic Creativity and Theft of Intellectual Property Act of 2011," S. 968, introduced on May 12, 2011 by Sen. Patrick Leahy (D-VT). PROTECT IP is a variation on an earlier bill titled the "Combating Online Infringement and Counterfeits Act" (COICA), which failed to become law in 2010.

11 For further discussion, see Abigail Phillips, "The 'PROTECT IP' Act: COICA Redux," Electronic Frontier Foundation, May 12, 2011, at https://www.eff.org/deeplinks/2011/05/protect-ip-act-coica-redux.

Fashion and Trademark Protection

Once a trademark is issued, it needs to be protected. In Charles Colman's CATWALK JUSTICE article, he discusses a recent trademark infringement case between Christian Louboutin and Yves Saint Laurent. The subject matter of the dispute is the color of the soles of shoes.

Everything You Need To Understand the Louboutin v. YSL Lawsuit

by Charles E. Colman, Esq.

* * *

Question: What's the difference between patents, copyrights, and trademarks, and which of these are relevant in the Louboutin case?

Answer: You've identified the "big three" in intellectual property. Patents cover novel inventions of useful products and processes, as well as certain ornamental aspects of functional goods. Copyrights protect non-utilitarian, original works of authorship. Only *trademark* protection (along with related, secondary areas of IP) is at issue in the Louboutin case. Trademarks protect words, symbols, and pretty much anything else that indicates the source of a good or service. But it's that "pretty much" that is the new thorn in Louboutin's side.

Q: Everyone knows that bright-red soles = Louboutin, so why is this a hard case?

A: Louboutin sued YSL for selling a variety of monochrome shoes that had bright-red soles (along with bright-red "uppers"). Along with the usual defenses to claims of trademark infringement—an insufficient percentage of consumers associate bright-red soles with Louboutin, consumers are not likely to be confused about the source of the shoes—YSL took the aggressive position that a single color on an article of apparel can never be a valid trademark. The U.S. Supreme Court has already ruled that color alone may serve as a trademark, provided there is an adequate level of consumer recognition and the color is not *functional*. (No one could, for example, claim trademark rights in the color red for stop signs.) The reason for this "functionality" bar is that it is *patent* law's job—and not that of trademark law—to grant monopolies on useful items. And when patent law does grant those rights, they're temporary—fourteen to twenty years, depending on the type of patent—whereas trademark protection can theoretically last forever.

YSL seized on this functionality rule, urging the district court to carve out what was essentially a special exception for fashion, taking the position that single colors are *always* functional in fashion because they are a basic design element that all labels need to have access to in order to compete in the marketplace. Many district court judges are wary of "making new law," as that is generally the role of appellate courts in the judiciary; but YSL's lawyers were likely emboldened to take such an aggressive stance because 1) YSL is a venerable design house with strong credibility; 2) Louboutin had (probably unwisely) sued over *monochrome* shoes, instead of shoes where the red sole contrasts with the upper; 3) Louboutin's trademark registration was quite vague, and judges don't like uncertainty in the law; and 4) the question "Is a single color inherently functional in fashion?" was posed during proceedings over Louboutin's requested preliminary injunction—an early stage of the case where a plaintiff has an extra burden to get what it wants from the court.

Q: So you're saying that if a trademark is found to be functional, it doesn't matter whether the trademark owner has secured a registration from the Trademark Office, or how many consumers associate the trademark with the owner?

A: That's right. Unlike some other challenges to trademark registrations, a challenge for functionality can be brought at any time. (Similarly, a challenge that a mark is, or has become, "generic" can be brought at any time, which is why companies like Chanel sometimes run ads instructing people not to use their brand names in a generic way; they're trying to avoid what trademark lawyers call "genericide.")

Q: But doesn't color *always* serve the "function" of making something more attractive?

A: In many instances, yes. But in many industries, the attractiveness of the product doesn't matter. The product at issue in the Supreme Court case I mentioned earlier, for example, was a dry cleaning pad with a distinctive green-gold color. Dry cleaners probably don't care what color their pads are; the customers never see them, anyway. But in fashion, color is a central feature that determines whether consumers will want to buy the product or not. YSL's lawyers argued, quite persuasively, that because of this, *fashion is just different*. And the judge accepted that argument.

Q: What do you mean, "fashion is just different"?

A: Judges generally don't like to draw industry-specific lines in their rulings, at least not where those lines aren't already laid out in statutes passed by Congress. They're under a lot of pressure not to "legislate from the bench," to use a phrase that has become popular—especially among conservatives—in recent years. But Judge Victor Marrero went ahead and drew an industry-specific line in his ruling on Wednesday, writing that "in the fashion industry color serves ornamental and aesthetic functions vital to robust competition[.]" As a result, it didn't matter that Louboutin's red sole was famously associated with the company; the functionality doctrine (specifically, the "aesthetic functionality" component of that doctrine) meant Louboutin's red sole could not serve as a *trademark*. One especially damaging piece of evidence for Christian Louboutin was an excerpt of a deposition of the namesake designer, in which he said he had decided to make his soles red because it "g[a]ve his line of shoes 'energy,'" and because the color was "'engaging, flirtatious, memorable and the color of passion,' as well as 'sexy.'" Sometimes, a single admission can lose a case, and this might very well have been that admission for Louboutin. The designer was basically admitting that his red soles served a *function* other than designating his company as the source of the shoes.

Q: What do you mean "lose a case"—the case isn't over yet, right?

A: That's true; all a judge decides on a preliminary injunction motion is whether the party seeking the injunction has a "likelihood of success" if the case moves forward. But it is pretty clear from the judge's decision, as well as his accompanying order for Louboutin to "show cause" why he shouldn't cancel the company's trademark registration, that he's made up his mind on the aesthetic functionality issue. In fact, his opinion even makes reference to an appeal to the Second Circuit Court of Appeals, which further suggests that the judge will stick to his guns Because the stakes are so high for Louboutin, it will very likely take this case as far as it can, perhaps even appealing to the Supreme Court if the Second Circuit turns out to agree with Judge Marrero. And the Supreme Court might actually take the case, since it hasn't *specifically* addressed colors-as-trademarks since the 1995 dry cleaning pad decision. Trademark lawyers see the prospect of a new Supreme Court opinion on this issue as something fun; the parties, however, may only see the cost of litigating a case that far up the court system, and—for Louboutin—the potentially disastrous result of bright-red soles becoming fair game for other purveyors of women's shoes.

Q: Okay, I get it, but this is obviously far more interesting for you than it is for me. Anything else I should know?

A: I just want to leave you with one especially florid quote from an unusually flowery opinion. The prose is remarkable because you usually find philosophical passages like this in Supreme Court opinions and occasionally in circuit court opinions, but very rarely in district court decisions. Enjoy:

"[Painting and fashion design] share a dependence on color as an indispensable medium. Color constitutes a critical attribute of the goods each form designs. Alone, in combinations, in harmonious or even incongruous blends, in varying patterns and shapes, the whole spectrum of light serves as a primal ingredient without which neither painting nor fashion design as expressive and ornamental art would flourish. For, color depicts elemental properties. As it projects expression of the artist's mental world, it captures the mutability, the fancy, the moods of the visual world, in both spheres working as a means to execute singular concepts born of imagination for which not just any other shade will do. Hence, color in this context plays a unique role. It is a feature purposely given to an article of art or design to depict the idea as the creator conceived it, and to evoke an effect intended. In ornamenting, it draws attention to itself, and to the object for which its tone forms a distinct expressive feature. From these perspectives, color in turn elementally performs a creative function; it aims to please or be useful, not to identify and advertise a commercial source."

The Constitution of the United States of America

We the People of the United States, in Order to form a more perfect Union, establish Justice, insure domestic Tranquility, provide for the common defence, promote the general Welfare, and secure the Blessings of Liberty to ourselves and our Posterity, do ordain and establish this Constitution for the United States of America.

Article. I.

Section 1.

All legislative Powers herein granted shall be vested in a Congress of the United States, which shall consist of a Senate and House of Representatives.

Section. 2.

Clause 1: The House of Representatives shall be composed of Members chosen every second Year by the People of the several States, and the Electors in each State shall have the Qualifications requisite for Electors of the most numerous Branch of the State Legislature.

Clause 2: No Person shall be a Representative who shall not have attained to the Age of twenty five Years, and been seven Years a Citizen of the United States, and who shall not, when elected, be an Inhabitant of that State in which he shall be chosen.

Clause 3: Representatives and direct Taxes shall be apportioned among the several States which may be included within this Union, according to their respective Numbers, which shall be determined by adding to the whole Number of free Persons, including those bound to Service for a Term of Years, and excluding Indians not taxed, three fifths of all other Persons. (See Note 2) The actual Enumeration shall be made within three Years after the first Meeting of the Congress of the United States, and within every subsequent Term of ten Years, in such Manner as they shall by Law direct. The Number of Representatives shall not exceed one for every thirty Thousand, but each State shall have at Least one Representative; and until such enumeration shall be made, the State of New Hampshire shall be entitled to chuse three, Massachusetts eight, Rhode-Island and Providence Plantations one, Connecticut five, New-York six, New Jersey four, Pennsylvania eight, Delaware one, Maryland six, Virginia ten, North Carolina five, South Carolina five, and Georgia three.

Clause 4: When vacancies happen in the Representation from any State, the Executive Authority thereof shall issue Writs of Election to fill such Vacancies.

Clause 5: The House of Representatives shall chuse their Speaker and other Officers; and shall have the sole Power of Impeachment.

Section. 3.

Clause 1: The Senate of the United States shall be composed of two Senators from each State, chosen by the Legislature thereof, (See Note 3) for six Years; and each Senator shall have one Vote.

Clause 2: Immediately after they shall be assembled in Consequence of the first Election, they shall be divided as equally as may be into three Classes. The Seats of the Senators of the first Class shall be vacated at the Expiration of the second Year, of the second Class at the Expiration of the fourth Year, and of the third Class at the Expiration of the sixth Year, so that one third may be chosen every second Year; and if Vacancies happen by Resignation, or otherwise, during the Recess of the Legislature of any State, the Executive thereof may make temporary Appointments until the next Meeting of the Legislature, which shall then fill such Vacancies. (See Note 4)

Clause 3: No Person shall be a Senator who shall not have attained to the Age of thirty Years, and been nine Years a Citizen of the United States, and who shall not, when elected, be an Inhabitant of that State for which he shall be chosen.

Clause 4: The Vice President of the United States shall be President of the Senate, but shall have no Vote, unless they be equally divided.

Clause 5: The Senate shall chuse their other Officers, and also a President pro tempore, in the Absence of the Vice President, or when he shall exercise the Office of President of the United States.

Clause 6: The Senate shall have the sole Power to try all Impeachments. When sitting for that Purpose, they shall be on Oath or Affirmation. When the President of the United States is tried, the Chief Justice shall preside: And no Person shall be convicted without the Concurrence of two thirds of the Members present.

Clause 7: Judgment in Cases of Impeachment shall not extend further than to removal from Office, and disqualification to hold and enjoy any Office of honor, Trust or Profit under the United States: but the Party convicted shall nevertheless be liable and subject to Indictment, Trial, Judgment and Punishment, according to Law.

Section. 4.

Clause 1: The Times, Places and Manner of holding Elections for Senators and Representatives, shall be prescribed in each State by the Legislature thereof; but the Congress may at any time by Law make or alter such Regulations, except as to the Places of chusing Senators.

Clause 2: The Congress shall assemble at least once in every Year, and such Meeting shall be on the first Monday in December, (See Note 5) unless they shall by Law appoint a different Day.

Section. 5.

Clause 1: Each House shall be the Judge of the Elections, Returns and Qualifications of its own Members, and a Majority of each shall constitute a Quorum to do Business; but a smaller Number may adjourn from day to day, and may be authorized to compel the Attendance of absent Members, in such Manner, and under such Penalties as each House may provide.

Clause 2: Each House may determine the Rules of its Proceedings, punish its Members for disorderly Behaviour, and, with the Concurrence of two thirds, expel a Member.

Clause 3: Each House shall keep a Journal of its Proceedings, and from time to time publish the same, excepting such Parts as may in their Judgment require Secrecy; and the Yeas and Nays of the Members of either House on any question shall, at the Desire of one fifth of those Present, be entered on the Journal.

Clause 4: Neither House, during the Session of Congress, shall, without the Consent of the other, adjourn for more than three days, nor to any other Place than that in which the two Houses shall be sitting.

Section. 6.

Clause 1: The Senators and Representatives shall receive a Compensation for their Services, to be ascertained by Law, and paid out of the Treasury of the United States. (See Note 6) They shall in all Cases, except Treason, Felony and Breach of the Peace, beprivileged from Arrest during their Attendance at the Session of their respective Houses, and in going to and returning from the same; and for any Speech or Debate in either House, they shall not be questioned in any other Place.

Clause 2: No Senator or Representative shall, during the Time for which he was elected, be appointed to any civil Office under the Authority of the United States, which shall have been created, or the Emoluments whereof shall have been encreased during such time; and no Person holding any Office under the United States, shall be a Member of either House during his Continuance in Office.

Section. 7.

Clause 1: All Bills for raising Revenue shall originate in the House of Representatives; but the Senate may propose or concur with Amendments as on other Bills.

Clause 2: Every Bill which shall have passed the House of Representatives and the Senate, shall, before it become a Law, be presented to the President of the United States; If he approve he shall sign it, but if not he shall return it, with his Objections to that House in which it shall have originated, who shall enter the Objections at large on their Journal, and proceed to reconsider it. If after such Reconsideration two thirds of that House shall agree to pass the Bill, it shall be sent, together with the Objections, to the other House, by which it shall likewise be reconsidered, and if approved by two thirds of that House, it shall become a Law. But in all such Cases the Votes of both Houses shall be determined by yeas and Nays, and the Names of the Persons voting for and against the Bill shall be entered on the Journal of each House respectively. If any Bill shall not be returned by the President within ten Days (Sundays excepted) after it shall have been presented to him, the Same shall be a Law, in like Manner as if he had signed it, unless the Congress by their Adjournment prevent its Return, in which Case it shall not be a Law.

Clause 3: Every Order, Resolution, or Vote to which the Concurrence of the Senate and House of Representatives may be necessary (except on a question of Adjournment) shall be presented to the President of the United States; and before the Same shall take Effect, shall be approved by him, or being disapproved by him, shall be repassed by two thirds of the Senate and House of Representatives, according to the Rules and Limitations prescribed in the Case of a Bill.

Section. 8.

Clause 1: The Congress shall have Power To lay and collect Taxes, Duties, Imposts and Excises, to pay the Debts and provide for the common Defence and general Welfare of the United States; but all Duties, Imposts and Excises shall be uniform throughout the United States;

Clause 2: To borrow Money on the credit of the United States;

Clause 3: To regulate Commerce with foreign Nations, and among the several States, and with the Indian Tribes;

Clause 4: To establish an uniform Rule of Naturalization, and uniform Laws on the subject of Bankruptcies throughout the United States;

Clause 5: To coin Money, regulate the Value thereof, and of foreign Coin, and fix the Standard of Weights and Measures;

Clause 6: To provide for the Punishment of counterfeiting the Securities and current Coin of the United States;

Clause 7: To establish Post Offices and post Roads;

Clause 8: To promote the Progress of Science and useful Arts, by securing for limited Times to Authors and Inventors the exclusive Right to their respective Writings and Discoveries;

Clause 9: To constitute Tribunals inferior to the supreme Court;

Clause 10: To define and punish Piracies and Felonies committed on the high Seas, and Offences against the Law of Nations;

Clause 11: To declare War, grant Letters of Marque and Reprisal, and make Rules concerning Captures on Land and Water;

Clause 12: To raise and support Armies, but no Appropriation of Money to that Use shall be for a longer Term than two Years;

Clause 13: To provide and maintain a Navy;

Clause 14: To make Rules for the Government and Regulation of the land and naval Forces;

Clause 15: To provide for calling forth the Militia to execute the Laws of the Union, suppress Insurrections and repel Invasions;

Clause 16: To provide for organizing, arming, and disciplining, the Militia, and for governing such Part of them as may be employed in the Service of the United States, reserving to the States respectively, the Appointment of the Officers, and the Authority of training the Militia according to the discipline prescribed by Congress;

Clause 17: To exercise exclusive Legislation in all Cases whatsoever, over such District (not exceeding ten Miles square) as may, byCession of particular States, and the Acceptance of Congress, become the Seat of the Government of the United States, and to exercise like Authority over all Places purchased by the Consent of the Legislature of the State in which the Same shall be, for the Erection of Forts, Magazines, Arsenals, dock-Yards, and other needful Buildings;--And

Clause 18: To make all Laws which shall be necessary and proper for carrying into Execution the foregoing Powers, and all other Powers vested by this Constitution in the Government of the United States, or in any Department or Officer thereof.

Section. 9.

Clause 1: The Migration or Importation of such Persons as any of the States now existing shall think proper to admit, shall not be prohibited by the Congress prior to the Year one thousand eight hundred and eight, but a Tax or duty may be imposed on such Importation, not exceeding ten dollars for each Person.

Clause 2: The Privilege of the Writ of Habeas Corpus shall not be suspended, unless when in Cases of Rebellion or Invasion the public Safety may require it.

Clause 3: No Bill of Attainder or ex post facto Law shall be passed.

Clause 4: No Capitation, or other direct, Tax shall be laid, unless in Proportion to the Census or Enumeration herein before directed to be taken. (See Note 7)

Clause 5: No Tax or Duty shall be laid on Articles exported from any State.

Clause 6: No Preference shall be given by any Regulation of Commerce or Revenue to the Ports of one State over those of another: nor shall Vessels bound to, or from, one State, be obliged to enter, clear, or pay Duties in another.

Clause 7: No Money shall be drawn from the Treasury, but in Consequence of Appropriations made by Law; and a regular Statement and Account of the Receipts and Expenditures of all public Money shall be published from time to time.

Clause 8: No Title of Nobility shall be granted by the United States: And no Person holding any Office of Profit or Trust under them, shall, without the Consent of the Congress, accept of any present, Emolument, Office, or Title, of any kind whatever, from any King, Prince, or foreign State.

Section. 10.

Clause 1: No State shall enter into any Treaty, Alliance, or Confederation; grant Letters of Marque and Reprisal; coin Money; emit Bills of Credit; make any Thing but gold and silver Coin a Tender in Payment of Debts; pass any Bill of Attainder, ex post facto Law, or Law impairing the Obligation of Contracts, or grant any Title of Nobility.

Clause 2: No State shall, without the Consent of the Congress, lay any Imposts or Duties on Imports or Exports, except what may be absolutely necessary for executing it's inspection Laws: and the net Produce of all Duties and Imposts, laid by any State on Imports or Exports, shall be for the Use of the Treasury of the United States; and all such Laws shall be subject to the Revision and Controul of the Congress.

Clause 3: No State shall, without the Consent of Congress, lay any Duty of Tonnage, keep Troops, or Ships of War in time of Peace, enter into any Agreement or Compact with another State, or with a foreign Power, or engage in War, unless actually invaded, or in such imminent Danger as will not admit of delay.

Article. II.

Section. 1.

Clause 1: The executive Power shall be vested in a President of the United States of America. He shall hold his Office during the Term of four Years, and, together with the Vice President, chosen for the same Term, be elected, as follows

Clause 2: Each State shall appoint, in such Manner as the Legislature thereof may direct, a Number of Electors, equal to the whole Number of Senators and Representatives to which the State may be entitled in the Congress: but no Senator or Representative, or Person holding an Office of Trust or Profit under the United States, shall be appointed an Elector.

Clause 3: The Electors shall meet in their respective States, and vote by Ballot for two Persons, of whom one at least shall not be an Inhabitant of the same State with themselves. And they shall make a List of all the Persons voted for, and of the Number of Votes for each; which List they shall sign and certify, and transmit sealed to the Seat of the Government of the United States, directed to the President of the Senate. The President of the Senate shall, in the Presence of the Senate and House of Representatives, open all the Certificates, and the Votes shall then be counted. The Person having the greatest Number of Votes shall be the President, if such Number be a Majority of the whole Number of Electors appointed; and if there be more than one who have such Majority, and have an equal Number of Votes, then the House of Representatives shall immediately chuse by Ballot one of them for President; and if no Person have a Majority, then from the five highest on the List the said House shall in like Manner chuse the President. But in chusing the President, the Votes shall be taken by States, the Representation from each State having one Vote; A quorum for this Purpose shall consist of a Member or Members from two thirds of the States, and a Majority of all the States shall be necessary to a Choice. In every Case, after the Choice of the President, the Person having the greatest Number of Votes of the Electors shall be the Vice President. But if there should remain two or more who have equal Votes, the Senate shall chuse from them by Ballot the Vice President. (See Note 8)

Clause 4: The Congress may determine the Time of chusing the Electors, and the Day on which they shall give their Votes; which Day shall be the same throughout the United States.

Clause 5: No Person except a natural born Citizen, or a Citizen of the United States, at the time of the Adoption of this Constitution, shall be eligible to the Office of President; neither shall any Person be eligible to that Office who shall not have attained to the Age of thirty five Years, and been fourteen Years a Resident within the United States.

Clause 6: In Case of the Removal of the President from Office, or of his Death, Resignation, or Inability to discharge the Powers and Duties of the said Office, (See Note 9) the Same shall devolve on the VicePresident, and the Congress may by Law provide for the Case of Removal, Death, Resignation or Inability, both of the President and Vice President, declaring what Officer shall then act as President, and such Officer shall act accordingly, until the Disability be removed, or a President shall be elected.

Clause 7: The President shall, at stated Times, receive for his Services, a Compensation, which shall neither be encreased nor diminished during the Period for which he shall have been elected, and he shall not receive within that Period any other Emolument from the United States, or any of them.

Clause 8: Before he enter on the Execution of his Office, he shall take the following Oath or Affirmation:--"I do solemnly swear (or affirm) that I will faithfully execute the Office of President of the United States, and will to the best of my Ability, preserve, protect and defend the Constitution of the United States."

Section. 2.

Clause 1: The President shall be Commander in Chief of the Army and Navy of the United States, and of the Militia of the several States, when called into the actual Service of the United States; he may require the Opinion, in writing, of the principal Officer in each of the executive Departments, upon any Subject relating to the Duties of their respective Offices, and he shall have Power to grant Reprieves and Pardons for Offences against the United States, except in Cases of Impeachment.

Clause 2: He shall have Power, by and with the Advice and Consent of the Senate, to make Treaties, provided two thirds of the Senators present concur; and he shall nominate, and by and with the Advice and Consent of the Senate, shall appoint Ambassadors, other public Ministers and Consuls, Judges of the supreme Court, and all other Officers of the United States, whose Appointments are not herein otherwise provided for, and which shall be established by Law: but the Congress may by Law vest the Appointment of such inferior Officers, as they think proper, in the President alone, in the Courts of Law, or in the Heads of Departments.

Clause 3: The President shall have Power to fill up all Vacancies that may happen during the Recess of the Senate, by granting Commissions which shall expire at the End of their next Session.

Section. 3.

He shall from time to time give to the Congress Information of the State of the Union, and recommend to their Consideration such Measures as he shall judge necessary and expedient; he may, on extraordinary Occasions, convene both Houses, or either of them, and in Case of Disagreement between them, with Respect to the Time of Adjournment, he may adjourn them to such Time as he shall think proper; he shall receive Ambassadors and other public Ministers; he shall take Care that the Laws be faithfully executed, and shall Commission all the Officers of the United States.

Section. 4.

The President, Vice President and all civil Officers of the United States, shall be removed from Office on Impeachment for, and Conviction of, Treason, Bribery, or other high Crimes and Misdemeanors.

Article. III.

Section. 1.

The judicial Power of the United States, shall be vested in one supreme Court, and in such inferior Courts as the Congress may from time to time ordain and establish. The Judges, both of the supreme and inferior Courts, shall hold their Offices during good Behaviour, and shall, at stated Times, receive for their Services, a Compensation, which shall not be diminished during their Continuance in Office.

Section. 2.

Clause 1: The judicial Power shall extend to all Cases, in Law and Equity, arising under this Constitution, the Laws of the United States, and Treaties made, or which shall be made, under their Authority;--to all Cases affecting Ambassadors, other public Ministers and Consuls;--to all Cases of admiralty and maritime Jurisdiction;--to Controversies to which the United States shall be a Party;--to Controversies between two or more States;--between a State and Citizens of another State; (See Note 10)--between Citizens of different States, --between Citizens of the same State claiming Lands under Grants of different States, and between a State, or the Citizens thereof, and foreign States, Citizens or Subjects.

Clause 2: In all Cases affecting Ambassadors, other public Ministers and Consuls, and those in which a State shall be Party, the supreme Court shall have original Jurisdiction. In all the other Cases before mentioned, the supreme Court shall have appellate Jurisdiction, both as to Law and Fact, with such Exceptions, and under such Regulations as the Congress shall make.

Clause 3: The Trial of all Crimes, except in Cases of Impeachment, shall be by Jury; and such Trial shall be held in the State where the said Crimes shall have been committed; but when not committed within any State, the Trial shall be at such Place or Places as the Congress may by Law have directed.

Section. 3.

Clause 1: Treason against the United States, shall consist only in levying War against them, or in adhering to their Enemies, giving them Aid and Comfort. No Person shall be convicted of Treason unless on the Testimony of two Witnesses to the same overt Act, or on Confession in open Court.

Clause 2: The Congress shall have Power to declare the Punishment of Treason, but no Attainder of Treason shall work Corruption of Blood, or Forfeiture except during the Life of the Person attainted.

Article. IV.

Section. 1.

Full Faith and Credit shall be given in each State to the public Acts, Records, and judicial Proceedings of every other State. And the Congress may by general Laws prescribe the Manner in which such Acts, Records and Proceedings shall be proved, and the Effect thereof.

Section. 2.

Clause 1: The Citizens of each State shall be entitled to all Privileges and Immunities of Citizens in the several States.

Clause 2: A Person charged in any State with Treason, Felony, or other Crime, who shall flee from Justice, and be found in another State, shall on Demand of the executive Authority of the State from which he fled, be delivered up, to be removed to the State having Jurisdiction of the Crime.

Clause 3: No Person held to Service or Labour in one State, under the Laws thereof, escaping into another, shall, in Consequence of any Law or Regulation therein, be discharged from such Service or Labour, but shall be delivered up on Claim of the Party to whom such Service or Labour may be due. (See Note 11)

Section. 3.

Clause 1: New States may be admitted by the Congress into this Union; but no new State shall be formed or erected within the Jurisdiction of any other State; nor any State be formed by the Junction of two or more States, or Parts of States, without the Consent of the Legislatures of the States concerned as well as of the Congress.

Clause 2: The Congress shall have Power to dispose of and make all needful Rules and Regulations respecting the Territory or other Property belonging to the United States; and nothing in this Constitution shall be so construed as to Prejudice any Claims of the United States, or of any particular State.

Section. 4.

The United States shall guarantee to every State in this Union a Republican Form of Government, and shall protect each of them against Invasion; and on Application of the Legislature, or of the Executive (when the Legislature cannot be convened) against domestic Violence.

Article. V.

The Congress, whenever two thirds of both Houses shall deem it necessary, shall propose Amendments to this Constitution, or, on the Application of the Legislatures of two thirds of the several States, shall call a Convention for proposing Amendments, which, in either Case, shall be valid to all Intents and Purposes, as Part of this Constitution, when ratified by the Legislatures of three fourths of the several States, or by Conventions in three fourths thereof, as the one or the other Mode of Ratification may be proposed by the Congress; Provided that no Amendment which may be made prior to the Year One thousand eight hundred and eight shall in any Manner affect the first and fourth Clauses in the Ninth Section of the first Article; and that no State, without its Consent, shall be deprived of its equal Suffrage in the Senate.

Article. VI.

Clause 1: All Debts contracted and Engagements entered into, before the Adoption of this Constitution, shall be as valid against the United States under this Constitution, as under the Confederation.

Clause 2: This Constitution, and the Laws of the United States which shall be made in Pursuance thereof; and all Treaties made, or which shall be made, under the Authority of the United States, shall be the supreme Law of the Land; and the Judges in every State shall be bound thereby, any Thing in the Constitution or Laws of any State to the Contrary notwithstanding.

Clause 3: The Senators and Representatives before mentioned, and the Members of the several State Legislatures, and all executive and judicial Officers, both of the United States and of the several States, shall be bound by Oath or Affirmation, to support this Constitution; but no religious Test shall ever be required as a Qualification to any Office or public Trust under the United States.

Article. VII.

The Ratification of the Conventions of nine States, shall be sufficient for the Establishment of this Constitution between the States so ratifying the Same.

Done in Convention by the Unanimous Consent of the States present the Seventeenth Day of September in the Year of our Lord one thousand seven hundred and Eighty seven and of the Independence of the United States of America the Twelfth In witness whereof We have hereunto subscribed our Names,

GO WASHINGTON--Presidt. and deputy from Virginia

[Signed also by the deputies of twelve States.]

Delaware

Geo: Read

Gunning Bedford jun

John Dickinson

Richard Bassett

Jaco: Broom

Maryland

James MCHenry

Dan of ST ThoS. Jenifer

DanL Carroll.

Virginia

John Blair--

James Madison Jr.

North Carolina

WM Blount

RichD. Dobbs Spaight.

Hu Williamson

South Carolina

J. Rutledge

Charles 1ACotesworth Pinckney

Charles Pinckney

Pierce Butler.

Georgia

William Few

Abr Baldwin

New Hampshire

John Langdon

Nicholas Gilman

Massachusetts

Nathaniel Gorham

Rufus King

Connecticut

WM. SamL. Johnson

Roger Sherman

New York

Alexander Hamilton

New Jersey

Wil: Livingston

David Brearley.

WM. Paterson.

Jona: Dayton

Pennsylvania

B Franklin

Thomas Mifflin

RobT Morris

Geo. Clymer

ThoS. FitzSimons

Jared Ingersoll

James Wilson.

Gouv Morris

Attest William Jackson Secretary

NOTES

Note 1: This text of the Constitution follows the engrossed copy signed by Gen. Washington and the deputies from 12 States. The small superior figures preceding the paragraphs designate Clauses, and were not in the original and have no reference to footnotes.

The Constitution was adopted by a convention of the States on September 17, 1787, and was subsequently ratified by the several States, on the following dates: Delaware, December 7, 1787; Pennsylvania, December 12, 1787; New Jersey, December 18, 1787; Georgia, January 2, 1788; Connecticut, January 9, 1788; Massachusetts, February 6, 1788; Maryland, April 28, 1788; South Carolina, May 23, 1788; New Hampshire, June 21, 1788.

Ratification was completed on June 21, 1788.

The Constitution was subsequently ratified by Virginia, June 25, 1788; New York, July 26, 1788; North Carolina, November 21, 1789; Rhode Island, May 29, 1790; and Vermont, January 10, 1791.

In May 1785, a committee of Congress made a report recommending an alteration in the Articles of Confederation, but no action was taken on it, and it was left to the State Legislatures to proceed in the matter. In January 1786, the Legislature of Virginia passed a resolution providing for the appointment of five commissioners, who, or any three of them, should meet such commissioners as might be appointed in the other States of the Union, at a time and place to be agreed upon, to take into consideration the trade of the United States; to consider how far a uniform system in their commercial regulations may be necessary to their common interest and their permanent harmony; and to report to the several States such an act, relative to this great object, as, when ratified by them, will enable the United States in Congress effectually to provide for the same. The Virginia commissioners, after some correspondence, fixed the first Monday in September as the time, and the city of Annapolis as the place for the meeting, but only four other States were represented, viz: Delaware, New York, New Jersey, and Pennsylvania; the commissioners appointed by Massachusetts, New Hampshire, North Carolina, and Rhode Island failed to attend. Under the circumstances of so partial a representation, the commissioners present agreed upon a report, (drawn by Mr. Hamilton, of New York,) expressing their unanimous conviction that it might essentially tend to advance the interests of the Union if the States by which they were respectively delegated would concur, and use their endeavors to procure the concurrence of the other States, in the appointment of commissioners to meet at Philadelphia on the Second Monday of May following, to take into consideration the situation of the United States; to devise such further provisions as should appear to them necessary to render the Constitution of the Federal Government adequate to the exigencies of the Union; and to report such an act for that purpose to the United States in Congress assembled as, when agreed to by them and afterwards confirmed by the Legislatures of every State, would effectually provide for the same.

Congress, on the 21st of February, 1787, adopted a resolution in favor of a convention, and the Legislatures of those States which had not already done so (with the exception of Rhode Island) promptly appointed delegates. On the 25th of May, seven States having convened, George Washington, of Virginia, was unanimously elected President, and the consideration of the proposed constitution was commenced. On the 17th of September, 1787, the Constitution as engrossed and agreed upon was signed by all the members present, except Mr. Gerry of Massachusetts, and Messrs. Mason and Randolph, of Virginia. The president of the convention transmitted it to Congress, with a resolution stating how the proposed Federal Government should be put in operation, and an explanatory letter. Congress, on the 28th of September, 1787, directed the Constitution so framed, with the resolutions and letter concerning the same, to "be transmitted to the several Legislatures in order to be submitted to a convention of delegates chosen in each State by the people thereof, in conformity to the resolves of the convention."

On the 4th of March, 1789, the day which had been fixed for commencing the operations of Government under the new Constitution, it had been ratified by the conventions chosen in each State to consider it, as follows: Delaware, December 7, 1787; Pennsylvania, December 12, 1787; New Jersey, December 18, 1787; Georgia, January 2, 1788; Connecticut, January 9, 1788; Massachusetts, February 6, 1788; Maryland, April 28, 1788; South Carolina, May 23, 1788; New Hampshire, June 21, 1788; Virginia, June 25, 1788; and New York, July 26, 1788.

The President informed Congress, on the 28th of January, 1790, that North Carolina had ratified the Constitution November 21, 1789; and he informed Congress on the 1st of June, 1790, that Rhode Island had ratified the Constitution May 29, 1790. Vermont, in convention, ratified the Constitution January 10, 1791, and was, by an act of Congress approved February 18, 1791, "received and admitted into this Union as a new and entire member of the United States."

Note 2: The part of this Clause relating to the mode of apportionment of representatives among the several States has been affected by Section 2 of amendment XIV, and as to taxes on incomes without apportionment by amendment XVI.

Note 3: This Clause has been affected by Clause 1 of amendment XVII.

Note 4: This Clause has been affected by Clause 2 of amendment XVIII.

Note 5: This Clause has been affected by amendment XX.

Note 6: This Clause has been affected by amendment XXVII.

Note 7: This Clause has been affected by amendment XVI.

Note 8: This Clause has been superseded by amendment XII.

Note 9: This Clause has been affected by amendment XXV.

Note 10: This Clause has been affected by amendment XI.

Note 11: This Clause has been affected by amendment XIII.

This information has been compiled from the U.S. Code. The U.S. Code is published by the Law Revision Counsel of the U.S. House of Representatives.

Updated September 20, 2004

Amendments to the Constitution of the United States of America

ARTICLES IN ADDITION TO, AND AMENDMENTS OF, THE

Amendments to the Constitution

CONSTITUTION OF THE UNITED STATES OF AMERICA, PROPOSED BY CONGRESS, AND RATIFIED BY THE LEGISLATURES OF THE SEVERAL STATES, PURSUANT TO THE FIFTH ARTICLE OF THE ORIGINAL CONSTITUTION (See Note 12)

Article [I.] (See Note 13)

Congress shall make no law respecting an establishment of religion, or prohibiting the free exercise thereof; or abridging the freedom of speech, or of the press; or the right of the people peaceably to assemble, and to petition the Government for a redress of grievances.

Article [II.]

A well regulated Militia, being necessary to the security of a free State, the right of the people to keep and bear Arms, shall not be infringed.

Article [III.]

No Soldier shall, in time of peace be quartered in any house, without the consent of the Owner, nor in time of war, but in a manner to be prescribed by law.

Article [IV.]

The right of the people to be secure in their persons, houses, papers, and effects, against unreasonable searches and seizures, shall not be violated, and no Warrants shall issue, but upon probable cause, supported by Oath or affirmation, and particularly describing the place to be searched, and the persons or things to be seized.

Article [V.]

No person shall be held to answer for a capital, or otherwise infamous crime, unless on a presentment or indictment of a Grand Jury, except in cases arising in the land or naval forces, or in the Militia, when in actual service in time of War or public danger; nor shall any person be subject for the same offence to be twice put in jeopardy of life or limb; nor shall be compelled in any criminal case to be a witness against himself, nor be deprived of life, liberty, or property, without due process of law; nor shall private property be taken for public use, without just compensation.

Article [VI.]

In all criminal prosecutions, the accused shall enjoy the right to a speedy and public trial, by an impartial jury of the State and district wherein the crime shall have been committed, which district shall have been previously ascertained by law, and to be informed of the nature and cause of the accusation; to be confronted with the witnesses against him; to have compulsory process for obtaining witnesses in his favor, and to have the Assistance of Counsel for his defence.

Article [VII.]

In Suits at common law, where the value in controversy shall exceed twenty dollars, the right of trial by jury shall be preserved, and no fact tried by a jury, shall be otherwise re-examined in any Court of the United States, than according to the rules of the common law.

Article [VIII.]

Excessive bail shall not be required, nor excessive fines imposed, nor cruel and unusual punishments inflicted.

Article [IX.]

The enumeration in the Constitution, of certain rights, shall not be construed to deny or disparage others retained by the people.

Article [X.]

The powers not delegated to the United States by the Constitution, nor prohibited by it to the States, are reserved to the States respectively, or to the people.

[Article XI.]

The Judicial power of the United States shall not be construed to extend to any suit in law or equity, commenced or prosecuted against one of the United States by Citizens of another State, or by Citizens or Subjects of any Foreign State.

Proposal and Ratification

The eleventh amendment to the Constitution of the United States was proposed to the legislatures of the several States by the Third Congress, on the 4th of March 1794; and was declared in a message from the President to Congress, dated the 8th of January, 1798, to have been ratified by the legislatures of three-fourths of the States. The dates of ratification were: New York, March 27, 1794; Rhode Island, March 31, 1794; Connecticut, May 8, 1794; New Hampshire, June 16, 1794; Massachusetts, June 26, 1794; Vermont, between October 9, 1794 and November 9, 1794; Virginia, November 18, 1794; Georgia, November 29, 1794; Kentucky, December 7, 1794; Maryland, December 26, 1794; Delaware, January 23, 1795; North Carolina, February 7, 1795.

Ratification was completed on February 7, 1795.

The amendment was subsequently ratified by South Carolina on December 4, 1797. New Jersey and Pennsylvania did not take action on the amendment.

[Article XII.]

The Electors shall meet in their respective states, and vote by ballot for President and Vice-President, one of whom, at least, shall not be an inhabitant of the same state with themselves; they shall name in their ballots the person voted for as President, and in distinct ballots the person voted for as

Vice-President, and they shall make distinct lists of all persons voted for as President, and of all persons voted for as Vice-President, and of the number of votes for each, which lists they shall sign and certify, and transmit sealed to the seat of the government of the United States, directed to the President of the Senate;--The President of the Senate shall, in the presence of the Senate and House of Representatives, open all the certificates and the votes shall then be counted;--The person having the greatest number of votes for President, shall be the President, if such number be a majority of the whole number of Electors appointed; and if no person have such majority, then from the persons having the highest numbers not exceeding three on the list of those voted for as President, the House of Representatives shall choose immediately, by ballot, the President. But in choosing the President, the votes shall be taken by states, the representation from each state having one vote; a quorum for this purpose shall consist of a member or members from two-thirds of the states, and a majority of all the states shall be necessary to a choice. And if the House of Representatives shall not choose a President whenever the right of choice shall devolve upon them, before the fourth day of March next following, then the Vice-President shall act as President, as in the case of the death or other constitutional disability of the President. (See Note 14)--The person having the greatest number of votes as Vice-President, shall be the Vice-President, if such number be a majority of the whole number of Electors appointed, and if no person have a majority, then from the two highest numbers on the list, the Senate shall choose the Vice-President; a quorum for the purpose shall consist of two-thirds of the whole number of Senators, and a majority of the whole number shall be necessary to a choice. But no person constitutionally ineligible to the office of President shall be eligible to that of Vice-President of the United States.

Proposal and Ratification The twelfth amendment to the Constitution of the United States was proposed to the legislatures of the several States by the Eighth Congress, on the 9th of December, 1803, in lieu of the original third paragraph of the first section of the second article; and was declared in a proclamation of the Secretary of State, dated the 25th of September, 1804, to have been ratified by the legislatures of 13 of the 17 States. The dates of ratification were: North Carolina, December 21, 1803; Maryland, December 24, 1803; Kentucky, December 27, 1803; Ohio, December 30, 1803; Pennsylvania, January 5, 1804; Vermont, January 30, 1804; Virginia, February 3, 1804; New York, February 10, 1804; New Jersey, February 22, 1804; Rhode Island, March 12, 1804; South Carolina, May 15, 1804; Georgia, May 19, 1804; New Hampshire, June 15, 1804.

Ratification was completed on June 15, 1804.

The amendment was subsequently ratified by Tennessee, July 27, 1804.

The amendment was rejected by Delaware, January 18, 1804; Massachusetts, February 3, 1804; Connecticut, at its session begun May 10, 1804.

Article XIII.

Section 1. Neither slavery nor involuntary servitude, except as a punishment for crime whereof the party shall have been duly convicted, shall exist within the United States, or any place subject to their jurisdiction.

Section 2. Congress shall have power to enforce this article by appropriate legislation.

Proposal and Ratification

The thirteenth amendment to the Constitution of the United States was proposed to the legislatures of the several States by the Thirty-eighth Congress, on the 31st day of January, 1865, and was declared, in a proclamation of the Secretary of State, dated the 18th of December, 1865, to have been ratified by the legislatures of twenty-seven of the thirty-six States. The dates of ratification were: Illinois, February 1, 1865; Rhode Island, February 2, 1865; Michigan, February 2, 1865; Maryland, February 3, 1865; New York, February 3, 1865; Pennsylvania, February 3, 1865; West Virginia, February 3, 1865; Missouri, February 6, 1865; Maine, February 7, 1865; Kansas, February 7, 1865; Massachusetts, February 7, 1865; Virginia, February 9, 1865; Ohio, February 10, 1865; Indiana, February 13, 1865; Nevada, February 16, 1865; Louisiana, February 17, 1865; Minnesota, February 23, 1865; Wisconsin, February 24, 1865; Vermont, March 9, 1865; Tennessee, April 7, 1865; Arkansas, April 14, 1865; Connecticut, May 4, 1865; New Hampshire, July 1, 1865; South Carolina, November 13, 1865; Alabama, December 2, 1865; North Carolina, December 4, 1865; Georgia, December 6, 1865.

Ratification was completed on December 6, 1865.

The amendment was subsequently ratified by Oregon, December 8, 1865; California, December 19, 1865; Florida, December 28, 1865 (Florida again ratified on June 9, 1868, upon its adoption of a new constitution); Iowa, January 15, 1866; New Jersey, January 23, 1866 (after having rejected the amendment on March 16, 1865); Texas, February 18, 1870; Delaware, February 12, 1901 (after having rejected the amendment on February 8, 1865); Kentucky, March 18, 1976 (after having rejected it on February 24, 1865).

The amendment was rejected (and not subsequently ratified) by Mississippi, December 4, 1865.

Article XIV.

Section 1. All persons born or naturalized in the United States, and subject to the jurisdiction thereof, are citizens of the United States and of the State wherein they reside. No State shall make or enforce any law which shall abridge the privileges or immunities of citizens of the United States; nor shall any

State deprive any person of life, liberty, or property, without due process of law; nor deny to any person within its jurisdiction the equal protection of the laws.

Section 2. Representatives shall be apportioned among the several States according to their respective numbers, counting the whole number of persons in each State, excluding Indians not taxed. But when the right to vote at any election for the choice of electors for President and Vice President of the United States, Representatives in Congress, the Executive and Judicial officers of a State, or the members of the Legislature thereof, is denied to any of the male inhabitants of such State, being twenty-one years of age,(See Note 15) and citizens of the United States, or in any way abridged, except for participation in rebellion, or other crime, the basis of representation therein shall be reduced in the proportion which the number of such male citizens shall bear to the whole number of male citizens twenty-one years of age in such State.

Section 3. No person shall be a Senator or Representative in Congress, or elector of President and Vice President, or hold any office, civil or military, under the United States, or under any State, who, having previously taken an oath, as a member of Congress, or as an officer of the United States, or as a member of any State legislature, or as an executive or judicial officer of any State, to support the Constitution of the United States, shall have engaged in insurrection or rebellion against the same, or given aid or comfort to the enemies thereof. But Congress may by a vote of two-thirds of each House, remove such disability.

Section 4. The validity of the public debt of the United States, authorized by law, including debts incurred for payment of pensions and bounties for services in suppressing insurrection or rebellion, shall not be questioned. But neither the United States nor any State shall assume or pay any debt or obligation incurred in aid of insurrection or rebellion against the United States, or any claim for the loss or emancipation of any slave; but all such debts, obligations and claims shall be held illegal and void.

Section 5. The Congress shall have power to enforce, by appropriate legislation, the provisions of this article.

Proposal and Ratification

The fourteenth amendment to the Constitution of the United States was proposed to the legislatures of the several States by the Thirty-ninth Congress, on the 13th of June, 1866. It was declared, in a certificate of the Secretary of State dated July 28, 1868 to have been ratified by the legislatures of 28 of the 37 States. The dates of ratification were: Connecticut, June 25, 1866; New Hampshire, July 6, 1866; Tennessee, July 19, 1866; New Jersey, September 11, 1866 (subsequently the legislature rescinded its ratification, and on March 24, 1868, readopted its resolution of rescission over the Governor's veto, and on Nov. 12, 1980, expressed support for the amendment); Oregon, September 19, 1866 (and rescinded its ratification on October 15, 1868); Vermont, October 30, 1866; Ohio, January 4, 1867 (and rescinded its ratification on January 15, 1868); New York, January 10, 1867; Kansas, January 11, 1867; Illinois, January 15, 1867; West Virginia, January 16, 1867; Michigan, January 16, 1867; Minnesota, January 16, 1867; Maine, January 19, 1867; Nevada, January 22, 1867; Indiana, January 23, 1867; Missouri, January 25, 1867; Rhode Island, February 7, 1867; Wisconsin, February 7, 1867; Pennsylvania, February 12, 1867; Massachusetts, March 20, 1867; Nebraska, June 15, 1867; Iowa, March 16, 1868; Arkansas, April 6, 1868; Florida, June 9, 1868; North Carolina, July 4, 1868 (after having rejected it on December 14, 1866); Louisiana, July 9, 1868 (after having rejected it on February 6, 1867); South Carolina, July 9, 1868 (after having rejected it on December 20, 1866).

Ratification was completed on July 9, 1868.

The amendment was subsequently ratified by Alabama, July 13, 1868; Georgia, July 21, 1868 (after having rejected it on November 9, 1866); Virginia, October 8, 1869 (after having rejected it on January 9, 1867); Mississippi, January 17, 1870; Texas, February 18, 1870 (after having rejected it on October 27, 1866); Delaware, February 12, 1901 (after having rejected it on February 8, 1867); Maryland, April 4, 1959 (after having rejected it on March 23, 1867); California, May 6, 1959; Kentucky, March 18, 1976 (after having rejected it on January 8, 1867).

Article XV.

Section 1. The right of citizens of the United States to vote shall not be denied or abridged by the United States or by any State on account of race, color, or previous condition of servitude.

Section 2. The Congress shall have power to enforce this article by appropriate legislation.

Proposal and Ratification

The fifteenth amendment to the Constitution of the United States was proposed to the legislatures of the several States by the Fortieth Congress, on the 26th of February, 1869, and was declared, in a proclamation of the Secretary of State, dated March 30, 1870, to have been ratified by the legislatures of twenty-nine of the thirty-seven States. The dates of ratification were: Nevada, March 1, 1869; West Virginia, March 3, 1869; Illinois, March 5, 1869; Louisiana, March 5, 1869; North Carolina, March 5, 1869; Michigan, March 8, 1869; Wisconsin, March 9, 1869; Maine, March 11, 1869; Massachusetts, March 12, 1869; Arkansas, March 15, 1869; South Carolina, March 15, 1869; Pennsylvania, March 25, 1869; New York, April 14, 1869 (and the legislature of the same State passed a resolution January 5, 1870, to withdraw its consent to it, which action it rescinded on March 30, 1970); Indiana, May 14, 1869; Connecticut, May 19, 1869; Florida, June 14, 1869; New Hampshire, July 1, 1869; Virginia, October 8, 1869; Vermont, October 20, 1869; Missouri, January 7, 1870; Minnesota, January 13, 1870; Mississippi, January 17, 1870;

Rhode Island, January 18, 1870; Kansas, January 19, 1870; Ohio, January 27, 1870 (after having rejected it on April 30, 1869); Georgia, February 2, 1870; Iowa, February 3, 1870.

Ratification was completed on February 3, 1870, unless the withdrawal of ratification by New York was effective; in which event ratification was completed on February 17, 1870, when Nebraska ratified.

The amendment was subsequently ratified by Texas, February 18, 1870; New Jersey, February 15, 1871 (after having rejected it on February 7, 1870); Delaware, February 12, 1901 (after having rejected it on March 18, 1869); Oregon, February 24, 1959; California, April 3, 1962 (after having rejected it on January 28, 1870); Kentucky, March 18, 1976 (after having rejected it on March 12, 1869).

The amendment was approved by the Governor of Maryland, May 7, 1973; Maryland having previously rejected it on February 26, 1870.

The amendment was rejected (and not subsequently ratified) by Tennessee, November 16, 1869.

Article XVI.

The Congress shall have power to lay and collect taxes on incomes, from whatever source derived, without apportionment among the several States, and without regard to any census or enumeration.

Proposal and Ratification

The sixteenth amendment to the Constitution of the United States was proposed to the legislatures of the several States by the Sixty-first Congress on the 12th of July, 1909, and was declared, in a proclamation of the Secretary of State, dated the 25th of February, 1913, to have been ratified by 36 of the 48 States. The dates of ratification were: Alabama, August 10, 1909; Kentucky, February 8, 1910; South Carolina, February 19, 1910; Illinois, March 1, 1910; Mississippi, March 7, 1910; Oklahoma, March 10, 1910; Maryland, April 8, 1910; Georgia, August 3, 1910; Texas, August 16, 1910; Ohio, January 19, 1911; Idaho, January 20, 1911; Oregon, January 23, 1911; Washington, January 26, 1911; Montana, January 30, 1911; Indiana, January 30, 1911; California, January 31, 1911; Nevada, January 31, 1911; South Dakota, February 3, 1911; Nebraska, February 9, 1911; North Carolina, February 11, 1911; Colorado, February 15, 1911; North Dakota, February 17, 1911; Kansas, February 18, 1911; Michigan, February 23, 1911; Iowa, February 24, 1911; Missouri, March 16, 1911; Maine, March 31, 1911; Tennessee, April 7, 1911; Arkansas, April 22, 1911 (after having rejected it earlier); Wisconsin, May 26, 1911; New York, July 12, 1911; Arizona, April 6, 1912; Minnesota, June 11, 1912; Louisiana, June 28, 1912; West Virginia, January 31, 1913; New Mexico, February 3, 1913.

Ratification was completed on February 3, 1913.

The amendment was subsequently ratified by Massachusetts, March 4, 1913; New Hampshire, March 7, 1913 (after having rejected it on March 2, 1911).

The amendment was rejected (and not subsequently ratified) by Connecticut, Rhode Island, and Utah.

[Article XVII.]

The Senate of the United States shall be composed of two Senators from each State, elected by the people thereof, for six years; and each Senator shall have one vote. The electors in each State shall have the qualifications requisite for electors of the most numerous branch of the State legislatures.

When vacancies happen in the representation of any State in the Senate, the executive authority of such State shall issue writs of election to fill such vacancies: Provided, That the legislature of any State may empower the executive thereof to make temporary appointments until the people fill the vacancies by election as the legislature may direct.

This amendment shall not be so construed as to affect the election or term of any Senator chosen before it becomes valid as part of the Constitution.

Proposal and Ratification

The seventeenth amendment to the Constitution of the United States was proposed to the legislatures of the several States by the Sixty-second Congress on the 13th of May, 1912, and was declared, in a proclamation of the Secretary of State, dated the 31st of May, 1913, to have been ratified by the legislatures of 36 of the 48 States. The dates of ratification were: Massachusetts, May 22, 1912; Arizona, June 3, 1912; Minnesota, June 10, 1912; New York, January 15, 1913; Kansas, January 17, 1913; Oregon, January 23, 1913; North Carolina, January 25, 1913; California, January 28, 1913; Michigan, January 28, 1913; Iowa, January 30, 1913; Montana, January 30, 1913; Idaho, January 31, 1913; West Virginia, February 4, 1913; Colorado, February 5, 1913; Nevada, February 6, 1913; Texas, February 7, 1913; Washington, February 7, 1913; Wyoming, February 8, 1913; Arkansas, February 11, 1913; Maine, February 11, 1913; Illinois, February 13, 1913; North Dakota, February 14, 1913; Wisconsin, February 18, 1913; Indiana, February 19, 1913; New Hampshire, February 19, 1913; Vermont, February 19, 1913; South Dakota, February 19, 1913; Oklahoma, February 24, 1913; Ohio, February 25, 1913; Missouri, March 7, 1913; New Mexico, March 13, 1913; Nebraska, March 14, 1913; New Jersey, March 17, 1913; Tennessee, April 1, 1913; Pennsylvania, April 2, 1913; Connecticut, April 8, 1913.

Ratification was completed on April 8, 1913.

The amendment was subsequently ratified by Louisiana, June 11, 1914.

The amendment was rejected by Utah (and not subsequently ratified) on February 26, 1913.

Article [XVIII].(See Note 16)

Section 1. After one year from the ratification of this article the manufacture, sale, or transportation of intoxicating liquors within, the importation thereof into, or the exportation thereof from the United States and all territory subject to the jurisdiction thereof for beverage purposes is hereby prohibited.

Section. 2. The Congress and the several States shall have concurrent power to enforce this article by appropriate legislation.

Section. 3. This article shall be inoperative unless it shall have been ratified as an amendment to the Constitution by the legislatures of the several States, as provided in the Constitution, within seven years from the date of the submission hereof to the States by the Congress.

Proposal and Ratification

The eighteenth amendment to the Constitution of the United States was proposed to the legislatures of the several States by the Sixty-fifth Congress, on the 18th of December, 1917, and was declared, in a proclamation of the Secretary of State, dated the 29th of January, 1919, to have been ratified by the legislatures of 36 of the 48 States. The dates of ratification were: Mississippi, January 8, 1918; Virginia, January 11, 1918; Kentucky, January 14, 1918; North Dakota, January 25, 1918; South Carolina, January 29, 1918; Maryland, February 13, 1918; Montana, February 19, 1918; Texas, March 4, 1918; Delaware, March 18, 1918; South Dakota, March 20, 1918; Massachusetts, April 2, 1918; Arizona, May 24, 1918; Georgia, June 26, 1918; Louisiana, August 3, 1918; Florida, December 3, 1918; Michigan, January 2, 1919; Ohio, January 7, 1919; Oklahoma, January 7, 1919; Idaho, January 8, 1919; Maine, January 8, 1919; West Virginia, January 9, 1919; California, January 13, 1919; Tennessee, January 13, 1919; Washington, January 13, 1919; Arkansas, January 14, 1919; Kansas, January 14, 1919; Alabama, January 15, 1919; Colorado, January 15, 1919; Iowa, January 15, 1919; New Hampshire, January 15, 1919; Oregon, January 15, 1919; Nebraska, January 16, 1919; North Carolina, January 16, 1919; Utah, January 16, 1919; Missouri, January 16, 1919; Wyoming, January 16, 1919.

Ratification was completed on January 16, 1919. See Dillon v. Gloss, 256 U.S. 368, 376 (1921).

The amendment was subsequently ratified by Minnesota on January 17, 1919; Wisconsin, January 17, 1919; New Mexico, January 20, 1919; Nevada, January 21, 1919; New York, January 29, 1919; Vermont,

January 29, 1919; Pennsylvania, February 25, 1919; Connecticut, May 6, 1919; and New Jersey, March 9, 1922.

The amendment was rejected (and not subsequently ratified) by Rhode Island.

Article [XIX].

The right of citizens of the United States to vote shall not be denied or abridged by the United States or by any State on account of sex.

Congress shall have power to enforce this article by appropriate legislation.

Proposal and Ratification

The nineteenth amendment to the Constitution of the United States was proposed to the legislatures of the several States by the Sixty-sixth Congress, on the 4th of June, 1919, and was declared, in a proclamation of the Secretary of State, dated the 26th of August, 1920, to have been ratified by the legislatures of 36 of the 48 States. The dates of ratification were: Illinois, June 10, 1919 (and that State readopted its resolution of ratification June 17, 1919); Michigan, June 10, 1919; Wisconsin, June 10, 1919; Kansas, June 16, 1919; New York, June 16, 1919; Ohio, June 16, 1919; Pennsylvania, June 24, 1919; Massachusetts, June 25, 1919; Texas, June 28, 1919; Iowa, July 2, 1919; Missouri, July 3, 1919; Arkansas, July 28, 1919; Montana, August 2, 1919; Nebraska, August 2, 1919; Minnesota, September 8, 1919; New Hampshire, September 10, 1919; Utah, October 2, 1919; California, November 1, 1919; Maine, November 5, 1919; North Dakota, December 1, 1919; South Dakota, December 4, 1919; Colorado, December 15, 1919; Kentucky, January 6, 1920; Rhode Island, January 6, 1920; Oregon, January 13, 1920; Indiana, January 16, 1920; Wyoming, January 27, 1920; Nevada, February 7, 1920; New Jersey, February 9, 1920; Idaho, February 11, 1920; Arizona, February 12, 1920; New Mexico, February 21, 1920; Oklahoma, February 28, 1920; West Virginia, March 10, 1920; Washington, March 22, 1920; Tennessee, August 18, 1920.

Ratification was completed on August 18, 1920.

The amendment was subsequently ratified by Connecticut on September 14, 1920 (and that State reaffirmed on September 21, 1920); Vermont, February 8, 1921; Delaware, March 6, 1923 (after having rejected it on June 2, 1920); Maryland, March 29, 1941 (after having rejected it on February 24, 1920, ratification certified on February 25, 1958); Virginia, February 21, 1952 (after having rejected it on February 12, 1920); Alabama, September 8, 1953 (after having rejected it on September 22, 1919); Florida, May 13, 1969; South Carolina, July 1, 1969 (after having rejected it on January 28, 1920, ratification certified on August 22, 1973); Georgia, February 20, 1970 (after having rejected it on July 24,

1919); Louisiana, June 11, 1970 (after having rejected it on July 1, 1920); North Carolina, May 6, 1971; Mississippi, March 22, 1984 (after having rejected it on March 29, 1920).

Article [XX.]

Section 1. The terms of the President and Vice President shall end at noon on the 20th day of January, and the terms of Senators and Representatives at noon on the 3d day of January, of the years in which such terms would have ended if this article had not been ratified; and the terms of their successors shall then begin.

Section. 2. The Congress shall assemble at least once in every year, and such meeting shall begin at noon on the 3d day of January, unless they shall by law appoint a different day.

Section. 3. If, at the time fixed for the beginning of the term of the President, the President elect shall have died, the Vice President elect shall become President. If a President shall not have been chosen before the time fixed for the beginning of his term, or if the President elect shall have failed to qualify, then the Vice President elect shall act as President until a President shall have qualified; and the Congress may by law provide for the case wherein neither a President elect nor a Vice President elect shall have qualified, declaring who shall then act as President, or the manner in which one who is to act shall be selected, and such person shall act accordingly until a President or Vice President shall have qualified.

Section. 4. The Congress may by law provide for the case of the death of any of the persons from whom the House of Representatives may choose a President whenever the right of choice shall have devolved upon them, and for the case of the death of any of the persons from whom the Senate may choose a Vice President whenever the right of choice shall have devolved upon them.

Section. 5. Sections 1 and 2 shall take effect on the 15th day of October following the ratification of this article.

Section. 6. This article shall be inoperative unless it shall have been ratified as an amendment to the Constitution by the legislatures of three-fourths of the several States within seven years from the date of its submission.

Proposal and Ratification

The twentieth amendment to the Constitution was proposed to the legislatures of the several states by the Seventy-Second Congress, on the 2d day of March, 1932, and was declared, in a proclamation by the Secretary of State, dated on the 6th day of February, 1933, to have been ratified by the legislatures of 36 of the 48 States. The dates of ratification were: Virginia, March 4, 1932; New York, March 11, 1932; Mississippi, March 16, 1932; Arkansas, March 17, 1932; Kentucky, March 17, 1932; New Jersey, March 21, 1932; South Carolina, March 25, 1932; Michigan, March 31, 1932; Maine, April 1, 1932; Rhode Island, April 14, 1932; Illinois, April 21, 1932; Louisiana, June 22, 1932; West Virginia, July 30, 1932; Pennsylvania, August 11, 1932; Indiana, August 15, 1932; Texas, September 7, 1932; Alabama, September 13, 1932; California, January 4, 1933; North Carolina, January 5, 1933; North Dakota, January 9, 1933; Minnesota, January 12, 1933; Arizona, January 13, 1933; Montana, January 13, 1933; Nebraska, January 13, 1933; Oklahoma, January 13, 1933; Kansas, January 16, 1933; Oregon, January 16, 1933; Delaware, January 19, 1933; Washington, January 19, 1933; Wyoming, January 19, 1933; Iowa, January 20, 1933; South Dakota, January 20, 1933; Tennessee, January 20, 1933; Idaho, January 21, 1933; New Mexico, January 21, 1933; Georgia, January 23, 1933; Missouri, January 23, 1933; Ohio, January 23, 1933; Utah, January 23, 1933.

Ratification was completed on January 23, 1933.

The amendment was subsequently ratified by Massachusetts on January 24, 1933; Wisconsin, January 24, 1933; Colorado, January 24, 1933; Nevada, January 26, 1933; Connecticut, January 27, 1933; New Hampshire, January 31, 1933; Vermont, February 2, 1933; Maryland, March 24, 1933; Florida, April 26, 1933.

Article [XXI.]

Section 1. The eighteenth article of amendment to the Constitution of the United States is hereby repealed.

Section 2. The transportation or importation into any State, Territory, or possession of the United States for delivery or use therein of intoxicating liquors, in violation of the laws thereof, is hereby prohibited.

Section 3. This article shall be inoperative unless it shall have been ratified as an amendment to the Constitution by conventions in the several States, as provided in the Constitution, within seven years from the date of the submission hereof to the States by the Congress.

Proposal and Ratification

The twenty-first amendment to the Constitution was proposed to the several states by the Seventy-Second Congress, on the 20th day of February, 1933, and was declared, in a proclamation by the Secretary of State, dated on the 5th day of December, 1933, to have been ratified by 36 of the 48 States. The dates of ratification were: Michigan, April 10, 1933; Wisconsin, April 25, 1933; Rhode Island, May

8, 1933; Wyoming, May 25, 1933; New Jersey, June 1, 1933; Delaware, June 24, 1933; Indiana, June 26, 1933; Massachusetts, June 26, 1933; New York, June 27, 1933; Illinois, July 10, 1933; Iowa, July

Amendment XXII

Section 1. No person shall be elected to the office of the President more than twice, and no person who has held the office of President, or acted as President, for more than two years of a term to which some other person was elected President shall be elected to the office of the President more than once. But this article shall not apply to any person holding the office of President when this article was proposed by the Congress, and shall not prevent any person who may be holding the office of President, or acting as President, during the term within which this article becomes operative from holding the office of President or acting as President during the remainder of such term.

Section 2. This article shall be inoperative unless it shall have been ratified as an amendment to the Constitution by the legislatures of three-fourths of the several states within seven years from the date of its submission to the states by the Congress.

Amendment XXIII

Section 1. The District constituting the seat of government of the United States shall appoint in such manner as the Congress may direct:

A number of electors of President and Vice President equal to the whole number of Senators and Representatives in Congress to which the District would be entitled if it were a state, but in no event more than the least populous state; they shall be in addition to those appointed by the states, but they shall be considered, for the purposes of the election of President and Vice President, to be electors appointed by a state; and they shall meet in the District and perform such duties as provided by the twelfth article of amendment.

Section 2. The Congress shall have power to enforce this article by appropriate legislation.

Amendment XXIV

Section 1. The right of citizens of the United States to vote in any primary or other election for President or Vice President, for electors for President or Vice President, or for Senator or Representative in Congress, shall not be denied or abridged by the United States or any state by reason of failure to pay any poll tax or other tax.

Section 2. The Congress shall have power to enforce this article by appropriate legislation.

Amendment XXV

Section 1. In case of the removal of the President from office or of his death or resignation, the Vice President shall become President.

Section 2. Whenever there is a vacancy in the office of the Vice President, the President shall nominate a Vice President who shall take office upon confirmation by a majority vote of both Houses of Congress.

Section 3. Whenever the President transmits to the President pro tempore of the Senate and the Speaker of the House of Representatives his written declaration that he is unable to discharge the powers and duties of his office, and until he transmits to them a written declaration to the contrary, such powers and duties shall be discharged by the Vice President as Acting President.

Section 4. Whenever the Vice President and a majority of either the principal officers of the executive departments or of such other body as Congress may by law provide, transmit to the President pro tempore of the Senate and the Speaker of the House of Representatives their written declaration that the President is unable to discharge the powers and duties of his office, the Vice President shall immediately assume the powers and duties of the office as Acting President.

Thereafter, when the President transmits to the President pro tempore of the Senate and the Speaker of the House of Representatives his written declaration that no inability exists, he shall resume the powers and duties of his office unless the Vice President and a majority of either the principal officers of the executive department or of such other body as Congress may by law provide, transmit within four days to the President pro tempore of the Senate and the Speaker of the House of Representatives their written declaration that the President is unable to discharge the powers and duties of his office. Thereupon Congress shall decide the issue, assembling within forty-eight hours for that purpose if not in session. If the Congress, within twenty-one days after receipt of the latter written declaration, or, if Congress is not in session, within twenty-one days after Congress is required to assemble, determines by two-thirds vote of both Houses that the President is unable to discharge the powers and duties of his office, the Vice President shall continue to discharge the same as Acting President; otherwise, the President shall resume the powers and duties of his office.

Amendment XXVI

Section 1. The right of citizens of the United States, who are 18 years of age or older, to vote, shall not be denied or abridged by the United States or any state on account of age.

Section 2. The Congress shall have the power to enforce this article by appropriate legislation.

Amendment XXVII

No law varying the compensation for the services of the Senators and Representatives shall take effect until an election of Representatives shall have intervened.

NOTES

Note 12: The first ten amendments to the Constitution of the United States (and two others, one of which failed of ratification and the other which later became the 27th amendment) were proposed to the legislatures of the several States by the First Congress on September 25, 1789. The first ten amendments were ratified by the following States, and the notifications of ratification by the Governors thereof were successively communicated by the President to Congress: New Jersey, November 20, 1789; Maryland, December 19, 1789; North Carolina, December 22, 1789; South Carolina, January 19, 1790; New Hampshire, January 25, 1790; Delaware, January 28, 1790; New York, February 24, 1790; Pennsylvania, March 10, 1790; Rhode Island, June 7, 1790; Vermont, November 3, 1791; and Virginia, December 15, 1791.

Ratification was completed on December 15, 1791.

The amendments were subsequently ratified by the legislatures of Massachusetts, March 2, 1939; Georgia, March 18, 1939; and Connecticut, April 19, 1939.

Note 13: Only the 13th, 14th, 15th, and 16th articles of amendment had numbers assigned to them at the time of ratification.

Note 14: This sentence has been superseded by section 3 of amendment XX.

Note 15: See amendment XIX and section 1 of amendment XXVI.

Note 16: Repealed by section 1 of amendment XXI.

This information has been compiled from the U.S. Code. The U.S. Code is published by the Law Revision Counsel of the U.S. House of Representatives.

Updated September 20, 2004

Credits

Excerpts from *People v. Voelker*. Copyright in the Public Domain.
Excerpts from *People v. Garcia*. Copyright in the Public Domain.
Excerpts from *Bueckner v. Hamel*. Copyright in the Public Domain.
Excerpts from *Federal Register*, vol. 76, no. 87, pp. 26–86. Copyright in the Public Domain.
Excerpts from *Freedom of Information Act Reference Guide*. Copyright in the Public Domain.
Excerpts from *Wyman v. Newhouse*. Copyright in the Public Domain.
Excerpts from *Burnham v. Superior Court of California, County of Marin*. Copyright in the Public Domain.
Excerpts from *International Shoe Co. v. Washington*. Copyright in the Public Domain.
Excerpts from *Kulko v. Superior Court of California*. Copyright in the Public Domain.
Excerpts from *Asahi Metal Industry Co. LTD. v. Superior Court of California, Solano County*. Copyright in the Public Domain.
Excerpts from *Calder v. Jones*. Copyright in the Public Domain.
Excerpts from *Boschetto v. Hansing*. Copyright in the Public Domain.
Excerpts from *Gulf v. Gilbert*. Copyright in the Public Domain.
Sample Legal Forms from uscourts.gov. Copyright in the Public Domain.
"The Difference Between Federal and State Courts," uscourts.gov. Copyright in the Public Domain.
"Maryland's Judicial System," mdcourts.gov. Copyright in the Public Domain.
Excerpts from *Cullison v. Medley*. Copyright in the Public Domain.
Excerpts from *Cohen v. Smith*. Copyright in the Public Domain.
"Testimony," *Snyder v. Turk*. Copyright in the Public Domain.
Excerpts from *Thoma v. Cracker Barrel Old Country Store, Inc*. Copyright in the Public Domain.
Excerpts from *Virden v. Betts and Beer Construction Co., Inc*. Copyright in the Public Domain.
Excerpts from *Herbert v. Enos*. Copyright in the Public Domain.
Excerpts from *Strange v. Entercom Sacramento*. Copyright in the Public Domain.
Excerpts from *Byrne v. Boadle*. Copyright in the Public Domain.
Excerpts from *Leikach v. Royal Crown Bottling Company of Baltimore, Incorporated*. Copyright in the Public Domain.
Excerpts from *Brandenburg v. Ohio*. Copyright in the Public Domain.
Excerpts from *Miller v. California*. Copyright in the Public Domain.

Excerpts from *Snyder v. Phelps*. Copyright in the Public Domain.
Excerpts from *Brown v. Entertainment Merchants Association*. Copyright in the Public Domain.
Excerpts from *Lemon v. Kurtzman*. Copyright in the Public Domain.
Excerpts from *Employment Division, Department of Human Resources of Oregon v. Smith*. Copyright in the Public Domain.
Excerpts from *Washington v. Glucksburg*. Copyright in the Public Domain.
Excerpts from *Craig v. Boren*. Copyright in the Public Domain.
Felix S. Cohen, "Excerpt of 'Dialogue on Private Property'," *Rutgers Law Review*. Copyright © 1954 by Rutgers Law Review. Reprinted with permission.
Excerpts from *Paset v. Old Orchard Bank and Trust Company*. Copyright in the Public Domain.
Excerpts from *Moore v. Regents of the University of California*. Copyright in the Public Domain.
Excerpts from *Shelley v. Kraemer*. Copyright in the Public Domain.
Excerpts from *Blevins v. Barry-Lawrence County Association for Retarded Citizens*. Copyright in the Public Domain.
Excerpts from *Kelo v. City of New London*. Copyright in the Public Domain.
Excerpts from *United States v. Causby*. Copyright in the Public Domain.
Excerpts from *Village of Euclid, Ohio v. Ambler Realty Co.* Copyright in the Public Domain.
Excerpts from *Penn Central Transportation Company v. City of New York*. Copyright in the Public Domain.
Excerpts from *Lucas v. South Carolina Coastal Council*. Copyright in the Public Domain.
Excerpts from *General Information Concerning Patents*, United States Patent and Trademark Office, pp. 1–4, 25–30. Copyright in the Public Domain.
Excerpts from uspto.gov. Copyright in the Public Domain.
Excerpts from *Diamond v. Chakrabarty*. Copyright in the Public Domain.
Excerpts from *State Street Bank & Trust Co. v. Signature Financial Group, Inc.* Copyright in the Public Domain.
Excerpts from *Bond v. Polycycle, Inc.* Copyright in the Public Domain.
Excerpts from *LeJeune v. Coin Acceptors, Inc.* Copyright in the Public Domain.
Excerpts from uspto.gov. Copyright in the Public Domain.
Excerpts from *Harjo v. Pro-Football, Inc.* Copyright in the Public Domain.
Excerpts from *Copyright Basics*, U.S. Copyright Office, pp. 1–7. Copyright in the Public Domain.
Excerpts from *Selle v. Gibb*. Copyright in the Public Domain.
Excerpts from *DeWitt Truck Brokers v. Flemming Fruit Company*. Copyright in the Public Domain.
Excerpts from *Baatz v. Arrow Bar*. Copyright in the Public Domain.
Excerpts from *Nursing Home Building Corporation v. DeHart*. Copyright in the Public Domain.
Excerpts from *Smith v. Van Gorkom*. Copyright in the Public Domain.
Excerpts from *Northeast Harbor Golf Club, Inc. v. Harris*. Copyright in the Public Domain.
"Commonwealth of Virginia State Corporation Commission, Articles of Incorporation of a Virginia Stock Corporation (SCC619)," scc.virginia.gov, pp. 1–2. Copyright in the Public Domain.
Excerpts from *Cantu v. Central Education Agency*. Copyright in the Public Domain.
Excerpts from *Hamer v. Sidway*. Copyright in the Public Domain.

"Press Release: Abercrombie & Fitch Proposes a Win-Win Situation". Copyright © 2011 by Abercrombie & Fitch, Brand Senses Department. Reprinted with permission.

Excerpts from *Cohen v. Cowles Media Company*. Copyright in the Public Domain.

Excerpts from *Shoemaker v. Commonwealth Bank*. Copyright in the Public Domain.

Excerpts from *Montes v. Naismith and Trevino and Construction Company*. Copyright in the Public Domain.

Excerpts from *Sokoloff v. Harriman Estates Development Corp*. Copyright in the Public Domain.

Excerpts from *Griswold v. Connecticut*. Copyright in the Public Domain.

Excerpts from *Eisenstadt v. Baird*. Copyright in the Public Domain.

Excerpts from *Lawrence v. Texas*. Copyright in the Public Domain.

Excerpts from *Loving v. Commonwealth of Virginia*. Copyright in the Public Domain.

Excerpts from *Goodridge v. Department of Public Health*. Copyright in the Public Domain.

Excerpts from *Roe v. Wade*. Copyright in the Public Domain.

Excerpts from *J.B. v. M.B.* Copyright in the Public Domain.

Excerpts from *Knussman v. State of Maryland*. Copyright in the Public Domain.

Excerpts from *Kassama v. Magat*. Copyright in the Public Domain.

Excerpts from *The Federal Court System in the United States, An Introduction for Judges and Judicial Administrators in Other Countries*, pp. 27–30. Copyright in the Public Domain.

Excerpts from *A Journalist's Guide to the Federal Courts*, pp. 15–23, 29–31. Copyright in the Public Domain.

Excerpts from *United States v. Jones*. Copyright in the Public Domain.

Charles Colman, "Everything You Need to Understand the *Louboutin v. YSL* Lawsuit". Copyright © by Charles Colman Law, PLLC. Reprinted with permission.

"United States Constitution." Copyright in the Public Domain.

"Amendments to the Constitution." Copyright in the Public Domain.

9 781609 276850

Printed by Libri Plureos GmbH in Hamburg,
Germany